America's Rogue Sheriffs: A Culture of Corruption

By

Tom Aswell

Copyright, 2023

by

Tom Aswell

ISBN: 978-1-7331968-5-7

All rights reserved

America's Rogue Sheriffs: A Culture of Corruption

Table of Contents

Prologue v
Introduction ix
Chapter 1   Sweet Home Alabama 1
Chapter 2   Arizona: From Earp to Arpaio 13
Chapter 3   Arkansas: Debit Cards, Conspiracy Theories 31
Chapter 4   California: A Virtual Nest of Corruption 39
Chapter 5   Colorado: Rocky Mountain Sex 59
Chapter 6   Delaware: First State, First Sheriff 63
Chapter 7   Florida: The No-Sunshine State 65
Chapter 8   Georgia on My Mind 81
Chapter 9   Idaho: We Don't Need No Stinkin' DNA 101
Chapter 10 Illinois: Cook County (More to the State than Chicago?) 105
Chapter 11 Indiana: Tow Truck Kickbacks (and Oh, Yeah, the Sex) 117
Chapter 12 Iowa: When You Can't Trust Fellow Officers... 121
Chapter 13 Kansas: Drugs, Bribery, and Guns 123
Chapter 14 Kentucky: Sheriff Brought Down by Reporters 129
Chapter 15 Louisiana: Anything Goes (But No Pimps) 141
Chapter 16 Maine: Sexting Between Adults Not Illegal 193
Chapter 17 Maryland: Bad Apples in Baltimore 195
Chapter 18 Massachusetts: Payroll Fraud, Theft, Extortion, Drugs, etc. 199
Chapter 19 Michigan: Quota and Bigotry 205
Chapter 20 Minnesota: No Discipline for Rogue Officers 209

Chapter 21	Mississippi: Hobbs and the Dixie Mafia	211
Chapter 22	Missouri: Suicide, a Threesome, and a Fry Cook	221
Chapter 23	Montana: Sex Scandals and a Write-In Winner	227
Chapter 24	Nebraska: Asset Seizure State	231
Chapter 25	Nevada: Sex, Porn, and More Asset Seizure	235
Chapter 26	New Jersey: Bribes, Double-Dipping	243
Chapter 27	New Mexico: False Arrests, Drug Trafficking	247
Chapter 28	New York: Drug Trafficking, Porn DVDs	255
Chapter 29	North Carolina: Poster Child for Abuse	259
Chapter 30	North Dakota: Steal, Deal Meth? Pay $500	273
Chapter 31	Ohio: Extortion, Tryst, Cocaine	275
Chapter 32	Oklahoma: Sex, Lies, and Drugs	283
Chapter 33	Oregon: Sex with the Governor's Wife	293
Chapter 34	Pennsylvania: $675K in Bribes, $35M in No-Bid Contracts	301
Chapter 35	South Carolina: Sex with Minor, Bribes, a State in Disarray	307
Chapter 36	South Dakota: Take Oath of Office, Go to Jail	319
Chapter 37	Tennessee: Cocaine, Prostitutes, and Buford Pusser	321
Chapter 38	Texas: Porous Border, Corrupt Lawmen	331
Chapter 39	Utah: Constitutional Sheriffs v. BLM	361
Chapter 40	Vermont: Sheriffs by Contract	365
Chapter 41	Virginia: Armored Vehicles for Sheriffs	369
Chapter 42	Washington: Payoffs to Protect Prostitution, Gambling	337
Chapter 43	West Virginia: America's Opioid Capital	383
Chapter 44	Wisconsin: Clarke a CSPOA Lightning Rod	387
Chapter 45	Wyoming: Sheriff Shoots, Kills Deputy	391
Index		399
Author's Notes		445

Prologue

Prison Legal News is a monthly online periodical and magazine that has been in existence since May 1990. A project of the non-profit Human Rights Defense Center, it is dedicated to reporting on criminal justice issues and prison and jail-related civil litigation, primarily in the United States. It draws upon numerous mainstream publications for much of the information published and in turn, I have, with its gracious consent, drawn on many of its stories about sheriffs for this book.

One of those stories, by writer Nicole Audrey Spector, was entitled "The 10 Worst Sheriffs in America." Spector, threw in the disclaimer to her list of whom she felt were the worst examples of law enforcement the suggestion to readers to prepare "for a lot of cowboy hats and moustaches!" And while I defer to her judgment of the credentials of each of her honorees, I know how difficult it was to winnow the list of bad sheriffs down to the ten worst. As is the case in compiling any such roster, we all have our personal favorites.

Spector's top ten, each of whom will be discussed in greater detail later in this book, include, in order:

- Bill Waybourn, Tarrant County, Texas;
- Scott Jones, Sacramento County, California;
- Steve Whidden, Hendry County, Florida;
- Gregory J. Ahern, Alameda County, California;
- Alex Villanueva, Los Angeles County, California;
- Bob Gualtieri, Pinellas County, Florida;
- Richard Jones, Butler County, Ohio;
- Donny Youngblood, Kern County, California;
- Tim Howard, Erie County, New York;
- Frank Reynolds, Cherokee County, Georgia.[1]

Spector's list is subjective and to her "top ten," I would offer for consideration, in no particular order, Louisiana's Louis Ackal of Iberia Parish (county), Louisiana; Oddie Shoupe of White County, Tennessee, and the infamous Joe Arpaio of Maricopa County, Arizona. If allowed to go back a few decades, I would have to also include Noah Cross of Louisiana's Concordia Parish and his chief deputy Frank DeLaughter.

There are many factors that contribute to making a very, bad sheriff. Money is almost always a big factor. Sheriffs are the county's designated tax collector in most jurisdictions and they preside over large budgets. Morgan County, Tennessee, for instance, devotes half its annual budget to maintaining the sheriff's of California fice's administrative expenses but the sheriff has sixteen other accounts over which the county has no authority. Alan Greenblatt in *Governing Magazine*, quoted Mirya Holman, associated professor of Political Science at Tulane University in New Orleans, as saying that a combination of large budgets and scant oversight contributes to an environment "where corruption is certainly possible, if not probable."[2]

Sheriffs generally can hold office as long as they want, or until they die. Their sweeping power is such that few potential rivals can offer a serious challenge at the polls. If sheriffs have any appreciable political skills, they solidify their base by doing the things politicians do best: help those in the best position to help them and then call in those chits when needed. It was that lack of term limits for sheriffs and district attorneys that former New Orleans FBI Special Agent in Charge Jeffrey Sallet warned about in his interview with the New Orleans Times-Picayune as he prepared for his transfer to Chicago in 2017. "Is it a healthy environment when the same family controls a parish through one of those means for decades?" he asked. "Do you really want to upset someone who has been in power for 30 years and may never get out of power?"[3]

Power, then, is perhaps the biggest driving force in a sheriff's morphing into something akin to a tyrant. The rise of the Constitutional Sheriffs and Peace Officers Association (CSPOA) has fed the notion that sheriffs are invincible, answerable to no one but the voters who put them in office. The CSPOA claims the U.S. Constitution shields sheriffs from the dictates of governors, legislatures, congress, even the President. Wielding such heady authority can feed a sheriff's insatiable appetite for unchallenged sovereignty.

That attitude is probably best summed up in a quote from Elhart County, Indiana, Sheriff Brad Rogers: "I'm answerable to the people. I have a face and a name. Try asking the federal government for a face and a name."[3]

Despite the fact that no elective office is less accountable or more reliable in producing scandal, that several Oklahoma counties were forced to raise taxes to pay off legal settlements arising from sheriff misdeeds, or that in South Carolina, one in four sheriffs were accused of law breaking, sheriffs' autonomy all too often is confirmed in the voting booth where incumbents are rarely challenged, much less defeated.[4]

A big reason for incumbent sheriffs' advantage at the polls is their control over local jobs. They have virtually unfettered authority in the hiring and firing of deputies who, in turn, usually campaign on their behalf come election time. Plus, there is a dearth of qualified candidates who could – or would – challenge the sheriff's reelection bid. Longtime Jefferson Parish, Louisiana, Sheriff Harry Lee, who claimed friendships with Bill Clinton and Willie Nelson, once dismissed the notion of running for governor, saying, "Why would I want to be governor when I can be king?"[5]

Another key to the aura of invincibility that sheriffs, along with the rest of our system of justice, enjoy is qualified immunity. An obscure judicially-created provision (not always codified into "law"), qualified immunity makes it almost impossible to hold sheriffs, cops, prosecutors or judges accountable for screw-ups like hiding exculpatory evidence, no- knock raids on wrong addresses, harassment, wrongful convictions, or other misconduct so long as such actions are performed in a reasonable manner, the term "reasonable," of course, being open to interpretation.

On April 7, 2021, New Mexico became only the second state to ban qualified immunity when Governor Michelle Grisham signed the state's Civil Rights Act, aka House Bill 4. The new law gave citizens the right to sue the state, a city or county when rights are violated.[6]

Ron Keine of New Mexico's Bernalillo County was one of four men wrongfully convicted of the kidnapping, rape and murder of a University of New Mexico student in 1974 and came within nine days of being executed for a murder he did not commit because of misconduct so severe that it led to the firing of several sheriff's deputies. Despite his exoneration, his lawsuit against the county and the sheriff's deputies who helped secure his wrongful conviction was dismissed. Keine and the other three exonerees eventually settled their case for $5,000 each, plus attorney's fees.[7]

Former New Mexico state legislator Stephanie Maez testified on behalf of that state's bill, tearfully telling of the arrest and framing of her eighteen-year-old son for murder by an Albuquerque homicide detective. Despite her son's vindication and release and the capture of the real killers, there was never any accountability for the detective.

Colorado, the only other state to enact similar legislation, ended qualified immunity in June 2020. Efforts in other states have failed, due mainly to the high-pressure efforts of law enforcement lobbyists and police unions who claimed that police officers would leave the profession en masse and those who stayed would be exposed to bankruptcy and the loss of their homes. Arguments that qualified immunity allows rogue offices to brutalize citizens fell on deaf ears in at least 35 states where bills to end or limit qualified immunity have died in recent years. Even the New Mexico law signed into law in April 2021 had been gutted by an amendment that inserted that prohibited an accuser from specifically naming an officer as a defendant in a lawsuit.[8]

But good or bad, and, in any case, immune from accountability, there is no question that sheriffs are powerful and unafraid to flex that power to their advantage.

I remain steadfast in my conviction that the vast majority of law enforcement personnel, sheriffs included, are decent, law-abiding public servants who strive to enforce laws equitably across demographic, racial, and gender lines and I would welcome those into my home at any time. They are dedicated and, though it may be a cliché to say this, they do put their lives on the line every day. Even as I write this paragraph, funeral services are being planned for a Louisiana State Trooper ambushed the day before by a crazed gunman who also shot four others, killing one of those as well. It was a senseless crime and neither the state trooper nor the other victim ever had a chance. These are not the men and women I write about in this book. It's the miscreants, unfortunately, who give the honest cops a bad name that I call out here.

Introduction

"We have to be responseful [sic] to the public, all the public, even the nuts. In short, this is kind of a kissass business, to put it bluntly."

--The Natchitoches Parish [Louisiana] Sheriff's Deputy Manual[1]

The office of sheriff is older than that of the president. Indeed, the position pre-dates the republic itself by more than a century, older even than the Magna Carta, signed in 1215. In fact, the office, which originated in England, dates back over a thousand years.[2] In this country, the first sheriff took office in Delaware in 1669—more than a century before the Declaration of Independence. (Ironically, it is in that state where efforts have been ongoing for several years to re-define the role of sheriff by revoking the office's arrest powers.)

The office gets its name from the term Shire Reeve, meaning the keeper of the county.[3] The sheriff, other than the town marshal and occasional police chief in some municipalities, is the only elected law enforcement official in America. More than ninety-nine percent of sheriffs in the U.S. are elected. In forty-two states, sheriffs are elected to four-year terms. In Massachusetts, the term is for six years. It's for a three-year term in New Jersey and for two years in Arkansas and New Hampshire. In Rhode Island, the governor appoints the sheriff and in two Colorado counties and Dade County, Florida, sheriffs are appointed by the county executive.[4]

There were 3,080 sheriffs in the U.S. as of January 2015, but three entire states—Alaska, which has no counties, Hawaii and Connecticut—do not have a sheriff. That doesn't mean the states are without serious problems with those who are sworn to uphold the law.

Even states that may have as few as ten counties, like New Hampshire, still seem to have captivating stories about their sheriffs – even as far back as its Pine Tree Riot of 1772. England, it seemed lacked a sufficient number of trees with which to build her Royal Navy's ships in 1721, so the king's surveyors traversed northern New England in search of the more plentiful tall white pines, which were marked with three slashes.

A second pine tree law, enacted in 1722, decreed that colonists were to be forced to pay for a royal license to cut trees on their own land.

In 1766, after settlers chased off a king's surveying party and sank their boat, King George II appointed John Wentworth governor of New Hampshire and his crackdown on violators led to the Pine Tree Riot. In April 1772, mill owner Ebenezer Mudgett refused to pay his fine for cutting the trees and was arrested by Sheriff Benjamin Whiting and Deputy John Quigley. He was released after promising to bring bail money the next day. Instead, Mudgett and about twenty men burst into Whiting's room at the Quimby Inn the next morning and held him down and beat him and Quigley, and forced both men to flee for their lives.

A sympathetic judge fined eight of the rioters only twenty shillings and court costs.[5] Sheriff Henry Plummer of Bannock, Montana, for the most extreme example, was hung by his own constituents in 1864 because of persistent stories that he commanded a "gang of robbers" even as he dispensed justice.[12] Plummer's actually began in 1856 Nevada City, California, where he was elected sheriff at the tender age of twenty-four. Re-elected the following year, he quickly found himself in trouble when he killed a man in a gunfight and was sentenced to ten years in San Quentin Prison.

Released after serving only seven months, he returned to Nevada City and soon joined a gang of outlaws who robbed area stagecoaches. By 1862, Plummer, suffering from tuberculosis decided to return home to Maine but ended up instead in Bannack, Montana, where he formed another gang calling themselves the Innocents.

By late spring 1863, the string of robberies and killings perpetrated by the gang had gotten so bad that the citizens advertised for a sheriff and Plummer was appointed on May 24, 1863. He immediately appointed two of his fellow gang members, Buck Stinson and Ned Ray, as deputies. Plummer's ascension to sheriff had the opposite of the desired effect as crime increased dramatically. More than 100 citizens were murdered over the next few months.

Meanwhile, Plummer expanded his authority to Virginia City in August 1863 after he was appointed Deputy U.S. Marshal for the eastern Idaho Territory.

A gallows Plummer had built served to hang only witnesses to the Innocents' crimes, which prompted the locals to form the Montana Vigilantes. The Montana Vigilantes employed the numbers "3-7-77," which remain unexplained today but which are still worn on the shoulder patches of Montana state highway patrolmen.

On January 10, 1864, a vigilante gang took Plummer, Stinson and Ray into custody and hung all three – Ray first, followed by Stinson and finally, Plummer. The vigilantes would go on to hang twenty-one men in January and February of that year but the robberies for which they were hanged continued unabated until 1867.[5]

Sheriffs' jobs in Rhode Island are largely ceremonial; they don't investigate burglaries, robberies, assaults or homicides. They don't even issue traffic citations. Their jobs are largely limited to security and to preside at governors' inaugurations and at commencement exercises at Brown University.

The state's sheriffs are not elected, but instead are appointed by the governor and once served at the governor's pleasure but now are appointed to ten-year terms at the dizzying salaries of about thirty thousand dollars per year.[6]

Sheriffs' offices range in size from one or two officers in small rural areas to the largest of them all, the Los Angeles County Sheriff's Office, with 16,400 deputies and 400 reserve deputies.[7] The last line of defense for the citizenry, the sheriff is the public's protector, the keeper of the peace, the guardian of liberty, and the protector of rights. He is responsible for keeping the peace and enforcing the law. In some states, such as California, certain law enforcement qualifications must be met before being able to run for sheriff. In most states, however, there are no such qualifications and anyone can run for the office. Moreover, the office is unique in that sheriffs are accountable directly to the U.S. Constitution and the constitutions of their respective states.[8] It is those last two factors—the general lack of qualifications (other than just being a good politician) and accountability solely to the federal and state constitutions, to the specific exclusion of the president, congress and the governor—that makes the sheriff the single most powerful person in a county, more powerful even than the district attorney or the judiciary in many cases.

That self-image of complete autonomy was never more evident than in 2013 when a Florida sheriff a few other vocal current and former sheriffs launched a resistance movement, vowing to resist federal efforts to enforce gun control laws, including the 1968 Brady Act that imposed a five-day waiting period before an unlicensed individual could purchase a handgun.

Liberty County Sheriff Nick Finch ordered a driver released after one of his deputies pulled the man over and discovered he was carrying a concealed pistol without a license, which is a felony in Florida. The driver's booking record was whited out. "I know what law rules the day," Finch said, "and it's the U.S. Constitution."

In a rare move, Florida Gov. Rick Scott suspended Finch. That's when a former sheriff from Arizona, Richard Mack, and the group he heads – the Constitutional Sheriffs and Peace Officers Association (CSPOA) – got involved with the backing of the John Birch Society, Gun Owners of America, and the Oath Keepers. Finch was eventually acquitted of charges of misconduct and falsification of records, reinstated as sheriff and awarded back pay and attorney's fees in excess of $160,000.[9]

Three years later, the man Finch's deputy had pulled over, Floyd Parrish of Bristol, Florida, was arrested for second degree murder in the shooting death of another man at Parrish's home.[10]

Finch served only one term as sheriff but his actions made him and Mack the darlings of the National Rifle Association and the Tea Party and the poster boys for a movement for sheriffs to "take back" the country from the federal government that Mack describes as "the greatest threat we face today."

Mack traveled around the country proclaiming that the constitutional sheriff movement is rooted in the historical definition of sheriffs as the most powerful law-enforcement officers within their respective counties and that sheriffs have unilateral power to decide which laws should be enforced and which ones could be ignored.[11]

In October 2021, Texas Attorney General Ken Paxton addressed a CSPOA conference in Mesquite, Texas, calling the CSPOA training being offered to and approved by the Texas Commission on Law Enforcement (TCOLE) "legitimate law enforcement training."

Mack and his CSPOA may even have been the inspiration for Montana State Rep. Gary Marbut's 2014 referendum that would have made any federal agent attempting to make an arrest of a Montana citizen for a federal crime subject to being arrested himself on charges of kidnapping.[12] That much power concentrated in the hands of a single individual, who often possesses no concept of basic human rights, is a recipe for abuse and greed. And sometimes the result is even outright lawlessness on the part of the very ones sworn to uphold the law. Intimidation supplants protection; liberty and rights are replaced by fear and persecution. And the sheriff, already all-powerful, becomes even more so.

The Louisiana Sheriffs' Association (LSA) is a case in point. "Prior to about 1978 or so, the office of secretary-treasurer was the power of the association," said Anthony G. "Tony" Falterman, retired sheriff of Assumption Parish, one of the original parishes of the Territory of Orleans located along the banks of Lafourche Bayou and the state's largest sugar cane producer.

Falterman said when he first became sheriff, the LSA "was located in a tiny hole in the wall on Third Street in downtown Baton Rouge." Today it's an ultra-modern, sprawling complex near the LSU campus. The LSA operates its own insurance pool, the Louisiana Sheriff's Law Enforcement Program, which covers more than three-fourths of the sheriffs' offices in the state in liability litigation.

"The LSA secretary-treasurer was provided an automobile and a credit card and represented the association at the legislature and at other functions and meetings," Falterman said. When he defeated Tangipahoa Parish Sheriff Frank Edwards as president of the sheriffs' association, use of a vehicle and credit cards were suspended. He also lobbied the state legislature successfully for what at the time was called hazardous duty pay, today known as supplemental pay. He got approval for the supplemental pay by agreeing that all recipients would undergo Police Officer Standards and Training (POST) certification. Falterman, as a member of the Louisiana Commission on Law Enforcement, also helped certify all the academies in Louisiana that applied to train recruits.[13] But even those reforms failed to prevent abuses.

With the rise of the sheriffs' influence, we have witnessed corruption, says DeKalb County, Illinois Sheriff Roger Scott, with some not living up to the "standards of the badge." That, naturally led to the indictment of some for various abuses, from drunkenness to corruption.

Falterman, who after retiring as sheriff, served as the district attorney for Louisiana's 23rd Judicial District which includes the parishes of Ascension, Assumption and St. James, agreed with Sheriff Scott. "It has always been my opinion that the longer an office holder remains in office, the greater the potential for committing absolutely egregious ethical or criminal violations. The aura of being untouchable and undefeated surrounding an elected official can lead to a tragic downfall and often prison, he said. A vast majority of the men and women in uniform are dedicated to their profession, and the potential for becoming an on-the-job fatality occurs every time a uniform is worn! We should all be thankful for the jobs being done by a mostly underpaid group of men and women that needs the public's support now—more than ever," Falterman said.[14]

About 70 communities in Alaska, nearly all of them Native Alaskans in demographic composition, and in areas with the highest poverty, sexual assault, and suicide rates in the U.S., have no local law enforcement. Even in some areas where there are police, rapists go unpunished and homicides go unsolved. When state police are called in on a crime, they are usually a half-hour flight away. Local police, when there are any, are often outnumbered by rapists by ratios as high as seven-to-one. Those remote areas have almost four times as many sex offenders, per capita, as the rest of the nation.

Villages are so desperate for law enforcement that they are forced to hire convicted felons because they are the only applicants. In Stebbins, a village of fewer than seven hundred residents, every cop, including the chief of police, has a criminal record. One officer was a registered sex offender. Altogether, the seven officers in Stebbins, had pleaded guilty or no contest in more than seventy criminal cases, including sexual abuse of a minor.

Village officials defend the practice, saying they have no choice because the job pays only $14 an hour and officers get no weapon with which to enforce the law.[15] It's not a new problem by any means. In 2005, Simeon Askoak testified to the plight of law enforcement before a group of congressmen assigned to fix Alaska's dearth of law enforcement officers. Askoak was the only cop in Russian Mission, his home town of 340 people. He called the situation "degrading." The village could not afford utilities for the police station, so he dug into his own pocket to purchase heating oil. When he could no longer afford to pay for the oil, the jailhouse pipes froze. "We are the first responders," he said in describing his duties to arrest drunk drivers, bootleggers, drug dealers, child molesters, domestic abusers and to pull bodies from the rivers.

Two days after his testimony, Askoak took his own life, leaving no one to carry out those duties in a region with the highest homicide rate and accidental death rate in Alaska. Russian Mission has not had a certified police officer since. Half the women in the village experience sexual assault or domestic violence but offenders are safe in the knowledge they can simply disappear when the visiting state troopers arrive.

When Askoak first began as Russian Mission's only cop, there were only 100 village public safety officers (VPSOs) in Alaska. By 2019, that number had shrunk to 38.[16] In the aftermath of Adam Lanza's shooting rampage at Sandy Hook Elementary School on December 14, 2012, in which 26 people – twenty of them children – were killed, many wondered where the sheriff's office was during the deadliest mass shooting at a school in America.

The answer is there was no sheriff.

Connecticut, as of December 1, 2000, joined Alaska and Hawaii as the only states with no sheriffs. Earlier, the House had approved the measure to abolish the eight sheriffs' offices by a 147-2 vote and the Senate followed suit by a 34-2 vote.[17] That sent it to voters who, on November 7, approved the referendum by a two-to-one margin.[18]

Part of the problem could have been the low salaries paid the state's eight sheriffs: $35,000 or $37,000, depending on the county. By comparison, Sheriffs in Louisiana, a relatively poor state, make nearly two hundred thousand dollars per year on average. In Connecticut, as in other states, deputies were entirely reliant upon the goodwill of their bosses, the sheriffs, for their jobs and could be fired on a whim. Such a system made sheriffs a source of patronage which in turn created an atmosphere ripe for corruption.

In the lead-up to the Connecticut referendum, the state's sheriffs had come under both state and federal investigations and several sheriffs were arrested in connection with embezzlement, racketeering and illegal possession of firearms.[18] Former New Haven County Sheriff Henry Healey, who died in 1997, for example, used his office to consolidate power and to make himself one of the state's most influential powerbrokers.[19]

But the catalyst in the move to abolish the office came in the testimony of thirty-three-year-old Sandra Caruso. Arrested in connection with a traffic violation, she was placed in a New Haven County sheriff's van in 1999 along with thirteen male prisoners. Shackled and handcuffed, she was helpless when the men broke through a partition and took turns raping her as she screamed in vain for help.[20]

The sheriff system in Connecticut was replaced by a statewide marshal system whereby appointed marshals would be accountable to state authorities as opposed to the old system where sheriffs answered only to voters. "All it does," said one opponent, "is change the name on the door" while substituting one form of patronage controlled by the legislature and governor for the old system of patronage controlled by the sheriffs.[21]

Following the historic vote, a letter went out to the deputies of the eight sheriffs' offices from the Connecticut Court Operations Division giving official notification that their offices would cease to exist at midnight on November 30. The letter, dated November 24, informed recipients that enclosed with the letter were four patches for two shirts identifying them as judicial marshals. "…You are hereby directed that effective December 1, 2000, you are to remove your existing deputy or special deputy patches from your clothing and that the enclosed judicial marshal patches are to be sewn on in their appropriate place," the letter said. "Not only will this help to ensure that your conduct is undertaken as a judicial marshal, and therefore assist in providing you the statutory protection…but it will also assist in enduring that only those persons authorized to work as a judicial marshal do so."[22] What started as a routine investigation of the theft of a mailbox belonging to Honolulu's police chief turned into one of the biggest political scandals in Hawaii's history and certainly the biggest involving law enforcement personnel. Before it was over, Police Chief Louis Kealoha and his deputy prosecutor wife Katherine were convicted of using their positions and power to frame a family member and to enrich themselves. It would go down as the single largest public corruption case in Hawaii's fifty years as a state.[23] In 2007, Katherine Kealoha was named trustee for her uncle Gerald Puana and her octogenarian grandmother, Florence. Six years later they sued her, claiming that she'd drained the $200,000 in their bank account. Katherine Kealoha was desperate to destroy her relatives' credibility before the case went to trial. On June 21, 2013, surveillance footage showed the Kealohas' mailbox being stolen from its pedestal. Katherine Kealoha told investigators the mailbox was worth $380, which set its value comfortably above the $300 level making the theft a felony, and her uncle Gerald Puana was charged with the theft.

There were two problems: the mailbox was actually cost only $150 and the perpetrator in the grainy video didn't fit the physical description of Puana. The entire thing, it turned out, was staged. And it also turned out that the Puanas weren't their only victims. To fund their lavish lifestyles—they lived in an exclusive gated community and she drove a Maserati, he wore a Rolex—they swindled more than $500,000 from banks, relatives and acquaintances. Katherine and Louis were charged with conspiracy, obstruction and false statements. Katherine and her brother, Rudolph Puana were also charged in a separate case with bartering opioids for cocaine.

Hawaii was one of only three states that allowed its police officers to actually engage in sex with prostitutes in order to make certain that they had a good case when they made an arrest.[24] Repeal of the exemption of that perk would have left Michigan and Alaska as the only states in the nation where law enforcement officers are still allowed to have sex in the interest of decency and morality.[25]

But all three states still permit police officers to have sexual contact with suspected prostitutes, according to *Justia*, an online legal analysis and commentary service. The rationale given was that undercover officers, in order to be able to catch a sex worker agreeing to exchange sex for money, need to be credible customers.[26]

On a much wider stages, sheriffs in at least 45 of the 50 states have virtually unlimited power to run their offices in any manner they choose, to appoint any political cronies as deputies and to seize private property unchallenged, all while answering to no higher authority.

That is the reason for this book. Abuse of power by those entrusted to protect the citizenry has come under a media microscope on a national scale. With the recent ambushes of law enforcement officers in Baton Rouge and Lake Charles Louisiana, it is understandable that there is an edginess and more than a little apprehension with the answering of each call for help or with each traffic stop. The headlines in all the newspapers and the TV news stories are ample evidence of this. This book does not dwell on the problem of deliberate attacks on police as weighed against the shootings of innocent victims by police (though some instances of senseless shootings by deputies are unavoidably included). Most often, these are events that involve snap judgments that result in tragic results which set off community protests and riots.

Nor is this about the vast majority of law enforcement personnel, including sheriffs and their deputies, who go about their duties and meet their responsibilities honestly and with respect for victims and perpetrators alike. Instead, it is the intent of this book to look at behind-the-scenes of wrongdoing, abuses of offices and of citizens that seem to have become a matter of policy for certain officials. Rather than isolated incidents, we will focus on trends that should—but only rarely do—cause the citizenry to rise up and say, "Enough!"

I first began taking notice of the problem of corruption with sheriffs in my home state of Louisiana. The resulting book, *Louisiana's Rogue Sheriffs: A Culture of Corruption*, led to this broader approach. In my research, I quickly came to realize that Louisiana, even with its obvious abundance of problem sheriffs, is not unique. The story of corrupt sheriffs is a nationwide one and it is more than just a problem: it's an epidemic.

Perhaps that's what prompted the Southern Poverty Law Center to address the growing trend of those "constitutional sheriffs" who are taking it upon themselves to promote open defiance of any federal laws they don't like, be it opposition to gun control proposals, public land use, or immigration policies. The SPLC noted that in 2014, the CSPOA published on its Web page a list of four hundred eighty-five sheriffs from Maryland to Washington State who, in the association's words, "have vowed to uphold and defend the Constitution against [President Barack] Obama's unconstitutional gun measures. The post was later taken down."[27]

Constitutional sheriffs claim to be the supreme law of the land with the unique legal authority to overrule state and federal laws, including the power to prohibit state and federal agencies from enforcing its laws. In June 2022, Barry County, Michigan, Sheriff Dar Leaf led an movement to enlist other sheriffs in seizing voting machines from local officials in an effort to prove there was widespread fraud in the 2020 presidential election. It wasn't Leaf's first rodeo. Prior to the election, he had appeared onstage at an anti-masking rally with three of the men later charged with plotting to kidnap and execute Gov. Gretchen Whitmer.[28]

Leaf's efforts appeared to be getting traction when the CSPOA fell in line in May when it called on sheriffs and police throughout the country "to come together in pursuit of the truth regarding the 2020 election." Mack openly supported Leaf's actions, saying that he would spread the word among the 300 sheriffs he claimed as members of CSPOA. Asked if seizure of voting machines by law enforcement might alarm people, Mack said, "Why, because we're trying to find the truth? If people think a legitimate investigation is a coup, then something's wrong with their brain waves."[29]

CSPOA's right-wing rhetoric was ramped up during the COVID-19 pandemic when many of the "constitutional sheriffs" refused to enforce masking or vaccine mandates. "Many sheriffs got on that bandwagon," said Mark Pitcavage, a senior research fellow at the Anti-Defamation League's Center on Extremism, adding that 2020 "was a very successful year for Richard Mack."[30] The principal intoxicants encouraging such confidence and defiance among these sheriffs are U.S. Code § 1983 and the Eleventh Amendment. Though never once invoking the term qualified immunity, U.S

Code § 1983 comes perilously close when it says:

> Every person who, under color of any statute, ordinance, regulation, custom, or usage, of any State or Territory or the District of Columbia, subjects, or causes to be subjected, any citizen of the United States or other person within the jurisdiction thereof to the deprivation of any rights, privileges, or immunities secured by the Constitution and laws, shall be liable to the party injured in an action at law, suit in equity, or other proper proceeding for redress, **except that in any action brought against a judicial officer for an act or omission taken in such officer's judicial capacity, injunctive relief shall not be granted unless a declaratory decree was violated or declaratory relief was unavailable** (emphasis added).

The second half of the dual protective measures for sheriffs, the Eleventh Amendment, also known as the Sovereign Immunity doctrine, reads in part:

The Judicial power of the United States shall not be construed to extend to any suit in law or equity, commenced or prosecuted against one of the United States by Citizens of another State, or by Citizens or Subjects of any Foreign State.

Sovereign Immunity, described as "anachronistic relic" that "should be eliminated from American law,"[18] is based on British common law which says that the King could do no wrong, though federal and state governments have the ability to waive immunity. While the text of the amendment would affect only diversity jurisdiction of the federal courts, the Supreme Court has interpreted it to prohibit federal suits against unconsenting states as well.

Karen Blum, professor of law at Suffolk University, in 2005 authored a fifty-two-page paper on the difficulties of suing sheriffs entitled *Support Your Local Sheriff: Suing Sheriffs Under § 1983* in which she noted that in claims against sheriffs, "the confusion has been compounded by the ramifications of the United States Supreme Court's decision in *McMillian v. Monroe County*."[31]

In that case, the court affirmed the decision of the Court of Appeals for the Eleventh Circuit which held that an Alabama county sheriff was not a final policymaker for the county in the area of law enforcement in a capital murder case in which the defendant and petitioner was convicted and sentenced to death. The conviction was reversed on appeal because the State had withheld exculpatory evidence. Because the petitioner had already spent six years on death row, he sued Sheriff Thomas Tate.

The Supreme Court ruled, however, that if a sheriff is determined to have been making policy for the state, the plaintiff is prohibited from suing the sheriff in his official capacity since that would be tantamount to a lawsuit against the state, forbidden by both the eleventh Amendment and the Supreme Court. On the other hand, a county, subject to legal action from violations caused by its own policymakers would not be liable for conduct attributed to a sheriff who is a state policymaker. Should a sheriff be found to have performed law enforcement or jail operations as a state official, plaintiffs would be forced to sue the sheriff only in his individual capacity. The county's insurers could refuse to defend or pay judgments against a sheriff in his individual capacity when the sheriff is considered a state, and not a county, official.

In the Alabama case, the district court dismissed claims against Monroe County as well as the official capacity claims against Tate and a deputy who were said to have intimidated a witness into making false statements to implicate the petitioner and to suppress exculpatory evidence.

The court held that Alabama counties lacked authority to make policy in the area of law enforcement and that Tate and his deputy could not represent Monroe County's law enforcement policy.

The decision was affirmed on appeal and then went to the U.S. Supreme Court which found that sheriffs were given "complete authority to enforce state criminal laws in their counties." Moreover, the Supreme Court said that while the sheriff's salary was actually paid by county, the county provides equipment for the sheriff's office, the sheriff's authority is limited to the county, and the sheriff is elected by voters of the county, it was not enough to offset the overriding fact that sheriffs' salaries were set by the legislature, not by county commissioners.

That interpretation drew harsh criticism from Justice Ruth Ginsburg, who when writing for the dissent, who said

> a sheriff locally elected, paid, and equipped, who autonomously sets and implements law enforcement policies op-

erative within the geographic confines of a county, is ordinarily just what he seems to be: a county official. Nothing in Alabama law warrants a different conclusion. It makes scant sense to treat sheriffs' activities differently based on the presence or absence of state constitutional provisions of the limited kind Alabama has adopted.

In Georgia, no opinion was reached by a majority of the Eleventh Circuit Court of Appeals sitting *en banc*, although a plurality did conclude that Georgia's State Constitution made the sheriff in *Greech v. Clayton County* a constitutionally-protected office independent from the defendant Clayton County, thus prohibiting the county from taking any action to affect the sheriff's office. The plurality said that Georgia sheriffs were state officials when carrying out any law-enforcement function.

The Eleventh Circuit, again meeting en banc, did reach a majority opinion on the status of Georgia sheriffs in setting use-of-force policies, ruling that sheriffs, while elected by county voters for the purpose of maintaining peace within the jurisdiction of the county, "directly represents the sovereignty of the State, has no superior in his county, and performs state functions for the sovereign in enforcing the laws and keeping the peace." The court's majority also concluded that neither the county nor the state would be obligated to pay a judgment against a sheriff in his official capacity. Such a judgment, it said would be paid from the sheriff's office's budget.[32]

If the Alabama and Georgia decisions were intended to clear the waters, they only succeeded in further confusion since they did nothing to address the disparate state laws and constitutional provisions of the remaining forty-eight states. The same Eleventh Circuit, for example, said in *Hufford v. Rodgers* that a suit against a Florida sheriff was not prohibited by the Eleventh Amendment because the Florida Constitution says that a sheriff is a county officer, and the sheriff's budget, salary and any judgment against him is paid by the county. Accordingly, while the state does retain control over sheriffs in certain circumstances, the sheriff cannot be considered as acting under the state's control in the enforcement of local ordinances. Because sheriffs' budgets are derived from county taxes and not from state funding, the state would not be liable for judgments against a sheriff.

Likewise, the Seventh Circuit Court of Appeals ruled in *Franklin v.*

Zaruba that an Illinois sheriff does not act for the state when engaged in general law enforcement and in *DeGenova v. Sheriff of DuPage County*, found that the sheriff is an independently-elected constitutional officer…has a legal existence separate from the county and the State, and is thus a suable entity. To even further muddy the waters, the sheriff subsequently settled the suit for $500,000 but in attempts to enforce the judgment, the plaintiffs became ensnarled in a classic *Catch-22* scenario: the sheriff's office received its budget from the county but lacked the authority to levy taxes to fund the judgment. The court agreed that the county was not responsible for payment, prompting an irate appeals court judge to determine:

> [A] state may not evade compliance by modeling its internal organization after a huckster's shell game, so that no matter which entity the plaintiff sues, the state (or its subdivisions) always may reply that someone else is responsible—and that power has been divided in such a fashion that the responsible person can't pay, and the entity that can pay isn't responsible for doing so.

Justices for the California State Supreme Court disagreed with the Alabama ruling in *McMillian* when it ruled in *Streit v. County of Los Angeles* that the sheriff acts for the county and not the state when administering county policy and as such, is subject to being sued. Even though the California Constitution places sheriffs directly under the supervision of the state attorney general, county boards of supervisors supervise the sheriffs, including law enforcement conduct, so long as the board does not obstruct the sheriff's criminal investigations. In essence, under California law, the sheriff is elected by county voters, the office is funded by the county, and the county is liable for tort judgments against the sheriff or his department.

By comparing the various state laws and contrasting state and federal courts within a single state, it's fairly easy to see inconsistencies in the application of Section 1983 jurisdiction. In the case of North Carolina, it is an even knottier problem because there is no method by which a federal court may certify an issue of state law (whether a sheriff is deemed by the state to be a state official) so that a determination may be made as to the ultimate federal issue (whether Eleventh Amendment immunity can be extended to the sheriff).

Blum argues that sheriffs elected by county voters, funded by county budgets and operating mostly within the jurisdiction of their respective counties should not be considered as an arm of the state unless:

the state has signaled its willingness to bear financial responsibility for constitutional harm caused by the particular function performed by a sheriff, through assumption of costs of defense or assumption of the obligation to indemnify the sheriff for any judgment rendered against him or her in his or her individual capacity, or

- the claim asserted by the plaintiff arises from constitutional harm resulting from the sheriff's enforcement of a nondiscretionary, ministerial duty imposed by a particular state court order or state law.[33]

She writes that *McMillian*'s biggest accomplishment was to create "a mess" that has resulted in "judicial opinions too much like mish-mash, - good in a soup, but not so good in legal doctrine," and that the various state and lower federal court opinions that have followed *McMillian* "reflect tedious exercises in sorting out myriad state constitutional and statutory provisions in search of abstract links connecting the sheriff's office to the state."

If a sheriff is acting in nondiscretionary, ministerial enforcement of state law, he is in fact, an agent for the state, and Eleventh Amendment immunity clearly applies, Blum writes. "When the policy is not the state's, the sheriff's office should be treated as an arm of the state only where the state has indicated its real and immediate concern in the matter by assuming the costs of defense or liability."[33]

Predictably, it is this lack of cohesiveness that encourages the mindset of the so-called constitutional sheriffs. If there is no consensus of whether they are agents of the state or the local county, how can there be any clear indication as to what their responsibilities are? The answer to some, like Richard Mack, is to simply enforce those laws with which they agree and ignore those with which they do not.

But the problems run much deeper than philosophical differences over edicts. Too many sheriffs are guilty of prisoner abuses, malfeasance, theft, or myriad other offenses for which they are seldom held accountable. Until sovereign immunity is repealed, until qualified immunity is a distant memory, law enforcement in general and sheriffs in particular, will see nothing to impede their continued trampling of citizens' rights. The fact that sheriffs in particular will see nothing to discourage their behavior is attributable to the ideology of the constitutional sheriff that springs from the provision that sheriffs answer to no authority other than the voters who far too often take far too little time property vet candidates other than from television sound bites. It is my fervent wish that this book might encourage closer scrutiny of those we elect to protect us. At the same time, I write this fully cognizant of the odds against that occurring.

To illustrate the futility of any hope that sheriffs' departments might make any legitimate attempt at improving the way things have always been done, consider this: of more than 3,000 sheriffs' departments in the U.S., only 122 participate in any formal national training standards. Texas, with 254 counties, for example, has precisely two counties enrolled in a national program like the Commission on Accreditation for Law Enforcement Agencies (CALEA). In fact, 33 states have three or fewer counties participating in such programs. Florida leads the pack with seventeen of its 67 counties (25 percent) participating in national accreditation programs.[34]

I support and applaud the many fine sheriffs, deputies and employees of sheriffs' departments throughout the U.S. who quietly go about doing their jobs every day of their working lives. They are to be commended and I would state unequivocally that these hard-working men and women are a solid majority of law enforcement personnel. It's the miscreants of the profession that I have attempted to call out for the defilements of their oaths of office, for their betrayal of our trust.

Because there was no one state that stood apart from the others in terms of abuses on the part of its sheriffs, and for ease of reference for the reader, it was decided that the best way to present my findings was to simply go alphabetically, state-by-state.

1

Sweet Home Alabama

IN 2018, twenty new sheriffs were elected in Alabama. Half of those succeeded incumbents who did not seek reelection and whose handling of the transition was described as professional and congenial. The other ten defeated incumbents. Seven of those had held their positions for 12 years, and another for 16. In only one of those did the transition go smoothly; Mark Pettway, the first Black to be elected sheriff of Jefferson County, which includes Birmingham, succeeded incumbent Mike Hale "without incident," according to Captain David Agee.

Missing or destroyed equipment, scamming a food bank and church, defiance of public records laws, purchasing a beach condo with funds earmarked for feeding prisoners, even allowing a high-risk prisoner to run his drug operation from a computer in the sheriff's office—all pretty much business as usual for the state that still proudly calls itself the "Yellowhammer State," a designation given a company of Mobile soldiers who fought with Confederate Gen. Bedford Forrest in the Civil War.

The most common complaint by the incoming sheriffs was claims of misuse, even misappropriation, of sheriffs' discretionary funds by their predecessors. "Discretionary" means precisely what the word implies, that funds may be used for whatever purpose the sheriff deems necessary to efficiently operate the office. In some cases, discretionary funds found their way into the private bank accounts of outgoing sheriffs. With state legislators typically unwilling to confront the powerful sheriffs, they answer to no one but voters who elect them—or turn them out of office. In 2016, an Alabama sheriff was convicted of corruption and removed from office, the first to leave office other than by death or electoral defeat in fifty years in that state.

In the northern part of the state, Phil Sims defeated twelve-year incumbent Sheriff Scott Walls in Marshall County in June 2018, but said he was barred from entering the sheriff's office by his predecessor until he officially took office at 12:01 a.m. January 14, 2019. What he found when finally allowed to enter was an office stripped bare. Government-issued Smart phones had multiple holes drilled through them, computer hard drives had been removed, records were missing, and more than $30,000 was missing from the jail's commissary fund. Moreover, he found that between December 2017 and August 2018, Walls had wired more than $81,000 from the sheriff's office's general fund into one of his personal accounts (more than $29,000 of that amount after his electoral loss to Sims), and that Walls had gone on a spending spree in the interim between his defeat and when Sims took office. More than $20,000 had been spent on 24,000 rolls of toilet paper, $9,000 on 450 boxes of garbage bags and ten huge drums of dishwashing liquid.[1]

It would be egregious enough if that was the only example of outgoing sheriffs leaving behind a path of destruction of public records and property, but it seems the practice is more the norm than the exception. Besides Walls, eight other incumbent Alabama sheriffs defeated for reelection opted to not cooperate with the new sheriff in town or to trash the place on the way out the door, or worse, both.

In Barbour County, in southeast Alabama, on the Georgia border, Leroy Upshaw who, like Scott in Marshall County, had held office for twelve years was ousted by Tyrone Smith. Upshaw did not go quietly into the night but did give Smith the silent treatment for "over a year," Smith said.

The outgoing lawman ceased issuing pistol permits and terminated the county's jail work-release program, depriving the county of revenue that Smith said he could have used for new body cameras and radar. Additionally, the sheriff's discretionary funds were nearly depleted and the jail food funding was about $6,000 in arrears, and there was little food in the jail's kitchen to feed prisoners when he took office.[2]

Danny Bond unseated incumbent Kenny Harden in Butler County in south-central Alabama, one county removed from the Florida panhandle. Bond said that he and Harden didn't speak between the June election and the following January when he took office. He said Harden and he also differed on the amount of money left in the office's discretionary fund and that the outgoing sheriff provided no transition instructions. "They don't tell you anything or show you anything," he said. "You just have to do it on your own."

Harden, asked about the discretionary funds, said Bond was "just new and don't know how the system works." He insisted he left about $80,000 of discretionary funds for his successor, which was more than the $15,000 he had inherited from his predecessor 12 years prior. He said he never spent discretionary funds on anything personal and that everything purchased was left for Bond.[3]

Covington is one of four counties nestled near the Florida panhandle in which outgoing incumbents made it difficult for their successors to effect a smooth transition. When Blake Turman took office after defeating incumbent Sheriff Dennis Meeks there, he quickly discovered a tangle of electrical cables dangling from a hole in the ceiling of the sheriff's office where a security camera system was supposed to be. "He (Meeks) spent $2,800 putting the closed-circuit camera system there, Turman said. "Now it's gone."

The camera system wasn't the only thing that Turman found to be missing. Records were destroyed or removed and public accounts were depleted in order to purchase a new computer system that the office could not use because of its incompatibility with the office's communications provider.

Even more serious was Turman's claim that more than $100,000 in military surplus equipment—part of more than $414,000 of military surplus transferred to the department under the federal 1033 program—was unaccounted for. "We looked high and low, all over our county properties," Turman said. "We called deputies that quit, people that are no longer with us and everything. We rounded up everything we could, but everything else we can't find." The missing military hardware included night-vision sniper scopes, ballistic eyewear, binoculars, and infrared illuminators.

He said he sought assistance in locating the missing equipment from his predecessor, but "they really couldn't care less."

Turman, a former Alabama state trooper, also discovered a $40,000 shortfall in the jail food fund. "I have no idea where it went," he said. Meeks, Turman added, denied his offer to help inventory the office following the election.

Meeks also spent $6,200 of sheriff's office discretionary funds on things like coloring books, Frisbees, pencils and other promotional items emblazoned with his name—after he'd lost the election to Turman. Turman said he could have used the discretionary funds to better equip his deputies who he said were armed with a variety of mismatched pistols, many of which required different caliber ammunition.

Meeks' response was to call Turman a liar. "Every bit of that (jail fund) money is in that account. I could've spent every bit of [it] if I wanted to, because I was the sheriff, but I didn't. Until January 14, I was still sheriff and I still had to operate the sheriff's office and had to spend money. I couldn't wait for his little butt to get here." Meeks also spent more than $7,400 in August 2018, after losing his reelection bid, on 41,000 rounds of ammunition which was several times the department's average monthly expenditure on ammunition. "You can't find those bullets," Turman said. "I searched and you can't find them."

He speculated that deputies may have used some of the ammunition at the gun range where each deputy would have been required to fire about one hundred fifty pounds yearly to re-qualify to carry pistols under Police Officer Standards and Training (P.O.S.T.). But since only about 20 deputies were authorized to carry weapons in 2018, that would account for only 3,000 rounds. The sheriff's office should have retained possession of the remaining ammunition, he said.

Another $1,500 was spent by Meeks following his defeat to pay for deputies' memberships to the Andalusia Health & Fitness, a gym owned by his daughter and son-in-law.[4]

In Crenshaw County, two counties removed from the neighboring Florida panhandle, Mickey Powell lasted only one four-year term before voters decided enough was enough. He was defeated by Terry Mears who received less than two hours of transitional assistance—on the day before he took office.

After taking office, Mears found that Powell had spent thousands of dollars of discretionary funds in his final months in office on purchases Mears felt were unnecessary and that the "upward of $73,000" in the discretionary fund remaining turned out to be closer to $20,000 or $30,000." He said he felt Powell "may have been just making up numbers."

To add insult to injury, Mears did not even have a badge during his first six weeks in office. Powell had badges made for every incoming sheriff's office employee—except for Mears.

Powell did not respond to repeated requests for comment.[5]

In north Alabama, Jim Underwood was ousted by challenger Nick Smith after only four years as the sheriff of Walker County. In what has become a familiar refrain, Smith said he was not allowed to enter the sheriff's office until two days before the election.

He also said his predecessor spent $62,000 more of discretionary funds in the three months following his defeat than was spent over the ten previous months. Purchases included $9,000 for rubber gloves, purchased at $70 per box and $13,000 for a new washing machine for the jail. Smith said he went online and found gloves for $10 a box and a similar washing machine for $1,800. He said Underwood also purchased four new vehicles for the sheriff's office, including a $33,000 Toyota Camry.

Contacted for a comment on Smith's allegations, Underwood acknowledged the prices for the gloves and washing machine seemed excessive but said a county employee, not he, decided which products to purchase. He said he only used the discretionary funds for legal purchases for the sheriff's department. "There's no way I would jeopardize a 45-year career in law enforcement for some monetary amount."[6]

Byron Yerby said he was not allowed into the Fayette County sheriff's office until 12:01 a.m. on January 14, 2019, six months after he defeated incumbent Rodney Ingle. He claimed the jail food fund was so exhausted that there was only enough food for one meal and that the county commission found it necessary to provide money to feed the inmates. Yerby said the day before the election that there were several thousand dollars in the accounts.

Not so, Ingle said while confirming that he and Yerby did not communicate for months. He provided copies of cashier's checks that showed where he paid Yerby $9,300 from a jail food account—in Ingle's name. He said he did not know precisely how much money was left in the discretionary accounts but said Yerby's claim that they were nearly depleted was "a joke" and added that money spent from the funds "was used for something legitimate."[7]

Only a few miles from Fayette County lies Lawrence County. Both are in northwest Alabama, near the border of northeast Mississippi. After he defeated incumbent Lawrence County Sheriff Gene Mitchell, Max Sanders was not allowed in the sheriff's office until 12:01 a.m. January 14, 2019. Between the June 2018 election and Sanders's inauguration, Mitchell used $215,000, more than half the office's discretionary funds, to purchase seven 2019 Chevy Tahoes for the department. Mitchell said the vehicles were not for anyone's personal use but for the department and would've been purchased "whether I stayed or not."

But on another, more controversial issue, Sanders said Mitchell sold nearly $6,000 of food from the jail's pantry to the county and personally kept the funds, further limiting resources available to Sanders upon becoming sheriff.[8]

A policy instituted by Governor Kay Ivey in 2018 actually made such practices legal but most incoming sheriffs said their predecessors chose not to take advantage of the loophole.

The same could not be said of outgoing Sheriff Todd Entrekin of Etowah County who made national headlines for the unabashed manner in which he took advantage of that loophole to redirect some $750,000 in funds earmarked to feed prisoners into his personal bank account over his final three years in office. Nearly $270,000 of that was transferred to Entrekin's personal checking account during his last six months in office.

After news broke in March 2018 about the manner in which he received legal additional "compensation" over and above his five-figure salary, he was denied a fourth four-year term when challenger Jonathon Horton, the Rainbow City police chief, defeated him in the June 2018 primary election.

Horton, like the other victorious challengers, said he had seven months between winning the primary and taking office "with zero transitional assistance from the past administration."

Entrekin's attorney denied the lack of cooperation, saying that Entrekin reached out to Horton on two different occasions but received no response. Entrekin earlier said he had a legal right to leftover jail food funds under a Depression-era law.

In September 2017, Entrekin and his wife Karen purchased a four-bedroom house in an upscale section of Orange Beach on Alabama's Gulf Coast, aka the "Redneck Riviera," as the Alabama-Florida stretch that includes Gulf Shores and Orange Beach in Alabama, and Destin and Panama City in Florida is known. The house purchased by the Entrekins included an in-ground pool and canal access. The $740,000 property is one of several properties owned by the couple either jointly or separately and assessed at a value of more than $1.7 million.

Entrekin supplemented his $93,000 sheriff's salary with the additional "compensation" from a source he identified in ethics disclosure forms as "Food Provisions." He even paid an Etowah County man to mow his lawn in 2015 via checks drawn on the "Sheriff Todd Entrekin Food Provision Account." (A similar effort by Shreveport, Louisiana Commissioner of Public Safety George D'Artois to pay reelection campaign consultant

Jim Leslie with a city check and Leslie's refusal to accept payment in that manner led to D'Artois' implication in Leslie's subsequent murder in 1976.)

The money in the food account was allocated by federal, state and municipal governments to feed inmates in the Etowah County jail, but was not used in that manner and instead was pocketed for Entrekin's personal use, according to a story written by Connor Sheets for AL.com.[10]

Entrekin, ever-defiant, defended the practice, saying, "This is a jail. This is not a bed and breakfast. If you're used to eating grandma's fried chicken, ordering pizza several times a week, you're not going to be happy. I haven't done anything wrong," he said. "If it's wrong, then somebody needs to change the law."[11]

The legislature, subsequent to the negative publicity about Entrekin's extravagant spending habits, did precisely that; it passed a law prohibiting sheriffs from keeping funds allocated to feed state inmates that weren't used for that purpose. Attorneys and law professors agree that while the sheriffs like Entrekin may have been in compliance with state law in keeping surplus funds for personal use, they may be in violation of federal law by also keeping federal jail food money.

Two civil rights groups filed lawsuits naming 49 Alabama sheriffs who the plaintiffs said converted jail food funds for their personal use. The two groups alleged the sheriffs abused state law in the practice.

That's 73 percent of Alabama's 67 counties in which sheriffs were incentivized to malnourish prisoners for the sake of being able to draw down excess food funds into their private bank accounts. In 2005, Mobile County Sheriff Jack Tillman was indicted for converting food funds to a retirement account for himself. He later pleaded guilty to perjury and an ethics violation and returned the money.

In 2009, Morgan County Sheriff Greg Bartlett was jailed by a federal judge for pocketing $212,000 from the fund while feeding prisoners stale corn dogs he purchased for $500. The inmates got the corn dogs for breakfast, lunch and dinner—for three months.

U.S. District Judge U.W. Clemon ordered court security to arrest "Sheriff Corndog" Bartlett at the end of a hearing that produced graphic testimony from underfed prisoners. Judge Clemon said the Alabama law allowing sheriffs to take home surplus meal money was "probably unconstitutional" and that Bartlett "makes money by failing to spend the allocated funds for food for inmates."

The law did not require that the money paid by the state be spent on food. At the hearing, ten prisoners said their meals were so meager they were forced to purchase snacks, sometimes at hundreds of dollars per month, at a for-profit store run by jailers and which generates profits for the sheriff's office. Some prisoners said they supplemented their meals by spending as much as $20 per week or more on chips, oatmeal pies and other junk food at the jail commissary.[13]

Morgan County remained under a federal court order to spend its jail food money on actual food even after Bartlett left office but his successor, Ana Franklin, invested $150,000 of the office's food funds in a used car lot operated by her boyfriend, a felon who had previously been convicted of bank fraud. Franklin was found in contempt of court for violating the consent decree and fined a mere thousand dollars, an amount hardly sufficient to discourage six-figure rake-offs.

Ripping off his department's food fund and using the money to purchase a luxury home on the Alabama Gulf Coast is bad enough if that were former Sheriff Todd Entrekin's only problem.

But it isn't.

Two bloggers posted stories in 2018 suggesting that he was under investigation for running a pedophile ring in the early 1990s when he was commander of the Etowah County Sheriff's Office's drug task force.

One blog post quoted a woman named Mary Elizabeth Cross, who said in 1992, when she was 15 years old, she had sex with Entrekin on four occasions and that he regularly had sex with multiple underage girls at "pedophile parties" attended by other law enforcement officers.

Huffingtonpost.com quoted Cross as saying she did not resist Entrekin's advances but did witness him rape another underage girl who said no. She said there were also drugs present at the parties given by Entrekin. "I was fifteen," she said. "It was right before my sixteenth birthday and I remember telling everyone I couldn't wait to turn sixteen so I could drive."

Entrekin denied the woman's claims. "I've never had sex with any fifteen-year-old girl or had drugs around or anything. I have never done drugs in my life," he said, adding he didn't even know Cross. "That's the most absurd thing I've ever heard of. Never, ever has anything like that happened before."[15]

When Monroe County Sheriff Thomas Tate opened his books, it was revealed he had converted $110,000 of food funds to personal use but at least he was compliant with Alabama's Open Records Act. The 49 sheriffs named as defendants in the lawsuits filed by the Southern Center for Human Rights and the Alabama Appleseed Center for Law and Justice weren't as cooperative as Tate. In a convoluted argument, they claim through the Alabama Sheriffs' Association that the moment they receive food money from the state, it becomes their personal money and that receipts, check registers, ledgers and canceled checks are personal information and not subject to public scrutiny.[14]

More than 30 years before the exposé that revealed Tate as one of those sheriffs who squirreled away money intended to feed inmates for their personal use, a revelation that he said "hurt his feelings," he was involved in a much more serious and higher profile transgression that wrongly placed a defendant on Alabama's death row for six years.

Tate's handling of the 1986 murder of eighteen-year-old Ronda Morrison, an employee of a Monroeville dry cleaners, could hardly have been more ham-handed and illegal. When he finally arrested Walter McMillian after a six-month investigation turned up no other suspects, the sheriff managed to have McMillian placed on death row before he was even put on trial, much less convicted of the murder.

Tate told McMillian, "I don't give a damn what you say or what you do. I don't give a damn what your people say, either. I'm going to put twelve people on a jury who are going to find your goddamn black ass guilty."[16]

Following his exoneration based on Tate's withholding exculpatory evidence in his initial trial, McMillian sued Tate and Monroe County. That's when McMillian learned another hard truth about justice: Sheriff Tate was protected from liability based on immunity laws. Despite overwhelming proof that Tate had suppressed evidence that would have cleared McMillian, the district court dismissed McMillian's claims, holding that Tate's unlawful acts were not reflective of Monroe County policy because in Alabama, the county has no authority to make law enforcement policy.

The case made it all the way up to the U.S. Supreme court where the lower court's decision was upheld in a rather convoluted 5-4 decision written by Chief Justice William Rehnquist that said that ruling, agreeing that a sheriff acting in his law enforcement capacity is not a policymaker for the county. Alabama sheriffs, when carrying out their enforcement duties, the court said, represent the State of Alabama, not their counties. The court rejected arguments that the result would create a lack of uniformity in Alabama by permitting sheriffs to be classified as state officials in some states and county officials in others.

Justice Ruth Bader Ginsburg wrote a scathing dissent in which she pointed out that Alabama law in several instances refers to sheriffs as county officials, noting that a 1991 amendment to the state constitution said that the "sheriff, a 'county officer,' shall be elected to [a] four-year-term" and that "sheriffs shall be compensated out of the county treasury in the same manner as 'other county employees.'"

She added that Tate "owes his position as chief law enforcement officer of Monroe County to the county residents who elected him, and who can unseat him." She again cited the state constitution which said, "A sheriff shall be elected in each county by the qualified electors thereof." Ginsburg said that on the ballot, candidates for the office of sheriff are grouped with candidates for other county offices, not with state office candidates. "Sheriff Tate, in short, is in vital respects a county official. Indeed, one would be hard-pressed to think of a single official who more completely represents the exercise of significant power within a county," she wrote. "Nothing in Alabama law warrants a different conclusion."[17]

The bottom line, then, in this tragic story is that an innocent man was subjected to six years on Alabama's death row because a sheriff knowingly withheld evidence that would have eliminated him as a suspect in the murder of Ronda Morrison. The sheriff was not only protected from liability based on the creative interpretation of immunity laws, but he was allowed to remain in office until his retirement in 2019.

In July 2016, Alabama Supreme Court justices found Sumpter County Sheriff Tyrone Clark guilty of willful neglect of duty and corruption in office, a decision that made Clark the first sheriff in that state to be removed from office for reasons other than retirement, death or electoral defeat in nearly half-a-century.

His removal from office came just five years after he was first elected in 2011 but his legal problems would continue for several more years.

Attorney General Luther Strange, who in 2017, was appointed to fill U.S. Sen. Jeff Sessions' unexpired term after Sessions was named U.S. Attorney General by President Donald Trump, said it was the first time in 44 years that an Alabama sheriff had been convicted after impeachment. "It's extraordinarily rare, but it's extraordinarily important because a violation of public trust by a law enforcement official is about the highest level of corruption I can imagine," he said.[18]

Among the charges brought against Clark was the granting of trustee status to prisoner Rodney Coats who was in jail under $675,000 bond on eight charges pending against him. Coats was granted access to the sheriff's laptop which he used to monitor his drug operations from jail, according to testimony given during his impeachment trial.

One woman testified that she had been held against her will in a trailer controlled by Coats and equipped with surveillance cameras that fed into the sheriff's laptop computer. She said she was repeatedly required to bring drugs to Coats in his jail quarters and that he and detention officers, including Clark, sexually assaulted her.[19]

Less than a year after his conviction, Clark was named in a lawsuit by a former female detention officer at the jail for sexual harassment.

Debra Hopson, who worked for the Sumpter County Sheriff's Department from May 2015 to February 2016, sued Clark, Clark's successor Sheriff Brian Harris and the sheriff's department in U.S. District Court for the Northern District of Alabama's Western Division in April 2017.

She said Clark began demanding oral sex only days after she started work at the jail, asking her if she "was ready to pay her debt for being hired," according to her petition. She said she testified against Clark in his impeachment trial. She claimed that she re-applied for employment to the department in writing, but that Harris did not re-hire her. She attributed the department's refusal to re-hire her to retaliation for her testimony.[20]

In November 2018, nineteen months after Hopson's lawsuit was filed and 30 months after his Supreme Court conviction, Clark was back in court where he pleaded guilty to eight criminal charges, including six felonies.

District Attorney Greg Griggers said, "We have been dealing with this case for three years. It was never my goal to send Tyrone Clark to prison. My goal was to remove him from office, hold him accountable for his crimes and to get rid of what had become a sickness on law enforcement in Sumter County."

The charges to which Clark pleaded guilty included:

- Two counts of unlawful employment of county inmates who did work on two houses owned by Clark;
- Three counts of ethics violations for using his office for personal

gain, including (1) charging inmates a portion of their earnings from working outside of jail without having an authorized work release program, pocketing the money they earned, (2) the work on his home, and (3) pocketing money from the sale of phone cards to inmates;
- Promoting prison contraband, including providing an inmate with a gun and keys to the jail that would allow the inmate to escape;
- Promoting prison contraband, including allowing the inmate to come and go and to access a room where he ran a drug operation and engaged in other illicit activities;
- Conspiracy to commit a controlled substance crime.

Perjury and human trafficking charges against Clark were dropped.[17]

2

Arizona: From Earp to Arpaio

ANY DISCUSSION of sheriff corruption in Arizona must necessarily begin and end with Joe Arpaio. But that's not to say there weren't others in the Grand Canyon State who didn't run afoul of the law or who failed to meet ethical standards.

Of course, that's not to say that with the likes of Cochise County Sheriff Johnny Behan and gunfighter Wyatt Earp, the state wasn't already steeped in the tradition of shady lawmen. Animosity erupted between the two men when Sheriff Behan did not follow through on his promise to appoint Earp as undersheriff. Behan ultimately befriended Ike Clanton whose brother was killed in the infamous Gunfight at Tombstone's O.K. Corral between the Earp brothers and the Clantons.

Behan, appointed in 1881 as the first sheriff of Cochise County, had signed as a guarantor of a loan to Ike Clanton and testified against the Earps in their trial following the gunfight. Rumored to be on the payroll of the Clantons, Behan was responsible for collecting prostitution, gambling, liquor and theater fees in Cochise County for which he received 10 percent of all proceeds. Seen as head of the so-called "Ten Percent Ring," a reputation for graft dogged him throughout his tenure as sheriff. He was eventually arrested and removed from office.[1]

But only Joe Arpaio would employ armored vehicles, a tank and actor Steven Seagal to raid a flock of chickens in March 2011.

The entire event was being filmed or staged, as the attorney for the property owner claimed, as part of Seagal's TV reality show, *Lawman*, and the actor was perched on the tank when it pushed over the wall of a building that Arpaio thought housed an illegal cockfighting ring. Seagal had been fired from his reserve deputy position in Jefferson Parish, Louisiana, and had moved his show to Maricopa County where Arpaio rolled out the welcome mat for him.

"Animal cruelty is one of my pet peeves," the actor said. Then, describing his role as if the entire affair had been a major operation, he said, "I came in on the 150 (tank) and we broke down the gate. I deployed out on the side of the house and guarded one side of the house, to see if anyone would run out."[2]

Arpaio and Seagal seemed made for each other, but Arpaio would subsequently be voted out of office, be found guilty of criminal contempt by a federal judge, and Seagal would move this reality show to New Mexico, all within a span of less than six years. But only a month after his conviction, Donald Trump, who won election the same night Arpaio was defeated, came to his rescue with a full presidential pardon.

The man who would come to personify a special contempt for Hispanics was born in Springfield, Massachusetts, of parents who had immigrated to this country from Italy,[3] an irony forever lost on the self-proclaimed "America's toughest sheriff."

After his discharge from the U.S. Army, he began his law enforcement career as a police officer in Washington, D.C. He migrated to Las Vegas, Nevada, in 1957 where he worked as a police officer for six months before his appointment as a special agent with the Federal Bureau of Narcotics, the forerunner of the Drug Enforcement Administration (DEA), where he would spend the next thirty years.[4]

Between the time of his retirement from DEA in 1987 and his election to his first of six terms as sheriff in 1992, Arpaio worked for his wife's travel agency where he sold passage on the Phoenix E space rocket which was scheduled to launch in 1992, on the 500th anniversary of Christopher Columbus's voyage to the new world. Though he claimed in 1988 that the first nineteen flights had been booked, no flights were ever made.[5]

Arpaio was notorious for forcing inmates to wear pink underwear and quartered them in Korean War-era tents in what he described as concentration camps under an intense Arizona sun that baked the state in temperatures of 118 degrees. Inside the tents, temperatures reached as high as 145 degrees.[6] He told complaining inmates, "It's 120 degrees in Iraq and the soldiers are living in tents and they didn't commit any crimes, so shut your mouths."[7] It earned the adoration of political conservatives, the combination of hatred and fear of Hispanics, and ultimately, the wrath of the federal courts.

Maricopa County is home to the Phoenix-Mesa-Glendale metro area, and with 4.4 million people, it is far and away Arizona's most populous county and the fourth-largest in the nation, larger even than twenty-three U.S. states. He quickly gained notoriety by:

- Banning girlie magazines;
- Feeding inmates Nutraloaf, moldy bread, rotten fruit, and other contaminated food recovered from food rescue;
- Limiting meals to twice daily;
- Keeping prisoners in overcrowded conditions,[8] and
- Handing down his pink underwear edict.

As he played more and more to the media spotlight, he seemed to focus less and less on his duties. He once boasted that he averaged 200 television appearances per month.[9] He became so enamored with his own reputation that he even began selling customized pink boxer shorts, complete with the Maricopa County sheriff's logo and "Go Joe" printed on them, as a fundraiser for the Sheriff's Posse Association. Arpaio refused to provide an accounting for money raised through the campaign despite allegations of misuse of funds.[10]

Arpaio, it seemed, could not escape legal problems, not that there was any evidence that he tried to avoid trouble and bad publicity. Federal Judge Neil V. Wake ruled in 2008 and again in 2010 that the sheriff and the Maricopa County jails had violated constitutional rights of inmates in issues of medical and other care.[11]

In 2011, a Maricopa County Office of Management and Budget found that he had misspent nearly a hundred million dollars over a five-year period. Money from a restricted detention fund, earmarked for the purchase of jail items like food, detention officers' salaries and equipment was used instead to pay employees to patrol the county. The analysis also showed that several sheriff's office employees whose salaries were paid from the fund were working job assignments that differed from what was recorded in their personnel records. Arpaio, it seems, kept a second set of personnel books detailing actual work assignments which varied from information contained in the county's official human resources records.

Money from the detention fund was also used to pay for a trip to Alaska where deputies stayed at a fishing resort, for trips to Disneyland, and for a $456,000 bus purchased in violation of county procurement regulations. Arpaio also used the detention fund to pay for investigations of political rivals and for activities of his human-smuggling unit.[12]

The year before, in September 2010, a devastating sixty-three-page internal memo written by Maricopa Deputy Chief Frank Munnell surfaced. It turned a harsh light on the department when it revealed that sheriff's department brass "willfully and intentionally" committed criminal acts by attempting to obstruct justice, tamper with witnesses, and destroy evidence.[13]

The memo prompted the FBI and Department of Justice to launch criminal investigations of the sheriff's department.[14]

Sometimes it took years for justice to prevail. In October 2007, Mike Lacey and Jim Larkin, founders of the *Phoenix New Times*, were arrested after publishing a news story on a grand jury investigation involving Arpaio's office. They were arrested by plainclothes detectives, handcuffed, put in SUVs with tinted windows and taken to jail. Only after a public outcry over the arrests were charges subsequently dropped.

The pair filed suit for violation of their civil rights and in 2012, five years after their arrests, the U.S. Court of Appeals for the Ninth Circuit ruled that they could proceed with their lawsuit against the sheriff's office. A year later, the Maricopa County Board of Supervisors voted to settle the suit for $3.75 million. They used the proceeds of the judgment to establish an endowed chair professorship at the Walter Cronkite School of Journalism and Mass Communication and to establish the Lacey & Larkin Frontera Fund which advocates for migrant rights and freedom of speech issues in Arizona.[15]

The two reporters were not the only ones Arpaio harassed. Between 2008 and 2010, he and former Maricopa County attorney Andrew Thomas subjected political opponents to numerous corruption investigations reminiscent of the Nixon years. The list of those investigated included judges, the Phoenix mayor, the Arizona attorney general, one of his election opponents, an ACLU attorney, county supervisors and administrators.[16]

The investigations resulted in criminal charges being filed against several individuals who the pair tried to get a grand jury to indict. Instead, Arpaio and Thomas lost every case either by adverse court rulings or by simply dropping the case and the grand jury, in a rare action, ordered the investigations terminated. Arpaio and Thomas's actions had cost the county nearly six million dollars – before the spate of lawsuits that followed. Their harassment also prompted the Arizona Supreme Court to disbar Thomas for having "outrageously exploited power, flagrantly fostered fear, and disgracefully misused the law," adding that had his actions been a criminal case instead of civil, "we are confident that the evidence would establish this [as a] conspiracy beyond a reasonable doubt."[17]

Arpaio in turn became the subject of an investigation for political motivated prosecutions, described by a former U.S. attorney as "utterly unacceptable." Phoenix Mayor Phil Gordon called Arpaio's actions a "reign of terror."[18]

No fewer than eleven targets of Arpaio's and Thomas's investigations subsequently filed lawsuits or legal claims. To underscore the recklessness of the pair, Maricopa County settled all eleven cases before any of the cases went to trial. The total tab for the eleven settlements was more than $12.1 million.

By June 2014, Maricopa County taxpayers had coughed up more than $44 million as a result of Arpaio's and Thomas's campaign of intimidation and retribution. Five years after Arpaio had been defeated, the county was still paying for his sins. In October 2021, Maricopa County approved a $5 million settlement with Uncle Sam's Restaurant owner Bret Frimell just weeks after another settlement of $400,000 with the restaurant manager, Lisa Norton. The two were arrested by Arpaio's deputies in January 2014 on employment-related identity theft charges that were dismissed when a judge ruled that a deputy recklessly disregarded the truth in affidavits used to obtain a search warrant. The judge found there was no probable cause to support the warrants. Nine employees of Uncle Sam's were arrested in the raid.

Frimmel and Norton claimed they were arrested after Frimell was asked by the U.S. Justice Department for assistance in a since-settled civil rights lawsuit accusing Arpaio's office of racial profiling, retaliating against the sheriff's critics and other civil rights violations.[19]

Arpaio's legal problems predated his arrest of the two reporters and the investigations. It had already been shown years before that Arpaio was not above orchestrating events to satisfy his unquenchable thirst for publicity.

In 1999, near the end of his second term in office, undercover deputies arrested eighteen-year-old James Saville, charging him with plotting to kill Arpaio with a pipe bomb. Arpaio, always on the lookout for a TV camera, quickly appeared in interviews to boast that plots to kill him were "not going to bother me."[20]

After languishing in jail for nearly four years, Saville was acquitted by a Maricopa County jury in 2003. Rather than seeing a plot to kill the sheriff, jurors were convinced that Saville had been entrapped by the sheriff's office as part of an elaborate publicity stunt by Arpaio. Jurors interviewed after the trial accused Arpaio of a "media ploy," a "publicity stunt at the expense of four years of someone's life," and "a big setup from the beginning."[21]

The following year, Saville sued Arpaio and Maricopa County for wrongful arrest and entrapment. In 2008 the county settled with Saville for $1.1 million, plus an unspecified amount from the county's insurer.[22]

In 2005, while the Saville lawsuit began winding its way through the legal system, Debra Braillard, a diabetic, was arrested and jailed on a minor drug-possession charge. Deputies ignored her pleas for medical treatment as she defecated and vomited on herself. She soon went into a diabetic coma and died while chained to a hospital bed. When her family sued, the county, in what would become a familiar trend, settled for $3.25 million—but only after spending an additional $1.8 million in legal fees.[23]

Two years after Braillard's death, in 2007, Manuel de Jesus Ortega Melendres, a Mexican tourist, was a passenger in a car stopped in Cave Creek in Maricopa County. Ortega Melendres claimed he was unlawfully detained for nine hours as a result of racial profiling. The ACLU filed suit on his behalf and the lawsuit was soon expanded when several other individuals joined with similar complaints. The lawsuit claimed that Arpaio and the sheriff's department engaged in a pattern of targeting Latino drivers and passengers in Maricopa County during traffic stops, and that practice discriminated on the basis of race in violation of the Fourteenth Amendment, which resulted in extended detentions in violation of the Fourth Amendment.[24]

The lawsuit was assigned to U.S. District Judge G. Murray Snow, and the case would eventually bring not only in a judgment adverse to Arpaio, but would also result in ramifications that surpassed the initial claim of profiling and rights violations.

Judge Snow on September 11, 2014, awarded more than $4.4 million in attorney fees to the four legal organizations that litigated the case.[25]

The decision came only three months after the *Phoenix New Times*, quoting an unnamed former detective with the sheriff's office's Special Investigations Division, reported on June 4 that Arpaio had launched a criminal investigation of Judge Snow and the U.S. Department of Justice.

Moreover, the former detective said Arpaio, convinced that Judge Snow and the DOJ had engaged in a conspiracy against him, was personally supervising the investigation.[26]

In an April 2015 civil contempt hearing, Arpaio testified that his attorney, Tim Casey, had hired a private investigator to investigate Judge Snow's wife and that the sheriff's office paid for an investigation by a Seattle computer expert to determine whether the DOJ had penetrated Arpaio's emails and those of local attorneys and judges, including Judge Snow.

Earlier, however, MCSO Chief Deputy Jerry Sheridan had testified there was no investigation into Snow, his wife or his family. The conflicting testimony created a potential ethics conflict for attorney Casey and he promptly withdrew as legal counsel for Arpaio and the sheriff's office.[27]

Judge Snow, during a status conference on May 14, said a court-appointed monitor had documents discovered from the "Seattle Operation" that revealed "an attempt to construct a conspiracy involving this court" and others, including the DOJ, former U.S. Attorney General Eric Holder, former Phoenix Mayor Phil Gordon and former MCSO Executive Chief Brian Sands.[28]

There followed unsuccessful attempts by Arpaio to remove Judge Snow from the case and Snow eventually ruled Arpaio in contempt, saying that he and others had made intentionally false statements about efforts to investigate him.[29]

In all, Arpaio and his office were named as defendants in dozens of civil lawsuits filed by those arrested by him and his deputies who ultimately cost Maricopa County taxpayers more than $140 million, an amount that included settlements, awards, and attorney fees. He was also made a defendant in federal litigation, one of which resulted in an injunction barring him from conducting further immigration roundups. In defiance of that injunction, his office continued to detain persons "without reasonable suspicion that a crime has been or is being committed. That ruling would not be handed down until after he left office.[30]

Perhaps Arpaio's greatest sin, however, was not in what he did as sheriff but instead, what he did *not* do.

In addition to his housing preferences, dress codes for prisoners, and racial profiling however, was a deeper, darker side that surfaced briefly in 2011 but which seemed to receive only passing attention. A financial audit revealed that he misspent $100 million on immigration sweeps and on investigations into anyone who questioned his policies, and the El Mirage police department claimed that he neglected to investigate 400 sex crimes dating back to 2007. The U.S. Justice Department launched an investigation of alleged racial profiling and the U.S. Attorney's office opened its own investigation into whether he abused his power by targeting judges and other elected officials who disagreed with his policies.[31]

The hiring practices of Arpaio's office also came under scrutiny in 2011 when it was revealed that eight family members of Chief Deputy David Hendershott, including his son, as well as several friends of family members, were given jobs with the department at Hendershott's insistence in violation of Maricopa County nepotism prohibitions.

The elder Hendershott, who was pulling down more than $260,000 annually as the result of his having already retired from one government position, would pressure the human resources director to find positions that would get friends or relatives "the most money."

In April 2011, following publication of an internal memo about the jobs Hendershott got for people who became known as "FODs," or "Friends of Dave," Arpaio fired Hendershott, but not before the chief deputy intervened in an investigation of three deputies deemed responsible for neglecting to pursue more than 400 reported sex crimes, including at least 32 cases of reported child molestation dating as far back as 2007.

In 2013, according to a story in the *Phoenix New Times*, Hendershott's successor, Chief Deputy Jerry Sheridan, said the investigation was wrapping up and that it centered on five deputies and two detectives, all of whom had since resigned.

But that contradicted a former lead investigator in the misconduct probe which indicated that the three principal leads were supervisors charged with overseeing the sex-crimes unit: Captain Steve Whitney, Lieutenant Hank Brandimarte, and then-Sergeant Kim Seagraves, who worked as the leader of the sex-crimes unit. All three were still employed by the sheriff's department at the time of the story.

That presented only two alternatives for Sheriff Joe, neither of them good: He either directed Hendershott to not only ignore, but to block the investigations, or he was oblivious to events occurring in his own office.[32]

That many of the cases involved Hispanic victims only served to underscore Arpaio's disdain for minorities. Elizabeth Ditlevson, then-acting director of the Arizona Coalition Against Domestic Violence, described the failure to follow through on the complaints as a matter of "political convenience within the department."[33]

In 2000, for example, it was claimed that the sheriff's office failed to properly investigate the reported rape of a fourteen-year-old by her classmates[34] or the rape of a fifteen-year-old girl committed by two unknown assailants.[35]

Both cases were reported as "exceptionally cleared" one without so much as an investigation, and the other without ever identifying a suspect. In the case of the fourteen-year-old, an identified suspect declined to appear for questioning and the entire matter was subsequently dropped. The fifteen-year-old's case was closed within a month of its being reported and before DNA testing was even completed.[36]

The guidelines for the *FBI Uniform Crime Reporting Handbook*, which are mandatory for all Arizona law enforcement agencies, specify that a case can only be cleared by exception when the perpetrator's identity and location is known and there is sufficient evidence to warrant prosecution but because of special circumstances, such as the suspect's death or the impossibility of extradition, an arrest cannot be made.[37]

"The sheriff's office has its own criteria for clearing cases," Arpaio said without bothering to explain what those criteria were.[38]

When asked by ABC's *Nightline* news program to explain why only 18 percent of cases were actually cleared, with the remaining 82 percent cleared by exception, Arpaio claimed the numbers were inaccurate. "We clear a higher percentage …We clear many, many cases—not 18 percent. But following that interview, statistics provided *Nightline* by the MCSO indicated that of 7,346 reported crimes, the sheriff's department had cleared only 944, or 15 percent, by arrest.[39] KPNX TV News in Phoenix said that under Arpaio, as many as 75 percent of cases may have been improperly cleared (reported as solved) without arrests or proper investigations.[40]

Even more egregious was the news that the Maricopa County Sheriff's Office failed to follow up on no fewer than 32 reported child molestations despite the fact that the suspected perpetrators were known by law enforcement in all but six of the cases. Most of the victims were children of illegal immigrants.[41]

In perhaps the most callous case of all, thirteen-year-old Sabrina Morrison, who suffered from a mental disability, was raped on March 7, 2007, by her uncle, Patrick Morrison. When she told her teacher the following day, the MCSO was notified and a rape test was taken. But the detective assigned to the case told Sabrina and her family there were no obvious signs of sexual assault—no semen and no signs of trauma.

Consequently, Sabrina's family turned on her, calling her a liar. All the while, her uncle continued to rape her, threatening to kill her if she told. She had an abortion after becoming pregnant by him. The family was not told that the rape kit had been tested at the state lab and that the presence of semen was detected. The lab requested a blood sample from the uncle but instead of following up on the request, and making an arrest, the detective filed the crime lab note away and closed the case for four years.

In September 2011, after Sabrina went public with details, the sheriff's office finally got around to obtaining a blood sample from Patrick Morrison. The sample proved to be a DNA match with the semen taken four years earlier. Patrick Morrison was arrested in February 2012 and pleaded guilty. He was sentenced to 24 years in prison.[42]

Arpaio offered a weak apology to "any victims," but in August 2012, Sabrina filed a claim of gross negligence against Maricopa County. In April 2015, the case was settled for $3.5 million.[43]

County supervisors, in response to the sheriff's office scandal over the 400 unsolved sexual assaults, had voted to approve more than $600,000 to fund six additional detective positions in fiscal year 2007 to investigate child abuse. But no new positions were added to the sex-crimes squad and sheriff's administrators were unable to account for where positions were added or what became of the funds after they were added to the budget.[44]

By 2015, Arpaio had taxed the patience of the judicial system to its limits. On June 24, the court ordered U.S. marshals to seize evidence related to contempt of court charges against the sheriff for his failure to stop racial profiling practices as ordered. On May 13, 2016, Arpaio was held in contempt and on October 25, 2016, just two weeks before the election in which Arpaio was seeking re-election to his seventh term, federal prosecutors announced they would press criminal contempt of court charges against him.[45]

On November 7, 2016, the real verdict was in. Paul Penzone, a twenty-one-year veteran of the Phoenix Police Department who had lost by six percentage points to Arpaio four years earlier, beat the long-term incumbent by nearly two hundred thousand votes, 861,757 to 665,581, or 56.3 percent to 43.5 percent, a 19 percentage-point swing from 2012.

But the story of "America's toughest sheriff," the man who promoted the "birther" movement, the insistence that President Barack Obama was not born in this country, was not over just yet. The criminal contempt decision was still pending and on July 13, 2017, the ax fell as U.S. District Judge Susan Bolton wrote that Arpaio "willfully violated an order of the court" by failing to ensure the compliance of his subordinates "and by directing them to continue to detain persons for whom no criminal charges could be filed." His sentencing was scheduled for October 2017.[46]

But then, President Donald Trump, who had earlier attempted to prevail upon then-Attorney General Jeff Sessions to intervene and close the criminal case against the former sheriff,[47] stepped in. On August 25, Trump, calling Arpaio an "American patriot" who had "kept Arizona safe,"[48] issued a full pardon[49], a decision that sparked immediate criticism from U.S. Senators John McCain and Jeff Flake and House Speaker Paul Ryan.[50]

In 2018, Arpaio entered the Republican primary to succeed the late Senator John McCain but received only 19 percent of the vote as Martha McSally won with 52 percent.[51] Later that year, he filed a $300 million defamation suit against *The New York Times*, the *Huffington Post*, *Rolling Stone*, and CNN. The suit was tossed by a federal judge the following year.[52]

Undaunted by the two election defeats and armed with a full pardon from President Trump, the eighty-seven-year-old Arpaio announced in August 2019 that he would seek his old sheriff's post in the 2020 election.

In making his announcement, he promised to re-open his Tent City Jail and renew his old jail policies and "Make Maricopa County Safe Again."[53] He lost the Republican primary by 6,000 votes.

To the immediate south of Maricopa County lies Pima County which abuts Mexico along its southern border. The county seat is Tucson where virtually all the county's one million people reside. One of four original counties in Arizona, it is named after the Pima Native Americans who are indigenous to the area but the American Indian population makes up only 3.3 percent of the population, compared to 74.3 percent white with Mexicans constituting the largest ancestry group. The county has an area of 9,189 square miles, 99.98 percent of which is land, with only 2.1 square miles of water.

As Joe Arpaio's reign of autocratic power was ending in adjacent Maricopa County, more than the hot Arizona climate was beginning to heat up in the adjacent Pima County sheriff's office. Before all was said and done, the FBI would initiate an investigation of the sheriff's office; the department's chief deputy would be indicted and would resign and later enter a guilty plea to misuse of federal funds; the sheriff's chief of staff would end his own life, and the sheriff would be defeated and would retire – sort of.

It all started in late 2015 when *The Arizona Daily Star* revealed that the niece of the sheriff's department's chief deputy was operating restaurants at headquarters and at the jail rent-free, without the requisite contract required of outside vendors, and with taxpayer-purchased equipment and labor.[54]

When the story ran, whistleblowers from within the department began coming forward, and what initially was a case of simple nepotism and violation of county regulations quickly evolved into a full-blown FBI investigation into an interdepartmental conspiracy of money-laundering involving half-a-million dollars of Racketeer Influenced and Corrupt Organizations (RICO) Act funds. Two of the whistleblowers were former

U.S. Surgeon General and long-time deputy chief for the sheriff's department, Dr. Richard Carmona, and Pima County Deputy Sheriff Association President Kevin Kubitskey.

When the department experienced problems with a previous food vendor, that vendor took her refrigerators and equipment with her.

Department officials then purchased twelve thousand dollars-worth of restaurant equipment. Officials initially said RICO dollars were used for the purchases, but later said the money came from the general fund.[55] RICO funds are monies seized from criminals and given to law enforcement agencies and designated specifically for enforcement purposes.

After purchasing the equipment, Chief Deputy Christopher Radtke suggested his niece, Nikki Thompson, a chef who was already known to several members of the department, as the new vendor.[56]

That $12,000 expenditure quickly expanded into a probe of the use of $500,000 in RICO funds inappropriately used to pay for entertainment, tuxedos, banquet food, flowers, furniture and rental of a banquet hall for the department's annual awards banquet. The law allows the purchase of food for deputies while on duty and for the purchase of awards but not for the other expenditures. The RICO funds were moved from the General Fund to the Sheriff's Auxiliary Volunteers (SAV) account from which the illegal purchases were made.[57]

The FBI investigation soon honed in on three top administrators within the Pima County Sheriff's Department: Sheriff Chris Nanos, Chief

Deputy Radtke, and Chief of Staff Brad Gagnepain.[58]

Gagnepain began his career with the department in 1978 as a reserve deputy while still serving in the U.S. Air Force. He was hired full-time as a patrol deputy in 1981 and crime-prevention programs he developed gained him national recognition, according to the *Arizona Daily Star*.

He continued to advance within the department and by 1998, he had been promoted to the rank of major and was named bureau chief, where he remained for nearly seventeen years. He retired in 2014, but only briefly. He returned to the department almost immediately as a special adviser to then-Sheriff Clarence Dupnik and in 2015 he was named by Nanos as chief of staff.[59]

Gagnepain, in 1992, was caught stealing campaign signs belonging to Dupnik's election opponents. The action cost him and a partner in the affair five-day unpaid suspensions. Considered as the driving force behind many of the more questionable practices within the department, Gagnepain oversaw the department's inner workings that came under investigation by the FBI.[60]

On the night of June 19, 2016, Father's Day, Gagnepain entered a neighbor's garage where he took his own life. The manner in which the investigation of the suicide was handled immediately came under question.[61]

Protocol dictated that had Gagnepain's death occurred in his home, it could have been investigated as a suicide. But since it happened in a neighbor's garage, it should have been treated as a homicide and turned over to another agency to investigate.[62]

Instead, Sheriff Nanos and Chief Deputy Radtke immediately took control of the investigation. The pair prevented investigators from reviewing items that might have been relevant, including Gagnepain's cell phone and papers contained in a manila envelope found on the front seat of his vehicle. Sources also later reported that crime scene logs could not be located.[63]

Sergeant Terry Staten, a deputy who was challenging Nanos in the 2016 election and who had been placed on administrative leave without pay because he was running against his boss, went on a local radio talk show to criticize the handling of Gagnepain's suicide. "…Sheriff Nanos showing up on scene, and Deputy Chief Radtke showing up on scene, these things concern me." He went on to say, "You have three people that are under investigation by the FBI. One decides to take his own life—not in his own house—and you have the other two named in the allegations showing up on scene and controlling the entire scene…and then not turning the scene over to another agency to investigate."

Staten said he had heard the crime scene logs did not reflect the presence of Nanos and Radtke, but said he could not confirm that report. "I have been cut from the herd," he said, referring to his being placed on leave for running against Nanos.

Staten, who had the endorsement of the deputies' union, was asked if other agencies would be brought into the investigation. "I don't know," he said. "I think it's probably too late now," adding he was unaware if the Pima County Sheriff's Office had maintained the scene and evidence. Efforts by news media to obtain copies of the investigation reports were unsuccessful.

"We lost one of the great leaders and visionaries in our department's history," Nanos said in an email to department employees the day after Gagnepain's death. "Brad Gagnepain was a behind-the-scenes leader, the man behind the curtain, who had his fingerprints on so many of the successful programs and events in our department…"

Unanswered were three important questions:

- Why was the investigation handled the way it was?
- Why did the sheriff and chief deputy have to come in and take control of the scene?
- Why was the investigation not handed over immediately to another agency?[64]

On October 10, 2016, four months after Gagnepain's death, Radtke, a thirty-year veteran of the Pima County Sheriff's Department and its second in command, was indicted by a federal grand jury for the misuse of RICO funds and promptly submitted his resignation.

Dr. Richard Carmona said he was confident that the FBI investigation would result in an indictment but that Nanos should not be allowed to shift blame. "You're responsible for everything [as sheriff]. Every procedure, and if you don't make sure they're correct, then you should be held accountable. And clearly there's a gap here—a big gap— especially when it results in an FBI investigation, because it's on your watch [that] all of these things occurred."

Union president Sergeant Kevin Kubitskey, who said he had faced retaliation for being a whistleblower, said he was counting on the FBI to dig deeper. "I encourage them to continue on with their investigation, which I know they're doing. I think you're going to see a lot more come from this than just one indictment."[65]

The indictment covered the five-year period from January 6, 2011 to July 11, 2016 and accused Radtke of conspiring with others to commit money laundering. The indictment, handed down by a Utah federal grand jury, said he would donate RICO funds to the Sheriff's Auxiliary Volunteers of Tucson. Then Radtke and others would make it appear that the RICO money was being used appropriately by the SAV by using SAV checks and credit cards to pay for items totaling $500,000 which were in reality, purchases for the sheriff's office.

In a news conference in which Nanos read from a prepared statement and afterward refused to take questions, he called the allegations blatant lies and attempted to turn the conversation away from the indictment and to direct blame on Carmona. "I will state it again," he said. "Dr. Carmona felt slighted that retired Sheriff Dupnik (Nanos's predecessor) did not hand the keys of this organization to him, or make him chief deputy through the years. That brings to question, what deal did Dr. Carmona make with my opponent (Mark Napier)?"

Napier called Nanos's accusations "laughable."[66]

On November 8, the same day that Maricopa Sheriff Joe Arpaio was defeated, Napier, a Republican, defeated incumbent Democrat Nanos in the sheriff's race in Pima County. Napier, who had lost to Clarence Dupnik by a 51-46 percentage point-margin four years earlier, pulled 56 percent of the vote to 44 percent for Nanos.[67]

Nanos, rather than remain on the job through the rest of his term, announced in December he would retire after 35 years in law enforcement, 32 of those in the Pima County Sheriff's Department. He left a budget that was $5.7 million in the red for Napier to deal with.[68]

Fewer than two months later, on February 16, 2017, Radtke, who was facing seven felony charges and substantial fines, entered a guilty plea to three misdemeanors in a plea deal that spared him a jail sentence and which drew the scorn of Kubitskey.

One of the original whistleblowers, Kubitskey expressed his disappointment when he said, "We know there's other[s] involved. And to see that the conspiracy charge was not addressed today raises some questions."

It was interesting to note that instead of the U.S. attorney's office and the FBI issuing a joint press release as is the tradition, the FBI remained silent on the issue. U.S. Attorney John Huber of the District of Utah said, "We have reached a just outcome in this case." He added in what seemed to be more a prediction than fact, "This investigation and prosecution has cleaned the Pima County Sheriff's Office of years of corruption and ensures it will not return. We recognize and commend the excellent work that the FBI in Tucson did on this important case."

The three misdemeanor counts to which Radtke pleaded guilty were:

- He admitted that on May 12, 2011, he participated in using a SAV check for $926.09 to reimburse the sheriff's department special awards fund. He admitted he requested part of that reimbursement for a $250 restaurant bill and tip and that other sheriff's department employees requested $109.09 in reimbursement for a new microwave oven for the sheriff's department's break room.
- Radtke admitted that on July 24, 2014, he participated in using the SAV credit card to purchase two model airplanes for himself and a colleague for $599.90 and to pay $90 for shipping. On July 29, 2014, he participated in using the SAV credit card to pay $50 for a rush shipping charge for the model airplanes.
- He admitted that on April 20, 2015, he participated in using a SAV check to pay an artist $500 to create a menu for the chalkboard at the café at the sheriff's department, even though the café was owned and operated by his niece, not by the sheriff's department.

Napier, who had run a campaign to clean up the department, issued a statement saying his department supported the deal "and understands prosecutorial discretion." He expressed disappointment that Radtke's "egregious criminal violation of public trust resulted in only a misdemeanor plea agreement with potentially an extremely light sanction. Mr. Radtke admits the existence of a sustained criminal conspiracy that spanned eighteen years, with his involvement being approximately six years. This activity shocks the conscience. It violates the honorable standards of law enforcement held by the 1,500 men and women of our department…This is simply unforgivable misconduct on the part of a few."[69]

Radtke received a sentence of one year of probation for each charge, to be served concurrently (meaning each of the three sentences would be lumped together and Radtke would serve only one year). He was fined $3,000 and ordered to complete one hundred hours of community service. The plea agreement also contained a stipulation that he was not to seek work in law enforcement or with Pima County.

Assistant U.S. Attorney David Backman told the court that even though no one else was charged in the case, the investigation revealed that several members of the sheriff's department were involved in schemes to divert RICO money. "We identified a person in the department's upper leadership who was probably more culpable than Mr. Radtke, but he is no longer with us," he said, referring to Gagnepain. "In this case, it's been a huge success. His (Radtke's) resignation was a significant moment, because it took care of the problem."

A furious Kubitskey accosted Backman in the hallway as soon as the courtroom had cleared, telling Backman the plea deal was not justice and that he (Backman) should be ashamed with the manner in which the case was prosecuted.[70]

Even after the dust had finally settled, information continued to leak out which indicated just how deeply the conspiracy to usurp the RICO funds ran. A 2013 memo that surfaced four months after Radtke's sentencing warned top commanders in the department about possible misuse of the funds.

The memo which emphasized the cost of the annual departmental awards ceremony "should not create the appearance of extravagance or impropriety" and that the department should "make changes as needed." A sheriff department official told KGUN-TV reporter Valerie Cavazos he removed the word extravagance when told the term was subjective. The annual awards ceremonies, which cost an average of $50,000, continued for two more years.

"Legal experts tell me dropping that line could show intent and could spell legal trouble," Cavazos said.

Lieutenant Joseph Cameron, who was in charge of the Records department said he believed the commanders who knew about the misuse of RICO funds should be held accountable. "I know that if myself or anyone else did these things we would be out of a job," he said.[71]

Napier appeared to just want the entire matter to go away and for him to run his department. Instead, he was secretly recorded by Cameron as saying, "A lot of people here did not follow the rules. I'm positive of that.

All of my chiefs didn't follow the rules. Many captains didn't follow the rules. That is absolute crystal clear."

But it also surfaced that Cameron may have had his own axe to grind with Napier, who had taken Cameron, then known as Joe Harvey, off patrol duty and put in charge of records 21 years earlier. Dupnik had wanted so badly to fire Harvey for alleged excessive use of force that he went to the Arizona Supreme Court to get him dismissed but the court ruled in favor of the merit commission that gave him his job back.

Harvey returned to work but only after he had his name legally changed to Joe Cameron to avoid being judged or targeted. Under his new name, he won two promotions, first to sergeant and then to lieutenant.

Napier said, "I have no reservation about the FBI investigation at all. I've spoken with them. I believe the investigation was thorough, complete. Quite obviously, if the AG (Arizona attorney general) were to come back and criminally charge five of my commanders, the administrative part is pretty clear, isn't it?"[72]

3

Arkansas: Debit Cards, Conspiracy Theories

PRIVATE PRISONS, prisoner work release programs and prison telephone services have received considerable ink in news reports, mostly negative, but another way to gouge prisoners unfairly received little attention until 2013.

A class-action lawsuit was filed against Benton County, Arkansas Sheriff Kelley Cradduck when prisoners processed into the county jail were issued involuntary prepaid debit cards in amounts identical to any cash taken from them when they were booked into the jail.

Benton County is in the extreme northwest corner of Arkansas and is the headquarters for the Walmart and Sam's Club corporations.

The problem with that procedure, the lawsuit claimed, was that the debit cards carried a weekly maintenance fee of $1.50—even if the card was not used—as well as other fees ranging from $1.50 to check the card's balance, $2.75 for using an ATM, three dollars to transfer money to a bank account, with some fees ranging as high as $38 per transaction.[1]

The lawsuit, which names Yves Adams as one of four lead plaintiffs, claimed that Keefe Commissary Network paid a 34 percent kickback to Cradduck on all gross sales from the commissary, also operated by Keefe. "This kickback is expressly identified and referred to as a 'service fee' in the contract between the two defendants," it said. The contract was signed in April 2012.[2]

A spate of similar lawsuits soon cropped up in Arizona where Bank of America held the vendor rights to the cards, Oklahoma, where Swanson Services Corp. issued the cards, Georgia (First Century Bank), Minnesota (Keefe), and Dallas County, Texas.

The Arkansas case apparently was the first to settle in 2014 on behalf of more than 2,200 people who were arrested or booked into the Benton

County Jail. The county agreed to pay $71,609 into a settlement fund which included $50,385 in legal fees and costs. The four lead plaintiffs received payments of $1,000 each.[3]

The debit card system was endorsed by the California State Sheriffs' Association. The association named Numi Financial on its website as a corporate partner.[4]

A 2018 settlement with Bank of America in Arizona stipulated the return of $168,000 in fees collected, commencing in 2012. BOA further agreed not to collect debit card fees in the future.[5]

The Arizona arrangement with the federal Bureau of Prisons (BOP) appeared to have originated from a no-bid contract between BOA and the U.S. Department of the Treasury. The cards were not reloadable and prisoners had no access to alternative methods of receiving their release funds. The lawsuit in that state claimed "unjust enrichment, conversions, and unfair and deceptive practices" and that the bank was "preying on a vulnerable population." One former prisoner who was a plaintiff in that lawsuit said he left prison with $120 on his card but could only retrieve $70 because of various fees he was charged.[6]

In Arkansas, the lawsuit filed by Adams said the debit card agreement between Keefe and Cradduck was "part of a quid pro quo for the kickback" that Cradduck received under the commissary agreement. "The agreement, the suit said, included "a schedule of fees that are involuntarily charged to inmates for the use (and failure to use) the prepaid debit card."

Adams had been arrested in February 2013 on suspicion of public intoxication and when he was booked into jail, $613 in cash that he had on him was seized by deputies. Following a night in jail, he was issued an "unwanted prepaid debit card rather than the currency he legitimately owned and possessed," the suit said, adding that he requested his cash but was told that the prepaid debit card was the only way for him to receive his money.[7]

The debit card matter was not the only controversy in which Cradduck found himself caught up.

On January 19, 2016, less than two years after the settlement of the debit card lawsuit, he was in trouble again, this time of a criminal nature. He was arrested on charges that he attempted to have a jail deputy paid for time that he did not work.[8]

Nineteen-year-old Gabriel Cox, a friend of his son, was hired by Cradduck as a prison guard on October 5, 2015. Cox lived with the Cradducks at the time. Lieutenant Robin Holt, one of two deputies to file a grievance against Cradduck, said he told her to backdate Cox's employee records by a week to give him pay for extra time he never worked. Holt refused Cradduck's order because she believed it to be "illegal and unethical," according to Captain Jeremy Guyll.

Cox lost his job the same month Cradduck was arrested after his arrest on drug charges.

Cradduck, who was campaigning for his third term at the time of his arrest, dismissed the charges as "political games," adding, "I will have my day in court and am very confident that I will be vindicated. I am not dropping out of the race."[9]

On January 21, Arkansas State Police, who had been investigating Cradduck for several months, suspended his registration to teach concealed-carry classes, "pending the final resolution of the charge."

Cradduck had retaliated against Guyll and Holt after they filed their grievances by demoting them but the grievance board ruled in favor of the whistleblowers and Cradduck was required to reinstate them.[10]

Despite his bravado at the time of his arrest, Cradduck entered a nolo contendere plea to a misdemeanor three months later, on April 29, 2016 one day after his successor was sworn in as the new sheriff. He was defeated in the March 1 Republican primary, finishing third against two opponents. He negotiated an $80,000 payout not to serve out the remaining nine months of his term. He was sentenced to six months' probation and ordered to pay a fine of five hundred dollars. He had served as sheriff of Benton County since 2013.[11]

In September 2017, it appeared he had landed on his feet when it was announced he had been hired by the Carroll County Sheriff's Office. Carroll County's eastern border abuts Benton County's western border, with both counties sharing a border with the state of Missouri. He was scheduled to start work there in October. He became eligible to work in law enforcement again when his record was officially expunged and the Arkansas Commission on Law Enforcement Standards and Training voted 4-3 on August 31 to allow him to retain his law enforcement certification.[12]

But Carroll County Sheriff Randy Mayfield and Cradduck later decided by mutual agreement that it would be "in the best interest of all" for Cradduck not to join the neighboring sheriff's department.[13]

Craddock was killed in an automobile accident in Oklahoma on January 5, 2020.

Lawmen are often portrayed on television and in movies as fearless protectors of the citizenry but when Faulkner County deputy sheriff Keenan Wallace shot a Chihuahua for being too aggressive, that fearless image took a serious hit.

The entire episode was captured on video by the homeowner, Doug Canady, who reacted to Wallace's actions by shouting, "Are you fucking kidding me? You're fucking kidding me!"

The video showed Wallace approaching Canady's home in Conway in central Arkansas in response to a complaint of an aggressive dog. Two small dogs could be seen on the front lawn and he could be heard threatening to shoot one of the dogs if it became too aggressive. Twenty seconds later, he did just that.

The video shows the two men arguing as the dog yelped in pain in the background. "I told you," Wallace told Canady as he approached the homeowner with taser in hand. Canady said the Chihuahua was not his but a neighborhood dog named Reeses that had been on his property and did not pose a danger to anyone.[14]

The dog suffered a broken jaw and shattered bones, but survived. She was treated at a Little Rock veterinarian after Canady rescued her. "She's doing well, considering all things," he said.

Wallace, ironically, was a K9 handler for the sheriff's department. He was fired by Sheriff Tim Ryals who, in something of an understatement, said, "I believe there were numerous opportunities to de-escalate the incident."[15]

In February 2006, the police chief, his wife and the mayor of Lonoke, Arkansas, were arrested in a corruption probe that included charges involving sex, drug-making, using prisoners to work on personal projects, burglary and tampering that shook the small town of fewer than 4,500 residents.

Such small-town shenanigans would not normally attract much attention but the police chief in this case was a former sheriff's deputy who was the central figure in a documentary that promoted a conspiracy theory that reached all the way to 1600 Pennsylvania Avenue in the nation's capital.

Lonoke police chief Jay Campbell was arrested for conspiracy to manufacture methamphetamine in an effort to lure a bail-jumper out of hiding. He was also charged with masterminding a criminal enterprise, hindering apprehension or prosecution, illegally employing state prisoners for personal gain, criminal conspiracy to commit residential burglary, theft by receiving stolen goods, and theft of services.

The town's mayor, Thomas Privett, admitted to using state prisoners for personal benefit by using prisoners to work on his home and for allowing Campbell to use one of his properties for prisoners to work on Campbell's boat.

Kelly Campbell, the police chief's wife, was charged with having sex with prisoners in her husband's office.[16]

Campbell was sentenced to 40 years in prison after his conviction on 23 counts and his wife was convicted and sentenced to 20 years on 26 charges but their convictions were overturned by the Arkansas Supreme Court and their cases remanded back to Lonoke County, Ark. Circuit Court.[17]

He was charged anew with 17 counts, pleaded guilty and was sentenced to 15 years with credit for nearly a thousand days already served. He was eventually released on parole on April 5, 2010 in apparent violation of two Arkansas state laws that required written notification of local law enforcement officials.[18]

So, what's the significance of this small-town police chief run afoul of the law?

Well, in 1987, he and another man, Kirk Lane, were deputy sheriffs in Pulaski County, the county in which the state capital of Little Rock is located. The governor of Arkansas at the time was Bill Clinton and the conspiracy theory alluded to earlier is the so-called great Arkansas railway mystery involving the deaths of two teenage boys.

The boys, seventeen-year-old Kevin Ives, and sixteen-year-old Don Henry, were run over by a train in 1987 in rural Saline County. The three counties, Saline, Pulaski and Lonoke, lie adjacent to each other in the dead center of the state with Pulaski flanked on the west by Saline and on the east by Lonoke. The boys' deaths were at first determined to have been caused by their falling into a marijuana-induced sleep on the tracks but out-of-state pathologists determined the deaths to be homicides, a rumor that launched the conspiracy theory that the boys were murdered to protect higher-ups after they accidentally witnessed a drug deal.

Deputies Campbell and Lane were investigating alleged drug trafficking by former district attorney Don Harmon who would, in fact, later be imprisoned on federal drug and racketeering convictions. The hunted became the hunter, however, when Harmon was named as special prosecutor to investigate the deaths of the teenagers and the two deputies would eventually claim in a lawsuit that when Harmon learned they were investigating him, he attempted to direct suspicion of the boys' murders onto the two lawmen, thus fanning the flames of what would become a full-blown conspiracy theory that eventually reached all the way to the White House, by then occupied by Clinton.

A one-hour 1996 documentary film entitled *Obstruction of Justice: The Mena Connection* was produced with the mother of one of the boys providing much of the film's conjecture that Campbell and Lane had killed the boys and dumped their bodies onto the railroad track in order to conceal evidence of their murder, and to make the conspiracy theory more palatable, with assistance from state and federal prosecutors—and then-Governor Bill Clinton.

The Wall Street Journal, also in 1996, even jumped into the fray with the publication of "The Lonely Crusade of Linda Ives," which was filled with conspiracy theories.

Linda Ives, Kevin's mother, and former Saline County deputy prosecutor Jean Duffy were given full editorial control over the documentary, according to producer Patrick Matrisciana, who had also produced an earlier "documentary," *The Clinton Chronicles*.

Despite his attempted deflection of responsibility for the film's content, a jury awarded Campbell and Lane nearly six hundred thousand dollars in damages.

The Jay Campbell saga came full circle when he was fired by the Pulaski County Sheriff's Office in 2000 when he attempted to employ his lieutenant's rank to intimidate subordinates over off-duty private security work. His appeal and reinstatement and back pay was denied in 2001 and the following year he became police chief for Lonoke.[19]

The Campbell matter wasn't the only time Lonoke County was in the headlines. On June 23, 2021, Michael Davis, a sergeant with the sheriff's office, shot and killed seventeen-year-old Huner Brittain. The teen had been working on his truck immediately prior to driving it down the road when Davis pulled him over. Brittain's family claimed that he exited his truck with a quart of oil in his hand and was shot by the deputy. Davis was convicted of negligent homicide and sentenced to a year in prison.

"He was never told to halt, he was never told to freeze, he was just immediately shot, Brittain's uncle, Jesse Brittain, said.[20]

A federal jury convicted Franklin County Sheriff Anthony Boen on two counts of deprivation of rights under color of law for using unreasonable force to punish pretrial detainees on two separate occasions in 2018, according to an August 9, 2021, news release by the U.S. Attorney's Office for the Western District of Arkansas.

On November 21, 2018, Boen slammed a detainee onto the floor and ripped his hair during an interrogation. Twelve days later, on December 3, he struck a detainee multiple times in the head with his closed fist while the detainee was sitting on the floor and shackled to a bench inside the jail. Both detainees suffered injuries as a result of Boen's actions.

The jury deliberated for more than ten hours before convicting Boen on two counts and acquitting him of one felony count of the same crime.[21]

In terms of pure flamboyance, bluster, controversy, and ambivalence, however, it would be difficult to beat former Sheriff Tommy Robinson, who parlayed his five years as Pulaski County's top cop into a six-year stint as a U.S. Representative before finally fading into oblivion.

A sheriff who favored gun control and who voted for Jesse Jackson at the Democratic convention and who ridiculed Ronald Reagan but who switched to the Republican Party the following year after falling out with Jackson, he switched parties again, this time to Independent, after losing the Republican primary election for governor of Arkansas as a Republican after having been picked as a potential candidate to unseat the incumbent governor, one Bill Clinton.

But it was as sheriff that he made his reputation as a maverick willing, even eager, to take on the establishment on any issue. He once protested overcrowding at the Pulaski County jail by transporting a group of prisoners to a state prison facility at Pine Bluff and chaining them to a fence outside the prison.[22]

In March 1982, Robinson had the county judge and the comptroller arrested on misdemeanor charges, and then a federal judge jailed Robinson for contempt after the sheriff ejected a special master named by the federal judge to oversee the jail. The county judge and comptroller, arrested after they refused to release money to pay the sheriff's bills after he had exhausted his budget, could have served as a red flag for his congressional tenure. As a member of Congress, he was one of 269 then-House members of the House to incur overdrafts with the House Bank, with 996 overdrafts totaling more than $250,000 in a sixteen-month period.[23]

Barry Lee Fairchild was convicted for the 1983 murder of Greta Mason. Fairchild, who had an IQ in the low sixties (considered to be mentally challenged), confessed during questioning following his arrest but recanted during his trial, claiming that Robinson and Major Larry Dill forced his confession by beating and threatening him during his questioning. A former deputy sheriff also testified that he saw Fairchild and his brother Robert tortured by Robinson and other officers. Following years of appeals, Fairchild was executed in 1995.

Robinson arrested attorney William McArthur for the murder of his wife, Alice McArthur, in their Little Rock home even though the prosecutor told Robinson he had no case. A grand jury ultimately cleared William McArthur who then sued Robinson. The lawsuit was dismissed because Robinson, like all in law enforcement, as well as prosecutors and judges, enjoyed qualified immunity that shielded them from responsibility for wrongful actions as long as the acts were carried out in the scope of their jobs.[24]

Robinson's deputies also raided a toga party being held in a Little Rock hotel being held by Central Arkansas society leaders led to a number of lawsuits and resulted in Robinson and his deputies being tagged as the "Keyhole Kops."[25]

4

California: A Virtual Nest of Corruption

IN LATE January 2019, the first calls went out advocating the abolition of sheriffs in California with at least three affiliated publications describing county sheriffs as a "problem child" among California elected officials.[1]

"No office is less accountable or more reliable in producing scandal," reporter Joe Mathews wrote for the *San Francisco Chronicle* on January 27. "Once elected, sheriffs in all fifty-eight counties have power over jails and policing, and act pretty much as they please."[2]

He quoted historian Andrew Isenberg, who said, "The power of sheriffs is inextricably tied up in the concept of a popular justice that is not bound by anything so mundane as the law."

Mathews had sufficient reason on which to base his advocacy for abolishment of the office as Connecticut had done nearly two decades earlier. There was a laundry list of sheriffs' scandals to cite in support of his advocacy on behalf of a state constitution change to do away with the office altogether.

In Santa Clara County, a sheriff's race devolved into a contest of which candidate could make the loudest claims against each other of excessive force, racist texts and sexual solicitations.

In Stanislaus County, the sheriff falsely blamed state law for the shooting death of a local police officer by an undocumented immigrant.

Sacramento Sheriff Scott Jones refused to submit to civilian oversight by literally locking the inspector general's office, blocking its investigation of excessive force.

Two of California's most powerful sheriffs were convicted felons at the time Mathews wrote his column.

When one sheriff was questioned about a series of actions he took upon winning election to his office, he explained in typical sheriff-speak: "The state Constitution lays out that the oversight of the sheriff is the voters."

"In other words," Mathews wrote, "you must wait four years before you can stop me, no matter what I do."[3]

One California Assemblyman, Kevin McCarty, a Sacramento Democrat, introduced Assembly Bill 1185 in early 2019 that would allow local counties to voluntarily establish citizen oversight of sheriffs. The bill passed both the House and Senate and was signed into law.

Three months after Mathews' column, *The Appeal*, a prison advocacy organization, published an editorial column in April 2019 asking if sheriffs are really necessary. The nineteen-hundred-word essay cited the multitude of problems with the Los Angeles County Sheriff's Office and also cited a series of corruption scandals that prompted Connecticut to abolish its eight county sheriffs' offices in 2000. The county of St. Louis took similar action way back in 1954 after the office of sheriff was removed from Missouri's constitution. Corruption scandals also prompted Miami-Dade County to consolidate sheriff's duties into a county police force. But in the case of Miami-Dade County, the politically-powerful Florida Sheriffs' Association in 2018 successfully lobbied the state legislature to pass a law requiring the re-establishment of the sheriff's office. Also in 2018, James Tomberlin advocated in the *Virginia Law Review* major changes. He wrote, "Policing requires robust regulation, and it is evident in studying sheriffs that elections alone are not sufficient to regulate law enforcement" and that what "made the sheriff attractive during westward expansion makes it obsolete at best and dangerously anachronistic at worst today" because of the inability of local governments to legally act as a check on sheriffs' power and authority or to hold them accountable. "In other words," he wrote, "it's not the Wild West anymore."[4]

Sheriffs' power was such a problem that California State Senator Richard Pan introduced a bill, SB-1303, that would have forced counties of 500,000 or more population which were not "charter" counties to create an office of medical examiner to investigate deaths.

California is one of only three states that allow counties to employ a sheriff-coroner system in which the sheriff oversees both law enforcement *and* death examinations. Forty-nine of the state's 58 counties use that system which raises fundamental civil-liberties issues. Steven Greenhut, writing for *Reason.com*, said the system created an "outrageous" conflict of interest, particularly in cases of officer-involved shootings. "Autopsies are often the basis for criminal charges and it is imperative that the public gains the necessary facts to determine fault and [to] deliver justice," Greenhut wrote. "Currently, sheriffs—who have an official, vested interest in these cases—make the final cause-of-death determinations."

Greenhut cited a case in which two forensic pathologists in San Joaquin County resigned over what they called intolerable interference by Sheriff-Coroner Steve Moore. He wrote that the county's chief medical examiner claimed in December 2017 that the sheriff interfered with his investigations.

Pan's bill passed both chambers of the California Assembly despite opposition from nearly every Republican member of each chamber but Governor Jerry Brown vetoed it, bowing to the opposition of the California State Association of Counties which argued the costs of such a law would be prohibitive.[5]

Two of the most high-profile scandals involving sheriffs' departments occurred coincidentally in two of the most high-profile counties in California which just happened to abut each other.

Little occurs in Los Angeles County or next-door Orange County that does not get national attention, whether the subject is politics, movie stars, or sports. The sheriffs' departments of the two counties certainly received their share, though it's a safe bet they'd have preferred to fly under the radar of the national—or local—news media.

On July 15, 2002, Orange County Sheriff Michael S. Carona glared into the TV camera and proclaimed to the then-unknown person responsible for the kidnapping and murder of five-year-old Samantha Runnion, "Don't sleep. Don't eat. We're coming after you." When a Lake Elsinore man was subsequently arrested, Carona was dubbed "America's Sheriff" by CNN's Larry King. He was honored at a White House ceremony and his name began getting serious mention as a future lieutenant governor or even a member of Congress.

But things were already beginning to take a bad turn in Orange County that same year and continued into 2019, with the unrelated scandals causing two dozen criminal convictions to be vacated, wrecking the careers of two sheriffs and numerous deputies along the way with one sheriff resigning after his criminal conviction, his successor opting not to run for re-election because of scandals in her own office. After the dust had settled, the sheriff she endorsed as her own successor appeared to be presiding over a department rampant in its use of excessive force.

The seeds for the Carona's problems were sown soon after he took office in 1999 when he convinced the Board of Supervisors to waive a requirement that top administrative positions in the office, called assistant sheriffs, have a minimum of two years' service at the rank of captain.

Armed with the board of supervisors' approval, he promptly appointed his campaign manager George Jaramillo, an attorney and one-time Garden Grove police lieutenant, and Don Haidl, a ninth-grade dropout who made a fortune auctioning government fleet vehicles, and who was one of Carona's top campaign fundraisers. Those appointments would ultimately lead to the indictment, resignation, and conviction of Carona on a single count of obstruction of justice—but not before details of public bribery, a sordid affair involving Carona and Jaramillo's law partner, Debra Hoffman, who was Carona's mistress, rocked Orange County, ground zero of Southern California political conservatism.

In 2002, Haidl's teenage son Gregory was accused along with two other youths of raping and videotaping themselves having sex with an unconscious girl during a party at the elder Haidl's Newport Beach home. When Newport Beach detectives began questioning the younger Haidl at his mother's home, Jaramillo, second-in-command of the 4,200-member sheriff's department, showed up in full uniform and advised the youth not to speak with investigators. That prompted immediate complaints from Newport Beach police, who pointed out Jaramillo was not there as Gregory's attorney, but as an officer of the law.

In October 2003, Gregory and two friends were caught allegedly in possession of a small amount of marijuana which, while not a serious crime itself, was nevertheless serious enough to have his bail for the rape charges revoked. Instead of arresting him, however, deputies drove him home and notified Jaramillo who agreed that the incident would not be recorded in the sheriff's department's activity log in the hopes the news media would not find out.

But the phone conversation between Jaramillo and a sheriff's department lieutenant was recorded and that recording would become instrumental in an investigation into whether Jaramillo and other sheriff's deputies obstructed justice by giving Gregory preferential treatment.

On March 17, 2004, Carona fired Jaramillo. Whether that was the reason for the firing or not, was never explained, but three days later, FBI agents removed unspecified evidence from his office. In a matter of days, it was learned that Jaramillo had been paid $25,000 in 2000 and in 2001 by the inventor of a laser device designed to shut off the engines of speeding cars to promote the device within the department.

Jaramillo was also hired as a management consultant for $15,000 a year. The problem was the inventor, Charles Gabbard, was convicted felon who had served time for armed robbery, grand theft and drug possession in the 1960s and 1970s.

What's more, the device did not perform well at demonstrations arranged by Jaramillo. But that didn't stop Gabbard from collecting money from investors in the gadget from places as far away as Ohio, Michigan and Pennsylvania—and convincing the investors to write thousand-dollar checks to Carona's campaign for which they were given 1,000 shares in his company, GHG.

GHG also kicked in $45,000 for a birthday bash and fundraiser for Carona, but no record of this expense on behalf of the campaign was ever listed in Carona's campaign finance reports.[6] Carona, in turn, did his part by writing a glowing letter of endorsement of Senate Bill 2004, which would have mandated that Gabbard's product be installed on all vehicles sold in California. The bill ultimately failed despite Carona's claim that "Our profession and our communities would be well-served" by the bill's approval.[7]

Meanwhile, other events were taking a toll on Carona's carefully-cultivated squeaky-clean public image:

- He accepted campaign contributions from and was seen partying with strip club owner and mob associate Rick Rizzolo, the subject of an FBI mob investigation who eventually went to federal prison for racketeering.
- A major donor, the owner of an Orange County liquor store chain and a secret major campaign donor of Carona's, was fined $200,000 for attempted bribery of a federal court official.
- A member of Carona's select dignitary-protection unit (in reality, the sheriff's spy squad) was arrested for solicitation in Las Vegas.
- Another member of the unit took his own life after being approached by investigators for information about the sheriff's office.
- A Carona drinking buddy who was the defense lawyer in the Haidl rape case was charged in the operation of an illegal inmate kickback

scheme inside the Orange County jail;
- Jaramillo wound up going to jail for public corruption and tax fraud.
- Don Haidl pleaded guilty to tax fraud and to making illegal payments to both Carona and Jaramillo.
- No fewer than 86 reserve deputies were removed by a supervisory board which said Carona had given badges to cronies who donated to his political campaign. Carona managed to get 56 of them reinstated.
- The California attorney general dropped 16 charges against Captain Christine Murray for illegally pressuring public employees to deposit money in her boss's campaign account.[8]

The shoe fell on October 30, 2007, when Carona was indicted by a federal grand jury on seven felony counts, including public corruption, witness tampering, and obstruction of justice. Indicted along with him were his wife, Deborah on one count of conspiracy and his mistress, Debra Hoffman, on eight counts of conspiracy.

The indictment accused the sheriff of accepting illegal payments, failure to report cash and gifts, including payments of a thousand dollars per month from Haidl, use of his yacht and private plane, at least $65,000 in payments to Hoffman by Haidl at Carona's behest, a $1,500 St. John Knit suit and a $15,000 gold and diamond Cartier watch for Deborah Carona, and a $5,000 boat.[9]

Apparently, Hoffman was not Carona's only extra-marital paramour. Erica Hill, Jaramillo's sister-in-law, testified she had a sexual relationship with the sheriff in the hope he would give her husband a job.[10]

Carona first met Debra Hoffman during his initial campaign for sheriff in 1998. She, along with Jaramillo, operated a struggling law firm. Soon after Carona took office, the two took frequent trips together to Las Vegas and Sacramento. Hoffman's husband was given a job as a painter on the sheriff's department's maintenance staff. She and her husband lived in a million-dollar Newport Beach home owned by a company controlled by David Gelbaum, a former hedge fund manager who contributed more than three million dollars to the Mike Carona Foundation, which sent underprivileged children to camp.[11]

Papers filed with the court by prosecutors said Carona either received or solicited cash and other things valued at more than $400,000.[12]

Carona officially stepped down as sheriff on January 14, 2008, two-and-one-half months after his October 30 indictment, to concentrate on fighting the corruption charges against him. By resigning, he became eligible to accept pro bono legal representation, something he could not do as a public figiure.[13]

On January 16, 2009, almost a year to the day after his resignation, he was acquitted on five counts of conspiracy, mail fraud and witness tampering, but was found guilty on a single count of witness tampering. Carona was in a celebratory mood, calling the outcome "an absolute miracle," but it was a hollow victory. Jurors interviewed after the trial indicated they believed the sheriff was guilty of illegally accepting cash and gifts but that the state's five-year statute of limitations did not allow them to consider acts committed before October 2002. "His hand was in the cookie jar," said juror Jerome Bell, a truck driver from Anaheim. "He was just quick enough to wipe the crumbs off his hands."

The jury heard testimony of influence peddling, bribes paid in envelopes stuffed with cash, hidden cameras in the sheriff's department, reserve badges given out to supporters, and sordid details of his relationship with Hoffman, including stories of a love nest, Las Vegas trips and secret bank accounts.

Carona had been caught on tape boasting that he was the "most lethal" politician in Orange County and he alluded to "untraceable cash...No trail anywhere...Not even close to being a trail."[14]

Three months after his conviction, on April 27, Carona was sentenced to 66 months in federal prison and ordered to pay a $125,000 fine by an irate U.S. District Judge Andrew Guilford, who was critical of Carona's celebration of his conviction on only one of six counts. "I cannot understand the unrestrained celebration and proclamations of innocence and complete vindication," he said. "I need a sheriff I can trust. Lying will not be tolerated in this courtroom, especially by the county's highest-ranking enforcement officer."[15]

Having failed to get a conviction of Carona on the five conspiracy counts, prosecutors decided not to pursue similar conspiracy charges against Deborah Carona and Debra Hoffman.

Details of cash in envelopes, influence peddling, consorting with organized crime figures, trysts with Hoffman, and doling out reserve deputy badges like so much Halloween candy was bad enough. But in February

2008, nearly a year prior to his conviction, word of a much uglier secret about his department was made public in the form of an eighty-six-page grand jury report on the operation of the Orange County jail under Carona.

Carona managed to keep the grand jury report secret for a time but reporters for the *Orange County Register* and the *Los Angeles Times* successfully sought a court order to get a copy. The investigation, precipitated by the particularly gruesome beating death of an inmate, revealed that Carona had taken the Fifth Amendment when questioned, even declining to admit he was sheriff at the time. He even declared that his department would conduct its own internal investigation of the death instead of the district attorney in violation of protocol.

On October 5, 2006, forty-one-year-old computer technician John Derek Chamberlain was sodomized, tortured and beaten to death by about twenty fellow prisoners as deputies who arranged for the assault watched television, sent text messages, played video games or slept while ignoring required jail walk-throughs—and then lied to conceal their complicity in the murder.

Chamberlain was a pre-trial detainee who had been arrested for possession of child pornography but guards lied to gang affiliated prisoner "shot callers" whom deputies used to maintain order by saying he was a child molester, for the express purpose of having him beaten.

"Shot callers" directed attacks on other prisoners at guard's direction and were rewarded with extra time out of their cells, clean uniforms, extra meals and hygiene products. Sometime between 5:50 p.m. and 6:50 p.m., Chamberlain was dragged to a spot in the unit that was out of sight of surveillance cameras. But just to be sure, deputy Phillip Le managed to "accidentally" erase surveillance video of the barracks for the time that Chamberlain was beaten to death. As Chamberlain screamed for help and pleaded for his life, he was stripped naked, sodomized, scalded with hot water, kicked, stomped, urinated on, and brutally beaten.

Guard station logs revealed entries noting "barracks secure" at 6:00 p.m. and "barracks secure, no problems," at 6:30. Yet, the coroner counted 43 displaced rib fractures. One prisoner hit Chamberlain in the head so hard it broke the assailant's hand.[16]

Carona began his sentence in January 2011 at Englewood Federal Correctional Institution near Denver. It was the same facility that housed former Enron executive Jeffrey Skilling and former Illinois Governor Rod

Blagojevich. With no reasons given, he was transferred to a Kentucky medical facility in November and was released to home confinement on May 13, 2015.

One of his partners in crime, Don Haidl died in 2012 at age 61 and spent no time in jail in connection to his tenure with the Orange County Sheriff's Office.

Sandra Hutchins, a retired Los Angeles County Sheriff's division chief, was appointed to succeed Carona on January 14, 2008, the same day Carona's resignation took effect. Seen as a reformer, she was subsequently elected to a full term in 2010 and re-elected in 2014, but as accusations of misconduct mounted, she said that she would not seek a third term in 2018.

She waded into controversy almost immediately. Saying the Carona administration "stretched good cause" for issuing concealed weapon permits, she immediately sent letters revoking more than six hundred permits.

Further controversy loomed on the horizon and in May 2015, Superior Court Judge Thomas Goethals took the unprecedented action of disqualifying all 250 prosecutors in the district attorney's office after it was learned that the DA had worked with the sheriff's office to set up a sophisticated jailhouse snitch network which allowed prosecutors to gather evidence against prisoners without the knowledge of their defense attorneys.

Goethals said that after years of alleged misconduct by prosecutors' withholding exculpatory evidence from defense attorneys may have placed dozens of cases in jeopardy. The scheme was discovered by public defender Scott Sanders who was defending mass murderer Scott Dekraai, who had pleaded guilty to killing his ex-wife and seven others in a beauty salon in 2011. Prosecutions collapsed in cases that involved informants who were eliciting illegal confessions and more were expected to follow. The sheriff's office had routinely coordinated with informants in order to circumvent a constitutional prohibition on eliciting incriminating statements from defendants who had legal representation and should not have been interrogated.[17]

Goethals wrote in his order that the discovery situation was "far worse than the court previously realized." In fact, he said, a trove of discovery material contained in a "computerized data base built and maintained by the Orange County Sheriff over the course of many years…remained secret, despite numerous specific discovery orders issued by this court…"

Yale Law School faculty member Laura Fernandez, who studied prosecutorial misconduct, said it was "amazing" that both the sheriff's office and the DA's office worked together to hide the misconduct.

The *Orange County Weekly* wrote, "For a quarter of a century, the Orange County Sheriff's Department (OCSD) operated one of the nation's longest frauds on the criminal-justice system through a secret, computerized records system called TREDS (Traffic Records Electronic Data System). In late 2014, Superior Court Judge Thomas M. Goethals forced a monumentally resistant OCSD to admit its existence. Why all the secrecy?"[18]

During a hearing at which Sheriff Sandra Hutchens was not in attendance, Goethals said to her attorneys, "I remind the sheriff that I've waited nearly four years—that's 200 weeks or 1,400 days. The entire Orange County community has been cheated," he added.

Even after an 1,157-page log surfaced giving the lie to claims, the sheriff's department continued to deny that a jail informant program existed, prompting and exasperated Judge Goethals to ask rhetorically, "What's going on over there?"[19]

The furor over the jail snitch program was still at full pitch when public defender Scott Sanders was at it again, this time accusing the sheriff's department of improperly recording inmate telephone calls.

It turned out he was correct. Global Tel Link (GTL), the vendor that oversaw the jail phone system, had indeed recorded more than a thousand inmate-attorney telephone calls over a three-year period and that fifty-eight of those calls were actually accessed by authorities.

GTL, in a July 27, 2018, letter to Hutchens, blamed the recordings on a "technical error" that occurred during a 2015 system update.

"They list about a thousand calls," Sanders said. "We think there's about 200,000 calls," adding that he believes OCSD and GTL removed thousands of inmate-attorney calls from the list. He said he filed a motion requesting access to the recorded calls of one of his clients but was told there was no record of any calls made by his client.[20]

As the Orange County Sheriff's Department transitioned to its third sheriff in a decade, the problems moved from the administrative offices and jail to the streets as deputies pulled driver from cars, beat and, in some cases, even shot them without provocation, prompting the *Orange County Weekly* to proclaim in a headline that Hutchens' successor Don Barnes ran a "toxic" agency.[21]

Immediately to the north of Orange County is Los Angeles County, the setting for such good-guy cop shows as *Dragnet* and *Adam-12*. As usual, the Hollywood treatment was in stark contrast to reality.

About the time things were starting to heat up for Hutchens in Orange County, things were also getting a little warm next door for L.A. County Sheriff Lee Baca. In August 2012, the department, already the subject of reports of extensive jailhouse brutality, was jolted by a federal investigation of a deputy serving as a liaison for a heroin-dealing white supremacist gang leader at the Men's Central Jail.

Even more damning was information that Lieutenant Greg Thompson, head of the Los Angeles County Intelligence Unit, had alerted the implicated deputy of the investigation and had given him the name of the inmate informant who was working with the FBI as well as the identities of the two deputies who initiated the report that had been given to Thompson, potentially putting the informant's life at risk and prompting a former FBI special agent to observe Thompson's action "smacks of corruption" and if done deliberately, constituted a criminal offense.

Another expert said the outing of the informant and the subversion of the investigation of the deputy was reminiscent of the way law enforcement operated in the developing world. "I do a lot of work in Mexico, and that's precisely the kind of thing you see happen there," said Dennis Kenney, a professor of criminology at John Jay College in New York.

"There's no question that …there is a culture of corruption," said Thomas Parker, a former special agent in charge of the FBI's Los Angeles field office. "It's been there for decades."[22]

Los Angeles Times reporter Robert Faturechi, speaking on National Public Radio (NPR) in late 2013, also noted that Baca's department had run a special hiring track whereby for years friends and relatives of department higher-ups had been given jobs and that "dozens" of officers with checkered pasts had "knowingly" been hired. One of those was a deputy who, when he was twenty-eight, had kissed and groped a fourteen-year-old girl. Another hire was the friend of the sheriff's driver who had been rejected by the Los Angeles Police Department because of a prior conviction of sexual battery after being charged with raping an unconscious woman.[23]

Though Baca had yet to be implicated in the ongoing investigation of his department, by mid-2014, he had to be feeling the pressure. Six deputies, including Thompson, had been indicted, accused of conspiracy and of obstruction, and on July 1, the six were found guilty on all counts.

Worse for Baca, the federal investigation had now reached as high as Undersheriff Paul Tanaka. The case dated back to 2011 when an inmate at the Men's Central Jail, Anthony Brown, was found in possession of a cell phone. Brown was working as an informant for the FBI in its investigation of jailhouse brutality by deputies. Deputies traced the numbers on his phone as well as calls made via the jail's phone system to the FBI's civil rights division.

To conceal his whereabouts from FBI agents, deputies started transferring Brown from jail to jail under aliases. They even brazenly ignored a federal court order to produce Brown for testimony, prosecutors said. Ratcheting up their efforts, deputies appeared at the home of FBI Special Agent Leah Marx, the lead agent in the jail corruption investigation, and threatened to arrest her for helping Brown acquire the contraband phone, even going so far as to videotape the confrontation.[24]

Thompson received the longest sentence of the six – 37 months. Other sentences ranged from 21 to 33 months. U.S. District Judge Percy Anderson said the six lacked "courage to do what is right" and failed to show "even the slightest remorse." He told them, "Blind obedience to a corrupt culture has serious consequences."[25]

It would eventually surface that Tanaka was central in the decision to thwart the FBI investigation and he would be sentenced to five years in a federal lockup for obstruction.[26]

As the FBI probe continued creeping ever upward in the department's chain of command, Baca, grasping the inevitable, resigned in 2014 and then in February 2016, reached a deal with prosecutors to fall on his sword by pleading guilty to a single felony count. He signed the plea agreement in which he admitted that he ordered deputies to intimidate Marx and to "do everything but put handcuffs on her," and later lied to federal prosecutors and investigators in denying that he was privy to discussions about attempting to derail the investigation into beatings by jailhouse guards. Baca's plea came after 17 members of his department had been convicted of federal offenses, including beating inmates, obstructing justice, bribery and conspiracy. He admitted that after he learned of the investigation, he met with Tanaka and others in September 2011 and instructed them to approach Marx, one of Brown's handlers.[27]

There was one problem with the plea agreement, however: the presiding judge in the case refused to accept the six-month jail sentence, saying it wasn't enough, given the severity of Baca's crime. Baca then withdrew his plea and prosecutors hit him with two additional charges of conspiracy and obstruction.[28]

A year after his plea deal fell through, Baca was convicted on March 15, 2017, of obstructing the federal investigation into jailhouse guards who accepted bribes to smuggle contraband into the L.A. County jails and brutally beat inmates. Assistant U.S. Attorney Lizabeth Rhodes said during closing arguments that the corruption "started from the top and went all the way down," and when Baca learned that a federal investigation was underway, "he obstructed and when he learned the FBI had turned its focus on him, he lied."[29]

Two months later, on May 12, U.S. District Judge Percy Anderson, the same judge who had sentenced the six deputies back in 2014, sentenced Baca to three years in prison and ordered him to pay a $7,500 fine. Repeating the same admonishment that he had leveled at the six deputies two-and-one-half years earlier, Anderson told Baca, "Blind obedience to a corrupt culture has serious consequences."

Baca, the judge observed, "knew what he was doing was wrong," but "had no problem using his office to further his own agenda."[30]

Carona and Baca were not the only California sheriffs to run afoul of the law or the court of public opinion.

Scott Jones (Sacramento County), T. Baxter Dunn (San Joaquin County), Stan Sniff (Riverside County), Laurie Smith (Santa Clara County), Frank Rivero (Lake County), Donny Youngblood (Kern County), and Ross Mirkarimi (San Francisco) each encountered problems of varying degrees of severity, largely of their own making, at some point in their tenures.

Nor were deputies spared of committing egregious acts, some of them criminal in nature, including drug trafficking, having sex with inmates and juveniles, grand theft, conspiracy, perjury, and falsifying records.

With Scott Jones, there were two concurrent controversies: his ability to talk out of both sides of his mouth and his apparently successful efforts to block an investigation into the fatal shooting of an emotionally disturbed man by sheriff's deputies.

In February 2018, he was touting statistics that reflected a 24 percent drop in Sacramento County's crime rate over the previous five years. A month later, he was at the White House where he told President Trump that California was rife with "spectacular failures" of law enforcement and plagued with dangerous criminal immigrants who stalked the public "every single day."

That prompted the *Sacramento Bee* editorial board to come out with guns blazing in an editorial on March 21 in which it reminded readers that Jones had earlier renounced Trump during his 2016 unsuccessful run for Congress from California's 7th Congressional District but now appeared to be looking for a job in the Trump administration.

"Jones' deputies can do plenty to make sure that immigrants convicted of serious crimes are deported," the editorial said. "They just can't run around rousting brown people and demanding their immigrant status.

"The situation here bears no resemblance to the epic pandering Jones put forth on Tuesday. Sacramento is many things, but it isn't some 'crimmigrant' hellscape.

"You know what is a 'spectacular failure,' though? An elected county official running for re-election, who goes to Washington and forgets whom he's representing—besides his own inexplicably star-struck self."[31]

The boiling point in the relationship between Jones and the Sacramento County Board of Supervisors came in August 2018 when former Inspector General Rick Braziel, who also had served as Sacramento police chief, was named to investigate use of force when deputies shot an emotionally disturbed African American man in May 2017.

Jones, in response to Braziel's appointment, literally locked him out of the department following the conclusion of his investigation in which he said deputies fired an "excessive" and "unnecessary" number of rounds at Mikel McIntyre. Jones called Braziel, who served as a police officer for 33 years, including four years as Sacramento's chief of police, a "layman."

"Literally, our sheriff locked the doors and didn't allow an inspector general to do his job anymore," said California Assemblyman Kevin McCarty of Sacramento in urging passage of his bill to create oversight boards equipped with subpoena and investigative powers.

The California State Sheriffs' Association, of course, was opposed to the bill, calling it "unnecessary."

A county grand jury, while saying Jones did not break the law, at the same time, endorsed calls for more oversight of the sheriff's department, including the creation of a separate commission to increase accountability of the department.[32]

In the central California county of San Joaquin, Sheriff T. Baxter Dunn pleaded guilty in January 2005 of one count of mail fraud and resigned from office over his part in a scheme to shake down two companies interested in constructing a power plant, a major inland deepwater port in Stockton, the San Joaquin County seat.

One of the companies, Calpine Corp., refused to deal with Dunn and two other county officials but the other, Sunlaw Energy Corp., agreed to pay a $2 million commission on the condition the company was selected to build the power plant.

Dunn, who had been sheriff for 14 years, accepted responsibility for his part in the kickback scheme, but wrote in a memorandum to his employees that he was involved in nothing more than a "harmless, legal business venture."[33]

Riverside County, near the Mexican border in southern California, with 2.3 million residents, is the fourth-most populous county in the state. Barely half-a-million voters turned out to defeat twelve-year incumbent Sheriff Stan Sniff in November 2018. Challenger Chad Blanco received 58 percent of the vote to only 42 percent for Sniff.

Sniff's decisive loss was attributable in large part to a cheating scandal in his department in which twenty-five deputies were caught cheating on a promotional exam and no one was fired. Some even got promoted.

But there were other factors that could have contributed to his loss. His department had experienced huge budget overruns and a mass exodus of employees led one of his supervisors to say Sniff was "unable to manage his organization in an effective way."

Riverside District Attorney Investigator Ian Anderson added, "There is no true leadership …and as a result, public safety is dangerously threatened."[34]

But it was the cheating scandal that took center stage in the campaign. The news of the cheating prompted a defense attorney to challenge the integrity and credibility of the deputy who arrested his client. Deputy Robert Cornett, a senior investigator for the sheriff's department, was identified as having shared secret test materials with several deputies during promotional exams. He arrested attorney Shaun Sullivan's client, a fellow deputy accused of threatening and harassing his ex-girlfriend.[35]

Laurie Smith became California's first female sheriff in 1998. In 2018, she was re-elected to a fifth term with 52 percent of the vote in a bitterly-fought election for sheriff of Santa Clara County. A big part of the reason for her relative difficulty was a decades-old allegation of sexual harassment and sex discrimination levied against her by subordinates who described alleged advances by Smith in somewhat graphic terms.

One former deputy who did not want to be identified said through his attorney that Smith was his supervisor at a jail when she allegedly touched herself in a way "that made him uncomfortable" and while they were working the 1994 World Cup at Stanford Stadium, she "suggestively" handled a police baton and sexually harassed him.

Another retired sheriff's sergeant, Gary Brady, also said in 1991 Smith "undressed and she got on top of me and she wanted me to do some things that I'm embarrassed to talk about now. He was an undercover narcotics officer at the time but after rejecting Smith's advances, he said she retaliated by removing him from an assignment with the Allied Agencies Narcotics Enforcement Team. He subsequently filed discrimination and sexual harassment complaints against Smith, both of which were denied.

Former correctional officer Ed Albanoski also said that Smith was four ranks above him when she came onto him during lunch at Elmwood Women's Jail in the 1980s. He said she had her uniform shirt unbuttoned "down to like the third button, not wearing a T-shirt, not wearing a bra, and kind of exposing herself to me."

Years later, Albanoski was injured on the job and later met with Smith about getting his job back but "she goes, 'Well, you should have been nicer to me at Elmwood.'"[36]

Lake County Sheriff Frank Rivero survived a recall attempt in 2013, but did not survive re-election less than a year later.

> Recall supporters said Rivero:
> - Was dishonest;
> - Had dishonored the sheriff's department;
> - Had incurred massive legal expenses from lawsuits against the department;
> - Had attempted to withhold information about false statements given by him;
> - Had alienated every law enforcement agency in the county as well as the Board of Supervisors;
> - Had managed to become the first sheriff in California history to be publicly classified as unethical, and
> - That his placement on the Brady List nullified him of his ability to

lead the sheriff's department. A "Brady List" is a list of law enforcement officers who were deemed to not be credible.

Recall supporters, needed 7,026 signatures but aimed at obtaining 9,000 signatures on the recall petition to give them sufficient cushion for signatures that might be invalidated. They were only able to get 7,762 signatures and enough of those were invalidated to cause an insufficient number to qualify to hold a recall election.[37]

Rivero responded by saying he was the victim of a vendetta by an "old boys' network" determined to thwart his campaign pledge to eliminate corruption in the county.

In June 2014, he faced two challengers: former sheriff's lieutenant Brian Martin and retired Clearlake Police Chief Bob Chalk. Martin eventually emerged victorious so the election accomplished what the recall petition could not—the removal of Rivero from office.

In something of a rebuke of the Constitutional Sheriffs & Peace Officers Association (CSPOA), the Orange County Sheriff's Office, reminding its deputies that "Your personal life can't interfere with your job," warned officers not to affiliate themselves with far-right extremist groups.

A sixty-six-page Power Point presentation, which also included a section on "the extreme left," suggested that sheriff's administrative officials were aware that deputies could be drawn to far-right groups and wanted to head off any racist or extremist social media postings that could embarrass the department and even lead to offenders' terminations.

A training session at which the Power Point presentation was shown warned employees to "exercise extreme caution and good judgment" in order to avoid personal or departmental liability for unprofessional or illegal activity, whether on or off duty.[38]

Following the resignation of Lee Baca after 16 years as sheriff, Los Angeles County saw three successors within the next five years. Baca resigned in 2014 before the end of his elected term and in 2017, he was convicted of felony obstruction and sentenced to three years in federal prison. He was the tenth member of the department convicted in the obstruction scheme. Undersheriff Paul Tanaka was sentenced to five years' imprisonment.[39]

John L. Scott was appointed interim sheriff upon Baca's resignation and served from January 30, 2014 to December 1, 2014 to finish out his predecessor's term. James McDowell was elected to succeed Scott and in 2018, McDowell was defeated for reelection by Alejandro Villanueva.

Within three years, Villanueva found himself in hot water when Cy Civilian Oversight Commission Executive Director Sean Kennedy wrote a ten-page report critical of what he said appeared to be "a pattern of LASD officials announcing they have opened 'criminal investigations' of various department heads, oversight officials and professionals." At the same time, Kennedy called for "an investigation to ascertain whether Sheriff Alex Villanueva is abusing his power or extorting public officials."

Villanueva and Undersheriff Timothy Murakami compiled some sort of enemies list that included, apparently, anyone who was ever critical of Villanueva or his department. Murakami even accused the FBI of assisting Inspector General Max Huntsman in his investigation of LASD even though, consistent with FBI policy, no representative of the FBI had ever confirmed that claim.

In his report, Kennedy noted that while Villanueva's "investigations" never resulted in charges being filed, they were nevertheless "invoked to chill oversight and criticism of the LASD" and hinted that his actions to thwart oversight of his department "may constitute extortion."

Michael Gennaco, a former federal prosecutor, called Villanueva's investigations "unconscionable."

"The Villanueva administration's pattern of announcing 'criminal investigations' of oversight officials and other perceived political enemies has persisted for over two years," Kennedy wrote in concluding his report. "While these heavily publicized criminal investigations have never resulted in the filing of any criminal charges, the targeted officials remain obligated to conduct oversight of the Department with a sword of Damocles hanging over their heads. The likelihood is high that such investigations have chilled meaningful civilian oversight of the LASD. To date, the COC has remained silent in the face of substantial evidence that the Sheriff is engaging in extortion or some other abuse of power. The COC should request an independent investigation by an entity unaffected by the announced investigations, such as the Office of the California Attorney General or the U.S. Department of Justice," he said.[40]

Villanueva and Murakami countered with a three-page letter dated July 14 in which they accused the COC of collaborating "to spread false accusations against Sheriff Alex Villanueva and the entire Los Angeles County Sheriff's Department." The letter further charged that the Office of Inspector General was using COC to obtain information about ongoing criminal investigations by the department and described Kennedy's accusations as "completely irresponsible."[41]

Finally, in November 2022, the voters of Los Angeles County had seen enough of the sheriff who derided "woke-ism," electing challenger Robert Luna by a margin of 60 percent to Villanueva's 40 percent. "He'll be remembered as the sheriff who went rogue, who operated as if he was above and outside of the law, who acted with impunity," said critic Mark-Anthony Clayton-Johnson of Villanueva.[42]

5

Colorado: Rocky Mountain Sex

WHILE SHERIFF of Arapahoe County, Patrick Sullivan once drove his jeep through a fence to rescue two of his deputies from a gunman. He also led a drive to convince the state legislature to ban assault weapons in an effort to cut down on the number of mass shootings. Aurora, the scene of a mass shooting in a movie multiplex in which twelve people were killed in 2012, is in Arapahoe County.

But on the afternoon of November 29, 2011, the man who was once named the nation's top sheriff was booked into the county jail that bore his name following his arrest for attempting to exchange methamphetamines for sex with a man.[1]

A judge, in an attempt to spare the sixty-nine-year-old Sullivan jail time, sentenced him to probation, but by June 2014, he had violated his probation a third time and was sentenced to 15 months in prison after a 911 caller said an "old man" was attempting to get three recovering addicts back on drugs. It turned out to be Sullivan, who was dealing meth to men in exchange for sex.[2]

Sullivan, who had retired in 2001 after 19 years as sheriff, was paroled from the Arkansas Valley Correctional Facility, a medium security prison in Ordway, Colorado, in March 2015.[3]

Sullivan wasn't the only Colorado sheriff to see his reputation sullied by a sex scandal, however.

Terry Maketa, Sheriff of El Paso County, was once considered a darling of the state's Republican Party until he became entangled in his own web of sexual misadventures in 2014. He was tried twice on various charges. When he was acquitted on several and deadlocked on others, he was retried. That trial also ended in a deadlocked jury and the presiding judge dismissed all charges against him.[4]

El Paso County, with 700,000 residents, is Colorado's most populous county and includes the cities of Denver and Colorado Springs.

Maketa, who was married, had been accused of having sexual relations with three subordinates, including his second-in-command, the sheriff's office's comptroller, and the head trainer for dispatchers. He was also accused of traveling with the women at taxpayer expense and of giving them raises and promoting them to positions for which they were unqualified. A formal complaint was filed by three commanders who also said he had used intimidation to keep people from reporting his removal of virtually all oversight of the department's $60 million annual budget. All three complainants were suspended by Maketa the following day.[5]

Maketa, as well as each of the three women, denied the reports of sexual relationships despite the discovery of "scores of sexually explicit text messages" to the three women from the sheriff. One of those included what appeared to be a "selfie" photo of Maketa nude from the waist up with the message, "wish you were here."[6] Among other things, Maketa was accused of threatening to terminate a $5.3 million contract with the county jail's health provider if it did not fire an employee who had refused to support term-limited Maketa's choice to succeed him.[7]

Sparsely-inhabited Sedgwick County (pop. 2,500) is nestled in Colorado's most extreme northeast corner abutting the southwestern corner of Nebraska.

Sheriff Thomas Hanna was arrested in August 2016 on charges that he sexually assaulted a developmentally disabled female inmate at his home before transporting her to jail. He was initially charged with sexual assault of an at-risk adult, sexual conduct in a correctional institute, prostitute-solicitation, and first-degree official misconduct. He was tried and found guilty of "official misconduct" on May 8, 2018 and the other charges were dropped. On July 13, was sentenced to seven months in jail with work release as a condition of twelve months' probation.[8]

(As an example of the disparity in sentencing, just a month later, a former special education assistant in Greely, Colorado, received 18 years following her conviction of sexually assaulting a fourteen-year-old student and sending nude photos of herself to other students.)

Hanna's conviction and sentence, did, however, carry the requirement that his Colorado peace officer certification be revoked, assuring that he would never again work in law enforcement.[9]

The Denver Sheriff's Office, not to be confused with the El Paso County Sheriff's Office, ran into a scandal of its own in 2017 when several embarrassing incidents became public:

- Sheriff Gary Wilson was forced to resign after it was revealed that he had a criminal record. His appointed successor, it turned out, had his own criminal record.
- Deputy Brad Lovingier was caught on video slamming a handcuffed inmate into a wall at a court hearing.
- Deputy Matthew Andrews assisted a prisoner's escape from jail by allowing him to wear his hat and coat as he walked out of the building.
- Michael Than, the second-highest-ranking member of the department, was accused of stealing nearly 1,300 copies of Turbo Tax software from several stores and selling them for more than $60,000 on eBay.[10]

6

Delaware: First State, First Sheriff

ON DECEMBER 7, 1787, Delaware was the first of the thirteen original colonies to ratify the U.S. Constitution, thus becoming the fledgling nation's first state. Delaware's first sheriff took office in 1669, one hundred eighteen years before that historic event and one hundred seven years before the Declaration of Independence.

And for more than 340 years, sheriffs in the state's three counties did little to attract unwanted attention.

All that changed in 2011 when the Sussex County administrator ordered Sheriff Jeff Christopher, a Tea Party Republican, to cease making traffic stops and taking people into custody unless ordered to do so by a court, and to remove emergency lights from all sheriff's vehicles.

Meanwhile, Delaware Attorney General Beau Biden, son of Vic President (and future President) Joe Biden, issued several non-binding opinions which concluded that sheriffs did not have police, or arrest, powers.

In June 2012, state lawmakers made it official by passing a law explicitly barring sheriffs and their deputies from making arrests. Christopher sued, falling back on the argument of the "constitutional sheriff" idea that federal and state governments are subordinate to local governing authority. He argued that lawmakers exceeded their authority and that they could not limit the power of sheriffs without passing a constitutional amendment. He said that because the Delaware constitution names sheriffs as "conservators of the peace," they have constitutional— not common law—powers, including arrest powers.

But the Delaware Supreme Court on October 7, 2013, in a twenty-six-page opinion, ruled that while the General Assembly could not abrogate a constitutional office or remove the core duties of a constitutional officer without a constitutional amendment, the sheriff's common law arrest power was not a fundamental or core duty of his role as "conservator of the peace," but rather was "merely incidental," and that the sheriff's arrest power "can be modified or even eliminated by the statute" and that the sheriff's argument to the contrary "is without merit." [1]

Christopher said he began to notice as far back as 2000 a reduction in funding and the chipping away of his office's powers. "Now my deputies and I have been relieved of all arrest powers and [we] can't even make a traffic stop," he said. "Delaware has only three counties. The other two sheriffs will not stand up with me."[2]

7

Florida: The No-Sunshine State

FROM DUMPING a paralyzed man from his wheelchair to planting drugs during routine traffic stops to mail fraud and tax evasion to failure adequately respond to a school shooting to just about every type of sex scandal you might imagine, Florida sheriffs' departments seemed to have it all.

News reports erroneously referred to Brian Sterner as a quadriplegic which, by definition means paralysis of all four limbs. Sterner, who had broken his neck in 1994 and drove a vehicle fitted with hand controls, was, in fact, a paraplegic since he had use of his arms.

But that seemed to be matter little to Hillsborough County sheriff's deputy Charlotte Marshall-Jones who unceremoniously dumped Sterner from his wheelchair when he didn't comply with her order for him to stand up while being booked for failing to appear in court to answer a traffic violation.

Marshall-Jones, a twenty-two-year veteran of the sheriff's office, was suspended without pay for the incident and three supervisors who stood by and did nothing after witnessing the incident were placed on administrative leave.

"I was appalled," said Joe +, chief deputy for the sheriff's department. "Obviously, the actions are indefensible at every level."[1]

Ken Jenne was a Broward County prosecutor and served in the Florida State Senate for 18 years before he was appointed in 1998 by then-Governor Lawton Chiles as sheriff of Broward County to succeed the late Ron Cochran. He presided over an office with 6,300 employees and an annual budget of $712 million in the state's second-most populous county.

Considered a likely candidate for higher office, possibly even governor, he resigned in disgrace less than ten years later when he pleaded guilty to federal tax evasion and mail fraud following a federal corruption investigation. In the end, it was revealed that he had sold his office, leaving his career in ruins in the process, for a paltry $151,625.[2]

An investigation that began as a probe into inflated crime statistics for the department soon evolved into revelations of money laundering and kickbacks from vendors. His former law firm was found to be paying for his Mercedes and auto insurance. When he obtained a desperation twenty-thousand-dollar loan, he had the money paid to his secretaries who would make deposits in increments of smaller amounts into his personal bank account. It was "nickel and dime stuff," as one observer described it. "That's not something the sheriff of Broward County should be doing," said prosecutor Matt Axelrod. "That's something drug dealers do."[3]

In 2004, the Broward County Sheriff's Office, the third-largest in the nation, touted statistics claiming that more than half of the crimes committed in 2003 had been solved. That was more than twice the national average and was also untrue.

Some of the crimes reported as solved were laid at the feet of people who were incarcerated or deceased at the time the crimes occurred. Other felonies were reduced to lesser misdemeanors in order to keep them out of official reports. A former aide to Jenne said he had been instructed to smear a reporter who was questioning the crime figures.

Two detectives were charged with criminal misconduct for falsely clearing cases and in the final analysis, actual numbers showed that crime was on the increase in much of Broward County.[4]

In all, 29 deputies were transferred in the wake of the phony crime statistics scandal that Jenne insisted occurred without his knowledge, prompting one of those who was transferred to observe, "Karma is a funny thing, isn't it? He was out there calling us bad apples."[5]

"…(H)e stayed too long, and in the end, he lost sight of what it means to serve the public," said U.S. Attorney Alex Acosta. "If as a community, we believe that public corruption and white-collar crimes cause as much harm as violent crime, we must insist on significant terms of imprisonment for public and corporate criminals."[5] (Ironically, Acosta's name would surface in the Jeffrey Epstein pedophilia scandal just a year later when he agreed to a plea bargain extremely favorable to Epstein.)

Broward County was rocked again on February 14, 2018, when Nikolas Cruz went on a shooting spree with a semi-automatic rifle at Marjory Stoneman Douglas High School in Parkland, Florida. The deadliest high school shooting spree in U.S. history left 17 people dead and another seventeen injured.

The mass shooting not only launched the most serious campaign for background checks to date, but set in motion events that would result in the end of Broward County Sheriff Scott Israel's career less than a year later.

The first and most visible indictment of the sheriff's office of course, was video that showed Broward County deputy Scot Peterson, armed and in uniform, hunkering down during Cruz's shooting spree instead of attempting to stop the shooter. Six days after the shooting, Peterson resigned in lieu of his being suspended without pay pending an internal investigation.[6]

But it quickly became evident that negligence on the part of school and law enforcement officials, including the sheriff's office and the FBI, went much deeper than Peterson's failure to confront Cruz. As early as the February 2016, two years before the shooting, Peterson was notified of complaints by Cruz's neighbors who said they feared he "planned to shoot up the school."[7] Moreover, a fellow student reported that he had used a school computer to research the making of nail bombs but the student said he was told by school administrators to mind his own business. School officials were also warned in the fall of 2016 that he threatened to kill a classmate.[8]

In the wake of those revelations, Israel steadfastly refused to resign in a confrontational interview with CNN host Jake Tapper. Asked if the killings might have been averted if Israel's department had acted on a number of tips about Cruz, the sheriff gave a curious response: "If ifs and buts were candy and nuts, O.J. Simpson would still be in the record books."

Tapper, incredulous, asked if Israel was "really not taking any responsibility for the multiple red flags that were brought to the attention of the Broward sheriff's office about this shooter before this incident?"

"Jake, I can only take responsibility for what I knew about. I exercised due diligence. I've given amazing leadership to this agency."[9]

Even as Israel was boasting of his "amazing leadership," Florida House Speaker Richard Corcoran on February 25, 2018, sent a four-page letter containing the names of 73 Republican House members calling on Governor Rick Scott to suspend Israel "immediately pursuant to …the Florida Constitution.[10]

Scott did not act on the letter but while he failed to act, his successor did not. On January 11, 2019, only days after taking office, new Governor Ron DeSantis suspended Israel, replacing him with former Coral Springs Police Sergeant Gregory Tony, who was skilled in active-shooter training. "I have no interest in dancing on Scott Israel's political grave, DeSantis said, "but suffice it to say the massacre might never have happened had Broward had better leadership in the sheriff's department."[11]

Abuses of office and betrayal of voters was not limited to Broward County by any means.

Charlie Morris appeared to have it all. After an eighteen-year career with the Air Force, he was first elected Sheriff of Okaloosa County in 1996 and won re-election in 2000, in 2004, and again in 2008 and served as President of the Florida Sheriffs' Association before it all came crashing down.

Okaloosa County is near the eastern end of the Florida Panhandle, bordered in the north by Alabama and on the south by the Gulf of Mexico and is home to some 200,000 residents. But in 2009, the county was poised to have six fewer inhabitants following the February arrest of Morris in Las Vegas. He had $30,000 in a hotel safe and $5,000 in his pocket at the time of his arrest.[12]

Within days of his arrest and hours before his scheduled appearance in federal court in Las Vegas on corruption charges, Florida Governor Charlie Crist suspended Morris from office. He had barely begun his fourth term as sheriff.

Morris and Teresa Adams, his office manager, were accused of paying "bonuses" from federal Homeland Security and Justice Training grants. Recipients were required to kickback part or all of their bonuses back to Morris in cash, ostensibly for charity. It turned out that Morris was the "charity," and he spent much of the money he received on gambling.

Pursuant to his guilty plea, Morris was sentenced on August 11, 2009, to six years in prison and ordered to pay $212,537 in restitution and to forfeit $194,000 in property. Federal Judge Lacey Collier said he had "tarnish(ed) the badge of every law enforcement officer in this entire area." The following month Adams pleaded guilty and was sentenced to three years in prison. Earlier, in January, Morris' chief of staff and mistress was found guilty following a trial, and three others in the sheriff's office faced racketeering charges in connection with the bonus scam.[13]

In the nine years from 2000 to early 2009, the Martin County Sheriff's Office paid out more than $1.33 million in lawsuit settlements over excessive force, falsified reports and wrongful arrests. A single case accounted for the bulk of that amount when an excessive force lawsuit was settled for $877,700 when Sergeant James Warren and four other deputies shot a man nine times for purse snatching. Dashboard camera footage showed the deputies as they continued firing at the man after he was face down on the ground.

But it was Deputy Steven O'Leary who appeared to bring the most embarrassment to the department for his handling of 80 arrests over an eleven-month period. Eleven people were released after substances that O'Leary claimed were narcotics in arrest after arrest turned out to be laundry detergent, sand, headache medicine and even simple rocks. He was fired by Sheriff William Snyder in January 2009 after he was notified by the Florida Attorney General's Office about the questionable arrests, though no criminal charges were brought against him.[14]

A deputy sheriff in Jackson County in the Florida panhandle took matters a step further than O'Leary. Instead of misidentifying substances as drugs, Zachary Wester would actually plant real drugs in the vehicles of cars he pulled over for minor infractions.

The former deputy was arrested on July 10, 2019, on 52 counts of racketeering, official misconduct, fabricating evidence, possession of a controlled substance and false imprisonment. In addition, he faced misdemeanor charges of perjury and possession of drug paraphernalia.

Wester, who was fired in September 2018, was accused of indiscriminately arresting innocent drivers after pulling them over for minor traffic violations and planting meth or marijuana in their vehicles while going through the motions of searching their cars.

No fewer than eleven victims were named in the affidavit charging Wester. One hundred nineteen cases involving him were subsequently dropped. A judge ordered eight inmates released from correctional facilities and 263 cases remained under review.

"There is no question that Wester's crimes were deliberate and that his actions put innocent people in jail," said Chris Williams, a Florida Department of Law Enforcement special agent. Ironically, while Wester was busy arresting innocent motorists for drug offenses, investigators discovered meth, marijuana and 42 pieces of drug paraphernalia in the trunk of his patrol vehicle.

Wester, who joined the Jackson County Sheriff's Department in 2016, came under suspicion in 2018 when a prosecutor noticed inconsistencies in what he wrote in his report and what was seen on his body camera—when, on the rare occasions he turned it on.

State Attorney William Eddins said investigators were attempting to learn Wester's motives. Eddins said any plea bargain with Wester was off the table and that the former deputy faced up to 30 years in prison for his actions.

Erika Helms, the sister of one victim who sued the sheriff's department over false arrest, said, "People are losing their lives, their freedom, their children, their marriages—all because of this one man. It's not just innocent men. It's innocent children. It goes a lot deeper than everyone realizes." She said her brother, Lance Sellers, was required to spend a year in residential rehab after his arrest for possession of meth. Charges against Sellers were later dropped. In addition to Sellers, more than a dozen of Wester's victims filed notices of intent to sue.[15]

Cheating on exams in college will get you expelled. Cheating to get into college might even get you unwanted headlines and a visit from authorities. Cheating to obtain a job where you have arrest powers over the general public is, well, disturbing.

But that's what occurred in Pinellas County, Florida, where Sheriff Bob Gualtieri hired 16 new deputies in November 2015 only to learn that seven of the 16 had been provided answers to training tests and foolishly raised red flags when they had perfect scores on their exams. "It shows their lack of a moral compass," Gualtieri said. "It shows their lack of a sense of right and wrong, and being willing to cut corners, and the ends justify the means, and they don't have to follow the rules. Well, in this profession, you have to follow the rules."

Gualtieri said training officer Eric Biddle knew one of the incoming recruits from their time together in nearby Pasco County. In text messages, Biddle told recruit Darold Cook, "It's not hard to be a rock star here," and offered to send Cook the test material.

In announcing the firing of the seven recruits and Biddle, Gualtieri said, "People who are cheats and liars don't belong working in law enforcement, and they're not going to work for the Pinellas County Sheriff's Office."

The irony, Gualtieri said, was that most of those implicated had prior law enforcement experience, had passed background checks, polygraphs and psychological evaluations, and should have easily passed the test without resorting to cheating.[16]

One common thread that seems to run through all political scandals, from town council to the presidency itself, is sex, more specifically, illicit sex. And it is quite apparent that sheriffs' offices are no exception.

LaVelle Pitts, sheriff of Bay County in the Florida panhandle from 1981-1989, was acquitted on four counts of perjury in May 1988 despite compelling testimony from several women who said they had either been demoted or fired for rejecting his demands for sex or who said they actually had ongoing sexual affairs with the sheriff. Five of the six jurors in his trial were convinced he was guilty but a lone holdout who had taught Pitts' granddaughter in Sunday School produced the not guilty verdict.

No fewer than eight women said that Pitts had demanded sex from them after being hired by his department. Some refused and paid for their refusals in the form of demotions or outright firings. Others acquiesced and were rewarded with gifts and favors—one was allowed to live rent-free in a mobile home he owned—from the married, born-again Christian sheriff, who would tell each woman she was the "only one he could trust."

First elected in 1980, Pitts, while celebrating his acquittal, vowed to seek a third term in the November election. But it was not to be. Guy Tunnell, police chief of Lynn Haven, was elected to succeed the fifty-four- year- Pitts.[17]

One might think that the negative publicity of having his deputies shoot fifteen rounds at a sixty-year-old unarmed man in his own driveway on August 2013 and a week later, climb through the window of a private residence without a warrant, pull a sleeping couple from their bed and shoot at their two dogs, one of which later died, would be sufficient cause for the sheriff of Escambia County to become somewhat introspective regarding to his department.[18]

But Sheriff David Morgan, who was given to wearing military ribbons on his uniform in violation of Defense Department regulations, was not a man who caved to public opinion. In fact, it seemed, the more criticism his office faced, the more defiant he became.

Escambia County is the westernmost county in the Florida panhandle, abutting Alabama to the north and to the west. It is home to Pensacola Naval Air Station, known as "The Cradle of Naval Aviation," where legendary baseball hall-of-famer Ted Williams trained during World War II. NFL hall of famer Roger Staubach, following a year's tour in Vietnam, also trained there and played on the base's Goshawks football team in 1967-68.

But by 2017, those were distant memories and the image in Escambia was vastly different for Sheriff Morgan and his department. It's one thing to defend your department against charges of excessive force. It's quite another to be accused of allowing a pedophile ring to operate openly within your ranks.

Two sisters, twins, filed separate lawsuits in federal court in October 2017, claiming that their mother and step-father, both employees of the Escambia County Sheriff's Office, had pimped them out to deputies in 2014 when both were minors. One of the suits named the sheriff's office, Sheriff Morgan, former Deputy Walter Michael Thomas Jr., and Deputy Mark Smith as defendants. The other sister's petition named only the sheriff's office, Morgan and Smith.

One of the lawsuits accused parents Leah and Douglas Manning of running a sex ring in which the sisters were sexually assaulted and said that Morgan "tolerated the sexual activities of his deputy sheriffs …because of his friendship and personal relationship with (Leah Manning)," who worked as a nurse for the sheriff's office at the time the abuse allegedly took place. Doug Manning was a deputy at the Escambia County Sheriff's Office at the time.

Both lawsuits claimed that Smith and other deputies would show up at the Manning home in uniform and in their patrol cars to engage in sex, sometimes remaining in uniform while assaulting the girls.

In related criminal charges, Smith was acquitted but Thomas was convicted in August 2016 and sentenced to 30 years in prison. Those charges stemmed from group sex with the Mannings and one of the girls, who was 17 at the time. Both Leah and Douglas Manning testified against Thomas, who will be a registered sex offender for 15 years after he is released from prison.

The Mannings said they had an open marriage in which each engaged in sex with multiple teenage girls, including the plaintiffs in the lawsuit. Leah Manning said her husband was jealous of her relationship with Thomas so he formed a relationship with one of his stepdaughters, which made Leah Manning jealous.

To resolve the festering jealousy, it was agreed that all four would have sex together. The two were convicted on lewd and lascivious behavior charges. Doug Manning, like Thomas, was sentenced to 30 years. Leah Manning was sentenced to 25 years. Both will be registered sex offenders for the remainder of their lives.[19]

The girls said they would come home from school and see different deputies' cars in the driveway. The lawsuit said as many as 40 deputies had sex with Leah Manning and she claimed that Sheriff Morgan was one of her sexual partners, a charge that Morgan vehemently denied. He claimed he had never met either Leah or Doug Manning, despite both having been employed in his department. "If I haven't met someone, how can I have sex with them?" he asked during a news conference.[20]

In her lawsuit, one of the girls said Morgan's sexual involvement with her mother created a conflict of interest as to the Escambia County's internal investigation of the sex ring.

Morgan was unsuccessful in his efforts to avoid giving a deposition as part of the girls' lawsuits. In a court filing what would seem to be a gift to standup comics were the subject matter not so sordid, he said a sheriff was not typically required to be a part of a deposition "and can designate a deputy to do it instead." Those claims notwithstanding, a federal judge ruled in July 2019 that because Morgan had voluntarily made public comments about the suit in his news conference, he had waived his right to exempt himself from giving a deposition. Morgan also filed motions to restrict access to cell phones and computers used in the prosecutions of the Mannings and Thomas.[21]

Clay County Sheriff Darryl Daniels, meanwhile, found it necessary to offer his apologies and regrets in May 2019 over his affair with a former co-worker and for the complexities such trysts often lead to when one or both parties are married to someone else. Everything started to come unraveled on May 14 when the sheriff of neighboring Duval County released a four-hundred-page internal affairs report that recommended that corrections officer Nicole Smith be fired. Among other things, the report revealed that Smith and Daniels had sex on duty in Daniels' office during the time when Daniels served as the Duval County jail director, before he was elected as Clay County's first black sheriff in 2016. Smith said in the report that she terminated the affair when she became engaged but continued her friendship with Daniels.

In addition to the internal affairs investigation, there were reports that Daniels' wife threatened Smith and that Daniels had ordered that Smith be arrested because she was stalking him. Meanwhile, Smith and her husband separated and Smith turned up pregnant, but the father was not immediately identified.[22]

An anonymous letter to Florida Governor Ron DeSantis, Attorney General Ashley Moody and the Florida Department of Law Enforcement

(FDLE) claimed that Daniels had threatened employees over leaks and asked that Daniels be removed from office. FDLE, meanwhile announced in June that it had begun a formal investigation, but stopped short of specifying just what it was investigating.[23]

LaVelle Pitts, David Morgan, and Darryl Daniels were the most high-profile cases of sex scandals in Florida sheriffs' offices. That's because they were the sheriffs of their respective counties. But there were other lurid stories involving illicit sex in other sheriffs' departments which involved deputies:

- In Broward County, a woman who claimed that because Prozac triggered a need for sex seven or eight times a day, her husband, a strapping six-foot-six deputy sheriff, couldn't keep up. The solution to Kathy and Jeffrey Willets was, quite obviously, prostitution. She ran personal ads to attract johns at $50 to $150 a session while her husband hid in a closet and took notes. The venture, which cost Fort Lauderdale decency crusader and Vice-Mayor John Danziger his job, worked until a "client" who allowed himself to become emotionally involved with Kathy heard Jeffrey Willets snoring in the closet and, fearing Kathy was being forced to turn tricks, called police. The deputy-pimp was subsequently suspended from the Broward County Sheriff's Office without pay and charged with living off the earnings of a prostitute. Both were later charged with wiretapping.[24]

- An Indian River County Sheriff's Deputy, James Cousins, resigned after rumors were confirmed that he received oral sex from a high school counselor as he drove her home from a high school football game in September 2018. He had been married only a few months and she had been married to a wildlife commission officer since 2007 and was the mother of two.[25]

- In Daytona Beach, Volusia County Sheriff Mike Chitwood said two of his deputies were forced to resign after an investigation determined the two, Bryan Scott Barnett, 50, and Jay Hawman, 47, were preying on women defendants participating in drug court programs. Chitwood said the two were in court when the presiding judge had personal conversations with the women who were later approached by the deputies who offered money or gifts in exchange for sex. Barnet resigned in December 2016 and Hawman was fired in July 2017 after at least ten women were interviewed by sheriff's investigators.[26]

- Marion County Sheriff Ed Dean announced in October 2012 that Undersheriff Dan Kuhn had resigned following allegations that Kuhn had met his mistress while on the job and in his office. The main problem for Kuhn was that he had won the Republican primary in the race for Marion County Sheriff. In making his announcement, Dean called on Kuhn to withdraw. "In view of the resignation of Dan Kuhn from the very office he seeks to be elected, coupled with admission of the extramarital affair …I believe it would be impossible for Dan Kuhn to effectively lead the sheriff's office. Kuhn, who dropped out of the race, admitted to an affair with the principal of a private school where his wife once taught. Two other deputies were suspended and demoted for unspecified involvement in Kuhn's affair.[27]

- Another sex scandal, this one in Walton County, cost five employees – a communications officer and four deputies – their jobs in January 2019. Sheriff Michael Adkinson, in announcing the firings, said, "None of these people should have been the least bit surprised. I've never been unclear about my expectations for conduct. If your personal life becomes a sheriff's office problem, it's going to end badly." And end badly it most certainly did. Communications Officer Mikaylah Coone was dating Investigator Aaron Ethridge. The only problem was, Sergeant Justin Tisdale and deputies Austin Bailey and Mat Williams were all having extramarital affairs with Coone, a fact that prompted Ethridge to threaten his three co-workers when he found out. Coone, for her part, was fired not only for the affairs, but also for lying about the trysts when questioned by investigators.[28]

- Scott Walker was interviewed, arrested and resigned following an investigation into claims that he solicited oral sex from a male employee he was training to write reports. Walker, it turns out was a deputy with the Polk County Sheriff's Office. Walker was arrested on October 5, 2018, on charges of sexual battery and false imprisonment. "We hold our people to a higher standard than we do members of the community," Polk County Sheriff Grady Judd said in a prepared statement." [29]

Sergeant Scott Lawson also worked for the Polk County Sheriff's Office. The department had been warned about a deputy preying on teenagers and Lawson had strip-searched a fifteen-year-old boy without reason. Still, the sheriff's office left him on the road. He loved to patrol the back roads late at night in search of bad boys.

Around 2:00 a.m. on May 31, 2002, he spotted a Volkswagen Passat and pulled in behind it in his unmarked Crown Victoria. When the Passat sped up, Lawson pursued, running stop signs and tearing around corners, but never employing his lights or siren. At 2:59 a.m., while going at speeds averaging 105 miles per hour, he rammed the Passat, causing it to hit a pine tree and split in two. The eighteen-year-old driver survived but his sixteen-year-old passenger, Miles White, did not. His body was found among the trees. Lawson immediately had his car removed from the scene in violation of department policy.

Lawson's report said dispatch told him the Passat was stolen (they did not), that he was never in pursuit (he was actually in pursuit for more than 15 miles), that he quit "surveillance" 2.7 miles before the crash and that he never exceeded 70 miles per hour.

A few days following the accident, a woman reported that she had seen photos of Lawson in news reports and realized he was the same one who had arrested her teenage son at a party and gave him a groin examination. A search warrant was obtained for Lawson's home and Detective Tom Page found rubber gloves, a stainless-steel examination table and a video called *Relax the Muscle, Please*. The detective interviewed 18 males, ages 16 to 28 and learned that Lawson had given most of them anal probes and genital exams – all while in uniform and in a department vehicle.

By the time investigators were finished, Lawson faced 36 charges that included nine counts of sexual battery, nine counts of battery and 18 counts of practicing medicine without a license. He resigned from the job he had held for 11 years and pleaded guilty to a single count of sexual battery and six counts of practicing medicine without a license. He was sentenced to 15 years in prison.

Detective Page initiated an investigation to determine if there was a link between the sex crimes and the crash that killed White but he halted the investigation. He told the *St. Petersburg Times* that he left the sheriff's office "because of how that investigation was done."[30]

A devastating seventy-two-page report by the FBI implicated members of the Fort Myers Police Department and at least one Lee County deputy sheriff in allegations of corruption.

The so-called Freeh Report, while heavily redacted, contained references to drug trafficking, information leaks by officers, murder and arranged hits. Besides noting that a potential witness was murdered it also twice referred to a Lee County deputy but did not specify if it was the same deputy. "It was reported that … sells narcotics under the protection of a Deputy…," and "…reported that the Deputy allowed … to use an LCSO [Lee County Sheriff's Office] vehicle to transport the narcotics."

At least three deputies were reportedly talking to the FBI about alleged corruption in the sheriff's office, including a report that at least one deputy was providing protection to a known drug trafficker. The three deputies said they had met with FBI agent James Rankine to report that:

- Opiates seized as evidence in previous cases was missing from the evidence room and other evidence showing criminal intent was either ignored or destroyed.
- A member of the sheriff's department was protecting a known drug trafficker who was the subject of a federal investigation.

The FBI, however, had no record of the May 2015 complaint by the three deputies and Agent Rankine, who retired from the FBI in February 2017, accepted a new one hundred thousand-dollar-per-year job—with the Lee County Sheriff's Office, the same agency he had declined to investigate.[31]

One of the most controversial cases in recent years concerned the manner in which the 2008 prosecution of sex predator Jeffrey Epstein was handled by Palm Beach County officials, including Sheriff Ric Bradshaw, whose office treated the registered sex offender more like a guest than a prisoner.

Not only was Epstein allowed out on work release in violation of Bradshaw's own policy, but he was alleged to have had sex with underage girls while he was supposedly working in the West Palm Beach office or at his home. Allowing him out on work release wasn't the only perk given him, however. Epstein's cell door was left unlocked and he was granted access to the jail's attorney meeting room where there was a television. He was even allowed to move to a separate non-staffed area of he jail after he agreed to pay for his own guards.

Bradshaw's department was in denial for more than a decade about its mishandling of Epstein's so-called incarceration and when State Senator Lauren Book, a survivor of childhood sexual abuse, called for the Florida Department of Law Enforcement to investigate the sheriff's office, Bradshaw announced, somewhat belatedly, that he was initiating his own internal investigation into whether his department properly monitored Epstein, who an Associated Press report said had "sexual contacts" with young women in Bradshaw's office.[32]

Pasco County Sheriff Chris Nocco thought he had a pretty good idea for preventing crime on his turf. Unfortunately, his method included harassment, intimidation, invasion of privacy and violations of constitutional rights that you might expect from an authoritarian regime, according to a July 26, 2021, story in the *Tampa Bay Times*.

Nocco's Office of Pre-Crime was created to compile a list of people it considers likely to break the law based on past criminal histories, social networks and outright surveillance. Deputies even showed up at subjects' homes repeatedly, often with no search warrant and no probable cause for arrests to write tickets for non-violations like overgrown grass and making arrests for vague or no reasons.

In some cases, letters were even sent to pre-criminals that read, "You may wonder why you were enrolled in this program. You were selected as a result of an evaluation of your recent criminal behavior using an unbiased, evidence-based risk assessment designed to identify prolific offenders in our community. As a result of this designation, we go to great efforts to encourage change in your life through enhanced support and increased accountability."

The agency even created a separate program that used schoolchildren's grades, attendance records and abuse histories to label them potential future criminals, a practice that national experts on policing compared to child abuse.

Not surprisingly, the tactic resulted in four subjects of increased scrutiny filing federal lawsuits against the sheriff's office.[33]

That would be bad enough if that was the only egregious action, but in 2019, more than 40 current employees of the Pasco County Sheriff's

Office were sued by 20 former employees who cited cases of extortion, coercion and wrongful termination. Most of the allegations in the 400-page lawsuit accused administrative officials of filing or signing off on false internal affairs complaints against employees, which created problems when they sought other employment.

One employee was accused of threatening to euthanize a K-9 and blame the death on his handler. To prevent the dog's death, the handler said he purchased the animal for $8,500. In another instance, a male employee reported a case of gender discrimination against women to his superiors. After reporting it, he claims false complaints were filed against him in retaliation and he was eventually terminated.[34]

A year before that lawsuit was filed, on August 2, 2018, Pasco Sheriff's Office deputies pulled over a vehicle in which Marques Johnson was a passenger on the pretense that the deputies were unable to see a part of the license plate on a trailer the vehicle was pulling. Johnson, whose father was driving the vehicle, refused to provide his identification and was arrested for resisting arrest even though Florida law stipulates that a law enforcement officer cannot arrest an individual for failure to identify himself if the request for ID was not reasonably related to the circumstances justifying the stop.

After arresting Johnson, deputies searched the vehicle for drugs despite the fact that the basis for the stop was the obscured license plate. No drugs were found and a judge subsequently dismissed the charges against Johnson who filed a federal lawsuit, claiming his civil rights were violated.[35]

Karla Bello claimed discrimination based on gender identity when she was held for eleven days in men's housing by the Pinellas County Sheriff's Office for unpaid parking tickets. Bello, who identifies as a female, filed suit in September 2020 in U.S. District Court in Florida's Middle District, claiming violations of her civil rights.[36]

Cited by USA Today Network, the Hendry County Sheriff's Department is one of Florida's worst, but no one could say that Sheriff Steve Whidden didn't believe in giving second – or third – chances to law enforcement miscreants.

In all, he hired 51 deputies between 2009 and 2021 who had histories of personal or professional misconduct. Of that number, 24 had been fired or resigned when accused of misconduct elsewhere and the remaining 27 had previously committed offenses that would have been considered to be violations of moral character had the acts been committed while employed as law enforcement officers. The offenses included DUI, theft, drug possession, falsification of records, making false statements, prostitution, subverting testing processes, misuse of position and discriminatory conduct.

At the beginning of 2021, of the department's 112 deputies, 32 remained employed who had tainted pasts that would conceivably disqualify them from law enforcement jobs anywhere else. That number represents 28.6 percent of the entire department – more than one in every four deputies. Seventeen current deputies, or 15 percent of the full-time roster, were either fired or resigned because of misconduct elsewhere. That's more than seven times the average rate for all other Florida law enforcement agencies, according to the *Yale Law Journal*.

Sergeant Nestor Echevarria, for example, was accused of pumping four bullets into Tyrone Reed as he lay in his own yard as other deputies sprayed about 30 bullets in all directions around the property when they responded to complaints about a block party. Scot Goldberg, Reed's attorney, noted that Echevarria had previously been fired from the Department of Corrections for using excessive force. "They take bad cops as a matter of custom," Goldberg said.

David Thomas, a former Gainesville police officer and currently an associate professor of forensic studies at Florida Gulf Coast University said there was "no excuse" for hiring deputies who had histories of misconduct. "The reality is that the person is ineffective and incapable of doing their job," Thomas said. "As a community member, I wouldn't want that. I would want quality service, quality employees and people I can trust."

As bad as Hendry County is, though, it's not the worst in Florida. The Gadsden County Sheriff's Office has nearly a third (32.9 percent) of its deputies who previously were either fired or resigned in the face of misconduct charges by other agencies.[37]

8

Georgia on My Mind

GEORGIA HAS 159 counties, second only to Texas' 254. Two theories arise when efforts are made to understand why there are so many counties. One story, which is not backed by any official action or edict, has it that counties were made deliberately small so that farmers in their mule-drawn wagons could get to the courthouse and back within a single day.

The other, more plausible explanation claims that the population of the state was so rural and dispersed, that by creating a structure of so many county governments, rural Georgia would be able to control the state. That's because in the late nineteenth century, there was something called the County Unit System whereby candidates won not by the number of votes they received, but by the number of counties they carried.[1]

But at least 32 of those counties have experienced some form of scandal or impropriety in their sheriffs' departments since 1950. That's 20 percent of the total counties – significant enough to cause concern, especially in a county like DeKalb, which includes part of Atlanta, the state's largest city, which has had at least seven separate cases of dishonor heaped upon the local sheriff's office. Three other counties, Fulton, Douglas and Clayton had two cases each of questionable or illegal practices.

Over the past 40 years, no fewer than three dozen sheriffs and deputies have been indicted and convicted of a multitude of offenses from sexual assaults to theft and embezzlement to taking payoffs from drug dealers.

The most flagrant and easily the most tragic occurred shortly after the sheriff's election in DeKalb County in 2000. In that election, challenger Derwin Brown, a veteran of more than two decades in law enforcement, defeated incumbent Sidney Dorsey, who was under investigation for racketeering and theft. It had been a bitter campaign and Dorsey was not about to go quietly.

On the night of December 15, 2000, Brown was in a good mood. He was three days from being inaugurated as sheriff of DeKalb County. But more important, it was his wife's birthday. He exited his car and started walking up his driveway. In his hand were a dozen roses for his wife Phyllis. Suddenly, the cold December night exploded with gunfire. Brown, struck by 12 bullets fell to the ground. His wife testified she knew he was dead as soon as she looked into his eyes.

District Attorney Tom Morgan immediately suspected Dorsey. His office had been investigating Dorsey for months, looking into his use of deputies for his personal business—he ran a private security firm—and administered contracts for the county's 3,700-bed jail, the largest in the South.

Dorsey had been sheriff for only one term before his defeat by Brown. He was elected in 1996, becoming DeKalb County's first African-American sheriff. But, prosecutors, said, he was power-obsessed. They got their first break when Patrick Cuffy was arrested for an unrelated killing of a man found outside his apartment. He negotiated a plea bargain whereby he would be given immunity in exchange for his testimony about Brown's murder. Cuffy testified that Dorsey wrote "Kill Derwin Brown" on a note and then the sheriff ate the note so as to leave no evidence.

Dorsey had killed two other people before. In 1965 he killed a man in a shootout while serving as an Atlanta police officer. He was cleared of wrongdoing in that case. In 1970, he killed a second man in a fight at a gas station. Charged with manslaughter, he was never tried after he said his gun discharged accidentally.

At both his trial at which he was convicted and at his sentencing, he continued to claim he was innocent. "I do not have the blood of Derwin Brown on my hands," he told the presiding judge who sentenced him to life in Georgia State Prison. He finally confessed in 2007 to having Brown killed.[2]

Dorsey's predecessor was Pat Jarvis, who served for 19 years, from 1976 to 1995.

Before becoming sheriff of DeKalb County, Jarvis for seven years was a pitcher for the Atlanta Braves where he won 83 games. He retired from baseball in 1974 and two years later ran to succeed Roy Bonner (more on him shortly).

He resigned in 1995 and the following year federal prosecutors began investigating his dealings with jail contractors and bonding companies.

They learned Jarvis had received as much as $200,000 in kickbacks. He eventually pleaded guilty to mail fraud and in 1999 started serving a fifteen-year federal prison sentence. U.S. District Judge Thomas Thrash also ordered him to pay a $40,000 fine.[3]

Incumbent Sheriff Jeff Mann faced a stiff challenge from Vernon Jones in 2016 with Jones charging that Mann used sheriff's office employees to perform campaign work on Mann's behalf and that he had failed to protect inmates from jailhouse violence.

Jones had his own political baggage. A special grand jury the year before had cleared him of wrongdoing in alleged bid rigging during his tenure as DeKalb County CEO.

Mann, a veteran of the U.S. Air Force and an attorney, would win that election but his tenure would be short-lived. In May 2017, just over two years after taking office, Mann was running again, while not for office, at least for his political life. An Atlanta police officer patrolling an area known for homosexual activity spotted a male—Mann, it turned out—as he fondled and exposed himself before walking toward him.

When the officer identified himself, the chase was on. The fifty-four-year-old Mann was no match for the younger officer and he was caught a couple of blocks later. The officer said he found two condoms in Mann's pocket.[4]

Mann was just the latest in a long line of DeKalb County sheriffs. Going all the way back to the early 1950s, there are four others besides Dorsey, Jarvis and Mann who generated negative headlines:

- Clem Jolly served only two years, from January 1951 to January 1953 before the seventy-five-year-old sheriff was accused of stealing funds from his office. Claiming politics was behind the charges, he nevertheless admitted to "bad judgment" on his part. A jury acquitted him in June 1951.
- Robert Broome succeeded Jolly and served eleven years, from January 1, 1953, to December 31, 1963, during which time he was sued for defrauding a "mentally incompetent" man in a land purchase deal. He was cleared of wrongdoing in 1957.
- Things got a little stickier for Broome's successor, J. Lamar Martin who nevertheless managed to hold office for nine years, from January 1, 1964 to December 31, 1972. Martin was convicted of accept-

ing four bribes from a bail bondsman in a bond kickback scheme that would eventually result in legislative action prohibiting sheriffs from participating in the bail bond business. In Martin's case, he was found guilty of accepting kickbacks totaling $12,905 and was subsequently fined an identical amount with no jail time.

- Martin's, successor, Rayburn L. "Roy" Bonner, served only one four-year term, from January 1, 1973, to December 31, 1976. Indicted in `1976 on two counts of perjury and a single count of mail fraud, he was accused of selling tickets to a fundraiser for a local hospital, but remitting only 25 percent of the money to the hospital. The indictment was subsequently thrown out but it apparently was enough to cost him re-election in 1976. Three months after leaving office, in March 1977, he was tried and acquitted for the murder of a sixteen-year-old boy he said was trying to break into his car.[5]

The campaign for sheriff of Forsyth County got especially ugly in 2016 when incumbent Sheriff Duane Piper questioned why challenger Ron Freeman didn't fire a deputy under his supervision in 2011 when it was learned that the married deputy had sex on multiple occasions with an eighteen-year-old girl while on the job.

Piper made the issue public in a graphic campaign flyer that contained a copy of the girl's handwritten complaint. The deputy was demoted, Freeman said, after he verbally recommended his termination. He ultimately wrote a memo recommending demotion and as a result, the deputy was able to work for other law enforcement agencies, which is what happened, Piper pointed out.

"As a result, this particular officer is now working at the campus of Georgia State University around other eighteen-year-old girls," he said.[6]

Piper's last-minute strategy didn't work as Forsyth County voters elected Freeman.

In Alma, Georgia, Bacon County Sheriff Mark Cothren found himself an inmate in his own jail following his arrest for battery after he grabbed a seventy-five-year-old man by the throat outside the sheriff's office on May 22, 2019.

Georgia Bureau of Investigation (GBI) agent Mark Pro said the man, John Daniel Melton, was walking up to the sheriff's office and was engaged in conversation with the sheriff when Cothren grabbed the elderly may by the throat. Pro said Melton was not an inmate or in custody, nor did he strike the sheriff. "The sheriff just released him and the guy (Melton) went on his way," Pro said.

Cothren, twenty-five years younger than Melton, was elected sheriff in 2016. He began his career with the sheriff's department in 1990 and rose through the ranks from jailer to investigator and chief deputy before his election.

Making matters worse from a public relations standpoint, the sheriff's office initially refused requests for a copy of Cothren's booking photo, a service it normally provides and which is considered a public record under Georgia law.

The Georgia Sheriffs' Association made a recommendation to Georgia Governor Brian Kemp to initiate an investigation of the incident and to determine if Cothren should be suspended with pay pending the outcome of the case.[7]

When Butts County Sheriff Gary Long took office in January 2013, he promised that he would not tolerate any type of unlawful drugs by his deputies. He had heard that deputies may have been using performance enhancing drugs. Upon taking office, he put out the word to his staff that no such conduct would be permitted.

A year later, six deputies became former deputies following an internal investigation initiated on January 22, 2014. Two deputies were fired outright and two days later four additional deputies submitted their resignations. Five of the deputies were holdovers from the previous sheriff's administration and one was hired by Long. None of the deputies' names were provided by Long.

The sheriff said no criminal charges were filed against the six but that he referred their cases to the Georgia Peace Officer Standards and Training (POST) Council. A revocation of their POST certifications would have meant they were not qualified to work for another law enforcement agency. There was no word of the outcome of the POST Council's investigation.[8]

Walker County Sheriff Steve Wilson said in 2019 that the installation of dash cameras for sheriff's department vehicles was too costly and not a priority.[9]

It's probably a good thing they weren't available three years earlier.

Deputy Wesley Holland was fired in May 2016 and was arrested on three felony counts of sexual assault by a person with authority, sodomy, and violation of oath, according to Wilson.

The charges stemmed from an investigation by the Georgia Bureau of Investigation that revealed that Holland was transporting a female prisoner from Fort Oglethorpe, Georgia, to Dunwoody, Georgia on April 30. While en route, Holland stopped his patrol car in Gordon County, which is immediately southeast of Walker County in the northwestern part of the state.

The female reported the assault to authorities in Dunwoody and they notified Wilson who requested the GBI investigate the matter. [10]

Two female employees of the Douglas County Jail were fired in 2002 after being accused of having improper sexual relations with inmates. Sheriff Phil Miller said corrections officer Belverly Arnold was observed entering a supply storage area with a male prisoner at the jail. The two were discovered shortly afterward as they were engaged in sex. A cook, Shirley Billinger, 61, was also found to have engaged in sexual relations with prisoners.[11]

Seven deputies in Rockdale County were suspended in September 2014 for possible cheating on an online test being offered by the Georgia Public Safety Training Center.

The seven were among 15 investigators assigned to general investigations in the Rockdale County Sheriff's Office. That represented more than half the total number of investigators in the office.

The cheating accusation affected more than test scores. Sheriff Eric Levett notified District Attorney Richard Read who said the scandal could affect cases pending before a Rockdale County grand jury where three of the suspended deputies had been scheduled to appear.[12]

A Richmond County deputy, whose responsibility it was to randomly certify coin-operated Georgia Lottery machines, was suspended and arrested because he didn't. Lieutenant Richard Elim was arrested in October 2018 when it was learned he was paid for inspecting a machine at a location that had not had a machine for "quite some time," according to Sheriff Richard Roundtree.

Deputies inspected the machines during their off-time as a special duty and are reimbursed by the Georgia Lottery. In Elim's case, he was charged with felony theft by deception after receiving $385 for work he did not perform. "Some of the stores that (Elim) claimed to inspect no longer had machines in them," Roundtree said.[13]

A reluctance to pursue sexual harassment complaints by female deputies eventually caught former Spalding County Sheriff Department Captain David Gibson up in an investigation of a cover-up and left the sheriff struggling to defend his lack of action, lending credence to the adage that the coverup is usually as bad as or worse than the original crime.

Gibson was indicted for multiple sex charges involving deputies he supervised in September 2015, but even more disturbing from a First Amendment standpoint was the revelation that a local attorney made an unprecedented offer to file a lawsuit to block a citizen from obtaining the department's file on Gibson, an offer that was accepted by the sheriff's office.

The indictment said that investigators noted several complaints from female deputies. Gibson, it said, exposed himself to one deputy, sent graphic photos to another deputy and solicited subordinates to have sex with him. It also said Gibson admitted to watching pornography on office equipment and on various websites.

Local truck driver Will Sanders made a public records request for a copy of the investigative file and instead, Sheriff Wendell Beam's secretary Ruby King sued to block him and incredibly, a judge granted her a temporary restraining order. That only served to pique Sanders' curiosity even more. "I knew there was more to the story than just them not wanting to release the records," he said.

Sanders made the same open records request to the Spalding County Board of Commissioners which gave him the records in compliance with the state's open records law. The report listed several employees who said they complained to Sheriff Beam about behavior on the part of Gibson. Beam said that he took no action because of the employees' reluctance to put their complaints in writing, prompting Sanders to opine that he believed the sheriff's failure to take action on the complaints was the reason the department attempted to shield the records from him.

"There is reference over and over inside the documents referring to Sheriff Beam knowing about what was going on and he took no action," he said.

Perplexed by the sheriff's department's resistance to releasing the records, Sanders made a second open records request—this time for department phone records. It turned out that all phone calls coming into the Spalding County Sheriff's Department are recorded.

Those recordings revealed that local attorney Johnnie Caldwell offered to file a lawsuit to block him from obtaining the Gibson file. King, worried that the victims' names would be made public, accepted Caldwell's offer.[14]

Sometimes the frustration of trying to do your job can lead you to commit actions you later regret. Such was the case of Treutlen County Sheriff Wayne Hook who was convicted in federal court in August 2003 of slapping two men he had just arrested.

It all began when Steven Tanner and Tony King led Deputy Ryan Griner (Hooks' first cousin) on a chase in 2001 that resulted in Griner wrecking his patrol car. The two were apprehended on October 27 at a Huddle House restaurant and Hooks later slapped each at the jail. Hooks' attorney, Jim Wiggins, described the incident as "merely the frustration of a very exhausted man who could not believe people could be so stupid. He could not deal with this kind of stupidity after the week he had."

The incident occurred around 2:00 a.m. Wiggins said Hooks had only about ten hours' sleep over three days because he was investigating a bank robbery and had been asleep only about an hour when he got a call that Griner had been in a wreck. The same jury acquitted Griner.

Some observers said the zeal with which prosecutors went after Hooks was a result of Hooks' assertion of his control of the county. "I'm sure Wayne irritated a lot of people, including the (FBI), because this was his place—his county—and he let people know," one local businessman said.[15]

Unlike another sheriff convicted of federal civil rights violations a decade earlier, Hooks was relieved of office and an interim sheriff appointed to serve until a special election could be held. In 1990, Oconee County Sheriff Terry Roach was similarly convicted of a federal civil rights violation in Georgia's Middle District but continued to hold office while incarcerated in a minimum-security prison in Alabama. He lost his bid for re-election in 1992 after only one four-year term.[16]

There is no room for argument that Clayton County Sheriff Victor Hill is skilled, albeit unintentionally, at making news. Clayton County, with more than a quarter-million residents, is fertile ground for enterprising newspaper reporters. Kem Kimbrough, who unseated Hill in 2008, directed deputies to investigate Hill in 2012 when he learned Hill, first elected in 2004, would oppose him for the second time in four years.

The result was that Hill, even while weighted down by a thirty-seven-count felony indictment, defeated Kimbrough. Prosecutors charged Hill with racketeering, theft, violation of his oath of office, making false statements and influencing a witness, though the latter charge was dropped during his trial. They said Hill, in his first term, was guilty of falsifying attendance records for an office employee and of taking county-issued cars on out-of-state vacations and used county gasoline or purchased fuel for personal travel with his county-issued credit cards.[17]

He was acquitted of all charges on August 15, 2013 but less than two years later he was back in the news when he accidentally shot a real estate agent he was offering defensive advice to. The woman, who was struck in the abdomen, testified that she did not believe he had harmed her intentionally. At the time of the May 2015 shooting, Hill refused to cooperate with investigators and declined to talk to Gwinnett County police.

He was arrested on a charge of reckless conduct, a misdemeanor. He pleaded no contest and was sentenced to twelve months' probation and fined one thousand dollars. In March 2017, nearly two years after the incident, his Georgia Peace Officer Standards and Training (POST) certification was placed on two-year probation, an action that required him to undergo additional training in order to become re-certified. The POST Probable Cause Committee determined that his actions were "unprofessional" and "indicative of bad moral character or untrustworthiness" and warranted disciplinary action.[18]

The very next year Hill was making headlines again, this time over a running feud he had with one of his former deputies. On August 27, 2018, Hill said that Deputy Robert Hawes had resigned in lieu of termination over a missing weapon that Hawes said he sold to a non-existent Atlanta police officer. Hill said Hawes had previously resigned in lieu of termination from the Atlanta Police Department, also for lying in an investigation. Hawes denied that he had resigned in lieu of termination from the sheriff's department but had simply resigned.

Hawes was released on $26,000 bail following his arrest for false official certificates, two counts of violation of oath as a public officer, and false statements in an ongoing battle with Hill. He had been charged in connection with what Hill described as a false report that he had sold his missing service weapon to an Atlanta police officer and for writing a fake ticket as cover for a stripper (no pun intended) who didn't want her boyfriend to know she'd been out all night.

Records provided by Hill indicated that Hawes was supposed to have turned in his missing pistol in October 2017 so that it could be replaced with a later model weapon. The serial number on the one he turned in did not match sheriff's office records. Hawes said he sold a Glock 42 to an Atlanta police officer and must have sold his service weapon instead. A check with the Atlanta Police Department indicated that no such officer by the name provided by Hawes ever worked there and that Hawes had fabricated the name.

Another weapon issued to Hawes was reported lost or stolen in 2014 after being left where his son and his son's friends had access to it. When Hawes' son became a suspect in the missing weapon, a second deputy tipped off Hawes of a fraud warrant against his son. As a result, Hill said one deputy was fired and another demoted and that the case would be reopened.

Additionally, Hill said a ticket was found in Hawes' patrol car after his resignation but there was no corresponding arrest record for the woman named. When contacted, she explained that she "was an exotic dancer and that Hawes wrote her the ticket so she could show it to her boyfriend to explain why she was out all night," Hill said.[19]

Former Telfair County Sheriff Jimmie Williamson was sentenced to three years in prison and fined $10,000 on June 29, 2009 after pleading guilty to charges of mail fraud and deprivation of honest services. Williams served two terms as sheriff, beginning in 2000 but by 2008, found himself facing multiple federal charges which could have resulted in up to twenty years' imprisonment and fines of up to $250,000.

Among the charges initially filed against Williamson:

- Embezzlement for his personal use fines and bond money received from individuals arrested in Telfair County;
- Acceptance of bribes from individuals arrested in exchange for reductions or dismissals of pending charges against them;
- Expenditure of public funds for the purchase of items for his own personal use.[20]

In one case, Williamson was accused of keeping $5,000 seized in a traffic stop. Federal prosecutors, however, said receipt books from the sheriff's office were never recovered, which prevented investigators from determining exactly how much county money was actually missing.[21]

In 2004, it had been only two years since several Dodge County officials, including a former sheriff, had gone to jail for voter fraud when Lawton Douglas found himself locked in a runoff election for the Dodge County Sheriff's job, so it would be reasonable to expect the candidates to run squeaky-clean campaigns. In an ideal world, that might be the case.

But for Douglas, the race had become something of a personal obsession. Both his grandfather and great-grandfather had run for sheriff and lost. Douglas, too, had run in 2000 and lost, so perhaps he felt family honor was at stake in 2004 when he ran again in 2004 and won by 400 votes only to be defeated for re-election in 2008.[22]

But it was his 2004 victory that was his ultimate downfall. On June 29, 2010, he was sentenced to 18 months in federal prison after it was revealed he, along with Dodge County Deputy Sheriff Olin Norman Gibson, had bought hundreds of votes with cash, liquor, and in some cases, drugs, in his 2004 runoff victory.

Prosecutors said that Douglas supporters paid voters for their blank absentee ballots and filled the ballots out with votes for Douglas. U.S. Attorney Edward Tarver said election fraud "strikes at the very heart of our democracy."[23]

After nearly four full terms in office, Wilcox County Sheriff Stacy Bloodsworth was sentenced to ten years in federal prison on May 8, 2013, for his part on the beating of three inmates and the subsequent attempt at covering up the incident.

Bloodsworth, who was first elected sheriff in 1994, resigned in February 2012, apparently in anticipation of a federal indictment which was handed down in May of that year.

It wasn't enough that he was forced out of office and sentenced to prison. He also took four others down with him—his son, Austin Bloodsworth (eighteen months), inmate-trustee Willie James Caruthers (eighteen months), former South Central Georgia Drug Task Force Agent Timothy King, Jr. (six months), and former Wilcox County Jailer Casey Owens (probation).

Sheriff Bloodsworth admitted during a plea hearing that on July 23, 2009, he was inside the Wilcox County Jail with the other defendants when, in his anger, he ordered the three prisoners out of their cells because one of them reportedly had a cell phone. Bloodsworth personally hit all three inmates and watched as the other participants hit and kicked them.

Incredulously, when it appeared that one inmate's jaw was broken,

Sheriff Bloodsworth attempted to put his broken jaw back in place with a wrench. It wasn't until a week later that the prisoner was taken to a hospital where his jaw was wired shut.

Compounding his poor judgment, Bloodsworth then concocted a story and instructed the others that if they were ever questioned, they were to say that Caruthers and the victim got into an altercation when the victim used a racial slur against Caruthers. He further instructed Caruthers and Owens to write the false cover story in a report.

Besides Sheriff Bloodsworth, Caruthers pleaded guilty to assaulting the inmate and to conspiring to cover up the assault. Austin Bloodsworth and Timothy King, Jr. each pleaded guilty to conspiring to cover up the assault and Owens pleaded guilty to misprision of a felony. [24]

Turner County Sheriff Roy Wiley probably had no idea his good deed might cost him his job and possibly even his freedom.

But on July 22, 2011, it was learned that Wiley had become the target of a criminal investigation that began on July 8 and by August 1, he had resigned after only two and one-half years in office. Twelve days later he entered a guilty plea and surrendered his police officer certification.

The charge? Wiley, who prior to his election in 2008 was the Sycamore, Georgia chief of police, was being investigated on connection with the removal of a bag of marijuana from the sheriff's office's criminal evidence room.

He was said to have instructed a deputy to remove "a small quantity" of marijuana that was being used to train drug sniffing dogs so that he could give it to a friend whose wife was suffering from cancer.

Craig Rotter, assistant special agent in charge of the Georgia Bureau of Investigation's Perry office, said Wiley thought the marijuana might help her in her chemotherapy treatment. The recipient of the marijuana also pleaded guilty to misdemeanor possession of marijuana. The deputies who were instructed to remove the weed from the evidence room were not charged, Rotter said, because "they thought it was official" and didn't know what it was to be used for.[25]

Jeff Davis County Sheriff Jimmy Boatright was much bolder in abusing his oath of office and tearfully pleaded guilty to wire fraud and bank fraud in federal court in September 2008. His plea cost him a year in jail, three years' supervised probation, a $5,000 fine, restitution in the amount of $9,148, and 150 hours of community service.

Boatright, who had been sheriff for sixteen years and who had already qualified as a candidate for re-election in the November 2008 election, was instead forced by law to resign as sheriff.

An FBI investigation revealed that he had illegally taken ownership of a pickup truck seized from a drug suspect, used the truck as collateral to secure a $16,518 bank loan for a relative, and used $1,182 in funds earmarked for the sheriff's department's D.A.R.E. (Drug Abuse Resistance Education) program toward the purchase of a new $2,182 wide-screen television set for his home.

Boatright, who had triple bypass heart surgery earlier in 2008, was facing a possible jail sentence of up to 50 years and fines as much as $1.25 million.[26]

The siren's song of public corruption, abetted by a cooperative sheriff, lured bootleggers and car thieves to Jackson County, Georgia, in the 1950s and 1960s. So bad was the county's reputation that Superior Court Judge Richard B. Russell, III threatened to petition the state's governor for help if Sheriff John Brooks continued to display an inability—or unwillingness—to bring offenders to justice.

Already saddled with more bootlegging cases than any other Georgia county, Jackson County by the 1960s was the epicenter for car thefts. Despite being a legally dry county, beer, wine and liquor were readily available at numerous bootleg houses and from stills that dotted the landscape. There were raids, but Brooks, for his part, claimed he couldn't locate many defendants to bring them to court to face charges.

Brooks, in a classic display of the autonomy enjoyed by sheriffs, simply refused to enforce laws against bootlegging, claiming those duties belonged to state and federal authorities.

A 1959 audit of the county uncovered widespread corruption among county officials and by 1963, a judge had been disbarred (to be replaced by Judge Russell) and Brooks had been arrested and convicted of car theft.

But even those actions didn't solve the county's problems, so into the void stepped Floyd Hoard. A lawyer by trade, he also served as editor of the local newspaper. In 1964, he became solicitor general, a position today known as district attorney. He immediately began leading raids on car theft locations and soon tightened the screws on bootlegging operations. In May 1967, he let law enforcement officials in on a raid on the operations of one Clift Park, just months before a new term of court was set to begin in

August.

On August 7, Hoard walked out the door of his home and got into his car. As he turned the ignition, the morning silence was shattered by the explosion of ten sticks of dynamite. A manhunt for Hoard's murderers resulted in the arrest and conviction of five men, including Park who had paid the others to kill Hoard. Park subsequently died in prison.

Jackson County would eventually be cleaned up, but it took the violent death of county prosecutor Hoard to accomplish what Sheriff John Brooks refused to do.[27]

Worth County Sheriff Jeff Hobby thought it would be a good idea to conduct a drug search at Worth County High School in April 2012.

It turned out to be a really bad idea after Hobby ended up serving six months in jail and five years' probation in addition to shelling out $3 million to be divided by 800 students as the result of a civil suit stemming from the infamous drug search.[28]

It seems that the search was a little too thorough—and personal.

Hobby and two of his deputies attracted unwanted national attention after they were accused of touching girls' vaginas and breasts and of groping boys' groin areas during the search which, incidentally, produced no drugs or arrests—unless one wants to count the sheriff and the two deputies.

Hobby was subsequently indicted on a single count of violating his oath of office and two counts of false imprisonment—all felony charges—and one count of sexual battery, a misdemeanor.

Deputy Tyler Turner was indicted on one felony count of violation of his oath of office and one misdemeanor count of sexual battery. Deputy Deidra Whiddon was indicted on one count of violation of her oath of office.

Hobby also pleaded to interfering with the Georgia Bureau of Investigation's criminal investigation of the incident. His plea also meant he had to resign from office.

Payments to the individual students varied from $1,000 to $4,000, according to how badly their civil rights were violated.[29]

The common thread that runs through countless southern sheriffs' offices is the controversy over prisoner work release programs that farm out inmate labor for profit. Georgia is no exception. Under a properly-run program, prisoners are paid a wage for working at private companies. The operator of the work-release program, be it a private jail or the sheriff, generally receives a percentage of those wages to offset the costs of housing and feeding the prisoners. Many times, the jail runs its own commissary which sells snacks and toiletries to prisoners at exorbitant prices, leaving prisoners with little of their earned income. There are even reported occasions of prisoners having a negative balance in their accounts at the end of their jail terms.

Proponents hold the practice up as a means by which prisoners are given the opportunity to learn a trade they can use for gainful employment once their jail terms are up. Opponents say it is nothing more than a poorly-disguised exploitation of prisoners for the profit of those who run the jails.

Sheriffs who run the work release programs can easily blur the lines between providing work opportunities and personally profiting from using inmate labor for personal gain. No fewer than six Georgia sheriffs have fallen into that trap since 1991.

Thirty-one prisoners and two former deputies told investigators that Sheriff Bobby Womack used prisoners from the Jenkins County Jail to work in his timber business, on more than a dozen mobile homes and houses he owns as rental properties, and on his personal home.

From operating chain saws on trees to repairing rental property to laying sod and cutting grass at the sheriff's residence, prisoners worked at enriching Womack. Sometimes he would pay them small amounts of cash. Others he allowed to leave jail on weekends and some would bring beer back to the jail to share with other prisoners.

Nor was Womack alone in the knowledge of his Jenkins County operation. Informants said the district attorney knew of the practice and did nothing to stop it and that the Georgia Bureau of Investigation initially appeared indifferent to reports of Womack's use of prisoner labor for personal gain. When the GBI finally did get around to conducting an investigation in 2004, Womack resigned.

But next door, in Screven County, Sheriff Mike Kyle had prisoners working on his campaign signs and performing work at his home and at area churches.

Dozens of prisoners and two deputies told the *Augusta Chronicle* during a three-month investigation by the newspaper that they poured cement for a patio and walkway, demolished a walk-in closet and installed a new shower at Kyle's home. They said they also paved driveways, installed sheetrock, tiled floors and installed plumbing in area churches in 2002 and 2003. Inmates also performed repair work on deputies' homes.

In 2004, a prisoner escaped from a work assignment, broke into a man's home, and attacked him with a machete, causing slashes to the man's back, arms, head and legs, three broken ribs and a punctured lung.

Kyle defended the use of inmate labor, claiming the practice was legal and that he had been using the labor for twelve years. While admitting he used prisoners to perform work at his home, he said it was permissible because he paid them for their labor.

Though one Georgia district attorney said he would have sought felony indictments against both Kyle and Womack had they been in his jurisdiction, a Georgia Sheriffs' Association panel only recommended that Kyle be reprimanded but not suspended.

Kyle was re-elected to a fourth term in 2004.

Other Georgia sheriffs found to have used prison labor for questionable purposes included:

- Coffee County Sheriff Rob Smith investigated by the Georgia Ethics Commission for using prisoners to work on his campaign signs;
- Early County Sheriff Jimmie Murkerson, investigated by the GBI for using prisoner labor at a paint and body shop and on a building he owned. A grand jury declined to indict him;
- Camden County Sheriff Bill Smith, investigated for using prisoner labor, theft and falsifying documents. Smith was indicted but the Georgia Attorney General's office subsequently dismissed the case;
- Former DeKalb County Sheriff Sidney Dorsey, indicted on 19 charges, including using prison labor for personal gain. Dorsey, however, faced far more serious charges involving the murder of his successor and was sentenced to life in prison.[30]

It took not an act of Congress but an act of the Georgia Legislature to force the state's sheriffs out of the sideline businesses of private security, private investigations, bail bonds and towing. It is relatively easy to see how a sheriff might be tempted to abuse his office by using it in any of those endeavors. In fact, we have already seen instances where Sheriffs Sidney Dorsey and Lamar Martin appeared to confuse their official duties with those of private security and bail bonds.

Senate Bill 117 was introduced and passed in 2003 at the urging of the Georgia Sheriffs' Association, which was understandably concerned with protecting the integrity of sheriffs in the Peach State. Sponsored by senators Charlie Tanksley, Steve Thompson, Daniel Lee, and Rene Kemp, the bill passed both chambers of the legislature but not without changes by the House Committee on Special Judiciary that traditionally originate in backroom deals and out of the public eye. Two major amendments to the bill effectively gutted the original intent of the bill.

First, the prohibitions of a sheriff's activities in the four arenas applied to *only* the county in which the sheriff had jurisdiction. That meant the sheriff in one county could actively engage in private security, private investigations, bail bonds, and/or towing in the next county over or, for that matter, in *any* of Georgia's remaining 158 counties.

The second change addressed the age-old political problem of nepotism in a way to make it palatable to sheriffs. Loopholes are always in demand in the passage of new laws, and that was especially true when it came to how sheriffs might be affected by SB 117. Accordingly, the House committee watered down that section of the bill by amending it to read that only a sheriff's un-emancipated children were prohibited from participating in the businesses of towing, bail bond, private investigations, or private security. Emancipated children i.e., those of the age of majority, were good to go – even in the county controlled by daddy.[31]

In March 2005, Georgia Federal District Judge Marvin Shoob found it necessary to assume supervision of the Fulton County Jail for the second time since 1999 because of deplorable conditions at the facility. Even Fulton County Jail Sheriff Jacquelyn Barrett told the judge it was a good idea for the court to take over the jail which housed more than 3,000 prisoners but which was designed for less than half that number.

Even before the 1,322-capacity-jail opened in the mid-1980s, it was already deemed too small to accommodate county requirements. The number of bunks was doubled but the number of showers, toilets and other utilities remained unchanged. One area provided twelve showers for 326 prisoners. Another housed 59 prisoners, 18 of whom slept on the floor.

There was plenty of finger-pointing. Barrett blamed the county for a hiring freeze and the Georgia Department of Corrections for failure to take custody of 200 prisoners, while the County Commission accused the sheriff of mismanagement. She invested $2 million of tax auction liens with Provident Capital which in turn lent the money to people who contributed about $40,000 to Barrett's political campaign.[32]

Barrett's successor, Myron Freeman, found himself on the proverbial hot seat two years later when he reinstated six of eight deputies whom he fired following the escape of a Fulton County Jail prisoner who went on a shooting rampage, killing four people, including a judge, a U.S. Customs agent, a court reporter and a sheriff's deputy.

Freeman had initially promised to crack down on deputies who did not perform their jobs and followed through with the firing of the eight deputies before reinstating six of them. An independent review found that each of the fired deputies had either failed to perform their duties or lied during the investigation. One deputy who had been in charge of monitoring the courthouse surveillance cameras, agreed to resign after being rehired.

By resigning, he not only received back pay and benefits, he also retained his state law enforcement certification.[33]

In November 2007, a federal grand jury indicted Clinch County Sheriff Winston Peterson for perjury, using forced prisoner labor, obstruction, and extorting former prisoners.

Peterson, who had served as Clinch County Sheriff for seventeen years, in 2000 began charging prisoners $18 per day for room and board in his jail. In the four-year period from November 30, 2000, and November 21, 2004, he collected thirty thousand dollars from 475 prisoners. That money was turned over to the County Commission. Those unable to pay the fees were forced to sign promissory notes before release with the warning they would be re-incarcerated for failure to pay.

On April 14, 2006, county officials agreed to repay the $30,000 collected from inmates, plus an additional $30,000 in attorney fees in settlement of a federal lawsuit brought by two former prisoners. The extortion count against Peterson was brought because he had no legal basis to charge the fees. The two obstruction counts related to testimony given by Peterson in June 2007 as it related to an FBI investigation of an unindicted co-conspirator, a judge. The forced labor count stemmed from Peterson's forcing a prisoner to work at a private business operated by Peterson's wife "by means of abuse or threatened abuse of law or legal process."

Apparently, the corruption in Clinch County ran deep.

Associate Magistrate Judge Linda Peterson, married to Sheriff Peterson's brother, was indicted two months earlier on charges of perjury and making false statements. She was accused of lying to a grand jury over whether she encouraged criminal defendants to use her father's bail bond company to obtain bonds.[34]

In August 2006, Berrien County Sheriff Gerald Brogdon entered a guilty plea to the illegal sale of a firearm to a felon. He was sentenced to five years' probation and ordered to pay a $2,000 fine.[35]

The 2019 whistleblower complaint by a U.S. intelligence official against President Donald Trump erupted in a political scandal that made international headlines. But more than three years earlier, a whistleblower complaint in the state of Georgia resulted in a blistering ruling against the Douglas County Sheriff's Office.

The complaint, actually filed back in 2011, typically took that long to make its way to the U.S. Court of Appeals' Eleventh Circuit where a three-judge panel took the sheriff's office to task for its retaliation against seventeen-year Douglasville police officer after he filed a complaint about alleged racial profiling by the sheriff's department.

Derrick Bailey, an African-American officer who had received above-average employee performance reviews between May 2010 and June 2012, said in his complaint that deputies made racially insensitive jokes about blacks and referred to the City of Douglasville's logo, which included a picture of a tree, as a "lynching tree." He suddenly found himself the subject of an effort to rid the department of him. Ordered to rewrite incident reports, he complained that to do so would violate department policy. He was fired.

At his appeal hearing, he argued that he was fired for speaking out against incidents he witnessed. The night of his appeal, he was followed home and stared down by two Douglas County Sheriff's deputies. The following day, Major Tommy Wheeler of the Douglas County Sheriff's Office issued a "be-on-the-lookout" (BOLO) advisory to local police, alerting them to consider subject Derrick Bailey a "loose cannon," who police should consider a danger, and to "act accordingly." Bailey sued, alleging retaliation and defamation.

The sheriff's office moved to dismiss the suit, claiming immunity but that motion was denied by the lower court and in a strongly-worded opinion, the Eleventh Circuit affirmed, noting that the BOLO gave all Douglas County law-enforcement personnel a "reasonable basis for using force—including deadly force—against Bailey."[36]

The court's opinion added, "Law-enforcement officers are sworn to protect and defend the lives of others. It is completely antithetical to those sworn duties for a law-enforcement officer to use his position to harness the power of an entire county's law-enforcement force to teach a lesson to—and potentially very seriously endanger—someone who had the temerity to speak up about alleged abuse." [37]

Victor Hill, the Clayton County Sheriff who received extensive mention earlier in this chapter, filed for bankruptcy two days before his term of office expired, claiming he could not afford to pay $1.7 million in damages stemming from several lawsuits, including a $475,000 judgment in favor of the brother of a former Clayton County sheriff who sued for false arrest. Subsequent to his bankruptcy filing, it was learned he had stashed $25,000 in an account he concealed from the bankruptcy court. He was ordered to turn the money over to be divided among his creditors.

He was also under investigation for the theft of weapons and other sheriff's department equipment prior to leaving office. The Clayton County Commission questioned a trip he made to Las Vegas that he charged to the county without the chairman's approval. He claimed he attended a conference during the trip.[38]

Captain Jay Baker, spokesperson for the Cherokee County sheriff's office, created a public relations flap in Marcy 2021 when he described the twenty-one-year-old shooter accused of killing eight people in a rampage across three Atlanta spas as "pretty much fed up and kind of at the end of his rope" and that "Yesterday was a really bad day for him."

Things only got worse when Internet readers and reporters discovered Baker's *Facebook* posts that promoted the sale of T-shirts emblazoned with wording that called the novel coronavirus an "IMPORTED VIRUS FROM CHY-NA." The reaction was immediate and predictable, with critics pointing out that everyone has bad days but it wasn't customary to go to Asian businesses and shoot Asian employees. Sheriff Frank Reynolds said he was unaware of the Facebook T-shirt post.[39]

9

Idaho: We Don't Need No Stinkin' DNA

IT WAS a fairly straightforward bill that came before the Idaho Legislature in 2016. Clinics would be required to use rape kits in all cases of alleged sexual assault, that the forensic evidence be forwarded for DNA testing, and that it be processed within 90 days. Additionally, the bill required that DNA samples were to be uploaded to a database in the hopes of finding a match that could potentially identify the attacker.

The bill further stipulated that law enforcement officials obtain prosecutors' approval to block DNA testing and allowed victims to request that DNA not be tested. Under the bill, Idaho crime labs would be required to conduct an audit of analyzed kits in an annual report that would be made public.

Bingham County Sheriff Craig Rowland, however, opposed the bill, arguing that the state should not intervene and that law enforcement officials should get to decide which kits get tested and which ones did not. The reason for his opposition, he said, was that rape kits were unnecessary because "the majority of our rapes that are call in are actually consensual sex."[1]

Idaho State Rep. Melissa Wintrow (D-Boise), sponsor of House Bill 528, was quick to describe Rowland's comments as damaging to women. "Many times, people are focused on a woman's behavior and the victim's response when we should be thinking about what are we teaching men in this society," she said. "What we are teaching young boys and men about how we should not initiate or cross any physical boundary without consent."

State Sen. Maryanne Jordan, a co-sponsor of the bill, said Rowland's approach goes far in addressing "the issue of backlogs of rape kits and sends a clear message that the crime of sexual assault is not taken seriously."

A 2015 investigation by the *Idaho Press-Tribune* revealed that several law enforcement agencies in the state sent fewer than half of its rape kits to DNA testing with one agency testing only 10 percent of its evidence.

Guidelines from the Department of Justice bring into sharp focus the reason attitudes like Rowland's discourage sexual assault victims in reporting attacks. "Acting on stereotypes about why women...are sexually assaulted, or about how a victim of domestic violence or sexual assault should look or behave," the guidelines say, "can constitute unlawful discrimination and profoundly undermine an effective response to these crimes."[2]

In Idaho County, the parents of a 16-year-old girl sued the sheriff's department in federal court after learning that a deputy, thirty-two- year-old Daniel Funderburg, had an ongoing sexual relationship with their daughter. Funderburg was sentenced in March 2013 to 90 days in jail, placed on six years' supervised probation, and fined $530.50 for having a sexual relationship with the girl.

The lawsuit said the relationship commenced and continued while Funderburg was working as a deputy for Sheriff Doug Giddings, Undersheriff Jim Gorges, and others, and that they knew he was spending time with the girl, including times while he was on duty.[3]

When a public official issues a public apology, it's generally because he finally got caught doing what he is now showing contrition for.

Former Jefferson County Sheriff Blair Olsen was no exception. Convicted on three felony counts of misuse of public funds, he issued the standard apology, saying, "I understand that being sheriff—a public official—that I am expected to hold myself to a higher standard. I honestly fee that I've tried to do that. In this case, I've failed by using poor judgment, and I'm sorry."

Not that his transgressions were really of such a serious nature. In fact, two of the counts for which he was convicted were overturned on appeal, leaving only one: allowing his wife to use a county-issued cell phone, hardly rising to the level of abuse by some of his contemporaries in other states. He received a sentence of 15 days in jail, a $2,500 fine, $1,023 in restitution, and 120 hours of community service.

But in a state like Idaho, where any news is big news, the state's attorney general took the occasion to give a mini-sermon on criminal activity. "Public corruption cases are serious for the simple fact that the offender holds a position of public trust and authority and then takes advantage of that position," said AG Lawrence Wasden. "This remains true if the crime results in the loss of even the smallest amount of public funds. But the real loss in these cases is to the erosion of trust and faith citizens have in their government."[4]

Two hundred miles to the west, Ada County officials in July 2021 were seriously considering the appointment of an anti-Semitic supporter of the extreme right-wing Constitutional Sheriffs and Peace Officers Association (CSPOA) before finally settling on Matt Clifford, a lieutenant in the sheriff's office to succeed Sheriff Steve Bartlett, who resigned suddenly in May, less than a year after winning reelection.

Steve Traubel, who worked in the Ada County Prosecutor's Office until 2019, was unapologetic about his support of CSPOA and his viewpoint that Jews were responsible for the communist regime in Russia because while they were Nazi victims, they were the "villain class in the Soviet Union" because they "led the Bolshevik revolution."

His conspiracy theory echoed the "Judeo-Bolshevism" propaganda promoted by Nazi Germany in the years leading up to and including the Holocaust, claiming that communism was a Jewish plot to undermine Germany. "What we don't often hear," Traubel told the Ada County Commission, "is how many hundreds of thousands of people were killed (in the Soviet Union) and what group actually started that."

Incredibly, Traubel had significant support from Republican officials for the sheriff's job despite Traubel's embracing the CSPOA position advocating absolute supremacy of the sheriff, even superior to Congress and the President. He indicated to the commission that the Boise municipal police should be placed under his command if he were to be chosen sheriff.

He authored a piece for the ultra-right *Gem State Patriot* website in which he said, "It is 2016! There is no longer black oppression in the United States. Police are good. Criminals are bad. It is not white versus black. It is police versus criminal. It is good versus evil. It is principles versus relativism. It is truth versus deception."[5]

10

Illinois: Cook County: There's more to the State than Chicago?

ANY DISCUSSION of miscreant sheriffs necessarily must include Cook County and Chicago. To assign Illinois to a secondary role behind say, New Jersey, in terms of sheer audacity in terms of public corruption would be an ironic injustice to the Land of Lincoln which has worked hard for more than two centuries to ensure its rightful place in the annals of official sleaze—from Chicago's ward leaders to the governor's mansion— and beyond.

The office of Cook County Sheriff is almost as old as Cook County itself, with John Kinzie being elected the first sheriff in 1831. Sheriffs served two-year terms until 1882 when Seth Hanchett became Cook County's first sheriff elected to a four-year term. In that fifty-one-year interim, the crime syndicates moved in with gambling, prostitution, and bail bond scams—all protected by the local sheriff.[1]

Bail bonds were provided by sheriff's agents who worked with the courts in the scheme. Bond forfeiture was widespread in Cook County and if someone was arrested for frequenting one of the sheriff's favored gambling establishments and subsequently skipped town, the bond money was simply divvied up between the arresting officer, the magistrate, the sheriff and gambling houses. The fact that the arrestee had skipped town was of little concern.[2] But sheriffs had other ways to supplement their income: skimping on the cost of feeding prisoners, a practice still held as acceptable in Alabama. Cook County Sheriff Chris Strassheim, who served a single term from 1906 to 1910, received 21 cents per prisoner per day by the Cook County treasurer but managed to feed prisoners for as little as 6 cents per day while pocketing the difference.[3]

Peter Hoffman, a one-time grocery clerk, was elected in 1922 and holds the distinction as the only Cook County Sheriff to serve prison time while simultaneously serving as sheriff after it was revealed that he was granting furloughs to inmates Terry Druggan and Frankie Lake so that they might attend to their bootlegging operations. They had, it turned out, cut a deal with Warden Wesley Westbrook whereby Westbrook was paid $2,000 per month by a Chicago ward political boss to allow conjugal visits from girlfriends, private rooms with their own baths and periodic furloughs. Westbrook subsequently received four months in jail and Hoffman was sentenced to 30 days in his own jail and ordered to pay a $2,500 fine but was allowed to complete his term as sheriff.[4]

Seventeen men held the office of Cook County Sheriff in the century following Hoffman, each, with rare exceptions, achieving varying degrees of notoriety. Despite repeated attempts at reform, greed and corruption held a tight grip on the office and the men who held it as Chicagoans appeared unable—or unwilling—to wrest the office from the control of those who ran the gambling and prostitution establishments or from crooked contractors and vendors. Encouraged by Chicago's history of graft, bribes and kickbacks and politicians who turned a blind eye to rampant vice, sheriff after sheriff either fell under the irresistible spell of personal enrichment or allowed their deputies to do so in their names.

Paddy Carr who took office in 1924, was the only one who never endured a scandal during his administration—and that was probably only because he died before he ever collected his first paycheck as sheriff.

Carr was succeeded by Charles Graydon whose corrupt tenure saw the expansion of slot machine gambling.

William Meyering followed Graydon in 1930, declaring, "I am not a reformer. I do not intend to become one." It was, for a change, a political promise kept. His chief benefactor was a highway patrolman named Matt Kolb who ran his own bootlegging operations. Kolb was murdered when he refused to cede his liquor operations to a gangster named Al Capone.

Next in line was John Toman (1934). Toman implemented reforms following repeal of the Volstead Act (Prohibition) and actually led the sheriff's office during a relatively scandal-free four years.

Thomas O'Brien changed all that when he took office in 1938. Having resigned from Congress to seek the sheriff's job, he allowed slot machine gambling and mob-run road houses to flourish. He earned the name "Blind Tom" because of the apparent inability of his hundred deputies to locate the names and addresses of 1,400 mob members from a handbook supplied by the Illinois Attorney General. Widely believed to be on the take, O'Brien was actually arrested himself in a Loop gambling raid in 1935, three years before he was elected sheriff. He returned to Congress after a single term as sheriff and remained there until 1964.

Peter B. Carey's (1942) tenure was marred by the suspension of five police captains and one lieutenant after someone in the sheriff's office tipped off operators of Cicero gambling houses of an impending raid. Carey was in the hospital in Milwaukee when Police Chief Hugh McCarthy was indicted on two counts of allowing gambling. When news of the indictment was published, Carey, who had presided over the most notorious police scandal in Chicago history to that point, promptly died.

Elmer Michael Walsh became sheriff in 1946 and in so doing, became Cook County's first Republican sheriff in a quarter-century as well as becoming the first Cook County office holder to go head-to-head against Mayor Richard Daley—and win. Walsh promptly issued 450 honorary deputy badges to political friends and campaign donors who used them as Get out of Jail Free cards and to otherwise flaunt their power and prestige. One of those recipients, John Gattuso, had his badge on his person when he was gunned down in a mob hit after botching his assignment to assassinate an informant.

In the wake of the honorary badge embarrassment, Sheriff John Babb (1950) promised to issue them only to press reporters and photographers. It's questionable if there were even 1,200 reporters and photographers in Chicago but that's how many Babb issued. He also hired former convicts as correctional officers in the notorious Cook County Jail. And despite repeated warnings from the Chicago Crime Commission, he allowed gambling and prostitution to prosper, continuing a time-honored tradition in the Cook County Sheriff's Office.

Joseph C. Lohman (1954), a University of Chicago sociology professor, was a true reformer brought down by subordinates and sloppy investigations. He opened the first training school for Cook County police officers, launched a Major Investigations Unit (MIU) following several high-profile murders. His administration was compromised by corruption charges brought against four officers accused of taking kickbacks. Additionally, the botched investigations of several murders—which were never solved—cost him his political future.

Frank Sain (1958) was next up. A former warden of the Cook

County Jail, like so many of his predecessors, he turned a blind eye to syndicate operations. In 1960, Virgil Peterson, executive director of the Chicago Crime Commission, turned over 207 addresses to Sain—addresses where illegal gambling violations had been observed. Sain in turn, raided only five of the addresses, prompting a furious response by Peterson: "During the entire four-year term of Sheriff Frank G. Sain, no effective action was taken by his office against wide-open syndicate gambling operations in either the suburban towns or in the unincorporated areas."

Illinois State Attorney Benjamin Adamowski added Sain "couldn't fine an elephant in a phone booth." Sain left the Cook County Police Department in total disarray.

As illustration of chaos found in the sheriff's office when Sain successor Richard B. Ogilvie took office in 1962, the new administration was unable to locate some of the county's squad cars which had simply been abandoned on the highways around Cook County by the outgoing administration. Ogilvie, who was a World War II veteran, having served under Gen. George Patton, successfully prosecuted gangster Tony Accardo on tax fraud charges, though the conviction was reversed on appeal. Telling a reporter that "Every police officer will be my personal appointment," he kept his word but made one major mistake in the appointment of Richard Cain (aka Richard Scalzetti), an ex-Chicago cop with questionable credentials, as his chief investigator within the department's Special Investigations Unit (SIU). Cain would be proven to be a mole within the department who was simultaneously shaking down illegal abortionists at $5,000 a pop. (An entire section will be devoted to Cain later in this chapter).

The biggest claim to fame for Joseph Woods was that his sister, Rosemary Woods was President Richard Nixon's personal secretary – the same Rosemary Woods of the infamous 18½-minute gap in the tape recording of a conversation between Nixon and H.R. Haldeman at the peak of the Watergate scandal. Sheriff Woods was also known for wearing Nixon's hand-me-down suits. He ordered 58 of his officers across the state line to help put down a racial disturbance in Gary, Indiana. When he subsequently made a record request of $200,000 for riot control, he received pushback from the Chicago Finance Committee chairman who suggested that unincorporated areas of Cook County should in the future call on the Illinois National Guard for assistance in riot control instead of the sheriff's office.

Richard Elrod (1970) was the first Cook County sheriff allowed to stand for re-election. As a result, he consolidated his power and held office for four full terms. He upgraded the crime lab and pistol range and centralized police headquarters, all badly-need reforms. But he also issued 1,200 deputy badges to politically-connected recipients, a widespread practice not limited to Cook County—or Illinois. The FBI's *Operation Safe Bet* investigation into organized crime and vice surfaced during his administration. The investigation revealed ongoing protection of owners of strip clubs and massage parlors. After the dust had settled, five current and former Cook County Sheriff's Office vice officers were indicted on charges of taking payoffs totaling $50,000 as protection for bookmakers and prostitution in the unincorporated areas of Cook County. Lt. James Keating, former head of CIU and Sgt. Bruce Frasch, who headed a vice control unit, were convicted on 18 counts of racketeering, extortion and tax fraud.

James O'Grady (1986) was appointed as Undersheriff by Elrod and promptly set about undermining his boss. When he succeeded Elrod as sheriff, he appointed Jimmy "The Bohemian" Dvorak as his Undersheriff and the office again became one of the most corrupt in Cook County. O'Grady hired 450 political cronies to sensitive jobs for which they were sorely unqualified and ghost employees – employees no one ever saw – proliferated. Advancement within the department was predicated solely on purchasing tickets to O'Grady-Dvorak fundraisers and merit tests, when administered at all, were rigged in favor of political allies. Many top campaign donors and hangers-on were deputized despite O'Grady's promise to end the practice. The Cook County Republican Party was hijacked by Dvorak and he and O'Grady extracted nearly $357,000 from correctional officers, Cook County police, and other employees during their first three years in office. Dvorak was eventually forced out as Undersheriff when it was revealed he received $10,000 per month in protection money in exchange for going easy on suburban gambling raids that would threaten the mob's bookmaking operations. He was indicted on income tax evasion and bribery charges. Charges that he received $175,000 from organized crime figures were dismissed but he was sentenced to 41 months in prison and fined $50,000. Added to O'Grady's woes were claims of improper actions taken by sheriff's investigators during six murder cases.[5]

In a city and county notorious for its corruption, the O'Grady administration took things to a new level of deceit, deception, and sham investigations of the mob. No fewer than two dozen "ghost" employees getting caught up in U.S. Attorney Jim Burns' net. They included Marie D'Amico, the daughter of former Chicago Alderman Anthony Laurino, who received nearly $83,000 to be a no-show employee of the sheriff's office. Even more egregious, Laurino's wife pulled in more than $300,000 in salary and benefits for doing little, if any, work for several municipal committees. Linda Holmes, the former girlfriend of Laurino's son, State Rep. William Laurino, was identified as a "ghost" assistant to Alderman Laurino, she agreed to cooperation with the investigation. But that ended when the car she was driving ran a red light and then slammed into a building, killing her.

O'Grady had barely taken office in 1986 when Sgt. Bruce Frasch and Lt. James Keating, former intelligence commander for the sheriff's office, were convicted of racketeering, extortion, conspiracy and income- tax fraud for shaking down bordello operators for protection money.[6]

While many of the cover-ups laid out in the Tribune story dated back to O'Grady's predecessor, Richard Elrod, by then a sitting judge, the protection continued well into O'Grady's tenure.[7]

As the noose tightened around O'Grady, he tried to limit the damage by firing deputies as their misdeeds became public but momentum proved to be a difficult train to stop. O'Grady belatedly moved for the firing of two deputies after a newspaper reported claims that the sheriff's office had suppressed investigations of murders and internal corruption. Lt. William H. Martin, a twenty-two-year veteran of the department, and Deputy Larry Geanes, who had six years' service with the Court Services Department, were suspended after being accused of a 1986 robbery of a drug dealer.

For two years after drug dealer and police informant Dwayne Henderson was murdered, high-ranking officials in the sheriff's office prevented investigators from pursuing the case, according to the *Chicago Tribune* which said Henderson's death was linked to a robbery and extortion ring that had been set up by Henderson, officers, and jail guards.

Near the end of his four-year term, it all came crashing down for O'Grady, once considered a viable candidate for mayor or even governor. When tapes surfaced of a reputed Chicago mobster's claims that James Dvorak, O'Grady's former undersheriff, and chairman of the Cook County Republican Party, was taking payoffs in exchange for protecting organized crime operations, it signaled the end of O'Grady's promising political career.

The tape surfaced during the trial of reputed mob leader Rocco Infelise who was among 20 people indicted on charges that they employed murder, extortion, and bribery to protect bookmaking and casino-style gambling operations in Cook County. In the tape, Infelise could be heard telling a bookmaker working as an informant that $35,000 a month was paid to law enforcement officials for protection and that $10,000 of that amount "goes to the sheriff" (actually Dvorak, not O'Grady).

Asked what the $10,000 paid monthly to Dvorak got him, Infelise replied, "Sheriff never bothers us, then we got a guy at the state's attorney's office. We got another guy downtown." He also implicated Chicago Police Superintendent LeRoy Martin and Mayor Richard M. Daley on the tape. Daley, Martin, Dvorak, and O'Grady vehemently denied Infelise's claims.[8]

By 1991, O'Grady, by now out office, could no longer blame the Elrod administration when one of his business associates was indicted for obstruction of justice. Daniel M. Davis, a former city police officer was vice president of Special Operations Associations, Inc. He was accused of obstructing a federal investigation into the firm's possible furtive dealings with a home incarceration company that provided electronic monitoring for inmates sentenced to home incarceration while O'Grady was sheriff.

The indictment of Davis, a twenty-year veteran of the Chicago Police Department, alleged that he obstructed justice by refusing to comply with a subpoena to produce documents pertaining to a proposed business deal in 1990 between his firm and Home Incarceration. The indictment said he caused an unidentified employee to conceal the requested document from a grand jury that was investigating possible concealed business and financial connections between Special Operations, Home Incarcerations, O'Grady, and Jimmy Dvorak.[9]

As an added embarrassment to the department, the *Chicago Tribune* reported there had not been an organized crime murder conviction in more than two decades despite an abundance of some 70 suspected mob killings.

Michael F. Sheahan (1990) was the first Cook County Sheriff allowed to serve successive terms and he managed to hang on for four straight four-year terms. His most significant achievement was the absence of a major scandal associated with his tenure but that did not stop the proliferation of interoffice politics in the sheriff's office.

Not so with his successor, Tom Dart (2006), who while more subtle, still managed to circumvent standard hiring procedures put in place to prevent the proliferation of "ghost" employees or the existence of deadhead positions. A so-called "merit board" created to oversee hiring, promotions and discipline for nearly 6,000 courtroom deputies, officers and correctional officers was better known for its political connections than its effectiveness.

The largely anonymous board, whose members received salaries ranging from $26,000 to $31,700 and credits toward taxpayer-funded retirements, was stacked with appointees better known for their political connections than for their qualifications.[10]

As the housing crisis peaked in late 2008, Dart came to the rescue of tenants when he announced he was suspending all foreclosure evictions in County. He said in countless cases, renters who had faithfully paid their rent were being evicted because they had not been informed that their landlord was in financial dire straits. He said mortgage companies had not met their obligations to identify and inform tenants in foreclosed properties. "These mortgage companies only see pieces of paper, not people." He said banks didn't care who got hurt and that he was "not going to do their jobs for them anymore. We're just not going to evict innocent tenants. It stops today."[11]

Not all the Illinois sheriffs who got themselves in legal jams were from Cook County.

On September 14, 2014, Rock Island County Sheriff Jeff Boyd submitted his resignation after pleading guilty to cyber-stalking after a formal complaint was filed charging him with sending repeated text messages in an attempt to intimidate and threaten a woman, an undocumented immigrant from Mexico who he met at a gym. Boyd, in resigning, forfeited the pension he would have received as sheriff although he retained eligibility for the pension he earned as a deputy for the Rock Island County Sheriff's Office.

"Mr. Boyd was elected by the people of Rock Island County to serve as its top law enforcement officer, but unfortunately he attempted to use his position to intimidate and stalk his victim," said Illinois Attorney General Lisa Madigan. "My office sought his resignation and criminal conviction to ensure he can no longer abuse the power that the people of Rock Island County entrusted in him."

Rock Island County is on the western-most border of Illinois, across the state from and slightly south of Cook County. Boyd's resignation took effect on September 12, 2014. He had run unopposed in 2014 after first being elected in 2010. The Rock Island County Elections Division had him as unopposed in the November 4 election that was less than two months from his resignation date. He was succeeded by Capt. Gerry Bustos, who was sworn in immediately upon Boyd's resignation.[12]

In 1998, Bureau County Sheriff Greg Johnson held a raffle for his re-election. First prize was a Harley-Davidson motorcycle or $12,000 cash. The drawing was originally set for August 23, but was put off until after the election. Months went by with no word of who the winner was until April 1999 when after repeated inquiries, Johnson identified the winner as one Lyle Rawson of Chicago.

The problem was, the Illinois Secretary of State had no records of any Lyle Rawson, nor did directory assistance in Chicago. To further clarify the issue, Johnson filed an amended campaign expenditure form in June with the Illinois State Board of Elections listing Urban Street in Chicago as Rowson's address. And while there is an Urban Street in Chicago, there was no street number corresponding to the address provided by Johnson.

One reporter who had been pursuing a tip that Johnson had pocketed the first-prize cash was Thetis "Scoop" Sims, a 55-year-old, part-time correspondent for the *Kewanee Star Courier*. On February 11, Johnson agreed to an interview with Sims but shortly after he arrived at her home, she suffered a fatal heart attack. Sims said the two were exchanging pleasantries when she suffered the heart attack.

"There were two people in that home, and one of them is dead," said Coroner Janice Wamhoff, who said Sims died of cardiac arrhythmia, which can be triggered by a stressful confrontation. "Stress is a big factor in a lot of this kind of thing. But we have no way of proving whether stress was the cause of her heart failure."[13]

The Kankakee County Sheriff's Office settled a class-action lawsuit in July 2017 that called on the county to pay nearly $1.5 million in damages to affected prisoners and their attorneys.

The lawsuit, initiated during the tenure of former Sheriff Tim Burkowski and settled during the administration of his successor, Mike Downey, stemmed from alleged excessive use of the Jerome Combs Detention Center's strip search policy and of the policy's not being applied in uniform fashion. Lead plaintiff was Darnell Fonder, who was arrested but never formally charged with any offense. As lead plaintiff, he received $25,000 while two other named plaintiffs each got $5,000. The remaining 1500 claimants received payouts ranging from $125 to $750 each while their attorney, Kenneth Flaxman, received $810,000 in fees.[14]

As a top law enforcement officer, a CIA operative who trained Cubans for the ill-fated Bay of Pigs invasion, the actual shooter in the JFK assassination (according to some conspiracy theorists)[15], FBI informant, confidant to mob boss Sam Giancana, it was perhaps appropriate that Richard Cain, aka Richard Scalzitti, met his demise at the hands of a shotgun-wielding assassin in a nondescript sandwich shop on Chicago's West Side.

Cain was all that—and more. A shady figure all the way back to his days as a Chicago cop, controversy followed him like the cloud that hovered perpetually over Al Capp's Joe Btfsplk, he was indisputably a brilliant person bordering, some said, on genius.

But even the smartest person can push his luck too far and that, apparently, is what Cain did when his face was blown away on Dec. 20, 1973. He was carrying no identification and the destruction was such that it took authorities hours to make an identity.

His star had started its ascent more than decade before when, after joining the Chicago Police Department in 1956, he had become chief investigator for Cook County Sheriff Richard Ogilvie by 1960. Even as he worked as Ogilvie's investigator, he was believed to have been working simultaneously for the Chicago crime bosses. It was believed that he forced suspected mob informants to take lie detector tests at taxpayer expense and then reported those who failed the tests to the mob.

In 1964, he was forced to resign and he was later convicted of robbery He served three years for bank robbery and for lying to a grand jury about a warehouse robbery.[16]

He claimed to have been deported from Mexico after training Cubans for the Bay of Pigs invasion, and after his parole from the robbery conviction, he returned there to work as courier for Giancana. He became a central figure in Giancana's money-skimming from casinos in Central America and Iran. As Giancana's financial advisor, he aided the mob boss in his attempt to control Chicago's illegal gambling operations. During this time, he began working as an informant for FBI agent William F. Roemer as a means of eliminating Giancana's rivals by exposing their operations to federal authorities.[17]

Several theories about Cain's violent death were offered up, all dealing with speculation of retaliation by one gang or another but the murder was never solved.

The northeast corner of Kane County abuts the northwest corner of

Cook County. Other than the proximity of the two counties, Kane, with a population of 130,000 and a population density of fewer than a thousand inhabitants per square mile has little in common with Chicago and Cook County (5.4 million people and a population density of 5,700 per square mile).

Despite its comparative rural Anglo-Saxon demographics, Kane in 2018 found it was not immune to corruption in its sheriff's office when Deputy Kimberly Zinke was arrested in April 2015 on felony charges of unlawful possession of a controlled substance.

Zinke came under suspicion of diverting seized prescription drugs destined for the sheriff's evidence locker. Illinois State Police obtained a search warrant for her home, finding several thousand prescription pills. She was sentenced to thirty days in jail plus twelve months' probation and fined $2,500 in March 2018.[18]

Less than two years later, in December 2019, Aaron J. Feiza, a sergeant with the Kane County Sheriff's Department, was arrested for possession of cocaine. Sheriff Ron Hain said when he was notified by state police that Feiza, a fifteen-year veteran of the department, was under investigation, "I immediately placed him on paid administrative leave pending the outcome of the investigation."[19]

A Cook County sheriff's deputy was found hanging from a bed sheet in his cell in Chicago's federal Metropolitan Correction Center in November 2014 following his arrest in an undercover drug sting. His death was called "a tragedy on multiple levels" by Cook County sheriff's spokesperson Cara Smith.

Stanley Kogut, 45, his 44-year-old partner, Robert Vaughan, and former Lyons police officer Jimmy Rodgers, also 44, were alleged to have conspired to use their positions as law enforcement officers to rob people of marijuana, contraband cigarettes and money, according to federal prosecutors. Kogut and Vaughan had been assigned to the federal High Intensity Drug Task Force.

Kogut and Vaughan were arrested after they ripped off an undercover FBI agent posing as a drug dealer, prosecutors said. Rodgers had earlier pleaded guilty to extortion as part of a plea agreement and was sentenced to five years in prison.[20]

11

Indiana: Tow Truck Kickbacks (and Oh, Yeah, the Sex)

THERE ARE no stories linking Indiana sheriffs to known mobsters, bootlegging operations, or illegal gambling. But the comparative lack of those vices doesn't necessarily preclude prostitution—or at least sheriffs cavorting with prostitutes. In the case of one former sheriff, he apparently didn't learn his lesson even after being forced from office.

In May 2017, Danny Rodden had just completed a two-year probation sentence following his arrest for paying a prostitute $300 for oral sex at a Louisville hotel when he was busted again for paying a different woman $300 on two separate occasions for sexual acts at his home in Sellersburg.[1] Rodden was the sixty-year-old incumbent sheriff of Clark County, Indiana, nestled on the Kentucky border in the extreme southeast area of Indiana, back in 2013 when he was accused of giving an unidentified prostitute a badge, uniform shirt and other clothing bearing the sheriff's department's insignia in order that she might obtain a government employee rate at area hotels. That same federal indictment charged him with counseling the destruction of evidence in a federal investigation and seven counts of making false statements to federal agents following the Louisville hotel encounter.

"As of now he's still the sheriff, said a senior litigation counsel for the U.S. Justice Department. He added that Rodden could be disqualified from office only if convicted of a felony.[2]

But Rodden, who had been married 29 years at the time of his arrest and who had two adult children, saved prosecutors the trouble when he resigned in disgrace from his $136,000-per-year job as Clark County's top cop. He was approaching the end of Indiana's consecutive term limit and had previously worked for 28 years as a Jeffersonville police officer and even serving at one time as the city's chief of police. He also served on the

Clark County Council for eight years prior to his election as sheriff in 2006.[3]

He faced up to 35 years in prison but instead was given only two years' probation in exchange for his resignation.

He was the second Indiana sheriff to be forced from office for an affair with a known prostitute. Both the Associated Press and the *Indianapolis Star* said Rodden and Boone County Sheriff Ken Campbell were involved with the same prostitute even though Boone County is in central Indiana and not near Clark County.[4]

Even though he stepped down after more than thirty years in law enforcement, Campbell insisted he did nothing illegal. "Certain allegations have recently arisen in regards to my conduct. While I believe I have committed no illegal acts, I must apologize for serious errors of judgment in my personal life. I have thoughtlessly and deeply hurt my family, friends, co-workers and those who placed their trust in me."[5]

When Jamey Noel succeeded Rodden as sheriff of Clark County he teamed with the A&E Network for a documentary entitled *60 Days In*, whereby seven innocent volunteers spent sixty days as undercover inmates in the problem-riddled Clark County jail. As a result of that undercover operation, five corrections officers were fired and four others resigned. A four-month employee of the jail was charged with sexual misconduct after he admitted to having sex with an inmate.[6]

Whenever any public official goes off the rails, legally and morally speaking, it generally can be traced back to at least of three motivating factors: greed (read: money), power or sex. Two examples in this chapter alone have shown how sex can destroy an otherwise unassailable political career. Sheriffs hold the reins of immense power from their first day in office but the desire for even more power can drive one to commit unfathomable acts that in the end bring them down.

In January 2017, the Lake County Council began plans to remove towing authority from the sheriff's department following the federal and state raid on the sheriff's department in November 2016.

The council, which previously controlled towing contracts, had given that authority to the sheriff in 2000.

Less than a year after that 2016 raid, in August 2017, John Buncich, two years into his fourth term as sheriff of Lake County, located in Indiana's northwest corner, on the southern tip of Lake Michigan, saw his career come to an abrupt end with his conviction of federal public corruption charges.

A veteran of 46 years in law enforcement, he was the first Indiana sheriff to leave office for public corruption since Rudy Bartolomel was forced to resign in October 1985 after pleading guilty to felony charges that he extorted campaign contributions from Lake County employees and ordered employees to work on his political campaigns.[7]

Buncich, whose salary was $146,000 and who presided over 475 county police and a $32 million budget, was convicted of federal bribery and wire fraud relating to an illegal towing scheme. He accepted bribes to help obtain jobs through the county for two operators. The bribes often were in the form of the purchase of campaign fundraising tickets.

Buncich was sentenced to 188 months in federal prison but also brought four others down with him.

William Szarmach, a tow truck operator, earlier pleaded guilty to bribery, wire fraud and tax evasion and agreed to testify for prosecutors. In a plea agreement filed in federal court, Szarmach testified that he purchased tickets to Buncich's fundraising events as well as making additional cash payments to Buncich to ensure that his operation got the business of towing vehicles for county police.

Szarmach, 61, and Timothy Downs, 67, former chief of the Lake County Sheriff's Police, and former sheriff's patrol commander Daniel Murchek, 56, were each sentenced to two years' probation. Additionally, Szarmach was ordered to pay restitution to the IRS and Downs was fined $6,000.[8]

Former Merrillville Town Council member Tom Goralczyk, 51, received a 15-month sentence in federal prison for accepting bribes in return for promises of a lucrative contract he made to an FBI informant. Murchek, third in command under Buncich, pleaded guilty to lying to FBI agents about accepting contributions from a tow operator for his own campaign to succeed the term-limited Buncich, according to the plea agreement filed in U.S. District Court in Hammond for the Northern District of Indiana. "Murchek abruptly dropped out of the race for sheriff earlier this year without comment," the plea agreement said.[9]

In handing down his two-year probation sentence, which also included a $3,500 fine, U.S. District Court Judge James Moody gave Murchek a tongue lashing, asking, "What the devil is wrong with you? Are you part of that corrupt culture? I want to know what makes people like you tick. You totally disappointed everyone."

"The case (against Murchek) is significant because it is the first in the towing scandal that marks a contribution that was not to the Buncich campaign and not to the Buncich boosters," the document said.

"The corruption in [the sheriff's office] destroys any integrity of good politicians and officials have in the rest of this state," Judge Moody said. Registering his disgust, he added, "They think everyone is corrupt. Most citizens feel the way I do. I've said it before, but they don't listen, they just take the place of those who leave."[10]

Perhaps Judge Moody had Kosciusko County Sheriff Aaron Rovenstine in mind when he said those words to Murchek.

Rovenstine's sins two years earlier in 2016 were not nearly as egregious as Murchek's but they did raise a few eyebrows around Kosciusko County, nestled in the northeastern part of the state, and they did result in a one-year suspended jail sentence and 250 hours of community service against the sheriff—all over a movie and book deal that never materialized.

Rovenstine, 56, was indicted on three counts of bribery, one count of intimidation, one count of assisting a criminal and five counts of official misconduct in connection with his accepting $40,000 from an inmate, Kevin Bronson, 56, and another man, 61-year- old Mark Soto, in exchange for special favors for Bronson who was attempting to market a movie and book about his life.

As if the bribery and special favors were not enough, Rovenstine also pleaded guilty to intimidating a Warsaw police detective who became suspicious of his activities, a move that effectively ended his career as a public official and law enforcement officer.

The investigation that eventually led to the end of a quarter-century of the Rovenstine family's hold on the Kosciusko County Sheriff's Office actually began in December 2014 when Warsaw police arrested Bronson on drug and gang charges. Bronson, skilled in the martial arts, but with a history of criminal gang activity, was seeking to sell the story of his life and had enlisted the help of Soto, a professor at Grace College in Winona Lake.

Bronson, in return for the $40,000, was housed in a special jail suite, allowed unrecorded, unsupervised phone calls and even allowed to leave jail with Rovenstine to dine at a local restaurant.[11]

12

Iowa: When You Can't Trust Fellow Officers…

CEDAR COUNTY, Iowa holds several unique claims to fame. Former President Herbert Hoover was born there, it was the epicenter for the Iowa Cow War of 1931 when distrustful farmers joined in attempts to block testing of cows for tuberculosis, and the Cedar County Sheriff's House and Jail is believed to have been the last jail and residence combination still in use upon its closure in 2001. Not even Mayberry possessed that kind of down-home congeniality.

But in May 2019, all pretense of cordiality ceased when Sheriff Warren Wethington let it be known that his jail would no longer honor arrests made by police officers in Durant nor would he allow Durant officers to set foot in the courthouse.

The action stemmed from numerous complaints coming out of Durant, community of about 1800 people about 165 miles east of Des Moines, about Robert Smith, one of the town's three full- time officers. Smith, it seems, had a reputation for being less than truthful, for using questionable force and of possessing a less than pleasant demeanor.

Wethington's action earned him plaudits from Durant's residents, who saw the directive as a rare public stand against police misconduct. At the same time, however, it exacerbated his long-running political feud with Cedar County Board of Supervisors Chairwoman Dawn Smith, who just happened to be Robert Smith's wife.

"I'm not saying they can't do their jobs," Wethington said of the Durant officers. "I'm just saying that I'm not going to vouch for their integrity. When you allow somebody to bring a suspect to your jail, you are saying, 'I believe this officer is credible and that there is probable cause this happened.' That's not the case here."

While Robert Smith said, "My record stands by itself," court records revealed that the Cedar County prosecutor's office routinely disclosed to criminal defendants that Smith's veracity as a witness could be called into question because of issues that surfaced during his 30 years as an Iowa state trooper.[1]

Two months after Wethington's directive was issued, Robert Smith was gone. Amid a growing chorus of misconduct claims, a video surfaced that showed him striking a motorcyclist during a 2017 traffic stop when he was still a state trooper.

Durant had hired Smith in 2018 following his resignation from Iowa State Patrol subsequent to an investigation into his arrest of biker Bryce Yakish. Video obtained by the Associated Press showed Smith pointing his gun at Yakish and then knocking him down.[2]

Former Chickasaw County sheriff's deputy Jeffery Athey, like Smith, lost his job but all in all, he considers himself fortunate. He could well have gone to prison but for the forgiving nature of his victim who argued successfully in court against the prosecution's recommendation of up to five years in jail.

Athey had worked as a deputy for the sheriff's office in Chickasaw, located in northeastern Iowa, near the Minnesota southern border, when he was arrested by New Hampton police in October 2014 for assault with intent to commit serious injury, assault with intent to commit sexual abuse or cause bodily injury, and indecent exposure.

He had become intoxicated at a party and lowered his pants and underwear several times before a co-worker, a female dispatcher, attempted to get him safely home. Once at his home, however, he grabbed the woman and tried to pull her into his bed. When a male dispatcher, James Diesburg, attempted to intervene, Athey struck Diesburg in the face and kneed him in the groin before putting him in a choke hold.

During sentencing, at which Athey said he was making no excuses for his action and was taking full responsibility, the female dispatcher said she did not see herself as a victim and considered Athey to be "like a brother," adding, "I forgave him the next day. He's one of the nicest people I've ever met."

Athey received a deferred judgment, meaning no jail time, though he was sentenced to two years' probation. Following his sentencing, he and his would-be victim embraced.[3]

13

Kansas: Drugs, Bribery, and Guns

AS LONG as mankind has existed on this mortal plane, there has been greed. From Esau's selling his birthright to Jacob to Judas and his thirty pieces of silver to the Teapot Dome scandal of the Harding administration, men have attempted to take shortcuts to riches. It can be as simple as charging a few thousand dollars on a stolen credit card. Other times it can be an intricate Ponzi scheme that can run into millions of dollars from hundreds of unsuspecting investors.

As often as not, however, greed manifests itself in no more complex fashion than kickbacks to a public official in exchange for a lucrative contract for some favored vendor.

But even more maddening can be the light punishment administered to such miscreants, especially when they're caught red-handed.

Reno County Sheriff Larry Leslie accepted $285,000 in bribes from attorney Gerald Hertach. In return for his "investment," Hertach's corrections company, MgtGp, Inc. was awarded a three-year $1.5 million contract to run the Reno County jail annex. That contract was later bumped up to a four-year, $2 million contract.

Hertach funneled the kickback money to Leslie through dummy Nevada corporations.

Leslie and Hertach were indicted in May 2001 on 21 felony bribery counts but were allowed to plead their charges down to two misdemeanor counts of conflict of interest, allowing them to receive only one-year jail sentences and an order to make restitution of $750,000 in October 2003. But even then, Hertach's attorney Steve Joseph argued that the punishment was "a little bit harsh for a class B misdemeanor."

Just how Leslie planned to make restitution was questionable at best. He told sentencing Judge Michael Barbera that the $285,000 bribe money, as well as his $60,000 annual salary was "all gone."

The bribery scheme was reported to the FBI and the Kansas Bureau of Investigation by Reno County narcotics detective Howard Shipley, a long-time friend of Leslie, after he became suspicious.[1]

Ten years later, Sandy Horton, head of the Kansas Sheriffs Association would publicly lament the arrest of three sheriffs and six deputies within a span of two years, a development he said was "offensive to every sheriff, and it should be."

The most serious case was that of the December 2011 arrest of Rooks County Sheriff Randy Axelson and a top deputy on drug charges. Rooks County is located in northwest Kansas, near Nebraska's southern border. Axelson was charged with distributing methamphetamine over a period of four months at the Rooks County Fairgrounds and within a thousand feet of a local high school. He pleaded guilty to four counts in July 2012 and was sentenced to more than four years in prison. Prosecutors dropped five other counts in exchange for his plea bargain.[2]

The case involving Jeff Curry of Franklin County, in eastern Kansas is far more lurid. Even as Curry was successfully running for re-election, authorities were undertaking a covert investigation into his relationship with Heather Jones, then the county attorney.

Records unsealed by the court on April 1, 2013, indicated that a confidential informant told a sheriff's deputy on May 20, 2012, that he saw Jones purchase meth from an associate of his on at least two occasions. The deputy, who was participating in a federal drug investigation, told Curry who instructed him to provide the information to federal authorities.

Meanwhile, Curry, who prosecutors said was engaged in an ongoing affair with Jones, warned her that she was under investigation. He gave her specific information about meetings and observations made by the informant.

Prosecutors dropped all charges against Curry and his chief deputy, Jerrod Fredricks, charged with interference with law enforcement, after they resigned their positions. Curry had been re-elected only four months earlier. Both Curry and Fredricks also surrendered their law enforcement licenses, which meant they could never work in a law enforcement capacity again. Jones resigned her position with Franklin County and began work as head of the sex crimes and child abuse division for the district attorney's office in nearby Johnson County.[3]

All the way across the state, on the Kansas western border next to Colorado, Hamilton County Sheriff Richard Garza was arrested on suspicion of aggravated assault in what was described as a "family matter." Because there was no physical violence, no charges were filed against Garza.

Still, Horton said he found incidents like Garza's "offensive."

"A sheriff's not above the law," he said. "They're charged to enforce the law. If there's a violation, they are subject to all the punishments and everything that falls within that. Integrity is a huge thing. We've got a lot of fine people out servicing in the office of sheriff, and they share in the disappointment."[4]

Sheriff Jeff Easter of Sedgwick County agreed, but took his concerns a step further. "What's more important is how those cases are addressed," he said. "If they're just kind of shoved under the carpet and nothing's really looked at, they really erode public trust."

Easter was speaking from first-hand experience. Four of his deputies were arrested on suspicion of criminal activity in the first year after his 2012 election, something Easter said he found "very frustrating."[5]

His frustration would surface again in 2019 and 2020 with the arrest of one deputy and the suspension if eight others. In 2019, Alexander Whiteman was arrested and placed on administrative leave on two counts of theft, including more than $300 from a coworker.[6]

The following year, eight deputies were suspended following reports of their using, distributing and selling steroids. All involved were with the detention bureau and included seven males and one female between the ages of 25 and 46. They had been employees of from three years to 16 years.[7]

A common trait common to many sheriffs throughout the U.S. is an affinity for guns and the irresistible urge to steal or sell weapons from their departments' evidence rooms.

A certain love for firearms is understandable, given the nature of the job, but it is difficult to comprehend why the chief law enforcement official of a county or any of his or her deputies would yield to the temptation of profiteering from weapons seized as evidence, knowing it could mean the end of their careers.

Even more puzzling is why Ness County Sheriff Bryan Whipple would knowingly sell a weapon to a convicted felon who was prohibited under federal law from possessing a firearm, let alone one purchased illegally.

Whipple, then 48, entered a guilty plea in October 2018 and agreed to resign as sheriff of Ness County, located in west-central Kansas. He had sold a .45-caliber pistol and ammunition to a man he knew was a convicted felon. Whipple also forfeited his law enforcement certification from the Kansas Commission on Peace Officers' Standards and Training (CPOST), according to U.S. Attorney Stephen McAllister.[8]

Robert Dierks, on the other hand, was removed from office for reasons of the heart, however misplaced those reasons may have been. And in the process of losing his job, he also lost his girlfriend.

While sheriff of Montgomery County, in the southeast corner of the state, adjacent to the Oklahoma state line, Dierks, 55, attempted unsuccessfully to persuade one of his deputies to abandon his January 2018 arrest of the sheriff's then-girlfriend. Alas, the girlfriend of two years broke up with Dierks when he couldn't get her out of her second offense DUI.

Dispatchers received a call on January 27 concerning a reckless driver suspected of being intoxicated. Deputy Ian Hurst pulled over a vehicle at 9:45 p.m. about five miles north of Independence. Driver Valerie Smith told the deputy to call Dierks, saying she was the sheriff's girlfriend. Hurst instead called his supervisor, and Smith called Dierks herself and handed her phone to the deputy.

Dierks said he would come pick Smith up if Hurst would just place her in handcuffs but Hurst and his supervisor decided to continue the DUI investigation and Smith was arrested. Dierks then called Hurst and asked if there was any way he could change his mind. Following the arrest, Dierks asked Hurst not to appear at Smith's driver's license hearing and further asked the deputy's supervisor and undersheriff to talk to Hurst about not testifying. He told them if Smith lost her driver's license, he would have to chauffer her children around, creating a hardship for him.[9]

Dierks was suspended from office in March 2019 and by the New Year, he had agreed to resign, to not seek public office for at least twelve months and not to discuss the merits of his case.[10]

The State of Kansas has a unique statute under which prosecutors may initiate ouster proceedings to seek the removal of a public official when the official engages in misconduct, neglects duties, or commits a violation involving "moral turpitude." The ouster statute was invoked in removing Franklin County Sheriff Curry in 2013.

Fourteen years earlier, the same law had been employed for the removal of Shawnee County Sheriff David Meneley when Kansas Attorney General Carla Stovall charged the sheriff with thirteen counts of willful misconduct or violations of moral turpitude. Following a seven-day trial, Meneley was found guilty of three counts and was ordered removed from office.[11]

Meneley's exit resulted from years of adverse publicity about drug use by an employee of the sheriff's department and about suspected tampering with drug evidence. A former narcotics officer with the sheriff's office testified at Meneley's trial that he had a cocaine addiction and had stolen cocaine from a drug investigator's office in 1994. The ensuing investigation by the Kansas Bureau of Investigation of that theft eventually led to the investigation that resulted in charges against Meneley.[12]

It's not that Kansas isn't trying to improve its image in law enforcement. It is.

The Kansas Commission on Peace Officers' Standards and Training (CPOST) increased the number of actions taken against law enforcement officers more than fourfold in the six-year period from 2011 to 2016—from about eight per year to 35. The offenses included such offenses as assault against ex-wives, taking advantage of children, showing up at work intoxicated, lying about internal investigations, road rage, stealing confiscated money, convictions of homicide and arson.

Bolstered by increased funding, CPOST initiated action against one of every 200 officers in 2015. That year, disciplinary action was taken against 93 officers, the majority of whom were either municipal officers or members of the Kansas Highway Patrol. Twenty-five of those, however, were deputies with four separate sheriff's departments. They included departments from Johnson County (ten), and Sedgwick, Reno, and Shawnee (five each).[13]

14

Kentucky: Sheriff Brought Down by Reporters

IN THE first decade of the twenty-first century, the state of Kentucky, like much of the rest of the nation, was suffering from a dual epidemic of prescription drug and crystal meth addiction. The drug problem was even more acute in Whitley County, the birthplace of Kentucky Fried Chicken. Embedded in the southeast corner of Kentucky on the Tennessee border, Whitley County is in the heart of poverty-stricken Appalachia. Making matters even worse were rumors that the local sheriff, Lawrence Hodge, was at the very center of the local drug trade.[1]

Samantha Swindler, the twenty-seven-year-old managing editor of the Corbin *Times-Tribune*, and twenty-year-old college sophomore/reporter Adam Sulfridge proved what federal agents had not been able to: Sheriff Hodge was dirty. He was suspected of trading guns, drugs and special favors.

Sulfridge had an advantage over reporters—three others had been assigned the story and each had come up dry—in that he was a local who was trusted by Corbin courthouse workers who began slipping him cryptic notes on scraps of paper instructing him which cases to look into.[2]

Swindler, a native of New Orleans, hired Sulfridge because he had written for his high school paper and because she was impressed with his knowledge of local government. But the clincher may have been the fact that Sulfridge's aunt had died of an overdose. He said his first reaction upon getting his assignment from Swindler was to wonder if she had obtained her drugs from someone being protected by the sheriff.[3]

Hodge was first elected sheriff on the campaign promise that he would clean up the drug problem in Whitley County. He even convinced the local CBS-TV station to cover a raid on one meth lab after which he said, "It put a dent in our drug problem here." But early on, there were the rumors that Hodge had gone bad. Todd Tremaine, a special agent with the Bureau of Alcohol, Tobacco and Firearms, told *60 Minutes*, "From about 2004, he (Hodge) just went downhill and was corrupt—involved with drug dealers, taking payoffs, extorting money from defendants." No matter what investigators knew, they were unable to build a case because of the impenetrable circle of drug dealers, crooked politicians and bad cops with which Hodge had surrounded himself. "He was very insulated," Tremaine said. "There was a lot of fear of what Lawrence might do if they cooperated."[4]

Undaunted, Swindler knew there had to be a paper trail somewhere. She began with the sheriff's department's evidence log. "There were months when nothing was checked in," she said. "I knew that this wasn't right because we had arrests every day in this area, particularly related to drugs. And when it's related to drugs, you know there's probably a gun. And it wasn't there."[5]

One morning as Sulfridge was taking a shower and getting ready for class, he got a chilling call from a federal agent who informed him there was a "credible" threat against his life. "Everything about (the threat) is just so surreal," he said. "You don't think a whole lot about it. Then later that night you start thinking, you're like, 'Geez, somebody wants to kill me. That's a little odd.' And it's the sheriff. The sheriff wants to kill you."[6]

Hodge was defeated for re-election and subsequently indicted. He pleaded guilty in 2011 to conspiracy to affect commerce by extortion under color of official right, conspiracy to distribute Oxycodone and conspiracy to commit money laundering. He was sentenced to 15 years in federal prison. But that didn't end his legal problems. He still had state charges to face, and in June 2013 he pleaded guilty to 18 counts of abuse of the public trust and three counts of tampering with physical evidence. He was sentenced to 17 years in prison to be serve concurrent to his federal sentence, meaning little additional jail time. He also was ordered to pay $355,188 in restitution.[7]

Hodge admitted that on at least three separate occasions between 2004 and 2007, he conspired with Roy Reynolds, a Williamsburg defense attorney, to extort money from defendants that the Whitley County Sheriff's Department charged with felony drug trafficking offenses. Reynolds pleaded guilty in connection with the case and served nearly two years in prison. He also was disbarred from ever practicing law again.[8]

Hodge appeared in court wearing a beige prison uniform, leg shackles and handcuffs that were attached to a chain around his waist. He replied "Guilty" when asked how he pled to each of the 18 individual counts but struggled to respond when asked by the judge to describe the criminal conduct contained in the charges listed in the indictment. The first eight counts dealt with checks written to Hodge and listed as being for undercover drug buys and for confidential sources from a drug and alcohol account the one-time sheriff maintained while in office. During the times the checks were written, few cases were sent to the grand jury involving undercover drug purchases, according to court testimony.[9]

Two counts of the indictment dealt with tampering with physical evidence charges related to 17 seized guns and knives. Hodge was also charged with two counts of abuse of the public trust relating to allegations that he converted 12 of the guns for his own use, sold three guns to a local attorney and gave two to his chief deputy. The final count of the indictment dealt with a tampering with physical evidence charge related to drugs and weapons that then Deputy Ronnie Bowling seized on Nov. 15, 2009, and turned over to Hodge as evidence. The physical material wasn't logged into evidence by Hodge, according to court testimony.[10]

He was ordered to make restitution in relation to those eight counts, four counts of abuse of the public trust dealing with missing money from Hodge's fee account, which covered general operating expenses, and three counts of abuse of the public trust listed in the indictment that dealt with shortages from the tax accounts of Hodge's office.[11]

"If they are elected as sheriff, the public expects a sheriff to do what he is elected to do and not go to the other side and be a part of the problem," Commonwealth Attorney Allen Trimble said.[12]

No story of Kentucky political corruption and strife could be written without including Harlan County. Earning the name "Bloody Harlan," the county burst onto the national stage during the turbulent 1930s when a dispute between coal miners and union organizers on one side and coal companies and law enforcement on the other. The number of casualties on each side remains unknown but miners, deputies and various company representatives lost their lives during the conflict which lasted from 1931 to 1939.

At the center of the labor discord was Sheriff J.H. Blair who said, "I did all in my power to aid the operators (owners)...there was no compromise when labor troubles swept the county and the 'Reds' came to Harlan County." That included illegally searching the home of striker Sam Reece and terrorizing his wife and children, prompting his wife, Florence Reece to write the lyrics to *Which Side Are You On*, which became an inspirational anthem for the miners.[13]

Half-a-century after the coal miner wars began, another Harlan County sheriff, Paul Browning, Jr., would again attract an unwelcome spotlight on Harlan County when he was sentenced in December 1982 to ten years in prison for conspiring to murder two political rivals.

Browning was acquitted on charges of attempting to burn down a house owned by a former deputy to collect fire insurance but was convicted of conspiring to murder a mining equipment dealer and a Harlan County magistrate with whom he had on ongoing political feud.[14]

He was released after serving fewer than three years. But as if the state convictions and the prison sentence were not bad enough for Browning, a more tragic fate lay ahead for him.

Twenty years after his conviction and sentencing, he was again seeking election to his former office when his body was found in his burned-out pickup truck in March 2002, less than a month after he was captured on videotape accepting money from an alleged drug dealer. He had been shot in the head.

On the tape, which was viewed by the Associated Press, Browning could be seen stuffing cash into his shirt pocket as another man counted it out. Browning also could be heard on the tape that he planned to kill a former deputy who had testified against him two decades earlier and that he also planned revenge against others who were involved in his arrest. Current Sheriff Steve Duff said the videotape had been given to him less than a month prior to Browning's murder but he refused to name the source of the tape.

The other man on the tape, Duff Said, was Dewayne Harris, who had been charged with trafficking in cocaine in 1998. That charge was subsequently reduced to possession of a controlled substance. Harris was later charged with cocaine trafficking again, but that charge was dismissed.

Browning could be heard telling Harris that the money, $2,500, was "all I needed to put me in that office. This is the best money you've spent in your life. You'll be the man with the powder...if someone moves in that's competition, let me know and they're busted," he said.

Browning said he wanted to send Duff, a former state trooper who originally arrested him, to prison and also said he wanted revenge on former Commonwealth's Attorney Ron John who had prosecuted his case. [15]

Four men were convicted or confessed to taking part in Browning's murder but it would be nearly eight years before the main instigator of the crime was finally brought to justice in 2009 but only after he was sentenced to federal prison in an unrelated matter nearly five years earlier.

If that's confusing, that's because it's a confusing case. Roger Hall, 41, a narcotics detective under former sheriff Duff, was sentenced to 30 years in prison in November 2009 for his part in Browning's 2002 murder. He pleaded guilty to two counts of criminal facilitation to murder and four counts of second-degree trafficking a controlled substance after being named by Dewayne Harris as the man who put the murder plan into action.

Harris, a major drug dealer who once paid Hall bribe money for protection, turned on the deputy after learning of an affair between his wife and Hall, which led to the three felony convictions earlier. Even as Hall's duties included investigating drug cases, he was taking thousands of dollars weekly from Harris in exchange for information on investigations and even for transporting drugs for him.

Harris said when Hall became concerned that Browning would fire him if he was elected, he decided he wanted Browning killed. When Harris's uncle, Raymond Harris, volunteered to do the deed, a plan was hatched to kill Browning in Tennessee and burn his truck in Virginia. That would involve agencies from three states which the plotters hoped would create difficulties in solving the killing.

Instead, Raymond Harris shot Browning prematurely while still in Kentucky and he and a cocaine addict named Johnny Epperson burned Browning's body in his truck in a secluded spot in Bell County.

It took the eternal triangle to break the case. Dewayne Harris was arrested on federal drug charges in 2003 and sent to prison. His wife, Edna, who had been involved in a sexual relationship with Hall, had recorded a conversation in which the two discussed their affair and during which they mentioned selling Dewayne Harris's baseball card collection.

Edna Harris later provided police the tape who in turn, played it for Harris who then turned on Hall. [16]

Besides Hall's thirty-year sentence, Raymond Harris was sentenced to life imprisonment while his nephew, Dewayne Harris was sentenced to 30 years and Epperson to 20 years.

Nearly five years earlier, in March 2005, Hall, then 37, was sentenced to 15 months in federal prison after he was convicted of providing the target of an investigation (Edna Harris) information about federal drug agents and agreeing to hide assets for her while she was in prison. Additionally, he lied to FBI agents about having a relationship with the woman.[17]

As a footnote to the entire affair, Browning's widow, Jayne Browning, eventually lost her lawsuit against Duff and Hall for the wrongful death of her husband.[18]

One might expect that Harlan County had experienced sufficient problems with its sheriff's department with the murder plots, killings, drug dealing, and general corruption but ex-sheriff Marvin J. Lipfird would run afoul of the law in November 2016 when he was indicted on federal charges of theft of public funds and property.

The former sheriff who was followed around by a camera crew from the *National Geographic* channel in 2013 and 2014 for its program about an Appalachian sheriff fighting drugs and "devoting his life to clean up the community," was sentenced to three months of weekends in jail, five months' probation and ordered to make restitution of more than $22,000.

Lipfird, who was married and who had a fourth-grade autistic son, was accused of spending public funds on food and alcohol, a massage, hotel rooms, and subscriptions to an online dating service and personal clothing. He eventually pleaded guilty to two felony charges.

U.S. District Judge Gregory Van Tatenhove said conduct like Lipfird's contributed to a creeping cynicism that causes people to question whether the system can be trusted.

Prosecutors recommended a nine-month sentence but Lipfird's attorney pointed to the bond between Lipfird and his son. Lipfird's wife, Carrie, said only Lipfird could calm the child during his emotional meltdowns.[19]

A sheriff, a former state police commissioner, and a state judge, and a county executive were among 12 people swept up in ten federal indictments containing 62 counts in connection with a drug smuggling investigation in northeastern Kentucky.

Morgan County Sheriff Roger Benton, former state police commissioner Marion Campbell, and Morgan County Judge-County Executive Gene Allen, were indicted and arrested on March 12, 1986, on charges of allowing loads of cocaine to be flown into Morgan County with their full knowledge and without interference. Additionally, Benton was charged with five counts of extortion and conspiracy to distribute drugs. They were introduced to a man known to them as Harry McBride who was said to have killed seven people and who "didn't talk." The local men accepted more than $10,000 so that McBride could fly cocaine into Morgan County with the full knowledge of and without interference from Benton.[20]

Despite Benton's claim that he was conducting an investigation of drug dealing in Morgan County and that it was "only natural" that he would have accepted bribes and drugs from those whom he was investigating, he was convicted on all counts.[21]

Benton wasn't the only Kentucky sheriff to fall from grace because of the temptation of fast money in the transition from bootlegging to drug smuggling in the Bluegrass State.

In August 1991, three sheriffs, a deputy sheriff, and a small-town police chief were all convicted of a total of 42 felony counts between them. Besides the count of conspiracy to commit extortion for which all five sheriffs were convicted, the other individual counts included:

- Former Lee County Sheriff Johnny Mann (convicted on 18 of 19 counts), Wolfe County Sheriff Lester Drake (guilty on 13 of 17 counts) and suspended Beattyville Police Chief Omer Noe (seven of 13 counts): conspiracy to distribute cocaine;
- Owsley County Sheriff Billy McIntosh (eight of 14 counts);
- Wolfe County Deputy Sheriff Wilson Stone (two of nine counts).

One other lawman, Sheriff Dean Spencer of Breathitt County, was acquitted of all charges against him.

The convictions came after twenty hours of deliberations over a three-day period and one year to the day after the five were arrested by FBI agents following a yearlong undercover investigation. During that operation, federal agents posing as drug dealers paid the lawmen bribes totaling $92,500.[22]

Evidence presented at trial revealed that the FBI initiated the undercover operation which was initially focused on Sheriff Mann who introduced the agents to the other officers who then "willingly advised and assisted the agents in the drug operation,"[23] which at one time saw packages of cocaine dropped by airplane on a farm owned by one of the lawmen.[24]

"What this particular situation does reflect is the absolute corrupting influence of drugs," said U.S. Attorney Louie DeFalaise.[25]

A news release issued after the arrests said official sheriffs' vehicles were used in the drug transactions and that FBI agents were seen taking hundred-dollar bills from an Owsley County vehicle. Following the arrests, five of the six men arrested were released on bail but bond was denied for Mann after an agent testified that at one point during the operation, he had promised to kill anyone who set him up.[26]

On appeal, several unique arguments were put forth by the officers, including Sheriff McIntosh's claim that he was participating in the operation only because he was conducting his own criminal investigation. "The jury, however, obviously did not believe McIntosh's story," the appellate court ruled.

The most original argument, also rejected by the appeals court, was offered up by Noe who said he should have been held accountable for only two kilograms of cocaine instead of twelve because the same two kilograms were used by the FBI in six separate transactions.[27]

It might seem reasonable to think the lessons would have been learned by the citizens of Breathitt and Lee counties from the arrest of sheriffs Spencer Mann. But less than a decade later, a familiar story rocked both counties. First, Breathitt County Sheriff Ray Clemons was sentenced to a year and a day in jail in 1997 for failing to report an ongoing drug enterprise by his daughter and son-in-law.

Five years later, he was back, seeking election to his former office but was rejected by voters. At the same time in Lee County, Doug Bramberg won his primary election for sheriff despite having previously pleaded guilty to a felony drug charge but lost the general election.

Even former Sheriff Roger Benton who had been caught up in that 1986 federal sting operation in which he was convicted and sentenced to prison for protecting drug dealers was seeking a political comeback. But like Bramberg and Clemons in Breathitt and Lee counties, he was turned back by the voters of Morgan County.[28]

By all accounts, Sam Catron was a pretty popular sheriff. After all, the voters of Pulaski County had already elected him four consecutive times and he was a heavy favorite for election to a fifth term. But on April 13, 2002, as the forty-eight-year-old Catron was preparing to leave a campaign rally in Shopville, a small town about 70 miles south of Lexington, his life was cut short by a sniper's bullet that slammed into his head.

It was easy enough to capture the shooter. Danny Shelley, 30, a local Oxycontin addict, was spotted by witnesses as he sped away. But he wrecked the motorcycle he was driving in his attempt to escape.

But then, it was quickly determined that the motorcycle he was driving was owned by Jeff Morris, Catron's former deputy and his opponent in the upcoming election. A third person charged with complicity was Kenneth White, 54.[29]

Shelly changed his initial not guilty plea in June 2013 and agreed to testify against Morris and White. White, a former DEA informant, convinced Shelley that he (Shelly) was about to be arrested by Catron. The plan, conceived by White, called for Shelley to meet with White and Morris after he had shot the sheriff. Unknown to Shelley, however, the other two had planned for Morris to kill Shelley under the pretense of self-defense, which he hoped would make him a hero and ensure his election. White's plan was to then run the county with Morris as his puppet.[30]

All three conspirators were sentenced to life in prison. White died in the Kentucky State Reformatory in La Grange in December 2018.[31]

Indicative of the political tension in eastern Kentucky at the turn of the twenty-first century was the fact that Catron was wearing a bulletproof vest at the time of his assassination. He wore the vest almost constantly when in public. In 1957, his father, Harold Catron, then the Somerset police chief, was gunned down in front of his house by three men as they drove past in a sedan. He survived the shooting and lived another seven years, until 1964 when a shotgun pellet that had remained lodged in his body shifted, causing a fatal heart attack.[32]

Former Barren County Sheriff Chris Eaton was sentenced to 18 months in federal prison in June 2015 following his conviction on a witness tampering charge. Eaton and four other law enforcement officers were initially indicted on federal civil rights violations stemming from an incident in which they were accused of beating a handcuffed man and then attempting to conceal the fact.

Arrested along with Eaton were deputies Aaron Adam Bennett, Danny McCown, and Adam Gene Minor and Barren-Edmonson County Drug Task Force Detective Eric Duane Guffey.

Eaton was indicted by a federal grand jury on two counts of deprivation of rights under color of law and one count each of witness tampering, falsification of a document, and providing a false statement to federal investigators.[33]

It would be difficult to find a more vivid illustration of the grip that the opioid epidemic has on the U.S. than Jamie Kinman.

Kinman was the sheriff of Carroll County, located in north-central Kentucky, adjacent to Indiana's southeastern border. Elected in part to keep the residents of the county safe from the influx of drugs, including opioids,

Kinman instead was forced to resign after pleading guilty in April 2017 to stealing painkillers from a terminally ill cancer patient—while in uniform.

Kinman's guilty plea to 11 counts of theft required him to participate in a one-year rehabilitation program and to resign from office. He also was sentenced to five years' probation.

The relatively light sentence was imposed despite Carroll County's status of sending people to prison at a highest rate of any county in Kentucky. Prosecutor James Crawford said he agreed to the plea deal because it required Kinman's immediate resignation. Had the case gone to trial and he result been appealed, Kinman could have remained in office through the end of his term in December 2018.

The criminal complaint filed against Kinman said that on February 10 and February 14, the sheriff, armed with a deadly weapon, unlawfully entered the home of a terminally-ill cancer patient and took hydrocodone pills from the home.[34]

It wasn't Kinman's first brush with the law as a defendant. Four months earlier, in December 2016, he was acquitted on charges of tampering with evidence in the alleged theft of painkillers in 2013 that were stored as evidence in the sheriff's department.[35]

Just down the road from Carroll County lies Bullitt County, which also abuts Indiana's southern border. It was there that David Greenwell was acquitted of five counts of abetting a drug dealer and of obstructing the federal investigation in November 2018.

Greenwell, who without explanation had abruptly resigned from office in February 2017, was accused of aiding former Bullitt County special sheriff's deputy Chris Mattingly's conspiracy to sell more than a ton of marijuana in Bullitt County and of obstructing justice by informing targets of the investigation.

Mattingly, who pleaded earlier to trafficking in pot and methamphetamine and money laundering, cut a deal to become the government's key witness in exchange for a reduced sentence. He subsequently testified that he was able to continue distributing drugs even while under federal investigation because Greenwell "had my back."[36]

The indictment, which was unsealed on May 3, 2017, said that in June 2014, Greenwell attempted to obstruct, influence and impede a federal criminal prosecution by informing Mattingly that his place of business was under photographic surveillance via a pole camera.

Then, on May 15, 2015, Greenwell disclosed to Mattingly the contents of intercepted wire communications that were part of the investigation, and in July 2015, he arranged a meeting with his deputy where Mattingly was provided with the names of three potential government witnesses in the federal prosecution.

Additionally, between July 2014 and July 2015, Greenwell allegedly aided and abetted Mattingly in a conspiracy to distribute a thousand kilograms or more of marijuana.[37]

15

Louisiana: Anything Goes (But No Pimps)

D. J. "CAT" DOUCET was one of the most colorful—and corrupt—in the history of colorful and corrupt Louisiana sheriffs. First elected in 1936 with the backing of the Huey P. Long political machine, he immediately encouraged illegal gambling and prostitution to flourish throughout St. Landry Parish. He soon earned the nickname "Cat," because of his personal role in the protection of prostitution along U.S. 190.

A 1939 FBI memo went even further in charging that Doucet "was operating all slot machines in St. Landry Parish." The following year, as his first term was nearing an end, both the St. Landry district attorney and the Eunice newspaper, the *Eunice New Era*, publicly appealed to the sheriff to clean up the vice in the parish.

He lost his bid for re-election in 1940 and that same year, he was indicted by a parish grand jury on charges he had embezzled $3,000. Even though seven of his former deputies testified against him, the charges were eventually dismissed because of "prosecution irregularities." Out of office for twelve years, he was again elected sheriff in 1952 and the following year, another grand jury investigated Doucet for unspecified activity but failed to indict him. He remained sheriff until 1968, winning four consecutive terms and surviving a December 11, 1958, *New Orleans Times-Picayune* article which cited "flagrant gambling law violations" in St. Landry Parish.

In 1956, in an interview with history professor and author Michael Kurtz, Doucet boasted that the election of Governor Earl K. Long, Huey's younger brother, in 1956 would enable him to "open up the cathouses again," adding that Long had promised to "let me get my fair share of the take."

Prostitution was so much a part of everyday life in St. Landry Parish that when the hookers raised their prices, representatives of the local business community called upon Doucet to complain that the fee structure was making life difficult for area college students who could ill-afford the new rate structure. Doucet, leaning back in his chair said, "You have a point. Maybe they could have special pricing, like kiddie plates at a restaurant."

Doucet, like Earl Long, was an astute politician. Both knew the days of Jim Crow segregation in the Deep South were numbered and, again like Long, Doucet could do the math when it came to taking advantage of the African-American vote. He became one of the first local white politicians in Louisiana outside New Orleans to endorse the growing civil rights movement by allowing blacks to register to vote.[1]

Doucet' successor, Adler LeDoux, was almost as tolerant of prostitution and gambling as Doucet had been but he did have his limits. John Maginnis, in his book *The Last Hayride*, wrote that in an interview following his 1979 retirement, LeDoux was asked why he had tolerated prostitution and pimps in St. Landry during his tenure. LeDoux was quick to correct the reporter. "No pimps," he said emphatically. [2]

St. Landry Parish deputy sheriff Joshua John Courville was charged with sexual battery, simple battery, and domestic abuse battery on New Year's Day 2023 after he fondled a woman in a bar and then followed her outside and ended up punching her in the face before finally climbing into his truck and passing out, according to a January 4 story in the *Opelousas Daily World*. He was placed on leave by the sheriff's department and subsequently resigned, according to the newspaper.

Concordia Parish, more specifically Ferriday, Louisiana, is best known as the birthplace of CBS and ABC newsman Howard K. Smith, General Claire Chennault, piano-pounding rocker Jerry Lee Lewis and his two cousins, televangelist Jimmy Swaggart and country singer Mickey Gilley.

But in the darkened corners away from the spotlight provided by the shared fame of those five favorite sons lies a shadowy side of Concordia Parish, a side that harbors whispered secrets of civil rights murders as well as the assassination of a suspected murderer in another case that implicated a powerful politician.

On two separate occasions Noah Cross was the sheriff of Concordia Parish, situated in Louisiana's delta farmland directly across the Mississippi River from historic Natchez. The contrast between Ferriday and Vidalia in

Concordia Parish and the Mississippi town could not be greater.

One of the oldest and most important European settlements of the lower Mississippi Valley, Natchez was founded by the French in 1716, more than a century before Jackson which replaced it as the state capital in 1822. An important cotton and shipping center, Natchez features many of the original antebellum homes that make the city a beautiful tourist attraction.

Across the river, Vidalia and Ferriday present quite a different picture. A wide four-lane concrete highway slices Vidalia in half before leading into Ferriday on the way northward to such towns as Clayton, Sicily Island, Winnsboro, Mangham, Wisner, Gilbert, Baldwin, Baskin, Archibald, and Rayville. Vidalia and Winnsboro come nearest to resembling real towns, with auto dealerships, farm supply franchises, and courthouses. The others, including Ferriday, stand in stark contrast with their run-down shops and deserted store fronts. Most feature the usual assortment of dollar stores, Walmarts, struggling furniture stores, liquor stores, rundown local police stations, used tire stores, the obligatory fast- food franchises and the vast array of Protestant churches. Some of these towns may have once been centers of local commerce but now are just waiting to die, their weary stores and shops long since boarded up and abandoned or quickly on their way to that ignominious fate. Poverty reigns supreme in the Delta and nowhere is that more evident than in the Louisiana farmland of cotton and soybeans that Concordia Parish calls home.

It was in 1944 that Cross was first elected sheriff, the same year that country and western crooner Jimmie Davis was elected to his first of two terms as governor. In 1948, Cross was ousted by Hartwell Love, the man he had defeated four years earlier. Cross would return in 1952 to beat Love and would remain in office until he reported to federal prison in 1973.[3]

Easily the most heinous act in Concordia Parish's sordid history occurred on December 10, 1964. The ominous presence of Cross's chief deputy, Frank DeLaughter was linked to the events of that night.

Shortly after midnight, Frank Morris, a black shoe repair shopkeeper, was asleep on a cot in the back of his store when he heard glass breaking. "He bolted to the front of the store and saw two men, one pouring gasoline on the outside of the building and the other holding a shotgun," local newspaper editor Stanley Nelson wrote years later. As a lit match dropped into the gasoline instantly turned the little shop into an inferno, the man behind the shotgun ordered Morris to "get back in there, nigger." By the time he exited the rear of the building, the shop was engulfed in flames, his feet were bleeding, his hair was on fire and the only remnants of clothing remaining were the elastic waistband of his boxer shorts and the shoulder straps of his undershirt. He was taken to a hospital by two police officers who happened to be nearby. Nurses who knew him said he was unrecognizable. Rev. Robert Lee, Jr., who visited Morris in the hospital, said, "Only the bottoms of his feet weren't burned. He was horrible to look at." Morris lived four days as friends, FBI agents, pastors, and family members attempted to get him to identify his attackers. Several witnesses would tell Nelson that they left believing Morris was holding back the identity of his assailants out of fear of reprisals against him or family members.

Potential witnesses soon began to disappear. One was a black man who happened to be walking by Morris's shop just before the attack. After his house was twice fired on by shotgun blasts, he received a visit from sheriff's deputies who advised him he was no longer welcome in Ferriday, his son told Nelson.

DeLaughter, in an apparent attempt to discredit the reputation and memory of Morris, started rumors that Morris was a bootlegger and drug dealer, saying that the arson was the result of a drug deal that went bad. No one was ever charged with the crime and, after 44 years, Morris's brutal murder faded from public memory. Those guilty of the crime continued to live freely, fearlessly, and with impunity – until Nelson began asking questions and writing story after story about the killing.

The Concordia Sentinel reported that a woman said in 2011 that she had been told by a man close to DeLaughter that the deputy and Arthur Leonard Spencer of Rayville had torched the shoe shop. The man, Ku Klux Klan member O.C. "Coonie" Poissot, told the FBI that he had been with DeLaughter only a few hours before the arson and that DeLaughter told him he was going to teach Morris a lesson for being "uppity."

Morris was 51 years old when he was murdered. His business catered to black and white customers alike, and many people of both races considered him a friend.

The Justice Department, however, was too preoccupied with three earlier civil rights murders to actively pursue Morris's killers. Only a few months earlier, the bodies of three civil rights workers had been discovered buried in a levee at Philadelphia, Mississippi (Neshoba County), and Attorney General Robert F. Kennedy directed the FBI's efforts to solving those murders.

So why was Frank Morris killed? A couple of theories exist and both are plausible for the time. One says because he was the only shoe repair shop in town and because families then could generally afford only a single pair of shoes, both blacks and whites patronized his shop. He waited on whites, particularly white women, outside, on the porch of his store. Still rumors started by local Ku Klux Klan members said he flirted with the white female customers. Another story has it that Morris refused to repair a deputy sheriff's boots at no charge and in so doing, offended the white lawman.

When all is said and done, the investigation of these cases ultimately relied on a single person: Nelson, whose book about the killings, entitled *Devils Walking: Klan Murders Along the Mississippi in the 1960s*, was published in 2016. Along the way, he was named in 2010 as one of three finalists for the Pulitzer Prize in the category of Local Reporting.[4]

Rather than the racial violence it was the payoffs to protect prostitution and gambling that turned out to be the downfall of Sheriff Noah Cross and his deputy/bag man DeLaughter.

Nelson wrote that Curt Hewitt, who had a lengthy rap sheet, moved to Concordia Parish in 1965 to replicate what he had done in St. Landry Parish: to operate the Morville Lounge as a gambling and prostitution hall for racketeering interests that included New Orleans mafia boss Carlos Marcello. But while he was well-versed in running gambling and whorehouses, his curriculum vitae did not include dealing with the Klan.

Hewitt, wrote *Sentinel* writers Nelson, Matt Barnidge and Ian Stanford, said he had experience running brothels in the St. Landry area where prostitution was widespread.

The Monterey Klan unit which threatened to burn down Hewitt's lounge was believed to have been involved in the beatings of at least three men in 1965: a white man and two black men. Despite the heavy influence of Marcello in gambling and prostitution operations in Concordia Parish, the Klan at the time remained a formidable foe so it became necessary for the club to protect its interests.[5]

Enter Noah Cross and deputy Frank DeLaughter.

In a bizarre twist, it turned out that, along with Marcello, the Morville Lounge, located about 15 miles south of Vidalia, had a second silent partner—the Klan itself. DeLaughter joined the KKK to keep tabs on the organization from a vantage point on the inside. He was assigned the duty of picking up the weekly payments of $150 to $250 from the clubs. The protection money, stuffed in white envelopes, was paid in cash.

FBI reports obtained by *The Sentinel* indicated that hookers were secreted in trailers near the lounge and at a Natchez trailer park. A fleet of cars to take prostitutes to and from the lounge was kept in a garage in Natchez.

In the early seventies, following a six-year federal investigation headed up by FBI agent John Pfeifer, the *Sentinel* reporters wrote, Hewitt, Cross, DeLaughter and others were prosecuted on federal racketeering, perjury and jury tampering charges. The FBI made the Concordia investigation a priority with three goals: to rid the parish of gambling and prostitution, to neutralize violent Klansmen and to remove Cross and DeLaughter from law enforcement.

On May 6, 1972, following a federal grand jury investigation, Cross was convicted on two counts of perjury for having lied to a grand jury about his acceptance of bribes to protect prostitution and gambling in Concordia Parish. In his trial, two bar owners testified that they made weekly protection payments to Cross or DeLaughter. One of the operators testified that he paid Cross $200 per month. Though Cross denied taking payments, he was convicted and sentenced to a four-year prison term. Re-elected despite his conviction, he petitioned the court for a re-trial a month before he took office for his seventh consecutive term.

Following his perjury conviction, he was charged with jury tampering and obstruction of justice. Again found guilty in 1973, he was sentenced to six years to be served concurrently with his perjury conviction.

After resigning from office, he reported to the federal correctional institution in Texarkana, Texas. He was released after serving half his term. He died in Ferriday on November 22, 1976.

Frank DeLaughter was as corrupt as Cross and even more prone to violence.

Once the Morville Lounge brought in gambling tables and hookers. DeLaughter quickly became a familiar—and frequent—visitor at the club.[6] In October 1965, DeLaughter was arrested along with two other

men, and later convicted in federal court, in the beating of William C. Davis, who had been accused of the theft.

Meanwhile, Morville Lounge prospered, thanks to the protection of Cross and DeLaughter. Hewitt ran a sophisticated operation, employing twenty prostitutes, some earning as much as $400 in cash per week. Peepholes were placed in doors at the lounge, and pit bulls and an arsenal of weapons were kept on the property to guard against unwanted guests.

But not all of the prostitutes were willing employees. A nearly naked teenage girl escaped from the lounge and was rescued by a minister and his wife. The girl said she had been taken to the lounge by force and forced to work as a prostitute.

Another woman testified before a federal grand jury that following her arrest in Shreveport, she was bonded out by a man who, unbeknownst to her, was a pimp. She was taken by force to the lounge where she was kept captive for nearly six weeks during time which she was made to "work a date" in Catahoula Parish before leaving. She said she was slapped around by two men while at the lounge.

DeLaughter was also believed to have been involved, at least indirectly, in the torture and drowning death of Joseph Edwards, a black employee of the Shamrock Motel in nearby Vidalia. His body was never found.[7]

Though DeLaughter was believed to have been involved in a multitude of other criminal acts, it wasn't until the 1970s that he and Cross were finally convicted in federal court not for the Morris murder, but for their roles in running prostitution and gambling operations at the Morville Lounge. Their convictions were based largely upon agent Pfeifer's unrelenting investigation.

DeLaughter, who stood six-feet-four and weighed 260 pounds, was sentenced to one year in prison after his racketeering conviction and for violating the civil rights of Davis. He was forever barred from working in law enforcement and was prohibited from carrying a firearm. He died in 1997.[8]

Jack Favor was a champion rodeo performer. In 1942, he won $18,000 (a lot of money for that period) riding the notorious bucking bronco Hell's Angel in the Gene Autry Rodeo in Madison Square Garden in New York City. He also held the bulldogging record on four separate occasions, once throwing a steer in 2.2 seconds in a Houston rodeo. By 1961, Favor had retired from the rodeo and was Regional Manager for Hydrotex Industries.

Willie Waggonner, older brother of U.S. Rep. Joe Waggonner, was the sheriff of Bossier Parish and his chief deputy and eventual successor was Vol Dooley. Louis H. Padgett, Jr. was the district attorney and O.E. Price was Twenty-Sixth Judicial District Court judge.

Mr. and Mrs. W.H. Richey operated a bait and tackle business near

Haughton in Bossier Parish across the Red River from Shreveport.

Floyd Edward Cumbey and Donald Lee Yates were a couple of hitchhikers whom Favor gave a ride from Tulsa to Bossier City during one of his business trips in 1964. The lives of these nine individuals would converge to produce tragic consequences for the Richeys and to test Favor's religious faith.[9]

Cumbey and Yates thought that the Richeys had $60,000 hidden in their possession. When the couple refused to admit that they had such holdings, they were murdered. The investigation dragged on for two years without a serious suspect. Meanwhile, Favor, a deeply religious man, had no knowledge of the Richey murders. He barely remembered Cumbey or Yates, he told investigators when he was lured in 1966 to Benton, the governmental seat of Bossier Parish. He thought he was returning to submit to a lie detector test to support his innocence in the murders. Instead, Waggonner arrested Favor on the spot, and District Attorney Padgett filed murder charges against the former rodeo star.

Following the Richey murders, Cumbey was tried in Missouri for armed robbery but was freed after a hung jury. Brought back to Bossier Parish, Cumbey pleaded guilty as an accessory to the murders and named Favor as the triggerman. Yates had already confessed to authorities his part in the murders but said that the third suspect was someone else, not Favor.

For whatever reason, Waggonner bought Cumbey's testimony while discounting that of Yates.

Following Favor's trial, Cumbey was allowed to change his murder pleas to manslaughter. Incredibly, he received suspended sentences on each count. Seven months later, Cumbey, on Waggonner's orders, was taken By Dooley to Texarkana, Texas, and released. Jurors who convicted Favor, however, were lied to. They were told Cumbey would serve hard time in the Louisiana State Penitentiary at Angola. Yates, meanwhile, was given life imprisonment in the case.[10]

Underscoring the manner in which the case was botched, Cumbey killed his former girlfriend and her roommate in Tulsa just two days after his release. Despite evidence to the contrary as to his whereabouts on April 17, 1964, Favor received a life sentence at the Louisiana State Penitentiary at Angola. When his attorney, former State Senator Joe Cawthon, died, his co-counsel, James B. Wells of Bossier City, who believed in Favor's innocence, began to work pro bono to procure a second trial. This required a lawsuit against Angola's then-warden, C. Murray Henderson.

During his seven years at Angola, Favor took the lead in turning the struggling prison rodeo into a professional production, which was first opened to the public in 1967 and which continues to attract thousands of spectators.

Wells filed a writ of habeas corpus on Favor's behalf, which the state courts denied. A federal judge, however, granted a second trial on the premise that Judge Price and D.A. Padgett, had conspired to convict Favor in his first trial. In the second trial, held seven years later, also held in Benton but with a different judge and prosecutor, Favor was quickly exonerated of the murders based on Yates' confession which had been blocked from admission by Judge Price in the first trial.[11] Favor filed a $7 million lawsuit against the State of Louisiana for wrongful imprisonment but settled for $55,000. The small settlement was a result of state officials having immunity in connection with their job duties, a law that gives prosecutors and investigators carte blanche to carry out false incrimination and warrantless prosecution with no fear of consequences.

Favor long contended that his conviction was the result of collusion among Price, Waggonner, Dooley, and Padgett, who by the time of Favor's suit, had been elected to a judgeship of the 26th Judicial District Court. Price was subsequently elected to the appeals court.

Favor died of pancreatic cancer on December 27, 1988, at the age of 77. Waggonner, who was first elected sheriff in 1948, remained in office until his death from a heart attack on May 9, 1976. He was succeeded by Dooley who remained in office until 1988. He died on August 11, 2014. [12]

Bailey Grant was an apparent master of the necessary political skills, remaining as Ouachita Parish sheriff for 32 years, from 1952 until his retirement in 1984.

On July 13, 1960, with Grant midway through the first year of his third term of office, the quiet of a seemingly routine summer morning was shattered by blasts from a shotgun wielded by one Zennie William Fuller, then 35. By the time the shooting was over just after 7:00 a.m., first with the shotgun and then with a pistol from point-blank range, four black men lay dead on his lawn. A fifth, though wounded, escaped on foot. All five were employees of Fuller.

Fuller claimed the five threatened him, but a heavily redacted FBI report on the cold case dated August 27, 2009, indicated that an agent interviewed a witness to the shooting who refuted that claim. Fuller was far behind in paying the men their wages and they appeared for work at his home and asked to be paid, the witness said.

The report said Fuller, who operated a sewer servicing business, "snapped" when the men demanded their back pay and opened fire with a shotgun, striking all five. "Four of them were lying on the ground but were not yet dead," it said. At that point, teenager William Herbert Fuller, identified as Zennie Fuller's son, "walked outside and shot four of the men in the head with a pistol. The fifth victim, Willie Charlie Gibson, had escaped on foot. [14]

Fuller, according to a November 30, 2009, story in the *Monroe News Star* about the FBI cold case, said the men came to his house with knives and that one of them swung at Fuller three times before he managed to retrieve his shotgun and began firing.

Zennie Fuller, the report said, then walked back into his house, took a drink of coffee and dialed Sheriff Grant. "Bailey, this is Robert," he is quoted as saying. "You better get down to my house. I just shot five niggers." Fuller and Grant "were known to be good friends," the report indicated. Fuller was taken into custody and initially charged with involuntary manslaughter but even those inconsequential charges were later dropped.

When Fuller, an active member of the Ku Klux Klan, began receiving threats following the shootings, he sought the protection of the KKK. (He eventually became the grand dragon of the organization.) Meanwhile, Fuller allegedly threatened the only survivor of the shooting, supposedly warning Gibson to corroborate his story and testify that he and the others had intended to kill Fuller.

The close bond of friendship between Fuller and Grant, along with Fuller's ties to the KKK, raises the logical question of whether Grant, like other Southern sheriffs in the mid-Twentieth Century, willingly turned a blind eye to the Klan as it employed every means of terrorism at its disposal—including threats, beatings, and even murder—in an attempt to stem the groundswell of non-violent activism that defined the civil rights movement.[15]

The Ouachita Parish Sheriff's Office entered a period of relative quiet during the three terms of Grant's successor Laymon Godwin. The same cannot be said for Royce Toney's single term in office. On February 25, 2012, Toney was arrested by federal authorities for conspiracy, computer fraud, identity theft and obstruction. Arrested with the 64-year-old Toney in the elaborate attempt at covering up Toney's extracurricular sexual affairs was a deputy, Major Michael K. Davis, who worked in the sheriff's IT department.

Additionally, the two were charged with a single count of obstruction for reformatting and installing a new operating system on a computer once Davis learned of the FBI probe. Finally, Toney was accused of obstruction by retaliating against a witness who was cooperating with the FBI investigation.[16]

On February 8, 2011, a team of FBI agents conducted a raid on the sheriff's office as a precursor to the indictments to come a year later. The raid was initiated at 4:00 p.m. and agents remained, gathering evidence until after 10:00 p.m.[17]

Toney had already been experiencing difficulties prior to the raid. He had been cited on numerous occasions in audits for violations of state public bid laws by using inmate labor on building projects that, because of their size, were mandated by law to be bid out. Inmate labor was used to renovate his office and for work at the sheriff's office's rifle range; Toney had also announced his intentions to again use inmate labor to renovate an old school building to be used to house the patrol division and the department's work release program.

Toney was also named as the "other man" in an acrimonious divorce proceeding after it was learned he was having an affair with the wife of a local attorney. While he may have survived his legal problems, it was the adulterous affair with a married woman that ultimately led to Toney's downfall. The details were simply too unseemly for a small town in the heart of the Bible Belt to ignore.

The divorce petition of Larry Glen Culp said his wife, Laurie Schween Culp, whom Toney had placed on his office's payroll at $80,000 per year, had been having an affair with Toney for at least two years. He said Laurie Culp and Toney had sex at a training facility inside the fence of Monroe Regional Airport, in Toney's home, in the parking lot of the Monroe Athletic Club and other parking lots throughout Ouachita Parish—including that of St. Francis Medical Center on the night Sheriff's Deputy J.R. Searcy was fatally shot.[18]

Even the most inured political observers found it impossible to get past that ethical and moral lapse. Some people take their politics a little more seriously than others. Take, for example, Cyrus "Bobby" Tardo. Elected sheriff of Lafourche Parish in 1971, he was defeated for reelection by Duffy Breaux in 1975. That he went on to be elected parish president in 1983 was of little consequence to Tardo. Losing in '75 to the man he had defeated four years earlier apparently was more than he could stomach. After all, he had given Breaux a job after Breaux, who finished third in that '71 election, endorsed Tardo over his runoff opponent—only to have Breaux run against him in the next election.

On December 15, 1988, Breaux and Deputy Daniel Leche were leaving a senior citizens' Christmas party at the Thibodaux Civic Center. A grocery bag was on the ground next to Breaux's vehicle and as he approached it, the sheriff kicked the bag with his foot. As he did so, an explosion rocked the still evening air as shrapnel and nails tore into Breaux's leg, nearly severing his foot.[19]

Marshall McClendon, a former police officer who had once worked for Tardo during his one term as sheriff as well as having served as an Ascension Parish sheriff's deputy, had detonated a bomb by remote control in an attempt on Breaux's life. Tardo had paid McClendon and John Tullier, Jr. $8,000 with the promise of another $12,000 if Breaux died. A third man, former Houma police officer Ralph Bergeron, was also charged.

An informant who admitted his involvement in the attempt on Breaux's life told federal agents that Tardo had supplied the money to have Breaux murdered, according to a federal affidavit that outlined allegations against the men. The informant said Tardo also gave McClendon an additional $2,000 for his participation in the bombing.

The affidavit released by U.S. Attorney John Volz said Bureau of Alcohol, Tobacco and Firearms (ATF) agents monitored a conversation between Tardo and the informant. It was during that meeting that Tardo affirmed his knowledge of the bombing, admitted to paying McClendon the extra $2,000, gave the confidential source $100 to help him get out of town, and admitted that he, Tardo, had entered into an agreement with McClendon that called for McClendon to maintain silence if arrested. [20]

Tardo, a retired state trooper, was sentenced to 29 years in prison but served less than three years of that sentence. He died of heart failure on April 30, 1992. He never left federal custody following his February 2, 1989 arrest. He was only 61 at the time of his death. Bergeron, Tullier and McClendon received sentences ranging from 11 years to 24 years' imprisonment.[21]

Breaux, meanwhile, would go on to serve as sheriff for 16 years, until 1992, when he, too, ran afoul of the law.

Breaux pleaded guilty in 1993 to mail fraud, conspiracy and obstruction of justice for deals in which he was involved while sheriff. At the center of the charges was a scheme to defraud Lafourche Parish of more than $100,000 through Shield Land, a company owned by Breaux and his Chief Deputy, Eddie Duet. The sheriff's office contracted with local banks which paid for the storage of mobile homes. Because Breaux and Duet owned the land where the trailers were stored, they profited directly from the transactions.

Breaux served more than four years in federal prison in Montgomery, Alabama, and was released in 1997. He died eight years later, on December 13, 2005, of complications from pneumonia. He was 77.[22]

In terms of bad luck with sheriffs, St. Helena Parish must hold franchise rights. Three consecutive sheriffs were carted off to jail between 1996 and 2008. Charges ranged from theft to mail fraud, conspiracy and money laundering to running a chop shop.

Sheriff Eugene Holland was found guilty in January 1997 and sentenced to 16 months in prison for misuse of government property and using prison inmates for personal labor and of misuse of government funds by paying personal bills totaling some $28,000 with public money.[23]

His arrest, conviction and imprisonment served as an ominous precursor for things to come. Less than a year later, in August, his successor, Chaney Phillips, who won a special election to succeed Holland, was indicted on 19 counts of conspiracy, mail fraud and money laundering. The charges were for actions federal authorities said occurred while he served as St. Helena Parish's tax assessor. Prior to the April election to succeed Holland, a state audit revealed the allegations of conspiracy, mail fraud and money laundering.

Phillips also was accused of spending nearly $2,000 from the assessor's office to buy suits and clothing for himself.[24] Phillips claimed he was innocent of all charges, but in April 1998, almost exactly a year after his election, he was found guilty on charges of conspiracy, mail fraud, theft and money laundering and was sentenced to eight years in prison.

Then it was Ronald "Gun" Ficklin's turn. Appointed sheriff after Phillips was forced from office, the former mayor of Greensburg would last eight years before he too, faced felony charges.[25]

Assuming office in April 1998, he became deeply involved in a more bizarre criminal operation than either Holland or Phillips: billing the Louisiana Department of Public Safety and Corrections (LDOC) for work-release prisoners in his charge who were in turn employed in an illegal chop shop run by a friend.

In February 2005 Ficklin was indicted on twenty-two counts of conspiracy, trafficking in motor vehicles with removed or altered vehicle identification numbers (VINs), removing or altering VINs, aiding and abetting the possession of a firearm by a convicted felon, misprision of a felony (the deliberate concealment by failing to report knowledge of a felony) for not reporting a felon with a firearm, and mail fraud.

The indictment charged that Ficklin employed state prisoners in a local car theft enterprise. His friend, convicted felon Barry Edward Dawsey, operated an illegal chop shop from B & D Auto Sales in St. Helena Parish.

The operation involved buying and selling salvaged and stolen vehicles. When Dawsey was arrested in a stolen pickup truck, officers found a gun and Ficklin's badge in the vehicle.[25]

Dawsey pleaded guilty in 2006 and received a three-year prison sentence. James Jackson, Mitchell Tidwell, and Kevin Simmons also pleaded guilty to their involvement in the car theft ring. Ficklin originally was arrested on a ten-count federal indictment. Twelve more counts were added as the investigation progressed.

He was accused of fraud for billing LDOC $140,000 by employing LDOC prisoners in Dawsey's chop shop from October 2000 to September 2001. LDOC paid the St. Helena Parish Sheriff's Office nearly $250,000 during that same time period. More than half of Ficklin's federal charges were for mail fraud.[26]

In February, he pleaded guilty to 17 of the federal charges. He was sentenced to 63 months in prison on each count, to be served concurrently, on October 30, 2007. He reported to prison to begin his sentence in November 2007.[27]

Ficklin, who served as mayor of Greensburg for 14 years before being appointed sheriff, died of cancer in federal prison in North Carolina in October 2011, less than a year before he was scheduled to be released in June 2012. He was 57.[28]

Early on, East Carroll Parish Sheriff Dale Rinicker saw that the private prison industry was on the cusp of an explosion in growth and he also saw dollar signs. Before it was all over, he would be $500,000 richer but would find himself a resident of a federal prison.[29]

In April 1990, Rinicker approached Lake Providence attorney and businessman Captain Jack Wyly. He wanted Wyly to finance the construction of a private prison in the parish to house state prisoners. The 72-year-old Wyly agreed and on April 11, East Carroll Correctional Systems, Inc. (ECCS), a subchapter S corporation, was chartered. One hundred shares of stock were issued to Wyly associates and family members. Thirty-five of the 100 shares were issued to 62-year-old Dorothy Morgel, who had worked as Wyly's legal secretary for 35 years. Wyly was listed in Louisiana Secretary of State corporate records as president and Morgel as secretary-treasurer. Only five of those 35 shares were hers, however. The other 30 were earmarked for Sheriff Rinicker in a maneuver that would lead directly to his downfall.[30]

An abandoned school building was purchased and renovations to convert it into the East Carroll Detention Center (ECDC) began. Simultaneously, a favorable lease agreement was executed whereby the East Carroll Sheriff's Office would pay ECDC rent of 25 percent of the funds paid by the Louisiana Department of Public Safety and Corrections to house state prisoners.

By August, the first state prisoners began trickling into the ECDC and the money was quick to follow. Construction loans were paid until May 1993 and only minimal shareholder distributions were paid out to cover tax obligations. After May, the money flow became a gusher.

Because Rinicker was personally profiting from an enterprise that did business with the sheriff's office, both an ethics violation and a conflict of interests, even in Louisiana, a convoluted—and necessary—scheme was hatched to conceal his interests. ECCS made payments, based on her 35 percent interest, to Morgel from May 1993 through August 1995.

Rather than launder the money through her own checking account at a bank in Lake Providence where she resided, she opened a second account in another bank in nearby Oak Grove. Her ECCS checks were deposited in the Oak Grove account and she wrote more than $286,000 in checks, most for less than the $10,000 amount that triggered the federally required transaction reporting.

Each of the checks was made payable to Rinicker friend Glen Jordan, who then cashed the checks at a Monroe bank. Rinicker's sister worked at the bank and helped facilitate the transactions. Rinicker then received the proceeds. Jordan was paid a small amount from each check for serving as the conduit. But then the participants got reckless, committing a blunder that sent up red flags to federal authorities. ECCS issued six checks totaling more than $54,000, payable directly to Rinicker.[31]

Jordan, Wyly and Morgel lied to state auditors and the FBI when asked to explain the payments but Jordan soon capitulated. He provided a detailed explanation of his part in laundering the money to Rinicker through ECCS, Morgel and Jordan—with an assist from Rinicker's sister, Myra Jackson. A federal grand jury indicted Wyly, Morgel, ECCS, Rinicker and Jackson on charges of mail fraud, conspiracy to launder money, and money laundering.

The indictment sought forfeiture of a certificate of deposit purchased by ECCS; the remaining balance in the ECCS bank account; all funds in Morgel's Oak Grove account; all ECCS assets and property, all rental payments from the sheriff's office, estimated at nearly $3 million, and approximately $340,000 in payments made to Rinicker.

Rinicker entered a pre-trial guilty plea in a deal in which he agreed to testify for the government at trial. In exchange for his cooperation, charges against his sister were dropped.[32]

Morgel claimed several times that she had not received any financial benefit from the scheme. Morgel and Wyly relied on their defense that they did not specifically intend to violate the law; that, instead, Rinicker extorted them and they, being much older, were afraid of him.

They claimed at trial that Rinicker had a violent temper and was the scheme's mastermind. They said he "extorted" them through fear and intimidation into abetting his scheme. But the prosecution said that rather than fearing Rinicker, they had cheated him out of $195,000. "There is no honor among thieves, obviously, because the thieves were stealing from the thief," they said.

Wyly received a sentence of 48 months imprisonment and ordered to pay a fine of $17,500. Morgel was sentenced to prison for one year and one day and fined $12,500. ECCS was fined $4.8 million. Moreover, Wyly, Morgel, and ECCS were ordered to forfeit their interests in the property described in the forfeiture verdict.[33]

Despite Rinicker's cooperation with prosecutors, the district court refused the government's request for lenience for Rinicker and sentenced him to five years imprisonment and ordered him to pay a $10,000 fine.

In 1992, Irvin "Jif" Hingle defeated two-term incumbent Sheriff Ernest Wooton for sheriff of Plaquemines Parish. Wooton would go on to serve in the Louisiana House of Representatives. Hingle would remain in office until his forced resignation in October 2011.

He got greedy while in office. The greed was fed by the easy money to be made with post-Hurricane Katrina cleanup contracts. Hingle would eventually plead guilty to bribery and conspiracy to commit wire fraud. He would receive only 46 months in prison because he cooperated with authorities by wearing a wire in August 2011 to trap Aaron Bennett of Benetech Software of Kenner, the person who bribed him.

On October 5, 2011, U.S. Attorney Jim Letten announced that Hingle had been indicted by a bill of information on charges of accepting bribes and conspiracy to commit mail fraud. A bill of information in lieu of a grand jury indictment is generally considered a strong indication that a suspect was cooperating with investigators.

Hingle accepted two payments of $10,000 each from Bennett in March and April 2008 shortly after he approved an invoice for $333,000 from Benetech for federally funded disaster recovery work. He was also charged with falsely reporting campaign expenditures of more than $100,000, which prosecutors say was used for personal purposes and not for campaign expenses.

At the same time, Bennett was charged with bribery and conspiracy.[34]

The bill of information charged that the Plaquemines Parish Sheriff's Office entered into a contract with Benetech to provide services relating to recovery from damages due to Katrina and future natural disasters. In early- to mid-2008, on two separate occasions, Hingle approved Benetech's invoices and issued checks to Benetech in connection with work purportedly done under the 2007 contract.

Besides the U.S. Attorney's office and the FBI, the case was also investigated by the Internal Revenue Service Criminal Investigation Division.

Within weeks of approval of the invoices, said the FBI, Bennett, owner of Benetech, twice made separate $10,000 cash payments to Hingle, paid with the intent of influencing him in connection with the contract. Moreover, charged the indictment, Hingle falsely listed more than $100,000 in expenditures as campaign-related when, in fact, they were for personal use.

"We place greater trust in our law enforcement officials, trust that they will maintain and display ethical and lawful conduct," said David Welker, Special Agent in Charge of the Federal Bureau of Investigation's New Orleans Field Office. "Conduct as detailed in the Bill of Information reduces the opportunity for fair business and severely reduces the public's trust in our elected officials."

Letten said the charges "reflect our sacred commitment in federal enforcement to maintain a zero tolerance for any public corruption." Those charges would be bad enough, but emails obtained by an investigative reporter for a New Orleans television station revealed that the shakedowns and influence-peddling were even more widespread.

New Orleans TV reporter Lee Zurik revealed the email chain that was first initiated in June 2009, prompting Rafael Goyeneche of the New Orleans Metropolitan Crime Commission to comment, "It's more of a horror movie, from Louisiana's point of view." [35]

Robert Isakson, managing director of the DRC Group, a disaster recovery company out of Mobile, Alabama, first wrote about an upcoming trip to Fort Lauderdale to attend the convention of the National Sheriffs' Association.

The DRC group had already made "tens of millions of Louisiana tax dollars" since Hurricane Katrina through lucrative disaster recovery contracts, Zurik said.

"Sheriff Jiff Hingle and we are hosting a formal dinner for about 30 or so sheriffs on Monday night at the nicest steak house in Fort Lauderdale," he wrote. Hingle, for his part, sent out invitations to the event sponsored by DRC. At least 34 invitees returned their RSVPs to the event, paid for by DRC.

Two weeks later, DRC and Isakson hosted a second dinner at the Louisiana Sheriffs' Association Convention in Destin. "If that was intended to influence the sheriff to continue to give him business, or to facilitate future contracts to that vendor, I think you may be approaching the criminal line with that," Zurik quoted Goyeneche as saying.

Meanwhile, Isakson sent separate emails on August 1 to Hingle and his driver, Maj. Brandon Mouriz. The subject of that email was Jails on Demand, a portable holding cell. It said Isakson's attorneys had determined if Hingle desired to lease portable jails from DRC, there would be "no obligation to follow the public bid law."

Two days after the BP Deepwater Horizon well blew up, Isakson received an email from Kristy Fuentes, DRC Group's Louisiana regional manager, who wrote that Mouriz "called today to see if we would sponsor a dinner in Destin during the Louisiana Sheriffs' Association Convention. Jiff is being inducted as president." An hour later, Isakson replied, "Absolutely, let's do this supper and anything else we can do to assist him in this honor."

The relationship between Hingle and Isakson was especially egregious because for a full decade Isakson, before forming the DRC Group, headed up the public corruption unit in the FBI's New Orleans office.

In 2009, DRC paid for Hingle and Mouriz to attend the LSU-Alabama football game in Tuscaloosa. Then, following the BP Deepwater Horizon catastrophic oil spill, Isakson and DRC gave Hingle and Mouriz a $100,000 loan to help start an equipment rental company and then DRC hired the company, paying nearly $500,000 with BP money. Additionally, DRC also paid a like amount to another Mouriz-affiliated company, Delta Security and paid Hingle's marina another $250,000. If that was not sufficient, DRC and Isakson separately hired Darren Angelo, Hingle's business partner at the marina, and paid $304,000 to him personally. Angelo's company, Fleet Intermodal, received $300,000.

And in return for all that largesse, DRC was paid $34 million by the Plaquemines Parish government between 2007 and mid-2012.

In January 2011, Hingle awarded DRC a $1.2 million contract to build a temporary 22-bed jail and a few months later gave DRC another contract for $1.9 million to construct a temporary facility for the sheriff's office.

Mouriz made $125,000 in 2010—almost $50,000 of that in overtime. Goyeneche said he wondered how Mouriz could earn that much money in overtime when, in the same year, Mouriz companies earned $912,000 from DRC for BP-related work. When Michael Lafrance was named acting sheriff after Hingle resigned in October 2011, one of his first acts was to fire Mouriz.

One month after his resignation from office, on November 30, Hingle entered a guilty plea to one count of conspiracy before U.S. District Judge Sarah R. Vance.[36]

Judge Vance, saying, "Corruption from the top leads to corruption all around," sentenced Hingle to a jail term of 46 months for conspiracy to commit mail fraud and bribery from Bennett whose company constructed the parish jail. She also fined him $10,000.

Hingle had been out of jail on a $50,000 bond since October 5, 2011, when he was charged with the felonies and simultaneously resigned from office.

Bennett had pleaded guilty to bribing Hingle that same October. Following Hingle's guilty plea the following month, U.S. Attorney Letten credited Hingle with stepping forward to help federal agents catch Bennett. The Justice Department, citing Hingle's cooperation with investigators, had recommended a sentence of two years and seven months but Judge Vance said, "I will not reduce the sentence to the extent requested by the government."

Hingle also admitted that he diverted more than one $149,000 from his political campaign for personal or sheriff's office expenses. Of that, Hingle claimed more than $100,000 in campaign expenses for personal or sheriff's office services was paid to a production company for promotional videos and other media. Those falsified reports were mailed by Hingle, prompting the mail fraud charge.

Hingle was still entitled to receive $104,000 per year in retirement benefits for the rest of his life, according to the state Sheriffs' Pension and Relief Fund. Louisiana voters passed a law in 2012 that gives state judges the latitude to deny retirement benefits to public officials who are convicted of felonies. Hingle's guilty plea, however, pre-dated passage of the bill. Moreover, the bill, a state law, applies only to state courts and Hingle pleaded guilty in federal court.[37]

Hingle died on January 9, 2018, of complications from pneumonia while being treated at M.D. Anderson Cancer Center in Houston.

It began in February 2011 with the first official word that Winn Parish Sheriff Albert D. "Bodie" Little was under investigation by the Louisiana Attorney General's office. What was not said at the time was that he was assisting his much younger girlfriend in her distribution of methamphetamines. The announcement came on the heels of the execution of warrants and the collection of evidence at Little's home and office by state police.

A year later, he stood convicted by a federal jury of drug trafficking charges.

He was sentenced to more than 14 years in federal prison after a jury found him guilty on one count of conspiracy to possess 50 or more grams of methamphetamine and two counts of facilitating drug trafficking through the use of a communication device.[58]

Little, 61 and married, was accused of helping his girlfriend cover up her drug deals as a means of preventing her arrest. A state trooper who testified in Little's trial, said, "It's clear he wanted everyone arrested except his girlfriend."

Federal charges resulted from an investigation by the Drug Enforcement Agency Task Force. The U.S. Drug Enforcement Agency, Louisiana State Police, the Caddo Parish Sheriff's Office, Shreveport police and Bossier City police participated in the investigation. Ten people were indicted along with Little, who was in his first term as sheriff.

U.S. Attorney Stephanie A. Finley said, "When law enforcement officers disregard the law it hurts all citizens. Former Sheriff Little knowingly chose to break the law and now he is paying the price for his betrayal of the trust the citizens of Winn Parish placed in him. We hope that this case, and the sentences imposed, sends a message that drug trafficking and corruption of those charged with protecting society from such crimes will not be tolerated and will be prosecuted to the fullest extent of the law."[59]

Harry Lee could be described as a lot of things: lawman, jailer, tax collector, process server, issuer of various licenses, attorney, power broker, and a confidant, pal to and sometimes business partner with some of the South Louisiana's shadiest characters, including the late New Orleans crime boss Carlos Marcello.

Article 39 of the Jefferson Parish Sheriff's Office operations manual says employees should avoid associating with criminals and those under investigation or indictment.

Lee, however, said the rule applied to deputies but did not apply to him.[40]

Accordingly, he felt no professional or moral restrictions that would have prevented him from continuing his personal and business relationship with Robert Guidry who had admitted to bribing former Gov. Edwin Edwards and others in order to obtain a license for a New Orleans casino. Nor would it, under Lee's unique moral code, have prevented him from associating with Frank Caracci, a convicted felon whom federal authorities linked to organized crime in New Orleans. In fact, Lee testified on Caracci's behalf during State Police hearings in 1994 on whether to pull Guidry's video poker license over Guidry's business association with Caracci.

Nor did Lee hesitate to spend the night as the guest of Marcello at the don's Grand Isle and Boutte camps—on several different occasions, according to a former State Police intelligence officer. The first word of Lee's stay at the Grand Isle camp leaked out during his initial campaign for sheriff.

At the time he first ran for sheriff Lee was a partner in the Jefferson Parish law firm of Lee, Martiny and Caracci. The other two partners were Daniel Martiny and Mark Caracci. Mark Caracci is Frank Caracci's son and Martiny would go on to election to the Louisiana State Senate.

No sooner did Lee take office as sheriff in 1980 than he retained his old law firm to defend his department. It wasn't until three years later, in 1984, when nearing the end of his first term, that he finally severed professional ties with the firm, though he was sold a one-third interest in the firm's office building for $65,000, a fee he was never required to pay. Nor was he required to pay his share of the firm's mortgage.

The Louisiana Board of Ethics, held a dog and pony show investigation of the arrangement that it concluded was in violation of Louisiana's code of ethics which prohibited Lee from having a contractual relationship with the law firm at the same time of the purchase agreement; another provision of the code prohibits public servants from receiving anything of economic value from any person who has or is seeking to obtain a contractual, business, or financial relationship with the public servant's agency.

The upshot of all the hoopla of the ethics hearings was the imposition of token fines of $1,000 each on Lee and the firm for the contractual agreement and additional $1,000 fines against Lee and the firm for the prohibited payments by the firm to Lee in the form of Lee's portion of the mortgage payments.

But the ethics board added somewhat incredulously, "No governmental purpose would be served by the execution of these fines and accordingly, they are suspended…because of the board's belief that the sheriff was acting in good faith."[41]

And while Lee was no longer officially associated with the firm, it did secure a profitable contract with the Louisiana Sheriffs' Association Risk Management Program. Lee, coincidentally, was a member of the board that ran the program.

Lee was never shy about his friendships with characters of questionable repute. He openly admitted during testimony in the hearing into Guidry's video poker license that he recommended to Guidry that he partner with Frank Caracci, convicted in 1970 for bribing an Internal Revenue agent, adding that while he did not know of Caracci's criminal background, it wouldn't have mattered to him even if he had known. "I'm not sure I knew Mr. Caracci had a conviction," he testified. "I would have no problem with that. I have a lot of friends convicted of felonies. A lot of people are uptight about that. I'm not."[42]

Other jewels to emanate from the mouth of Harry Lee:

- "The sheriff (of Jefferson Parish) is the closest thing there is to being a king in the U.S. I have no unions, I don't have civil service, I hire and fire at will, I don't have to go to (the parish) council and propose a budget. I approve the budget. I'm the head of the law-enforcement district and the law-enforcement district only has one vote, which is me."
- "My job is to catch crooks. My hobby is to expose hypocrites."
- "I'm old enough and ornery enough that I don't have to appease anybody."[43]

The year 2016 was not especially good to Lee's successor, Newell Normand.

Jefferson Parish is a mostly white suburb of majority black New Orleans, situated immediately west of the Crescent City. Normand, as chief deputy to the hugely popular Lee, literally inherited the office upon Lee's death from leukemia on October 1, 2007, less than three weeks before he was to stand for election to his eighth consecutive term. Because state law requires qualifying for election to reopen if a candidate dies before an election, Normand was able to qualify to run against three challengers. He easily overwhelmed his opponents with 91 percent of the vote.

Barely two years into his administration as Lee's successor, Normand faced his first public relations hiccup, brought on by actor Steven Seagal, a pal of the late Harry Lee. He had an A&E Network television reality show called, appropriately enough, *Steven Seagal, Lawman*, which entitled him to carry a special sheriff's deputy badge and to ride with Jefferson Parish deputies as they patrolled the parish, busting prostitutes and drug dealers.

Lee often buddied up to celebrities, singing with Willie Nelson, dining with Bill Clinton, and making Seagal a reserve deputy after their friendship was cemented by a mutual fondness for firearms. He recruited Seagal to train his deputies in shooting and martial arts, brought him along to charitable events, and to go on patrol with his deputies, which eventually led to the A&E series.

But then Kayden Nguyen entered the picture, filing a lawsuit against Seagal in which she accused him of holding her against her will and using her as a sex slave during the second season of filming his show. Before the merits of Nguyen's lawsuit could be determined, Normand, by now sheriff, pulled the plug on the show and invited Nguyen to file a criminal complaint, saying, "I will treat Mr. Seagal no differently than any other employee of the Jefferson Parish Sheriff's Office."[44]

Eleven months later, Seagal popped up again, this time as a special reserve deputy for the infamous Maricopa County (Arizona) Sheriff Joe Arpaio. Normand apparently had no problem with that until Seagal said in an interview that he was "on loan" to Arpaio "out from Louisiana."

Seagal made the claim in an interview immediately following a massive raid by the Maricopa County Sheriff's Office on a home in Laveen, Arizona, which netted exactly one subject suspected of promoting cockfighting.

Normand said Seagal "was facing an internal affairs investigation immediately following the outcome of his lawsuit. And he refused to return to Jefferson Parish, at which time he tendered his resignation." Nguyen's complaint was later dropped but pursuant to his resignation, Seagal was no longer affiliated with the Jefferson Parish Sheriff's Office, Normand said.[45]

No sooner had Normand laid to rest news reports that the FBI and the IRS were investigating him and a company in which he was part owner than another story cropped up. That story involved his wife's selection as legal counsel for the Louisiana Stadium and Exposition District, more commonly known as the Superdome Commission, whose members are appointed by the governor.

Near the end of 2016, Normand appeared to face his biggest crisis over a road rage incident that began on the bridge connecting New Orleans to Jefferson Parish's west bank area and ended in the shooting death of a former NFL player.

Joe McKnight, 28, played on three state championship football teams at John Curtis High School in River Ridge, suburb of New Orleans before starring at Southern California. He played for the Kansas City Chiefs and the New York Jets before an injury derailed his professional career. He was working for a New Orleans mental health clinic when he became involved in an altercation with Ronald Gasser on the Crescent City Connection, the Mississippi River bridge connecting New Orleans to the west bank of Jefferson and Orleans parishes west bank. Both drivers exited the elevated extension in Gretna and when McKnight approached Gasser's vehicle, Gasser fired three shots from inside his car, striking McKnight once in the hand and twice in the upper body.

The real controversy erupted when Normand's office declined to book Gasser for the shooting. The decision not to arrest Gasser proved to be a major PR snafu for Normand as protests erupted almost immediately and Normand's response to the protests during a press conference didn't help assuage feelings among the African American community.

The sheriff attempted to explain his office's lack of action with several puzzling pronouncements. "If you rush to judgment from the beginning and make a strategic error," Normand said, "it makes it very difficult to recover later." He then acknowledged that Louisiana's "stand your ground" self-defense law might come into play. He also said, somewhat incredulously, that there was no evidence that the shooting was racially motivated—McKnight was black and Gasser white. His threat to arrest protesters only made a bad situation worse. [46]

Normand's controversial tenure came to an end in mid-2017 when he abruptly announced that he was stepping down after 37 years with the Jefferson Parish Sheriff's Office, the last ten as sheriff, to move into his new career as a talk show host for a New Orleans radio station. Making his announcement on July 25, he set his retirement date as August 31. Normand insisted the timing of his announcement was "a coincidence at best," and had nothing to do with the federal indictment of his veteran chief deputy Craig Taffaro.

Taffaro, father-in-law of Louisiana Lt. Gov. Billy Nungesser, was indicted by a federal grand jury just five days earlier, on July 20, for tax evasion and for filing a false tax return in connection with CTNN, an offshore supply company that he co-owned with Normand. His indictment in turn, came a little more than a month after his retirement following nearly 50 years with the Jefferson Parish Sheriff's Office.

CTNN (Craig Taffaro, Newell Normand) apparently did little but collect commissions on sales between two other companies. Equipment and goods were actually purchased by Harvey Gulf, a billion-dollar marine transportation enterprise owned by Republican donor Shane Guidry. They were purchased from a company called Pelican Marine which was owned by Taffaro's son-in-law Nungesser, who upon his election as lieutenant governor, placed Pelican's assets in a blind trust assigned to Taffaro. Guidry, for his part, also served as special assistant to Attorney General Jeff Landry, who once served as Guidry's personal attorney. Guidry was hired to oversee the attorney general's criminal investigations unit at a salary of $12,000 per year.[47] Landry in turn served as a salaried member of the Harvey Gulf board.

What began as a federal investigation into a work-release program took a bizarre turn on June 11, 2019, with the arrest of former St. Tammany Parish Sheriff Jack Strain on state charges of rape, incest and indecent behavior with a juvenile.

A St. Tammany Parish grand jury indicted Strain on two counts each of aggravated rape and aggravated incest and single counts of sexual battery and indecent behavior with a juvenile. He was convicted by a jury of six men and six women on all six counts on November 8, 2021.

Two of his alleged victims were under the age of 12 and the alleged incidents dated back as far as 1975, to when Strain himself was as young as 16, according to 22nd Judicial District Attorney Warren Montgomery. One of his victims claimed he was only six when Strain anally raped him.

At least five persons testified at trial that they were molested by Strain, one of whom said he was raped as late as June 2004. Strain was related to two of the victims, documents indicated. Strain, 56, was first elected sheriff in 1995, serving until his defeat in 2015 by challenger Randy Smith.[48]

The federal investigation that precipitated his arrest by state authorities stemmed from Strain's privatization of the parish jail, which he turned over to two of his friends. Those two, Skip Keen and David Hanson, subsequently pleaded guilty in February 2019 to conspiracy to solicit bribes and to commit wire fraud. Ironically, Keen was one of those who testified that Strain had raped him as a youth.

In 2013, the Slidell Work Release Center was losing money with expenses up by a third. Strain decided he needed to sell the 18-year-old facility to a private operator.

To make sure he would be able to unload it, he poured nearly half-a-million dollars into renovations of the center just a year before it was transferred to private operators. Sheriff's Department Maj. Clifford "Skip" Keen, who served as facilities manager for the sheriff's office, oversaw the renovation that included construction of a newer, larger kitchen. Partial renovations were performed by contractor Allen Tingle, who was paid $4,240 for his work.

Then, eschewing public bids on the proposed takeover, Strain signed a three-year contract with newly formed St. Tammany Workforce Solutions. One of the principals of the company was 21-year-old Jarret Keen, son of Maj. Skip Keen. Manager of St. Tammany Workforce Solutions, according to Louisiana Secretary of State corporate records, was Tingle. Brandy Hanson was also listed as a director for the company. She was a former sheriff's office employee and was described by the *New Orleans Advocate* as "the daughter of another member of Strain's inner circle."

Strain told *The New Orleans Advocate* that he met with four potential operators but declined to identify them. None of them submitted a formal proposal to take over the facility. In fact, records would seem to suggest that Strain may have planned for St. Tammany Workforce Solutions all along. Secretary of State corporate records show that the company, which had no other business, filed its incorporation papers on March 23, 2013, less than two weeks before Strain indicated to a local newspaper that he was considering privatization of the center. The address given on the original incorporation papers was 141 Production Drive. That's the same address as the work release center.[49]

Twenty-two-year-old Victor White III was stopped by Iberia Parish deputies on March 3, 2014. The deputies said marijuana and cocaine were found on White and he was placed in a sheriff's department patrol car, his hands cuffed behind his back. While cuffed, deputies said, he somehow managed to get a gun and "committed suicide" by shooting himself in the back.

A coroner's report released five months later, however, said White shot himself in the chest, a feat that would seem to defy the laws of physics.

That White's hands were never tested for gunpowder residue only served to cast further doubt on the official version of events. Still, the parish coroner, Dr. Carl Ditch, insisted White's death was a suicide.

W. Lloyd Grafton, an expert retained by the White family, weighed in on the evidence in an interview for this book. He said the entry wound was more to the right side than frontal area and that the bullet exited from White's left side. "There is no way he could have shot himself the way they (officials) described it, with his hands cuffed behind his back," Grafton said.

On May 19, 2015, U.S. Rep. Cedric Richmond of Louisiana's Second Congressional District, wrote a gut-wrenching three-page letter to then-U.S. Attorney General Loretta Lynch in which he requested an investigation into the deaths of eight people who were in the custody of the Iberia Parish Sheriff's Office.

Richmond also asked that the U.S. Justice Department look into other incidents of beatings and the violations of prisoners' civil rights, including at least ten cases of civil lawsuits which resulted in settlements totaling more than a million dollars.[50]

In March 2016, ten months after Richmond's letter, Sheriff Louis Ackal and one of his top deputies, Lieutenant Colonel Gerald Savoy, were indicted by a federal grand jury on charges of conspiracy and civil rights violations over the alleged multiple beatings of detainees in the jail's chapel where there were no security cameras.

The indictment said it was the "plan and purpose of the conspiracy that IPSO officers and supervisors would punish and retaliate against inmates and pretrial detainees by taking them to the chapel of the (Iberia Parish Jail), where there were no video surveillance cameras, to unlawfully assault them."

One inmate would be beaten for an alleged offense and if he blamed another inmate, the second inmate would also be beaten with no apparent effort being made to ascertain who was telling the truth. In at least one case, a second inmate beaten over another's accusation (after the first had been similarly beaten) blamed a third who was then brought in and beaten like the others, the indictment said.

In another case, when it was learned that an inmate was in jail as an accused sex offender, a deputy held his baton between his legs as if it were his penis and forced it down the inmate's throat, causing him to gag.

Ackal, incredibly, was acquitted at trial. Meanwhile, more than one hundred criminal cases involving those deputies have been tossed as a result of the investigation of the sheriff's office, which stretched back to 2008 during Ackal's first term of office.[51]

Former Deputy Jason Comeaux said after deputies got drunk at a party, they wanted to find someone to beat up so they targeted two young black men, ages 16 and 21. Ackal was later furious—not over the beatings, Comeaux testified, but over the fact the deputies were caught and a written report made.

Prior to his trial, the sheriff was secretly recorded as he made threats against federal prosecutor Mark Blumberg, including threats to kill him, court filings revealed. Court transcripts show Ackal threatening to shoot the prosecutor, who was a special litigation counsel in the Justice Department's Civil Rights Division in Washington, D.C.

Recounting a conversation in which Ackal said he was told by an unidentified person, presumably from the Justice Department, that he could help the government: "You know these people, you can give them to us," he quoted the person as saying. "I said, 'the only thing I'm gonna give you, [is] fucking shoot you right between your goddamn Jewish eyes, look-like-an-opossum bastard,'" Ackal also called Blumberg a "sorry, son-of-a-bitch Jew bastard in Washington."

Victor White, Jr., father of Victor White, III., said he felt anger as he watched Ackal spit tobacco juice into a cup in the courtroom during testimony in his trial. White said trial testimony "validated everything that he was hiding and the things that we knew." He said he and his wife drove from their home in Alexandria, 100 miles from the trial in Shreveport so he could "look at him (Ackal) face-to-face and let them say they didn't do those types of things."

But upon hearing the verdict he could only feel sick.

For his part, Ackal claimed he was "totally exonerated," accusing those who testified against him as lying "about the whole thing." He said the investigation of his office ferreted out bad lawmen from his agency who, he said, hurt "innocent people." He added that he was going back to New Iberia "and make sure my house is very clean." He said deputies' testimony shook him "to the core. I guess it's because I'm very nice."

Seven of Ackal's former deputies received sentences in U.S. District Court in Lafayette on March 28, 2017. Each of the seven had testified in Ackal's trial four months earlier. The sentences ranged from 87 months in federal prison for Chief Deputy Gerald "Bubba" Savoy[11] and 54 months for Byron Benjamin LaSalle and Bret Broussard to six months for one-time canine handler Robert Burns who pleaded to a single count of deprivation or rights for his failure to intervene when fellow deputies beat inmate Anthony Daye in August 2011 in the parish jail chapel.

Federal Judge Donald E. Walter, who said he never liked sentencing those who appeared before him in court, told the deputies that they were "the worst. So many law enforcement officials are out there risking their lives for little pay. All I can say is you had lousy leadership," he said. "How sad this is for all concerned." [52]

Donald Broussard of New Iberia learned the dangers of crossing a vengeful sheriff like Ackal. On July 8, 2016, Broussard was rear-ended by a hit-and-run driver In Lafayette Parish who minutes later collided head-on with an 18-wheeler in adjacent Iberia Parish and was killed. Yet it was Broussard who was indicted on a charge of manslaughter by an Iberia Parish grand jury on March 19, 2017, just nine days before the seven deputies were sentenced.

So just how did Broussard find himself in Ackal's crosshairs? On July 1, a week before the auto accident, Broussard committed the unpardonable sin when he became the impetus behind a recall of Ackal. Broussard, an African-American, was one of the organizers of The Justice for Victor White III Foundation which filed a petition on July 1 to force a recall election.

A story in the March 19, 2017, *Daily Iberian* read, "A New Iberia man who was instrumental in the drive to recall Iberia Parish Sheriff Louis Ackal last year has been indicted for manslaughter in the aftermath of an alleged road rage incident that left a Bossier City man dead in July."

Moments before the fatal crash, Rakeem Blakes, 24, rear- ended a Cadillac driven by Broussard at the corner of Ambassador Caffery Parkway and U.S. 90 in Lafayette Parish. Broussard said he followed Blakes into Iberia Parish when Blakes fled the scene after Broussard had approached his car but denied that he chased Blakes. "The guy hit me," Broussard said. "I got within 20 feet of him so I could get his license plate number. I gave it (the license number) to the (911) dispatcher and they told me to fall back, so I fell back." Broussard said reports that he had a gun were ridiculous. "I don't even own a gun," he said. "I told the State Police they could search my car. They just handed me my license and let me go on my way."

Broussard said Blakes was driving erratically, causing a hazard for other drivers.

Iberia Parish District Attorney Bo Duhé said the case involving Broussard was turned over to his office for review in November following completion of the LSP investigation. In what has to be one of the most convoluted reviews of the investigation, Assistant District Attorney Janet Perrodin presented the case and the grand jury returned a true bill indicting Broussard for manslaughter and "aggravated obstruction of a highway," which led to Blakes' death.

It was a scenario tailored just for Broussard who had the temerity to take on a powerful sheriff whose proclivity to extract revenge against those who would dare stand up to his authority was already well-established. Broussard, for his part, vowed to fight the "malicious and unwarranted" prosecution. "I welcome their witch-hunt. The truth will come out at trial. They like to keep niggers in their place in Iberia Parish because most of the time, that's what they're used to dealing with. But they're dealing with an educated black man who has never been, nor will I ever be, scared to speak truth to power—especially in instances when those in power abuse that power. They picked the wrong one to go to war with." [52]

In March 2018, Ackal quietly settled a federal lawsuit brought by the family of Victor White III—almost exactly four years after his March 3, 2014, shooting death while in the custody of deputies. As has become more and more common in such cases, terms of the settlement were sealed and White's family was prohibited by a confidentiality clause from disclosing the settlement amount, believed to be about $600,000.

In an interview with the author, White's father, Victor White, Jr., said he was unhappy with the judge's order that terms of the settlement not be disclosed. "The judge says we can't talk about the settlement amount, but I believe the people of Iberia Parish have a right to know how much the sheriff department's actions cost them," he said.[53]

The Victor White case was not the only case in which Iberia Parish Sheriff Louis Ackal had to make substantial payouts.

Christopher Butler sued after he was beaten while handcuffed by a deputy Cody Laperouse in 2013. Ackal fired Laperouse who promptly went to work as an officer for the St. Martinville Police Department. Ackal's office paid out $350,000 in that case.

Ackal also paid out $175,000 to the family of 16-year-old Daquentin Thompson who hanged himself while being held in Iberia Parish's adult jail in 2014.

In a case that displayed the ugly side of Ackal's idea of justice, the sheriff instructed two of his deputies to "take care of" Howard Trosclair after Ackal had been told Trosclair assaulted one of his (Ackal's) relatives, according to appeal documents filed by deputy David Hines with the U.S. Fifth Circuit Court of Appeals. When Trosclair was arrested, the court records say he was "compliant and followed the officers' commands." Hines nevertheless used his knee to strike Trosclair "several times in the side" and struck him "two to three times" with his baton in the back of his legs. Hines continued to knee Trosclair in the abdomen or groin even after he was restrained. Hines then filed a false police report to cover up the wrongful assault, the appeal record says.

That episode cost the sheriff's office $275,000.

Additionally, Ackal's office is the only sheriff's office in Louisiana to make use of a special Louisiana Sheriffs' Law Enforcement Program (LSLEP) set up to pay sexual harassment and discrimination claims—and he had to use the program twice.

The Iberia Parish Sheriff's Department paid more than $400,000 to the plaintiff in a 2015 lawsuit filed by a female deputy who claimed that Ackal did nothing to stop retaliation from Bert Berry, chief of the criminal department, who "egregiously" harassed her for ten months.

The other complaint was filed by three female employees in 2009. They claimed that chief deputy Toby Hebert sexually harassed them. Their claims were eventually settled for $7,500 each.

In 2004, the New Iberia Police Department was dissolved and law enforcement within the city limits was taken over by the sheriff's department (the department was reinstated on July 1, 2018 after 14 years of inactivity). Ackal became sheriff in 2008 and since that time, not a single homicide has been solved and in 2015, none occurred, according to FBI crime data.

And that is precisely the problem: Reporting is voluntary and homicides are simply not reported by the Iberia Parish Sheriff's Department. The sloppy reporting practices only contribute to continued killings, according to Thomas Hargrove who runs the non-profit Murder Accountability Project. He called the sheriff's office's reporting record "God-awful…the worst reporting I've ever heard. First of all, you haven't a clue whether murders are being solved. This is literally a matter of life and death.

In December 2004, Nelson Landry, Jr., left home in a new car and never returned. A missing person report was filed but when his car was found two days later, the sheriff's office had no record of the missing person report. Landry's body was not found until February 2005 and his murder remains unsolved after nearly 14 years.

On December 4, 2015, Terry Delahoussaye, Sr., was shot in his vehicle in an apparent robbery-murder. Gold jewelry he was wearing and a "significant amount" of money he had in his wallet were missing. After nearly three years, the investigation into his death appears to have hit a dead end. "Ackal did not do his job," said Delahoussaye's brother, Ricky. "They were too busy looking for drugs on him while he was lying there fighting for his life.

"If you call and say, 'There's a drug deal going on,' they'll come right away. But if you call and say, 'Someone's dying at the end of the street,' they'll be here in forty minutes, an hour," he said. "It feels like they're just saying, 'Let the niggers kill the niggers. It's a black-on-black crime, so who cares?' When a white guy gets shot, they treat it differently. Yeah, I'm pissed off and I'm going to stay pissed. I used to think my brother was in the wrong place at the wrong time. Now, my opinion is different."

Both Landry and Delahoussaye were African-American.

"African-American murders are much less likely to be cleared than any other kind of murder," Hargrove said while acknowledging that because they are more likely to be drug- and gang-related, they are statistically more difficult to solve. "But that doesn't begin to explain the depth of the racial divide. We are not providing sufficient resources to African-American murders," he said.[54]

Community activist Robbie Bethel-Carrier said blacks are reluctant to talk to the sheriff's department because it "has proven not to be a friend of the community. When the head of your department (Ackal) says it's okay to call the residents monkeys, it's okay to turn a dog loose on somebody, it's okay to shove a stick down their throat to sexually violate them—who would talk to them?"

Along with the breakdown in relations between the sheriff's department and the residents of New Iberia it was contracted to protect, the absence of an accurate FBI reporting system, keeps the public in the dark about community safety. That, said Hargrove, lowers public accountability and hinders criminology research.

Ackal's problems continued into 2019 when his office agreed to a $2.5 million settlement to bring to an end a lawsuit filed by Derrick Sellers who was beaten senseless by deputies in 2013. Another $275,000 was paid to Marcus Robicheaux, the prisoner who was subjected to police dog attacks as he lay face-down during a jail shakedown in 2012.

Sellers, a former U.S. Marine from Abbeville, once ran 15 miles a week but today cannot even pick up trash without falling. His left cheekbone was broken up to his eye socket, causing the eyeball to shift outward. He was left crawling across the floor of his cell following the beating. He wears darkened frames cupped around the sides, like racehorse blinkers, in order to train his focus. He wears a lanyard around his neck which holds a device that pulses electric current to his cranium through a pair of wires clipped to his earlobes. He wears a back brace because of three ruptured discs. He no longer can drive a car or ride a bicycle. "I have a tricycle," he said.

What's even worse is the deputy who inflicted the most damage, Eric Blanchard, was still employed by the sheriff's office at the time Sellers was interviewed.[55]

The LSLEP has since terminated the Iberia Parish Sheriff's Office from participating in the insurance pool because of the mounting number of lawsuits against the department.

A multitude of lawsuit judgments and settlements has cost the department almost $6 million, an average of about $50,000 for every month of Ackal's ten years in office.

In early 2015, the head of the Metropolitan Crime Commission (MCC) in New Orleans said his organization might undertake a study of the St. Bernard Parish criminal justice system. And while Rafael Goyeneche, III, head of the citizens' organization dedicated to exposing public corruption, said the purpose of such a study would be to "raise the level of accountability and efficiency in the criminal justice system," he stopped short of making any direct reference to shady deals involving then-Sheriff Jack Stephens following the disastrous BP Deepwater Horizon rig explosion and ensuing oil spill in the Gulf of Mexico.

St. Bernard, situated below New Orleans and along the eastern bank of the Mississippi River in the toe of the Louisiana boot, was the site of the historic Battle of New Orleans in 1814 in which Gen. Andrew Jackson defeated Gen. Edward Packenham's British forces. What the British could not do, Hurricane Katrina accomplished nearly 200 years later in 2005.

Obliterated by Katrina, its population was nearly halved as thousands of victims simply decided not to return. Fire protection, mosquito control and garbage collection ceased when the parish's tax base dried up. Five years later, disaster would strike again with the April 20, 2010, BP Deepwater Horizon oil spill that wiped out the parish's shrimping and fishing industry.

Additional damage was inflicted by the politically-connected who put their own enrichment before the general welfare of their fellow citizens—and at considerable expense to BP. And St. Bernard Parish Sheriff Stephens was right in the thick of all the financial exploitation.

Local companies with ties to the parish power structure reaped profitable cleanup contracts and then charged BP for every conceivable expense. The prime cleanup contractor, which had no oil-spill experience to go with its history of bad debts, submitted bills with little or no documentation. A subcontractor charged BP more than $15,000 per month to rent a generator that usually cost only a tenth as much. And a firm owned in part by Sheriff Stephens charged more than a million dollars per month for land it had been renting for less than $1,700 per month.

While there was money to be had, the bulk of the cash influx flowed to companies and individuals who had the right connections to the parish power structure, including Parish President Craig Taffaro, Jr., the son of Jefferson Parish Chief Deputy Sheriff Craig Taffaro, Sr. The junior Craig was the brother-in-law of Louisiana's Lt. Gov. Billy Nungesser. It was also the younger Taffaro who doled out jobs and contracts to personal friends, political cronies and relatives.[56]

Amigo Enterprises Inc., which for years leased land to one of the busiest marinas in the parish, got in at the outset. BP based its cleanup operation at the marina at an astronomical cost. Amigo had previously leased the land for less than $1,700 a month from the Arlene & Joseph Meraux Charitable Foundation Inc. Amigo sub-let the facility to BP, which was billed for more than $1.1 million a month.

Amigo wasn't just any company. One of the owners was 26-year sheriff Jack Stephens, who, it happens, also sat on the board of the Meraux Foundation. According to the most recent ethics form Stephens filed with the state, he earned more than $100,000 from Amigo the year before the BP spill.

Stephens's cousin, Anthony Fernandez, Jr., formerly worked as Stephens' chief deputy and was one of Stephens's two partners in Amigo. Fernandez said BP paid less than the $1 million a month in rent to Amigo claimed by critics.

Fernandez also got substantial revenue from BP for another company, Parish Oilfield Services LLC. Parish Oilfield hired off-duty sheriff's deputies to provide security for the spill.

The sheriff's office signed an eviction notice for BP on August 31 because BP had not paid some $3 million in rent to Amigo. The message on the eviction notice was terse: "Landlord wants possession of his property." Not said was notification that the sheriff's company was the landlord. BP paid Amigo and the work on the cleanup resumed.

Unfortunately, the study proposed by Goyeneche never took place. "We never received the funding for it," he explained nearly three years later.[57]

Goyeneche's words in January 2015, however, may well have been prophetic. Less than seven months after that address, on August 4, 2015, St. Bernard deputy sheriff Jarrod Gourgues was indicted for felony theft, perjury and three counts of malfeasance in office for allegedly receiving pay while on duty for the sheriff's office and at the same time collecting pay for work as the parish's road director. He also was accused of accepting more than $10,000 from a parish IT contractor, ParaTech, according to the indictment. His perjury count was for lying to a grand jury.[58]

Additionally, he was charged with two malfeasance counts which stemmed from his being a de facto co-owner of a lawn care and debris removal company that had a contract with the parish. Parish employees are barred by law from doing business with the parish, said a spokesman for the Louisiana attorney general's office. Gourgues was accused of accepting about $50,000 through the lawn care business and from the owner of a parish waste and recycling contractor.

Eleven months later, a parish judge threw out all five counts of the indictment in a decision that only served to enhance the image of a parish which, like Plaquemines, its neighbor across the Mississippi River, pretty much does as it pleases, conflicts of interests and ethics—and the law itself—be damned.

Thirty-Fourth Judicial District Judge Jeanne Juneau granted a motion by Gourgues to quash the five-count indictment because the sheriff's office had provided copies of two subpoenas to a New Orleans television station. The copies had been provided in response to a formal public records request by WWL-TV. Juneau, in her ruling, said the station reported on the grand jury investigation the day before the actual indictment. And that, she said, violated the prohibition against disclosure of secret grand jury materials, thereby exerting "prejudice and influence on members of the grand jury."[59]

Stephens, at the completion of his seventh term, did not seek reelection in 2011, ending the second-longest tenure of any St. Bernard Parish Sheriff after 28 years. He said he decided against seeking an eighth term because of increased scrutiny and a growing bureaucracy following Hurricane Katrina. Mostly, though, he said, he had "seen it all."[60]

The Civil Rights Division of the U.S. Justice Department delivered a stunning blow to the Evangeline Parish Sheriff's Office and the Ville Platte Police Department in a 2016 scathing report that left the door open to a flood of lawsuits against and criminal prosecution of the two departments for civil rights infringements through unconstitutional incarceration, intimidation and extortion.

The report's findings also cast a cloud of legal doubt that potentially tainted an undetermined number of past criminal convictions that resulted from such practices.

In its report dated Dec. 19, the Justice Department concluded "that there is reasonable cause to believe that both the Ville Platte, Louisiana, Police Department [VPPD] and the Evangeline Parish Sheriff's Office [EPSO] have engaged in a pattern or practice of unconstitutional conduct" that dated back "as far as anyone (at either department) can remember."

The 17-page report went on to say, "Both VPPD and EPSO have arrested and held people in jail—without obtaining a warrant and without probable cause to believe that the detained individuals had committed a crime—in violation of the Fourth Amendment to the Constitution. We have additional concerns that these unconstitutional holds have led to coerced confessions and improper criminal convictions. These findings reflect the results of an investigation into both agencies, which have engaged in nearly identical practices within overlapping jurisdictional boundaries."[61]

The arrests, called "investigative holds," were used routinely by both VPPD and EPSO as a part of their criminal investigations during which threats of continued wrongful incarceration were employed to induce arrestees to provide information. Authorities also threatened their family members and potential witnesses, the report said.

"The arrests include individuals suspected (without sufficient evidence) of committing crimes, as well as their family members and potential witnesses," it said.

The report included claims that individuals improperly arrested were:

- Strip-searched;
- Placed in holding cells without beds, toilets, or showers;
- Denied communication with family members and loved ones;
- Commonly detained for seventy-two hours or more without being provided an opportunity to contest their arrest and detention;
- Held and questioned until they either provide information or the law enforcement agency determines that they do not have information related to a crime.

The report further said there were "concerns that some people may have confessed to crimes or provided information sought by EPSO and VPPD detectives, apparently to end this secret and indefinite confinement." It said that the practice is "routine at EPSO and VPPD" and that both agencies acknowledged that they used holds to investigate criminal activity for as long as anyone at the agency can remember. The number of holds used in recent years was described as "staggering."

"Between 2012 and 2014, for example," it said, "EPSO initiated over 200 arrests where the only documented reason for arrest was an investigative hold. In that same period, VPPD used the practice more than 700 times. The number of holds by EPSO and VPPD is likely even higher; both agencies use such rudimentary arrest documentation systems that the total number of arrests for investigative hold purposes is likely underreported."

Following the onset of its investigation in April 2015, "leadership of VPPD, EPSO and the City of Ville Platte admitted that the holds are unconstitutional" and have taken steps to begin eliminating their use, the report says, adding that still more work "remains to be done." The agencies' policies, procedures, training, and data collection and accountability systems "must ensure that investigative holds are eliminated permanently," it said, adding that local officials "must work to repair community trust, because many people may still be justifiably reluctant to provide information to law enforcement for fear that doing so could subject them to an unconstitutional detention."

The report was the culmination of an investigation of a cross-section of community residents, some of whom were subjected to the investigative holds.

Detectives from both agencies violated individuals' Fourth Amendment rights when, "lacking probable cause, they instructed officers to 'pick up' an individual and 'bring him in' for questioning rather than making an 'arrest,'" the report's narrative said. "Indeed, there can be little doubt that the Fourth Amendment's probable cause requirement applies where suspects are involuntarily taken to the police station. This practice subjects individuals to arrest and detention without cause and erodes the community trust that is critical to effective law enforcement in Evangeline Parish and Ville Platte."

The investigative holds are made "without a warrant, without any showing that the testimony is essential and that obtaining it via subpoena is impracticable, and without any attempt to obtain prior judicial approval," the report says.

"EPSO and VPPD officers have used unlawful investigative holds as a regular part of criminal investigations for more than two decades. Most holds operate as follows:

- When a detective at either agency wanted to question someone in connection with an ongoing criminal investigation, the detective instructed a patrol officer to find that individual in the community and bring him or her in for questioning.
- The patrol officer commanded the individual to ride in a patrol vehicle to either the City or Parish jail, where pursuant to the jail's standard procedures, jail personnel strip-searched the individual and placed him or her in a holding cell until a detective is available to conduct questioning.
- Detainees were not permitted to make phone calls to let family or employers know where they were. They were allowed access to bathrooms and showers only when taken into the jail's general population area.
- Similarly, EPSO's investigative holds often lasted for three full days. During that time, detainees were forced to sleep on the Parish Jail's concrete floor. One EPSO deputy reported that he saw someone held without a warrant or a probable cause determination for more than six days.

The investigative holds were not supported by probable cause. Both EPSO and VPPD detectives acknowledged that they used investigative holds where they lacked sufficient evidence to make an arrest, but instead had a "hunch" or "feeling" that a person may have been involved in criminal activity. One VPPD officer noted that they used investigative holds specifically where the officer needed more time to develop evidence to support a lawful arrest. Similarly, an EPSO detective described using investigative holds when he had "a pretty good feeling" or a "gut instinct" that a certain individual was connected to a crime.

The report indicated that officers at both agencies admitted that they use the time that a person is "on hold" to develop their case, either by gathering evidence or by convincing the detainee to confess. One EPSO detective told investigators that he experimented with investigative holds by testing whether a crime wave subsides while a particular person is in jail. He explained that if the crimes continue during the hold, the presumably innocent person is released but if the crimes cease during the detention, the detective investigates the person further.

VPPD officers explained that holds assist their investigations by inducing people to talk to investigators and by allowing detectives to gather evidence while the individual they suspect is in custody and cannot communicate with people on the outside. Moreover, both agencies confirmed that they used holds to detain individuals whom they did not suspect of involvement in criminal activity, but who instead had the misfortune of being related to suspects, may have witnessed crimes, or otherwise might have knowledge of criminal activity.[62]

Incredulously, Ville Platte Police Chief Neal Lartigue professed not to know the indiscriminate use of the investigative holds may have been in violation of the Fourth Amendment which requires authorities to have probable cause to detain citizens.[63]

In an ominous warning of the perils of investigative holds, the report said, "The willingness of officers in both agencies to arrest and detain individuals who are merely possible witnesses in criminal investigations means that literally anyone in Evangeline Parish or Ville Platte could be arrested and placed 'on hold' at any time."

Terrebonne Parish Sheriff Jerry Larpenter apparently never read the First Amendment. Neither, it seems, did Thirty-Second Judicial District Court Judge Randal Bethancourt. Nor does it seem that either ever checked into the constitutional status of Louisiana's criminal defamation statute.

Larpenter made national news on August 2, 2016, when he sent a posse of six deputies to the home of a suspected blogger and hauled away two laptop computers because the blogger said bad things about the sheriff. The blogger, Houma police officer Wayne Anderson, posted critical observations about Larpenter, Parish President (and former State Rep.) Gordon Dove and others. The gist of the story was that certain connected entities evaded their responsibility to pay nearly $400,000 in parish taxes and that local officials committed malfeasance by not pursuing the collection of the delinquent taxes. Those same officials, it said, were guilty of nepotism, committing ethics violations, and violating environmental regulations.[64]

Anderson, who had worked as a Terrebonne Parish sheriff's deputy before going to work for the Houma Police Department, had documents and links to documents to support claims in his post and yet all that apparently made no difference to the two officials who went after him with a vengeance. Overlooked by Sheriff Larpenter was the guarantee under the First Amendment of the U.S. Constitution of Anderson's right to free speech. Even more astonishing was that Bethancourt, supposedly something of a legal scholar by virtue of his position as a sitting judge, went along with the sheriff's scheme.

Relying upon an obscure state criminal defamation statute designed to discourage freedom of speech and enacted during the last term of former Gov. John McKeithen (1964-1972), Bethancourt said he had to stay within the "four corners" of the warrant and affidavit.

The only problem with the judge's interpretation of the state's defamation statute is that it is non-existent. Anderson's attorney correctly pointed out that Bethancourt made a mistake in approving the warrant to raid his client's home because the defamation statute was declared unconstitutional in 1981. Since the law was held unconstitutional, it would seem that neither Judge Bethancourt nor the sheriff—nor anyone else, for that matter—had any right to Anderson's computers. That, simply put, constituted an invasion of privacy.

After a federal judge dressed down Bethancourt and Larpenter by familiarizing them with the First Amendment and ordered that Anderson's computers be returned, Anderson and wife Jennifer promptly filed suit against Larpenter and Dove. The litigation cost Larpenter's office around $200,000 and Dove another $50,000.[67]

Then there is the story of the "Mysterious X" that first catapulted

Larpenter into the Sheriff's Office. At the beginning of April of that year, Charlton P. Rozands was still the sheriff, but at that particular point in time, he was:

- Under federal indictment;
- Dying of cancer.

Rozands and his two sons, along with Chief of Detectives Aubrey Authement and deputy Elmore Songe were all indicted on charges ranging from malfeasance in office, improper removal of weapons from the sheriff's office, unauthorized and illegal personal use of weapons being held as evidence, and the disposal of weapons being held as evidence but which had been in Authement's possession.[68]

The sheriff's cancer was so advanced, in fact, that he was said to have been heavily medicated on morphine and thus, unable to perform the simplest of tasks—even as simple as signing his name. Rozands died on April 19. Six days before his death, on April 13, Larpenter supposedly signed the required oath of office as Rozands' Chief Criminal Deputy. On the second page of that document, in the left-hand margin, is the signature, "C.P. Rozands, Sheriff."

Except it's not Rozands' signature. A comparison of that signature with a document actually signed by Rozands makes that abundantly clear. Several people who were in positions to know said that Rozands would have been physically unable to sign anything because of the advanced stages of his cancer and because he was heavily medicated with morphine. What is not clear is who actually did sign his name.

In fact, at some point prior to Larpenter's signing his oath of office, a meeting was reportedly held to discuss a successor. Said to have been at that meeting were Rozands' wife Mae, his two sons, and Houma attorney William F. Dodd, legal counsel for the sheriff's office and son of a former Louisiana state politician and Earl Long contemporary. The year was 1987, and at the time, state law allowed an official's widow to assume his seat but Mrs. Rozands let it be known she wasn't interested in the job. Nor were either of their sons. The choices were quickly eliminated until there was only Larpenter who, when asked, said he would take the job.

The affidavit was quickly drafted, presumably by Dodd, that named Larpenter as Chief Criminal Deputy, which would make him next in line for the office of sheriff. But to make the appointment official, Rozands was required to sign it. Despite being described as being in no condition to do so, he supposedly signed the document with an "X."

But did he? One person close to the series of events said, "I don't think Rozands would have waited until he was that sick to appoint Jerry Larpenter. They were close, but I think if Rozands had wanted Larpenter as his Chief Criminal Deputy, he would have appointed him while he was well enough to know what he was doing."

Besides the job promotion and salary boost that came with Larpenter's ascension into the sheriff's chair, it also gave him the decided advantage of running as an incumbent in the next regular election only months away in October. In that election, the incumbency proved beneficial, all right. Larpenter, running against eight opponents, got a whopping 44 per cent of the vote, a full 30 points more than his closest competitor, who got 14 percent. In the November runoff, he received 69 per cent of the vote to win his first of seven terms, interrupted only by his unsuccessful run for Parish President in 2007.

Each one of his elections were won by wide margins and he ran unopposed in 2015. But the details of how he went from obscure deputy to sheriff for those few months in 1987 remain murky and clouded with questions of whether Rozands actually scrawled that "X" or it was done by someone else in his name.[69]

Finally, there are the unanswered questions that persist, three decades after his death, concerning Rozands' heavy-handed control over local bars, gambling and prostitution—and rumors of ties to organized crime during his tenure as Terrebonne's chief law enforcement officer.

Now a municipal judge, a man who worked for Rozands as an 18-year-old deputy while attending college shared some revealing stories about Rozands. During his tenure with the Terrebonne Parish Sheriff's Office, the young deputy witnessed some interesting practices, which included, among other things, Rozands' insistence that bar owners in the parish keep an eight-by-ten photo of him hanging over their bars' cash registers. Whenever a parish bar owner applied for a liquor license or a renewal, he was provided along with his license, a photo of the sheriff. He was instructed to hang it in a conspicuous location, preferably over the bar. The bars were regularly checked by deputies for compliance and if it was found that the photo was not where is was supposed to be, Rozands would promptly pull the bar's license and order it closed.

But an even more disturbing revelation was that of Rozands' making regular payoffs to New Orleans Mafia boss Carlos Marcello. "Carlos controlled the pinball machines and all the pool tables in Terrebonne Parish," said the former deputy. "They were owned by Lafourche Novelty Company but Carlos controlled the entire coast from Texas to Florida at that time. All the bars had to have their cigarette machines from CNL Cigarettes. CNL ran the bookie business in the parish, along with prostitution and pinball.

"A.B. Pereira was the bag man for Marcello. Everyone called him Abe. He would pick up the payoff money from the bars and of course, Rozands was getting a take for himself. A man named George Saadi put Rozands and Marcello together. All the sheriff department uniforms had to come from Saadi Haberdashery. "

The former deputy said every Wednesday, a briefcase full of cash would be placed in the trunk of a sheriff's department vehicle which would then be driven to Mosca's Restaurant in Westwego in Jefferson Parish. "The driver of the sheriff's car would park next to one of Marcello's Cadillacs in the parking lot. Marcello got all his Cadillacs from Pontchartrain Cadillac and the sheriff got his from Cournoyer Cadillac in Houma."

Inside the restaurant, keys would be exchanged and one of Marcello's men would go to the cars and open the trunks. "The full bag of money would be taken out of the sheriff's vehicle and placed in the trunk of Marcello's car. An empty briefcase would be taken from the Marcello car and placed in the trunk of the sheriff's car. Back inside the restaurant, the keys would swap hands again."

A naïve kid at the time, the deputy had not even started law school. "Looking back, there was so much going on in that office, it would curl your hair," he said.[70]

In terms of pure corruption, greed and violent reprisals against anyone who might stand in his way, the saga of former Shreveport Commissioner of Public Safety George D'Artois stands alone. His story underscores the undeniable argument that unrestrained autonomy can ultimately lead only to a bad ending for everyone involved.

D'Artois served as a deputy under Caddo Parish Sheriff J. Howell Flournoy from 1952 until his resignation in 1962 to run for Public Safety Commissioner under Shreveport's city commission form of government, a five-member body that exercised combined executive and legislative functions for the city with the mayor serving as the commissioner of administration. D'Artois, a Democrat, upset two-term incumbent J. Earl Downs. He was re-elected in 1966, 1970 and 1974. Far more power was enjoyed by commissioners, each of whom ran his own fiefdom, than under the mayor-council form of government which was established with the 1978 elections when single-member legislative city council districts and an executive mayor were elected.

As public safety commissioner, D'Artois frequently lectured in Baton Rouge at the LSU Law Enforcement Institute and at the Southwestern Legal Foundation at Southern Methodist University in Dallas. He was cited by the National Police Officers Association of America in 1973 for outstanding work in law enforcement.

But all was not what it appeared to be. When several hundred thousand dollars earmarked for financing a synchronized traffic system by D'Artois's department disappeared in 1968, none of the Shreveport commissioners could ever account for it. Mayor Calhoun Allen was dismissive, speculating in a somewhat cavalier manner that the money was used for other "needed projects."[71]

Even as D'Artois was running not only the Department of Public Safety, but the entire city of Shreveport "with an iron fist" without the niceties of a velvet glove, New Orleans organized crime boss Carlos Marcello was making regular visits to Shreveport. [72]

The 1970 election served as a wake-up call for D'Artois. Though he received 59.8 percent of the vote in defeating Republican William Kimball, the election was too close for D'Artois who was accustomed to polling much higher numbers against token opposition. For his 1974 re-election campaign, he hired advertising executive Jim Leslie who had previously worked as a reporter for *The Shreveport Times*. It would prove to be a fateful move for both men. Following his easy victory, D'Artois, in a crass and arrogant gesture, paid Leslie for his work on the campaign with a check drawn on city funds. Leslie returned the check and asked that he be paid from D'Artois's campaign funds. Instead, D'Artois told Leslie to keep the city check and to keep the matter between the two of them. Leslie again returned the check, along with a threat to go public if he was not paid properly. From that point forward, Leslie was a marked man.[73]

Leslie subsequently contracted with the Louisiana Association of Business and Industry (LABI) to spearhead its push for passage of the hotly contested right to work bill pending before the Louisiana Legislature. The bill, thanks largely to Leslie's work, narrowly passed the legislature. He joined other proponents of the bill to celebrate the victory into the early morning hours of July 9, 1976. As he exited from his car in his hotel parking lot about two a.m., he was killed instantly by a blast from a twelve-gauge shotgun fired from behind a wooden fence. He was 38.[74]

There had been a labor-related killing at a Lake Charles petro- chemical plant only a few weeks before, which those in the labor movement felt expedited passage of the right to work bill, so the immediate speculation was that Leslie's killing also was attributable to the raw emotions on the part of organized labor that accompanied the right to work movement. That theory was quickly dismissed and all eyes turned toward Shreveport and the fallout from the ongoing D'Artois-Leslie dispute over a $3,500 city check.[75]

On August 6, 1976, less than a month after Leslie's murder, a Baton Rouge judge issued a warrant charging D'Artois for his alleged part in the killing. Though he was soon released for lack of evidence, D'Artois was forced to resign from office.

Two months later, D'Artois was ordered to appear in a Shreveport court to face charges of theft of $300,000 and intimidation of witnesses for a grand jury investigating him. D'Artois's attorneys told the judge their client, who was suffering from heart disease, was too ill to appear in court.[76]

The slide in D'Artois's fortunes continued in April 1977. He was arrested a second time in the Leslie murder. Later that month, he was ordered to stand trial for felony theft of $30,000 in municipal funds which D'Artois said was paid to informants. His attorneys questioned how he could stand trial in light of his deteriorating heart condition. In response, Judge William J. Fleniken instructed prosecutors to have doctors and medical equipment in place during the trial which had been postponed several times already.

D'Artois died during heart surgery ten months later in San Antonio. The allegations against him, including any part he may have played in Leslie's murder, were never resolved. [77]

That was not the end of the story, however. An associate of D'Artois, a man named Rusty Griffith, was eventually identified as the trigger man in the Leslie murder. But before he could face trial, he was himself assassinated on October 15 or 16, three months and a week after Leslie was murdered. He was apparently lured to the Three Rivers Wildlife Management Area in Concordia Parish. As he stood next to a car unknowingly talking to his killers, he peered into the back seat through an open window. He was hit in the face by a blast from a twelve-gauge shotgun fired first from only three feet away and a second from about eight feet away.

Shreveport political consultant Elliott Stonecipher called D'Artois "the most powerful ever public official [in Shreveport] ... who dragged the citizenry through the deep ditch of a corruption scandal which forever stained our city." He wrote that after Leslie twice refused the city check from D'Artois and threatened to go public, D'Artois "went to work looking for someone to kill him." He said D'Artois solicited the hit from Shreveport police officers, a city department head and at least one 'professional' killer "well-known to law enforcement."

In the spring of 1976, months before the Leslie murder, Shreveport Police Chief T.P. Kelley and Captain Sam Burns approached *The Shreveport Times* on a furtive mission to get the newspaper to investigate public corruption which was spreading like a cancer under D'Artois, Stonecipher wrote, adding that both the informal Dixie Mafia and the real Mafia operated with impunity in Shreveport. The two law enforcement officers shared the belief with many others that D'Artois had too much power, that he ran both Mayor Calhoun Allen and the city itself.

The Times assigned a four-member "Enterprise Team" of reporters led by one of the paper's more capable reporters, Marsha Schuler. The reporters' first story broke like a bombshell over Shreveport on April 25, 1976.

"An incomparable frenzy of local and state news coverage yielded some outstanding journalism about what had happened to us," Stonecipher wrote. "Only three weeks after *The Times'* opening barrage, Caddo Parish District Attorney John Richardson handed his concurrent criminal investigation over to Louisiana Attorney General William Guste.

The Caddo Parish grand jury first met on June 6. One month and three days later, Leslie was dead. Three months and one week after that, his accused killer was dead.[78]

One of the most sordid indictments of law enforcement came in October 2019 with the arrest of a Livingston Parish deputy and his schoolteacher wife on charges of child pornography, rape, video voyeurism and obscenity. The arrests set off a chain reaction of lawsuits as more details emerged and served to cast doubts on the sheriff's department's methods of background checks.

It took more than three years before Perkins, in January 2023, would finally plead guilty and was sentenced to 100 years in prison just before his trial on 78 counts was scheduled to begin

Dennis Perkins, 44, was head of the department's SWAT team and his wife Cynthia, 34, was a junior high school teacher when the pair was indicted on a combined 150 counts, including first-degree rape, attempted rape, sexually battery of a child under the age of 13, video voyeurism, mingling harmful substances, obscenity, possession of child pornography, producing child pornography and sexually abusing a dog. Cynthia Perkins, who subsequently divorced her husband, pleaded guilty in 2022 in a deal that called for her to testify against Dennis Perkins and was sentenced to 41 years in prison.[79]

Stories broke with subsequent reports, of equal parts incredulity and revulsion, that Perkins had ejaculated on various pastries and into bottles of energy drinks that were then ingested by his wife's fifth-grade students. As if that were not enough, those same reports told of his having sex with a dog.

Perkins had been employed as a deputy since 2002. He was hired on the recommendation of then-deputy Jason Ard who vouched for Perkins's "good character." Ard was elected sheriff in 2011. Ard, upon Perkins's arrest, called his former deputy "monstrous."

Perkins had previously served as a municipal police officer for the Livingston Parish town of Walker but resigned from that position after admitting to stealing property from the Walker Police Department as well as admitting to theft of merchandise from a local store while shopping. He had been described at the time as a "high risk" employee.[80]

Following allegations of Perkins's debauchery, several lawsuits were filed by irate parents against the Livingston Parish School Board. The lawsuits claimed the school board was negligent in allowing Cynthia Perkins to bring homemade goods and serve them to children. They also claimed the school board failed to employ a safe and competent teacher, failed to properly check her background and failed to employ proper precautions to ensure the safety of students.[81]

Immediately to the south of Livingston Parish lies Ascension Parish. There, Todd Eric Tripp, a former sheriff's deputy was fired in 2013 following his arrest for attempted child pornography possession and indecent behavior with a juvenile. He was convicted and was sent to prison. Released in 2019, he was placed on probation but in 2020, he became a fugitive after becoming wanted on three counts of carnal knowledge of a juvenile, computer-aided solicitation of a minor and unlawful use of social media over allegations of his solicitation of a teenage boy in another parish, law enforcement officials said.

Tripp, a native of the Ascension Parish town of Sorrento, was captured in South Carolina in October 2020, the Ascension Parish Sheriff's Office said. [82]

About the same time as the arrest of Perkins and his wife, reports were emerging 120 miles to the west of a sex trafficking ring run by sheriff's deputies dating back more than a decade. Three Jefferson Davis Parish deputies were charged in a 2002 corruption case after at least a half-dozen women told authorities that deputies raped and trafficked them to male inmates inside the Jefferson Davis Parish jail, according state and FBI records. [83]

The allegations surfaced in the aftermath of the unsolved case of eight slain prostitutes in Jefferson Davis Parish following a documentary on *Showtime* which examined the so-called Jefferson Davis 8. Former Sheriff Ricky Edwards said at the time that two deputies had been arrested for taking bribes to arrange sex between inmates.

At least a half-dozen women had said deputies ran a jailhouse sex-trafficking ring in which female inmates were repeatedly coerced into having sex with male inmates. One of the deputies implicated in the scandal who was subsequently fired was Allarate "A.J." Frank, who pleaded no contest to a misdemeanor count of criminal mischief. Frank later worked more than a decade for the Eunice Police Department in Acadia and St. Landry parishes and ran unsuccessfully for police chief there. After losing that election, he turned up as a police officer in the neighboring town of Basile. [84]

The Ascension Parish Sheriff's Office in February 2021 agreed to pay $50,000 in damages to a Baton Rouge man who said the department held him in jail for four days on the false assumption that he was in the country illegally even though a judge had ordered him released.

Despite the agreement to pay the settlement – plus attorney's fees – Sheriff Bobby Webre denied his office had done anything wrong, claiming instead that Ramon Torres had been legally detained on orders of a different judge and "not on the whim of any deputy."

"No court ruled that this office violated any law or policy. My deputies handled this situation in accordance with our policies and procedures and by order of a judge," he said.

The ACLU of Louisiana's attorney, Bruce Hamilton, disagreed. "This incident should be a cautionary tale to very community in the state: when local law enforcement agencies take it upon themselves to enforce federal immigration law, everyday citizens pay the price."[85]

The December 15, 2016, FBI raid of the Tangipahoa Parish Sheriff's Office and the Hammond, Louisiana, Police Department was the culmination of an almost year-long investigation of a member of a Drug Enforcement Agency task force suspected of stealing cash from drug dealers, selling confiscated narcotics and witnesses tampering.

It would be nearly five years before Chad Scott a high-profile, highly-decorated DEA agent would be convicted and sentenced to 160 months in federal prison. Before his June 2021 conviction, Tangipahoa deputies Karl Emmett Newman and Johnny Domingue, also members of the task force, would plead guilty to an assortment of charges.

Karl Emmett Newman, pleaded guilty in July 2017 to unlawfully carrying a firearm in furtherance of an August 2015 robbery that was disguised as the execution of a search warrant and of misappropriating money confiscated by the DEA during another search. Domingue pleaded guilty in February 2018 to possession of cocaine and of misappropriating money confiscated by the DEA. In exchange for his guilty plea, Domingue received a lighter sentence of 20 months for testifying against Scott.[86]

Domingue, however, couldn't resist the lure of easy, albeit illegal, money. Less than three years following his guilty plea, he was re-arrested in Texas in September 2020 for negotiating to purchase four kilos of cocaine for about $100,000. In a scheme that began in July, the

U.S. Attorney's office in Houston said Domingue also agreed to transport another four kilos of cocaine in a plan to sell the drugs in Houston and Louisiana.[87]

The refusal by former Rapides Parish Sheriff William Hilton to comply with federal Americans with Disabilities Act resulted in his successor's settling a federal discrimination lawsuit brought by a former deputy for $187,500, although it was too late to help the plaintiff, who died prior to the settlement.

Twenty-year department veteran Jerry McKinney, Sr., a former Army officer, suffered a stroke in 2017 and could not pass his required firearm recertification when he returned to work. Hilton moved him to a 12-hour shift at the jail that did not require firearm certification. But the 12-hour shift brought on other health issues so McKinney's doctor recommended that his schedule be modified to eight-hour shifts.

The sheriff's office refused, suggesting that if he could not work the

12-hour shift, he should retire. When McKinney refused to retire, he was fired. Incredibly, Hilton testified in his deposition that his office had never provided accommodations to employees with disabilities, saying to do so would have "disrupted the operation of the department" and created an appearance of special treatment for McKinney."[88]

Problems continued for the Rapides Parish Sheriff's Department under new Sheriff Mark Wood. First, an unmonitored drug sting in September 2022 during which an informant was raped resulted in a lawsuit by the victim against the department four months later.[89]

About the same time that lawsuit was being filed in January 2023, a traffic stop over tinted windows and modified muffler resulted in the shooting death of motorist Derrick Kittling, who had only recently purchased the vehicle. The stop by a Rapides deputy underscored the lack of consistency in laws regulating tinted windows. Kittling had not modified the truck's windows or mufflers from the condition that existed when he purchased it and it had a new inspection sticker at the time that indicated that the vehicle had passed inspection.[90]

Caldwell Parish is located in Louisiana's Mississippi Delta region, the most economically-challenged area of the state. So, the alleged theft of $35,000 by the Caldwell Parish Sheriff Office's Chief Civil Deputy was pretty big news for the area that former Louisiana Gov. John McKeithen called home.

Deborah Dollar was arrested September 14, 2021, by Louisiana State Police on a single count of malfeasance in office and one count of felony theft. State police detectives said she had taken the money from the cash drawer over a period of 18 months.

Sheriff Clay Bennett said the arrest did not reflect on the values or dedication of the men and women of his department. "I want to make sure that our community understands that I will not tolerate any misconduct by the people that are sworn to uphold the law and protect the citizens of Caldwell Parish," he said.[91]

When Sojourner Gibbs suffered familiar symptoms of diabetic coma while pulling out of a parking space, she slammed on her brakes and called out for help. A bystander called 911 and four Jefferson Parish sheriff's deputies arrived just ahead of the paramedics. She said she told deputies she was diabetic but the sheriff's department report said she told them, "Go away." She remembers hearing one deputy say, "This bitch is lying. She's high on something."

When deputies surrounded the car, a white woman, Alicia Dardar, was passing by. She had bad vibes about what was taking place, so, with the memories of George Floyd still fresh in her mind, she stopped and started filming with her camera as deputies threw Gibbs to the ground. "I think the cops saw a Black person and instantly assumed she's on drugs," Dardar said. "If it was me in that vehicle, it would have been a very different moment."

The four deputies dragged Gibbs out of the vehicle and one deputy grabbed one of her legs, pulling it from beneath her, sending her crashing face-first to the pavement. The tied her hands behind her back with zip ties until paramedics arrived and took her blood sugar level. It was seventeen milligrams per deciliter. Anything below forty is considered critical and sometimes fatal. One of the paramedics told her, "You could have died." As she remained in the ambulance, deputies combed through her belongings in her SUV, a search that appeared to have been done without probable cause.

Gibbs filed a complaint with the sheriff department's internal affairs division but the sheriff's office neglected to adhere to its own internal investigations policy: no one ever interviewed her or Dardar before the officers were exonerated of all wrongdoing. Nor did the sheriff's office ever respond to inquiries about her case. Dardar possessed the only recorded footage of the encounter. That's because the Jefferson Parish Sheriff's Department remains one of the few major law enforcement agencies in the country that does not use body cameras.[92]

Even as the Jefferson Parish Sheriff's Department was facing multiple lawsuits involving allegations of wrongful death, excessive force, and racial discrimination, it was revealed in January 2023 that the department routinely destroyed deputies' disciplinary records over a ten- year period, action which *ProPublica* noted made it more difficult to hold deputies accountable in a court of law or to track problem officers moving from one department to another.

The department has no records retention policy even though state law requires all public agencies, including the sheriff's department, to secure approval from the Louisiana State Archives in the Secretary of State's Office prior to destroying any public records.

In fact, the same source noted that almost half of all Louisiana sheriffs routinely violate the state's public records laws. Twenty-three of the state's 64 parishes (counties) have never obtained state approval for their records retention policy as required by law.[93]

16

Maine: Sexting's Between Adults Not Illegal

WHEN THE HEAT was turned up on Oxford County Sheriff Wayne Gallant after it was learned that he'd sent sexually-explicit photographs to a woman while in his office—and in uniform—his unlikely defense was that he had broken no laws. "I did nothing illegal," he told the *Bangor Daily News*. "It was an adult thing that happened two years ago."[1]

Illegal or not, the news did not sit well with the Maine Sheriffs' Association, of which Gallant was serving as president. Even as he defended his actions, he did the prudent thing and stepped down as head of the association but stopped short of resigning as sheriff, saying, "I was elected by the people of Oxford County."[2]

"This is unbelievable if it's true," said York County Sheriff William L. King, Jr., who served as secretary of the association.[3]

One day after Oxford County commissioners demanded that the three-term sheriff step down, Gallant resigned when it became apparent there would be an official effort to remove him.[4] But his resignation did not end his legal problems.

Seven months later, in July 2018, it was learned that the FBI was investigating Gallant and his former Chief Deputy Hart Daley over allegations of sexual harassment and attempts to cover-up Gallant's actions after then-current Chief Deputy Chris Wainwright told a judge the entire story "could take hours to tell."

The short version started with the arrest of Oxford County detective Brian Landis on a domestic violence charge in June 2017. Four days after his arrest, Gallant was accused of soliciting oral sex from Landis, and Gallant allegedly wanted his girlfriend to watch.

Wainwright said investigators decided to wait until Gallant was removed from office before seizing the department's computers and cellphones when they would be turned over to the FBI. But Daley became aware of the plan, Wainwright said, and by the time Gallant left, all the devices were wiped clean.[5]

Even as the Gallant investigation was ongoing, Kenneth Hatch, a former Deputy-of-the-Year with the Lincoln County Sheriff's Office, was fired following an internal investigation after being accused of sexually abusing three underage girls.[6]

17

Maryland: Bad Apples in Baltimore

IN SOME STATES, public corruption is more the bailiwick of municipal law enforcement than county sheriffs. Maryland would appear to be one of those states, though the Old Line State is not without its disreputable sheriffs' departments.

In February 2018, two members of an elite Baltimore plainclothes police unit were convicted of racketeering, robbery and fraud but not until one officer testified that he had stolen money with a detective later gunned down the day before he was scheduled to give his own testimony against his fellow officers.

The Gun Trace Task Force was disbanded in 2017 after some of its members were charged with robbing drug dealers, conducting illegal searches, claiming unearned overtime, and then attempting to cover up their illegal activities. Of eight members indicted, six pleaded guilty and four of those testified against the remaining two, Daniel Hersl, 48, and Marcus Taylor, 31, who were fired immediately after the verdicts came down. Two others who entered guilty pleas did not testify. Those pleading guilty included Thomas Allers, Momodu Gondo, Evodio Hendrix, Wayne Jenkins, Jemell Rayam, and Maurice Ward.[1]

The two-week federal trial produced testimony that exposed the depth of corruption within the unit charged with reducing the number of illegal guns on Baltimore streets. Testimony by the four who had agreed to testify revealed they stole hundreds of thousands of dollars in cash, drugs, guns, and luxury items, doing so under the guise of seizing the merchandise for legitimate enforcement purposes. They manufactured probable cause to chase and search suspects or to enter houses without proper warrants to go through goods they desired, covering up their involvement in car crashes when pursuits went south.²

Testimony also had offers peddling garbage bags filled with drugs looted during Baltimore's 2015 riots, selling seized drugs and guns, committing armed home invasions and carrying pellet guns to plant on suspects.

But Gondo provided the most drama when he testified that Detective Sean Suiter was among several officers who, along with Gondo, stole money in 2008 and 2009. Suiter was fatally shot with his own gun on Nov. 15, 2017, the day before he was scheduled to testify against the others. His killing has remained unsolved and Baltimore police officials have denied any evidence that he participated in the crime spree.³ But the exposure of the Gun Trace Task Force was just the culmination of a long string of Baltimore police corruption stories:

- 1999: An unidentified police officer provided warnings to bookmakers of search warrants and impending raids. No city officer was ever indicted in the matter.
- 2001: A secret Internal Affairs office that only a few in the department knew even existed was burglarized and ransacked. Sensitive information on up to six files involving police misconduct were compromised when they were stolen or tampered with, along with a list of citizens who had lodged complaints against officers. One file was that of an officer under investigation and who was later charged with falsely arresting a man on drug charges.
- 2003: A Baltimore police officer was indicted on charges of trying to alert suspected drug dealers of impending arrests during a sting operation.
- 2006: FBI agents arrested a pair of Baltimore officers for masterminding an illegal drug-dealing and robbery ring.
- 2012: An officer was suspended after a gun used to shoot a 13-year-old girl was found in his personal vehicle; another officer was charged with dealing heroin from a police precinct parking lot, and about 60 officers were implicated and fifteen were sentenced to federal prison terms when a kickback scheme was uncovered which revealed that officers were paid by an auto body shop to direct business to the shop. Some of the officers submitted fraudulent insurance claims and falsified police reports.
- 2013: A Baltimore officer was arrested on human trafficking charges

after his 19-year-old wife agreed to have sex for cash with an undercover officer;[4] Freddie Gray, a 25-year-old black man was arrested for possession of a "switchblade" which turned out to be legal. Forty-five minutes after being placed inside a police van, he was found unresponsive, his spinal cord nearly severed. After seven days in a coma, he died. Six officers were charged in his death but over a two-year period, four trials produced no convictions and charges were eventually dropped. Many top- ranking officials in the Baltimore Police Department, however, retired, quit or were fired and many inconsistencies in the official version of Gray's death have since been uncovered.[5]

All the problems with Baltimore Police notwithstanding, deputies from three separate Maryland county sheriffs' offices still managed to grab headlines for themselves.

In Frederick County, deputy Sam Allen Bowman, 41, was arrested in March 2011 for having sexual contact with a 14-year-old female student who attended the school where he was assigned as a resource officer. Court documents said he had an inappropriate relationship with the ninth-grade student, including having sex with her in his patrol car and in the girl's home. Sheriff Chuck Jinkins said the most shocking part to him "is that this is a person who was hired as a law enforcement officer, and in this case, someone who was trusted to protect students in the school system."[6]

In Carroll County, former sheriff's department major Nicholas Plazio entered a guilty plea to charges that he willfully and knowingly gave false information to the state's attorney office and gave false testimony in court in connection with a homicide case. He was given a one-year suspended prison sentence, three years supervised probation, and was ordered to pay a $5,000 fine and to complete 500 hours of community service.[7]

Kevin John Nagyiski, a 17-year Caroline County sheriff's deputy, was charged with sexual assault in March 2019. According to Sheriff Randy Bounds, the assault was said to have taken place on a boat in the Choptank River. The incident was referred to the Maryland Natural Resources Police.[8]

18

Massachusetts: Payroll Fraud, Theft, Extortion, Drugs, etc.

GETTING ELECTED as sheriff in one of Massachusetts's 14 counties is tantamount to a guarantee of a lifetime appointment, it must seem to some. Michael Ashe Jr., for example, retired in 2016 after 42 years – seven full six-year terms – and Berkshire County Sheriff Carmen Massimiano Jr. served 32 years and didn't step down until forced to do so for health reasons in 2010. He was succeeded by Detective Thomas Bowler who spent 24 years on the Pittsfield police force.

Extended tenures such as those of Massimiano and Ashe carry with them considerable power, say critics: power with little to no oversight. "I think there are sheriffs around the state who have built up empires, said State Rep. William "Smitty" Pignatalli. "I wouldn't call it abuse of power, but I would call it flexing of muscle."[1]

But the safeguard of job security can also lend itself to a false sense of invulnerability, as evidenced by the case of suspended Middlesex County Sheriff John McConigle, who was sentenced to nearly five years in prison on federal racketeering and tax evasion charges in February 1995.

McConigle, pleaded guilty in December 1994 to taking as much as $30,000 in illegal payments from deputies whose jobs he controlled. Judge Patti Saris sentenced him to 57 months in prison and ordered him to pay a fine of $10,000 and to serve two years' probation at the end of his prison time. He entered his guilty plea under an agreement whereby three additional extortion counts were dropped. He earlier was convicted of tax evasion. He initially claimed in his defense that what he had done was "acceptable because it's been done this way by others."[2]

From 1985 to 1993, McConigle was a fixture at Harvard as, astride a white horse, he led commencement at the school each June.[3]

Even though his conviction was in 1994, it took more than six years for the Massachusetts attorney general's office to get around to issuing a demand that the Middlesex County Retirement Board cease pension benefits for the convicted lawman. The local board had accepted the advice of retired district court Judge Paul Menton who said a state pension forfeiture law that required retirement board to deny or rescind pensions of any public employee convicted of a crime related to his or her duties was a violation of the First Amendment.[4]

A decade after McConigle's conviction, the Middlesex sheriff's office was back in the news with the arrest of Stephen Donnelly Jr., a former sheriff's captain on embezzlement and drug charges.

The 37-year-old Donnelly spent the morning of Nov. 22, 2004, in East Boston District Court where he entered a not guilty plea to charges that he sold cocaine to undercover state troopers across the street from a local high school which triggered additional charges because of the proximity to a school. Later that day, he stood accused of embezzling money from the Middlesex County Sheriff's Office during the time he worked there.

Donnelly's boss, Sheriff James DiPaola, initiated the investigation of the missing funds by retaining the services of national accounting firm DeLoitte & Touche to audit his office's books.[5]

Ironically, DiPaola himself would come under a corruption investigation that would end in tragedy after he became the subject of an ethics investigation. In November 2010, after being questioned by *The Boston Globe* about his plans to collect a state pension while continuing to serve as sheriff, he announced he would retire in January 2011.

A week later he was dead from a self-inflicted gunshot wound. DiPaola, 57, was found dead in a resort hotel room in Wells, Maine, after *The Globe* reported that he had implemented a scheme whereby he could collect $98,500 in retirement income in addition to his sheriff's salary of

$123,000, a move that, while legal, raised ethical questions. At the same time, a Boston television station aired a story that he had used political campaign funds for his personal use and that he had summoned sheriff's office employees to use official vehicles to give him rides on occasions when he had been drinking.

The next day, DiPaola acknowledged that the State Ethics Commission was investigating his office to determine whether workers in the sheriff's office raised money for his reelection, a practice forbidden by state law. First elected in 1996 in a special election, he was reelected to six- year terms in 1998, 2004 and 2010. Prior to his reelection, he had found a loophole in state law that allowed him to legally collect his salary and pension simultaneously.

After being confronted by *The Globe*, he had a change of heart, saying he didn't want his career to end in such a way. Instead, he announced despite just having won reelection, he would resign on Jan. 6. But his death on Nov. 27 changed those plans as well.[6]

Fourteen months after DiPaola's death, Massachusetts Attorney General Martha Coakley announced she was closing her "pay to play" investigation into public corruption that produced no criminal charges despite interviews of sheriff's employees that reveal a perception of favoritism of employees who made donations to DiPaola. Coakley's investigation, however, did result in an agreement by DiPaola's campaign treasurer Patricia Covelle to pay a $4,000 fine, that she turn over more than $295,000 in remaining campaign funds and that she never again work as the treasurer of any political committee.[7]

On Sept. 17, 1996, suspended Essex County Sheriff Charles Reardon pleaded guilty to federal influence-peddling charges in a plea agreement under which the government drooped other pending charges against him. He resigned from office the following day and was subsequently sentenced to a year and a day in federal prison.

Reardon and three aides were indicted on charges that Reardon took $3,600 in campaign contributions, charitable donations and tickets to entertainment events from a process-serving company that depended on the sheriff for $100,000 a year in business.[8]

In becoming the second Massachusetts sheriff in two years to plead guilty to corruption charges – Middlesex County Sheriff John McConigle was the other – Reardon issued a formal statement saying, "In light of my guilty plea, I feel I could no longer continue as an effective sheriff."[9]

Fifteen years later, the Essex County Sheriff's Office was again fending off negative publicity under a new sheriff, Frank Cousins.

Cousins, considered a rising star in the Massachusetts Republican Party, came under investigation by a Boston TV station over reports that he used intimidation to extract campaign contributions from employees of the sheriff's office. One unnamed employee told WBZ-TV, "You won't lose your job, but you won't get promoted, you won't get anywhere" if you don't contribute to Cousins' campaign. Between 2005 and February 2012, the date of the report, more than 300 department employees and their immediate family members had contributed more than $400,000 to Cousins.

The previous May, Cousins was fined $10,000 for accepting undocumented contributions to his campaign. While denying any wrongdoing, Cousins said following the report that he would no longer accept donations from union employees in his department. That reduced his donor pool from 502 to 27.[10]

The WBZ report was followed by a December 2017 report by the *Newbury Port Daily News* that Cousins encouraged more than 80 of his employees to call in sick on days when they were not ill, often using the time to work other jobs, and to claim holiday and vacation time to which they were not entitled. Over a seven-year stretch, from 2009 to 2016, a State Inspector General report said the practice cost state taxpayers nearly $1.1 million.

The report said Cousins authorized the sick leave abuse sometimes as a reward to "favored members of his staff," and at other times as part of deals with "problem employees" who had filed labor grievances against the department or threatened lawsuits. The report noted that work logs revealed sick time for some employees was entered into the system months in advance.

Even as the report was being prepared by the inspector general's office, the Greater Newburyport Chamber of Commerce was touting Cousins as the chamber's new president, effective Jan. 3, 2018.[11]

News reports in December 2020 revealed that Bristol County Sheriff Thomas Hodgson's office had illegally turned dogs on two dozen federal immigration detainees in May of that year. Massachusetts Attorney General Maura Healey's report said Hodgson's office displayed "callous disregard" for the detainees' well-being.

Healey's investigation learned that 25 detainees were inside Unit B of the Bristol detention center when ten detainees complained about potential contamination at the jail, where a number of staffers had tested positive for coronavirus. Hodgson rejected their request to be tested in the immigration facility because, he said, he was concerned they could infect their fellow residents. Attorneys for the detainees said they were attacked by dogs, pepper-sprayed and denied access to legal counsel. The detainees said it was Hodgson himself, along with his officers, who attacked first and that jail staff broke glass and caused damage to facilities.

Hodgson, described by *The Boston Globe* as a "fervent supporter" of immigration enforcement, in 2017 had offered inmate labor to build Donald Trump's wall on the U.S. border with Mexico.[12]

By May 20, 2021, exactly five months after Joe Biden was inaugurated as President, Hodgson's contract with the Immigration and Customs Enforcement (ICE) was terminated for its' "unacceptable" treatment of the prisoners. "[W]e will not tolerate the mistreatment of individuals in civil immigration detention or substandard conditions of detention," said Secretary of Homeland Security Alejandro Mayorkas.[13]

19

Michigan: Quotas and Bigotry

WHEN, IN THE DAYS leading up to the 2020 election, six militia members were arrested by federal authorities for plotting to kidnap Michigan Gov. Gretchen Whitmer, one Michigan sheriff took the unusual step of defending the plot, described as domestic terrorism.[1]

Barry County Sheriff Dar Leaf, himself a member of the Constitutional Sheriffs and Peace Officers Association, and who had refused to enforce Whitmer's social distancing guidelines as a means of mitigating the effects of the coronavirus pandemic, acknowledged he knew two of the men, brothers Michael and William Null. He described the pair as "nice and respectful." Leaf took it a step further when he suggested that the men might have been justified in their actions, apparently overlooking allegations that the group had planned on taking Whitmer to another state to put her on trial and to possibly execute her.[2]

Leaf had even shared a stage with William Null and was a guest speaker during an anti-shutdown protest in Grand Rapids in May 2020. He said at the time that the COVID-19 shutdown was comparable to being arrested and that the government was taking away people's free will.[3]

Grand Traverse County Sheriff Tom Bensley was approached by the Michigan Department of Transportation regarding safety concerns in a construction zone along a U.S. highway. Drivers, prohibited from making left turns in the construction zones, were cutting through private property and Bensley instructed his deputies to start issuing tickets.

But he didn't stop with those simple instructions. He told deputies that if they issued five citations in the stretch of road in question, he would give them a day off.

The only problem with that was that it was considered a quota and quotas are illegal.

"Today, the prosecutor told us that we went about this the wrong way," Bensley said, noting that tickets issued in the construction zone would be voided.[4]

This was a minor infraction, to be sure, when discussing corrupt or problem cops. *The Detroit Free Press* in 2017 conducted an in-depth investigation of the ability of problem cops to remain on Michigan streets. Its findings were disturbing. Twenty-six states may revoke an officer's license simply for misconduct but Michigan is one of 19 states that can only remove an officer for a felony conviction. The remaining five – California, New York, Massachusetts, Rhode Island and Hawaii – have no revocation authority in place for wayward cops.[5]

"Police officers are among the most protected public employees in the state," the paper reported. "Laws, unions, judges and city leaders where the cops work often shield their disciplinary records and, in some cases, basic information like their names. Judges overseeing civil lawsuits routinely agree to seal records."[6]

Officers who were terminated for offenses like having sex on duty, assaults, drugs, leaking information to felons, and other misconduct regularly turned up working for other law enforcement agencies. A deputy in Oakland County landed another job in law enforcement after being fired for his conduct during a narcotics investigation that resulted in prosecutors having to drop seventeen criminal cases. Another deputy in Eaton County who resigned when his run-in with a motorist was caught on video, was promptly hired by another sheriff's office that was aware of the earlier incident. William Melendez, known as "Robocop," beat a motorist so severely in 2015 that a Detroit judge handed down a prison sentence of from 13 months to ten years.

Like at least ten other cops who landed in trouble, Melendez was working for the Highland Park police department. Highland Park, population 11,000, is a suburb of Detroit and seems to be the landing spot for rogue cops. Former Gladwin County sheriff's deputy Eric Freier was one of those. Leaving after only three months with the sheriff's department, he popped up in Ann Arbor for 18 years, Fowlerville for seven months and Highland Park for a year-and-a-half before getting into a fight with bouncers at a nightclub.

Tiffany Lipkovitch worked for the Wayne County Sheriff's Office for ten years, from May 30, 2000, until May 24, 2010, before she was shown the door following accusations of assisting felons in state prisons who were accused of smuggling drugs. She was hired by Highland Park on November of 2011 and was still with the department at the time of the *Free Press* stories.[7]

Accidentally exposed court records supposedly revealed the names of several officials, including Wayne County Sheriff Benny Napoleon, who were targets of a federal investigation. But less than two weeks after the late December 2017 revelation, Napoleon denied that he was a target. Napoleon, a former Detroit police chief and sheriff since 2009, said he was unaware he was named in a court filing which was temporarily unsealed in federal court.[8]

But by August 2018, Napoleon, who ran unsuccessfully for mayor of Detroit, was back in the news with reports of his misuse of campaign funds. *The Detroit Metro Times* reported that the sheriff had spent $27,071 on Detroit Lions tickets, $4,745 at a Washington, D.C. steakhouse, and $3,934 at an upscale hotel in San Francisco, continuing a trend of at least six years in which he was found to have spent campaign funds on hotels, concerts and sporting event tickets, a massage parlor in California and a strip club in Chicago. He even spent $521 on a single Uber ride. Other expenditures included $541 for tabs at Hooters, $4,353 on dry cleaning, $7,096 on florists, $1,440 at the Detroit Yacht Club, $1,379 at Best Buy, and $1,502 at Bed Bath & Beyond.

Campaign funds were also used for a gym membership, for payments to SiriusXM, and ClubCorp., a Dallas-based operation of private golf clubs.

Despite Michigan Campaign Finance Network Director Simon Schuster's assertion that the expenditures constituted "some of the most egregious misuse I've personally seen, Napoleon defended the expenditures were "work-related or campaign-related." The expenditures for sporting events, for example, were work-related, he said, because he had to show his support for local teams. "They are in Wayne County, and they are sports teams, and I support them. I need to be seen supporting the sports teams in the county."

He said he conducted business over lunch and dinner and that he refused to accept a free meal. "I don't take free shit," he said. "It gets you in prison."[9]

Complete autonomy notwithstanding, the Jackson County Board of Commissioners wasn't bluffing when it threatened in January 2019 to yank Sheriff Steven Rand's county-owned vehicle and nearly $11,000 a year in benefits unless he resigned by May 1.

The official threat was made after Rand was named in a federal lawsuit accusing him of being a "multi-faceted bigot" because of his derogatory remarks about women, blacks, the LGBT community and anyone else he found who didn't measure up to his discriminatory standards.

Among the allegations against him in the lawsuit, filed in February 2018, were claims that he called a county judge a "scatter-brained cunt," referred to a black former deputy a "dumb nigger," and labeled black suspects in a criminal case as "fucking monkeys."

Besides his vehicle, specific benefits taken away from Rand included:

- Medical insurance – Rand paid $4,529 per year in premiums and the county paid $8,071;
- Short-term disability insurance – Rand paid $83 per year and the county paid $78 dollars;
- Long-term disability insurance – the county paid $2,393 per year;
- Basic life insurance – the county paid one $135 per year;
- 2017 Ford Interceptor – the county paid $32,311 for the vehicle in 2017.

Rand purchased five months' retirement in March 2017 for almost $16,000, making him eligible for full retirement as early as March 4, 2018. After having received a 22 percent raise in January 2017, his salary was $107,000 per year.[38]

In January 2021, Judge Stephanie Dawkins-Davis of Michigan's Eastern District Federal Court granted a partial dismissal of the suit against Rand who, by that time had stepped down. Judge Dawkins-Davis allowed the county's litigation against the former sheriff to proceed, however.[39]

20

Minnesota: No Discipline for Rogue Officers

JACK KEECH, for eight years the sheriff of Watonwan County, admitted to authorities on Sept. 15, 2017, that he once inappropriately touched a juvenile girl while he was giving her a massage. He reportedly admitted he did so intentionally, knowing it was wrong, but denied ever abusing a second, younger girl. The 83-year-old Keech was found dead later that same day, the victim of an apparent suicide.

Investigator Brian Martin wrote in his report that he would have recommended that Keech be charged with two counts of criminal sexual conduct after a sheriff's investigator interviewed both girls on Sept. 6. The girls, by then teenagers, told the investigator that Keech had molested them multiple times when they were visiting his home in Madelia when one was in the fourth grade and the other in the second. The abuse had occurred over several years, they said, but family members had not believed them.

One of the girls said Keech also requested that she touch him and that he forced her to look at pornography. The other child said Keech once told her he wished she was older and that he was younger so they could get married.

Years before George Floyd's death at the hands of Minneapolis police, Police Chief Medaria "Rondo" Arradondo met with community activists who urged him to adopt a peer intervention training program developed by the New Orleans Police Department designed to redefine police culture and to prevent the very actions that result in Floyd's tragic death.

The program, called Ethical Policing Is Courageous (EPIC) was never adopted and the image of officer Derek Chauvin's knee on Floyd's neck touched off days of demonstrations and rioting by Blacks fed up with bearing the brunt of overzealous police misconduct. EPIC was born of a federal consent decree in 2016 after widespread misconduct was uncovered inside the New Orleans Police Department and the program was soon being considered in Baltimore, Washington, D.C., Philadelphia, Fayetteville, N.C., Boston, and Wilmington, Del.

Basically, EPIC is designed for officers to intervene when they witness another officer engaging in excessive force on someone. Jonathan

Aronie, who oversees the New Orleans consent decree, said there was "no guarantee," but had EPIC been in place in May 2020, "it is more likely that Mr. Floyd would be alive today. The officers on the scene would have felt empowered to take action, they would have been more confident to take action, and they would be more likely to take action."[2]

And while municipal police departments are separate from sheriff's departments in both their origins and their missions, they are inextricably linked in the minds of John Q. Citizen because of the way personnel move from one to the other with such apparent ease. To the casual citizen observer, authority is authority and there are really no lines of distinction to be drawn in the layman's eyes.

Where 26 states may revoke an officer's license for misconduct, Minnesota, like Michigan and 18 other states, has no procedure in place to pull a rogue law enforcement officer's license short of the officer's being convicted of a felony. That makes it difficult to hold officers to a higher standard and in turn allows wayward cops to escape state discipline and should they be fired from one agency, often turn up working for another one in a nearby county or municipality.

Take Richard Ohren, for example. A deputy with the Mahnomen County Sheriff's Office, he first came to the attention of the Peace Officer Standards and Training (POST) Board's attention way back in 1998 when he was convicted of DWI and disorderly conduct. The board suspended his license for three years but following his reinstatement, he received a second DWI in 2000 and a third in 2015. He pleaded guilty to misdemeanor drunken driving, but that offense does not trigger a POST Board review. The county fired him nonetheless and he and the police union fought the case and in 2016, an arbitrator ordered Mahnomen County to reinstate him. Adding insult to injury, the county was forced to apply for a state waiver so that he could drive public vehicles without an ignition interlock device, which he is required to have on his personal vehicle.

And then there's the case of Michael Ficken. While on duty and in his Prior Lake Police Department uniform, he kicked in his ex-fiancée's locked bedroom door and verbally assaulted the woman and a companion. He was subsequently convicted of disorderly conduct and fourth-degree property damage. The Prior Lake police chief fired him but the Post Board didn't take action on his case because it doesn't consider such misdemeanors grounds for discipline. He next turned up as a deputy for the McKenzie County Sheriff's Office in North Dakoka.[3]

21

Mississippi: Sheriff Hobbs and the Dixie Mafia

ANY DISCUSSION of sheriffs and corruption in Mississippi has to begin with the so-called Dixie Mafia and former Harrison County Sheriff Leroy Hobbs, Sr.

Founded in the 1940s, the Dixie Mafia was a loose collection of car thieves, drug dealers, bootleggers, pimps, gamblers, con artists and ruthless killers scattered throughout the southern states from Texas to Florida and into the Carolinas, Virginia, Arkansas and Tennessee. Headquartered in Biloxi, it hit its stride in the 1960s under the loose leadership of Mike Gillich. With no connections to the more infamous La Costa Nostra, its members are neither "family," nor of any particular ethnic lineage.[1]

Hobbs was first elected sheriff in 1971 and remained in office 12 years before being arrested on June 16, 1983 for bribery, extortion, conspiracy to commit murder and conspiracy to import and distribute cocaine. He was convicted of racketeering in 1984 and sentenced to 20 years in prison. He served almost 12 years in prison before his release.

It was during and immediately following Hobbs's reign as Harrison County's top cop that the Mississippi Gulf Coast went through some of its most tumultuous times that included a bogus lonely-hearts club run out of Louisiana's Angola State Penitentiary and the brutal murder of a state circuit judge and his wife, a candidate for mayor of Biloxi at the time of their deaths.

But the murders occurred after Hobbs had already entered a federal prison, so what was his connection to their deaths?

For the answer to that question, you have to start with retired FBI Special Agent Keith Bell, who says the level of corruption in Biloxi and Harrison County was so "out of control" that federal authorities in 1983 designated the entire Harrison County Sheriff's Office as a criminal enterprise. "They were doing anything and everything illegal down here," Bell, who grew up on the Gulf Coast, said. "For money, the sheriff and officers loyal to him would release prisoners from the county jail, safeguard drug shipments and hide fugitives. Anything you can think of, they were involved in," he said.[2]

Around this same time, Dixie Mafia prisoners incarcerated at Angola were running a multi-million-dollar scam from within prison walls in the form of a "lonely hearts" club aimed specifically at gays from as far away as New Zealand who would give prisoners Kirksey McCord Nix and Bobby Joe Fabian money which was entrusted to their attorney Pete Halat back in Biloxi. Halat, who spent the money, blamed his former law partner, Circuit Judge Vincent Sherry, of stealing the funds which resulted in a contract being put out on Sherry and his wife, mayoral candidate Margaret Sherry, who were gunned down in their home on Sept. 14, 1987.

Hobbs, meanwhile, was experiencing his own legal problems. Four years earlier, on June 16, 1983, six months into his final year in office, a federal task force apprehended him, his chief deputy Craig Monroe and eight others as they waited on a farm in north-central Harrison County for what he anticipated to be an airdrop of cocaine. The farm was owned by Dixie Mafia member D.J. Venus, III, one of those also arrested that night. The airdrop was a sham, a sting by federal agents. That incident led to his 20-year prison sentence.[3]

In addition to the charges for which he was convicted, Hobbs was also accused of offering protection in the contract killing of strip-club owner and alleged Dixie Mafia member Dewey D'Angelo and of plotting to assassinate then-Gulfport Police Chief Larkin Smith to prevent Smith from running against Hobbs for sheriff. He was never officially charged for either, however.

If observers thought that was the last they'd heard from Hobbs, they were mistaken.

Seven years later, in January 2007, the 72-year-old former sheriff and pal of New Orleans crime boss Carlos Marcello, filed papers to run for his old job, saying his prior arrest and conviction "was all political."[4] But it was not to be. Melvin T. Brisolara was elected over Hobbs and incumbent George Payne. Hobbs died on March 3, 2008 of natural causes.[5]

The incumbent he was running against the previous year had his own problems. In August 2007, a federal jury convicted former corrections officer Ryan Michael Teel for his part in abusing inmates at the Harrison County Adult Detention Center in Gulfport. Teel was convicted of conspiracy to violate the civil rights of inmates, specifically in connection with the beating death of prisoner Jessie Lee Williams, Jr. in February 2006. Williams died from severe brain trauma after he was beaten by Teel in the jail's booking room. Teel was also convicted of obstructing justice by writing a false report in an attempt to cover up the Williams beating.

In all, eight corrections officers pleaded guilty to civil rights violations pursuant to the federal investigation. Former Deputies Dedri Yulon Caldwell, Daniel Lamont Evans, William Jeffrey Priest, Karl Walter Stolze, Morgan Lee Thompson, and Preston Thomas Wills all pleaded guilty to conspiring to abuse inmates at the jail. Former Deputies Regina Lynn Rhodes and Timothy Brandon Moore also pleaded guilty to civil rights crimes and obstruction of justice.[6]

Teel was given two life sentences by U.S. District Judge Louis Gulrola in November 2007.[7] In the civil lawsuit that followed, Harrison County agreed to a $3.5 million wrongful death settlement with Williams's family.[8]

Even though Sheriff Payne cooperated with investigators and was not charged, it's difficult to imagine such widespread abuse was occurring in his department without his knowledge. And while he was not directly implicated in the abuse, the investigation and convictions must surely have contributed to his defeat by Brisolara.

Right down U.S. 190 from Harrison County is Jackson County, Mississippi. It's where singer Jimmy Buffett grew up in county seat Pascagoula. It's also where Sheriff Mike Byrd found himself in deep trouble with the feds. Even the conservative *Christian Science Monitor* was given to acknowledging the extent of power – and abuse – under which America's sheriffs operate in a story it did on Byrd in 2013, noting that he joined "dozens of sheriffs from New Mexico to Georgia who have faced indictments for malfeasance while in office over the last decade for everything from destroying incriminating court documents to murder."[9]

Byrd was initially indicted by the State of Mississippi on 31 counts, including fraud, embezzlement and extortion. He was accused of abusing the power of his office by refusing to pay for lawnmower repair, ordering surveillance on a man who objected to the location of a hotel in Ocean Springs, dispatching deputies to stake out a Mexican restaurant because it refused to accept a check from him, and of ordering a detective to file murder charges against an innocent man for political purposes, specifically that the four-term sheriff was running for re-election and wanted to boast that there were no unsolved murders in his county.[10]

A breakdown of the charges included ten counts of embezzlement, ten counts of fraud, two counts of hindering prosecution in the second degree, two counts of tampering with a witness, one count of perjury, two counts of attempted subornation of perjury, two counts of intimidating an officer in the discharge of his duties, and two counts of extortions.[11]

But the charges against him soon escalated to federal offenses. He admitted he twice kicked a patrol car theft suspect in the groin after the man was handcuffed and "unresisting." He further ordered a deputy to delete his patrol car's dashcam footage of the assault and later ordered an employee to drill a hole in his hard drive to ensure no one could ever recover any data from Byrd's office computer. Byrd resigned from office on Dec. 11, 2013, after pleading guilty to one count of witness tampering in federal court and to one count of witness intimidation in state court in exchange for the dismissal of the remaining twenty-nine counts. He was sentenced to six months of house arrest, three years of post-release supervision, $5,000 in fines and ordered to pay an additional $5,000 in investigative costs.

But even then, his troubles were far from over. Former deputy Kristan Seibert filed a sexual harassment lawsuit against Byrd, claiming unwanted touching by Byrd and solicitations of oral sex. When she rejected his advances, she was transferred to a remote outpost and Byrd later texted her with the message, "In life, there are winners and losers and you have to pick sides. If you pick the losing side, you die." He would ultimately be ordered to pay $260,000 in damages to Seibert.[12]

Occasionally, sheriffs and sheriffs' deputies get into trouble for actions outside the scope of their official duties.

Forrest County is home to the University of Southern Mississippi in Hattiesburg, a couple of counties north of Harrison County. Chief Deputy Charles Bolton was terminated in September 2016 after he and his wife Linda were convicted of five counts each of filing false federal income tax returns. Bolton was also found guilty on four counts of tax evasion in connection to returns filed for tax years 2009-13.[13]

The Boltons allegedly received food stolen from the jail which was subsequently used at a restaurant the couple owned. Additionally, they were accused of attempting to conceal income by cashing tens of thousands of dollars in checks purportedly issued in payment for liquor, wine and catering services to prevent those payments from being recorded on the business's bank statements.

Charles Bolton was sentenced to 45 months in prison for tax evasion and filing false tax reports. His wife received a 30-month sentence. Additionally, Charles Bolton and Linda Bolton were fined $10,000 and $6,000, respectively. The couple was also ordered to make restitution to the Internal Revenue Service in the amount of $145,849.78.

Jerry Woodland also was sentenced to a year in prison and three years of post-release supervision for his part in the scheme. He also was ordered to repay $443,395.61 to the Forrest County Board of Supervisors. He and fellow jail employee Allen Haralson were accused of mail fraud for drafting and submitting purchase requisition forms for food and food-related items that were "purchased by invoices and payments sent through the United States Postal Service or other common carriers," according to their indictment. Haralson pleaded guilty in November 2014, but died before he could be sentenced.[14]

Charles Rinehart, who served as sheriff of Alcorn County from 2008 to 2015, was sentenced to 20 years in prison but had that sentence reduced to two years' house arrest in December 2016 after he and two others pleaded guilty to conspiracy to defraud and fraud against the county in a case stemming from the purchase of several vehicles by the sheriff's department.

Rinehart had purchased six autos from a used car dealership run by Teddy and Pamela Denise Null. An investigation that resulted in the arrest of the three in June 2015 revealed that the Nulls created fraudulent quotes from other dealers which were then submitted to the Alcorn County Board of Supervisors. Both Nulls also received 20-year sentences but Teddy Null's sentence, like that of Rinehart, was reduced to two-years' house arrest while Denise Null's sentence was lowered to one-year house arrest.[15]

Besides the apparent bid manipulations, State Auditor Stacey Pickering said the cars were salvaged vehicles and may have been rebuilt with stolen parts. The conditions of the salvaged cars were not disclosed to the county, he added.

Four days before his June 23 arrest, Rinehart was issued an unrelated civil demand for more than $181,000 for funds his department allegedly misappropriated in connection with the Alcorn County Regional Correctional Facility's Technology Fund, the Alcorn County Sheriff's Commissary Account, and the Alcorn County Regional Correctional Facility.[16]

Pickering applauded the sentences, saying no one was above the law. But given the light sentences in such a case of public corruption when compared the more severe penalties imposed for lesser crimes committed by those not in a position of influence, one has to wonder about the supposed even-handedness of justice.

Bobbie Gentry made the Tallahatchie Bridge famous with her 1967 blockbuster hit *Ode to Billie Joe*. Half-a-century later, a former sheriff would attract legal attention of another description to the county of the same name.

William Brewer, for 21 years the sheriff of Tallahatchie County, was arrested in August 2018 and charged with allowing the robbery of a drug dealer and for drug distribution in exchange for bribes over a 15-year period. He entered a guilty plea to extorting a bribe in April 2019 and was sentenced to a six-year federal prison term.

Evidence shows that a drug dealer informed Brewer of plans to rob another dealer of drugs and cash and Brewer did nothing to stop the robbery. The robbery took place and the perpetrator, who cooperated with the FBI in its investigation, paid Brewer $6,500 of the money taken. In addition to the six-year prison term, Brewer was also ordered to serve three years of supervised probation following his release and to forfeit $42,500.[17]

Just a couple of counties to the southeast of Tallahatchie lies Webster County where Sheriff Tim Mitchell pleaded guilty to two counts of trafficking in stolen firearms and two counts of embezzlement less than two months after Brewer's conviction. He was sentenced to 15 years' imprisonment in July 2019, seven months after his arrest and a month after his guilty plea. He was originally indicted on ten counts that also included charges of seeking sex from two female county jail inmates, ordering deputies to steal guns and drugs from evidence, and threatening to bury a subordinate if she told anyone.

Two others were also accused of abetting Mitchell. Former Chief Deputy Landon Griffin was arrested on two counts each of embezzlement and trafficking firearms, and former jailer Santana Monshea Townsend was charged with two counts of sexual activity with an inmate, furnishing contraband to an inmate, and sale and possession of a controlled substance.[18]

Mississippi is unique in that convicted felons can – and do – get themselves elected sheriffs. It happened not once, but three times in the

Magnolia State in 1995. In each case, the candidates were allowed to take advantage of a legal loophole that allows those convicted of federal crimes or certain state crimes prior to November 1992 to be elected to public office.

Jacob Cartlidge was elected sheriff of Sharkey County in the Mississippi Delta in 1995 despite having served a year in a federal penitentiary for taking bribes from undercover DEA agents posing as drug dealers in 1986. Cartlidge did not explain how he could serve as sheriff when he was prohibited by law, as a convicted felon, from carrying a weapon.[19]

He was Sheriff Joe Ford's chief deputy back then but because Ford was also a full-time farmer, he delegated the authority to run the office and supervise four other deputies to Cartlidge. When Neal Wade, a local known user of controlled substances, told Mississippi Bureau of Narcotics agent Bill Marshall that Cartlidge had solicited money from Wade in return for providing protection for drug deals, Marshall equipped Wade with a wire monitor for a meeting with Cartlidge.

Marshall and another agent heard Cartlidge demand $500 a month for protection. Two days later, Wade, again wearing a wire, paid Cartlidge $250 provided him by the agents. Eventually, Cartlidge was introduced to the two agents who told the deputy that he would be paid $1,000 to protect planes flying thousand- pound loads of marijuana into Sharkey County. Cartlidge was paid $500 with a promise of another $500 when the first load arrived.[20]

Gary Mauney was elected sheriff of Tippah County on November 7, 1995, despite having been convicted in 1974 of selling amphetamines. He was given a one-year suspended sentence at the time. The same judge who heard his case, by then retired, had his record expunged in 1995, just six months before his election, retroactive to 1976 and another judge issued him a certificate of rehabilitation which, unlike Cartlidge, allowed him to carry a weapon.

The Mississippi Supreme Court ruled on February 26, 1998, that "The fact that his sentence was suspended does not remove his conviction from the status of an infamous crime." Based on that interpretation, the state's high court upheld a lower court decision disqualifying Mauney from holding office.[21]

The case of Warren County Sheriff Paul Barrett did not involve drugs but was considered more serious than those of Cartlidge or Mauney because he had commissioned Virginia resident J.C. Herbert Bryant as a

Warren County deputy sheriff and Bryant had ingratiated himself with the U.S. Marshal's Service. Bryant was co-founder of the Armored Response Group of the United States (ARGUS), a company established to provide military armaments to local sheriffs' departments in times of urban uprisings.

ARGUS had indirect ties to then Vice-President George H.W. Bush and National Security Advisor Oliver North and his Iran-Contra operation. Barrett would be convicted on two counts of making "a false material declaration" under oath to federal agents (see chapter on Virginia).

Barrett's conviction was eventually overturned on appeal.[22] He died on July 1, 2014.

The Noxubee County Sheriff's Office settled a lawsuit filed in 2020 by a woman incarcerated at the jail who said deputies gave her special privileges in exchange for sex. Elizabeth Layne Reed claimed in her petition that deputies Vance Phillips and Damon Clark provided her with a cellphone and other perks, including a sofa in her cell in exchange for sexual encounters with her.

She claimed that then-Sheriff Terry Grassaree was aware of the arrangement but did nothing to stop them. She said that initially, the liaisons took place outside the jail but eventually moved to the jail's interrogation room and even her cell.

Additionally, she said that Grassaree "sexted" her, demanding that she use the phone deputies had provided her to send him "a continuous stream of explicit videos, photographs and texts" and touched her in a "sexual manner" while she was in jail.

Grassaree, who was defeated for reelection in 2019, was named defendant in an earlier lawsuit, in 2007, by four former inmates who accused the sheriff of violence, including claims that he choked or beat them while there were in his custody. One plaintiff said he pinned her against a wall and threatened to let a male inmate rape her.

In 2006, when jail cell keys were left hanging openly on a wall, male inmates opened the doors to the cell of two women inmates and raped them, according to claims the women made. One of the women said Grassaree subsequently pressured her to sign a false statement to cover up the rapes, according to a state police report that, inexplicitly, was never made public.

In all, at least eight men, including four deputies and Grassaree himself, have been accused of sex abuse of women inmates who were being held in the jail during Grassaree's tenure. A federal indictment accused the former sheriff of committing bribery in 2019, near the end of his second – and last – term, and of lying to federal agents when he was questioned about whether he requested sexually explicit photos and videos from Reed.[23]

Despite the years of complaints against Grassaree, no higher authority has ever reviewed how he ran his jail or whether his policies endangered women because, like so many other states, Mississippi leaves rural sheriffs to police themselves and their jails with no outside authority, all of which raised another issue.

Calling county supervisors "willfully blind," Jackson attorney Ron Welch, who represents inmates in Mississippi jails who filed a class action suit more than half-a-century ago against the superintendent of the Mississippi State Penitentiary at Parchman.

Saying that there was no system of inspections of jails, Welch said, "It's giving sheriffs a free pass. They can do as they wish."

An investigation by the Mississippi Center for Investigative Reporting at *Mississippi Today* and *The New York Times* indicated that in addition to the lack of inspections, there is a chronic lack of oversight in that no state regulator has the authority to fine a sheriff for endangering people in custody or for failing to train staff who operate the jails.[24]

22

Missouri: Suicide, a Threesome, and a Fry Cook Sheriff

THE DECADE from 2011 to 2019 was an especially bad one for eight Missouri sheriffs.

The story actually begins as early as 2008, when 28-year-old Tommy Adams decided to challenge incumbent Carter County Sheriff Greg Melton. Only weeks before the election Melton, who was rumored to be corrupt and into methamphetamine use, was found in his garage with a bullet in his brain. His death was ruled a suicide.

That left Adams, who had previously worked as a fry cook, an auto mechanic and the one-man, part-time police department for the town of Ellsinore (pop. 446), head of a three-man sheriff's department with the responsibility for the safety of the county's 500-square miles and its 6,265 residents.

It didn't take long for rumors about Adams to surface. Rarely showing up for work, he began spending on cars, building a cabin in the woods and paying for expensive elective medical procedures – on a meager salary of $37,000. His relationship with a local meth kingpin raised eyebrows, especially when Adams hired the man's daughter, Steffanie Kearbey, as a deputy despite her lack of experience in law enforcement. She would eventually be arrested for her part in assisting Adams in stealing and selling guns from the sheriff's office's evidence room.

Adams himself would be arrested in April 2011 in a drug sting and it was revealed that he was involved in meth use.[1]

He was sentenced in July 2012 to ten years in federal prison on two felony counts of possession of stolen firearms and a single felony count of sale of a stolen firearm and Kearbey received a sentence of five years.[2]

Eight months after Adams's arrest, Perry County Sheriff Keith Kellerman, who had been sheriff since 1998, was cited by police after being caught engaging in sex with another man in a parked vehicle.[3]

In May 2017, former Mississippi County, Missouri, Sheriff Cory Hutcheson's peace officer license was revoked at the request of Attorney General Josh Hawley. Three months after that, a federal grand jury returned a 28-count indictment on charges from fraud to assault to his involvement in an inmate's death, and in another year, he was sentenced to six months in federal prison.[4]

It was a quick fall from grace for Hutcheson who in 2016, was elected after promising to clean up crime in the county of 14,000 people in southeastern Missouri. Hutcheson, 34, was already facing robbery charges and a wrongful death suit when he was indicted. He had served as a sheriff's deputy prior to his election as the county's top cop.

Federal prosecutors said that over a three-year period from when Hutcheson was a deputy through the first few months during his tenure as sheriff, he uploaded fraudulent documents to a law enforcement database in order to obtain the location by "pinging" of more than 200 cellphone users, including a judge, a former sheriff and several other law enforcement officials.[5]

He pleaded guilty to two charges: wire fraud and identity theft. He resigned following his guilty plea and was forbidden from ever working in law enforcement again.

During his brief tenure as sheriff, two prisoners died in custody and another prisoner who gave birth to a stillborn baby while shackled. One of those deaths resulted in a $270,000 settlement with the prisoner's family. In the other custody death, Hutcheson gave a "burner" cell phone to a deputy so they could coordinate their stories in an effort to avoid liability.[6]

Jackson County, Missouri, is the home of Independence and its favorite son, former President Harry Truman. Christine Lynde was an administrative assistant in the sheriff's office there. The beneficiary of several promotions and pay raises, she became the highest-paid civilian employee in the department and received perks not available to other county employees, including a bi-weekly $240 car allowance and permission to work from home. She made frequent trips courtesy of Jackson County taxpayers.

The only problem with that was she was also the girlfriend of Sheriff Mike Sharp and the pair had an ongoing romantic and financial relationship. They even owned a house together and Sharp, Lynde and the sheriff's ex-wife had sex together – all while Lynde had a harassment lawsuit pending against the county, a suit that cost Jackson County more than $325,000. When details of their relationship became public, Sharp resigned on April 19, 2018.[7]

Like Sharp, Texas County, Missouri, Sheriff James Sigman had an ongoing romantic relationship with a subordinate that would ultimately cost him his job. Unlike Sharp, however, the Texas County sheriff and his girlfriend Lt. Jennifer Tomaszewski were arrested for assault, robbery, child endangerment, unlawful use of a weapon, harassment, abusing prisoners and misuse of official information by a public servant. Additionally, Tomaszewski was charged with misrepresenting herself as a peace officer and putting residents at risk. Both were married to someone else while involved in their romantic relationship.

More than one-fourth of sheriff's office employees were fired or quit during the months leading up to the pair's indictment on July 2018.[8]

A Missouri Highway Patrol trooper reported that Tomaszewski struck a man with the mental capacity of a nine-year-old in the face with her elbow after he was already unconscious, saying that she was "trying to bust his eardrum out." "If we hadn't been there, they would have killed that boy," a deputy said. "He was completely unconscious and his lips were turning blue."[9]

Sigman was present at the time and reports about what occurred were removed from the inmate's file as was a grievance filed by an inmate after Tomaszewski threatened to put a bullet in his head.

She also went on ride-alongs, acted as an undercover officer during stings and served search warrants, detained suspects, searched residences and performed duties reserved for commissioned officers. Occasionally, she would be armed with an AR-15 rifle issued to Sigman and she wore a uniform that was indistinguishable from that of other deputies.

Once, while serving a search warrant, she pointed a firearm at several subjects, including a one-year-old who lived across the street from the residence being searched after she confronted the residents because she thought they were video recording officers and taking pictures under the mistaken assumption that video and photos were not allowed.

One officer said that he pushed her away when he observed her pointing a gun at the back of a man as she was attempting to handcuff him while he was lying on the ground.[10]

On Feb. 9, 2016, Former Saline County Sheriff Wallace Newman George, Jr., age 70, pleaded guilty to a single count of stealing from an organization that receives federal funds.

First appointed acting sheriff in November 1979, he was elected to a full term the following month and held the office for 36 years to become the longest-serving sheriff in Missouri history until his resignation the day before his guilty plea.

George would assign deputies to transport prisoners extradited or voluntarily returned from outside Saline County between Jan. 28, 2010, to June 30, 2015, and then submit claims for reimbursement for himself. Checks paid George totaled $97,083, of which about 75 percent, or $71,994 was for mileage with the remainder being for meals and other expenses. He paid $51,162 in restitution to Saline County and $27,749 to the state.[11]

He was sentenced to nine months in Federal Prison Camp, a minimum-security facility in Yankton, South Dakota.[12]

For Lincoln County Sheriff's Detective Scott Edwards, the punishment was considerably worse. But then, so was the crime. Edwards was indicted on November 8, 2011, by a federal grand jury on sexual abuse and sexual contact charges.

The Lincoln County Drug Court had contracts with the sheriff's office to employ part-time "drug court trackers" to monitor the whereabouts and curfews of drug court participants. Edwards, one of those who served as a "drug tracker" until his termination in December 2010, was accused of aggravated sexual abuse of two of the female victims and of engaging in acts that included sexual contact with three others. Additionally, the indictment said Edwards restrained and confined one of the female victims by force, intimidation and deception.The victims were under the court-ordered supervision of Edwards, age 50, who used his official position to commit acts of sexual assault, prosecutors said. He pleaded guilty in July 2012 to two felony counts of deprivation of rights including aggravated sexual abuse, a single felony count of deprivation of rights including kidnapping, and two misdemeanor counts of deprivation of rights including sexual contact. He was sentenced to ten years in prison followed by three years' supervised release.[13]

A Nodaway County, Missouri homeschooling family reached an out-of-court settlement with the local sheriff's office after Sheriff Darren White and Chief Sheriff's Deputy David Glidden raided their home without a warrant, tasered and pepper-sprayed the couple and their dog, and threatened to shoot the family dog, all over the family's refusal to submit an inspection of their home.

The Nodaway County Sheriff's Department had been summoned on Sept. 30, 2011, after Laura and Jason Hagan declined a request by a child protective service caseworker to conduct a follow up inspection of a report of a messy house.

When White and Glidden showed up without a court order, they, too, were denied entrance to the Hagan home. As Jason Hagan turned to go back inside, Glidden sprayed him with pepper spray at the back of his head and then directly to his face. He then sprayed Laura Hagan. He then shot Jason Hagan in the back with his taser. As he fell, Laura closed the front door. Sheriff White then came to the door and with Glidden, forced the front door open to find the couple lying on the floor. Glidden then proceeded to spray Laura in the face a second time and Glidden slapped her, knocking her glasses off, as White sprayed Jason. The officers then sprayed the family dog and threatened to shoot the animal if it didn't stop barking.

Finally, White and Glidden handcuffed and arrested the couple, charging them with resisting arrest and child endangerment – all in the presence of the Hagans' three young children who were transported to a hospital emergency room for evaluation for exposure to prepper spray, thus raising the question of just who was actually endangering the children, ages eight through 12.

All charges against the Hagans were subsequently dismissed by a judge who wrote in his ruling, "The State has not offered sufficient, if indeed any, evidence of an exception that would justify a warrantless entry. The court will not allow [an] exception to sanction warrantless entry into a private residence by pepper spray and taser. If the officer had a warrant in hand and such force was necessary, that is a different story, but those are not the facts of this case."[14]

23

Montana: Sex Scandals and a Write-In Winner

IN ONE OF THE more bizarre sheriff elections ever in the State of Montana, a write-in candidate was elected sheriff of Valley County after sex scandals doomed two other candidates.

Sheriff's deputy Tom Boyer entered the race as a write-in candidate in August 2013 and quickly gained the endorsements of several former sheriffs, including longtime former sheriff Glen Meier. He defeated Glasgow police officer Joe Horn, the only one of his two opponents who remained in the race.

Horn, who had pointed to his 27 years' experience in law enforcement, including 14 years with the Glasgow Police Department, was accused of sexual and physical abuse by two of his daughters.

The third candidate, former Undersheriff Luke Strommen, dropped out of the race in August after the Montana Department of Justice's Division of Criminal Investigation charged him with sexual abuse of a child.[2]

Strommen was convicted of raping a teen in July 2020 after his victim testified that he had raped her about 50 times between 2009 and 2011, beginning when she was 14 years of age. She testified that most of the encounters occurred in Strommen's patrol car while he was on duty and in uniform.[3]

He had previously been charged with having a sexual relationship with a 17-year-old girl and of transferring sexual images. In October 2019, he entered a guilty plea to one count of sexual abuse of children for soliciting a 17-year-old to email him sexually explicit images.[4]

In Lake County, in Northeast Montana, the outcome of charges lodged against the local sheriff's office was either a lot of smoke and mirrors or a coverup of major proportions that extended all the way to the State Capital in Helena.

When drawn-out investigations by the Montana Attorney General's Office, the Montana Police Standards and Training (POST) Commission and Montana Fish, Wildlife and Parks failed to produce the desired results of whistleblowers, they filed a lawsuit against Sheriff Jay Doyle and three of his officers, Undersheriff Dan Yonkin and officers Dan Duryee and Mike Sargeant.

By the time the dust had settled over the charges of poaching, lying about military experience (probably the more serious of the charges, it would turn out), an illegal search, obstruction of justice, and lying about experience, two deputies would resign after the attorney general's office found no reason to prosecute those accused.

Deputies Ben Woods and Patrick O'Connor were cited by the attorney general's office. In a twist to the plot, Woods was one of those filing the lawsuit but the attorney general's office implicated him in illegally recording conversations with Doyle and Sargeant, but declined to prosecute him.

Likewise, the POST Commission and FWP were slow to bring charges against Doyle, former undersheriff Karey Reynolds and deputy Dan Duryee, who was said to have lied about his military experience. His misrepresentation of his military experience, it would turn out, helped get him appointed as a head of the department's Special Response Team and as a sniper without attending any formal training.[5]

One deputy said in a sworn statement to POST that he began entertaining doubts about Duryee's military experience after being ordered by him into an unsafe position during an armed standoff. The deputy said he was threatened when he approached Duryee about his discovery. For his trouble, the deputy was disciplined for using a department computer to run a check on Duryee's military history.

A sergeant in the department also provided a sworn affidavit in which he said he witnessed Duryee bag up skull fragments from a suicide victim. Duryee, he said, was collecting the fragments for a female deputy he was dating because she wanted them to train her cadaver dog for search and rescue.[6]

The lawsuit also said that former deputy Terry Leonard's personal computers were seized and illegally searched and the hard discs downloaded onto a department computer after he posted claims during a contentious sheriff's election campaign. The suit said the department kept all his hard drive information even though no charges were ever filed against him.[7]

By January 2012, however, Reynolds would resign[8] and in March 2014, Duryee followed suit.[9]

24

Nebraska: Asset Seizure State

ON CHRISTMAS EVE, 1993, Teena Brandon, a twenty-one-year-old woman who preferred dressing as a man, attended a Christmas party where she was brutally raped by two ex-convicts.

Despite their threats to kill her if she told anyone, she reported the assault to Richardson County Sheriff Charles Laux. But rather than consider the evidence from the rape kit, Laux instead focused his interview of Brandon by questioning her gender identity ("Did you ever put a folded sock down in your pants to try and pass yourself off as a man?"), her sexual orientation and his belief Brandon either enjoyed or even participated in the rape.

Believing that Laux had arrested her assailants, John Lotter and Tom Nissen, Brandon remained in the general area. But warrants were never issued for the pair's arrest and on Dec. 31, the two made good on their promise, killing Brandon and two other innocent people who had the misfortune to be with her at the time.

Only after the three murders were Nissen and Lotter finally arrested by Laux, who was in his third term as sheriff of Richardson County. Nissen testified against Lotter and received life in prison. Lotter was sentenced to death.[1]

Teena Brandon's mother, JoAnn Brandon, filed a civil lawsuit against the sheriff and Richardson County which claimed it was nearly broke from the cost incurred in prosecuting Nissen and Lotter. A local judge awarded her only $17,360.97 but the Nebraska Supreme Court, in a scathing, 20-page opinion, increased the award to $100,000.[2]

Actress Hilary Swank would win the 1999 Academy Award for her portrayal of Teena Brandon in the movie *Boys Don't Cry*.[3]

The presumption of innocence is the cornerstone on which the American system of justice is based. In criminal cases, the prosecution is required to prove its case against a defendant beyond a reasonable doubt.

Unless you are a motorist just passing through.

In the wake of the Sept. 11, 2001, terror attacks, the government turned the nation's police forces into modern-day Robin Hoods with the passage of sweeping asset seizure laws that put many itinerant motorists in the unique position of having to prove their innocence as opposed to requiring prosecutors to prove their guilt.

In the 14 years from 2001 and 2014, police seized $2.5 billion in cash by making on-the-spot decisions that the money was crime-related even though no one was ever charged with a crime. The incentive was obvious: under the Equitable Sharing Program, local and state law enforcement agencies received much of that seized cash back - $1.7 billion over that same 14-year period.[4]

Nebraska is no exception to the abuse that has grown out of asset seizure laws. Douglas County, where Omaha is located, took part in 159 such traffic stops from 2001 to 2014 and seized $16.2 million in cash, receiving $11.5 million back under the Equitable Sharing Program.

In December 2012, David Frye, a part-time Seward County sheriff's deputy, pulled over John Anderson of San Clemente, California, on I-80 near Lincoln. Frye issued a warning ticket to Anderson for failure to signal when changing lanes. The entire encounter lasted 13 minutes. By law, once that process is completed, the driver has a right to leave if he is not placed under arrest but they are never told they have that right.

In Anderson's case, Frye said he noticed indicators of possible suspicious activity: an air freshener, a radar detector and inconsistencies in Anderson's explanation of his travels – something any motorist might be guilty of, but certainly no crime.

When Anderson declined to give permission for Frye to search his car (again, within one's rights), Frye said, "I'm just going to, basically have you wait here," and he radioed for a drug-sniffing dog. Thirty-six minutes later, the dog arrived and soon indicated the presence of drugs. But when officers searched Anderson's vehicle, there were no drugs, just $25,180.

That's when the pressure was applied to Anderson. Frye suggested that he might not have known the money was in his car and began pushing for Anderson to sign a waiver relinquishing the cash. A minimum of five times Frye pressed Anderson to deny the cash was not his and to sign the waiver. "You're going to be given an opportunity to disclaim the currency," he said as he again suggested that Anderson "sign a form that says, 'That is not my money. I don't know anything about it. I don't want to know anything about it'" and that unless he signed the waiver, he would be charged with a crime and that "you'll go to jail."

More than an hour later, Anderson finally acquiesced and signed the waiver but later sued to get the money back, claiming he signed the waiver only because he felt intimidated by Frye.[5]

Anderson requested that he be provided legal counsel because he could not afford an attorney, but the court refused, explaining that he had no such right because the proceeding was a civil one, not criminal.[6]

It wasn't until 2016 that the State of Nebraska revised it standard for asset seizure from beyond a reasonable doubt to require a criminal conviction before any assets could be seized.[7]

It's not every day that someone in law enforcement files a complaint of wrongful prosecution and discrimination against a law enforcement agency, but that's exactly what happened in Sarpy County in eastern Nebraska in 2001.

Richard Rivera, a former West New York, New Jersey, police officer, was working as a consultant on law enforcement and security matters in the Omaha area. He was conducting a survey to determine how local police departments responded to requests for information on procedures to file complaints on police officers' conduct.

When he attempted to obtain information from the Sarpy County Sheriff's Department, deputy Joe Eaton threw him against a car and handcuffed him. He was released two hours later after being issued a citation for "false reporting," which the Sarpy County attorney subsequently refused to prosecute. The entire sequence of events was recorded by an Omaha television reporter who was accompanying Rivera as he conducted his survey.

To make matters worse, Sarpy County Sheriff Pat Thomas contacted the West New York Police Department back in New Jersey to let them know he had arrested their former employee. Thomas even went out of his way to contact Rivera's hometown newspaper, which ran a Page One story about the arrest.

Rivera and the ACLU of Nebraska filed a lawsuit against the sheriff's department, claiming that his rights had been violated because of his Hispanic national origin and that his First Amendment rights of free speech had also been violated when the sheriff's office retaliated against him for attempting to speak out about the matter.[8]

When Dennis Wever became the third suicide in five years in the Lincoln County Jail, it proved too much for Federal Judge Laurie Smith who ruled that Sheriff James Carmen could not be shielded from liability in a lawsuit brought by Wever's mother, Nancy Wever.

When sheriff's deputies responded to a 911 call from Dennis Wever on Dec. 8, 2001, Wever consented to go to a hospital peacefully if deputies agreed not to handcuff him, saying he would kill himself if jailed. Deputies proceeded to wrestle him to the ground and handcuff him anyway. He was arrested and put in the back of a squad car where he promptly kicked out the back window. Officers dragged him from the car, again threw him on the ground and put him in leg chains.

He was then taken to the Lincoln County Jail and placed in an isolation cell where he requested a blanket. Despite his having threatened suicide, he was given a blanket at approximately 5:14 p.m. At 5:30, he was discovered hanging from the blanket he had been given.

When Wever's mother sued, Sheriff Carmen claimed qualified immunity as a matter of law because he had no personal involvement in Wever's arrest and subsequent death but did not address the issue of supervisory liability. Wever held that Carmen was aware of two prior suicides, one in 1999 while he was sheriff and one in 1996 prior to his tenure.

Carmen argued that as a matter of law, one or two suicides were insufficient to put him on notice that his training and supervision was constitutionally inadequate. "Under his proposed rule," a federal appeals court wrote in its decision of Nov. 4, 2004, "a sheriff may sit idly by until at least a third inmate known to be suicidal takes a blanket from an officer and hangs himself, only then ordering his officers not to place a suicidal person in an isolation cell and hand him a blanket. We decline to so hold."

The lawsuit was settled in 2005 for an undisclosed sum.[9]

25

Nevada: Sex, Porn, and More Asset Seizures

STOREY COUNTY, located near Reno in western Nevada, is the smallest county in terms of area (264 square-miles) in the state. It is the location of the Comstock Lode silver discovery of 1859, but its biggest claim to fame is that it also is the location of the infamous Mustang Ranch. And therein lies some of the problems that helped lead to the recall efforts against Storey County Sheriff Gerald Antinoro in April 2017.

Antinoro survived the contentious vote, defeating the recall effort by a 883-601 count.[1]

Though Antinoro survived the recall effort, the support of then- Republican Attorney General Adam Laxalt may have ultimately cost Laxalt the governorship of Nevada. He lost that race to Democrat Steve Sisolak the following year by 39,700 votes despite the endorsement of President Donald Trump.[2]

Laxalt in July 2018 issued a 28-page report in which he declined to pursue criminal charges of sexual misconduct against Antinoro,[3] who had endorsed Laxalt's gubernatorial bid on Laxalt's Web page. Antinoro also had the support of his former top deputy Wes Duncan who was a heavy favorite to succeed Laxalt as attorney general, but like Laxalt, wound up losing to Democrat Aaron Ford.[4]

Melanie Keener, a former chief deputy in Antinoro's office, sued the sheriff for sexual harassment when she was fired from her job after 15 years because she filed the complaint against her former boss.

The Nevada Commission on Ethics eventually found insufficient evidence to open a formal hearing on the complaints by Keener and Antinoro political foe Lance Gilman, owner of the Mustang Ranch, a well- known brothel even though the ethics commission did acknowledge there was a "perception of impropriety" that fell short of any law violation.[5]

The decision to dismiss the complaints was made despite an independent investigation three years earlier which found that Antinoro violated

Storey County's sexual harassment laws on two separate occasions.[6]

No matter if it was the smallest county in Nevada or the largest (Nye County, at 18,159 square miles), claims of sexual impropriety and sexual harassment in sheriffs' offices played no favorites.

In January 2017, two separate lawsuits were filed against the Nye County Sheriff's Department by current and former deputies who described a pattern of hostile work environment through years of sexual harassment that superior officers ignored. Nye County Sheriff Sharon Wehrly, who said it would be inappropriate to comment on pending litigation, did say, however, that the ones accused in the lawsuits were no longer with the department.

Sergeant Kelly Jackson, one of the plaintiffs, said she faced explicit sexual harassment that included obscene verbal abuse, inappropriate emails from colleagues, being shown pornography on work computers, being propositioned for sex and being groped and fondled by male co-workers.[7]

Only ten months earlier, in March 2016, the Nye County Sheriff's Department and former sheriff Tony Demeo, Captain William Becht,

Sergeant David Boruchowitz and ten unnamed officers were named defendants in another lawsuit that claimed department public information officer Boruchowitz seized plaintiff Jaysan Gal's laptop computer from Gal's then-girlfriend as part of a criminal investigation.

Boruchowitz, the lawsuit said, found a number of pornographic videos on the laptop, including one of Gal, 37, and his girlfriend having sex. Boruchowitz called the girlfriend to the station to have her help identify people featured in videos on the laptop, including the one of her and Gal and later called her to tell her he enjoyed the videos.

He passed the video around the squad room and held "pornography matinees" at the station and downloaded the video to his cellphone, the lawsuit said, adding that the videos were Gal's "intellectual property" and the department did not have the authority to show them publicly for nonofficial police business. It said that Demeo knew about the viewings and that that Brecht, Boruchowitz's supervisor, encouraged the behavior by participating.[8]

It was not the first disciplinary action involving Boruchowitz. As far back as 2010, he was arrested after a complaint that accused him of burglary and assault in an effort to harass candidates seeking public office.

The 2010 charges accused then-Detective Boruchowitz of targeting Nye County sheriff candidates Scott Cobel and Ted Holmes and District

Attorney Robert Beckett by kicking in a door and forcing entry into a residence where Cobel's daughter and some friends were and subjecting the teens to searches, including breathalyzer tests, without a warrant. The incident appeared to stem from an ongoing political feud between Beckett and Sheriff Tony De Meo.

In what seemed like a parody of law enforcement, Boruchowitz issued a news release announcing his own arrest. The release was accompanied by his jail booking photo. Beckett then attempted to appoint his own special prosecutor to investigate charges of misconduct in the sheriff's office. But a judge later rejected the charges, saying that Beckett lacked the authority to appoint a special prosecutor, so Beckett refiled the charges himself.[9]

No discussion of corruption and duplicity among Nevada sheriffs' offices could take place without Clark County taking center stage.

With the city of Las Vegas accounting for the bulk of the county's 2.3 million residents, Clark is easily the most populous county in the state. In Vegas, where prostitution is legal and where casinos thrive, it should be no surprise that Clark would be a breeding ground for unethical behavior on the part of those appointed to protect its citizens.

In 2012, a local pimp named Ocean Fleming was sentenced to life in prison with the possibility of parole after five years for first-degree kidnapping and twenty-two other felony counts in connection with a sex-trafficking investigation. The prosecutor in his case was Elizabeth Mercer, who had requested life with parole eligibility after 22 years.

The problem with all that was that Mercer was married to Chris Baughman, the lead detective in the case against Fleming. Baughman and fellow vice detective Albert Beas were said to have been having sex with prostitute Jessica Gruda, the primary witness against Fleming. Moreover, Fleming said that Baughman was also having a romantic/sexual relationship at the same time with his supervisor, Vice Lieutenant Karen Hughes.

But the most damning accusation leveled by Fleming's attorneys was that Baughman and other detectives were taking payoffs from Jamal "Mally Mall" Rashid, a local prostitution kingpin who wanted Fleming's pimping operations shut down. When deposed in 2017, Baughman pleaded the Fifth on all questions relating to Fleming's prosecution, including the direct question if he had taken bribes from Mall to set up Fleming.

Prostitute and Fleming girlfriend April Millard would subsequently sign a sworn affidavit in which she said Baughman threatened her with jail unless she testified against Fleming. Another prostitute who was Millard's friend, also gave a sworn affidavit in which she said she was sexually involved with Detective Beas and that she likewise was pressured to give testimony that Fleming also physically attacked her. "DA [sic] Mercer told me that if I testified that Ocean had put his hands around my throat, strangling me, that she could put him away for a longer period of time," she said.

When Fleming appealed his sentence, a special prosecutor, after meeting with District Attorney Steve Wolfson, worked out a deal with Fleming whereby he would be released from prison in 2020 rather than allow Fleming's accusations to be made public in open court, according to a publication located more than 2,400 miles away which said the settlement was the result of the joint effort by Sheriff Joe Lombardo and DA Steve Wolfson to halt an inquiry into allegations of police and prosecutorial misconduct.

The now-defunct *Baltimore Post-Examiner* wrote in February 2019 that Lombardo and Wolfson got "nervous about the exposure of corruption in their respective departments and (did) what government officials often do when instances like this surface and dirty laundry is about to be exposed."

The publication added, "…[O]ne can make a convincing argument that the prosecutor was corrupt, the cops were corrupt and the district attorney and the sheriff both took measures to ensure further corruption would not be exposed in the countroom.[10]

Baughman, author of several books, left the sheriff's department in 2013 to star in a TV reality show that was soon canceled. He attempted unsuccessfully to return to the department and was last seen working for a local strip club. Hughes was reported to be retired and living in Brazil. Beas was given a 40-hour suspension, the most severe disciplinary action short of termination and was assigned to patrol. Mercer became the Chief Deputy District Attorney.[11]

For two decades, the Las Vegas Metro Police Department, headed by the sheriff, ranked third behind Houston and Chicago in the U.S. in officer-involved shootings per capita. Of the 310 shooting incidents during the period from 1990 to 2011, 115 were fatal, including three officers killed in the line of duty.[12]

Following is a year-by-year (1995-2012) compilation of incidents of misconduct that resulted in convictions, confessions, plea bargains or disciplinary action taken against members of the Las Vegas Metropolitan Police Department/Clark County Sheriff's Office.

- **1995**: Officers Brian Nicholson and Robert Phelan and Sergeant James Campbell received jail sentences and were fired by the department after they pleaded no contest to charges related to the beating of a suspected coin thief. Campbell and Nicholson received nine months each and Phelan was sentenced to six months in jail.
- **1996:** Officer Michael Ramirez, a former officer of 30 years, was arrested in October 1996 and pleaded guilty in 1998 to having used his badge, gun, and the threat of arrest to force a couple to engage in sex in front of him two years earlier.
- On December 28, off-duty officer Ron Mortensen killed Daniel Mendoza in a drive-by shooting and was sentenced to life imprisonment. Officer Christopher Brady, who was driving at the time, received a nine-year sentence.
- **1997:** Officer Art Sewall was arrested on February 8 for attempted sexual assault and oppression. He was arrested following an undercover sting at a local motel after the department received a complaint that he was engaged in criminal conduct. He resigned from the department the following month. In June 1999, he pleaded guilty to two felony counts of oppression and charges of kidnapping and sexual assault were dropped.
- **2004:** The department's Fiscal Affairs Committee recommended a $295,000 settlement after Keith Tucker, 47, died after being tased while handcuffed and on his stomach.
- **2006:** Officer Eric Barros left the department after being sentenced to three years' probation for theft and falsifying evidence during a drug raid.
- **2007:** On March 27, the department was ordered to pay $1.48 million after officers gave special treatment to a fellow officer's wife who had struck and killed a bicyclist in 1994. Janet Wagner killed Erin DeLew who was riding her bicycle home from a supermarket. The resulting lawsuit said that Wagner's husband, officer David Wagner, and his fellow officers knew she had been drinking but covered it up and delayed calling the Nevada Highway Patrol.
- In July, officer Jared Wicks struck and killed Raymond Yeghi-

azarian while pursuing another vehicle through an intersection with no emergency lights or siren. A judge reduced a $2.2 million jury award in 2011 to two hundred fifty thousand dollars.
- **2008:** Officer William Miller left the department after being covicted on charges of domestic violence and coercion.
- **2009:** The department's Fiscal Affairs Committee approved a $120,000 settlement with Calvin Darling over the four days he spent in jail following a collision with officer James Manor, who was not wearing a seat belt and was killed in the accident. Manor was driving his patrol car at 109 miles per hour when he struck Darling, who was attempting a left turn. Sheriff Doug Gillespie said that Manor and a vehicle driven by another officer had their lights and sirens on but this was later proven to be untrue. Darling was arrested at the scene and charged with DUI. His blood alcohol content was tested at .035 and the Clark County District Attorney's office dropped the DUI and failure to yield charges.
- A settlement of one million dollars was approved on May 23, 2011, for the family of Dustin Boone following the November 2009 choke-hold death of Boone.
- Former Lieutenant Benjamin Kim was implicated in the widespread Homeowners Association multi-million-dollar scandal. He pleaded guilty in federal court on May 4, 2012, to a charge of misprison of felony "for the concealment of an attempt to commit bank fraud." He was sentenced on February 4, 2013, to three years' probation.
- **2010:** The department approved a settlement of $1.7 million with the family of Trevon Cole, who was fatally shot by Detective Bryan Yant on June 11, 2010, after it was shown that Yant violated several departmental policies regarding the preparation and serving of a warrant on Cole.
- **2011:** Mitchell Crooks was video recording a police investigation of a reported burglary on March 20, 2011, when officer Derek Colling approached him, beat him, arrested him on charges of obstructing a police officer and assault/battery on a police officer. Crooks' complaint to Internal Affairs of excessive force was upheld and the department settled with Crooks, who had no criminal record, for $100,000.

- A seven-figure settlement figure was anticipated after Sheriff Doug Gillespie and Assistant Sheriff Ray Flynn admitted that switched DNA samples had mistakenly sent an innocent man named Dwayne Jackson to the Nevada State Prison for four years.
- A federal jury awarded $2.1 million to Charles Barnard on August 11, 2011, for excessive force used by officers Gary Clark, Greg Theobald and Steven Radmanovich. The award was reduced to $1.6 million by a federal judge.
- Officer Jesus Arevalo killed unarmed Stanley Gibson on December 12, 2011, in a standoff at an apartment complex. Gibson, a Gulf War veteran suffering from psychological distress, had been circling an apartment complex when the report of a burglar was called in. As officers prepared to extract Gibson from his SUV, he gunned his engine and Arevalo responded with four shots from an AR-15 assault rifle. In October 2013, at the recommendation of two separate review panels, Arevalo became the first officer in the department's history to be fired as a result of an on-duty shooting. The department settled with Gibson's family for $1.5 million in 2013.
- **2012**: On June 25, 2012, less than two weeks after his resignation from the department, former officer John Norman pleaded guilty to two gross misdemeanors and was required to register as a sex offender. He was arrested on February 1, 2012, on felony charges of coercion and oppression after he detained and/or arrested two women who he made to expose their breasts and one of them who he fondled. The investigation of the charges began in late 2011 when he was advised of the possible charges and he refused to cooperate with investigators.

Officer Jacquar Roston was suspended for forty hours because of poor judgment after the November 2012 wounding of a man he thought was involved in a domestic disturbance. The victim, in fact, was just sitting in a car.[13]

An investigative story by a *Washington Post* team of reporters in 2014 showed among other things, the Las Vegas Metropolitan Police Department/Clark County Sheriff's Office participated in 243 such seizures between 2000 and 2013. Those 243 raids/traffic stops netted $18 million in seized property and cash, $7.3 million of which was rebated back to the Humboldt County Sheriff's Department by federal agencies.[14]

In Humboldt County in northern Nevada, the oldest county in the state, sheriff's deputy Lee Dove pulled Tan Nguyen over for driving three miles per hour over the speed limit. When he asked to search Tan's vehicle, Tan declined. Dove then claimed he smelled marijuana but couldn't find any drugs. A search of Tan's car turned up a briefcase containing $50,000 in cash and cashier's checks, money Tan said he won at a casino. Tan was not arrested nor was he charged with a crime – not even a traffic citation but Tan said in a lawsuit that Dove threatened to seize and tow his car unless he "got in his car and drove off and forgot this ever happened."

Less than three months later, Dove pulled Ken Smith over for speeding. A warrant check found a warrant for a Ken Smith, and on that basis, Dove detained Smith. The Ken Smith on the warrant, it turned out, had a different date of birth and was black. The Ken Smith whom Dove pulled over was white. Smith was "unarrested" and "allowed" to leave with his vehicle if he signed a waiver to surrender $13,800 in cash and a .40 caliber Ruger handgun he had in the vehicle. Both drivers sued the Humboldt County Sheriff's Department, claiming violation of their Fourth Amendment rights against unreasonable search and seizure.[15]

A report, *Policing for Profit*, published by the Institute for Justice, said the incentives behind civil forfeiture led to abuses by law enforcement. "Nevada has scant protections for property owners against forfeiture abuse," the report said. "Police can seize property under a legal standard lower than the beyond-a-reasonable-doubt standard used in criminal convictions. Owners bear the burden of proof, meaning they have to prove their innocence in court." And while law enforcement agencies are required to keep records on forfeiture, Nevada refused to provide such information to the Institute for Justice.[16]

In 2015 Nevada adopted reforms to its civil forfeiture laws that raised the standard of proof to clear and convincing evidence and a criminal conviction before property could be forfeited in connection with a crime, but the overriding financial incentive to seize cash and property did little in the way of actually protecting owners. Statewide between 2000 and 2013, $37 million in cash and property was seized by authorities, of which $13 million went back to state sheriffs' departments as equitable sharing funds.[17]

26

New Jersey: Bribes, Double-Dipping

THINK NEW JERSEY and, fair or not, visions of organized crime come automatically to mind.

Michael Mordaga was Chief of Detectives for Bergen County making $177,000 when reputed mobster Frank Lagano was gunned down outside a restaurant owned by Lagano in April 2007.

Ten years later, the murder would remain unsolved but memos that surfaced in a lawsuit filed by state investigator James Sweeney's estate following his death alleged a long-standing association between Mordaga and Lagano as well as the claim that Mordaga and others in the Bergen County Prosecutor's Office were responsible for Lagano's execution-style murder by intentionally blowing his cover as a state informant.[1]

Sweeney claimed in his memo to his superiors at the state attorney general's office that not only did Lagano and Mordaga have a personal relationship, but that Lagano even provided Mordaga with construction plans of his family room so that Mordaga could replicate it in his own 5,000-square-foot, $1.3 million home he was building, courtesy of contributions from Bergen County builders.

Sweeney's estate claimed in its lawsuit that Mordaga owed Lagano money and also feared a lawsuit referral scheme he had with an attorney whose name was redacted from the memo would be revealed because Lagano was serving as an informant to Sweeney.

Mordaga retired from the sheriff's office in the months following Lagano's death and next turned up as civilian police director in Hackensack, a post he left in 2016.[2]

Joseph C. Spicuzzo, the former sheriff of Middlesex County, and two of his deputies ran a jobs-for-cash bribery scheme from 1996 to 2008 in which seven applicants for sheriff's investigators were required to pay bribes ranging from $5,000 to $25,000 for their jobs and an eighth paid $12,000 in exchange for two promotions within the sheriff's office.

Spicuzzo, 68, who served as sheriff of Middlesex County for nearly thirty years, was sentenced in September 2013 to nine years in state prison, two years of which he was required to serve before becoming eligible for parole. He pleaded guilty to collecting about $112,000 in bribes from individuals seeking jobs or promotions in his department. He was also ordered to pay a $55,000 fine and permanently barred from public employment in New Jersey. Even more severe, he forfeited his entire state pension.

Former sheriff's investigator Darrin P. DiBiasi, 45, was sentenced to 364 days in county jail as a condition of five years' probation, ordered to serve 200 hours of community service and was likewise prohibited from future public employment in the state. DiBiasi pleaded guilty in June 2013 to a third-degree charge of conspiracy to make illegal gifts to a public servant and for assisting Spicuzzo in collecting the bribes.[3]

A second deputy, Paul Lucarelli, 48, who admitted to collecting $25,000 in bribe money for Spicuzzo, was sentenced in October 2013 to three years' probation, fined $2,500, ordered to perform 500 hours of community service and also barred from future public employment.[4]

"Sheriff Spicuzzo's decades as a political power broker in Middlesex County corrupted him to the point that he viewed jobs in the sheriff's office as personal assets he could sell for his own enrichment," said Acting Attorney General John Hoffman. "Spicuzzo clearly thought he was above the law, because that is the only way to explain his brazen demands for bribes from new recruits. With this prison sentence, we affirm that nobody is above the law in New Jersey."[5]

Bergen County Sheriff Michael Saudino resigned on Sept. 21, 2018, ending 46 years in law enforcement after being caught on tape casting disparaging remarks about African-Americans, gays and the state's first Sikh attorney general.

A public radio station obtained the tape on which Saudino could be heard saying that Attorney General Gurbir Grewal was appointed to his post because of "the turban," and saying that Gov. Phil Murphy's policies would allow blacks to "come in, do whatever the [expletive] they want, smoke their marijuana, do this, do that. And don't worry about it…" He could also be heard on the tape wondering aloud if Lt. Gov. Sheila Oliver, who was unmarried, was gay.

Executive Undersheriff George Buono and Undersheriffs Robert Colaneri, Brian Smith, and Joseph Hornyak also resigned along with Saudino.[6]

In 2016, a New Jersey blogger named Mark Lagerkvist conducted a survey of state sheriffs and found that of the 21 counties 16 had sheriffs who were collecting not only their sheriffs' salaries, but state pensions as retired law enforcement officers, as well.

It may have come as news to Lagerkvist, but this practice is not at all unusual. Louisiana has several parish (county) sheriffs who are retired state troopers drawing generous retirement benefits in addition to their equally generous salaries.

Heading up Legerkvist's 2016 list, ironically, was then Bergan County Sheriff Spicuzzo whose guilty pleas to bribery cost him both his $138,000 sheriff's salary and his $130,000 pension as a retiree from the Emerson Borough Police Department – more than a quarter-million dollar per year combined income.

Others on Lagerkvist's list included:
- Passaic County Sheriff Richard Berdnik: $253,957 ($151,887 in sheriff's salary, plus $102,070 as a retiree from the Clifton Police Department);
- Ocean County Sheriff Michael Mastronardy: $234,309 ($110,244 salary and $124,065 as a Toms River Township Police Department retiree);
- Mercer County Sheriff John Kemler: $233,330 ($148,199 salary, $84,831 as a retiree from his own Mercer County Sheriff's Office);
- Somerset County Sheriff Frank J. Provenzano: $211,227 ($135,206 salary, $76,021 as Bridgewater Township Police Department retiree);
- Warren County Sheriff David P. Gallant: $210,636 ($128,149 salary, $82,487 as a New Jersey State Police retiree);
- Essex County Sheriff Armando Fontoura; $210,187 ($147,794 salary, $62,393 as a retired Essex County undersheriff);
- Middlesex County Sheriff Mildred S. Scott: $204,095 ($142,754 salary, $61,341 as a Middlesex County Sheriff's Office retiree);
- Morris County Sheriff Edward V. Rochford: $200,838 ($139,203 salary, $61,545 pension as a Morris Township Police Department retiree);
- Hunterdon County Sheriff Frederick W. Brown: $197,796 ($133,740 salary, $63,449 pension as a retiree of the Raritan Township Police Department);

- Gloucester County Sheriff Carmel M. Morina: $197,189 ($133,740 salary, $63,449 pension as a Greenwich Township Police Department retiree);
- Salem County Sheriff Charles M. Miller: $195,452 ($119,386 salary, $76,066 pension as a retiree from the Salem County prosecutor's office);
- Camden County Sheriff Gilbert Wilson: $195,136 ($144,753 salary, $50,383 pension as a Camden City Police Department retiree);
- Sussex County Sheriff Michael Strada: $172,033 ($125,060 salary, $46,973 pension as a Mount Olive Township Police Department retiree);
- Cumberland County Sheriff Robert Austino: $166,938 ($107,250 salary, $59,688 pension as a Vineland Police Department retiree), and
- Cape May County Sheriff Gary Schaffer: $161,654 ($107,500 salary, $54,154 pension as an Ocean City Police Department retiree).

Altogether, the sixteen sheriffs received about $3.3 million in public pay - $2.1 million in sheriffs' salaries, plus $1.2 million from various retirement programs. Lagerkvist said the average sheriff in the 16 counties received $207,000 per year - $131,000 in salaries and $76,000 in retirement.

Lagerkvist did a deeper dive and found that sheriffs also often hired retired law enforcement officers for key positions in their departments. He found 33 retirees working as undersheriffs in 18 counties. Together, they were paid $6 million per year - $3.3 million in salaries and $2.7 in pensions.

In all, the 49 sheriffs and undersheriffs were paid $9.3 million a year in 2016 -- $5.4 million in salaries and another $3.9 million from pensions.

Lagerkvist said he obtained his information through Open Public Records Act requests and the New Jersey State Treasury's online pension database.[7]

27

New Mexico: False Arrests, Drug Trafficking

NEW MEXICO in early 2013 became another in a string of locations where actor Steven Seagal would take his traveling road show.

Having worn out his welcome in Jefferson Parish, Louisiana, the martial arts specialist-turned-lawman reappeared in Maricopa County, Arizona, when he was deputized by then-Sheriff Joe Arpaio. He next turned up in Hudspeth County in West Texas before Doña Ana County, New Mexico, Sheriff Todd Garrison administered the oath to him in Las Cruces on Jan. 22.[1]

Not to be outdone, Socorro County Sheriff William Armijo would deputize Incredible Hulk actor Lou Ferrigno seven years later.[2]

Perhaps it was the perception that New Mexico needed an image makeover though in reality, the state is probably no worse than most other states when it comes down to corruption in government in general and law enforcement in particular.

But one unsolved case that continues to haunt the Las Cruces area after more than seventy years is that of Ovida "Cricket" Coogler, a vivacious if promiscuous 18-year-old waitress whose violent death in 1949 has been linked to then- Doña Ana County Sheriff Alfonso Luchini "Happy" Apodaca who waited a full week before publicizing her disappearance and who some at the time believed attempted to destroy evidence at the scene where her decomposed body was discovered.[3]

Apodaca, who had once been a New Mexico state policeman, had a reputation of his own. Parents reportedly instructed their daughters to "never get alone in a car with Happy Apodaca."

When he arrived at the scene, he walked over and lifted up her skirt and said, "Yeah, that's her," according to Gerald Smith, one of those who had discovered the body. Smith said the sheriff did not rope off the crime scene and could have even run over some of the vehicle tracks in an attempt to obliterate evidence.[4]

What came next, however, was even worse, and landed Apodaca in trouble. Already rumored to have been involved with Coogler, the sheriff picked up and detained in isolation two men who turned out to be no more than scapegoats. One was a New Mexico A&M student named Jerry Nuzum, who played for the Pittsburgh Steelers and attended the university in the off-season in order to obtain his degree.

The other was an African-American World War II veteran named Wesley Byrd. Byrd was tortured by law enforcement officials in an effort to force a confession out of him. He was driven to Coogler's gravesite where officers attached a bicycle lock to his testicles and forced him to walk. They threatened to bury him at the same location if he didn't confess, but he never did.

Because of Coogler's association with persons suspected of involvement with illegal gambling, a full-scale investigation into organized crime and public corruption was launched that resulted in raids on gambling establishments, including some that were paying state politicians, a judge and Apodaca for protection.

Apodaca and State Corporation Commissioner Dan Sedillo were tried and acquitted of charges of gambling and morals violations but Apodaca was eventually convicted of civil rights violations in connection with the arrest and torture of Byrd. Apodaca, New Mexico State Police Chief Hubert Beasley and state police officer Roy Sandman were sentenced to a year in La Tuna federal prison in Anthony, Texas.[5]

Former Colfax County Sheriff Vidal Sandoval was sentenced to more than seven years in federal prison for drug trafficking and theft of government property.

Federal District Judge Judith Herrera sentenced the 50-year-old former sheriff to 87 months in prison in February 2020, more than three years after he entered a guilty plea without benefit of a plea agreement in July 2016.[6]

The FBI and the New Mexico State Police arrested Sandoval on March 13, 2015, on an indictment charging him with aiding and abetting an attempt to possess cocaine with intent to distribute in Colfax County, New Mexico, on Feb. 28, 2015. The indictment included forfeiture provisions seeking a money judgment in the amount of $17,500, the proceeds Sandoval obtained through his unlawful conduct. The indictment was superseded on April 14, 2015, to add two theft of government property offenses charging Sandoval with stealing money belonging to the FBI on Dec. 15, 2014, and

Jan. 25, 2015.

Sandoval was employed as a deputy sheriff by the Colfax County Sheriff's Department between December 2014 and February 2015, during which time he received training on how to properly handle evidence. Sandoval knew that he was forbidden to keep money and other property he seized while executing his official duties.

While on duty on December 15, 2014, Sandoval stole money from two motorists whom he believed to be drug traffickers transporting the proceeds from the sale of illegal drugs. After Sandoval found $8,000 in cash in the motorists' vehicle during a traffic stop, he called Leon Herrera and enlisted him to tell the motorists that he (Herrera) was a law enforcement officer. At the conclusion of the traffic stop, Sandoval retained $7,500 for his personal use and did not turn it into the Colfax County Sheriff's Department; he returned $500 to the motorists. Sandoval later learned that the cash belonged to the FBI and that the two motorists whom he suspected of being drug traffickers were actually undercover officers.

On February 28, 2015, Sandoval accepted $10,000 in cash to escort a load of illegal drugs through Colfax County into Colorado. Sandoval traveled to Wagon Mound, New Mexico, in his patrol car and while wearing his uniform, where he met a motorist whom he believed to be a drug trafficker. Sandoval accepted $5,000 from the motorist. During their conversation, the motorist displayed a box containing cocaine and Sandoval understood that the motorist was going to Colorado with the intention of selling the cocaine. After instructing the motorist to drive a few car lengths behind him, Sandoval drove through Colfax County and into Colorado, where he again met with the motorist and received another $5,000. Sandoval retained the $10,000 for his personal use instead of turning it into the Colfax County Sheriff's Department. Sandoval later learned that the $10,000 belonged to the FBI and that the motorist whom he suspected of being a drug trafficker was actually an undercover officer. Sandoval also learned that the box displayed by the undercover officer that he believed contained two kilograms of cocaine and three kilograms of "sham" cocaine.[7]

"When law enforcement officers betray the communities they swore to protect, it overshadows the heroic work the majority of police, deputies, and agents perform on a daily basis," said Special Agent in Charge James C. Langenberg of the FBI's Albuquerque Division. "The FBI, working with partners like the New Mexico State Police and Colfax County Sheriff's

Office, will pursue anyone who dishonors the badge and puts the public at risk."

"I am proud of the role we played in identifying this defendant's criminal behavior and holding him accountable," said Tim Johnson, Chief of the New Mexico State Police. "His actions were an egregious violation of public trust. Thorough investigation and continuing cooperation between agencies again yielded just results."[8]

Heath White was once the sheriff of Torrance County but by the time he was accused of embezzling more than $20,000 in equipment and storing county property at his home in May 2019, he was a sitting magistrate judge.

To no one's surprise, those charges were dismissed by fellow Judge Charles Brown in a 16-page order in October 2019, but not before White was suspended from the bench.[9]

On Jan. 2, 2020, the state attorney general's office filed an appeal of Brown's ruling.[10]

An investigation into White's activities was initiated in early 2019 after items purchased by the sheriff's department during his tenure turned up missing. Investigators said he purchased more than $150,000 worth of items, including night vision goggles, auto parts and numerous guns, all of which were kept by White. Some of the items were found in a store he owned.[11]

Former Rio Arriba County sheriff Tommy Rodella got the bad news from U.S. District Judge James Browning on Jan. 22, 2020, that he would not be getting out of prison early.[12]

Rodella was sentenced to ten years in federal prison in January 2015 following his conviction on criminal civil rights and firearms charges. He was sentenced to thirty-seven months imprisonment for his conviction on deprivation of rights charges and an additional 84 months for brandishing a firearm while committing the civil rights offense. He also ordered to pay a $200,000 fine and will be on supervised release for three years following the completion of his prison term.[13]

Rodella and his 26-year-old son Thomas had become involved in a confrontation with a motorist on March 11, 2014, and had attempted to provoke the driver to fight them before pursuing him after he drove away and dragging him from his vehicle. Sheriff Rodella was not wearing a uniform at the time and was brandishing a pistol. The federal indictment said Rodella slammed his sheriff's badge into the victim's face. "Sheriff

Rodella chose to abuse his power rather than uphold his oath to protect the public," said U.S. Attorney Damon Martinez.[14]

"The Justice Department will continue to vigorously investigate and prosecute officers who cross that line because they discredit the noble service of every other law enforcement officer and weaken the public's trust in those who are sworn to protect them," Martinez said. "I commend the prosecutors and investigators for their outstanding work on this case."

"The American people hold their law enforcement officers to high standards, and those standards are even higher for the leaders of public safety agencies. Although the FBI realizes the majority of officers perform their duties in an exemplary and even heroic manner, we will not hesitate to investigate those who betray the public's trust," said Special Agent in Charge Carol K.O. Lee of the FBI's Albuquerque Division. "I want to thank the FBI Special Agents and support staff who worked on this investigation, as well as the U.S. Attorney's Office for a successful prosecution in this case."

The Bernalillo County Sheriff's Department also had its share of problems:

- Deputy Darryl Burt, senior officer in the sheriff's department Gang Unit, was found guilty in 1995 of drug trafficking charges and charged with kidnapping, criminal sexual penetration, and other felonies in connection with the traffic stop of a 24-year-old male, as well as 34 counts of sexual assault and extortion of a 16-year-old boy. He was acquitted in November 1992 of sex-related charges, was indicted on 34 counts of sexual assault and extortion of a 16-year-old boy over a number of months and a number of different encounters. (These charges were unrelated to the sex charges filed against him previously.) Burt was placed on unpaid leave from BCSO. He later pled guilty to two misdemeanor charges and was sentenced to two years in jail.

- A year later, Burt, a former undercover narcotics agent, and Michael Disney were taken into federal custody as the result of drug raids in their homes, after being videotaped selling drugs in a parking lot across from Eldorado High School. Both men were working at The Wild Side, Disney's drug paraphernalia shop. At the time of the raid at Burt's house, Burt and a 17-year-old male, wearing only boxer shorts, fled through the bedroom window. A loaded 45- caliber handgun, a Fix-A-Flat can filled with cocaine, and a BCSO badge and credentials were among the items found in Burt's garage. Both Burt and Disney later pled guilty to possession with intent to distribute. The men were described as partners in a heavily armed El Paso-to-Albuquerque drug trafficking operation. Burt was sentenced to 33 years and nine months on a cocaine distribution conviction in U.S. District Court.

- In 1997, Bernalillo County Sheriff's Deputy Joseph Estrada was convicted of embezzlement for taking more than seven hundred thirty dollars' worth of shirts from Dillard's Department Store where he was moonlighting as a security officer.
- In June 2001, when sheriff's deputy Tom Lujan and other unnamed deputies, seized and arrested Michael Bradford, 16, as he and his sister Robin, fifteen, waited for their mother to pick them up after a concert. There had been fights at the concert, but the Bradford children were not involved. Deputies arrested and handcuffed Michael, threw him onto the hood of a squad car, kneed him in the groin, knocked him to the ground and kicked and beat him until he lost consciousness. They grabbed Robin, tore her shirt off, and called her a "whore." A civil rights suit contended the assault occurred "because Michael was a young black man close enough for officers to grab." The charges against Michael were later dropped. The Bradfords' civil suits claiming excessive use of force, false arrest, malicious prosecution and negligence were settled for $45,000.
- Bernalillo County deputies were called to the home of activist Gilbert Elizondo and his wife after the death of his mother-in-law, who died of natural causes. Sgt. Natalie Jasler tried to prevent Mrs. Elizondo from viewing her mother's body, and when Elizondo stepped in to block a blow by Jasler to his wife, Jasler slapped and kicked the couple. Elizondo was then arrested on a charge of aggravated assault on a peace officer. Jasler kneed Elizondo in the groin several times while he was handcuffed and other deputies held him. Jasler's charges against Elizondo were later dropped.
- When 80-year-old Harvey Bell was ordered by Bernalillo County Sheriff's Deputy Paul Chavez to evacuate his home because of a fire, Bell refused because he had earlier been told he did not have to evacuate and none of his neighbors were evacuating. Chavez forci-

bly handcuffed Bell, then took him down so violently with a leg-sweep maneuver that Bell's kneecap was broken. He then left him unconscious, handcuffed and bleeding, on the curb.[16]

28

New York: Drug Trafficking, Porn DVDs

GOV. FRANKLIN D. ROOSEVELT removed New York County Sheriff Thomas M. Farley from office in 1932 following the Seabury investigations that also took down the mayor of New York City and the powerful Tammany Hall political machine.[1]

The investigation was launched as the result of persistent reports that working-class women were being arrested on trumped-up charges. Unable to afford attorneys, they were told by prosecutors that their convictions and jail time were certain unless they paid protection money to prosecutors and judges.

Farley had been called as a witness by the Hofstadter Committee, which had appointed former Judge Samuel Seabury to lead its investigation into corruption among law enforcement, prosecutors, judges and bail bondsmen. The sheriff, a Tammany Hall associate, was owner of a gambling club that was consistently tipped off before raids of his establishment. He was unable to explain his possession of bank deposits of more than $350,000.[2]

The first casualty of the Seabury investigation, Farley, died two years later.[3]

Saratoga County Deputy Sheriff Charles E. Fuller was sentenced in June 2014 to five years in federal prison after entering a guilty plea to accepting $5,000 in exchange for aiding and abetting the possession with intent to distribute a controlled substance.

He accepted a total of $5,000 from an FBI-supervised confidential source as payment for transporting the source and what Fuller believed to be cocaine but which was actually imitation cocaine. Fuller made trips from Albany to Warren County on February 19, 2014 and on February 27, 2014.

During the first trip, the defendant drove the source with what he believed to be 250 grams of cocaine in return for $1,000, and during the second trip, he transported the source with what he believed to be one kilogram of cocaine in return for $4,000.[4]

Fuller, who was president of the Saratoga County Deputy Sheriff's Police Benevolent Association, said gambling and alcohol abuse had left him with debts and desperate for cash. He was off-duty but carried his personal handgun when he drove the female informant on the two trips. The five-year sentence was mandatory because he was carrying a gun in connection with his efforts to protect a drug trafficker.[5]

"Corrupt law enforcement officers insult the many honorable officers who serve with integrity," said FBI agent Andrew W. Vale. "Any law enforcement officer who violates his oath to protect the community and instead takes part in criminal activity should expect the same outcome as a criminal. The public has the right to be assured of the integrity of its public servants, in particular those charged with enforcing the law. Today's arrest serves as a reminder that no one is above the law and that the FBI is committed to working with the law enforcement community to prevent the erosion of public trust that accompanies such incidents.

Saratoga County Sheriff Michael H. Zurlo added, "The allegations against Fuller are an affront to and undermine the integrity of the hardworking men and women of the Saratoga County Sheriff's Office. We will not tolerate corruption among our ranks."[6]

Seneca County Sheriff Leo Connolly's two-year jail sentence was overturned and he was acquitted in his 2010 retrial two years after his conviction on two misdemeanor charges, but one of his deputies, Undersheriff James R. Larson was sentenced to twenty-one months at the same time after pleading guilty to second-degree rewarding official misconduct.[7]

Larson had paid another deputy overtime to concoct charges against a Fayette couple who had been critical of Connolly. Several other charges against Larson were dropped in the plea bargain. He had also been charged with possession of more than $5,000 in stolen equipment, including a shotgun, tires and wheels, a laptop, a GPS, a Pepsi machine, a Shop-Vac and headlamps.

He also was initially charged with working at side jobs when he was supposed to be on duty, for having staff members charge blank DVDs to a county credit card and then drive to his house to pick up pornographic

DVDs for copying – all while the staff members were also supposed to be on duty.[8]

Connolly's conviction was in 2008 but was reversed on appeal based largely on the fact that Larson, who Connolly's attorney said was "completely discredited because of his own crimes," was the key witness in the sheriff's prosecution. A jury needed only 90 minutes to find him not guilty in his second trial. Connolly did not seek reelection in 2007.[9]

Erie County Sheriff Tim Howard is among the 140 or so active sheriffs in the U.S. who consider themselves "constitutional" sheriffs and not obligated to enforce laws with which they disagree. As a member in good standing of the Constitutional Sheriffs and Peace Officers Association (CSPOA), he feels no legal obligation for him to abide to mandates that prisoner suicide attempts be reported as "life-threatening situation." Nor does he see the need to adhere to mandated procedures to timely and effectively address allegations of sexual misconduct between his deputies and individuals incarcerated at the Erie County Holding Center and the Erie County Correctional facility.

That defiance to follow procedures might explain why more than two dozen prisoners have died during his tenure and why the New York attorney general saw fit to name Howard as a defendant in a lawsuit over allegations of sexual misconduct at correctional facilities.

Attorney General Letitia James said in her lawsuit that there were eight instances in which Howard refused to comply with directives that required his office to report allegations of sexual misconduct to the New York State Commission of Corrections in a timely manner and that he only finally did so after reports of his refusal to comply appeared in the media.

Of the 28 prisoner deaths between 2005, when he took office, and October 2019, Howard said, "We're not a hospital. The person most responsible for a suicide is the person that commits the suicide."[11]

29

North Carolina: Poster Child for Abuse

WHEN, IN 1768, Sheriff Hawkins, whose first name has been lost to history, seized a farmer's horse because he was unable to pay his taxes, about 80 residents of Sandy Creek, North Carolina, as a way of protesting unfair tax rates, set out in search of the sheriff. When they found him, they forced Hawkins sit backward on the horse while riding through town. It was a punishment symbolic of a practice called skimmington imported from England as a means of ridiculing a henpecked man.[1]

Hillsborough Sheriff Edmund Fanning responded by declaring the protesters to be rebels and insurgents to be shot or hanged "as mad dogs." Six of the group's leaders were subsequently arrested and hanged in 1771.[2] The consequences of malfeasance and other wrongdoing have gotten less severe in the ensuing 252 years, but North Carolina still has had its moments with sheriffs and sheriffs' deputies running afoul of the oaths they took to uphold the law and to protect the citizenry.

For example, between 1988 and 2016, there were 366 deputy sheriffs in 87 of the state's 100 counties who had their certifications as law enforcement officers revoked by the state for disciplinary reasons.

Twenty-eight counties had five or more revocations.[3]

Of the 366 revocations statewide during that time period, 35 were deputies of the Wake County Sheriff's Department.[4]

There are a number of reasons for which a law enforcement officer's certification may be revoked under North Carolina law. These include:

- Any felony unless granted an unconditional pardon of innocence;
- Any crime for which the authorized punishment could have been imprisonment for more than two years;
- Conviction of a Class B misdemeanor after the date of initial certification;

- Conviction of a Class B misdemeanor within a five-year period prior to the date of certification;
- Four or more convictions of Class B misdemeanors regardless of the dates of commission;
- Four or more convictions of a Class A misdemeanor, each of which occurred after the date of initial certification;
- Any combination of four or more Class A or Class B misdemeanors regardless of the date of commission or conviction;
- Finding of a lack of good moral character;
- The officer fails to meet any of the required standards;
- The officer has been terminated from employment for which he was commissioned;
- The officer has committed any prohibited act;
- The certification for the agency with which he is employed is terminated, suspended or revoked;
- If the officer knowingly makes a material misrepresentation of any information required for certification, and
- If the officer has been denied certification or had such certification suspended or revoked by the North Carolina Criminal Justice Education and Training Standards Commission, the North Carolina Sheriff's Education and Training Standards Commission or a similar North Carolina, out-of-state or federal approving, certifying or licensing agency.[5]

If ever there existed a poster child for abuse of authority and an argument in favor of term limits, it would have to be Alamance County Sheriff Terry Johnson.

Johnson no sooner had a federal lawsuit for racial profiling dismissed in August 2020 than he found himself again immersed in controversy when he accused a woman of violating the law and of being affiliated with Antifa after she asked why Johnson and his deputies were not wearing masks in violation of the governor's order to do so.

On August 14, Johnson spoke to a friendly group in Siembra, North Carolina, that was protesting a local referendum to move the city's Confederate monument and to repeal the sheriff's agreement with Immigration and Customs Enforcement (ICE) to detain illegal immigrants when local activist Lindsay Ayling walked up to the sheriff and asked why he and his deputies were not wearing face masks in accordance with the Gov. Roy

Cooper's directive.[6]

"Ma'am, you're breaking the law," Johnson responded, apparently in reference to an ordinance requiring any protest of two or more people to obtain a permit and then proclaiming no more permits would be granted for the "foreseeable future," the protest against removal of the Confederate monument notwithstanding.

Johnson was incorrect about Ayling's First Amendment right because the North Carolina ACLU had obtained a temporary restraining order that blocked the ordinance.[7]

In August 2015, U.S. District Judge Thomas Schroeder, appointed by President George W. Bush, dismissed a lawsuit against Johnson which had claimed that the sheriff was targeting Latinos during traffic stops and checkpoints in order to expedite their deportation and, in the process, to generate revenue for the sheriff's office.

The Department of Justice had brought the lawsuit, claiming that Latino drivers were as much as ten times more likely to be stopped by Alamance deputies who created "a pattern of discriminatory law enforcement activities…"

Several activists alleged that Johnson was directing his deputies to "go out there and get me some of those taco eaters" by arresting Latino drivers for offenses for which whites would not be arrested. The arrests in turn would allow the victims to be processed through the immigration database which in turn facilitated the partnership between Johnson's office and ICE that allowed Johnson's deputies to act as immigration officers and to incarcerate Latinos in the local jail for which Johnson's office received $3.6 million from ICE in 2019.[8]

The ACLU of North Carolina condemned Judge Schroeder's dismissal, characterizing it as a "miscarriage of justice," while urging the DOJ to file an immediate appeal. The ACLU statement said the decision "flies in the face of a mountain of evidence that Sheriff Johnson and the Alamance County Sheriff's Office engaged in discriminatory policing."[9]

Five years later, Johnson was again defending himself against a defamation lawsuit filed by a Texas couple whom Johnson obliquely referred to as human traffickers.

Aris Lamont Hines and Brandi Kauilani Thomason, formerly of Mebane, North Carolina, but living in Texas at the time of their lawsuit claimed the sheriff's department wrongfully investigated and charged them for enrolling an ineligible student athlete in Alamance-Burlington schools.

In May 2016, Johnson held a press conference and made public statements voicing suspicions while Kingsley Jonathan, known as Johnathan Kingsley was enrolled in the local school that Hines and Thomason were involved in a larger, multistate human-trafficking operation that also involved three girls the couple was alleged to have attempted to enroll as well. "This has the smell of a human trafficking organization," Johnson said at the time.

The couple was eventually charged with obstruction of justice and obtaining property by false pretenses, charges that were later dropped. The three girls were found in the Dominican Republic, New York and Texas just weeks after the charges were filed. Hines and Thomason were never charged with trafficking but claimed that their reputations were damaged to such an extent that they had to leave North Carolina. Jonathan went on to play defensive end for Syracuse University.

In a confusing ruling, Judge William Osteen, Jr. dismissed Alamance County from the litigation, ruling that Johnson's deputies are not legally employees of the county even though the county government approves the sheriff's department's budget.[10]

For violence, including murder, political corruption, and unabashed targeting of minorities by the local justice system, one need look no further than Robeson County, North Carolina, located on the state's southern border it shares with South Carolina.

Robeson is where 22 members of the sheriff's department, including the sheriff himself, were convicted of various crimes ranging from pirated satellite TV to arson, kidnapping and robbery of drug dealers. It's also where a former sheriff was suspected of involvement in drug trafficking, where a Native American attorney was a rising local political star until he was gunned down, and where doubts continue to linger as to the true identity of the killers of both the Native American attorney and former NBA star Michael Jordan's father three decades ago.

First, there was the March 26, 1988, shotgun murder of Julian Pierce, the Georgetown-educated Native American who was running for Superior Court Judge against District Attorney Joe Freeman Britt. Britt was listed in the Guinness Book of World Records as the World's Deadliest Prosecutor with 47 death-penalty convictions, the vast majority of whom were African-American or Lumbee Indians. The county population was about evenly split between whites, African Americans and Lumbees.

Maurice Geiger, an attorney whose nonprofit monitored Robeson's courts, said in 1991 that a review of thousands of cases from the 1980s forward revealed that an estimated 1,000 innocent people were wrongfully convicted *every year* [emphasis author's]. He said Britt's office employed several tactics to force guilty pleas. The court calendar was manipulated as defendants waited for their cases to be called. Others were tricked into signing forms that waived their rights to counsel (an easy task, given the county's adult illiteracy rate of 30 percent).

Killings of Lumbee men by sheriff's deputies were frequent – including one by 23-year-old deputy Kevin Stone, the sheriff's son. A coroner's inquest presided over by a funeral director with zero legal training took all of 12 minutes to find that the shooting was "an accident and/or self-defense."

Pierce's daughter, Julia Pierce, herself an attorney, is convinced that then-Sheriff Hubert Stone was somehow involved in her father's murder. The elder Pierce had campaigned against drug trafficking, racism in the local justice system and corruption in the county and Stone was rumored to be involved in all three – and personal friends with Britt.[11]

Moreover, Hubert Deese, a Robeson County drug dealer later convicted and sentenced to federal prison, was said to be Stone's unacknowledged son, though his name was not among the survivors listed in Stone's obituary in 2008.[12]

Three days after Pierce's murder, Stone called a press conference and announced that a 24-year-old Lumbee named Johnny Goins, who had been dating the daughter of Pierce's ex-girlfriend, was the killer. Unfortunately, Stone said, Goins, while hiding in a tiny closet, had committed suicide by placing a shotgun in his mouth and pulling the trigger. That pronouncement instantly changed the official cause from a political killing to a domestic dispute.

The autopsy report, however, said the shotgun was placed against the right side of Goins' head, near his ear. Researcher Nicole Lucas Haimes, who produced a documentary about the killing 29 years after the murder, noted that it would have been difficult, if not impossible, for Goins to have placed a bulky shotgun against the side of his head in such a confined space.

When Haimes asked Stone if the gun was open, the sheriff said, "No, it was closed. It had just been fired."

Crime scene photos showed the shotgun in Goins' lap and the gun was broken open.

The local medical examiner said Goins left a suicide note admitting that he shot Pierce and that a companion named Sandy Chavis was present. The note was never produced.[13]

African American and Lumbee residents were so distrustful of local government and Robeson County's justice system that five weeks after Pierce was killed, they elected the dead man by a 2,000-vote majority.[14]

The second murder, that of James Jordan, occurred five years later, on July 23, 1993. Daniel Green and Larry Demery were convicted of the crime but in 2016, attorneys for Green said there was reason to believe that Stone, sheriff at the time of the murder, attempted to steer the investigation away from a drug investigation to kidnapping and robbery.

Investigators said at the time they were led to Green and Demery by tracking calls made from the cell phone in Jordan's vehicle. One of those calls was made to Hubert Deese, Sheriff Hubert's illegitimate son and a convicted drug trafficker. At the time of Green's 1996 trial, Green's defense team attempted to introduce evidence of that call but was prevented from doing so by the presiding judge. Demery, who admitted shooting Jordan, had worked with Deese at a mobile home dealership about a mile from where Jordan's body was found two weeks after the murder.

Green's attorneys believe that Jordan may have been killed after he stumbled upon a drug deal and they further believe that had the jury known about the connection between Demery and Deese, they may have arrived at a different verdict. The defense lawyers claim that the Robeson County Sheriff's Department failed to pursue that angle in order to protect Deese, who also was a friend with the lead investigator on the case.

Deese spent considerable time at the sheriff's department answering telephones and going on ride-alongs with deputies and former police officers told federal agents in 1997 that Deese paid deputies for information about ongoing drug investigations.

While Stone, who served as sheriff from 1978 to 1994, was never implicated, his successor Glenn Maynor was among the 22 sheriff's department personnel who were indicted on charges from pirating satellite television signals to kidnapping, perjury, arson, drug trafficking, armed robbery and money laundering.

Green's attorneys said that reports from the sheriff's office, the

State Bureau of Investigations and the federal Drug Enforcement Agency revealed that Stone was aware of his son's cocaine trafficking and that he took extraordinary steps to protect him.

"If the jury had known that the sheriff's office had a strong motive to conceal evidence of drug motive," defense attorneys said, …they would have been less likely to conclude that the murder transpired in the course of a carjacking" as prosecutors claimed at the trial of Green and Demery.[15]

Maynor, who succeeded Stone as sheriff and served until 2004, was sentenced to six years in prison in June 2008 following a six-year-long federal and state investigation known as Operation Tarnished Badge. He pled guilty in September 2007 to lying to a grand jury and misuse of federal funds. He received a one-year sentence on the former charge and five years on the second, with sentences to be served consecutively. He was also ordered to pay restitution of $17,550 and to spend three years on supervised release following completion of his sentence.

U.S. Attorney George Holding said, "We started with the lowest of the low. Basically, the investigation started with drug dealers who were telling us they had been robbed or abused in some manner by law enforcement. From those witnesses, we worked all the way up to the sheriff."[16]

Two years after Maynor left office, in 2006, a *Fayetteville Observer* reporter wrote, "The rumors persisted for years: some Robeson County deputies were beating up drug dealers and stealing their money."

He also wrote that Maynor and the district attorney's office knew about the corruption by defense attorneys, but "their attitude was, 'Well, [the defense attorneys'] clients are drug dealers and we are not going to put any stock in what they say,'"

But finally, on June 9, at the end of a lengthy investigation, a 29-page indictment was returned against three former drug enforcement deputies, accusing them of stealing tens of thousands of dollars seized during traffic stops for drugs. Further, the three, Roger Hugh Taylor, Charles Thomas Strickland, and Steven Ray Lovin, were accused of firebombing homes and of kidnapping drug dealers and holding them for ransom.

The indictments – six additional sheriff's deputies and two Lumberton police officers had been brought up on charges earlier – were so bad that even former Sheriff Hubert Stone, the subject of considerable speculation in his own right, was prompted to call them "one of the worst black marks that we can have against us here in the county."

It became apparent that things were going south when, in March 2005, federal and state agents appeared at the sheriff's office with a Ryder-rental truck and spent the next four hours loading documents and computers from the sheriff's office into the vehicle.

District Attorney Britt said instead of seized drugs having been packaged, tagged and given to an evidence custodian for safekeeping until trial, drugs were found in deputies' desks, in their cars and out in the open and some drugs were missing. Within a week, five members of the Drug Enforcement Division had turned in their badges and resigned.

Britt said of former Sheriff Maynor, who had resigned in 2004, citing health reasons, "Officially, he is not a suspect. I think …there are certain questions about what Sheriff Maynor knew and how much he knew and was he involved in any of this?"[17]

That would change soon enough.

Federal officials in 2004 canceled the Equitable Sharing Program that allowed local law enforcement to share in the cash and other assets seized from criminals because of the indictments over traffic stops and ensuing robberies. But by 2019, deputies in Robeson County had resumed the practice under probationary status.[18]

Derek O'Mary, a lieutenant with the Durham County Sheriff's Office, was responsible for managing the department's account used for undercover drug buys.

On June 7, 2011, he was sentenced to 42 months in prison after pleading guilty to embezzling nearly $98,000 of the department's Anti-Crime Narcotics Unit funds over a six-year period from July 2003 to March 2009.

In exchange for his guilty pleas, additional charges of obstruction of justice and cocaine possession involving the theft of drug evidence from the department were dismissed.[19]

At the time of his September 2010 arrest his attorney, Joe Cheshire said, "Mr. O'Mary had a long and substantial career serving the people of Durham County, and no one should forget his sacrifices as we work through the process of this case."[20]

O'Mary wasn't alone in yielding to the temptation of assessable cash from undercover drug buy money. Little more than a year later former Franklin County Sheriff Pat Green received a sentence of up to 62 months in prison for embezzling $221,000 from the county through a bogus drug investigation that he said involved a county commissioner and two senators. The theft of the funds occurred over a three-year period, from October 2007 to December 2010. Of the total embezzled, $203,000 was earmarked for undercover drug buys and the remaining $18,000 was confiscated drug money which was supposed to have gone to Franklin County schools but which was instead taken from the sheriff's office evidence room.

As part of his plea bargain, Green also agreed to repay all money to the county.[21]

Officially, former Buncombe County Sheriff Bobby Lee Medford went to prison for his conviction on federal bribery, conspiracy, mail fraud and money laundering charges but his biggest crime was when he pressured witness testimony in the wrongful convictions of five African-American for murder in a case that cost one of the defendants 11 years behind bars and the county $8.2 million in settlements, only $2.8 million of which was paid by insurance.

During his 12 years as sheriff (1994-2006) Medford developed a kickback scheme whereby he allowed illegal video poker machines to operate in exchange for cash payments with some of the money coming from biannual golf tournaments he sponsored, tournaments that attracted large donations from video poker interests. While some of the money from the video poker operators was spent on his campaigns, he pocketed up to $300,000 in bribe money, prosecutors said. Two dozen people involved in the illegal video scheme had already pleaded guilty by the time Medford was convicted in June 2008.[22]

A 2000 state law charged North Carolina sheriffs with the supervision of video poker operations. Donations from the golf tournaments were used for Medford's reelection campaigns and paid into credit union accounts controlled by Medford or his girlfriend.

Medford was convicted on charges of controlling a multimillion-dollar gambling scheme following jury deliberations of less than two hours. He was sentenced to concurrent terms of 15 years in federal prison.[23]

But the worst transgression was the coercion by Medford and deputies Samuel Constance, George Sprinkle, Michael Murphy, and John Elkins of false statements from suspects that implicated Kenneth Kagenyera in home invasion and murder of Walter Bowman in Fairview, North Carolina, that occurred when three African-American men burst into his home and shot him through a bedroom door.

It took 11 years but in September 2011, it was determined that Medford and his deputies had destroyed and/or concealed exculpatory evidence that would have exonerated Kagenyera. Three North Carolina Superior Court judges unanimously declared him innocent of the murder.[24] Medford died of coronavirus in June 2020, just 16 months before his scheduled Oct. 11, 2021 release date.[25]

Brunswick County, nestled in the southernmost part of the state, holds the distinction of having two sheriffs sentenced to prison terms. Only one came out alive.

In June 1983, Sheriff Herman Strong was sentenced to 14 years in federal prison following his conviction on drug smuggling and conspiracy charges. He would serve only four years before being released in June 1987.[26]

On June 30, 1983, just two days after Strong's successor, John Carr Davis, was sworn in as sheriff, Ronald Hewett took the oath as a Holden Beach police officer on his twentieth birthday. Ten years later, Hewett was named D.A.R.E. officer of the year and a year after that became the youngest sheriff in North Carolina when, at the age of 31, he defeaed he defeated James Brown at the age of thirty-one.

But by the time he ran for his fourth consecutive term, the stories of questionable behavior were being repeated throughout the county. They included reports of his requiring deputies to paint campaign signs for him, allowing his son to accompany him on calls, showing up intoxicated at crime scenes, jeopardizing his son's safety and that of hostages by kicking in a door during a SWAT response, and having a deputy guard his residence while his driveway was being paved.

By June 2007, the U.S. Attorney's Office was issuing subpoenas seeking documents and testimony concerning more than thirty people as "relevant parties." A second wave of subpoenas was issued in January 2008 and on March 27, 2008, the local district attorney's office announced that Hewett was suspended from office on the grounds of habitual neglect, willful misconduct or maladministration, extortion and intoxication.

Four days later, a Brunswick County grand jury indicted him on three felony counts of embezzlement and one count of obstruction of justice. Hewett resigned on April 15 and on June 2 pled guilty to one count of obstruction of justice and was sentenced to up to sixteen months in prison, followed by two years of supervised release and a fine of ten thousand dollars.[27]

Hewett served about 14 months of that sentence but by July 2014, found himself in hot water again when he was arrested on federal firearms charges. [28]

Three days later he was dead.

An autopsy report released on Dec. 3, 2014, said Hewett, fifty-one, died of a heart condition following an altercation with jailers.[29]

Gaston County Sheriff's Reserve Captain Wesley Clayton Golden was sentenced to 20 months in prison, a year of probation and a fine of $200 in February 2014 after he pleaded guilty to extortion and conspiracy a year earlier.

Golden, along with Mark Ray Hoyle was recruited by Frankie Dellinger, a 20-year veteran of law enforcement, in 2012 to provide protection for transports of what they thought were stolen goods valued at $160,000 but expected to be resold for $400,000. In reality they were being caught up in a sting operation run by federal agents.

Dellinger was a reserve officer with the Cherryville Police Department, having formerly worked in the department's narcotics division. Hoyle was a civilian brought into the scheme by Dellinger and provided with a badge and gun. The three men were to have safeguarded loaded trailers in exchange for cash payments.

Dellinger was sentenced to three years in prison, two years' probation and a $400 fine while Hoyle was sentenced to 21 months in jail, two years' probation and ordered to pay a $300 fine.[30]

Eight Northhampton County sheriff's deputies received federal prison sentences ranging from two to ten years in June 2017 following their convictions in a massive drug sting operation on charges ranging from conspiracy to distribute illegal narcotics, firearms and bribery charges.

"Operation Rockfish" was initiated after reports that rogue Virginia corrections officer, Lann Tjuan Clanton, was extorting criminals he stopped and keeping their contraband for himself. FBI agents infiltrated Clanton's operation, gave him a $9,000 Rolex watch and more than $41,000 in bribes in exchange for Clanton's transporting what he believed was more than 100 kilograms of cocaine and heroin and more than $2 million in drug money.

As Clanton expanded his operations along the I-95 corridor through Maryland and North and South Carolina, he recruited correctional officers,

Virginia prison employees, a North Carolina 911 dispatcher and eight current or former Northhampton County deputies – all while undercover FBI agents watched and listened.

When the shoe fell, it fell hard. In late April 2015, 13 current and former law enforcement officers and two civilians were indicted for their participation in the drug trafficking conspiracy. Two years later, the sentences were handed down by Senior U.S. District Court Judge Malcolm Howard of the Eastern District of North Carolina.

Clanton received a sentence of 192 months (more than 16 years). Northhampton deputies receiving sentences included Ikeisha Jacobs (ten years), Jason and Curtis Boone (eight years each), Jimmy Pair, Jr., Thomas Jefferson Allen II, and Cory Jackson (seven years, three months each), Wardie Vincent, Jr. (six years), and Tosha Dailey (two years).[31]

In North Carolina, sheriffs may cooperate with Immigration and Customs Enforcement (ICE) at their own peril, as former Mecklenburg County Sheriff Irwin Carmichael learned in May 2018. Other sheriffs apparently took Carmichael's experience as their cue to refuse cooperation with ICE. Carmichael had chosen to cooperate with President Donald Trump's deportation policy by participating in a controversial ICE program to form partnerships with state and local law enforcement through the 287(g) program which delegated immigration roles to the local authorities. According to ICE, the Mecklenburg County Sheriff's Office's participation in the program led directly to some 300 deportations in fiscal year 2017. Carmichael's opponent, Democrat Garry McFadden, said, "287(g) does not create a trusted working relationship between law enforcement and many of the community.

McFadden captured the Democratic nomination with 52 percent of the vote while Carmichael polled a distant third place with just over 20 percent. Because no Republican qualified for the election, McFadden was the sheriff-elect of North Carolina's second-largest county, which includes the greater Charlotte metropolitan area.[32]

By February 2019, the sheriffs of three other counties were publicly distancing themselves from ICE and 287(g).

Said Orange County Sheriff Charles Blackwood: "Orange County has never been a participant in the 287(g) program. Our position is and continues to be that, if we receive documentation that provides the necessary legal basis to satisfy the Fourth Amendment, we will hold the individual.

Absent the necessary legal basis to hold someone, they will be released."

Durham County Sheriff Clarence Birkhead said his decision not to honor ICE detainers was "to help all of Durham's people feel safe and encourage our residents to feel like they can trust my deputies – and law enforcement in general."

In Wake County, Sheriff Gerald Baker said it made "no difference whether a person is in this country legally or illegally. If he or she breaks any law in this county, they will be arrested and prosecuted." On the other hand, he said, "Any individual released from the Wake County Detention Center has met requirements of bail set by the courts. We release individuals by order of the courts."[33]

Granville County Sheriff Brindell Wilkins was suspended from office in September 2019 following his indictment for allegedly helping to plot the killing of a deputy who had a recording of him using "racially insensitive language." Charles R. Noblin, Jr. was appointed to succeed Wilkins in January 2020. The suspension was moot inasmuch as he had already resigned, effective more than a year earlier, on July 9, 2018.[34]

Before he could go to trial on the initial charges, he indicted again in June 2021 on two counts each of obstruction of justice and failure to discharge his duties while still in office. One count of each charge was connected to his office's drug unit while the remaining charges were for improper approval of gun permits.

Soon after his 2019 indictment, investigators began looking at operations of the drug unit, tracking money seized and used by investigators in drug cases. More than 100 criminal cases had to be dismissed in 2017 because the drug unit didn't document its interactions with a frequent informant, including agreements with him, how much he was paid or who was being targeted in undercover drug buys. Sergeant Chad Coffey, a member of the drug unit, was indicted in 2020 on charges of obstruction of justice, conspiracy to deliver cocaine, embezzlement and altering or destroying evidence.[35]

Wilkins, who was first elected sheriff in 2009, said in a conversation that former deputy Joshua Freeman would soon release an audio recording of him using "racially insensitive language" to state authorities in Raleigh. Wilkins, court records said, told the person he was speaking with to "take care of it" and said "the only way you gonna stop him is kill him." He added instructions on how to carry out the murder without being identified, court records said.[36]

Gates County Sheriff Randy Hathaway received a 45-day suspended jail sentence, was ordered to pay a $500 fine and perform 100 hours of community service after pleading guilty to a misdemeanor charge of failing to discharge his duties while sheriff.

The sentence was imposed in September 2018 after Gates and three deputies were charged with embezzlement in January.

Hathaway was arrested along with deputies Glenda Parker, Levar Newsome, and Tobe Ruffin. Each was charged with obtaining property by false pretense. Former deputy Brandon Hawks was also arrested on two counts of embezzlement of public property by a public officer and a single firearm count. His father was also arrested on two counts of possession of a stolen firearm.[37]

30

North Dakota: Steal, Deal Meth? Pay $500

IF YOU ARE A SHERIFF in North Dakota, your penalty for using and distributing meth and the theft of three-quarters of a million dollars is to simply repay the money, pay an additional fine of $500 and serve 25 days of home confinement.

Johnny "Zip" Lawson, former sheriff of Wells County, was originally indicted in May 2017 on felony charges of conspiracy to deliver methamphetamine and bribery and three misdemeanor charges of providing false information to a law enforcement officer, neglect of duty and ingesting a controlled substance (methamphetamines). He was accused of consuming methamphetamine prior to his April 25 resignation. He got the meth in exchange for not investigating residential burglaries in Wells County. His supplier, Blake Lail, was also charged with six felonies in connection to an investigation by the North Dakota Bureau of Criminal Investigation.[1]

The two felony counts were eventually dropped and he pled guilty to two misdemeanors, filing false reports to police and ingesting meth. Judge Daniel Narum sentenced the former sheriff to 25 days of home confinement.

Two years later, Lawson was back in trouble, this time accused along with his wife of converting for their personal use $751,000 in overpayments made from the North Dakota Department of Human Services.[2] Lawson again avoided prison time. This time U.S. District Judge Daniel Traynor ordered full restitution from the pair, parents of 13 children. Additionally, the Lawsons were ordered to pay $100 in special assessments and to serve three years of supervised release.[3]

A former McKenzie County sheriff's deputy received a suspended sentence in March 2019 after being convicted of having a sexual relationship with an underage boy.

Bryton Dahl, 24, was also a substitute teacher and had worked from November 2015 to March 2017 as a Williston police officer before going to work as a deputy with the McKenzie County Sheriff's Department until his arrest in August 2017 on charges of corruption or solicitation of a minor.

He was convicted in November 2018 but Northwest District Judge Benjamen Johnson found that Dahl did not directly abuse his role as a police officer because there was no testimony that he used his position to coerce anyone.

He sentenced Dahl to three years in prison with all but the time he spent in jail awaiting sentencing suspended.[4]

The sheriff of Ward County was allowed to resign to avoid prosecution after he allowed Dustin Irwin, a 25-year-old member of the Mandan, Hidatsa and Arikara Nation died in custody in 2014 when he was not transported to a hospital to receive medical attention.

Sheriff Steven Kukowski, who had been operating the Ward County jail under state oversight since December 2014 for failure to keep the facility in proper condition, was scheduled to appear at a removal hearing in April 2017, but worked out an agreement with county commissioners whereby he would resign and would receive $75,000 from the county while waiving the right to pursue any action against the county.

Ward County reached an undisclosed settlement with Irwin's family in separate negotiations in April 2016.[5]

31

Ohio: Extortion, Tryst, Cocaine

DELAWARE COUNTY Sheriff Walter Davis, unopposed for re-election in November 2012, abruptly resigned from office on April 9 and withdrew his name from the upcoming ballot after it was learned that he used county money to pay for an out-of-state rendezvous with a female deputy.

Davis had spent the previous weekend removing items from his office in apparent preparation for his resignation. Earlier, the Delaware County Republican Central Committee voted 65-8 to rescind its endorsement of him.

More repercussions followed his resignation as the deputy he spent the night with, Janine Senanayake, was fired and subsequently filed a sexual harassment lawsuit against the department. Previously known as Janine England, Senanayake had resigned under a similar cloud in 2009 from the Perry Township Police Department after a video surface showed her in an intimate scene in a patrol car with the police chief.[1]

In 2016, Pike County Sheriff Charles Reader obtained national prominence as the public face of the investigation of the execution-style murders of eight members of the Rhoden family in Ohio's Appalachia region known mainly for its extreme poverty and illegal marijuana.[2]

Four years later, Reader was sentenced to three years in prison and barred from holding public office in Ohio after pleading guilty to five counts of theft in office and tampering with records related to allegation that he stole money seized in drug cases and attempted to replace it when an investigation was initiated in 2018.[3]

Reader was appointed sheriff in May 2015 and less than a year later, eight members of the Rhoden family were found murdered in their homes in rural Pike County. The dead included Dana Rhoden, 37; her former husband, Christopher Rhoden Sr., 41; their daughter, sons Christopher, 16;

Clarence "Frankie," 20, and Kenneth, 44; their cousin, Gary, 38; and Hanna Gilley, 20, who was in a relationship with Clarence. Three children, including Hanna Rhoden's four- day-old daughter, were unharmed.

Following an investigation that spanned several states, Billy and Angela Wagner and their two sons, Jake and George, were arrested on aggravated murder charges in November 2018.[4]

Only days before the four were arrested for the murders, the Ohio state auditor's office received an anonymous tip that Reader had misused funds, borrowed money from employees and allowed his daughter to drive a car from the sheriff's impound lot.

Court documents would ultimately indicate that Reader had misappropriated about $15,000 in seized funds, borrowed another $6,000 from his employees and circumvented rules at his department's auctions that allowed family members to obtain impounded vehicles.

He was initially indicted on 18 counts but eventually entered pleas on five counts.[5]

Found guilty on February 12, 2015, on 18 of 25 separate counts, including the first-degree felony of engaging in a pattern of corrupt activity, Athens County Sheriff Pat Kelly was sentenced a month later to seven years in prison by Judge Patricia A. Cosgrove who noted that Kelly showed no remorse for his actions.

Cosgrove, who could have sentenced Kelly to ten years just for the count of engaging in a pattern of corrupt activity, sentenced him to three years for that, two years for perjury and two years for multiple theft convictions, and further ordered that the terms run consecutively for the seven-year total. He was also ordered to pay about $6,000 in restitution to Athens County, with the money to be taken from his Ohio Public Employees Retirement System pension.[6]

The jury deliberated for about 16 hours before convicting him of corrupt activity 12 of 13 theft-in-office charges, three of four theft counts, perjury and failure to keep a cashbook. He was acquitted of money laundering, tampering with evidence, tampering with records and the misdemeanor charges of obstructing official business and dereliction of duty.

Judge Cosgrove noted that he had misspent public money on restaurant meals even as the sheriff's office lacked sufficient cruisers and other equipment, and that he had sold county property for scrap and pocketed the cash proceeds.[7]

Three years after federal agents entered his office armed with a search warrant, former Allen County Sheriff Sam Crish was sentenced to more than 11 years in prison after he pleaded guilty to federal charges of extortion, intimidation, bribery and other strong-arm tactics in an attempt to get out from under more than $600,000 in gambling debts.[8]

Investigators revealed a six-count indictment of Crish in June 2018 for extortion, soliciting bribes and making false statements to the FBI.

Crish first joined the Allen County Sheriff's Office in 1991 where he held several positions, including commander of the office's Investigative Division and the West Central Ohio Crime Task Force (WCOCTF). He was first elected sheriff in 2008 and was reelected in 2012 and 2016.

The federal indictment charged that Crish had solicited $8,000 from an individual who gave him the money in cash in an alley behind the sheriff's office in 2012. Two months later, that same individual applied for the position of nurse at the county jail, which Crish oversaw. Crish solicited $42,000 from that person, ostensibly to pay debts and the individual took out a home equity line of credit and again passed the money to Crish in that same alley.

A year earlier, the WCOCTF was investigating a second person for drug offenses. No charges were ever filed in connection with that investigation but in February or March 2013, that person gave Crish a $20,000 loan which was later forgiven after Crish promised to "take care of" an uncover operation in which that person, identified by federal authorities as "person 2," was "going to get indicted." Person 2 in 2014 pleaded guilty to drug trafficking and was sentenced to 24 years in prison.

Crish later demanded that prostitution charges against a used car dealer be dropped after the man paid Crish $7,000 in September 2015. The charges were subsequently dismissed.

Crish also obtained ten thousand dollars in cash from another used car dealer who was under investigation for prostitution and also in 2015, Crish told a grocery store owner that for two thousand dollars, he could make an investigation into illegal gambling operations go away. The store owner gave Crish a $2,000 loan in October 2015, which Crish repaid at no interest.[9]

A two-year undercover sting operation resulted in the arrests of 44 law enforcement officers in the Cleveland area in 1998, including Cuyahoga County sheriff's deputy Michael Joye who boasted to undercover agents that he had eight other deputies available to serve as members of a "security detail" to protect future drug transactions.[10]

In all, law enforcement officers from three departments worked to ensure that there would be no interference in the sale of hundreds of pounds of purported cocaine, the FBI said, adding that they were paid more than $120,000 to protect the fake drug deals – at times wearing uniforms and handguns as they did so.

Joye, also known as Guido, told an undercover agent, "My guys take care of business. If someone touches you, they're gonna get the hand snapped off ...When the cops come, they say what happened, and we show 'em our badges ...They'll listen to a badge."

The only problem for Joye and the others was that the FBI was also listening and videotaping the exchange. The lone undercover agent went incognito in March 1995 as the investigation of organized crime was launched. He posed as a criminal who made a living dealing drugs. About a year and a half into the investigation, Joye approached an undercover agent and sold him crack cocaine, saying at the time that he knew many law enforcement officers willing to assist the agent in illegal activity.

"This is something we do it right," Joye told the agent. "We do it precise ...military type. We're in. We're out. It's all over ...covert operation." He said jail guards would do the work because they felt underpaid in their jobs. Asked if his associates were trustworthy, Joye said, "We're a family ...and not one of us wants to get busted. Nobody wants to get caught."

The first deal was when six men unloaded 20 gambling machines from a truck into a storage locker on November 13, 1996, as an FBI video camera recorded the entire operation. The second was on February 27, 1997 and involved eight guards who helped drive 600 pounds of marijuana to the Lost Nation Airport in Willoughby, loaded the drugs onto an airplane and watched a second undercover agent trade fake bearer bonds and supposed cocaine for the marijuana. Joye assured agents that any police officer who pulled over the load of marijuana would go away once the jail guards showed their badges.

Joye's men also protected other deals and once escorted supposed cocaine from an Interstate 71 hotel to the county airport.[11]

Joye, as organizer of the rogue officers would ultimately receive the most severe punishment – a sentence of nine years and four months.[12]

Jefferson County Sheriff Fred Abdalla's biggest problem was that he appeared to be too protective of the fabled Steubenville Big Red football team – especially after two players on the team were accused of raping a 16-year-old girl (both were ultimately found guilty).

Abdalla did the same thing other sheriffs have done: he went after the messenger instead of the perpetrators, declaring in an interview that he was "coming after" Anonymous, a fellow Steubenville High School athlete who posted the video of the assault on social media. Abdalla was subsequently booed when he appeared to speak at an Occupy Steubenville rally the day following his threat to seek reprisals against Anonymous.[13]

Abdalla was unaware that he was sharing the stage with Anonymous, who, like others on the stage, was wearing a Guy Fawkes mask. At that rally, Anonymous, later identified as Deric Lostutter, posted, "I wonder if Sheriff Abdalla knows that I can reach out and tap him on the shoulder right now." Soon after, police began pulling over anyone in Guy Fawkes masks in an attempt to ferret out the real Anonymous – to no avail.[14]

Youngstown served as a footnote to the indictment of Michael Joye and 44 other law enforcement officers in Cuyahoga County when Mahoning County Sheriff Phil Chance found himself caught up in the same sweeping roundup of rogue cops in the Cleveland-Youngstown area.

Youngstown sits on the Pennsylvania border almost exactly halfway between Cleveland and Pittsburgh, placing the town in the middle of a struggle between mafia families in the two larger cities for control of Youngstown's gambling operations. It was there that Chance first ran for sheriff against incumbent Ed Nemeth in 1992 – and lost.

But he did garner 40 percent of the vote and encouraged by those numbers, ran again in 1996. This time, however, he turned to Youngstown Mafia boss Lenine "Lenny" Strollo for help in his campaign. A member of the Pittsburgh branch of La Cosa Nostra, Strollo was having his own problems after a falling out with Nemeth who refused to protect Strollo's rackets. He also was experiencing competition from independent gambling operators as well as from the Cleveland mob.[15]

It proved to be a fateful union that also figured John Chicase, Lawrence "Jeep" Garono, and Charles O'Nesti into the equation that would eventually lead to Chance's downfall. Chicase was a former deputy sheriff who ran a legitimate security business while also participating in Strollo's criminal enterprise.

Strollo's long-time friend O'Nesti was an aide to U.S. Rep. James

Traficant, himself a former sheriff of Mahoning County who, despite admitting as much on tape, nevertheless was acquitted of accepting more than $100,000 in bribes from organized crime figures while sheriff, arguing at trial that he was running his own sting operation when he took the bribes. He made national headlines while sheriff by refusing to execute foreclosure orders on unemployed homeowners after the collapse of the area's steel industry.

In 2002, Traficant was indicted on ten felony counts of racketeering, bribery and fraud and following a two-month trial, was convicted on all ten counts. On July 24, 2002, by an overwhelming vote of 420-1, he became only the fifth member of the House and second since the Civil War to be expelled from Congress.[16]

Strollo dictated that Chicase be hired by Chance. Chicase, Garono, and O'Nesti were used as go-betweens for Strollo to funnel money to Chance, who reciprocated by closing down competing gambling operations identified by Strollo while allowing Strollo's enterprises to operate without interference.

In addition to taking payoff money from Strollo, Chance also strong-armed Youngstown businesses to contribute to his campaign or face repercussions from the sheriff's office. One of those was a fireworks business run by millionaire Bruce Zoldan, who had supported Chance's opponent in the 1996 election.

Chance was eventually indicted on five counts by a federal grand jury charging him with conducting the affairs of an enterprise in violation of the Racketeer Influenced and Corrupt Organizations (RICO) Act with conspiracy to commit a RICO violation, violations of the Hobbs Act (extortion), and obstruction of justice.

He was convicted on one count of violation of the RICO statute, two counts of violation of the Hobbs Act by conspiring to obstruct, delay or affect commerce through extortion, and one count of conspiring to obstruct of justice in relation to "intent to facilitate an illegal gambling business."

U.S. District Judge Kathleen O'Malley sentenced Chance to 71 months' imprisonment and two years of supervised release. In sentencing him to the 71 months, the judge increased the sentence by three levels from standard sentencing guidelines on the basis that Chance's conduct was undertaken as chief law enforcement officer of Mahoning County.[17]

Two former Lucas County Sheriff's deputies were sentenced on January 28, 2011, to prison terms followed by two years' supervised release for federal civil rights violations and records falsification following the in-custody death of a pretrial detainee at the Lucas County Jail in 2004. John E. Gray received a prison sentence of two years while Jay M. Schmeltz was sentenced to one year and one day and fined $6,000.

The two were found guilty by a federal jury in connection with the death of inmate Carlton Benton. Evidence presented at trial showed that Gray assaulted Benton on May 30, 2004, in a cell at the Lucas County Jail and left him lying unconscious without seeking medical help. Gray and Schmeltz then wrote false reports in an attempt to conceal the incident. Lucas County Sheriff James Telb and Internal Affairs Investigator Robert McBroom were acquitted on charges related to allegations of a subsequent cover-up.[18]

Butler County Sheriff Richard K. Jones has been described as "Ohio's mini-Trump." It's not a description he rejects. Not only did he refuse to enforce mask mandates during the coronavirus pandemic he also refuses to equip his deputies with FDA-approved Narcan which law enforcement officers and firefighters elsewhere spray up victims' noses to reverse the effects of opioid overdoses.

"We don't do shots for bee stings; we don't inject diabetic people with insulin. When does it stop?" he said in an interview with *The Washington Post*. "I'm not the one that decides of people live or die. They decide that when they stick that needle in their arm."[19]

He is said to have been Trump before Trump, calling for immigration reform as far back as 2006. In 2016, Jones led a crowd in chanting "Build that wall" during a Donald Trump rally and then went on to pull a higher percentage of votes (72 percent) than any other Republican on the ballot that year, including Trump's 61 percent.[20]

In 2010, he faced federal charges of violating the constitutional rights of an undocumented immigrant, Luis Rodriguez Trevino, who alleged that the sheriff infringed on his Fourth and Fourteenth amendment rights. Rodriguez Trevino, who had lived in Butler County for eleven years, was arrested by Jones in 2007, charged with providing false identification and deported to Mexico. He was later acquitted on the basis that sheriff's deputies had no authority to enforce federal immigration law and that they had neglected to read Rodriguez his Miranda rights. Rodriguez Trevino filed suit.[21]

Jones ended up paying him $100,000 to settle the civil rights suit in 2011.[22]

32

Oklahoma: Sex, Lies, and Drugs

IN TERMS OF REALLY BIZARRE BEHAVIOR, it would be difficult to eclipse the exploits of Milton Anthony, former sheriff of Carter County. When twenty-six-year-old Kelli Denney, an employee in Anthony's sheriff's department, asked Anthony to hire her husband, Anthony, 65, responded by asking Denney to marry him. She rejected that offer but took Anthony up on his request for sex in exchange for hiring her husband. Their sexual relationship began in July 2015 and continued for several months but when she attempted to end their trysts, he threatened to alter her work hours and even fire both her and her husband if she did not continue their relationship.

Denny then began to record their conversations, and she saved text messages between them and he was arrested on June 2, 2016, on one count each of corruption in office and felony bribery.[1]

He entered a guilty plea in November to the bribery count in exchange for avoiding jail time. He received a two-year deferred sentence and agreed not to serve in law enforcement anywhere in the future.[2]

Joe Russell, former sheriff of Love County, avoided jail time with his own plea bargain in March 2017, but his son wasn't so lucky.

A young couple last seen in the company of a relative of Russell in July 2013 in Love County remained missing and the girl's family finally declared her dead in January 2021. Russell refused to involve his department in trying to apprehend the sheriff's relative who was driving the car in which the two were passengers when last seen.

Russell, meanwhile, got off with the proverbial slap on the wrist: a guilty plea to willful omission to perform a duty, which carried a penalty of a year of unsupervised probation and $300 in court costs.[3]

Among his transgressions as sheriff:

- He allowed a fugitive, the girlfriend of his son, to stay at his home even though he knew she had four outstanding warrants for her

arrest. (She was, in fact, arrested three days after she broke up with the sheriff's son and moved in with another man.)
- He allowed several individuals to use meth inside his own home in his presence.
- He allowed his son to deal meth from his home.
- He arrested women in bikinis on public intoxication charges but instead of taking them to jail, he took them to his home and had them strip for him.
- He allowed his nephew, James Conn Nipp, the driver of the vehicle in which the missing couple, Misty Miller, 17, and Colt Haynes, 21, were passengers when last seen, to visit with family members unsupervised in a deputy's office where evidence was stored.[4]

A month after his own arrest and seven months before his plea bargain, in August 2016, Russell's son, George "Willie" Russell, was sentenced to 40 months in federal prison after pleading guilty to methamphetamine distribution. He was arrested in May 2015 after selling meth to an undercover officer.[5]

Things were already tight in Delaware County, but when residents were forced to approve a sales tax increase in order to pay a $13.5 million settlement between the county and more than a dozen female inmates who suffered sexual assaults at the hands of sheriff's deputies, it was too much. Sheriff Jay Blakfox resigned in the scandal's wake, citing personal reasons but denying any wrongdoing.

To the southwest only three counties away, another sheriff was forced out of office in the aftermath of the accidental shooting death of a jail inmate by a reserve deputy who, in addition to being friends with the sheriff was a major contributor to his election campaign.

Robert Bates, seventy-four, was what was described as a play-for-pay cop who was an inadequately-trained reserve deputy who was allowed to ride with deputies during an illegal gun sales sting in 2015 when he mistook his gun for his taser and shot suspect Eric Harris, an unarmed black man who died from his wound.

Instead of cooperating with investigators looking into charges of corruption and favoritism given toward Bates in training, however, Sheriff Stanley Glanz attempted to block a grand jury investigation of his department. Glanz, for his part, received a one-year suspended sentence while Bates was sentenced to four years in prison for second-degree manslaughter.⁶

Former Latimer County Sheriff Melvin Holly wasn't so lucky. He was sentenced to 25 years in federal prison after being convicted on 14 of 15 counts after he was indicted for making sexual advances or having sexual contact with eight female inmates of the Latimer County Jail, which he called his "Hollyday Inn."⁷

A federal appeals court overturned four of the aggravated sexual assault charges, ruling that the trial court had "erroneously instructed the jury on the definition of aggravated sexual abuse," but the appeals court ruling did not subtract any time from his sentence.⁸

He was also convicted on one count of lying to federal investigators and for witness tampering after he allegedly told one of his victims she would wind up "floating face down in a river" if she divulged details of his sexual advances toward her. That inmate later settled a civil case against the county for $85,000.

The 63-year-old Holly, who was married, had sex with at least three female inmates and groped several other females, including the 16-year-old daughter of a jail employee, according to federal charges.⁹

Love County Sheriff Moses Wesley Liddel, Jr. in 1989 was heard on tape saying, "Sometimes you have to break the law to help the law."

Despite that damaging evidence, a jury in Sherman, Texas, acquitted Liddell and his son-in-law, police officer Roger Ray Hilton of plotting to kidnap and torture a suspected drug dealer who, in fact, had no record of drug-related arrests.

Prosecutors said Liddel and Hilton conspired to kidnap suspected drug dealer Pearl "Sonny" Cornett who lived across the state line in Gainesville, Texas. The plan was, prosecutors told jurors, for the lawmen to torture Cornett by forcing a hot curling iron into his anus until he revealed where drug labs were located in Oklahoma and Texas.¹⁰

For those who claim there are two standards of justice – one for the those who can afford costly legal representation and another for those who cannot, the prosecution of former Wagoner County Sheriff Robert "Bob" Colbert and one of his deputies represents a textbook case.

In April 2016, Colbert and his deputy, Jeffrey T. Gragg, were indicted by a multicounty grand jury for taking $10,000 in illegal drug money during a 2014 traffic stop under civil asset forfeiture laws and then allowing the driver and his passenger to go free, in essence, agreeing not to pursue criminal charges in return for handing over the cash. By 2017, three felony charges involving the alleged bribery were dropped and the two lawmen were allowed to plead guilty to a misdemeanor charge of "public officers willful neglect to perform duty" for unlawfully neglecting or refusing to take motorist Torrell Wallace into custody for possession of drug proceeds.[11]

Colbert subsequently received a five-year deferred sentence from Judge Matt Orendorff, who dismissed extortion charges against the former sheriff and another judge tossed the remaining two charges. Gragg received a two-year deferred sentence in exchange for his guilty plea on a reduced charge of willful neglect or refusal of duty.[12]

Also in Delaware County, Sheriff Jay Blackfox resigned in November 2011 after nearly 12 years in office after the county agreed to pay $13.5 million to settle a lawsuit brought by several women who said they were raped and sexually assaulted in the county jail. The settlement was three times the county's $4.5 million annual budget.[13]

Blackfox was never personally accused of any sexual wrongdoing – jail administrator Lonnie Hunter and deputy Bill Sanders, Sr. were the principal offenders who allegedly raped and sexually assaulted the female inmates, the lawsuit said. His crime, according to the lawsuit, was covering for his employees and ignoring prisoners' complaints. Sanders, a volunteer jailer, was dismissed from the sheriff's office and died in November 2008. No charges were ever brought against Hunter, who was placed on administrative leave in April 2011 and later fired.

"We alleged the sheriff permitted his jail to be a sexual romper room," said attorney Thomas Seymour, who represented 15 former female prisoners who were held at the Delaware County Jail between 2004 and 2010.[14]

Former Custer County Sheriff Mike Burgess wasn't as lucky as Blackfox. Like Blackfox, he resigned after being indicted on 35 counts involving an alleged sex-slave operation at his jail and the county also reached a $10 million settlement on behalf of fourteen female prisoners who claimed the Burgess used prisoners or those under his supervision of a drug court to commit sex acts for his own gratification.[15]

The similarities end there, however. Where Blackfox, who was never accused of sexual wrongdoing himself – his crime was covering for his employees who were so accused – was allowed to simply resign, Burgess was hit with a 79-year jail sentence and fined $15,000 after being found guilty on 13 felony counts, including five counts of second-degree rape. He was acquitted on 23 other counts that included charges of second-degree rape, forcible sodomy, and rape by instrumentation.

Besides the five counts of second-degree rape, he was also convicted of three counts of bribery by a public official, two counts of forcible sodomy and one count each of kidnapping, sexual battery and engaging in a pattern of criminal offenses.

Burgess, 56 and married, was actually sentenced to 94 years in prison but Judge N. Vinson Barefoot ordered him to serve 15 years concurrently with other sentences, thereby reducing the total sentence to 79 years. The jury that convicted him had recommended 94 years.[16]

Convicted of racketeering in December 1995, former Choctaw County Sheriff J.W. Trapp was sentenced in March 1996 to 51 months in federal prison for demanding bribes from drug dealers. The sentence of more than four years was the maximum possible under the federal sentencing guidelines.

He was convicted of soliciting bribes totaling tens of thousands of dollars from marijuana growers and a night club owner who operated a dice game and sold alcohol without a license and also sold methamphetamine.

The club owner testified that Trapp charged $400 per week in protection money for allowing the club owner's craps game to continue but then raised the rates when business was prospering. Another witness said Trapp demanded $20,000 to protect his marijuana operation.

Trapp was first arrested in September 1995 and then was arrested a second time in mid-October for allegedly tampering with a federal witness in connection with his original indictment. His second arrest occurred on October 18, 1995, in Sherman, Texas. He was among nine people arrested by federal authorities and resigned from office shortly after his initial arrest. The original charges stemmed from a 1993 domestic dispute when

Loyd Sales was revealed by his wife to be growing a large plot of marijuana. Trapp told the woman to leave the property and that he would take no further action. Trapp was accused of accepting more than one $150,000 in bribes to remain silent about the marijuana cultivation which netted millions of dollars in sales.[17]

Joe Hogan was appointed sheriff of McIntosh County in June 2009 to succeed Sheriff Terry Jones, along with his Undersheriff, Mykol Brookshire, was sentenced to prison for pocketing cash taken in May 2009 traffic stop. Less than a year later, Hogan was forced to resign.

Hogan had been investigated by the Oklahoma State Bureau of Investigation at the request of the local district attorney's office into reports that his wife, Jeane, a convicted felon, may have illegally carried a firearm and worn a badge and uniform. The couple had married in October 2009.

Questions also were raised about a reserve deputy who had moved from Las Vegas with Hogan's wife and lived with the couple.[18]

Hogan came to power after Jones and Brookshire were each sentenced to 27 months imprisonment followed by 24 months' supervised release after entering guilty pleas to extorting thousands of dollars in cash from motorists under Oklahoma's asset forfeiture program.

On May 21, 2009, the pair confiscated a sum of money from a vehicle driven by an undercover federal agent who had six $5,000 bundles. Brookshire took one of the bundles to his patrol car and then placed the remaining five on the dashboard of his patrol unit, telling the undercover agent that he would be jailed if he failed to complete a release of currency form.

When Jones subsequently informed the Drug Enforcement Administration, he advised that he had seized only five bundles of currency. "The defendants stole a portion of the confiscated cash," U.S. Attorney Sheldon J. Sperling said.[19]

Oklahoma County Sheriff John Whetsel was reelected to a sixth consecutive term in November 2016 despite a scathing audit that reflected instances of possible embezzlement, bribery and corruption.

Among findings of the audit:

- The Sheriff's Office did not pay for inmate healthcare even though funds were available to do so at the time the contracts were due.
- The Office spent about $900,000 to purchase Sheriff vehicles, even though the Office's other financial obligations were unmet.
- The office used subsequent year funds to pay obligations from the previous fiscal year in violation of state law.
- Unallowable costs may have been charged against the 'Aggregate Limit' of the Armor Correctional Health Services, Inc. contract.
- Two outside organizations, HOPE Team and FOP Lodge #155 activities are managed by Sheriff Office employees during county work hours.

- Donations received by the County Sheriff's Office were not presented and accepted by the Board of County Commissioners.
- For the FY2015, the Oklahoma County Reserve Deputy program cost $263,855.39. There is some question about whether there is an inappropriate relationship between individuals granted a Special or Reserve Deputy position and campaign contributions made by the individual to the Sheriff's campaign fund. The audit shows that donations were not properly presented or approved by the Board of County Commissioners, and that the Sheriff's Office allowed use of facilities for unauthorized groups.
- The Oklahoma County Sheriff's Office accepted a donation of Sheriff Whetsel's personal vehicle, after a $28,000 payment was made to a trust in Whetsel's wife's name. This and two other vehicle donations were neither handled appropriately nor approved by the Board of County Commissioners.

The audit of the sheriff's office, coming at a time when the Oklahoma County Jail was under national scrutiny for chronic overcrowding and overcharging prisoners, was requested when it was discovered that the Oklahoma County jail inmates were expected to pay not only their costs of incarceration, but were also being overcharged to accommodate indirect costs of incarceration, including sentencing programs, court clerk and juvenile justice salaries and payroll of the Oklahoma County public defender's office and that inmate incarceration fees were invoiced and collected by the sheriff's office rather than through the court clerk's office as required by state law.[20]

On March 19, 2019, the entire staff of the Nowata County Sheriff's Department resigned over what Sheriff Terry Sue Barnett termed Eighth Amendment violations and "blatant corruption" on the part on at least one judge.Barnett gave the reason for the mass walkout as the refusal of the county to do anything to repair conditions at the aging county jail which had been closed since high levels of carbon monoxide had sent four employees to the emergency room the previous February.

Despite the report and the ongoing problems, a judge had threatened to hold Barnett in contempt of court if she didn't immediately reopen the building and bring all the inmates back.

Instead, the entire department walked out.[21]

A federal class action lawsuit was filed in November 2017 against every sheriff in the State of Oklahoma as well as against judges, court officials and the Oklahoma Sheriffs' Association over a procedure that turned unpaid court fees and fines into a collection "extortion" racket.

The complaint, filed in Tulsa by seven plaintiffs, claimed that one of the plaintiffs, Ira Lee Wilkins, pleaded guilty to a criminal charge in 2015 but failed to pay court costs and was arrested and sent to state prison.

Attorneys representing the plaintiffs said Wilkins and others like him were "victims of an extortion scheme in which the defendants have conspired to extract as much money as possible through a pattern of illegal and shocking behavior."

Aberdeen Enterprizes II, Inc., a private collection company also named as a defendant, is responsible for what plaintiffs claimed were violations of their rights and acts of corruption when collecting unpaid court costs and fines. Aberdeen had an exclusive contract with the Oklahoma Sheriffs' Association which it used to threaten defendants with jail time for non-payment of fees and costs.[22]

The plaintiffs' complaint was dismissed by U.S. District Judge Terence Kern on March 12, 2021, due to the court's "lack of subject matter jurisdiction".[23]

Coming on the heels of the September 2022 stabbing death of Las Vegas Review-Journal reporter Jeff German, a recorded conversation involving McCurtain County Sheriff Kevin Clardy and other county officials on March 6, 2023, took on chilling undertones when the discussion turned to killing two news reporters with at least one member of the group also lamenting the fact that hanging African Americans is illegal.

The discussion was apparently precipitated by an eight-part series of stories by reporter Chris Willingham that cast the sheriff's office in a bad light. One of his stories was about the death of a jail prisoner who died at a hospital in March 2022 after he was shot by deputies with a stun gun.

In the conversation among officials, recorded by Chris Willingham McCurtain Gazette-News following adjournment of an official meeting because he suspected county business was being considered in private, County Commissioner Mark Jennings said to Clardy and sheriff's Captain Alicia Manning, "I know where two deep holes are dug if you ever need them," apparently a reference to killing Chris Willingham and his father Bruce Willingham, the paper's publisher. "I've got an excavator," Clardy replied.

Jennings then said he knew "two or three hit men" in Louisiana and that "they're very quiet guys." Jennings also complained of the inability to hang Black: "They got more rights than we got," he added.[24]

The episode prompted Oklahoma Gov. Kevin Stitt to call on the participants in the conversation to resign. Jennings did so, but not Clardy, at least not by the time this book went to press. Instead, his response to the entire affair was to indicate that he felt the recording was illegal.[25]

33

Oregon: Sex with the Governor's Wife

THE SORDID STORY of former Multnomah County Sheriff Bernie Giusto is one of the more sensational tales of malfeasance and outright debauchery in the annals of Oregon governance that ultimately spelled an ignominious end to a twenty-four-year in law enforcement.

Giusto, the subject of a 2007 investigation by the U.S. Department of Justice over systemic problems at the county jail, was cleared of any law violations but that probe morphed into the largest and most expensive investigation of an Oregon law enforcement officer's ethics by the Board of Public Safety Standards and Training (BPSST).

In the end, a BPSST Police Policy Committee comprised of fellow sheriffs, chiefs of police and officers from throughout Oregon, on May 13, 2008, voted overwhelmingly to revoke Giusto's badge based upon evidence of a 20-year-old lie.

The lie occurred when he was as an Oregon State Trooper. He joined the security detail of then-Gov. Neil Goldschmidt in 1987. In 1989, he untruthfully denied to his state police supervisors that he was having an affair with Goldschmidt's wife.

Then it got really sleazy. It turned out that while working as Goldschmidt's driver, he was aware that the governor had repeatedly sexually abused a young teenage girl and then paid her hush-money to keep the abuse secret. Giusto, at the time an Oregon State Police lieutenant, did nothing to halt the abuse, the BPSST committee noted.

Almost overshadowed in all the sensationalism involving the governor, his wife and the teenage girl was Giusto's violation of state law in September 2006 when he drove a county-owned SUV on a weekend getaway to Seattle with his girlfriend and her daughter.

The Goldschmidts divorced in 1990. Giusto, first elected sheriff in 2002, resigned, effective July 1, 2008.[1]

Teresa O'Brien, who had served as a deputy in the Josephine County Sheriff's Department for 24 years, filed a lawsuit in federal court against her boss, Sheriff Dave Daniel and four other sheriff's department employees in 2019, claiming that the office had a culture of "sexual banter and innuendo" and that the office discriminated against female employees. She claimed that she and other women had been "subject[ed] to frequent and ongoing sexual harassment by male employees, deputies and/or higher- level management and command staff."

O'Brien said the fact that many of those who engaged in the ongoing practice were in higher levels of supervisory authority made it difficult to report complaints. She said when she did make a formal complain to the human resources department of the sheriff's office in January 2018, she was retaliated against. She said a disciplinary letter was placed in her file at the direction of Daniel and Undersheriff Travis Snyder for "alleged inappropriate treatment of a co-worker."

She said that on "hundreds" of occasions, her immediate supervisor, Sgt. Ray Webb, sent inappropriate text messages to her, including a photograph of a bed with stained sheets. Other examples of texts from Webb to O'Brien:

- "I don't have a muscular body but I could still rub my junk on you."
- "I think we should be curled up on the couch in our jammy's watching Netflix."
- "Do you want to know what I would do with you to keep you satisfied or leave it in the wind?"

She said at times, Webb would appear at work in an intoxicated state and proposition her for sex.

She also claimed that another deputy, Lt. Edward Vincent, regularly made sexually-charged comments to her and other employees.[2]

Further to the north, in Marion County, Sheriff Russ Isham resigned after an investigation found evidence of official misconduct, in this case an attempt to interfere in the investigation of an extramarital affair.

Isham described the relationship as personal and having nothing to do with his office, but Tony Green of the Oregon Attorney General's office said Isham attempted to use his office in an effort to pressure a subordinate who then reported the sheriff's activity to another supervisor.

"My decision to resign comes out of a personal relationship that I had with an adult female other than my wife," Isham said in a prepared statement. "This involved person was not an employee or anyone that has anything to do with the sheriff's office. This relationship, while personal, was discovered by an employee. While this was strictly personal, it has impacted my ability to do the job I was elected to do."[3]

Former Klamath County sheriff Frank Skrah was sentenced to 120 hours of community service, a year's probation and fined $3,000 after his conviction in May 2017 on five misdemeanor charges in connection with the use of excessive force against suspects.

Prosecutors had sought a jail sentence of 60 days, two years' probation and $8,000 in fines but Judge Roxanne Osborne said there would be "no purpose" in sending him to jail.

His conviction came just four months after his term of office ended. He was convicted of holding a flashlight to the throat of one suspect, striking a second and choking a third. He was acquitted of strangulation and official misconduct related to the third suspect.[4]

Malheur County Sheriff Brian Wolfe received an unusual request in August 2019 that called on him to offer a legal opinion on whether a local newspaper had engaged in criminal conduct.

What made the request so unique is that it came from county legal counsel Stephanie Williams, the person whom it would seem to be the more appropriate party to make such a call. Wolfe was ambivalent about opening an investigation in the matter, which involved reporters sending emails to the personal email addresses of local economic development officials after being asked to limit correspondence to office hours and to a single county email address.

"Suggesting that professional journalists are behaving as criminals in gathering vital information for the community appears to be an effort to silence and intimidate *The Enterprise*," newspaper publisher Les Zaitz said.

Adam Marshall, an attorney for the National Reporters Committee for Freedom of the Press, agreed. "I'm not aware of any law limiting when people can email public officials or let alone how there could be one," he said, adding that if Malheur County officials were investigating use of email, "it seems like an intimidation tactic that is deeply disturbing."[5]

The Washington County Sheriff's Office was racked by two separate scandals over a three-year period that saw three deputies fired and placed on probation for periods ranging from eighteen months to two years while a fourth was facing the possibility of nearly six years' imprisonment after the department reached a $625,000 settlement after a prisoner suffered a fractured skull in a jailhouse beating at the hands of deputies.

Surveillance video showed that Albert Molina, forty-five, while being booked on suspicion of riding a bicycle while intoxicated on March 30, 2018, was slammed against a wall and pinned to the ground by jail guard Rian Alden who was then joined by three other deputies who helped Alden hold Molina face-down on the floor.

During the booking process, Molina was instructed by Alden to stand against the wall for his booking photo. Molina saluted Alden and the two exchanged more gestures before the much-larger Alden ran out from behind a desk and attacked the prisoner. Molina remained in intensive care for a fractured skull for five days, incurring medical bills of $135,000.

The Washington County District Attorney's Office at first refused to prosecute Alden for misdemeanor second-degree official misconduct but in the wake of the May 2020 killing of George Floyd by Minneapolis police, Washington County Sheriff Pat Garrett was informed of a 2003 email in which Alden, then not employed by the sheriff's office, referred to himself as a racist and used ethnic slurs against Mexicans.

On May 31, six days after the Floyd killing, Alden was placed on administrative leave and his racist email was revealed by the media and the district attorney's office seemed to find its moral outrage. A grand jury indicted Alden on a misdemeanor charge of official misconduct but a second grand jury was then shown Molina's heretofore undisclosed medical records and the surveillance video previously considered of "minimal value." Taken together, they were sufficient to warrant additional felony indictments against Alden, two for second-degree assault and one each for unlawful use of a weapon and first-degree official misconduct.

"I own this," said Garrett. "I will not be pointing fingers at anybody else. Part of being responsible is taking steps to fix it."[6]

Just a year before the Molina beating, three deputies were fired and/or convicted of charges, received varying terms of probation for their sexual harassment and a female deputy filed a federal lawsuit against the sheriff's department, claiming sex and gender discrimination, retaliation, sexual harassment, battery and negligence within the department.

Deputy Angela Branford asserted that male sergeants openly speculated on her underwear in front of prisoners, asked to see her breasts and in one case, a sergeant pulled his genitals out of his pants while both were on duty, asking, "Don't you want to play with that?"

She said fear of retaliation prevented her from reporting that she was a coerced into a sexual relationship by sheriff's corporal, Jon Christensen who she said choked her in an effort to force her to remain in a relationship with him. Christensen was fired in December 2015 for his coercion of Branford. He was indicted that same month and sentenced in September 2016 to two years' probation, 80 hours of community service and other sanctions.

Two other former deputies were also convicted of charges stemming from an anonymous letter received by the department in August 2015. Former Sgt. Dan Cardinal received two years' probation in January 2016 for official misconduct for engaging in sexual activity while on duty. Specifically, he was accused of asking to see Branford's breasts and of exposing himself to her.

Former deputy David Bergquist received 18 months' probation in March 2016 for sexual harassment after he allegedly pulled a co-worker's breast out of her clothing and placing his mouth on it at a union party in winter 2015.[7]

Terry Schrunk was appointed sheriff of Multnomah County following the 1949 recall of Sheriff Mike Elliott who had made misrepresentations during his campaign. Schrunk was elected in his own right and in 1956 ran successfully for mayor of Portland despite allegations that he was linked to organized gambling. He was indicted in 1957 on charges of bribery and perjury. Accused of taking a bribe during a gambling raid at a North Portland nightclub in 1955 while he was sheriff, he took – and failed – a lie detector test. He was subsequently acquitted following a two-week trial after the jury deliberated less than two hours.[8]

Glenn Palmer ranks as one of the most controversial sheriffs to ever hold office in the state of Oregon. First elected sheriff of Grant County in 2000 after serving ten years as a patrolman with the John Day Police Department, he was elected by default when the incumbent he was challenging died a week before the election.

He may well have remained an obscure local sheriff had it not been for the takeover of the Malheur National Wildlife Refuge in January 2016 by armed militants led by Ammon Bundy, son of Nevada rancher Cliven Bundy. Palmer's support of the splinter group boosted his reputation as a "constitutional sheriff" who subscribe to the theory that the U.S. Constitution bestows a status on them as supreme to the laws of the U.S. government.[9]

When *The Oregonian* newspaper began to delve into his appointment of more than 65 people as special deputies, a number far exceeding the single digit appointments of other nearby counties, Palmer simply stopped responding to records requests or claimed they were unavailable. Two of his appointees were convicted felons. He could not produce any applications or background checks on any of his deputy appointees. Some in Grant County feared that Palmer was creating his own secret police force.

Richard Mack, a former sheriff from Arizona who encouraged sheriffs to apply the U.S. Constitution on their own terms, to challenge federal jurisdiction and to assume that they were the ultimate authority in their respective counties, held special training sessions for Palmer and referred to him as having the courage "to stand for what's right." He even named Palmer as the first "Sheriff of the Year" for the newly-formed Constitutional Sheriffs and Peace Officers Association, an organization on the Southern Poverty Law Center's (SPLC) radar.[10]

Palmer reciprocated by criticizing the U.S. Forest Service for its restrictions on grazing, mining and logging and the closing of roads. He made unsubstantiated claims of witnessing excessive use of force and of "people getting guns pointed at them by federal officers for wood permit and road closure violations."

The Oregonian could find no record of any such confrontations and Palmer's own second-in-command, Undersheriff Todd McKinley, said the sheriff had not shared reports nor had he briefed his staff on such allegations. Neither had the Forest Service received any complaints from Palmer.

Yet in 2011, Palmer terminated a contract that called for the Forest Service to patrol its campgrounds and forest roads, claiming that the Forest Service had never explained its authority under the Constitution to patrol public lands. Five years later, he submitted his own Grant County Public Lands Natural Resources Plan to county commissioners at which time the county attorney reported that there was nothing in the Constitution or federal law that gave Palmer the power he obviously thought he had.[11]

Retired state police lieutenant Gordon Larson said Palmer should never have worn a badge, adding that the sheriff bore "the bulk" of responsibility for the influx of new faces in Grant County, whom most residents felt were tied to the militia.[12]

That sentiment gained traction with a May 3, 2016, *Facebook* post by the militant organization The Oath Keepers, later identified as participating in the January 6, 2021 U.S. Capitol insurrection. The post was in support of an organization called the Oregon Firearms Federation for its support for Palmer. Both the Oath Keepers and The Oregon Firearms Federation, like the Constitutional Sheriffs and Peace Officers Association, have come to the attention of the SPLC.[13]

Despite being cleared in ethics and criminal investigations, Palmer was defeated in his bid for a sixth term in 2020 by McKinley, bringing an end to his controversial 16-year tenure.[14]

Douglas County Sheriff John Hanlin attempted to one-up Palmer in 2012 when he posted a video on *Facebook* that suggested the Sandy Hook shootings that killed 20 children and six adults in Newtown, Connecticut, may have been staged and that the parents of the slain children were "crisis actors."[15]

Ironically, Hanlin would be the face of law enforcement in the wake of the Umpqua Community College shootings just three years later that claimed the lives of ten people as he called on the media "not to glorify and create sensationalism" for the shooter.[16]

A month after the Sandy Hook shooting, he fired off a January 13, 2013, letter to then-Vice President Joe Biden in which he vowed that "any federal regulation enacted by Congress or by executive order of the President offending the Constitutional right of my citizens shall not be enforced by me or by my deputies, nor will I permit the enforcement of any unconstitutional regulations or orders by federal officers within the borders of Douglas County, Oregon."[17]

For all his bluster over the rights of sheriffs, he got caught with his uniform pants down, literally, three years after his letter to Biden.

A photo of him – sans pants – was posted on *Facebook*, supposedly, he said, by an ex-girlfriend in what apparently was a case of revenge porn. Hanlin said he and his girlfriend had recently ended their relationship and that he "did not authorize the photo." Another photo posted at the same time which he did not address showed the sheriff giving the middle finger to the camera.[18]

34

Pennsylvania: $675K in Bribes, $35M in No-Bid Contracts

JOHN GREEN, who was the longest-serving sheriff in Philadelphia history, holding office for 22 years, from 1988 to 2010, was sentenced to five years in prison on August 1, 2019, nearly a decade after leaving office, for selling his position as sheriff and running an office that was basically corrupt and dysfunctional.

Prosecutors said Green, 71 at the time of his sentencing, received more than $675,000 in bribes, kickbacks and other benefits that ranged from a secret job for his wife to huge amounts in campaign contributions in exchange for awarding $35 million in non-bid work to a man who became the sheriff's office's largest vendor. Co-defendant Jim Davis was permitted to run the sheriff's office's foreclosed property sales in exchange for bribes and illegal campaign contributions paid by Davis. The contractor was convicted of fraud and income tax offenses.

He and Green were tried in federal court in February and March 2018. A 2015 ten-count indictment accused Green of negotiating corrupt agreements with Davis.

A former police officer, he won election on a promise to end favoritism and incompetence in the sheriff's office. He won national acclaim when he imposed a temporary moratorium on sheriff's sales to assist distressed homeowners but resigned abruptly midterm in 2010 when reports of sweetheart contracts surfaced in the media.

Davis, who hired Green's wife at $89,000 over six years, also purchased and renovated a Philadelphia home for Green, selling it to him at a $39,000 loss and gave the sheriff a non-interest loan of $258,000 for a retirement home near Orlando, Florida.

The resignation of Green didn't end the problems of the sheriff's office, however. His successor, Jewell Williams, was plagued by sexual-harassment lawsuits and one suit was settled for $127,500 in 2018. Williams also continued the questionable practice of spending millions of dollars purchasing advertisements for sheriff's sales in community newspapers. He bought more ads than were legally required and some of the newspapers were owned by people with close ties to the Democratic Party.[1]

Green's was the second five-year sentence handed down against a sheriff's officer within a four-year period. Earlier, in May 2015, a former Hudson County sheriff's officer, William Chadwick, 59, was sentenced to five years in prison for signing fake documents for a bounty hunter in exchange for cash.

Chadwick had pleaded guilty on July 14, 2009, to second-degree official misconduct and was ordered to forfeit $5,500 in illegal cash gifts that he admitted receiving from bounty hunter Adel Mikhaeil, 50. Another Hudson County sheriff's detective, Alberto Vasquez, 46, was sentenced to 90 days in jail as a condition of four years' probation and was ordered to forfeit $3,500 in illegal cash gifts after pleading guilty in 2010 to third-degree official misconduct.

Mikhaeil paid Chadwick and Vasquez for their signatures certifying that certain fugitives had been apprehended by the bounty hunter when in fact, they were captured by law enforcement officers. The signatures of Chadwick and Vasquez enabled Mikhaeil to higher fees from companies that insured the fugitives' bail bonds but reduced the amounts of the bail forfeitures, meaning a savings to bail bond insurers but a loss to the counties where the fugitives had jumped bail and fled the state, which divided forfeited funds.[2]

A jury of seven men and five women found former Bucks County sheriff's deputy Gary Browndorf guilty in June 2012 of hitting a handcuffed suspect and then lying about it. At the same time the jury acquitted Browndorf of five counts of falsely imprisoning Philip Romanek, 29, while serving an arrest warrant in July 2011.

Browndorf claimed that Romanek kicked him but former deputies who testified against Browndorf indicated that Browndorf lied about being kicked. Sheriff Edward Donnelly said the ruling "hurts everyone involved in law enforcement. People look at us with jaundiced eyes," he added.

Testimony in the trial indicated that deputies went to the apartment of Romanek's girlfriend, Samantha Doneker, to serve a warrant on Romanek for a parole violation on a DUI conviction. Doneker denied Romanek was at the apartment, but deputies found him in her attic. He was handcuffed and lowered to two other deputies who testified that Romanek was cooperative and did not resist.

Browndorf was suspended in September pending an investigation and later fired. Three other deputies were also subsequently fired for failing to report the assault.[3] Two years after the verdict, Bucks County paid a settlement of $85,000 to Romanek and Doneker.[4]

In criminal law vernacular, macing means to attack someone with a chemical spray that serves as an eye irritant and which temporarily disables an individual. In politics, macing is a relic of bygone days when incumbents would require public employees to contribute to political campaigns. The practice was supposed to have been abolished with the rise of civil service rules, unions and a public tired of subsidizing politicians.

Pennsylvania Governor George Howard Earle, III, was indicted for the practice in the 1930s and Westmoreland County political leader Egidio Cerilli went to jail in 1980 for macing, which by that time was called extortion.[5]

Someone apparently forgot to inform Allegheny County Sheriff Pete DeFazio.

DeFazio pleaded guilty in federal court in November 2006, ending a five-year investigation of the sheriff's office by federal authorities that centered on officials who applied pressure on workers to purchase tickets to DeFazio fund-raising events. Those who declined to purchase tickets found themselves saddled with undesirable assignments or were denied vacation requests.

Former Allegheny County Chief Executive Jim Roddey said the sad thing was that DeFazio "probably didn't think he was doing anything wrong." Franklin & Marshall College political science professor G. Terry Madonna said the tactic "was a real common practice in courthouses around the state" until the 1960s.[6]

DeFazio was sentenced to five years' probation in February 2007. His sentence included six months on electronic home monitoring and an order to pay a $5,000 fine.[7]

Two others in DeFazio's office, including chief deputy Dennis Skosnik, received federal prison sentences and a third was placed on one year's probation.[8]

Twelve years later, a former clerk with the Allegheny County Sheriff's Office, Erika Romanowski, entered a guilty plea to a single count of obstruction of justice four months after she was indicted on two counts that also included a charge of making false statements to federal investigators. The federal charges said she disclosed sensitive law enforcement information related to active federal investigations to two individuals suspected of involvement in a large-scale, violent drug trafficking operation in an effort to protect them from prosecution.[9]

Despite the seriousness of the charges against her, Romanowski was sentenced to only one day in prison, followed by three years of supervised release. She was also ordered to perform one hundred hours of community service.[10]

By contrast, Martha Stewart was sentenced to five months in jail and two years' probation following her conviction of obstruction of justice and lying to investigators.[11]

Westmoreland County Sheriff Jonathan Held was found guilty, but when a member of the jury disagreed that there was a unanimous verdict, the judge declared a mistrial and prosecutors said they would try him again for theft and conflict of interests. In the interim between the mistrial and any further prosecution, Held was defeated for reelection and moved to Florida, perhaps making the entire matter moot.

So, what was all the fuss about that brought him to trial in the first place?

It all started in February 2018 when the Pennsylvania Attorney General's Office filed charges against Held, then serving his second – and last – term in office, accusing him of ordering his staff to campaign for him while on duty.

Investigators said Held directed his subordinates to solicit gift cards and merchandise from gun shop operators beginning in 2015 for his annual campaign fundraiser, "I Out-Shot the Sheriff." Deputies said the sheriff made use of office records to identify potential donors and ordered deputies to drive county sheriff's patrol vehicles to collect items while in uniform and to use county computers on which to log all donations.[12]

Held was convicted in December 2018 and the presiding judge ultimately declared a mistrial. After the jury reached a verdict, the jury foreman handed the judge a slip of paper which indicated that the jury's finding was unanimous. During a routine polling of the jury, the judge asked each individual juror if they agreed with the verdict and one of them answered that he did not. The judge, following a conference with attorneys for each side, ordered the jury to resume deliberations but about a half-hour later, he called the jury back and declared a mistrial.[13]

Prosecutors immediately voiced their intentions to re-try Held but before that could take place, retired Greensburg District Judge James Albert, a Democrat, defeated Republican Held's bid for a third term.[14]

Before Sean Kilkenny became sheriff of Montgomery County in 2015, he plied his trade as an attorney under contract to municipalities across southeastern Pennsylvania and was tied to a growing political scandal involving Allentown Mayor Ed Pawlowski.

Kilkenny and a business partner treated Pawlowski to a $5,000 night on the town that included tickets to a sold-out Eagles playoff game and dining at an upscale steakhouse and also contributed $14,000 to Pawlowski's election campaign in an effort to land a $3 million tax-collection contract they eventually won.[15] Kilkenny was never charged with a crime but Pawlowski, a former

Democratic candidate for governor and who also made an unsuccessful run for the U.S. Senate, was eventually charged, tried and convicted on federal bribery and extortion charges. He was sentenced in October 2018 to fifteen years in prison to be followed by three years of supervised release. He also was ordered to pay almost $94,000 in restitution.[16]

Pawlowski's attorney Jack McMahon argued that if taking Eagles game tickets constituted a bribe, "then the bribers should be culpable, also."[17]

Under cross-examination, Kilkenny admitted that Pawlowski never requested a bribe, nor were conditions attached to any requests he made for contributions. At the same time, he said he "felt pressure" to contribute to the mayor's Pawloski's gubernatorial campaign since his law firm was bidding on a lucrative contract with the City of Allentown at the time.[18]

35

South Carolina: Sex from Minor, Bribes, a State in Disarray

SHERIFFS OR SHERIFFS' DEPUTIES in at least 23, or exactly half of South Carolina's 46 counties have run afoul of the law over the past half-century. The offenders included eight who were recognized by the South Carolina Sheriffs' Association as "Sheriff of the Year." The father of one of the recipients of the honor was not only bestowed with that same distinction 21 years earlier, but also once served as president of the association.

Offenses ranged from simple DUI by a sitting sheriff to embezzlement to taking kickbacks and bribes to sexting and sexual harassment to seizures of property and cash from innocent motorists to soliciting sex from a minor.

Sheriffs' departments in South Carolina appeared to be in a state of disarray. And while the offenses and convictions are enough to shake the public's confidence in law enforcement anywhere, it's important to remember that the Palmetto State, rather than being the exception, instead represents the norm across the nation – from ocean to ocean and border to border.

A five-month investigation by the *Charleston Post and Courier* found that some of the sheriffs' transgressions included:

- Funneling public funds into sham credit union accounts in order to purchase a $72,000 motor home for himself. His actions weren't discovered until after his death;
- Booking four first-class airline tickets to Reno, Nevada, for a National Sheriffs' Association annual conference for the sheriff, his chief deputy and two ranking deputies – only the two ranking deputies did not go and the wives of the sheriff and his chief deputy went instead, on the public dime;
- Suborning perjury by trying to get a witness to lie to the FBI;

- Protecting a massive drug and fraud enterprise from the sheriff's office;
- Taking kickbacks on the cost of repairs to county vehicles;
- Aiding a bogus credit repair business by falsifying records.

The McCormick County Sheriff's Office was rocked in 2019 when five of its deputies were charged with taking bribes for falsifying immigration documents and protecting drug dealers.[1] It was the second time in seven years that the sheriff's office personnel had been caught up in a scandal. In May 2012, it was discovered that former Sheriff Larry Williams, who had been dead for a year and a half, and his girlfriend, Ivadella Walters had funneled public funds into bogus accounts at the South Carolina Federal Credit Union where Walters was employed.

A lawsuit filed against Williams' estate by Orangeburg County said the pair spent $72,000 on a motor home for themselves, though they later changed the registration from their name to the country's.[2] It was never made clear just how much money was diverted in the scheme, but Walters and the credit union paid the county $70,000 in a settlement of the lawsuit.[3]

George Reid, a semi-literate deputy, was elected sheriff of McCormick County by defeating the county coroner who was facing bribery charges in February 1987 to complete the term of former Sheriff Jimmy Gable who had earlier been convicted of embezzling U.S. Treasury checks.[4]

Reid, who had failed the police officers' basic training course at the South Carolina Criminal Justice Academy while serving as Gable's chief deputy, was himself convicted of felony grand larceny in 1974 but received a pardon the day before he filed to run for sheriff.

The only candidate with an apparent clean record was Don Neal, a former law enforcement officer who had retired from a career in Polk County, Florida. He finished third in the December 1986 Democratic primary behind Reid and coroner Jack Keown.[5]

Five years earlier, in October 1981, seven persons, including a former sheriff, pleaded guilty in federal district court to conspiracy to violate voting laws, specifically, attempting to bribe voters to cast absentee ballots for former Sheriff Roy Lee. Included among those entering guilty pleas were Dillon County Democratic Chairman Alan Schafer, Lee, and former deputy sheriff William P. Jones.[6]

That same year, former Berkeley County Sheriff James W. Rogers was indicted on federal charges of protecting illegal gambling operations and in 1982, he was sentenced to 15 years in prison.[7]

In 1972, Anderson County Sheriff James H. Williams entered a guilty plea to a single count of conspiracy following his seven-count federal indictment for his involvement in an auto theft ring. He was initially charged with conspiring to the interstate transportation of stolen motor vehicles, interstate transportation of falsely-made and forged securities, selling merchandise valued at more than $5,000 and aiding and abetting in the commission of the aforementioned crimes.[8]

Chester County Sheriff Alex "Big A" Underwood and two of his deputies were convicted on a combined 23 counts following a nine-day trial in Columbia in April 2021 in what *The Columbia Post and Courier* described as "one of the largest public corruption cases brought against [South Carolina] law enforcement officials in recent memory" and which shone a spotlight on "South Carolina's history with crooked sheriffs."[9]

Underwood, who was suspended from office in 2019 amid a federal civil rights investigation and lost re-election the following year, was convicted along with deputies Johnny Neal and Robert Sprouse. Underwood was convicted by a federal jury on seven corruption and abuse of power charges. He was acquitted of tampering, falsifying records and making false statements during a federal investigation.

Underwood was accused of using public funds to pay for first-class plane tickets for him and his wife to a sheriffs' convention in Las Vegas, of forcing deputies to construct a "party barn" on his property, of skimming money deputies had earned working after-hours DUI checkpoints, of having deputies conduct surveillance and arrest political opponents, and then lying in attempts to cover up his actions.

But the most egregious accusation was that he and his deputies unlawfully arrested, roughed up and jailed a man, Kevin Simpson, who taped and live-streamed deputies who were responding to a wreck in front of his home in 2019. The jury heard testimony that Neal shoved a handcuffed Simpson to the ground and Sprouse seized Simpson's phone after illegally entering his home with other deputies. Simpson and his mother subsequently spent several days in jail. Deputies did not write a report on the incident for two months and then only after an FBI agent called asking about the encounter.[10]

That was Chester County. Just two counties to the east lies Chesterfield County, where Sheriff Sam Parker was convicted in 2014 and sentenced to two years in prison on charges of misconduct in office, embezzlement and providing contraband to prisoners. He served one year before being released on good behavior. He served three more years on probation.

Parker gave weapons to friends, allowed prisoners out to attend Halloween and Christmas parties and allowed them other privileges and even flew one inmate in the sheriff's helicopter to visit his ailing mother. He also was found guilty on two counts of embezzling public funds under $10,000.[11]

Former Colleton County Sheriff Andy Strickland avoided jail time when he plea bargained to three charges, down from fifteen charges he had been indicted on nine months earlier. Sheriff for seven years before resigning after the charges were filed, he was initially arrested in November 2019. More charges were added in February when he was accused of beating his girlfriend, forcing deputies to work on his properties and using county resources to run what prosecutors described as an "inappropriate relationship," entailing embezzlement, corruption, and illegally dispensing drugs.

On October 23, 2020, he entered guilty pleas to the first three charges and was sentenced to five years' probation and was ordered to resign as sheriff, to permanently relinquish his law enforcement credentials, to perform 200 hours' community service, and to submit to random drug testing.[12]

Former Florence County Sheriff Kenney Boone was sentenced to one day in jail after pleading guilty on January 8, 2020, to embezzlement and misconduct in office. He was also sentenced to five years' probation, subject to a reduction to 18 months provided he repay the $17,000 he stole from various accounts, that he close his campaign account, and complete substance abuse and mental health treatment.

Boone admitted to misappropriating Florence County funds and drug seizure money to purchase groceries, window tinting, and other personal items. Money from his federal narcotics fund, the county general fund and his campaign fund were used at restaurants, Sam's Club, Best Buy, and on out-of-state trips.[13]

Two years after the South Carolina State Law Enforcement Division (SLED) began its investigation, Greenville County Sheriff Will Lewis was sentenced in October 2019 to one year in prison after being convicted on a single count of misconduct of a public officer and acquitted on another charge.

But the case was considerably more complicated than that one offense. Lewis was accused of using public resources to perpetuate an adulterous affair with a former assistant who was convicted earlier of separate charges against her. Sixteen months later, in February 2021, after Lewis was released from jail, 12 remaining criminal charges against the former sheriff were dismissed.

A 2017 investigation initiated by SLED after former assistant Savana Nabors filed a sexual harassment lawsuit against Lewis in 2017 turned up cameras hidden in smoke detectors in Lewis's office. Nabors claimed in her petition that she was wrongfully terminated from her job at the sheriff's office because she "refused to tolerate Lewis's sexual advances."[14]

Lewis wasn't the only South Carolina sheriff to face the wrath of a former lover. Laurens County Sheriff Ricky Chastain admitted to having an affair and settled a lawsuit filed by Allison Haley Manley who claimed that her affair with Chastain resulted in two pregnancies.

The woman, an employee of the Laurens County Sheriff's Office, claimed that Chastain convinced her to terminate the first pregnancy and even drove her to a clinic in Charlotte and paid for her abortion. She said she decided to keep the second child. She said Chastain demanded that she resign her job and when she refused, he had his subordinates exert pressure on her to quit. She did finally resign in October 2010.[15]

Chastain apparently didn't learn from the affair and ensuing lawsuit, which he said was settled for $35,000. Four years later, in 2016, more than 6,600 texts exchanged between Chastain and a second woman, sent between October 2015 and April 2016 were leaked to a number of media organizations in South Carolina.

Some of the text messages were innocent enough – messages about job interviews and Chastain's impending reelection campaign, other contained explicit language about sex acts and dozens of nude photos of the woman. Moreover, hundreds of the messages were exchanged during normal weekday business hours.[16]

Chastain was defeated for reelection in 2016 by Don Reynolds but four years later, he was back seeking a return to office.[17] Reynolds defeated a field of three challengers, including Chastain, in the June Republican primary with 51.85 percent of the vote. With no Democratic challenger, he was assured of a second term and Chastain's career in law enforcement appeared to be over.[18]

Edward Jerome "E.J." Melvin was sentenced to 17 years in federal prison in March 2011 following his November 2010 conviction on 30 counts of drug conspiracy and for racketeering, ending ten years of tyrannical rule as sheriff of Lee County.

Prosecutors said Melvin repeatedly received hundreds of dollars in bribes to help drug dealers avoid jail. Authorities said he also received kickbacks for catering barbecue dinners for county functions and contracts.[19]

A federal jury deliberated 15 hours before returning with guilty verdicts on trafficking and conspiracy counts.

Melvin resigned in May 2010 after he and 11 others were charged with conspiring to deal drugs. During his two-week trial prosecutors played conversations recorded from a wire worn by Lee County drug investigator Johnny McCutchen, who, beginning in June 2009, cooperated with the FBI in its investigation. McCutchen testified that Melvin repeatedly thwarted ongoing investigations of known drug dealers.[20]

Melvin was arrested along with 13 other defendants in May 2010 on federal warrants that charged that the 14 had engaged in conspiracy since 2006 to possess with intent to distribute five kilograms or more of cocaine and 50 grams or more of crack. Melvin was the only one to request a trial. The others each pleaded guilty to various drug conspiracy charges and then testified against Melvin.

Melvin was also ordered to pay total restitution of $22,470 for the tax dollars he stole during the conspiracy. That amount included $5,300 he extorted from convicted drug dealers. Melvin will start paying the restitution sixty days after his scheduled release date in March 2026.[21]

South Carolina's longest-serving sheriff was sentenced to a year and a day in federal prison in April 2015 after pleading guilty to conspiring to harbor and conceal illegal aliens.

James Metts was sheriff of Lexington County for 42 years before he was suspended from office in June 2014 following his indictment on ten criminal counts. Prosecutors said he accepted money from a restaurant owner in exchange for keeping the establishment's employees from being arrested for being in the country illegally.

Prosecutors and defense attorneys agreed that Metts, age 68, did not need to go to jail but the presiding judge said it bothered him that the former sheriff would not face any prison time.[22]

When the Richland County Sheriff's Office set up an undercover sting operation to catch sexual predators who used social media and online chat rooms to hook up with minors or prostitutes for sex, there was no reason to believe deputies would nab one of their own. But that's exactly what happened when deputy Derek Vandenham, on duty, in his patrol car and in uniform, communicated to have sex with a 15-year-old.

Vandenham, 34, who had been with the department, for four years, was arrested and immediately fired, Sheriff Leon Lott said at a news conference in August 2019. "One of the most disgusting things that I've been having to deal with is to have a deputy do something like this," Lott said. Vandenham was charged with solicitation of a minor and second degree attempted criminal sexual conduct with a minor.[23]

Like Chester County's Alex Underwood, Saluda County Sheriff Jason Booth wanted a party shed constructed on his property. Unlike Underwood, he did not force his deputies to do the work, choosing instead to recruit his labor from an inmate of the county jail.

For his transgression, Booth was sentenced to a year in jail in August 2012. The jail sentence was suspended on the condition he paid a $900 fine.

Details of the plea bargain of the man who was once Saluda County's top lawman, were kept secret. The only details available to the public were the indictment, the sentencing sheet and Solicitor Strom Thurmond Jr.'s review of the facts of the case – a review that took less than six minutes. Unanswered were questions of whether or not Booth may have impeded the investigation or misused other inmates in the past.

Moreover, a report compiled by the State Law Enforcement Division (SLED) agent who investigated the case, normally released under the Freedom of Information Act, was not made public.

What is known is that Booth pleaded guilty to a misdemeanor instead of a felony, which meant he could work in law enforcement in South Carolina again.[24] Sure enough, Booth, who had resigned in 2012, was back in 2016 as he sought to return to office but he fell woefully short, losing the Republican Party primary to Robin Freeman by more than a two-to-one margin.[25]

A federal undercover investigation targeting public corruption in Union County resulted in the 2009 indictments and subsequent guilty pleas of a number of officials, including Sheriff Howard Wells. The investigation involved cocaine distribution, bribery, kickbacks, lying to investigators, witness tampering. Others caught up in the investigation included Union

County supervisor Donald Begenbaugh, Union Mayor Bruce Morgan, former Union County Tax Assessor Willie Randall, Jr., and local residents Darnell Beacham and Willard Dee Farr.

Wells pleaded guilty to lying to federal investigators in January 2010 and was sentenced to three months' imprisonment, three years of supervised release, $2,500 in restitution, a fine of $5,000 and a special assessment of $100.[26]

Former Williamsburg County Sheriff Theodore "Big Mac" McFarlin had served only four years of his sentence of more than 24 years in federal prison before he died in October 2002 at the age of 70.

McFarlin, South Carolina's first black sheriff since Reconstruction and Williamsburg County's first black sheriff ever, was convicted in February 1998 of drug conspiracy and perjury following a three-day trial and sentenced to 292 months in prison.

Key witnesses to McFarlin's role in an ongoing drug conspiracy with convicted drug dealer Thomas Lee "Ty" Williams included several current and former sheriff's deputies. Williams had fired on deputies when they attempted to arrest him following a controlled undercover drug buy in September 1990 that was carried out without McFarlin's knowledge or consent. No one was injured in the shootout and Williams was arrested within ten minutes.[27]

A co-defendant, Clarence Edward Cyrus, who was allowed to deal drugs with the blessings of McFarlin, pleaded guilty to a single count of conspiracy to distribute more than five kilograms of cocaine and one count of distribution of crack cocaine and was sentenced to life in prison without the possibility of parole.[28]

It wasn't the first time McFarlin had found himself in legal trouble. He was suspended from office in October 1982 when he was indicted on 22 counts on claims from three white prisoners that they were beaten and sexually assaulted by seven black inmates while in McFarlin's jail. McFarlin was charged with obstruction of justice, misconduct in office and official misconduct. Five black prisoners and two black trustys were also indicted on charges that ranged from criminal conspiracy and criminal sexual conduct to aggravated assault and battery.[29]

That trial ended in a mistrial as did a second trial in May 1983 when two separate juries were unable to reach a verdict and he returned to office until his conviction 15 years later.[30]

A credit repair scam landed former Williamsburg County Sheriff Michael L. Johnson in federal prison for 30 months and his accomplice for 33 months in March 2015. Additionally, Johnson and co- defendant Lester L. Woods were ordered to make restitution and to submit to three years' supervised release when they were released from prison.

The pair had concocted a scam credit repair enterprise whereby Woods would charge as much as a thousand dollars to raise clients' credit scores. He would then contact Johnson who would prepare police reports or incident reports that said the client Woods was working with had been the victim of identity theft.

Woods then would prepare a cover page of accounts that supposedly were fraudulent, attach the incident report and fax it to Equifax. Equifax, relying on the information provided by Johnson, would delete the defaulted debts and other derogatory information from the client's credit history, making it possible for the client to obtain additional credit on which he or she was also likely to default. In all, Johnson and Woods collaborated to expunge more than $11 million in credit information.[31]

Spartanburg County Sheriff Chuck Wright told the county council and members of the community on September 21, 2020, "I don't owe you an apology for doing my job" following his earlier assertion that his deputies had every right to shoot two young black men accused wrongly of shooting at deputies.

Wright, notorious for his reputation as an overly enthusiastic proponent of asset seizures via Operation Rolling Thunder along I-85 and I-26, had made the remark after the two, Akymzee Holbert, 22, and Tarus Mallory, 23, were accused of shooting at deputies. The two said they were not aware deputies were in the area and charges against them were eventually dropped. "I want the community to know, these were two young black males that the liberals are trying to say we're after to try to kill all the time," Wright told the *Spartanburg Herald-Journal*. "We're not trying to kill anybody; we're not trying to hurt anybody."

There may not have been any controversy if Wright had stopped there. Instead, he added, "We had every opportunity to kill two young black men and we did not do it." That prompted County Council member Michael Brown, who also served as chairman of the local NAACP chapter, to call for Wright to apologize. "I know he's in a tough position, but you have to know that you represent everyone in this county, not just a certain segment,"

Brown said.

Resident TyQuian English was less charitable. "You didn't say he had the right to kill two citizens, he said he had the right to kill two black males. How am I supposed to feel about that? I'm not a liberal, I'm not a Republican, either. I'm just a black man trying to survive in America. And I don't know if I can live with Chuck Wright."[32]

In January and February 2019, *Greenville News* reporters Nathaniel Cary, Anna Lee and Mike Ellis wrote at least half-a-dozen stories about the manner in which Wright and his deputies terrorized motorists on interstate highways by seizing property and money through asset forfeiture laws, even seizing $6,000 sent by FedEx by a man to a friend who was down on his luck because it was believed erroneously to be related to the illegal drug trade.

Maintaining that South Carolina highways equated to "rivers of cash," the newspaper's reporters noted that civil forfeiture errors and delays only served to hurt victims and enrich law enforcement by millions of dollars.

Between 2014 and 2016, Spartanburg County seized nearly $3.5 million – more than any other agency in the state. The sheriff's office also confiscated 21 vehicles, 19 guns and other property, including a $50,000 Aximum watch. In one case, a 2012 Ford Raptor, also valued at $50,000, seven other vehicles, a business and $3 million were seized in a single haul.
Wright said he took some of the forfeiture money to pay off the remaining $20,000 owed on the truck and then outfitted it with a siren and blue lights and turned into a patrol unit. "It runs about 185 mph," Wright said. "It will absolutely fly."[33]

The reporters' stories were perhaps prompted by a 2016 lawsuit filed by a victim of Operation Rolling Thunder.

A North Carolina man, Eamon Hugh Cools-Lartigue, was pulled over for speeding and ordered out of his vehicle. His lawsuit said that drug-sniffing dogs were brought to the scene on I-85 in Spartanburg but did not alert deputies to any illegal substances in the vehicle. Cools-Lartigue told deputies that he had cash in a retail bag in his vehicle. He claimed in his lawsuit that he managed musical artists and that he never attempted to conceal the money, adding that he was in rightful possession of everything in the vehicle.

He said deputies seized the $29,000 that was in a bag "despite having no legal rights" to the money and "coerced" him into sighing an affidavit in which "he appeared to relinquish control over the monies."[34]

Former Berkeley County Sheriff Wayne DeWitt, who had resigned in February 2015 after being charged with driving under the influence and leaving the scene of an accident, was sentenced to three years' probation, 60 hours of community service and two Alcoholics Anonymous meetings per week in January 2016 after being arrested a second time for DUI following a high-speed chase at speeds of a 100 miles per hour.[35]

36

South Dakota: Take Oath of Office, Go to Jail

KOREY J. WARE, 28, was given a seven-year suspended prison term but was required to spend thirty days in jail, perform 100 hours of community service and pay more than $1,100 in fines – all after he was sworn in as sheriff of Roberts County.

In the order of occurrence, Ware got into a barroom fight in Aberdeen, was elected sheriff, was charged with felony aggravated assault, was sworn in as sheriff while charges were pending, and eventually was convicted. Prior to being elected sheriff, he had punched out one Taylor Kwas who had approached his former girlfriend, who was dating Ware at the time.

The punch broke Kwas's jaw and charges were filed against Ware after he was elected sheriff but before he took his oath of office. After being sworn in, his duties were restricted through an agreement reached with the South Dakota Law Enforcement Standards and Training Commission and he later agreed to decertification as a law enforcement officer and instead of performing law enforcement duties, focused on administrative work.[1]

Things got even weirder on Bon Homme County, which rests hard on the Missouri River that forms the border between southeastern South Dakota and northeastern Nebraska. It was in this sparsely-populated county that deputy sheriff Mark Maggs decided to run against his boss, Sheriff Lenny Gramkow. It was a rout, with Deputy Maggs pulling in 72.6 percent of the vote as he defeated incumbent Gramkow, 878-331. Gramkow waited for a full minute after the polls closed before he fired Maggs, posting his time-stamped termination notice, signed by the defeated sheriff, on *Facebook* but giving no reason for his action. But South Dakota is a right- to-work state where employees may be fired without cause and where sheriffs have total autonomy in the hiring and firing of personnel.[2]

37

Tennessee: Cocaine, Prostitutes and Buford Pusser

THE EARLY- AND MID-1980S were tumultuous times for sheriffs in Tennessee, particularly in the eastern part of the state as no fewer than ten top county law enforcement officers were either arrested or implicated in narcotics, prostitution, bootlegging and gambling activities.

In 1984, Anderson County's Dennis Trotter received the maximum sentence of 15 years in federal prison and ordered to pay a $5,000 fine after entering a guilty plea just three weeks before his scheduled trial on a 27-count federal indictment charging him with conspiring to sell cocaine from a roadside tavern where drugs and prostitutes were said to be "freely available."

Trotter was accused of taking monthly bribes of at least $1,000 in return for overlooking drugs and prostitution said to be "freely available" at the Lakefront Tavern. Federal agents discovered bank certificates worth $70,000 and nearly $1,100 in cash in the sheriff's safety deposit box and seized another $1,600 from him when he was arrested.

Just four years earlier, in 1980, Trotter was named Tennessee's "Outstanding Sheriff of the Year."[1]

In early 1986, former Hamblen County Sheriff John C. Brock was arrested in Florida on charges of possession of marijuana, cocaine, and narcotics paraphernalia and in March, Claiborne County Sheriff Billy Wayne Smith and Scott County Sheriff Marion Carson, along with Grundy County sheriff's deputy Ronnie King and Harriman City Judge Glenn Langley were arrested on charges ranging from illegal gambling with video poker machines to accepting bribes in exchange for protecting gambling devices to guaranteeing a safe landing for a planeload of cocaine. In Langley's case, he was charged with issuing false search warrants so that a co-conspirator could confiscate a pound of cocaine from an undercover agent posing as a drug dealer.[2]

Just three months later, in June, White County Sheriff John McGhee was arrested and accused of participating in a scheme to take planeloads of cocaine into a rural airport. He was arrested in a Nashville hotel by federal authorities after he allegedly accepted a $20,000 payoff from undercover agents. He would eventually plead guilty to two counts of a nine-count indictment but he subsequently appealed a district court's denial of a motion to arrest judgment, indicating a defect in the indictment, and the appellate court reversed the lower court and remanded the case back to the district court.

The nine-count indictment stemmed from McGhee's involvement with individuals who wanted to operate a nightclub in White County that offered prostitution and high-stakes gambling. One of the individuals involved later became a government informant.[3]

Less than four months later, Roane County Sheriff Giles Narramore was charged with selling high-grade Colombian marijuana he had confiscated months earlier and in cases not involving drugs, one former sheriff entered a guilty plea to taking bribes to protect the illegal operation of video gambling devices and another was sentenced to five years in prison for inmate beatings, firearms violations and fraud.[4]

There could be no discussion of Tennessee sheriffs without including the legendary Buford Pusser in the conversation. Pusser, who once wrestled under the name "Buford the Bull," was the sheriff of McNairy County for only six years (1964-1970), but gained a reputation of near mythical proportions, thanks to the 1973 movie *Walking Tall*, starring Joe Don Baker, and several sequels, a TV movie and a short-lived TV series depicting the career of Pusser.

Try as it might, Hollywood must have found it a challenge to embellish his story. In his first run for sheriff his opponent, incumbent James Dickey, was killed in an auto accident, handing Pusser an electoral win by default. The youngest sheriff in state history at age 27, he immediately set about trying to eliminate the Dixie Mafia, aka the State Line Mob.

McNairy County sits on Tennessee's southern border with northeast Mississippi. US 64 cuts east-west through the county, connecting New York City and San Francisco. US 45 runs north-south from Lake Superior to Mobile, Alabama, on the Gulf coast through McNairy. The intersection of the two major routes was well before completion of the interstate high system and thus created an ideal base of operations at the time for smuggling drugs, booze and women.

Nashville U.S. Attorney Joe Brown said Tennessee became the go-to state for drug smugglers and human traffickers after federal authorities stepped up enforcement efforts in Florida. "Tennessee, with its small airports and big highways, was particularly susceptible," he said, pointed out that in Tennessee's 95 counties, sheriffs' salaries ranged from $21,000 to $56,000 per year. "Drugs generate a lot of cash. Lay cash out and you'll soon find someone willing to break the law to get some," he said.

"I can't see anything but greed," added Lawson White, director of the Tennessee Sheriffs' Association.[5]

On August 12, 1967, just before dawn, Pusser received a call about a disturbance on a side road outside of town. His wife Pauline decided to ride along when he went to investigate. As he drove, a second car pulled alongside and the occupants opened fire, blowing away part of the left side of his jaw but killing his wife. Eighteen days and several surgeries later, Pusser was no longer just the sheriff, but a man bent on revenge[6]

Convinced that Kirksey McCord Nix was the triggerman, Pusser also was certain that Carl Douglas "Towhead" White, Geore McGann, and Gary McDaniel were also directly involved. Within three years all but Nix were dead. White was gunned down outside a Mississippi motel in 1969. It was widely thought that Pusser had pulled the trigger. The following year, McDaniel and McCann were shot dead in Texas.

Nix was imprisoned in the Louisiana State Penitentiary at Angola for the murder of a New Orleans grocer and was later found to be involved in the killing of Biloxi, Mississippi, Judge Vincent Shelley and his wife Margaret, who was a candidate for mayor of Biloxi at the time of her death. Her opponent, incumbent Mayor Pete Halat was later found to have worked with Nix in plotting the murders of the Shelleys.

No one was ever prosecuted for the killings of White, McDaniel or McCann. In 1974, Pusser himself was killed when he was thrown from his car when it slammed into a roadside embankment at 100 miles per hour.[7]

It would be a mistake to assume corruption of sheriffs' offices in Tennessee only began with the federal crackdown on smuggling in Florida just as it would be wrong to assume that it ended with the defeat of the so- called Dixie Mafia. The sad truth is tainted offices existed well before Pusser and long after his death.

In 1936, Memphis political boss Edward Hull "Boss" Crump appointed Paul Cantrell as his candidate for sheriff of McMinn County all the way across the state near the North Carolina line. Cantrell won in what would become known as the "vote grab of 1936." Cantrell instituted a merit pay system whereby deputies were paid per arrest which, of course, led to widespread abuses. Shaky arrests for public drunkenness and "fee grabbing" from tourists and travelers flourished, generating fees in excess of $300,000 over the next ten years.

For the 1946 elections, some 3,000 World War II veterans had returned home and formed a non-partisan political association fielding their own candidates to oppose Crump's machine. Knox Henry, a decorated veteran of the North African campaign was picked to oppose Cantrell. Even with their own poll watchers looking on, violence still erupted. When an elderly African-American attempted to vote, he was insulted by a deputy who hit him with a brass knuckle and then shot him in the back as he tried to flee.

Another poll watcher was brutally beaten by deputies when he protested when an underage girl was brought in by deputies to vote. Besides being too young, she had no poll tax receipt and was not listed in the voter registration. After the poll watcher was beaten, he was arrested, handcuffed and hauled off to jail in the town of Athens.

But the veterans weren't giving up so easily. They lay siege to the county jail where deputies were caught counting the votes without the presence of a second party. The GIs occupied the second floor of a bank building across the street. Their higher ground gave them a strategic advantage. Eventually, the deputies surrendered and sporadic violence broke out all over town and when the votes were finally counted, Knox Henry had defeated Cantrell.

The GI-backed government, however, collapsed within a year and was replaced by a clique similar to the one they had fought so hard to defeat.[8]

When FBI agent Thomas Farrow transferred from Miami to the Knoxville division, he began contacting state prosecutors who kept steering him back to Cocke County hard on the North Carolina border in eastern Tennessee. "[I]n their (prosecutors') minds, it was such a bed of corruption that the tentacles went throughout the county and throughout the sheriff's department," he said.

Operation Rose Thorn began in 2001 and culminated in 2008 with forty-eight arrests on federal charges, including eight local law enforcement officers with the Newport Police Department and the Cocke County Sheriff's Department.

Farrow said the most unnerving aspect of his investigation was meeting potential informants – police officers – in cemeteries at midnight "knowing that when they show up to talk to you, they're going to have a gun" because they were in uniform. "You don't know if two or three of his buddies are hiding with rifles," he said, adding that on most occasions, "there was another agent with me."

He said deputies expressed the sentiment that they began with good intentions but soon were told, "Hey, stay away from the chicken fights because those are the sheriff's. Stay away from the poker machines, those are the chief deputy's."

Sheriff D.C. Ramsey resigned for health reasons in 2006, two years before the FBI said it had records showing he had received thousands of dollars to protect illegal gambling and cockfighting, but he was never charged even though the investigation uncovered drugs, chop shops, prostitution and illegal liquor sales.[9] Ramsey had been arrested by federal agents as far back as 1970 but his conviction was subsequently overturned. His nephew, chief deputy Patrick Taylor was known to be associated with video poker rings and was said to have participated in the movement of drugs and stolen property

"There were seven different undercover agents who floated in and out" of the investigation," Farrow said. "Their safety was my primary concern in the entire investigation. It was fairly dicey at times for them, but their participation was paramount to the case."[9]

Though Ramsey was never prosecuted, his nephew, Taylor, was sentenced to two years in federal prison in April 2008. Additionally, he was ordered to serve three years of supervised release after completion of his prison sentence, ordered to pay a $5,000 fine and forbidden to hold any position of trust during his supervised release.[10]

Chuck Arnold, the disgraced former sheriff of Gibson County avoided jail by pleading guilty to 23 separate felony counts in October 2016, eleven months after he and eleven other former sheriff's office employees were indicted on 113 counts.

Arnold was sentenced to ten years' probation and ordered to make restitution of more than $8,000 after pleading guilty to one count of conspiracy to obtain a controlled substance by fraud, one count of forgery, five counts of obtaining a controlled substance by fraud, one count of extortion, two counts of theft of property over $1,000, five counts of facilitation of theft, and eight counts of official misconduct. Multiple counts of similar charges were dismissed by prosecutors as part of his plea deal.[11]

Discrepancies in the department's payroll, prescription medication funding and pharmaceutical records were discovered by an audit ordered by Arnold's successor, Sheriff Paul Thomas. The audit led to the discovery of a scheme by Arnold and Chief Deputy Jeff Maitland to steal money from the county by allowing employees to log overtime hours that they did not work. Also, department nurse Renea Terrell was found to be filling prescriptions in the names of prisoners who never received them. Other employees of the office caught up in the investigation cut their own deals with prosecutors.[12]

Another Arnold, former Rutherford County Sheriff Robert, was unable to avoid jail, however. He was sentenced to 50 months in prison in May 2017 after entering a guilty plea in January to wire fraud, wire services fraud and extortion for his role in a scheme to sell e-cigarettes to inmates.

Robert Arnold, along with his uncle John Vanderveer and his chief administrative deputy Joe Russell, II, formed JailCigs, LLC to sell electronic cigarettes to Rutherford County Jail inmates. The three principals invested $3,000 each and prosecutors say that investment netted Arnold $60,000 profit between October 2013 and April 2015.

Arnold was arrested in September 2016 and was suspended from office two months later. In addition to his four-plus-years' sentence, Arnold also agreed to pay $52,500 in restitution to Rutherford County and to forfeit $66,790 he made from the enterprise. Vanderveer and Russell also entered guilty pleas in their own plea agreements.[13]

Russell was sentenced to 15 months in November 2017 after pleading guilty in January. He, like Arnold, was ordered to pay $52,500 in restitution and to forfeit $66,790 in profits made through the e-cigarette scheme. Vanderveer was sentenced in September to a year and a day in prison.[14]

Arnold completed his reduced prison sentence on April 15, 2020 and was placed on three years' supervised release.[15]

Arnold, despite his guilty plea, called himself a political prisoner in a telephone interview in 2019, saying his sentence was "all politics."

He sought a pardon from President Donald Trump but there was no indication that Trump ever considered his appeal for an executive grant of clemency for a full and unconditional pardon.[16]

While other Tennessee sheriffs were involving themselves in money-making schemes involving drugs, prostitution, illegal booze, gambling and even e-cigarette sales to inmates, Fentress County Sheriff Charles Cravens was using his considerable power to grant special privileges to female inmates in exchange for sex.

Some of the special favors he granted included transportation of inmates by Cravens from the jail to visit relatives, allowing them to go outside the jail to smoke cigarettes and even providing money to relatives for deposit into inmates' jail commissary accounts.

Besides driving female inmates from the jail and engaging in sex in a vacant trailer and in his vehicle, Cravens also was charged by federal authorities with kicking a male inmate in the backside and placing him in a headlock while another officer handcuffed him and then struck the inmate in the back of the head.

Cravens, on Aug. 23, 2017, entered a plea of guilty to three counts of honest services fraud and a single count of deprivation of rights under color of law. At the same time, he announced his resignation as sheriff. He was sentenced to 33 months in prison, followed by two years of supervised released.[17]

"The women here could not consent, not in any meaningful way," said Assistant U.S. Attorney Katy Risinger, who portrayed Cravens as the most powerful man in the county who coerced the women into having sex with him and took advantage of his position of authority. "They were reliant on defendant for their safety, their food, their clothing, their well-being," she said.[18]

Shelby County Sheriff Jack Owens was a decorated Army veteran, having served in both Korea and Vietnam, where he served two tours of duty. He assumed office as sheriff of Shelby County (Memphis) in August 1986 and in 1990, he announced his intention to run for reelection.

But then, on May 5, as his office was the subject of an investigation of civil rights violations, he purchased gas for his patrol car with his credit card at a Memphis service station and cleaned and oiled his 20-gauage, county-issue pump shotgun in the parking lot. When he was finished, he raised the weapon to his head and squeezed the trigger.

Two weeks earlier, a grand jury had handed down indictments against three of his deputies for the beating death of 28-year-old Michael Gates during an undercover sting operation during which deputies posed as drug dealers. Seventeen deputies were suspended following the incident.

In an unrelated investigation, a grand jury had heard testimony from several of Owens' top deputies into financial matter involving the department.[19]

Nicole Audrey Spector, writing in *Prison Legal News*, left White County Sheriff Oddie Shoupe off her list of America's ten worst sheriffs, but there's a good argument that he deserved a spot on that dubious list.

Shoupe left office in September 2018 after opting not to seek reelection. It's just as well, considering his penchant for excessive force – including shooting unarmed suspects – in chase situations, instructing his deputies to lie to investigators about the details, and even erroneously informing a mother that deputies had shot and killed her son.

On May 4, 2017, body and dash cam video clearly showed deputies surrounding a disabled vehicle of a suspect who had refused to pull over earlier in the day in neighboring Putnam County. When the suspect, Teddy Lee Dodd, who was standing outside his car, reached back inside the vehicle, a deputy, fearing he was reaching for a gun, drove his SUV into Dodd's car, breaking Dodd's leg.

When Shoupe arrived at the scene, he was informed that Dodd's car had been rammed. "With what?" he asked. Told that it was a sheriff's patrol car, he said, "Oh, shit. I told them not to use those cars. A few minutes later, he returned to the deputies, and thinking that all body cams were turned off, instructed deputies to change their stories to the effect that it was Dodd who rammed the deputy's vehicle.

With the body cam recording him, he said as he stared at his deputies, that the Tennessee Highway Patrol "is going to fill out an incident report. It's not a wreck report since there's no damage to the cars – very little, minor – since he hit the patrol car."

Putnam County Sheriff David Andrews, who was also a past president of the Tennessee Sheriffs' Association, was upset at Shoupe's effort to distort the facts by telling his deputies to lie, calling his actions "uncharacteristic and not representative of Tennessee sheriffs."

White County Deputy Nate Theiss refused to go along with the misrepresentation, saying the other deputy, Richard Lynch rammed Dodd's driver side door, adding, "I will never sacrifice my credibility or reputation to fit a narrative that is fundamentally false."[20]

The incident with Dodd occurred only a couple of months after deputies shot and killed another driver, Michael Dial, in a pursuit after Shoupe gave the order over the radio to "take him out. Don't ram him. Shoot him. Fuck that shit. You're gonna tear my cars up." After the chase and Dial had been shot in the head, Shoupe said of the chase, "I love this shit. God, I tell you what, I thrive on it."

Afterward, even though Dial had been identified on police radio dispatches, Dial was incorrectly identified by deputies as Jason Kirby. Accordingly, Kirby's mother was summoned to the hospital where Shoupe told her that her son was dead. "He shot at us and we had to take him out," the sheriff lied. Dodd had not shot at officers and Jason Kirby was alive and well, but away from his phone.

"He's proud of killing that guy – thinking it was me," Kirby said. When he was reunited with his mother he said, "I went in and hugged her and she just cried for, like, hours, you know," Kirby said.[21]

38

Texas: Porous Border, Corrupt Lawmen

AS ONE MIGHT IMAGINE, the state of Texas is fraught with examples of sheriffs gone bad. There are several contributing factors for this. The state is huge. There are 254 counties, as varied in their demographic makeup as they are numerous. While there are those, like Harris County (Houston), with more than four million people, the vast majority are rural, sparsely-populated jurisdictions - like Loving County on the Mexican border with barely 100 residents. The average annual salary for a sheriff in Texas is just over $41,000 – about a hundred thousand dollars below that of neighboring Louisiana. An added disadvantage is the state's proximity to Mexico and Mexican drug cartels, which offer strong incentives for cash-strapped sheriffs and deputies to either look the other way or to actively participate in revenue-generating enterprises, even those that are plainly illegal.

Four counties nestled together in the southern tip of Texas, Zapata, Starr, Hidalgo and Cameron, with a combined population of more than 1.2 million people, represent the very worst of the worst in trying to separate law enforcement from the law breakers.

It was that participation that led directly to the downfall of six sheriffs and a couple dozen deputies of these four separate Lone Star State border counties, including one that earned the unenviable title of a smuggler's paradise. Mexican drug cartels did not stop at the Rio Grande, but spilled over to the north side of the border between the two countries. One estimate puts the drug influence of the Gulf Cartel headquartered in Matamoros on the Rio Grande economy at between 10 and 20 percent.

"There's a lot of dirty money in the Rio Grande Valey," said Chad Richardson, emeritus sociologist at the University of Texas Pan American in Edinburg. "And that money is available to corrupt public officials, including officers at the border, including sheriffs, including judges."

Starr County, Texas' very own "Little Colombia," located at the southernmost tip of the state is 97 percent Latino and 100 percent poor. Two of the county's sheriffs and three deputies would be caught up in the drug trade and be handed prison sentences in a 17-year span.

In the case of Sheriff Eugenio "Gene" Falcon, Jr., the problems actually started eight years before his 1998 guilty plea to federal bribery charges and carted off to prison for two years. The year was 1986 and the battleground was not in Starr County, but across the shallow river that divides the two countries. The warrant issued by Mexican authorities said Falcon, clad in camouflage fatigues and leading a four-man commando squad into Reynosa, 40 miles inside the Mexican border, pumped seven rounds from an Uzi machine gun into a convicted drug runner while he was handcuffed to a bed in a hospital room.

The shooting of Margarito Piedra fueled long-held rumors of Falcon's own possible involvement in moving marijuana and cocaine across the border into the U.S. Falcon, who never made more than $38,000 a year as sheriff, was first elected in 1981 when the job paid only $24,000.[1]

Ironically, it wasn't drugs that proved to be Falcon's undoing. With the feds wondering how he could live in a $90,000 house, they set a trap in 1997. Thinking, he was meeting with the owner of a bail bond company, he was in fact meeting with undercover agent Homero Arturo Longoria, who received more than $109,000 over two decades as a paid confidential informant. In exchange for referring inmates to Longoria, Falcon received about a dozen payments totaling $11,000. The sting would ultimately cost him two years of his life behind bars.[2]

Eleven years after Falcon was sentenced, his successor, Sheriff Reymundo Guerra was sentenced to more than five years for using his position as sheriff of Starr County to facilitate a drug cartel in exchange for cash. U.S. District Judge Randy Crane handed down a sentence of 64 months without benefit of parole and a four-year term of supervised release upon completion of his Guerra's prison term.

Guerra's arrest and conviction was the culmination of Operation Carlito's Weigh, a joint investigation carried out by the FBI, DEA, the IRS, the Houston Police Department's Criminal Investigation Division and the Hidalgo County High Intensity Drug Trafficking Area Task Force. Guerra, since January 2007, had been tipping off Jose Carlos Hinojosa on increased law enforcement activity and searches and seizures of stash locations and on at least one occasion, gave investigators false information in order to deflect suspicion from one of Hinojosa's associates. On another occasion,

Guerra even shut down a case involving one of Hinojosa's associates.[3]

Three Starr County deputies, eying the opportunities afforded their bosses by the drug smugglers must have decided their bosses shouldn't be able to monopolize the opportunities before the deputies.

In July 2012, two deputy sheriffs, Nazario Solis III and Jason Michael Munsell were arrested by federal authorities on charges that they accepted cash payments in exchange for protecting drugs and gambling in the county.

A federal indictment charged Solis with one count each of conspiracy to commit bribery and extortion, federal programs bribery, extortion, conspiracy to possess with intent to distribute marijuana, possession with intent to distribute marijuana, and attempt to possess with intent to distribute cocaine. The same indictment charged Munsell with one count each of conspiracy to commit federal programs bribery and extortion, federal programs bribery, and extortion.

Solis was also charged with attempting to distribute cocaine and cash in exchange for semi-automatic and fully-automatic firearms as well as for participating in extensive negotiations with another individual to obtain the firearms which Solis intended to send to his "boss" in Mexico. The individual with whom he was negotiating, however, turned out to be an undercover agent.[4]

Two years later, in November 2014, another Starr County deputy, Amy Reyes, was arrested along with her civilian brother, Bobby Lee Reyes, when they attempted to smuggle 75 pounds of marijuana bundles across the border at Hebbronville. Both subsequently entered a guilty plea, admitting that they were to be paid $1,000 to move the drugs from Rio Grande City to Houston. She was fired as soon as the arrests were announced.[5]

Sandwiched between Starr and Cameron counties is Hidalgo a county which, like its next-door neighbor, experienced its own problems with law enforcement with two sheriffs and a pair of deputies suffering the same fates as their contemporaries along the Rio Grande. With a population of 775,000, according to the 2010 census, it is easily the largest of the three (Cameron had 406,000 residents, and Starr, the smallest, had only sixty-one thousand). The county seat is McAllen which served as the retirement home of the late author H. Allen Smith. McAllen would later become notorious as a detention center for illegal aliens where children were held in cages by the Department of Homeland Security.

Sheriff Guadalupe "Lupe" Treviño, a fixture in the Rio Grande Valley's Democratic Party, was one of the most powerful lawmen on the border. But in April 2014, he pleaded guilty to federal charges of money laundering and in June was sentenced to five years in federal prison and fined $60,000. Prosecutors said he took thousands of dollars in campaign contributions from a drug trafficker named Tomas "El Gallo" Gonzales.[6]

A year earlier, in March 2013, his son, Jonathan Treviño, a former Mission police officer, and several other members of his street-level narcotics task force called the Panama Unit – including five Hidalgo County deputies – were indicted for conspiring to possess with intent to distribute cocaine, marijuana and methamphetamines.

Jonathan Treviño had been running the task force since 2006 and by the time of Sheriff Treviño's resignation and guilty plea, the younger Treviño and his task force members were already serving time in federal prison.[7]

In December 2013, Sheriff's Office Commander Jose Padila was indicted on charges involving the alleged trafficking of marijuana and money laundering.[8]

A decade earlier, in November 1994, Hidalgo County Sheriff Brig Marmolejo, Jr. was sentenced to seven years in federal prison for taking $151,000 in payoffs in exchange for giving special privileges to drug dealer Homero Beltran Aguirre, an inmate in the Cameron jail. The special privileges for Aguirre including allowing him to have family picnics in jail and sex with his wife and his 25-year-old girlfriend in the sheriff's own office.

Aguirre testified at Marmolejo's trial that he gave the sheriff $5,000 each month, plus an additional $1,000 for each conjugal visit conjugal visit with his wife, Maria. Prosecutors said Marmolejo also accepted gifts of fried goat meat, thousand-dollar watches, a $10,000 sports car for his daughter and a non-interest loan to build a pavilion at his ranch for his daughter's wedding reception.

While awaiting sentencing but still in office, Marmolejo approved the release on bond of a woman's brother who had just been convicted of a barroom killing. The woman had contributed a thousand dollars to the sheriff's campaign but upon the man's release, he fled to Mexico before he could be sentenced for the killing. The incident forced Marmolejo's resignation.[9]

Cameron the southernmost of the three counties, is situated at the very bottom of the Texas map, between Mexico and the Gulf of Mexico.

With a 2010 population of 406,000, its county seat is Brownsville. That's where singer-actor Kris Kristofferson grew up. It was also the home of Sheriff Conrado Cantu who in 2005, was sentenced to 24 years in federal prison and hit with a $5,000 fine for using his office to lead a criminal enterprise that extorted money from drug dealers and other criminals.[10]

Captain Rumaldo Rodriguez, Cantu's chief of criminal investigations, was also sentenced to fourteen months in federal prison and Geronimo Garcia who ran the county's jail commissary under a no-bid contract, was sentenced to nine years, six months and fined $5,000.

Cantu's guilty plea came as the result of a 45-page federal indictment handed down in 2005, charging him with ten counts of extortion, drug trafficking, obstruction of state and local law enforcement, witness tampering and bribery. Ironically, he wasn't indicted until after he had been defeated for reelection, but before he was scheduled to leave office.

Shortly before his defeat at the polls, sheriff's deputies stopped a truck and seized $25,000 in purported drug profits. Later that same day, the driver made a telephone call to a man he knew could help him: Jerry Garcia, the same person who ran the jail commissary. He asked Garcia if he could find out which law enforcement agency had provided the tip that had led to the seizure. Five days later, Garcia came through with the information.

The driver soon received a second call from Garcia who said if he wanted to avoid future problems, he could pay the sheriff $4,000. There were several more calls, leading to more deals. Small amounts of money changed hands. At their next meeting, the sheriff was present. The driver offered $5,000 in cash for the tips he had received and to secure future unimpeded movements of drug money. Cantu told him to give the payment to Garcia. Cantu and Garcia met later that day at a restaurant, and the money changed hands as a camera clicked nearby. Neither man had any idea that the truck driver was a government informant.[11]

Of the four counties on the southernmost Texas border, Zapata, with only $14,000 residents, is easily the smallest in population. The county abuts and is immediately northwest of Starr County and is only 47 miles downriver from Laredo. It was there, in 1994, that Zapata County Sheriff Romero R. Ramirez pleaded guilty to federal drug-related charges after being caught up in Operation Prickly Pear, a sting operation that also resulted in the conviction of Zapata County judge (the Texas equivalent to a county commissioner in other states) Jose Luis Guevara on several public corruption counts.

Ramirez, who said his indictment was an effort by the FBI to repair its image after the Branch Davidian debacle in Waco the year before, was accused of accepting $20,000 in drug profits in exchange for allowing a smuggler to use his ranch on Falcon Lake as a marijuana holding area. Ramirez said he thought the money was legitimate payment for hunting, fishing and camping rights on his property.[12]

Not nearly as visible to outsiders and not as lucrative for sheriffs – or as tinged with the danger element as conspiring with drug kingpins is the flourishing business of no-bid contracts between vendors who operate commissaries for prisoners in county jails in the 254 counties spread across the Texas landscape.

Scant scrutiny is given these contracts that allow enormous profits for the operators who are often politically-connected to the incumbent sheriff who in turn most likely receives generous campaign "contributions" from the operator.

While there is little information as to how money is generated through the county jail commissaries, the 160,000 inmates in the Texas state prison system spend about $100 million a year on snacks, clothes, stamps, soft drinks, cigarettes and even Mother's Day cards.[13]

Jail commissaries, along with work-release programs, present an opportunity for sheriffs to shift the cost of incarceration to inmates and their families while enriching the private vendors in the process. The secret of the success of commissaries lies in the exploitation-laden combination of monopoly operation and price gouging. Ramen noodle soup, the most popular item sold in the commissaries, cost vendors fourteen cents and sell for twenty-five cents, a 44 percent markup.[14] Other prices included:

- Soft drinks: $2.35;
- Coffee (regular): $2.70
- Coffee (decaf): $3.30
- Hot chocolate: $3.75
- Hershey's Chocolate Bar (with or without almonds): $1.70
- Bottled water (six-pack of half-liter bottles): $3.75
- Nacho Cheese Chips: $1.50
- Aspirin, generic (limit 2); $1.60
- Chapstick: $3.70[15]

But in September 2007, one such arrangement led to the indictment and resignation of longtime Bexar County Sheriff Ralph Lopez and a felony theft guilty plea by his campaign manager John Reynolds. Part of Lopez's plea bargain to three misdemeanor charges called for his cooperation with authorities in the investigation of the relationship between Texas sheriffs and Premier Management Enterprise of Prairieville, Louisiana.

The charges against Lopez stemmed from his acceptance of an all-expense-paid golf vacation in Costa Rica from Premier in exchange for his assistance in obtaining the lucrative Bexar County jail commissary contract and subsequently neglecting to report the trip and $600 in unrelated campaign contributions.

As part of his plea bargain agreement, authorities agreed to drop the investigation of Lopez's wife, Nancy, who had helped him launder campaign contributions.

Reynolds pleaded guilty to a single count of third-degree felony theft for his diversion of $32,000 in Premier funds into his own accounts. Former Premier CEO Ian Williamson testified that Renolds demanded charitable donations of $27,500 that he claimed were for scholarship funds for the Optimists, a charitable group, and campaign contributions in exchange for the contract. The campaign contributions were to consist of 1 percent of gross commissary sales and deposited in Lopez's campaign, which was controlled by Nancy Lopez. She also was involved with Systems Analysts, a company which received thousands of dollars in consulting fees from Premier.[16]

The scheme had even deeper roots. Lopez had established the Benevolent Fund corporation board several years earlier to run the jail commissary. The board's vice chairman, John E. Curran III, owned a temporary worker company that supplied employees for the commissary operated by Premier.[17]

The investigation of the relationship between Premier Management and Texas sheriffs quickly spread to two other counties and even swept up another, larger vendor in the profitable jail commissary business.

Former Kleberg County Sheriff Tony Gonzales, on his way out the door, approved a Premier food commissary contract for his jail. Coincidentally, either before or after Gonzalez left office in late 2004, he accepted private consulting work from Premier's owners.

Gonzales also made the original connections that helped Premier get a commissary contract in Nueces County (Corpus Christi). An associate of former Sheriff Larry Olivarez, another Lopez friend, benefitted after helping Premier win a jail commissary contract there in 2005. In his position as a commercial real estate broker who was appointed by the sheriff to an ad hoc committee that awarded the contract, the friend earned a commission on the sale of 56 acres where LCS Corrections Services Inc., another company owned in part by Premier's principals, was building a private detention center.

The former sheriff's chief deputy then won political backing from LCS when he ran as a candidate to replace Olivarez, who had stepped down to run for county judge.[18] When Corporal Armando Treviño was arrested on charges of bribery, possession of heroin – in uniform and armed – in May 2019, he became the 30th deputy arrested from the Bexar County Sheriff's Office since 2018 and the eighth during 2019.

Authorities had set up surveillance after becoming suspicious that Treviño had been smuggling drugs into the Bexar County jail for much of his five-year tenure with the department. The surveillance team quickly observed a narcotics transaction taking place between Treviño and a man identified as Rudy Anthony De La Cruz.

Bexar County Sheriff Javier Salazar called Treviño's arrest "insulting" and "an affront to the other 1,500 deputies that I have in this agency that just want to come to work and protect and serve and do a great job and provide for their families. Folks like [Treviño] are totally disrespecting everybody that wears that badge with honor and distinction."[19]

Salazar had run successfully to unseat incumbent Sheriff Susan Pamerleau in 2016, saying that it was the culture of the sheriff's department that prompted him to run in the first place.

It didn't take long after Salazar was elected for deputies to begin leaving the department – for jail. On April 17, 2018, Leonard Lopez, a 15-year veteran of the department was charged with sexual assault in connection with a two-year-old allegation. He was the third deputy to be arrested in a week's time. Six days earlier, deputies Michael Gomez and Joseph Anthony Hernandez were indicted for official oppression for allegedly punching an inmate in the face and hitting him with a stick while trying to handcuff him at the Bexar County jail.

In February, 14-year-veteran Deputy Adelaida Adams was charged by prosecutors with defrauding the federal Medicaid and SNAP programs out of as much as $100,000. In August 2017, Deputy Rita Alvarez was charged for collecting drug debts and depositing them digitally in an account for inmate Cristobal Perez.

Salazar placed seven members of the jail's Special Emergency Response Team on administrative leave less than two weeks later after six of the members used handcuffs, shackles and a stun gun to haze the seventh member and videotaped it.

On Christmas Eve 2017, Jesse Aaron Massey, who had resigned from the department only weeks earlier, was arrested on charges he choked and suffocated his girlfriend, a San Antonio police officer, with a pillow.[20] One of the stories that led Salazar to run for sheriff was a sex scandal that cost four deputies their jobs and saw a fifth resign while under investigation for behavior that involved sex in a patrol car, salacious text messages and at least one ruined marriage.

A lieutenant who had been with the department for 37 years resigned in November 2015 within days of learning he was under investigation for having sex in a patrol car with Deputy Melissa Campbell who also was sexting with three other employees, all sergeants.[21]

Federal authorities were investigating possible corruption in the Bexar County Sheriff's Office as early as 2010 when it was suspected that some deputies may have been unlawfully taking evidence or stealing money and property from detainees. The investigation began into possible civil rights violations but soon expanded into questions of how deputies could live beyond their county pay scale with group trips to Las Vegas and the purchase of expansive property in South Texas.

Complaints ranged from deputies moonlighting in private security jobs at apartment complexes and using excessive force and threats to shaking down residents, to running roughshod, arresting people without cause and stealing money.[22]

Sex also was the root of many of the problems in the Harris County (Houston) Sheriff's Department with no fewer than 15 deputies being implicated in various scandals involving sex over a nine-year stretch. It became such a problem, in fact, that in 2016, an otherwise assumed prohibition of sexual relations between deputies and witnesses and/or victims had to be issued as a formal policy after a sergeant assigned to investigate a high-profile murder of fellow Deputy Darren Goforth slept with a key witness in the case – who, it turned out, had had a fifteen-month affair with the murder victim before his death. The sergeant, Craig Clopton, was fired over his indiscretion.[23]

Before the dust had settled following Clopton's firing, two more deputies were terminated – one for also having sexual relations with the woman and a second for having "inappropriate communications" with two witnesses related to incidents he responded to. One of those witnesses was involved in the murder investigation of Goforth.

If that's confusing, here's the chronology of events that led to a burgeoning sex scandal within the Harris County Sheriff's Department:

On August 28, 2015, Goforth was fueling his vehicle at a Chevron station just outside of downtown Houston when a man identified as Shannon Miles walked up to him and shot him in the back of the head and then pumped 15 more rounds into Goforth's body.

Following Goforth's murder, it was revealed by prosecutors that a woman who had witnessed the shooting and who was seen crying over his body the night he was shot, had been having an affair with Goforth, who was married. Homicide Detective Clopton was assigned to interview her, and Clopton ended up having consensual sex with the woman at her home on September 10, less than two weeks following Goforth's death.

Clopton, a veteran with the department whose actions were described as "unethical and inexcusable" by Sheriff Ron Hickman, who described the department's interactions with witnesses as "like a doctor-patient relationship," was fired in October.[24]

All that would have been embarrassing enough for Hickman's department but in February 2016, the axe fell on two more deputies tied to the Goforth investigation.

Deputy Marc De Leon, a 14-year veteran of the department, was fired on February 10 after being accused of having sex with the same woman while on duty and then lying about it. Two days later, Deputy Jason Goodrich who had worked on the Patrol Bureau for two years after having previously served as a reserve deputy in Bexar County, was fired for "inappropriate communications" with two witnesses of incidents he had investigated. One of those was, it turned out, the same former mistress of the slain Goforth.[25]

Just three years earlier, in 2013, deputies Adam Wright, Michael Medina, and Robert Johnson were fired for having sex in their patrol cars with a married teacher in the Pasadena Independent School District. Both the woman and her husband were reserve deputies, volunteers who participated in ride-alongs with full-time deputies.[26]

Hickman called the sexual episodes "the gift that keeps on giving." His immediate predecessor, Sheriff Adrian Garcia might have agreed. In October 2012, six Harris County jail employees were fired for sexual misconduct, specifically, having sex with female inmates.

The six terminations brought to more than twenty officers and civilian employees of the sheriff's department who were either suspended without pay or fired outright for having inappropriate relations with inmates, providing contraband, or both since 2007.[27]

But it does not seem to matter when it occurs or who is sheriff at the time. Sexual offenses continued unabated in the Harris County Sheriff's Office well into the year 2021.

Deputy Kenneth Reed was fired and charged with sexual assault in July 2020 following an investigation of a complaint by a woman who reported a uniformed deputy assaulted her in March. She said Reed had started a conversation with her and instructed her to put her daughter back inside her vehicle. He then called her to his patrol car where she said he sexually assaulted her.[28]

Some sexual abuse cases involving deputies are far worse than others, though, because they didn't always involve adults. In May 21, 2021, two employees, dispatcher Christina McKay, and deputy Chonda Shalett Williams were fired from the department, arrested and charged for their involvement in another person's sexual assault of a child. That person, Deputy Constable Robert Johnson, committed suicide following a standoff with police that lasted several hours.

During the standoff, Johnson made several telephone calls and confessed to allegations of sexually assaulting a minor and implicated McKay and Williams before taking his own life.

McKay was charged with aggravated sexual assault of a child and Williams was charged with sexual assault of a child. Court documents said Johnson and Williams had sex with a minor while the child was unconscious from ingesting pills and alcohol provided by Johnson. The minor later came forward to share recollections from one of the incidents that occurred in December 2020.

McKay admitted to witnessing Johnson sexually assault a passed-out minor in a hotel room, according to records obtained by a Houston television station. McKay said she provided Johnson with pills so that he could sedate the underage victims, according to court documents. McKay made reservations at the same hotel twenty times in one twelve-month period, authorities said.[29]

Three Harris County female deputies filed suit against the sheriff's department on May 24, 2021, claiming that they had been the victims of sexual assault at hands of their superior officers.

Ironically, the three were working on a task force to fight human trafficking after they were picked for "undercover operations" where their superiors used so-called "bachelor-party" prostitution stings in an attempt to arrest pimps running call girls.

Instead, the attempted stings were little more than a "booze-fueled playground for sexual exploitation" where the female deputies were subjected to abuse, their lawsuit said. They said they were molested by intoxicated male commanding officers during the undercover operations.

They said when they raised concerns with their superiors, they were ridiculed, retaliated against and demoted to less prestigious assignments. In addition to Harris County, the suit named as defendants Constable Alan Rosen, Assistant Chief Chris Gore, and Lt. Shane Rigden. A fourth plaintiff, Jacquelyn Aluotto, a female human trafficking advocate, said she was fired one day after reporting the alleged misconduct to Internal Affairs.[30]

It wasn't all about sex, of course. In April 2021, 11 Harris County Sheriff's Office employees were fired and six more were suspended without pay following the death of a detainee in the Harris County jail during the February winter storm.

Twenty-three-year-old Jaquaree Simmons died as the result of multiple blows to his head. He had been booked into the jail on a felony murder charge on Feb. 10. On Feb. 16, he received a "closed strike," and fell to the floor during an altercation with guards in his cell. He was struck several more times after the initial blow but none of the jail personnel present at the time documented the second use of force, a policy violation, said Sheriff Ed Gonzalez. Simmons died the following day.[31]

Former Harris County deputy sheriff George Wesley Ellington was sentenced to five years in federal prison in August 2011, followed by two-years supervised release, after pleading guilty to accepting a $500 bribe. The bribe was for him to access confidential information from secured law enforcement databases and for providing security and protection in his official capacity to an individual he believed was transporting Ecstasy.

Ellington's wife, Tania Katrisse Ellington, was also sentenced to a year and a day in federal prison, to be followed to a one-year supervised release for knowingly concealing her husband's criminal activities. George Wesley Ellington entered his guilty plea on April 14, 2011 and Tania followed suit on April 26.[32]

Former Swisher County sheriff Emmett Benavidez was sentenced in August 2011 to thirty days in jail, to be followed by one year of probation, thirty hours of community service and mandatory attendance of a "rational behavior" class and a fine of five hundred dollars after pleading guilty to charges of official oppression in connection with allegations he sexually harassed a former Swisher County employee in a neighboring county.

Benavidez's fondling himself in front of Cassie Pointer not only resulted in his resignation, his sentencing, and a $300,000 settlement of a federal lawsuit, but also tainted two other officials, including a county judge and Benavidez's successor as sheriff.

Pointer, who recorded Benavidez during the trip into Randall County, complained to Swisher County officials, including County Judge Harold Keeter and Benavidez's eventual successor, Sheriff Burnie Wells. Both denied the allegations and Keeter, whose position is akin to county commissioners in other states, retaliated against Pointer and another female companion for reporting the incidents.

"If people would have listened to us in the beginning, there wouldn't have been a federal lawsuit," Pointer said. Ultimately, she prevailed in a $300,000 settlement and Benavidez resigned. And while Swisher County officials did not act on the women's complaint, prosecutors in Randall County, where the offense occurred, did. "It took another county to step forward and do the right thing," said Pointer who, along with her family, moved from Swisher County.[33]

Cody Grubb was appointed by Keeter as Benavidez's immediate successor but soon resigned when health and safety issues at the county jail were ignored by county officials. Wells was then brought in even though he did not possess a Texas peace officer license as required by state law. A former police officer in Happy, Texas, he had been allowed to resign after he allowed an unlicensed teenager to drive and then violated the youth's civil rights. His tenure as sheriff was marked by repeated incidents that reflected poorly on his abilities as an administrator and peace officer:

On December 30, 2013, Ramiro Rutiaga was involved in a single-vehicle accident and when Tulia police attempted to contact Wells because the accident was in his jurisdiction, he was nowhere to be found. He had left his department unmanned and did not reroute calls to his home in another county. Forty-five minutes after the initial call, Rutiaga was struck and killed by a delivery truck.

In June 2014, a black family from Tulia was driving around looking for junk cars to purchase. A white man who was a personal friend of Wells began following the family. When the family pulled over to ask why he was following them, he pulled a shotgun on them. Wells arrived shortly after that and told his friend to leave whereupon Wells immediately began brutalizing the father and threatening the mother with further violence.

In October 2014, Wells hired a new deputy ostensibly for the formation of a K-9 unit but in reality, to recruit her to conspire against the Pointer woman who was suing Benavidez. When she refused, she became a target of his wrath. When she attempted to resign, Wells fired her and the K-9 unit was disbanded. Another employee who had agreed to testify in Pointer's behalf also was fired.

Before Wells and before Benavidez fondled himself, county jail inmate Terry Borum attempted suicide. That was in 2010 and injuries he suffered in his attempt left him in need of special feeding devices. Keeter, not wanting to spend the eighty dollars per day required for proper care, recommended that jailers feed him honey and lemon juice. Objections by jailers were ignored and Borum eventually lost consciousness because of malnutrition and fell. He suffered head injuries that proved fatal two days later, prompting a lawsuit by his family.

A year after Borum's unsuccessful suicide attempt, another inmate, Louis Garcia, Jr., successfully hung himself in his Swisher County jail cell, prompting a lawsuit that claimed improper surveillance equipment and protocols prohibited officials from detecting his efforts and preventing his suicide.[34]

Swisher County also made national headlines in July 1999 when it became public that forty-three people in Tulia, the county seat, had been arrested by the Swisher County Sheriff's Department on suspicion of dealing drugs. Of that forty-three, forty were black, leading many to suspect the real root of the problem was racism and bigotry.

The lead investigator, an undercover agent who built the cases, was subsequently charged with perjury in a case that ultimately cost the county

$6 million and ruined the lives of innocent people. He received minimal punishment in being sentenced to ten years' probation.

In 2003, Texas Gov. Rick Perry pardoned thirty-five of the thirty-eight who went to trial or accepted plea agreements.[35]

Asset forfeiture laws, while applicable in every state, do vary in the degree of severity. The Institute for Justice in 2010 published a 123-page study of the law as it applies in each state. The study, titled *Policing for Profit*, revealed that twenty-nine of the fifty states scored a D in its grading system which was based on each state's forfeiture law itself and what the institute called its "Evasion Grade," which rated each state on its ability to circumvent its own asset forfeiture laws in order to seize private property for little or no cause.

Delaware, Wyoming, Alaska, Montana, and Massachusetts each got an F in its Law Grade while four others – California, New York, Georgia, and Texas – received an F for their Evasion Grade. Five states – New Mexico, North Carolina, Nebraska, Wisconsin, and Massachusetts – have since instituted reforms to their asset forfeiture laws to make them more equitable to innocent citizens. Still, a 2021 investigative report by *ProPublica* revealed that Massachusetts prosecutors can still hold on to seized money indefinitely even when no one is charged with a crime.[36]

Between 2001 and 2013, forfeiture proceeds in the U.S. totaled nearly $540.7 million, the report said. Texas, between fiscal year 2000 and FY 2008, received $201.4 million in asset seizure proceeds returned to the state by the U.S. Department of Justice under an agreement between the states and feds.[37] In 2017 alone, the state received more than $50 million by seizing cash, cars, jewelry, clothing, art and other property authorities claimed were linked to crime.[38]

Texas had the third-worst overall grade of all the states, beating out only Virginia and West Virginia. In Texas, the asset forfeiture law is civil, not criminal, and the property, not the owner, is charged with involvement in a crime.[39] That accomplishes two things that favor local governments that abuse the law to fatten their operating budgets: it makes a far easier for authorities to seize private property and because it assumes guilt on the part of the property, it shifts the burden of proof to show guilt from law enforcement to the owner who must prove innocence in order to get his property back. At the same time, it serves as a powerful tool of intimidation to be used to persuade the owner to waive his rights.

In Texas, four counties – Smith, Reeves, Harris, and Webb – stand out as the worst of the worst, but it was no picnic in San Jacinto County, seventy miles north of Houston, as far back as 1983.

In March that year, San Jacinto County Sheriff James C. "Humpy" Parker pleaded guilty to two felony civil rights counts and one extortion count after admitting in federal court that he tortured prisoners, subjected blacks, women, and rock music fans to strip-searches on a local highway and demanded kickbacks from a bail bondsman over a period of six years.

He was sentenced to ten years in federal prison and ordered to pay a $12,000 fine and his chief deputy, John Glover, was sentenced to two years imprisonment and five years' probation. Sheriff Parker was later given two additional one-year sentences to run concurrently with the ten-year sentence for water torture he admitted performing on prisoners. Sheriff Parker's son, Gary Parker, bail bondsman James Browder, and Herbert Atwood, who participated in the water torture practices, all received probated sentences. Gary Parker was sentenced to thirty-five years in the Texas prison system in 2007 for kidnapping and other first-degree felonies.

Sheriff Parker and his deputies had carried out a practice of terrorizing motorists along Highway 59 by searching the insides of women's bras and forcing male drivers and passengers to drop their pants for searches in open view alongside the highway. Targeted victims included blacks, any car with a bumper sticker promoting a Houston rock music radio station, drivers and passengers whose hair was long enough to touch their collars, and cars with Louisiana license plates with a "G" on them, signifying State Police Troop G, headquartered in Shreveport, a city Parker considered especially corrupt because he considered it run by the Dixie Mafia.[40]

Trial records showed that motorists' vehicles were often tampered with, such as disconnecting tail lights, in order to create probable cause for pulling them over. More than a thousand such arrests were made, resulting in more than $300,000 in fines finding its way into the county coffers. Parker also collected thousands of dollars from bondsmen, particularly Browder, who split the prisoners' money with him.[41]

Potter County Sheriff Mike Shumate was facing up to life imprisonment in June 2008 after a 12-woman jury found him guilty of engaging in organized crime activity, specifically, accepting bribes from a vendor who supplied food for the county jail.

Instead, he was sentenced to only six months followed by eight years' probation and a fine of $5,000. Shumate, who only three months earlier had lost his bid for reelection, was removed from office immediately following the verdict and taken into custody.[42]

Testimony presented at his trial indicated that Shumate accepted bribes from Mid-America Services, a Dallas-based company, to provide food service and commissary contracts at the Potter County jail. Mid-America President Robert W. Austin, Jr., and his predecessor, Elbert Madera, began planning a comprehensive bid for the food services contracts seven months before Potter County, located in the Texas panhandle, requested bids for the service.

The contract, however, was awarded to a competing company in January 2003. Soon afterward, Shumate began receiving gifts and meals from Mid-America. The sheriff subsequently notified the winning bidder that its services were no longer needed and began working to have the contract assigned to Mid-America. Because three parties – Shumate, Austin, and Mid-America – were alleged to have organized a scheme committee several bribery offenses, each defendant was charged with a first-degree felony which, under Texas law, can carry a life sentence and a $10,000 fine.[43]

Potter County wasn't the first flirtation between Mid-America and a Texas sheriff. As early as 2001, Dallas County Sheriff Jim Bowles was reported to have accepted several gifts and favors from Mid-America between 1999 and 2001, including thousands of dollars in meals for Bowles and paying nearly $1,900 to a construction company to pave a driveway at the sheriff's home. Bowles said travel expenses that Mid-America President Elbert "Jack" Madera also paid for him were reimbursed.[44]

Between the time Bowles took office in 1985 and 2003, five contracts worth millions of dollars were signed between the sheriff's office and Mid-America. The department received a portion of the $4 million in annual revenue generated by the contract even though Madera's bid was worth only about $600,000 in annual revenue to the sheriff's department as compared to a minimum of $1 million offered by other bidders on the contract.

The relationship between Bowles and Madera was unusually close, records show. Bowles even occasionally acted on behalf of the company, accompanying Madera on visits to other Texas sheriffs in an effort to solicit commissary business for Mid-America.[45]

Though no charges were ever brought against Bowles despite his appearance before a Dallas County grand jury, it nevertheless all came crashing down in March 2004 when a former chief deputy named Danny Chandler defeated Bowles in the Republican primary. Chandler was in turn upset in the general election by Democrat Lupe Valdez, former senior agent for the Department of Homeland Security.[46]

In 1955, Presidio County, Texas, was used as the backdrop for the George Stevens epic movie *Giant*, starting, James Dean, Rock Hudson, Elizabeth Taylor, Carroll Baker, Dennis Hopper, Sal Mineo, Earl Holliman, and Chill Wills. It was a story of how the oil changed Texas and Texans. The irony was that Presidio County never produced a drop of oil. Still, it was pretty heady stuff for a county of fewer than 10,000 residents.

At an elevation of 4,800 feet, the county sits in the Big Bend of the Rio Grande, a national park about the size of Rhode Island, and shares one hundred fifty miles of Rio Grande shoreline with Mexico. Marfa, the county seat, sits at an altitude roughly the same as Denver and its evening temperatures in July average about a degree lower than in Anchorage, Alaska. *Texas Monthly* magazine, in a lengthy profile on the county in 1977, described Marfa as "the last frontier," proclaiming that "what Texas once was, Marfa still is."[47]

But like Starr, Hidalgo, Cameron, and Zapata counties, it shares a common border with Mexico, separated only by the shallow Rio Grande. The fifth-longest river in the U.S., It forms 1,255 miles of an international border between the U.S. and Mexico, every inch of it in Texas.[48]

Vietnam veteran Richard Dee Thompson became sheriff of Presidio County in May 1973 after his predecessor, Hank Hamilton, was shot to death. During his ensuing four terms in office, which paid only $22,657 a year, he would lead a regional drug task force, film anti-drug TV spots for U.S. Customs and even served as president of the Sheriffs' Association of Texas. He would claim $1.5 million in seized narcotics when in truth, only $5,000 was seized. He boasted of 147 arrests when in reality, fewer than 50 were made – and three of those were for illegal purchases of beer.

All that came crashing down on Feb. 14, 1992, when he entered a guilty plea to his role in a cocaine-smuggling operation that moved tons of the drug across the Rio Grande into the U.S. As early as 1976, city police officer Manny Rodriguez, who challenged Thompson in his bid for his first full term, warned associates privately that Thompson was involved in the drug business, but no one believed him.[49]

Glyn Robert Chambers, who owned a ranch in Presidio County

across the river from San Antonio del Bravo, described as a hotbed of narcotics activity in Mexico, pleaded guilty to a single count of federal drug trafficking in exchange for his testimony against Thompson. Chambers once picked up a load of cocaine in Mexico but when the truck broke down after crossing the border, he called for help on a walkie-talkie and it was Thompson who appeared to give the truck a jump start, court records said.[50] In the early morning hours of Dec. 3, 1991, based on information provided by an informant, federal agents were staking out a red horse trailer parked at the county fairgrounds when at about 1:15 a.m. a green Suburban was seen driving on the Fairgrounds Road with its lights off. It was the vehicle normally driven by Sheriff Thompson. Upon closer inspection of the trailer, it was discovered that beneath the bales of hay and empty feed sacks were forty heavy sacks, each marked with the blue polo player, the signature of a Colombian drug cartel. Contained in the sacks was 2,421 pounds of cocaine that graded out at 93 percent pure and which had an estimated street value of $50 million. Thompson and Chambers stood to make $500,000 each had the shipment reached San Antonio or Houston safely.

After initially claiming he was only transporting cocaine seized in a narcotics investigation, he ultimately entered his guilty plea to federal drug trafficking charges and was given two life sentences in federal prison in May 1992 after the presiding judge noted that he and Chambers together had been responsible for smuggling more than twenty tons of cocaine and marijuana through Big Bend. His sentence was later reduced to 30 years and he would serve 26 years before he was released in 2018.

In return for his cooperation in Thompson's trial, Chambers also got life but was released after serving 18 years.[51]

Hudspeth County Sheriff Arvin West could be described as flamboyant and controversial and no one would argue. He had a knack for attracting national attention to the second-westernmost county in the state despite its population of fewer than five thousand residents scattered across the county's 4,572 square miles (approximately one person per square mile).

He told local farmers to arm themselves against drug smugglers from Mexico. He also boasted of a standoff between himself and alleged Mexican soldiers who he said were protecting drug runners. Sheriff West even testified before a congressional committee that drug cartels were planning to rig their illicit loads with detonators set to explode if seized Finally, he made assertions to a California newspaper that the cartels had hired hit men to kill U.S. lawmen, West has never passed up an opportunity at seeking publicity if it could bring more federal enforcement dollars into his county that shares about a hundred miles of the Rio Grande as the common border between the county and Mexico.[52]

West even joined several other sheriffs, from Louisiana to Arizona, in making movie star Steven Seagal a reserve deputy, saying that the Hollywood tough guy would bring "a wealth of tactical experience and dedication as a peace officer" and teach martial arts to members of the sheriff's department.

But what really set West apart from the typical white-hat, cowboy-boot-wearing, gun-totin' Texas sheriff was his bizarre link to an obscure but rogue Navy intelligence office at the Pentagon back in Arlington, Virginia., and an attempt by the intelligence unit to funnel military equipment to Hudspeth County in proximity to the Mexican border.

Even more curious, David Landersman, the former director of the intelligence unit, his son, and the spouse of one of the intelligence officers served as deputies to Sheriff West. Two of Landersman's former subordinates also moonlighted as reserve deputies. Many questions about why Pentagon officials and their relatives were employed as deputies 1,600 miles away in a remote county about the size of Connecticut in the parched Rio Grande basin but many of the answers were sealed to protect national security.

Civilian Navy employee Sterling Gill, who served in Hudspeth County, was questioned by prosecutors as to whether she and Landersman had attempted to establish a military training center in Hudspeth County, complete with new roads, an airstrip and $14,000 in radio equipment at the thirty-two-thousand-acre Circle Ranch, owned by her in-laws. Gill, who was subsequently suspended indefinitely without pay, said the radios were for use by the sheriff's office. She denied, without elaborating, allegations relating to the training center and airstrip.

But when a *Washington Post* reporter wrote about the operation in 2013, Navy security officials burned and shredded sensitive documents. A Navy security officer who supervised the document destruction said he was merely purging old files in accordance with Navy regulations.

The supervisor, Richard Kent Ford, originally testified in 2014 that he was unaware that Landersman, Gill, and others from the intelligence unit were under investigation or that there had been news coverage of the case.

But when an email he had written warning several Navy officials of the *Post's* front-page coverage shortly before he oversaw the file destruction, he said he had "forgotten" about the *Post* story. The Navy fired Ford from his job after concluding that he was untruthful in his original testimony in the silencer case.

Among the revelations of reporter Craig Whitlock was an account that the intelligence unit had arranged for the unauthorized, sweetheart contract for the purchase of AK-47 silencers from Landersman's brother, Mark, who profited more than $1.5 million on the deal. Details about the silencers have remained under a cloud of mystery because of the court-ordered sealing of testimony, but there were indications that they were part of a top-secret operation to arm guerrillas or commandos overseas.

A bankrupt California auto mechanic, Mark Landersman produced three hundred forty-nine homemade, unmarked silencers in a machine shop at a cost of less than $10,000 under a contract that paid him $1.6 million. Three Navy officials testified that they had approved David Landersman's request to spend the money on intelligence studies, not a weapons deal.[53]

Mark Landersman and Lee M. Hall, a man who helped arrange the contract, were each convicted of conspiracy in October 2014. Mark Landersman was sentenced to sixty days in prison and Hall received a six-month sentence. David Landersman was also indicted but suffered two seizures in four days while on trial for theft and conspiracy and Federal Judge Leonie M. Brinkema dismissed the indictment against him.[54]

Sheriff West was never charged in the convoluted scheme.

It could have been that the deputy sheriffs in Maverick County were camera shy, but their reactions to being videotaped appeared more than a little excessive to witnesses. When Ernesto Flores asked deputies for their names as he was videoing them after being told that his sister and her boyfriend were being arrested on Oct. 14, 2020, the deputies charged him and "took me down against the car," Flores said, adding that one of the deputies attempted to pepper spray him.

Multiple federal appeals courts have affirmed that the First Amendment gives citizens the right to record members of law enforcement in public as long as they are not interfering and are standing a safe distance away from the scene. Flores said the unidentified deputies kept him handcuffed for several minutes before releasing him without charging him with any offense.

Maverick County Sheriff Tom Schmerber refused media requests to provide copies of bodycam footage of the incident but recordings made by witnesses appeared to support Flores' allegations.[55]

Former Travis County sheriff's deputy Nicholas Broderick was ordered held without bail after a three-count indictment charged him with the shooting deaths of his ex-wife, his stepdaughter and the stepdaughter's boyfriend in a domestic dispute about ten miles from the Texas State Capitol in Austin on April 18, 2021.

The only survivor was the Brodericks' nine-year-old son. Ironically, the two adults were supposed to be meeting so that Broderick could visit with his son. Instead, Broderick rammed his ex-wife's vehicle and opened fire. The boy escaped, flagged down a driver and climbed into the car that stopped for him. He told the driver to call 911, explaining that his father was angry about the divorce from his mother.[56]

Ten months earlier, Broderick, who investigated property crimes as a Travis County deputy, was placed on administrative leave after being charged with sexual assault of a child. He was released on $50,000 bail after that incident and he was ordered not to contact or go within two hundred feet of the child and ordered to wear a GPS tracking device.[57]

In his 1969 book *The Peter Principle*, Laurence J. Peter observed that people in a hierarchy tend to rise to their "maximum level of incompetence" and that personnel are promoted based on their success in previous jobs until they reach a level at which they are no longer competent because skills in one job do not necessarily translate to another.

Peter could well have been writing about former Fort Bend County Sheriff Troy Nehls. Nehls, who bears a resemblance to former University of Oklahoma and Dallas Cowboy coach Barry Switzer, parlayed a mediocre record as a member of the Richmond, Texas, police department, where he was fired for destruction of evidence, to election as Fort Bend County sheriff in 2012 and 2016 and finally to his election as U.S. Representative from Texas's 22nd District as an unapologetic supporter of President Donald Trump.

Even before his election to congress, his support for Trump went so far as to utilize unpaid labor of jail prisoners to implement a program of giving free disinfectant to residents after Trump had touted disinfectant on national television as a cure for coronavirus.

Of his 1998 termination by the Richmond Police Department, Nehls said on *Fox and Friends*, "It didn't prevent me to get where I am today, now, did it?"

Houston attorney John T. Floyd, a vocal opponent of Nehls, posted a laundry list of transgressions by the Fort Bend County sheriff on Oct. 22, 2020. Among those listed was Floyd's claim that Nehls lied on his job application with the Richmond Police Department when he signed a form attesting that he'd never been arrested or charged with a crime. In 1988, he had been arrested for underage drinking and obstructing police as they attempted to arrest him.

Floyd also listed other disciplinary problems encountered by Nehls while employed by Richmond police:

- Jan. 31, 1997: he was disciplined for failing to contact a victim for additional information in an investigation;
- March 3, 1997: he failed to properly handle evidence after having earlier received specific instructions in a written memo about previous mishandling of evidence;
- June 3, 1997: destroyed evidence after being instructed to enter the evidence as found property;
- Sept. 26, 1997: failed to return property to owner after being ordered to do so;
- Oct. 22, 1997: three-day suspension without pay for disregarding written directive denying an extra job request and then misleading a superior about the circumstances of the incident;
- Dec. 29, 1997; one-day suspension for making an improper arrest;
- Jan. 14, 1998: disciplined for working an extra job without securing proper approval as required.

These were just eight of more than 20 disciplinary incidents found on his Richmond Police Department personnel record.

Additionally, while he was sheriff, the Texas Commission on Jail Standards warned him to take "corrective measures" after two inmates died in less than two months while in his custody.

The Houston Chronicle, Floyd wrote on his blog, published an article claiming that a special narcotics task force under Nehls' supervision was guilty of racial profiling of Hispanics in the county and that in 2019, nearly 90 percent of motorists stopped by deputy Todd Ganey, a member of the task force, were Black or Hispanic.

Kathleen Wall, a fellow Fort Bend County Republican, accused Nehls of being weak on enforcement of human sex trafficking laws in the county. The father of one sex trafficking victim said to Nehls, "I'd love to look you in the eye and have you tell me how you can possibly sit there and not do your job and not protect my family because that's what you've done for years."

During his congressional campaign, Nehls proclaimed that he would "stand with President Trump to defeat the socialist Democrats, build the wall, drain the swamp, and deliver on pro-economy and pro-American policies." But after winning the Republican primary, he quietly removed the pledges from his website, "underlining," said Floyd, "his willingness to say anything to be elected."[58]

Nehls' brother, Trever Nehls, sought to succeed Troy Nehls as sheriff upon the latter's election to congress but the voters of Fort Bend County gave former Houston police officer Eric Fagan, a black Democrat, a seventeen-thousand-vote victory as he defeated Trever Nehls by five percentage points, 52.6 percent to 47.4 percent.[59]

If you wished to create a female caricature of the prototypical, militia-supporting, authoritative, all-powerful former sheriff who acted as the last line of defense against a federal government bent on usurping the rights of American patriots, you might begin with Pamela Elliott, who served as sheriff of Edwards County for eight years. Perhaps it was more than coincidental that Elliott began her law enforcement career with the Gilbert Police Department in Maricopa County, Arizona, the home turf of former Maricopa Sheriff Joe Arpaio who oversaw the worst pattern of racial profiling in U.S. history until his eventual defeat at the polls.

Elliott fit right in the so-called patriot movement, led by former Graham County, Arizona, Sheriff Richard Mack. Mack and Arpaio jointly founded the Constitutional Sheriffs and Peace Officers Association (CSPOA), a far-right organization that embraces civilian militias, anti- government rhetoric, conspiracy theories, Christian end-times theology, and a conviction that sheriffs are the highest law enforcement authority in the land.[60]

During her eight years as sheriff, Elliott, a Republican, attempted to barge her way into a meeting of the local Democratic Party in a private home by claiming the meeting fell under the Texas Open Meetings Act (it didn't; the act does not apply to a local party's executive committee meeting). Austin attorney Buck Wood called the effort harassment. "It's intimidation and illegal use of the sheriff's office powers. It may even be abuse of office, and if so, could be a criminal offense."

First elected in 2012, she arrested local officials and declared war on David Velky, the superintendent of the local independent school district, leading Velky to suspect that the sheriff and her Republican allies planned "to get rid of me and certain board members" in order to take control of the school system. "I think they want control over the hiring of the teachers and staff members," Velky said. "I think they want to be able to bypass the procedural safeguards of the law – to arrest people without the grand jury; to bring charges without consulting the district attorney; to decide who is on the grand jury."

And while Velky may have sounded like some sort of tinfoil hat conspiracy theorist himself, Elliott lent some validity to his claims when she had deputies stake out every voting precinct in the 2014 midterm elections – contrary to election law – in an effort to intimidate Hispanic voters.

Elliott botched a local murder investigation but it should not have come as a surprise to the citizens of Edwards County. She arrested four "suspects" in the brutal 1996 stabbing murder of a local woman. The murder became a featured cold case on the television show *Unsolved Mysteries* in 2014, and she reopened the case. In the summer of 2015, the four arrests were made. One of those arrested was Neri Garcia who it turned out was already in jail at the time of the murder. Elliott persisted, nevertheless, insisting that Garcia had escaped the night of the murder and that robber was the motive.

Finding a flimsy case backed by an affidavit written at a middle-school level, District Attorney Tonya Ahlschwede, in conjunction with the Texas attorney general, dismissed the charges against all four, saying the case needed "further investigation."

Even that wasn't the worst of Elliott's misdeeds. Before moving to Texas and while serving as a member of the Gilbert, Arizona, Police Department, Elliott, then known by her still unmarried name Pamela Brock, was instrumental in sending the wrong woman to prison for seven years for a bank robbery she did not commit. In 2012, the same year Elliott was elected sheriff of Edwards County, the federal government settled a wrongful conviction with the woman for a million dollars.[61]

By 2020, the residents of Edwards County, all two thousand of them, had seen enough of Elliott. Former Texas Game Warden J.W. Guthrie defeated Elliott in the March Republican Primary. Because there were no Democrat candidates, Guthrie became the new sheriff in town.[62]

Hal Bynum, a former deputy sheriff in Kimble County, was appointed sheriff in June 1990 upon the resignation of former Sheriff Pat Davis. Four years later, Bynum and his wife would be dead, the victims of an apparent murder-suicide that shook the county of fewer than five thousand residents.

Davis resigned in the wake of a minor scandal involving a 1980 Cadillac seized by the sheriff's department and purchased by the sheriff for two hundred dollars without having gone through the required public auction procedure.[63]

On May 28, 1994, Bynum called 911 at 4:50 a.m. to report that he had found his wife, Connie, 43, nude and dead of an apparent heart attack outside their home at the local airport, near the couple's dog pen. Thinking it degrading to be found that way, he said he dragged her body into their mobile home and laid her on the sofa before calling 911.

But details of his story didn't add up. What eventually emerged were bizarre stories of an extramarital affair and bestiality. She had what appeared to be a bite mark on her left breast, ligature marks on her wrists, bruises on her legs from her ankles to her groin, abrasions on her back that were consistent with carpet burns, and two penetrating horizonal stab wounds to the vaginal cavity.

Bynum's explanation of the stab wounds was that his wife had probably been having sex with their Rottweiler dog and the animal inflicted the wounds. He said he and Connie had been walking earlier and that they'd been drinking and had an argument about a previous affair she had with a pilot who flew out of the local airport the Bynums managed. He said he later fell asleep and upon waking, could not find Connie in the house.

The couple had migrated to Kimble County and Junction from Muleshoe in Bailey County in the Texas Panhandle. He was a deputy in Bailey County and before they married, Connie was a confidential assistant who aided him with drug investigations. Rumors that Bynum was under investigation for sexually molesting a juvenile female followed the couple to Kimble County. As sheriff, Bynum routinely brought female trustys home with him from the Kimble jail.

Connie, something of a freethinker, cited her religion as Wicca, the white magic witchery.

On May 29, the day after Connie's death, the medical examiner in San Antonio discovered more signs of trauma, including marks at the base of her neck, more bruising on the legs and the bite mark on her breast was more visible. The medical examiner said the bruises on her legs were consistent with rape, though no official cause of death was given.

When Texas Rangers showed up at Bynum's residence, they found that the 51-year-old sheriff dead with a self-inflicted shotgun wound to the chest, a department-issue twelve-gauge pump shotgun lying on his torso.[64]

A Llano County grand jury in August 2018 handed down three-count indictments of Llano police officer Mark Burke and Llano County sheriff's deputy Duncan Roberts for their part in trying to pick a lock at a home and then kicking the door in and arresting the man inside the home.

On June 9, Roberts and Burk responded to a domestic violence complaint. Burke's body cam video showed the two officers shining flashlights into the home of Clay Holley, who refused to respond when Roberts knocked on the front door.

Burke tried unsuccessfully for several minutes to pick the lock with a kit from his police vehicle before Roberts gave Holley a final warning before he said he would kick the door in. "I'm not playing with you, man," Roberts said as he began kicking at the door. He forced the door on the fourth kick and entered the residence to arrest Holley. "You're going to jail," Roberts told Holley before holding him in the back of a patrol unit for nearly an hour and later releasing him without ever charging him.

Llano County Sheriff Bill Blackburn disciplined Roberts, stripping him of his police powers and putting him on paid administrative leave when the indictment came down. But Blackburn would not allow Roberts to draw a salary while sitting out his suspension. Instead, he assigned the deputy to work in the county jail until the criminal charges were resolved. "I think for the citizens of the county, if he's going to be on paid leave, he should be working for it," Blackburn said.

Blackburn said Roberts was a good deputy. "He may have made a mistake; I can't say one way or another. That's for a jury to decide," he said. "If I ever had a bad officer that I thought was working for me, he wouldn't be working for me, I'd fire him. I don't want people bringing disgrace on the office, and I don't think my officer brought disgrace on the office."[65]

In March 2006, *The Los Angeles Times* described Smith County, Texas, in rural East Texas, as a haven for meth labs, virtually free to "operate unnoticed." Misdemeanor drug charges "are as common as drunk driving arrests."

But a quarter-century earlier, Smith County Sheriff J.B. Smith was the center of attention following his 18-count indictment on charges of official misconduct, attempted arson and a laundry list of other charges. Smith was charged with dousing a car belonging to Charles Everett Wintters with gasoline and attempting to ignite the fuel. He also was accused of using county vehicles and gasoline for personal use, including numerous trips to nearby Louisiana.[67]

But Smith was never convicted and went on to serve as sheriff for 36 years (1976-2012), making him one of the longest-tenured sheriffs in Texas history. Along the way, he also established himself as a better- than-average humorist, authored two books and even hosted a *Discovery Network* reality show, *Lone Star Justice*.

Not a bad comeback from an official misconduct indictment.[68]

In Leon County, three sheriff's deputies were indicted in March 2017 for the misuse of official information.

Sheriff Kevin Ellis said he turned the matter over to the Texas Rangers as soon as he learned of the involvement of deputies Christian Negron, Dustin Bresko, and Brandon Monk.

The men were accused of sending sensitive information to Normangee Police Officer Matthew Cowan, who was under investigation by the sheriff's office for assault. All three deputies were initially placed on suspension with pay and later terminated after Texas Rangers presented the case to the Leon County District Court.[69]

The shine from his new badge had not even faded when Panola County Sheriff Ron Clinton found himself arrested, and on his way out of office after entering a guilty plea to tampering with a government document.

Only two months after being sworn into office, Clinton was arrested on charges stemming from expenses related to travel to a new-sheriff school in Austin in December 2012 and his misuse of county funds and abuse of his authority to repay the expenses.

After he failed to account for a $900 cash advance to attend the school for new sheriffs, he requested funds from the sheriff's department's seizure and forfeiture fund to cover the expense. That request was denied, so the following day, Jan. 11, he received $1,000 from the department's confidential informant fund, saying it was to be used "to pay an informant," the arrest warrant said. On that same date, he repaid the outstanding balance of $810.58 to the Panola County Treasurer's Office in the same monetary denomination as the confidential informant fund.

He then provided the name of a "confidential informant" who, when interviewed by Texas Rangers, said Clinton had asked him to say he had received the thousand dollars in return for Clinton's helping the informant with a probation issue. But in the end, the informant, James Ingram, decided he didn't want to lie, so he revealed the plot behind the alleged bribe – and Clinton went to jail.

In essence, Clinton had failed to repay the money before coming up with a scam in which the county paid itself to resolve his debt.[70]

Prisoners die in his custody, inmates' life-saving prescriptions have gone unfilled, there is an inadequate number of caseworkers or psychologists, prisoners with minor offenses are not released in the face of a deadly pandemic, undocumented immigrants are targeted for arrest for minor offenses and immediately turned over to ICE, and deputies are allowed to enforce federal immigration law which would seem to contradict the very concept of the constitutional sheriff.

Still, Bill Waybourn was reelected sheriff of Tarrant County (Fort Worth) by a 52.7 percent to 47.3 percent margin over his Democratic opponent.

Just between January 2020 and election day in November, ten prisoners – one a month – died in his custody. The Tarrant County Sheriff's Office reported that 67 percent of its deaths over the past 15 years were from natural causes but Krishnaveni Gundu, executive director and co-founder of the Texas Jail Project, isn't buying it. "If your blood pressure meds are delayed or you have diabetes and you die, they say it's a natural cause. That's not true," she said. "It's negligence."

And because of the way health care is administered, patients often do fall through the cracks. "I've gotten complaints from inmates saying their medication has run out and they can't get any more," said a former jail supervisor.

Working with ICE, Tarrant County deputies gather up undocumented immigrants on minor charges such as marijuana possession. Many of those so arrested are immediately handed over to ICE before even being charged in a court of law.[71]

39

Utah: Constitutional Sheriffs v. BLM

IT WAS TOUCH AND GO for about six months, but in the end, charges against San Juan County Sheriff Richard Eldredge and two of his deputies were dismissed after a district court judge ruled that the Utah Attorney General's Office did not meet its burden of proof to hold the defendants over for trial.

Eldredge had been charged in May 2017 with retaliation against a witness (a third-degree felony), reckless endangerment, obstruction of justice, and official misconduct after then-deputy Todd Bristol said Eldredge pointed an unloaded assault rifle at his back at a shooting range. Also charged were Chief Deputy Alan Freestone who investigated the 2015 incident after Bristol reported it, and Deputy Robert Wilcox, who Bristol said was standing next to Eldredge at the time.

Bristol said he heard "the click of a dry firearm" as he walked past the other three at the shooting range and turned to see the rifle pointed at his back. Wilcox told investigators that he had unloaded it and despite the sheriff's not verifying that it was unloaded, Judge George Harmond ruled that it was not a deadly weapon at the time.

"As a matter of law, the mere pointing of the weapon cannot create a substantial risk of death or serious bodily injury without proof the firearm was loaded and capable of discharging," Harmond said in his curious ruling. In February 2017, two years after the firing range incident, Eldredge recommended Bristol's termination and Bristol subsequently resigned on April 21.[1]

Piute County Sheriff Marty Gleave said in February 2016 that he would "deputize every man, woman and child in the county," if necessary, to stop the U.S. Bureau of Land Management and the Forest Service from taking grazing permits on Monroe Mountain from local ranchers, one of whom was his uncle. The two agencies combined to control 74 percent of the land in Piute County.[2]

The Monroe Mountain controversy mirrored similar disputes ove- access to federally-owned land in several other western states which in turn gave rise to the rise of the so-called "Sagebrush Sheriffs," and the formation of the Constitutional Sheriffs and Police Officers Association (CSPOA) by former Graham County, Arizona, Sheriff Richard Mack.

Mack, with the endorsement of sheriffs like Eldredge, led the movement whereby local sheriffs refused to enforce federal and state laws that the sheriffs deem unconstitutional, whether they involve road closures by the Bureau of Land Management, gun control, drug laws, or bans against selling unpasteurized milk. Mack called it a fight to rescue the country from the "cesspool of corruption" that he said Washington, D.C., had become.[3]

Davis County Sheriff Todd Richardson, something of a lightning rod for controversy, announced in March 2018 that he would not seek a third term but instead, would walk away from law enforcement after a career that spanned more than a quarter-century.

He made his announcement on the heels of confrontations with other county leaders and after enduring five internal audits, but just before two other controversies surfaced that tarnished his eight years as sheriff.[4]

Two months after he announced that he would not seek reelection, Richardson announced that five department staffers had been placed on leave following a sexual harassment investigation that had begun back in January. That investigation revealed that the five employees of the county corrections department had either sexually harassed six female employees themselves or had failed to intervene to prevent the harassment.

"I am deeply saddened by the actions of these employees, and offer my sincere apology to the public and the rest of the employees in the Davis County Sheriff's Office," Richardson said in a prepared statement, adding that he took "full responsibility of the mishandling of the situations as it occurred during my tenure."[5]

Eleven days following that statement, on May 22, it was learned that a criminal investigation had been initiated into the handling of deposits of $126,000 by the sheriff's office. Davis County Auditor and Clerk Curtis Koch said his staff found thirty-four thousand dollars in cash and checks stashed in drawers in one staff member's cubicle.

Much of the mishandled money was from deposits made to the accounts of county jail inmates. Sloppy record-keeping allowed double credits to one inmate's account, giving him enough money to bail himself out of jail.[6]

Sheriff Kelly Sparks, who succeeded Richardson, said in February 2020 that the financial mess left by Richardson had been cleaned up. "A very small dollar amount could not be reconciled, under four hundred dollars," added auditor Curtis Koch.

The April 2018 audit also found that Richardson used department employees to perform work for private organizations on county time and that Richardson ignored auditors' instructions to cease co-mingling public and private funds.[7]

A federal judge refused in October 2018 to dismiss a four-year-old lawsuit against Millard County, law enforcement officers, and the local sheriff's office after police and sheriff's deputies shot a man six times and tased the man who had fled officers and, following the thirty-minute chase, rammed his truck into patrol units.

The man, George Finlinson, was diagnosed as suffering from mental illness and, after his release from the hospital for treatment of his gunshot wounds, was placed in isolation for six weeks in the Utah County jail under suicide watch.

After the slow-speed car chase ended with Finlinson ramming police patrol units, officers, including sheriff's deputies, fired forty rounds at him, striking him in the torso five times and once in the neck. He continued struggling with officers after the shooting and was tased by officers.

"From beginning to end, the officers treated Mr. Finlinson as a dangerous criminal subject, and never as a man in the throes of a mental health crisis," U.S. District Judge Tena Campbell wrote. "A reasonable jury could conclude that the officers' actions before shooting and tasing Mr. Finlinson – both their plan and the resulting chase – were reckless and caused the ultimate use of force."

40

Vermont: Sheriffs by Contract

VERMONT IS SOMETHING of an anomaly in that the state's fourteen sheriffs, in addition to receiving taxpayer dollars to provide certain state-mandated law enforcement services, obtain at least part of their funding through contracts they enter into with individual state agencies, private business, towns, schools, courts and other entities. In most cases, the local sheriffs personally pocket a percentage of that contract income for their personal use.

And while the percentage varies from sheriff to sheriff, it's all legal and in some cases, it allows some sheriffs to nearly double their base salary. An investigation by the *Seven Days* Blog in 2018 revealed that Windsor County Sheriff Michael Chamberlain had fifty-eight outside contracts in fiscal 2017. In one of those contracts, the State Department of Mental Health paid Chamberlain's department $217,736, most of which was for "sit watches," staying at a hospital bedside of mental health patients. That, along with his $77,672 state salary, brought his income for the year to $145,623, not counting healthcare and retirement benefits.

State law allows sheriffs to keep up to 5 percent of their departments' contract revenue for themselves, though not every sheriff took the full percentage. Washington County Sheriff Samuel Hill's office took in about $564,400 in contract revenue, legally entitling him to more than $28,200, but he took home only $12,830 – approximately 2 percent. That, along with his $77,672 state salary and $30,912 in benefits, brought his income for the year to $121,414.

Franklin County Sheriff Robert Norris topped the fourteen sheriffs in outside income - $17,914 from contracts and $52,922 in overtime pay, for a total of $70,836 over and above his state salary. He was followed closely by Lamoille County's Robert Marcoux ($67,951) and Windsor County's Michael Chamberlain ($67,325), who took the full 5 percent. With contract income, benefits and salary, Chamberlain made $144,997 in 2017.

Chamberlain said that early in his career he took contracts as a dancehall security guard, picking up a job "for three to four dollars an hour.

The owner would pay you at the end of the night, often in cash," he said.

Essex County Sheriff Trevor Colby, with only $4,302, took home the smallest amount in personal income from outside contracts.

State Human Resources Commissioner Beth Fastiggi was less than charitable about the (legal but perhaps questionable) double-dipping, saying she was "unaware of any other arrangement" in state government allowing public servants to take a share of their earnings.

There are other ways, of course. Orange County Sheriff Bill Bohnyak did not take any money from the contract revenue his office earned but he did perform his own contract work at fifty dollars per hour for an additional $27,117, bringing his total 2017 compensation package to $163,157, including benefits.

And while the state forbids employing family members within "the same department, institution or organizational unit," sheriffs are not state employees, so they are not bound by that provision – and they take full advantage of that loophole. Eleven incumbent sheriffs employed parents, siblings, children and other family members, *Seven Days* reported.

Kevin McLaughlin worked for his father when the elder McLaughlin was sheriff of Chittenden County and then employed his father when he became sheriff in 1987. He also employed his mother and a brother. Likewise, Colby grew into his job by answering phone calls as a teenager for his sheriff father while his mother ran the office. When his father retired, he gave out almost $25,000 in bonuses, including $2,500 to his wife and $1,500 to his daughter, both of whom were on his office's payroll. When the younger Colby became sheriff on his own in 2011, he hired his dad.

Grand Isle County Sheriff Ray Allen served as chief deputy under his sheriff wife until her suicide in 2011. Appointed to succeed her, he hired sons Blake and Brandon as deputies.[1]

Four years after *Seven Days* reported that Allen supplemented his personal income by more than $29,000 from outside contracts, Allen forced closure of the Grand Isle County Courthouse for three days a week after he cut security services at the building because of the department's inability to pay competitive salaries to security personnel. While legal, the action could have (and perhaps did) hinder defendants' constitutional right to a speedy trial.

Without full-time security, the courthouse closed for in-person services on Mondays, Wednesdays and Fridays, effective August 1, 2021.[2] The story was much the same elsewhere. In Washington County, Sheriff Hill said his inability to replace deputies lost by attrition forced him to turn down some transports of those in custody and to cut screening services at the courthouse. In Windham County, the sheriff's department halted security operations for the court because it felt it wasn't being paid enough to continue the service.[3]

In April 2004, Washington County Sheriff Donald Edson resigned after entering a guilty plea to a felony fraud charge in connection with a convoluted loan transaction and an attempted coverup of what became of the money.

Edson borrowed twenty-five thousand dollars from the neighboring Lamoille County Sheriff's Office with a promise to repay the money in ninety days. When Lamoille County officials came calling for their money, he said the money had been used in an undercover drug operation when in fact, it had been deposited in the bank account of Edson's sister. The State Attorney General's Office had initiated an investigation into the loan in July 2002 after a state audit discovered the transaction. He was able to avoid jail time with his plea bargain by agreeing to perform two hundred fifty hours of community service and to make restitution of thirty-two thousand dollars.[4]

Two years after Edson's fall from grace, another sheriff was forced to resign after the discovery of widespread financial abuses that included departmental expenditures for personal purchases. Windham County Sheriff Sheila Prue pleaded guilty to embezzling thousands of dollars after an audit found that she had charged her department with purchases of airfare and meals for her domestic partner and child, groceries, pet supplies, clothing, exercise equipment, household goods, a banjo, and other personal items.

In addition to resigning, her plea bargain agreement required her to perform eighty hours of community service and to make restitution of $36,000.[5] In 2006, she attempted to get her record expunged from a political ad when State Auditor Randy Rock, seeking reelection, used old newspaper clippings about his investigation of Prue to bolster his claim of having helped expose fraud and waste while in office[6]

A former deputy in Caledonia County resigned after three women came forward to claim that he had sought – and in some cases, successfully obtained - sexual favors from them in exchange for leniency. Captain Stephen Bunnell, 47, resigned after coming under investigation for seeking nude photographs and/or sex in exchange for money from women involved in the criminal justice system.

The investigation began in April 2020 after *Facebook* messages were discovered that suggested an accused female drug dealer was seeking favors from the deputy and providing nude photos in return. Bunnell was placed on leave after he admitted to giving another woman money in exchange for photos. A third woman also came forward to say that Bunnell promised to make her tickets disappear and that he would help her get her license back in exchange for sex. His patrol vehicle was taken away in August and he resigned in October, but in August 2021, it was learned that he still faced charges of prostitution and prohibited conduct.[7]

41

Virginia: Armored Vehicles for Sheriffs

VIRGINIA, with its proximity to the nation's capital, found itself perfectly positioned in the 1980s for a major public relations debacle involving former Loudoun County Sheriff John R. Isom. Isom, almost on cue, accommodated the skeptics by plunging his department into a neck- deep morass of intrigue and inappropriate involvement with a Mississippi sheriff, a wannabe millionaire lawman, a paramilitary organization and the U.S. Marshal's Office.

With a median household income of $136,268, the county ranked first in the U.S. in that enviable statistic among jurisdictions with a population of 65,000 or more. Loudoun, with an estimated population of more than 415,000, is included in the Washington, D.C.- Arlington-Alexandria Metropolitan Statistical Area.

By 1992, Loudoun County officially severed ties with the Armored Response Group of the United States (ARGUS), but by then, the damage had been done. Before it was all over, Warren County, Mississippi, Sheriff Paul L. Barrett would be convicted of perjury (though his conviction would be overturned on appeal), and ARGUS co-founder, J.C. Herbert Bryant, a deputy in Barrett's department, would be convicted of one count of impersonating a federal official.[1]

For his part, Isom escaped any criminal charges but his entanglement with ARGUS did prompt a federal investigation of the ARGUS Foundation and its financial relationship to Isom and his office:

- Isom and Bryant co-founded ARGUS in 1985 to provide armored vehicles to law enforcement agencies during crises.
- Bryant was a major contributor to Isom's election campaigns.
- ARGUS shared and donated office space to the sheriff's department in Leesburg, the county seat.
- ARGUS's office was located in the same building as the Sterling

substation of the Loudoun County Sheriff's Department.
- Captain John Sealock, head of the Loudoun Sheriff's Department's SWAT team, was a member of ARGUS.

But Isom's ties to the nation's shadowy "secret government" go back much further than his association with ARGUS. He was linked to illegal CIA domestic actions dating back to the early 1970s when he worked at the McLean substation of the adjoining Fairfax County Police Department. In 1975, the Rockefeller Commission disclosed that the CIA had utilized the County police to conduct illegal domestic political surveillance.

To that end, law enforcement and intelligence officials believe that ARGUS itself was an "off-line" creation reflective of that "secret government" network and was a component of Oliver North's Iran-Contra operation.[2]

It's not that Bryant did not attempt to thwart Loudoun County's move to cut ties with his organization. In fact, he cited the 1992 riots that rocked Los Angeles in the aftermath of the police beating of Rodney King as an example of what could happen elsewhere. "You may think that what happened in Los Angeles is something that just happened on the spur of the moment, Bryant told county supervisors. "That was all pre-planned. That was all timers, incendiary devices, which blew up most of those buildings."

In the end, the U.S. Justice Department investigation determined that the Marshals' Service was guilty of "serious misjudgments" in giving a badge and arrest authority to Bryant but found no evidence of criminal wrongdoing. Nor was Mississippi Sheriff Barrett of any help to Bryant when he said Bryant's status as a sheriff's deputy carried no weight "outside Warren County."[3]

Problems continued for the Loudoun County Sheriff's Office into 2019, but to a far lesser degree, during Sheriff Mike Chapman's campaign for a third consecutive term when it was revealed his campaign had accepted money from a vendor after the company had been awarded a major contract with Chapman's office.

In September of that year, Wellpath, LLC, a private healthcare provider, contributed nearly $15,000 to the sheriff since he took office in 2012, including $5,000 in September 2019, only months after the company had been awarded a $4.7 million contract to provide healthcare services to inmates of the jail overseen by Chapman.

The contract was awarded by the Loudoun County Board of Supervisors and a spokesperson for the board told *The Washington Post* that Chapman was not involved in the decision. Wellpath was formed in October 2018.

Chapman's Democratic opponent, Justin Hannah, called the donations "ethically questionable." Criminal justice reform advocates, moreover, said when sheriffs can outsource healthcare at jails they run, it becomes difficult for the public to trust that sheriffs are accountable for the well-being and safety of detainees and staff. "It does create this perverse incentive to scrimp on the care," said Corene Kendrick, a staff attorney at the Prison Law Center in California, "because for every lab test not run or a specialist visit not done, that's just additional profit that the company can pocket."[4]

Wellpath was formerly known as Correct Care Solutions (CCS) before a 2018 name change brought about by a merger with Correct Care with another prison healthcare provider. Two years before the controversy over Wellpath's contributions to Chapmen, a federal investigation was initiated into the awarding of a contract to Correct Care by the Norfolk County Sheriff's Office despite Correct Care's bid that was about two hundred thousand dollars higher than a competitor. Correct Care had contributed $36,500 to Sheriff Bob McCabe's election campaign.

Reports indicated that McCabe, in a private meeting, had suggested contacting Correct Care to alert them to the bid difference. When told that would be illegal, he was said to have dropped the issue but Correct Care later revised its bid to undercut the competing firm. In that contract award in Loudoun County, Correct Care's bid was about six hundred thousand higher than the lowest bid.[5]

CCS, which provides medical and behavioral health services for a quarter-million patients at local, state, and federal prisons, jails, hospitals and civil commitment centers in about forty states, was the target in no fewer than three dozen federal lawsuits in Virginia. Federal prosecutors issued two grand jury subpoenas seeking documents related to the sheriff's office and CCS. The subpoenas were issued months after McCabe's name surfaced in a public corruption case. McCabe, who had served as sheriff since 1994, abruptly stepped down after announcing earlier that he would seek re-election.[6]

If McCabe thought his resignation would make his problems go away, he was mistaken.

He announced in December 2016 that he would step down from his

$178,000-a-year position, effective February 1, 2017. By mid-April, the Norfolk *Virginian-Pilot* had completed an investigation into the sheriff's twenty-year tenure and the newspaper launched its own investigation in November 2016 after a star witness in a federal trial told authorities that he had bribed McCabe.

Reporters interviewed more than sixty current and former sheriff's department employees and found an undercurrent of resentment and distrust on the part of employees who said they were required to campaign for their boss, ordered to perform non-official duties while on the clock. "You were just expected to work [campaigns]," said one former employee. You volunteered to be in favor with the sheriff."

It was a common practice for the sheriff to call deputies late nights from bars and have them pick him up and drive him home. "That's the reason I had a sheriff's car," said former Sergeant Kenneth Darling. "I've driven him home many a night." Another deputy was said to have driven McCabe and a date to a restaurant in downtown Norfolk on New Year's Eve in the late 1990s and waited outside while the couple dined.

Norfolk builder Ronnie Boone, Sr., who pleaded guilty to bribing then-Norfolk Treasurer Anthony Burfoot, was an associate of McCabe and McCabe's wife worked for Boone's wife as a real estate agent and later at a restaurant owned by Boone. When McCabe's wife was attempting to open a sports bar in a building owned by Boone, McCabe had one of his captains to help manage the restaurant while the captain was on medical leave from the Sheriff's Office in violation of a state law that prohibits sheriff's employees on medical or sick leave from working elsewhere.

A woman named Lorraine Snyder, who oversaw food services at the jail for ABI Management, the company contracted to prepare meals for inmates, was simultaneously identified as a manager for the restaurant in health department inspection reports.

Former sheriff's office employees told of McCabe's using deputies and inmates alike to perform personal projects at McCabe's home and at the townhouse then owned by his future wife, then Janet Torres.

An inmate, John Field, served as both an inmate and a sheriff's office employee. While doing time for drunken driving in 1994, he landed a job as a maintenance worker for the department, remaining on the payroll for more than three years. One of his jobs was to convert McCabe's garage into a "party place," former Sergeant Darling said.

McCabe was also cited by several female employees, including two sisters who worked in the department, who said the sheriff would come on to them. He settled with the two sisters for $12,500 while not admitting any wrongdoing. Another female employee said she was harassed for a decade. McCabe at first started off with seemingly innocent flirting but then he began making promises. He also hired waitresses from his favorite bars and hired numerous relatives to work in the department.[7]

Former Loudoun County sheriff's deputy Terry Daniel was cited in a 2012 federal civil rights lawsuit stemming from a November 2009 encounter during which Daniel knocked plaintiff Charles Garcia unconscious by striking him in the back of the head in what Garcia's attorney described as an unprovoked attack.

Ironically, it was Garcia who ended up being charged with assaulting a police officer even though footage from a patrol car camera clearly shows Garcia talking to another deputy as Daniel approached from behind at a full sprint and struck Garcia, who immediately collapsed to the ground. While insisting he had not assaulted anyone, he nevertheless pleaded guilty to a reduced charge and received a suspended sentence in order to avoid a felony trial, his lawsuit said.

Garcia, who claims the blow left him with permanent brain damage, including headaches, memory loss, and general confusion, said he had been celebrating his wife's birthday at a restaurant with family in Sterling, Virginia. The family called for a taxi but the taxi driver said he could not take the entire party and Garcia and his family were told to exit the vehicle.

As the taxi left, a dispute ensued between a deputy and members of the group. When Daniel arrived at the scene, Garcia was standing with his hands in the air as his wife was being arrested, pleading that his wife be treated with care, the lawsuit said. Daniel approached at a dead run and struck Garcia and then stepped on his face.[8]

Chesapeake Sheriff's Deputy Jenis Leroy Plummer, Jr. was sentenced to thirty months in prison after pleading guilty in April 2019 to federal charges that he smuggled heroin, cocaine, cell phones, e-cigarettes and other contraband into the Chesapeake city jail between July 2017 and January 2019 in exchange for more than $6,500 in cash. He faced a possible sentence of up to twenty years.[9]

Former Henry County Sheriff H. Franklin Cassell was sentenced to eight months in prison and fined $15,000 in September 2007 after pleading guilty to making false statements to investigators about a scheme to resell drugs and guns seized from criminals.[10]

Cassell and 12 current and formers members of his department were charged in November 2006 with taking part in the enterprise following a lengthy investigation by the U.S. Attorney's office in Roanoke. Henry County, described as a struggling, rural county, abuts North Carolina on Virginia's southern border.

"It is disgraceful corruption that they (the 13 defendants) would take narcotics seized from the community and then members of law enforcement would put them right back out there," said U.S. Attorney John Brownlee.

Federal investigators became suspicious that the sheriff's department was involved in drug trafficking as early as 1998 when drug enforcement officials in Philadelphia intercepted a package containing the drug ketamine that had been mailed to Philadelphia address by a sergeant with the Henry County Sheriff's Office. The sergeant, James A. Vaught, had also been involved in a money laundering scheme "to disguise the source of monies represented to have been derived from the distribution of cocaine," the federal indictment charged.

Brownlee said in addition to reselling seized drugs, deputies with the department worked with a drug ring to take other items seized from criminals, including firearms, cash, automotive equipment and lawn mowers.[11]

Former Page County Sheriff Daniel W. Presgraves was sentenced in 2009 to nineteen months in federal prison, fined a $1,000, and ordered to forfeit another $75,000 after pleading guilty to racketeering charges that included illegally using prisoner labor for personal work and attempting to suborn witnesses to perjure themselves.

Presgraves, who served eight years before resigning in November 2008, had been indicted in October 2008 on 22 federal counts that charged him with accepting a $500 bribe to protect cockfighting, sexually harassing a dozen female employees, using inmates from the jail to perform work on property owned by him and his relatives, conspiring to deal marijuana, tipping off a local company about a federal investigation, embezzling more than $86,000 – including money he allegedly extorted from the jail's pay phone vendor – and attempting to launder about two hundred thousand dollars through complex bank transactions.

Witnesses told investigators that Presgraves routinely made lewd comments to female employees, groped them, told one woman that he was thinking of her while he was having sex with his wife, and dropped his pants for another as he asked her to "take care of things." Once an investigation was launched into the allegations, Presgraves told the women that they should take his secret "to the grave."[12]

From questionable contracts with vendors to skimming profits from those vendors to using prisoners for personal work to simply abusing and brutalizing prisoners, county jails have frequently brought down powerful sheriffs across the American landscape.

Richmond County Sheriff Michelle B. Mitchell was no exception. A 2002 investigation revealed that Mitchell had spent money earmarked for the benefit of prisoners on social club memberships, photographs of herself and parties and gifts for her deputies.

Virginia state law mandates that inmate store profits from the sale of food, toiletries and clothing to prisoners are to be used "within the facility for education, recreational or other purposes for the benefit of the inmates. Instead, Mitchell spent $834 for meals and a membership at a local social club and restaurant, $596 for photographs of herself to be used in her re-election campaign, $525 to purchase a Palm Pilot and $5,000 of store profits as a donation to the Historic Richmond Foundation. In return for the donation, she and another jail official received free tickets to a dinner.

She also utilized store profit funds to purchase $144 in gourmet food and wine for jail staff, $513 for gourmet coffee for staff and visitors, $300 for retirement gift certificates, $120 for guards to attend a barbeque, and $246 to give a painting of a lighthouse to Richmond Circuit Judge Learned Barry. Canteen profits also went to pay for parties, movie tickets and trophies for jail employees, memberships in trade associations, and trips to a law enforcement job-fair, meetings, and conferences.

Sheriff Clarence Williams, Jr., of nearby Chesterfield County said his office used canteen profits on things that directly benefitted prisoners. "The law is right there in front of you," he said. "There [are] no ifs ands or buts about it."[13]

Mitchell was never prosecuted for the apparent misuse of prisoner funds, but she was defeated for re-election to a fourth term to her $114,000-per-year job in 2005. She was then hired in 2007 by Henrico County Sheriff Mike Wade to work as an inmate classification specialist, an entry-level position that paid $35,000 per year.[14]

Warren County Sheriff Daniel McEathron abruptly resigned from the job he'd held for sixteen years on May 1, 2019 – seven months before his term was set to end. On Friday, May 24, his business partner, local economic development authority director Jennifer McDonald, was indicted on four felony counts in connection with the embezzlement of at least $2.7 million – part of $21 million that allegedly went missing. The following Tuesday, May 28, McEathron parked in front of his family's secluded mountainside home, took his weapon, stuck it in his mouth, and pulled the trigger.

McEathron was never officially implicated in the property development scam before his death, but *The Washington Post* theorized that he "may have felt the tide turning against him" as a number of high-ranking county officials were swept up in the federal investigation of his and McDonald's involvement in a real estate investment company called DaBoyz LLC.

Their company used $3.5 million in development authority funds to purchase four separate properties, including a three-bedroom house in Virginia Beach which was in turn rented to McEathron's son and daughter-in-law.

In another transaction that development authority officials said smelled like money laundering, DaBoyz paid a construction company $1.9 million for a large tract of land and then sold it back a month later for $1.3 million.

McDonald allegedly billed the authority more than fifty thousand dollars to pay for the renovation of a vacant inn but then used those funds instead to pay personal credit card bills. She was also accused of doctoring invoices to obtain $4.6 million for purchasing tax credits and then embezzling the money.

A plumbing company owned by her husband, Sammy North, also collected more than $62,000 in secret payments, an audit review reported. North was arrested along with family friend Donald Poe, accused of conspiring with McDonald to funnel $841,409 to Poe's solar panel installation company.[15]

42

Washington: Payoffs to Protect Prostitution, Gambling

IN NOVEMBER 2020, voters in Pierce County voted overwhelmingly to return the local sheriff's office to an elective position after 40 years of an appointed sheriff. The county had moved to an appointed sheriff in 1980 following the 1978 federal indictment of Sheriff George Janovich and 14 others on racketeering charges. In the end, twelve were sentenced to a combined 170 years in federal prison and fined a collective $398,000.

Despite his conviction following a four-month trial in U.S. District Court in San Francisco, Janovich refused to resign from office until he was officially sentenced to 12 years in prison for accepting payoffs to protect a bail bond syndicate, illegal gambling, and prostitution at night clubs. He served six years before being paroled.

With Pierce County being the only county in the entire state of Washington with an appointed sheriff, supporters of proposed amendment No. 1, which had called for reverting the office back to an elective one maintained that an elected sheriff would be more accountable to citizens.[1]

In 2011, Daryl C. McClary, writing for *HistoryLink.org*, wrote an essay about the 1978 racketeering trial to which six defendants entered guilty pleas before trial, seven were convicted, one was acquitted and charges against a fifteenth defendant were dismissed.[2]

Janovich, who was moved from prison to prison about 30 times and kept in protective custody because of his law enforcement background, was released after six years. He died on June 19, 2005, when his appendix burst during a Father's Day celebration with his family. He was 77. Sheriff's Detective Ed Troyer, who would be elected sheriff in 2020, said, "[T]here's no hiding the fact that he disgraced our department. The guys have been trying to live that down for 25 years. There's no soft-coating that."[3]

Troyer could have possibly applied those words to himself in January 2021 after he confronted a Black newspaper carrier in his neighborhood around 2:00 a.m. The carrier, Sedrick Altheimer, had approached Troyer's unmarked car in front of Troyer's house after noticing that Troyer had been following him on his route for several blocks. A call by Troyer to 911 in which he said Altheimer had threatened to kill him resulted in about 40 officers responding to the scene.

Troyer later retracted that claim when speaking with the Tacoma Police Department and in June 2021, Altheimer slapped Pierce County with a five-million-dollar lawsuit, claiming his constitutional rights had been violated, causing him "severe emotional distress."

Washington Governor Jay Inslee subsequently directed the state attorney general to conduct an investigation of the confrontation between Altheimer and Troyer, a thirty-five-year veteran of the sheriff's department, for any potential criminal violations.[4]

In June 2014, the King County Sheriff's Office was racked when one of its deputies was arrested for his involvement in drug distribution, theft of sheriff's office property, and an escort service in which his wife, a former exotic dancer, actively participated in prostitution with her husband taking most of the money.[5]

The online story posted by a Tacoma TV station did little justice to the extent of crimes Deputy Darrion Keith Holiwell was accused of. Senior Prosecuting Attorney Gary Ernsdorff, in a bill of information formally charging Holiwell, laid out a sordid scenario in which the deputy was accused of using steroids, providing drugs to his wife to keep her energy level high so she could work her day job and her evening escort service, and of stealing for resale as much as forty-five thousand dollars in live ammunition from the King County Sheriff's Office firing range and using the money to purchase tactical gear and firearm-related parts and gear. Some of the ammunition was placed on the shelf for resale at a business owned by Holiwell.[6]

Ernsdorff, saying there were "significant concerns for the safety of the community and the many witnesses who have cooperated in the investigation," requested that bail for Holiwell be set at $150,000, a relative low figure considering the charges against him. "By all accounts, the defendant is a highly-skilled marksman," Ernsdorff said. "He is the chief firearms instructor for the King County Sheriff's Department, selected for that position for his demonstrated skills with weapons. He is a proficient competitive shooter on a national level. The side business he owns and operates, Praetor, provides firearms instruction and firearm accessories.

Firearms are not just a routine part of the defendant's day-to-day life; they are an essential part of his existence.

A conviction for anyone of the charged counts will prohibit him from possessing firearms."

The prosecutor said Holiwell was said to possess "a minimum" of six "various high-quality personal firearms," which he described as "a mix of military-style rifles and handguns. Some witnesses put the figure much higher." He said witnesses said Holiwell stored his weapons in a large gun safe in his home. "Yet, when the search warrant was served, detectives did not locate a single firearm in the residence; the gun safe was empty. Nor did they locate even a single round of ammunition. Investigators know that Holiwell was tipped off about the investigation," Ernsdorff said, asking that, as a condition of his release on bail, "that he surrender any firearms that he owns or has access to, that he be prohibited from possessing firearms and that he be prohibited from contact with Alicia Holiwell (his third and then-estranged wife) and other witnesses…"

In the twenty-one-page Certification for Determination of Probable Cause filed as part of the bill of information, Alicia Holiwell was quoted as telling investigators that when Darrion Holiwell learned of her extramarital affairs, he told her, "If you're going to have sex, you might as well get paid for it."

That's when they began planning to run an escort service together with him reaping 80 percent of the proceeds and anticipating an income of ten thousand dollars as his share of the proceeds. Holiwell, who was a small business owner himself, began giving marketing ideas to Alicia, telling her how she could establish "high net worth clients," the certification said. As she began to become exhausted from working a full-time day job and the escort service at night, he would provide her with Adderall, HGH (human growth hormone), marijuana and Ecstasy. Holiwell, meanwhile, was using steroids, HGH and Clenbuterol, a beta2-adrenergic antagonist used for bodybuilding.

They were living apart at the time in what she thought would be a one-year trial separation, but he would soon show up with a younger girlfriend. Alicia, angry that he was violating the terms of their so-called open relationship, filed for divorce and ceased giving Holiwell money from the escort service.

A search warrant executed on his home turned up bottles of steroids in injectable form, methylone (a stimulant psychoactive designer drug also known as MDMA), amphetamines, and Anastrozole (a breast cancer treatment but a drug used by some athletes and body builders to counter the estrogen-like effects of steroids).

Holiwell, who served as an instructor at the King County Sheriff Office's firing range, also was accused of removing brass casings from the firing range and turning it in for credit to local vendors and using the money from the sale to create an off-the-books "slush fund" account that he used for equipment and trades. The thefts occurred over a five-month period in 2007 "when ammunition was in very short supply" because of the ongoing U.S. military action in Afghanistan, court filings said. Overall, from 2007 through April 2014, he obtained off-the-book credits of as much as forty- five thousand dollars in exchange for more than nineteen thousand pounds of brass casings, and during this same time period, he sold used King County-owned equipment and provided credit to those accounts for another four thousand dollars.[7]

Holiwell, who was fired a month after his arrest because Sheriff John Urquhart said, "He does not deserve to be a police officer," was sentenced to a year and a day in jail on August 4, 2014 after pleading guilty to promoting prostitution, theft and drug dealing.[8]

That relatively lenient sentence became even more controversial only three weeks later when it was alleged that Holiwell had defrauded the court with his plea of poverty. During sentencing, his attorney told the court he was destitute but investigators said on August 25 that he had cashed in his retirement for one hundred eighty thousand dollars just weeks earlier. Holiwell had pleaded poverty in an effort to get a lighter sentence and the court had accepted his story and used it in determining the appropriate sentence.[9]

The aftershock of the arrest of Holiwell brought the entire administrative structure of the King County Sheriff's Office into question for its self-righteousness and self-claimed obliviousness, prompting the *Seattle Post-Intelligencer* to rip Urquhart for not being able to detect the fact that something was amiss in his department – something like the disappearance of SWAT equipment, along with nineteen thousand pounds of brass ammunition casings; rumors of steroid use by his deputies, steroids purchased from Holiwell, and someone in his department – a major crimes investigator – who apparently tipped Holiwell of the pending raid so he could move his weapons and ammunition from his home. That "someone," an unnamed female, was subsequently placed on paid administrative leave pending the outcome of an investigation into whether she rendered criminal assistance to Holiwell. Two other deputies were also placed on administrative leave while the investigation ran its course. Urquhart declined to identify the three deputies who were under investigation.

The newspaper editorial noted that Urquhart had said the worst part of the whole thing was "the culture that allowed this to happen in the first place," and then pointedly noted, "That would be you, Sheriff. You are responsible for the culture of your office. Clueless."

While the *Post-Intelligencer* noted that the sheriff's office was working to determine whether Holiwell dealt steroids to Urquhart's deputies, it pointed out that the office, per state law and union agreements, was not allowed to screen its employees for steroids, nor was it permitted to research whether employees who were on steroids obtained them by prescription or through illegal means. "One of the gravest curiosities within law enforcement," the editorial said, is that rules exist…that give cops protections trumping all laws that would apply to the rest of us.[10]

43

West Virginia: America's Opioid Capital

AUTHOR TIMOTHY SNYDER in 2018 described Mingo County as "one of the places in America most touched by opioids. A town in Mingo County with a population of 3,200 was shipped about two million opioid pills per year.[1]

Snyder's assertion is a difficult claim to dispute.

Mingo County, so beset by economic blight that one local mayor said, "[T]his is where President Kennedy invented poverty." Better known as the home of the infamous long-running feud between the Hatfields and McCoys, it was pretty much controlled by the Preece family by the mid-1970s. By 1987, eight Preeces, in-laws, and associates were packed off to jail on various charges. Between 1984 and 1986 the family was bringing in about a million dollars a year. Other means of fraudulent income was not unheard of. Kermit, a town of 700 people, had a hundred business and residential fires in a single year, generating millions more in insurance claims.[2]

West Virginia's youngest county, Mingo County was created in 1895 and named for the Iroquoian Mingo Native American tribe and abuts Kentucky's eastern border.

Drugs and arson weren't the only means of graft. In 1988, former Sheriff Johnie Owens, a local power broker, was convicted of tax evasion and selling the county sheriff's job to Eddie Hilbert in 1982 for $10,000 and was sentenced to 14 years in federal prison. Why would someone pay that much for a local office in a poverty-stricken county? To assist relatives and business associates in illegal activities, according to *The New York Times*.[3]

Hilbert drew a seven-year sentence for misusing the sheriff's office after being indicted by a federal grand jury on 13 felony counts of buying his office, helping protect a drug ring in return for illegal campaign contributions, and buying and selling marijuana out of his office.[4]

In all, 14 others were indicted in the sweep that netted Hilbert, and normally, that would be sufficient to set local government on a straighter and narrower path. But this is Mingo County where the wheels of reform turn slowly, and 15 years later, it appeared that the political landscape had changed little, if at all.

In 2012, it was more of the same as "Team Mingo" – a sheriff, a judge, a prosecuting attorney, a county commissioner and a magistrate – took a sudden fall from grace after they conspired to engage in corrupt activities ranging from covering up a sheriff's drug addiction to denying defendants their constitutional rights to framing the husband of a woman with whom the judge was having an affair.

The short story of what happened is that Circuit Court Judge Michael Thornsbury and County Commissioner David Baisden learned that a drug defendant was going to testify that Sheriff Eugene Crum was purchasing prescription painkillers from him. Instead of paying the $3,000 he owed for the illegal drugs, Crum, Baisden, Thornsbury and County Prosecutor Michael Sparks at first pressured the drug defendant into firing his defense attorney who Crum learned was providing information to federal agents and hiring one handpicked by Team Mingo, then pleading guilty to a lesser charge and dropping his allegations against Crum. When he did so, he was sentenced to 15 years in prison.

Thornsbury was later charged with attempting to plant drugs in the truck of the husband of a woman with whom he was having an affair. When that attempt failed, he then arranged to have him arrested for stealing scrap metal for which he'd been given permission to take.

When the dust finally settled, Thornsbury was sentenced to 50 months in federal prison for denying citizens their constitutional rights, Baisden received 20 months.[5] Former Mingo County chief magistrate Dallas Toler was sentenced to 27 months in prison for falsifying a voter registration application during the 2012 primary election so that a convicted felon, still on probation and ineligible to vote, could cast a ballot for the Team Mingo faction.[6]

By the time the black SUVs carrying federal agents came rolling into Mingo County, however, Sheriff Crum was dead, shot while he was eating lunch in his cruiser in the town of Williamson, across the street from an alleged pill mill pharmacy he was said to have been watching. Tennis Maynard was charged with the murder. Some said the sheriff was shot because he had angered drug dealers with his crackdown on their activity.

Maynard's family, however, said Crum, who at one time was Maynard's boxing coach, had sexually abused him when Maynard was a teenager, though Sparks said there was no evidence to support abuse allegations.[7]

Bo Williams was elected Sheriff of Roane County in November 2016. By early January, he was arrested for stealing methamphetamine from the evidence locker of the Spencer Police Department where he worked prior to his election. He was placed on leave and resigned from the Spencer department in December, about a month after he was elected sheriff and was arrested on January 3, just two days after taking office on New Year's Day.

He was sentenced in March to up to ten years of home confinement after acknowledging he was a meth addict and had taken more than a thousand dollars' worth of the drug from the Spencer evidence room.[8]

Lincoln County Sheriff Jerry Bowman was sentenced in August 2012 to one year and a day in federal prison, three years of supervised release, and fined $5,000 after pleading guilty to conspiracy against rights in connection with a 2010 primary election fraud scheme.

Bowman admitted that he falsified more than a hundred absentee ballot applications on behalf of voters who had no legal basis to vote absentee. After the fraudulent applications were processed, he then returned to the homes of many of the voters and accompanied them as they voted, instructing them as to which candidates he supported. He even marked at least six voters' ballots himself, he admitted.

Bowman's co-conspirator, former Lincoln County Clerk Donald Whitten, was sentenced to a year and six months in prison, three years of supervised release and also fined $5,000 after pleading guilty to making a false statement to investigators in connection with the fraud scheme.[9]

Former Hancock County Sheriff's Lieutenant Mark Cowden was sentenced in U.S. Federal District Court to 18 months in prison and three years of supervised release after being convicted in October 2016 of depriving of rights under color of the law, a felony offense that a jury determined resulted in bodily injury to his victim, a drunk driving suspect. He was acquitted of the second count of his indictment that charged him with falsifying a record.

Video surveillance from within the lobby of the Hancock County Courthouse showed Cowden push the suspect face-first into a wall and punch him in the back of his head.

Because Cowden, a 26-year veteran of the sheriff's department, was unable to pay fines, U.S. District Court Judge Frederick Stamp ordered him to pay more than $3,000 in restitution to his victim, who filed a civil lawsuit against Cowden.10

Another excessive and wrongful force lawsuit was filed by a one-armed former state senator who said Clay County deputies handcuffed his one good wrist to his ankle in September 2018.

Andy Schoonover, who served ten years in the West Virginia Senate before serving 14 months in prison for accepting bribes for a business arrangement, said deputies decided to detain him after questioning him repeatedly after he drove to his brother's home to take him to a hospital after he experienced chest pains earlier in the day.

Schoonover, who lost his left arm in an ATV accident in 2014, said deputies Michael Patrick Morris and Jonathan Holcomb cuffed his right wrist to his right ankle but never told him why he was being arrested or read him his Miranda rights. He was never charged with anything.[11]

Logan County Sheriff Johnny "Big John" Mendez knew how to go about getting elected. Unfortunately, he got caught. Twice. Mendez pleaded guilty on July 19, 2004, to buying votes and resigned his office – again.

He was convicted in 1993 of paying off poll workers during his 1988 campaign for magistrate. He resigned then and was fined $15,000 but regained the office in 1994.

Federal investigators said that in conspiring to buy votes both in 2000 and again in 2004 primary elections, he paid between $10 and $100 for votes with the higher number going to heads of households who could deliver multiple votes.

A condition of his plea bargain, he was forced to resign from office and barred for life from ever seeking public office again.[12]

44

Wisconsin: Clarke a CSPOA Lightning Rod

IF THERE IS A SHERIFF – or former sheriff – who could give former Maricopa County, Arizona, Sheriff Joe Arpaio a run for the title as America's most controversial sheriff, it would have to be former Milwaukee County Sheriff David Clarke.

On August 31, 2017, two months after he vowed to remain in office until his term expired in January 2019, he abruptly announced his resignation, ending 15 mostly contentious years as sheriff of Wisconsin's most populous county. The announcement by one of the country's most prominent "constitutional sheriffs" also followed word that his anticipated appointment as assistant secretary for the U.S. Department of Homeland Security under the Trump administration.

His resignation did not mean Clarke would fade away. Instead, if anything, he became even more vocal and controversial in retirement with his Twitter account, TV appearances and personal speaking appearances. In March 2020, he urged his 900,000 followers to "take to the streets" in defiance of early coronavirus preventative measures, calling the virus "the damn flu."

"GO INTO THE STREETS FOLKS," he tweeted. "Visit bars, restaurants, shopping malls, CHURCHES and demand that your schools re- open. NOW! If government doesn't stop this foolishness…STAY IN THE STREETS. END GOVERNMENT CONTROL OVER OUR LIVES. IF NOT NOW, WHEN? THIS IS EXPLOITATION OF A CRISIS," he tweeted on March 15.[1]

Elected as a Democrat he was an avid Trump supporter and was particularly critical of the Black Lives Matter movement, even though he himself is black.

"I want to thank Sheriff Clarke for his decision to step down," said Wisconsin State Sen. Lena Taylor (D-Milwaukee). "After years of abuse at his hands, the people of Milwaukee can sleep soundly tonight."[2] *The Mil-*

waukee Journal-Sentinel said Clarke left "many unresolved issues" behind with his resignation, including the deaths of at least five persons at the Milwaukee County Jail since 2016.

A public inquest into the death of Terrill Thomas, a mentally ill man who died of dehydration in a solitary cell in 2016 found probable cause to hold seven jailers accountable for committing criminal abuse, neglect, or ill-treatment of inmates after determining that Thomas was deprived of water for seven days.

Two federal lawsuits were filed against Clarke over Thomas's death and another suit was filed over the death of an infant born while her mother was an inmate being held alone in a cell.[3]

A long-time devotee of Richard Mack's Constitutional Sheriffs and Peace Officers Association (CSPOA), he was named the organization's "Sheriff of the Year" in 2013 and in 2016, he was presented the "Leadership Award" by the militant patriot organization Oath Keepers.

On accepting the latter award, he told the audience, "I'm one of those that believes that only a citizen uprising is going to allow We the People to resume our rightful place in this republic. Our government has been co-opted. Our government is corrupt. All of our institutions of government are corrupt. The White House is corrupt. The Congress is corrupt. Our courts are corrupt."

Shortly after the 2016 election, he posted on *Twitter* his proposals on halting protests against Trump, saying "It's showdown time. Pushback time. Are you ready? I am." Among the proposals he posted:

- Declare state of emergency
- Impose early curfew
- Mobilize National Guard
- Authorize ALL non-lethal force
- Tear gas.

He was a regular on Fox News before the network dumped him after he failed to land a job in the Trump administration. He also appeared on conspiracy monger Alex Jones' *Infowars* radio program where he made the Trumpian prediction that an attempt by the federal government to confiscate guns would prompt "the second coming of an American Revolution, the likes of which would make the first Revolution pale by comparison."[4]

His political rhetoric aside, Clarke also came under criticism in 2012 for promoting one of his deputies to the rank of captain despite an internal investigation that found she committed a "clear act" of misconduct when she awarded thousands of taxpayer dollars to an account that she created for a man with whom she had an extramarital affair.

Investigators said the case fell short of a criminal act because there was no evidence that Nancy Evans benefitted personally even though most of the money was spent by her boyfriend, Jevon Terry, while the two attended her work-related jail conference in Reno, Nevada.

The investigation found that Evans had awarded three no-bid contracts to Midwest Wood Flooring for nearly $6,000 even though county purchasing regulations banned the stringing together related deals with a collective cost exceeding $2,000.

Since 1990, Terry had been convicted of four crimes: stealing a car in 1990, battery for hitting a man in the head with the butt of a gun in 2005, failing to pay $23,000 in child support in 2012 and disorderly conduct for hitting a child in 2012.

The Milwaukee County Deputies Union filed a lawsuit claiming that Clarke illegally promoted Evans. The suit claimed that Evans lacked law enforcement certification and that Clarke did not follow proper procedures for filling a vacancy in the sheriff's department.

Clarke said of the investigation by his own department, "This is what a real war on women looks like. I find it sad that these misogynistic attitudes in law enforcement now come masked as lawsuits. I thought we were past thinking that women cannot do this job."[5]

45

Wyoming: Sheriff Shoots, Kills Deputy

SUBLETTE COUNTY Sheriff Stephen Haskell only wanted his deputies to look professional. That effort to discard random western wear in favor of uniforms resulted in one deputy retiring rather than conform and Haskell was forced from office and nearly went to jail.

Haskell's problems began after he was elected in 2014, but before he took over as sheriff on January 5, 2015, when he ordered more than $11,000 in uniforms and equipment for his deputies-to-be but then attempted to change the invoices so as to make it appear he made the purchases after he took office so that the county would pay for them.[1]

The new dress code would have included Pinedale, which was named by *True West* magazine as a true Western town where deputies wore cowboy hats, cowboy boots and vests. "I'm very much for the Western way of life and the look. However, for a professional outfit, I like everybody to look the same."

Uniformity notwithstanding, Deputy Gene Bryson immediately announced his retirement, saying, "I've had a cowboy hat on since [I was] 19. It's Western. It's Wyoming. I am not going to change. I've been here for forty-odd years in the sheriff's office and I'm not going to go out and buy combat boots and throw my vest and hat away and say, 'This is the new me.'"[2]

Haskell was arrested in January 2016, a year after taking office and he was convicted on three counts in February 2017 and in July, he was given a suspended sentence for his successful completion of a nine-month work- release treatment facility program and placed him on five years' probation. He was ordered to resign from office and to pay restitution of $11,798 to the county treasurer, $3,345.98 to the county attorney's office and $360 in other court fees.[3]

Mike Rosa was an undercover agent recruited by Rock Springs Director of Public Safety Ed Cantrell in 1977 to clean up the boom town of Rock Springs of drug trafficking when he was shot and killed the following year – by Cantrell.

Rosa, the 29-year-old Puerto Rican who grew up in New York City's Spanish Harlem, and the 51-year-old Indiana-born Cantrell were a mismatch from the outset. Rosa had knocked around several law enforcement agencies while Cantrell found steady employment with the Wyoming State Police before becoming undersheriff to Sweetwater County Sheriff James Stark prior to being hired for the Rock Springs job.

Rosa reportedly was preparing to testify before a grand jury about what he'd uncovered in Rock Springs, and his supervisor, Sergeant James Callas, was concerned his testimony might include a disputed $90 expense item. So, on July 15, 1978, two days before Rosa's scheduled grand jury testimony, Callas and Cantrell met with Rosa outside a downtown bar. Described as "in worse shape than Serpico," because the famous

New York cop turned whistleblower "at least had some personal friends in the department," Rosa was out of his element as a Puerto Rican from New York in a western town like Rock Springs.

The meeting took a bad turn at the outset, but details became sketchy and conflicting. One version had Rosa still holding a cocktail glass when the shooting took place; another had him reaching for his weapon and simply being too slow on the draw against the quicker Cantrell. Either way, Rosa took a bullet between the eyes and Cantrell was arrested for first-degree murder. He was tried in nearby Pinedale, but acquitted after only three hours' deliberation by the jury. A $7 million lawsuit by Rosa's widow, Rebecca, was dismissed as was a $63 million lawsuit against CBS and *60 Minutes* newsman Dan Rather.[4]

Besides *60 Minutes*, the gripping saga of the last wild west gunfight caught the attention of *Harper's* and *Life* magazines, both of which did features on the shooting and trial. A book entitled *The Last Western* was also written by Rone Tempest who said the story held elements of irony and inevitability reminiscent of Greek and Shakespearean tragedies. He described Cantrell as an "intense scholar of Old West lore and legend" and said he was the man most likely "primed to react with lethal speed to perceived threat."

He wrote that though acquitted, Cantrell later struggled with alcoholism and became "just a guilty man that the system didn't catch."[5]

Cantrell died on June 11, 2004, in Salt Lake City. He was 76.

Qualified immunity for law enforcement officers is said by its proponents to be necessary in order for officers to carry out their duties. Opponents say it is just a way for cops to hide behind their badges for unwarranted beatings and other misdeeds.

It's an ongoing debate that has received increased attention in recent years as cell phone and body cams have become more prevalent in the recording of events like the killing of George Floyd of Minneapolis or Ronald Greene of Monroe, Louisiana.

The Uinta County Sheriff's Department received the benefit of qualified immunity when sued over a jail guard's sexual assault in 2006 and that decision by the Wyoming Supreme Court did little to dissuade opponents of the law from calling for change.

The state's high court ruled that a lower court improperly denied qualified immunity on claims that a guard in the sheriff's employee sexually assaulted a female prisoner despite the sheriff's knowledge of the deputy's drug addiction and history of theft.

Todd Hoover underwent back surgery while working as a jail guard in Utah and became addicted to pain pills, a by now familiar pattern in the story of a national opioid addiction problem. To feed his habit, he stole prisoners' medication. He then moved to Wyoming and was hired as a detention officer by Uinta County Sheriff Louis Napoli in 2006. Napoli knew nothing of Hoover's drug habit or theft history at the time of the hiring.

Hoover overdosed while on duty which led to an internal investigation which revealed that history. Napoli, instead of terminating Hoover, only suspended him without pay for two weeks, had him undergo counseling and urinalysis testing and serve an extended probational period and provide full disclosure of his medical records as part of his disciplinary plan.

Some would call the sheriff's actions a show of compassion and label him as an advocate of rehabilitation, not an altogether bad image for any administrator. But after returning to work, Hoover met detention center prisoner Judee Pennington, who had been terminated from a drug court program and was awaiting placement in a treatment program. Instead, Hoover gave her drugs and sexually assaulted her.

He was terminated, prosecuted, and given a prison sentence. Meanwhile, Pennington filed suit, and the trial court denied qualified immunity to the sheriff and county. They appealed. and the Wyoming State Supreme Court reversed, finding that "the good faith and reasonableness depend on whether Sheriff Napoli should have anticipated that Hoover was likely to assault an inmate. [T]he record contains nothing that should have alerted the sheriff to this risk, Sheriff Napoli was supervising and training an employee, which is a discretionary act."[6]

– Colorado, New York, Montana, Nevada, and New Mexico – have banned or curtailed qualified immunity in any form while some three dozen states have tried and failed, thanks to the power of the law enforcement lobbyists who have beaten back nearly every attempt. It's long past time for a change.

Asset forfeiture is another area of abuse employed far too often by law enforcement, particularly sheriffs. Only four states have abolished the practice of civil asset forfeiture. Those states are North Carolina, New Mexico, Nebraska, and Maine. Other states should consider following suit.

When speaking of change, it is appropriate to call for a change in the manner in which sheriffs rule their turf with complete autonomy. At the county level, there is no one more powerful than the sheriff – not the local prosecutor, not the judge, not the governor, not Congress, nor even the President of the United States. No one in a democratic republic such as ours should hold sway with such a jurisdictional club. The concept of the so-called "constitutional sheriff" must be addressed and the issue of responsibility and accountability settled once and for all. No law enforcement officer should be able to cherry-pick the laws he or she chooses to enforce and ignore those with which there might be a philosophical difference.

Acknowledgements

No project such as this could be undertaken without the support and encouragement – and scrutiny – of many people. First, and most important of all, is Betty, my wife of more than half-a-century. We embarked on our journey together in 1968, surviving on my GI Bill, her $60-a-week job and my $125-per-week full-time job with The Shreveport Times while attending Louisiana Tech University full-time. Looking back, they were both the best of times and the wasted years for me as I spent all my free time playing softball, baseball and tennis, and dirt- biking, giving little serious consideration to my chosen vocation. Through it all, Betty persevered, raising three beautiful daughters, until I finally (I think) grew up and began taking my career seriously. She is a thorough proofreader for my manuscripts, with able support from others like Steve Winham and retired Louisiana State Trooper and fellow author John Rigal, Jr. My cousin Jeanette Herren has been one of my biggest fans dating back to my childhood. She has always encouraged me and told me to believe in myself. It should be noted that as a creative graphic artist, she also designed the covers for several of my other books, including this one.

Perhaps no one outside my family has been more of an inspiration to me than several people who are, unfortunately, no longer with us. Mrs. Mary Alice Garrett, Miss Charlotte Lewis, and Miss Maggie Hinton were my Ruston High School English teachers and each of them, in her own way, prodded, encouraged, goaded me, taking an underachiever under their wings and nurturing some glimmer of talent that they alone could see. Earvin Ryland was my civics and history teacher at RHS and lit the fire of curiosity in me about how government works (and why it sometimes doesn't), a fire that still burns brightly after sixty years.

John Hays was a maverick, old-school journalist who came from Texas to our town of Ruston unannounced, became disenchanted with local government and launched his own weekly newspaper, the *Morning Paper*. It was that publication that stirred things up in Ruston and forced the locals to begin to think for themselves and to see that there were alternatives to the status quo. He showed me that one writer, swimming against the current can indeed effect change. I had the journalism degree but he had courage.

He taught me a lot about perseverance.

Tom Kelly gave me my first job in newspaper when he hired me off the street to sell advertising for the *Ruston Daily Leader*. When I couldn't hack it as a sales rep, he "promoted" me to sports editor where I was fortunate enough to photograph high school quarterback Terry Bradshaw in his Shreveport living room as he signed his scholarship to Louisiana Tech. *Monroe Morning World* Editor Jimmy Hatten and *Baton Rouge State-Times* Editor Jim Hughes each taught me a lot about what it takes to be a probing, successful reporter who takes what sources say with a grain of skepticism and listens for what they *don't* say for the real story. Jim Hughes could administer withering criticism and unmerciful verbal discipline. He once asked me, following a major reporting error, what he had to do to protect the newspaper from me but through it all, he was a hard-nosed professional.

Wiley Hilburn who, as head of the Louisiana Tech Journalism Department, made it his mission to convince a talentless, sports editor to abandon his fantasy of becoming a baseball coach and to switch his major to journalism. For that, I will forever be grateful, for it changed my life.

Any writer, no matter how skilled, is perhaps the worst one to critique a manuscript, especially one of this length. If smart, the writer will always ask a trusted professional to check spelling, syntax, punctuation and grammar. The task for this effort fell to retired attorney and friend Fred Mulhearn and to him I owe my deepest gratitude

Most of all, there are my paternal grandparents who took me, an 18-month-old malnourished infant, from a hospital in Galveston, Texas, where I had been abandoned when my mother left for the West Coast. They gave me a home life that, while poor in worldly possessions, was oh, so rich in love and guidance. How could I ever adequately express my appreciation for their sacrifice?

Nearly all of the aforementioned are gone now and I often find myself wishing they were still alive so I could thank them personally but I guess this will have to do.

"Enterprise Team," *The Shreveport Times*, 187
"Bloody Harlan," Kentucky, 131
"Buford the Bull", 322
"constitutional sheriff", 298
"constitutional sheriffs", *387*
"Hollyday Inn", 285
"I Out-Shot the Sheriff.", 304
"Little Colombia", 319
"Mysterious X", 182
"pay to play" investigation, 201
"Sagebrush Sheriffs", *362*
"Sheriff of the Year.", 288, 307, 388
"Shot callers", 46
"Team Mingo", *384*
"The Lonely Crusade of Linda Ives,", 36
60 Days In, 118
60 Minutes, 130, *392*
A&E Network, 118, 163
Abbeville, Louisiana, 174
ABC, 142
Abdalla, Sheriff Fred, 278
Aberdeen Enterprizes II, 290
Aberdeen, South Dakota, 309
ABI Management, *352*
Accardo, Tony, **110**
Ackal, Sheriff Louis, 168, 169— 174
ACLU, 16
ACLU of Louisiana, 189
ACLU of Nebraska, 233
Acosta, U.S. Attorney Alex, 66
Ada County Commission, **103**
Ada County, Idaho, **106**
Adam-12, 48
Adamowski, Illinois State Attorney Benjamin, **108**
Adams, Adelaida, 338
Adams, Sheriff Tommy, 221
Adams, Teresa, 68

Adams, Yves, 31
Adkinson, Sheriff Michael, 75
Afghanistan, *380*
Aguirre, Herman Beltran, 334
Ahern, Gregory J., v
Ahlschwede, District Attorney Tonya, *355*
Alabama, 1, 68, 71, 88 **108**
Alabama Appleseed Center for Law and Justice, 9
Alabama Sheriffs' Association, 9
Alabama Supreme Court, 10
Alabama, University of, 159
Alabama's Open Records Act, 9
Alamance County Sheriff's Office, 260
Alamance County, North Carolina, 260
Alamance-Burlington, North Carolina, 262
Alameda County, California, v
Alaska, ix, xiv, xvii, 345
Albanoski, Ed, 54
Albany, New York, 255
Albert, Sheriff James, 305
Albuquerque, New Mexico, 249
Alcorn County Board of Supervisors, 215
Alcorn County Regional Correctional Facility, 215
Alcorn County Regional Correctional Facility's Technology Fund, 215
Alcorn County Sheriff's Commissary Account, 215
Alcorn County, Mississippi, 215
Alden, Rian, 296
Alexandria, Virginia, *353*
Allegheny County Sheriff's Office, 303
Allegheny County, Pennsylvania, 303

Allen County Sheriff's Office, 277
Allen County, Ohio, 277
Allen, Blake, *366*
Allen, Brandon, *366*
Allen, County Judge Gene, 134
Allen, Mayor Calhoun, 185, 187
Allen, Sheriff Ray, *366*
Allen, Thomas Jefferson, II, 270
Allentown, Pennsylvania, 305
Allers, Thomas, 195
Allied Agencies Narcotics Enforcement Team, 54
Alma, Georgia, 84
Altheimer, Sedrick, *377*
Aluotto, Jacquelyn, 342
Alvarez, Rita, 338
American Revolution, *388*
Americans with Disabilities Act, 190
Amigo Enterprises Inc., 175
Anaheim, California, 45
Anchorage, Alaska, 348
Andalusia Health & Fitness, 4
Anderson County, South Carolina, 309
Anderson County, Tennessee, 309
Anderson, DA Investigator Ian, 53
Anderson, John, 232
Anderson, U.S. District Judge Percy, 51, 52
Anderson, Wayne, 181
Andrews, Matthew, 61
Andrews, Sheriff David, 328
Angelo, Darren, 159
Angola State Penitentiary. *See* Louisiana State Penitentiary at Angola
Ann Arbor, Michigan, 206
Anthony, Sheriff Milton, 283
Anthony, Texas, 248
Anti-Crime Narcotics Unit, 266
Antifa, 260

Antinoro, Sheriff Gerald, 235
Apodaca, Sheriff Alfonso Luchini "Happy", 247
Appalachia, 129
Appalachian, 134
Arapahoe County, Colorado, 59
Archibald, Louisiana, 143
Ard, Sheriff Jason, 188
Arevalo, Jesus, 241
ARGUS, *369*
Arizona, 13, 298
Arizona Coalition Against Domestic Violence, 20
Arizona Daily Star, 24
Arizona Supreme Court, 16, 30
Arkansas, ix, 31—38, 211
Arkansas Commission on Law Enforcement Standards and Training, 33
Arkansas State Police, 33
Arkansas Supreme Court, 35
Arkansas Valley Correctional Facility, 591
Arlene & Joseph Meraux Charitable Foundation Inc., 175
Arlington, Virginia, *350*
Armijo, Sheriff William, 247
Armored Response Group of the United States (ARGUS), 218, *369*
Arnold, Belverly, **86**
Arnold, Sheriff Chuck, 325
Arnold, Sheriff Robert, 326
Aronie, Jonathan, 210
Arpaio, 13—27, 247, 387
Arpaio, Joe, v, 21, 164
Arpaio, Sheriff Joe, 247, *354*, *387*
Arradondo, Police Chief Medaria "Rondo", 209
Ascension Parish Sheriff's Office, 189
Ascension Parish, Louisiana, xiii,

188
Ashe, Sheriff Michael, Jr., 199
Askoak, Simeon, xiv
Associated Press, 78, 118, 122, 132
Assumption Parish, Louisiana, xiii
Aswell, Betty, *397*
Athens County, Ohio, 276
Athens, Tennessee, 324
Athey, Jeffery, 122
Atlanta Braves, 84
Atlanta Police Department, **89**
Atlanta, Georgia, 83, 84
Attorney General's Office, Pennsylvania, 304
Attorney General's Office, Vermont, *367*
Atwood, Herbert, 346
Augusta Chronicle, **95**
Aurora, Colorado, 59
Austin, Robert W., Jr., 347
Austin, Texas, 352, 354, 358
Austino, Sheriff Robert, 246
Authement, Aubrey, 182
Axelrod, Matt, 66
Axelson, Sheriff Randy, 124
Ayling, Lindsay, 260

B & D Auto Sales, 154
Babb, Sheriff John, **107**
Baca, Sheriff Lee, 49—51
Backman, U.S. Attorney David, 29
Bacon County, Georgia, 84
Bailey County, Texas, *356*
Bailey, Austin, 75
Bailey, Derrick, **99**
Baisden, David, *384*
Baker, Carroll, 348
Baker, Jay, **100**
Baker, Joe Don, 322

Baker, Sheriff Gerald, 271
Baldwin, Louisiana, 143
Baltimore Police Department, 197
Baltimore Post-Examiner, 238
Baltimore, Maryland, 195, 209
Bangor Daily News, 193
Bank of America, 31
Bannack, Montana, x
Barbour County, Alabama, 2
Barefoot, Judge N. Vinson, 287
Barnard, Charles, 241
Barnes, Sheriff Don, 48
Barnett, Bryan Scott, 74
Barnett, Sheriff Terry Sue, 289
Barnidge, Matt, 145
Barren County, Kentucky, 137
Barren-Edmonson County Drug Task Force, 137
Barrett, Sheriff Jacquelyn, **97**
Barrett, Sheriff Paul, 217
Barrett, Sheriff Paul L., *369,370*
Barros, Eric, 239
Barry County, Michigan, 205
Barry, Richmond Circuit Judge Learned, *375*
Bartlett, "Corndog". Bartlett, Sheriff Greg, 7
Bartlett, Sheriff Steve, **103**
Bartolomel, Sheriff Rudy, 119
Basile, Louisiana, 189
Baskin, Louisiana, 143
Bates, Robert, 284
Baton Rouge, xiii, 185, 186, 189
Baton Rouge, Louisiana, xvii
Battle of New Orleans, 174
Baughman, Chris, 237
Bay County, Florida, 71
Bay of Pigs, **114**
Beacham, Darnell, 3145
Beam, Sheriff Wendell, **87**
Beas, Albert, 237

399

Beasley, Chief Hubert, 248
Becht, William, 236
Beckett, District Attorney Robert, 237
Begenbaugh, Donald, 314
Behan, Sheriff Johnny, 13
Bell County, Kentucky, 133
Bell, FBI Special Agent Keith, 211
Bell, Harvey, 252
Bell, Jerome, 45
Bello, Karla, 79
Benavidez, Emmett, 343
Benetech Software, 157
Benevolent Fund, 337
Bennett, Aaron, 159, 161
Bennett, Aaron Adam, 137
Bennett, Sheriff Clay, 191
Bensley, Sheriff Tom, 205
Benton County Jail, 32
Benton County, Arkansas, 31
Benton, Carlton, 281
Benton, Louisiana, 148, 149
Benton, Sheriff Roger, 134, 136
Berdnik, Sheriff Richard, 245
Bergan County, New Jersey, 245
Bergen County Prosecutor's Office, 243
Bergen County, New Jersey, 243, 244
Bergeron, Ralph, 152
Bergquist, David, 297
Berkeley County, South Carolina, 308, 317
Berkshire County, Massachusetts, 199
Bernalillo County Sheriff's Department, 251
Bernalillo County, New Mexico, vii, 251, 252
Berrien County, Georgia, **99**

Berry, Bert, 172
Bethancourt, District Court Judge Randal, 180
Bethel-Carrier, Robbie, 173
Bexar County jail, 325
Bexar County Sheriff's Office, 337—339
Bexar County, Texas, 324, 325, 328 340
Biddle, Eric, 70
Biden, Attorney General Beau, 64
Biden, Joe, 63
Biden, Vice President Joe, 299
Big Bend, 348, 349
Billinger, Shirley, **86**
Biloxi, Mississippi, 211, 323
Bingham County, Idaho, **101**
Birkhead, Sheriff Clarence, 272
Birmingham, Alabama, 1
Black Lives Matter, *387*
Blackburn, Sheriff Bill, *357*
Blackwood, Sheriff Charles, 270
Blagojevich, former Illinois Gov. Rod, 47
Blair, Sheriff J.H., 131
Blakes, Rakeem, 170
Blakfox, Sheriff Jay, 281
Blanchard, Eric, 174
Blanco, Sheriff Chad, 53
Bloodsworth, Austin, **91**
Bloodsworth, Sheriff Stacy, **91**
Blumberg, federal prosecutor Mark, 169
Board of County Commissioners, Oklahoma County, 284
Board of County Commissioners, Oklahoma County, Oklahoma, 289
Board of Public Safety Standards and Training (BPSST), 293
Boatright, Sheriff Jimmy, **92**
Boen, Franklin County, Ark. Sheriff

Anthony, 37
Bohnyak, Sheriff Bill, *366*
Bolton, Charles, 214
Bolton, Linda, 216
Bolton, U.S. District Judge, 23
Bon Homme County, South Dakota, 319
Bond, Sheriff Danny, 2
Bonner, Roy, 82
Bonner, Sheriff Rayburm L. "Roy", 84
Boone County, Indiana, 118
Boone, Curtis, 270
Boone, Dustin, 240
Boone, Jason, 270
Boone, Ronnie, Sr., 3*72*
Boone, Sheriff Kenney, 310
Booth, Sheriff Jason, 313
Boruchowitz, David, 236
Borum, Terry, 344
Bossier City police, 161
Bossier City, Louisiana, 148, 170
Bossier Parish, Louisiana, 147
Boston Globe, The, 200, 202
Boston, Massachusetts, 200, 209
Bounds, Sheriff Randy, 197
Boutte, Louisiana, 162
Bowler, Sheriff Thomas, 199
Bowles, Sheriff Jim, 347
Bowling Ronnie, 131
Bowman, Sam Allen, 197
Bowman, Sheriff Jerry, *.85*
Bowman, Walter, 267
Boyd, Sheriff Jeff, **112**
Boyer, Tom, 227
Boys Don't Cry, 231
BP, 159, 174
Bradford, Michael, 252
Bradford, Robin, 252
Bradshaw, Sheriff Ric, 78

Brady List, 54
Brady, Christopher, 239
Brady, Sgt. Gary, 54
Braillard, Debra, 18
Bramberg, Doug, 136
Branch Davidian, 336
Brandimarte, Maricopa County Lt. Hank, 20
Brandon, JoAnn, 231
Brandon, Teena, 231
Branford, Angela, 296
Breathitt County, Kentucky, 135
Breaux, Sheriff Duffy, 152
Bresko, Dustin, *358*
Brewer, Sheriff William, 216
Bridgewater, NJ, Township Police Department, 245
Brinkema, Judge Leonie M., 351
Brisolara, Sheriff Melvin T., 212
Bristol County, Massachusetts, 202
Bristol detention center, 202
Bristol, Todd, *361*
Britt, District Attorney Joe Freeman, 262
Brittain, Huner, 36
Brock, Pamela, *355*
Brock, Sheriff John C., 321
Broderick, Nicholas, 352
Brogdon, Sheriff Gerald, **99**
Bronson, Kevin, 120
Brooks, Sheriff John, **93, 94**
Brookshire, Undersheriff Mykol, 287
Broome, Sheriff Robert, 83
Broussard, Bret, 169
Broussard, Donald, 170
Broward County, 65
Broward County Sheriff's Office, 65—74
Broward County, Florida, 65—74

Browder, James, 346
Brown University, xi
Brown, Anthony, 50,
Brown, California Gov. Jerry, 41
Brown, Judge Charles, 250
Brown, Michael, 315
Brown, Sheriff Frederick W., 245
Brown, Sheriff James, 268
Brown, Sheriff-elect Derwin, 81
Brown, U.S. Attorney Joe, 323
Browndorf, Gary, 305
Browning, Jayne, 134
Browning, Sheriff Paul, Jr., 132
Browning, U.S. District Judge James, 250
Brownlee, U.S. Attorney John, *374*
Brownsville, Texas, 335
Brunswick County, North Carolina, 268
Bryant, J.C. Herbert, 217, *369*
Bryson, Gene, *373*
Bucks County, Pennsylvania, 302, 303
Buffett, Jimmy, 213
Bullitt County, Kentucky, 138
Buncich, Sheriff John, 118
Buncombe County, North Carolina, 269
Bundy, Ammon, 297
Bundy, Cliven, 297
Bunnell, Stephen, *368*
Buono, Executive Undersheriff Buono, 244
Bureau County, Illinois, **113**
Bureau of Alcohol, Tobacco and Firearms, 130
Bureau of Alcohol, Tobacco and Firearms (ATF), 152
Bureau of Criminal Investigation, North Dakota, 273
Bureau of Land Management, U.S., *361*
Bureau of Prisons, 32
Burgess, Sheriff Mike, 286
Burke, Mark, *356*
Burkowski, Sheriff Tim, **113**
Burns, Robert, 169
Burns, Sam, 189
Burns, U.S. Attorney Jim, **110**
Burt, Darryl, 251
Bush, President George W., 261
Bush, Vice President George H.W., 218
Bustos, Sheriff Gerry, **112**
Butler County, Alabama, 2
Butler County, Ohio, v, 281
Butts County, Georgia, 86
Bynum, Connie, *356*
Bynum, Sheriff Hal, *356*
Byrd, Sheriff Mike, 213
Byrd, Wesley, 248

Caddo Parish grand jury, 187
Caddo Parish Sheriff's Office, 161
Caddo Parish, Louisiana, 187
Cain, Richard, **114**
Caldwell Parish Sheriff Office, 191
Caldwell Parish, Louisiana, 191, 194
Caldwell, Dedri Yulon, 213
Caldwell, Johnnie, **87**
Caledonia County, Vermont, *367*
California, xi, xii, 39– 57, 206– 345, 349, 371
California Attorney General, 44, 56
California State Association of Counties, 41
California State Sheriffs' Association, 32, 51
Callas, James, *392*

402

Calpine Corp., 56
Camden County, Georgia, **99**
Camden County, New Jersey, 246
Camden, NJ, City Police Department, 246
Cameron County, Texas, 331–334, 348
Cameron, Pima County Lt. Joseph, 29
Campbell, James, 239
Campbell, Jay, 34–36
Campbell, Kelly, 35
Campbell, Marion, 134
Campbell, Melissa, 339
Campbell, Sheriff Ken, 118
Campbell, U.S. District Judge Tena, *363*
Canady, Doug, 34
Cantrell, Ed, *391*
Cantrell, Sheriff Paul, 323, 324
Cantu, Sheriff Conrado, 335
Cape May County, New Jersey, 246
Capitol, U.S., 299
Capone, Al, **106**
Capp, Al, 114
Caracci, Frank, 161
Caracci, Mark, 162
Cardinal, Dan, 291
Carey, Sheriff Peter B., **107**
Carmen, Sheriff James, 234
Carmichael, Sheriff Irwin, 270
Carmona, Dr. Richard, 24, 26
Carona, Deborah, 44
Carona, Sheriff Michael S., 41–51
Carr, Sheriff Paddy, **106**
Carroll County, Ark. Sheriff's Office, 33
Carroll County, Arkansas, 33
Carroll County, Kentucky, 138
Carroll County, Maryland, 197

Carson, Sheriff Marion, 310
Carter County, Missouri, 221
Carter County, Oklahoma, 283
Cartlidge, Sheriff Jacob, 218
Caruso, Sandra, xv
Caruthers, Willie James, **91**
Cary, Nathaniel, 316
Casey, Tim, 19
Cassell, Sheriff Franklin, *373*
Catahoula Parish, Louisiana, 147
Catron, Harold, 137
Catron, Sheriff Sam, 136
Cavazos, Valerie, 29
Cave Creek, 18
Cawthon, State Sen. Joe, 148
CBS, 142, *392*
CBS-TV, 130
CCS, *356*
Cedar County Board of Supervisors, 121
Cedar County Sheriff's House and Jail, 121
Cedar County, Iowa, 121, 122
Central America, 114
Cerilli, Egidio, 303
Chadwick, William, 302
Chalk, Bob, 58
Chamberlain, John Derek, 46
Chamberlain, Sheriff Michael, *365*
Chambers, Glyn Robert, 348
Chance, Sheriff Phil, 279
Chandler, Danny, 348
Chapman, Sheriff Mike, *370*
Charleston Post and Courier, 307
Charlotte, North Carolina, 270, 311
Chastain, Sheriff Ricky, 311
Chauvin, Derek, 209
Chavez, Paul, 252
Chavis, Sandy, 264
Chennault, Gen. Claire, 142

Cherokee County, Georgia, v, **100**
Cherryville Police Department, 269
Cherryville, North Carolina, 269
Chesapeake city jail, *313*
Chesapeake, Virginia, *373*
Cheshire, Joe, 266
Chester County, South Carolina, 309, 313
Chesterfield County, South Carolina, 309
Chesterfield County, Virginia, *375*
Chicago Crime Commission, **107**
Chicago Finance Committee, **108**
Chicago Police Department, **110**
Chicago Tribune, **110**
Chicago, Illinois, vi, **105—115, 207, 238**
Chicase, John, 279
Chickasaw County, Iowa, 122
Chiles, Gov. Lawton, 65
Chittenden County, Vermont, *366*
Chitwood, Sheriff Mike, 74
Choctaw County, Oklahoma, 287
Choptank River, 197
Christensen, Jon, 297
Christian Science Monitor, 213
Christopher, Sheriff Jeff, 63
CIA, **114**, *370*
Cicero, Illinois, **107**
Circle Ranch, 350
Civil Rights Division, U.S. Dept. of Justice, 169
Civil Rights Division, U.S. Justice Department, 177
Civil War, 280
Claiborne County, Tennessee, 321
Clanton, Ike, 1
Clanton, Lann Tjuan, 269
Clark County District Attorney, 240 Clark County Sheriff's Office, 239, 241
Clark County, Indiana, 117
Clark County, Nevada, 237
Clark, Gary, 240
Clark, Sheriff Tyrone, 11
Clarke, Sheriff David, *387—389*
Clay County, Florida, 73
Clay County, West Virginia, *386*
Clayton County Commission, **100**
Clayton County, Georgia, 88, **100, 103**
Clayton, Louisiana, 143
Clearlake, California, 55
Clemon, US District Court Judge U.W., 7
Clemons, Sheriff Ray, 136
Cleveland, Ohio, 277
Clifford, Sheriff Matt, **103**
Clifton, NJ, Police Department, 245
Clinch County, Georgia, **101**
Clinton, Arkansas Gov. Bill, 35—37
Clinton, Bill, vii, 164
Clinton, Sheriff Ron, *358*
Clopton, Craig, 339
CNL Cigarettes, 184
CNN, 23, 41, 67
Coakley, Massachusetts Attorney General Martha, 201
Coats, Rodney, 11
Cobel, Scott, 236
Cochise County, Arizona, 13
Cochran, Sheriff Ron, 65
Cocke County Sheriff's Department, 324
Cocke County, Tennessee, 324
Coffee County, Georgia, **96**
Coffey, Chad, 268
Colaneri, Undersheriff Robert, 245
Colbert, Sheriff Robert "Bob", 281
Colby, Sheriff Trevor, *351*
Cole, Trevon, 240

Colfax County Sheriff's Department, 248
Colfax County Sheriff's Office, 249
Colfax County, New Mexico, 248
Colleton County, South Carolina, 310
Collier, U.S. District Judge Lacey, 68
Colling, Derek, 240
Colorado, iii, 59, 249
Colorado Springs, Colorado, 60
Columbia Post and Courier, The, 309
Columbia, South Carolina, 309
Comeaux, Jason, 168
Commission of Corrections, New York State, 257
Comstock Lode, 235
Concordia Parish, Louisiana, vi, 142, 144, 186
Confederate, 260
Congress, 280, 299
Connecticut, ix, xv, , 39, 299, 350
Connecticut Court Operations Division, xv
Connolly, Sheriff Leo, 256
Constance, Samuel, 267
Constitutional Sheriffs & Peace Officers Association (CSPOA), 55
Constitutional Sheriffs and Peace Officers Association, 103
Constitutional Sheriffs and Peace Officers Association (CSPOA), vi, xii, xviii, 103, 257, *354, 362, 388*
Constitutional Sheriffs and Police Officers Association (CSPOA), *354*
Coogler, Ovida "Cricket", 247
Cook County Jail, **107**
Cook County Republican Party, **109**

Cook County Sheriff's Office, **105**, 107, 109
Cook County, Illinois, **105, 107, 115**
Cook, Darold, 70
Cools-Lartigue, Eamon Hugh, 308
Coone, Mikaylah, 75
Cooper, Gov. Roy, 261
Coral Springs, Florida, 68
Corbin *Times-Tribune*, 131
Corcoran, Florida House Speaker Richard, 67
Cornett, Deputy, 53
Cornett, Pearl "Sonny", 285
Corpus Christi, Texas, 337
Correct Care Solutions (CCS), *371*
Cosgrove, Judge Patricia A., 276
Cothren, Sheriff Mark, 84
Cournoyer Cadillac, 184
Cousins, James, 74
Covelle, Patricia, 201
Covington County, Alabama, 3
Cowan, Matthew, *358*
Cowden, Mark, *385*
Cox, Gabriel, 34
Cradduck, Benton County, Ark. Sheriff Kelley, 31—34
Craig Taffaro, Newell Normand (CTNN), 186
Crane, U.S. District Judge Randy, 332
Cravens, Sheriff Charles, 327
Crawford, James, 138
Crenshaw County, Alabama, 4
Crescent City Connection, 1657
Criminal Investigation, Montana Dept. of Justice Division of, 227
Criminal Justice Education and Training Standards Commission, North Carolina, 260
Crish, Sheriff Sam, 277

Crooks, Mitchell, 240
Cross, Mary Elizabeth, 8
Cross, Noah, vi
Cross, Sheriff Noah, 145—147
Crum, Sheriff Eugene, *367*
Crump, Edward Hull "Boss", 323
Cruz, Nikolas, 66
Cuffy, Patrick, 82
Culp, Larry Glen, 151
Culp, Laurie Schween, 151
Cumberland County, New Jersey, 246
Cumbey, Floyd Edward, 148
Curran, John E., III, 337
Curry, Sheriff Jeff, 124—126
Custer County, Oklahoma, 286
Customs, U.S., 348
Cuyahoga County, Ohio, 277
Cyrus, Clarence Edward, 314

D.A.R.E., 93, 268
D'Amico, Marie, **112**
D'Angelo, Dewey, 212
D'Artois, George, 6, 184
D'Artois, Public Safety Commissioner George, 184, 185
DaBoyz LLC, *376*
Dade County, Florida, ix, 40
Dahl, Bryton, 270
Dailey, Tosha, 270
Daily Iberian, 170
Daley, Hart, 193
Daley, Mayor Richard, **111**
Dallas County, Texas, 334
Dallas Cowboy, 352
Dallas, Texas, 185, 207, 347
Daniel, Sheriff Dave, 294
Daniel, Terry, *373*
Daniels, Sheriff Darryl, 73, 74

Danziger, John, 74
Dardar, Alicia, 192
Darling, Calvin, 240
Darling, Kenneth, *372*
Dart, Sheriff Tom, **111**
Davis County Sheriff's Office, *362*
Davis County, Utah, *362*
Davis, Daniel M., **111**
Davis, Gov. Jimmie, 143
Davis, Jim, 301
Davis, Lonoke County Sgt. Michael, 36
Davis, Michael K., 151
Davis, Sheriff John Carr, 268
Davis, Sheriff Pat, *356*
Davis, William C., 146
Dawkins-Davis, Judge, 208
Dawsey, Barry Edward, 154
Daye, Anthony, 169
Daytona Beach, Florida, 74
De La Cruz, Rudy Anthony, 338
De Leon, Marc, 340
De Meo, Sheriff Tony, 237
DEA, 14, 137, 190, 217, 332
Dean, James, 348
Dean, Sheriff Ed, 75
Deepwater Horizon, 159, 174
Deese, Hubert, 263, 264
DeFalaise, U.S. Attorney Louie, 136
DeFazio, Sheriff Pete, 303
Defense Department, 71
DeKalb County, Georgia, 81, 83, **96**
Dekraai, Scott, 47
Delahoussaye, Ricky, 175
Delahoussaye, Terry, Sr., 175
DeLaughter, Frank, vii, 145, 147, 148
Delaware, xi, 63, 64, 332
Delaware County, Oklahoma, 279
Delaware General Assembly, 64
Delaware Supreme Court, 64

DeLew, Erin, 239
Dellinger, Frankie, 269
Delta Security, 159
Demeo, Sheriff Tony, 236
Demery, Larry, 264
Democratic Party, 302
Denney, Kelli, 283
Denver Sheriff's Office, 61
 Denver, Colorado, 46, 60, 348
Department of Corrections, Florida, 80
Department of Homeland Security, 333
Department of Homeland Security, U.S., 387
Department of Human Services, North Dakota, 273
Department of Justice, U.S., 18, 56, 261, 293, 345
Department of Justice, U.S., 18
Department of Mental Health, Vermont, *365*
Department of Public Safety, 185
Des Moines, Iowa, 121
DeSantis, Florida Gov. Ron, 73
DeSantis, Ron, 67
Destin, Florida, 6, 158
Detroit Free Press, The, 206
Detroit Lions, 207
Detroit Metro Times, The, 207
Detroit Yacht Club, 207
Detroit, Michigan, 206
Devils Walking: Klan Murders Along the Mississippi in the 1960s, 145
DeWitt, Sheriff Wayne, 317
Dial, Michael, 328
DiBiasi, Darrin P., 244
Dickey, Sheriff James, 322
Dierks, Sheriff Robert, 126
Diesburg, James, 122

Dill, Pulaski County, Ark. Maj. Larry, 38
Dillon County, South Carolina, 308
DiPaola, Sheriff James, 206
Discovery Network, 358
Disney, Michael, 251
Ditch, Dr. Carl, 167
Ditlevson, Elizabeth, 20
Dixie Mafia, 187, 211, 322, 346
Docobo, Joe, 65
Dodd, Teddy Lee, 328
Dodd, William F., 182
Dodge County, Georgia, **90**
Dollar, Deborah, 191
Domingue, Johnny, 190
Dominican Republic, 262
Doña Ana County, New Mexico, 247
Donald Trump, President, 10, 99, 202
Doneker, Samantha, 302
Donnelly, Sheriff Edward, 302
Donnelly, Stephen, Jr., 200
Dooley, Sheriff Vol, 147
Dorsey, Sheriff Sidney, 81, **96**
Doucet, Sheriff D.J. "Cat", 141
Douglas County Jail, **86**
Douglas County Sheriff's Office, **99**
Douglas County, Georgia, 81
Douglas County, Nebraska, 232
Douglas County, Oregon, 299
Douglas, Lawton, **91**
Douglasville, Georgia, **99**
Dove, Lee, 241
Dove, Parish President Gordon, 181
Downey, Sheriff Mike, **113**
Downs, Commissioner of Public Safety J. Earl, 185
Downs, Timothy, 119
Doyle, Sheriff Jay, 228

Dragnet, 51
Drake, Sheriff Lester, 135
DRC Group, 158
Drug Enforcement Administration, 288
Drug Enforcement Administration (DEA), 14
Drug Enforcement Agency, 190, 269
Drug Enforcement Agency Task Force, 161, 190
Druggan, Terry, **106**
Duet, Eddie, 153
Duff, Sheriff Steve, 132
Duffy, Daline County prosecutor Jean, 36
Duhé District Attorney Bo, 170
Duncan, Wes, 235
Dunn, Sheriff T. Baxter, 51—53
Dunwoody, Georgia, **86**
Dupnik, Pima County Sheriff Clarence, 25
Durant, Iowa, 121
Durham County Sheriff's Office, 266
Durham County, North Carolina, 266, 271
Duryee, Dan, 228
Duval County, Florida, 73
Dvorak, Jimmy "The Bohemian", **109**

Eagles, Philadelphia, 305
Earle, Gov. George Howard, III, 303
Early County, Georgia, **96**
Earp, Wyatt, 13
East Boston District Court, 200
East Carroll Correctional Systems, Inc. (ECCS), 155
East Carroll Detention Center (ECDC), 155
East Carroll Parish, Louisiana, 155
East Carroll Sheriff's Office, 154
Easter, Sheriff Jeff, 125
Eaton County, Michigan, 206
Eaton, Joe, 233
Eaton, Sheriff Chris, 137
ECCS. *See* East Carroll Correctional Systems
ECDC. *See* East Carroll Detention Center
Echevarria, Nestor, 80
Eddins, State Attorney William, 70
Edinburg, Texas, 331
Edson, Sheriff Donald, *367*
Edwards County, Texas, *354, 355*
Edwards, Gov. Edwin, 161
Edwards, Joseph, 147
Edwards, Scott, 224
Edwards, Sheriff Frank, xiii
Edwards, Sheriff Ricky, 189
El Paso County Sheriff's Office, 61
El Paso County, Colorado, 59
El Paso, Texas, 252
Eldorado High School, 251
Eldredge, Sheriff Richard, *361*
Elhart County, Indiana, vi
Elim, Richard, **86**
Elizondo, Gilbert, 252
Elkins, John, 267
Ellington, George Wesley, 342
Ellington, Tania Katrisse, 342
Elliott, Pamela, *354*
Elliott, Sheriff Mike, 297
Elliott, Sheriff Pamela, *354*
Ellis, Mike, 316
Ellis, Sheriff Kevin, *358*
Ellsinore, Missouri, 221
Elmwood Women's Jail, 54
Elrod, Richard, **108**

England, Janine, 275
Englewood Federal Correctional Institution, 46
English, TyQuian, 316
Enron, 46
Enterprise, The, 295
Entrekin, Karen, 6
Entrekin, Sheriff Todd, 6, 9
Epperson, Johnny, 133
Epstein, Jeffrey, 69, 77
Equitable Sharing Program, 232, 266
Erie County Correctional facility, 255
Erie County Holding Center, 257
Erie County, New York, v, 259
Ernsdorff, Gary, *378*
Escambia County Sheriff's Office, 72
Escambia County, Florida, 71
Essex County, Massachusetts, 201
Essex County, New Jersey, 245
Essex County, Vermont, *366*
Estrada, Joseph, 252
Ethical Policing Is Courageous (EPIC), 200
Ethics, Louisiana Board of, 162
Ethridge, Aaron, 75
Etowah County, Alabama, 6
Eunice New Era, 141
Eunice Police Department, 189
Eunice, Louisiana, 141, 189
Evangeline Parish Sheriff's Office, 177
Evangeline Parish, Louisiana, 180—213
Evans, Daniel Lamont, 213
Evans, Nancy, *389*

Fabian, Bobby Joe, 212
Facebook, **100**, 299, 319, *368*

Fagan, Sheriff Eric, *354*
Fairchild, Barry Lee, 38
Fairchild, Robert, 38
Fairfax County Police Department, *370*
Fairfax County, Virginia, *370*
Fairview, North Carolina, 267
Falcon Lake, Texas, 336
Falcon, Sheriff Eugenio "Gene," Jr., 319
Falterman, Anthony G. "Tony", xviii
Fanning, Sheriff Edmund, 259
Farley, Sheriff Thomas M., 255
Farr, Willard Dee, 314
Farrow, Thomas, 324
Fastiggi, Beth, *366*
Faturechi, Robert, 49
Faulkner County, Arkansas, 34
Favor, Jack, 147, 149
Fawkes, Guy, 279
Fayette County, Alabama, 5
Fayetteville Observer, 265
Fayetteville, North Carolina, 209
FBI, vi, 16, 23, 42, 56, 67, 77, 88 **93**, **98**, **109**, 124, 135, 141—156, 164, 173, 189, 216, 248, 251, 256, 277, 307, 312, 324, 336
FBI Uniform Crime Reporting Handbook, 21
FDA, 281
Federal Bureau of Narcotics, 15
Federal Prison Camp, South Dakota, 225
Feiza, Sgt. Aaron J., 118
Fentress County, Tennessee, 316
Fernandez, Anthony, Jr., 178
Fernandez, Larry, 50
Ferriday, Louisiana, 144, 148
Ferrigno, Lou, 247
Ficken, Michael, 212

Ficklin, Sheriff Ronald "Gun", 153, 154
Field, John, *352*
Fifth Circuit Court of Appeals, U.S., 172
Finley, U.S. Attorney Stephanie A., 161
Finlinson, George, *363*
First Amendment, 87, 180, 200, 233, 351
First Century Bank, 31
Fiscal Affairs Committee, Nevada Police Department's, 239
Flake, U.S. Sen. Jeff, 23
Flaxman, Kenneth, **113**
Fleet Intermodal, 159
Fleming, Ocean, 237
Fleniken, District Court Judge William J., 186
Florence County, South Carolina, 310
Flores, Ernesto, 351
Florida, v, ix, xxi, 2—7, 40, 65—73, 80, 184, 211, 301, 321
Florida Attorney General's Office, 69
Florida Department of Law Enforcement, 69, 73, 78
Florida Department of Law Enforcement (FDLE), 74
Florida Gulf Coast University, 80
Florida Sheriffs' Association, 40, 68
Florida State Senate, 65
Flournoy, Sheriff J. Howell, 184
Floyd, George, 192, 209, 296, *393*
Floyd, John T., 353
Flynn, Assistant Sheriff Ray, 241
Fonder, Darnell, **113**
Fontoura, Sheriff Armando, 245
FOP Lodge #155, 288

Ford, Attorney General Aaron, 235
Ford, Richard Kent, 135, 350
Ford, Sheriff Joe, 217
Forest Service, U.S., 298, *361*
Forrest County Board of Supervisors, 215
Forrest County, Mississippi, 216
Forrest, Gen. Bedford, 1
Forsyth County, Georgia, 84
Fort Bend County, Texas, 352, 353, *354*
Fort Lauderdale, Florida, 74, 158
Fort Myers Police Department, 77
Fort Myers, Florida, 77
Fort Oglethorpe, Georgia, **86**
Fort Worth, Texas, *359*
Fourth Amendment, 18, 176, 242, 270
Fowlerville, Michigan, 206
Fox and Friends, 352
Fox News, *388*
Frank, Allarate "A.J.", 189
Franklin & Marshall College, 303
Franklin County, Arkansas, 37
Franklin County, Kansas, 124
Franklin County, North Carolina, 266
Franklin County, Vermont, *365*
Franklin, Sheriff Ana, 8
Frasch, Sgt. Bruce, **109**
Frederick County, Maryland, 197
Fredricks, Jerrod, 124
Freedom of Information Act (FOIA), 315
Freeh Report, 77
Freeman, Joshua, 271
Freeman, Sheriff Myron, **97**
Freeman, Sheriff Robin, 313
Freeman, Sheriff Ron, 84
Freestone, Alan, *361*
Freier, Eric, 206

Frimell, Bret, 17
Frye, David, 232
Fuentes, Kristy, 159
Fuller, Charles E., 255
Fuller, William Herbert, 150
Fuller, Zennie William, 149
Fulton County Jail, **97**
Fulton County, Georgia, 81, **97**
Funderburg, Daniel, **102**

Gabbard, Charles, 43
Gable, Sheriff Jimmy, 308
Gadsden County Sheriff's Office, 80
Gadsden, Florida, 80
Gagnepain, Pima County Sheriff's Dept. Chief of Staff Brad, 25
Gainesville, Florida, 80
Gainesville, Texas, 285
Gal, Jaysan, 236
Gallant, Sheriff Wayne, 193
Ganey, Todd, *353*
Garcia, Charles, *373*
Garcia, Geronimo "Jerry", 325
Garcia, Louis, Jr., 344
Garcia, Neri, *355*
Garcia, Sheriff Adrian, 341
Garden Grove, California, 42
Garono, Lawrence "Jeep", 279
Garrett, Mary Alice, *397*
Garrett, Sheriff Pat, 296
Garrison, Sheriff Todd, 247
Gary, Indiana, **108**
Garza, Sheriff Richard, 125
Gasser, Ronald, 165
Gaston County, North Carolina, 269
Gates County, North Carolina, 272
Gates, Michael, 327
Geiger, Maurice, 263
Gelbaum, David, 44

Gem State Patriot, **103**
Gene Autry Rodeo, 147
Gennaco, Michael, 56
Gentry, Bobby, 216
George, Sheriff Wallace Newman, Jr., 224
Georgetown University, 262
Georgia, xxi, 81, 86, 345
Georgia Bureau of Investigation, **84, 92, 95**
Georgia Bureau of Investigation (GBI), 84
Georgia Department of Corrections, **97**
Georgia Ethics Commission, **96**
Georgia House Committee on Special Judiciary, **97**
Georgia Legislature, **97**
Georgia Lottery, **86**
Georgia Peace Officer Standards and Training (POST), **86**
Georgia Peace Officer Standards and Training (POST) Council, **87**
Georgia Public Safety Training Center, **87**
Georgia Sheriffs' Association, 85, **96**
Georgia State Prison, 82
Giancana, Sam, **114**
Giant, 348
Gibbs, Sojourner, 191
Gibson County, Tennessee, 325
Gibson, David, **87**
Gibson, Olin Norman, **91**
Gibson, Stanley, 241
Gibson, Willie Charlie, 150
Giddings, Sheriff Doug, **162**
Gilbert, Arizona, Police Department, *354, 355*
Gilbert, Louisiana, 143
Gill, Sterling, 350

411

Gillespie, Sheriff Doug, 240
Gilley, Hanna, 276
Gilley, Mickey, 142
Gillich, Mike, 211
Gilman, Lance, 235
Ginsburg, Supreme Court Justice Ruth Bader, xx, 10
Giusto, Sheriff Bernie, 293
Gladwin County, Michigan, 206
Glanz, Sheriff Stanley, 284
Glasgow Police Department, 227
Glasgow, Montana, 227
Gleave, Sheriff Marty, *361*
Glidden, David, 226
Global Tel Link (GTL), 48
Gloucester County, New Jersey, 246
Glover, John, 246
Godwin, Sheriff Laymon, 150
Goethals, Superior Court Judge, 48
Goethals, Superior Court Judge Thomas M., 47
Goforth, Darren, 339
Goins, Johnny, 263
Goldberg, Scot, 80
Golden, Wesley Clayton, 269
Goldschmidt, Gov. Neil, 293
Gomez, Michael, 338
Gondo, Momodu, 195
Gonzales, Sheriff Tony, 337
Gonzales, Thomas "El Gallo", 334
Gonzalez, Sheriff Ed, 342
Goodrich, Jason, 340
Goralczyk, Tom, 119
Gordon County, Georgia, **86**
Gordon, Pheenix Mayor Gordon, 17
Gordon, Phoenix Mayor Phil, 19
Gore, Assistant Chief Chris, 342
Gorges, Undersheriff Jim, **102**
Gourgues, Jarrod, 176
Governing Magazine, vii

Goyeneche, Rafael, 158
Goyeneche, Rafael, III, 174
Grace College, 120
Grafton, W. Lloyd, 167
Gragg, Jeffrey T., 285
Graham County, Arizona, *354*, *362*
Gramkow, Sheriff Lenny, 319
Grand Isle County Courthouse, *366*
Grand Isle County, Vermont, *366*
Grand Isle, Louisiana, 162
Grand Rapids, Michigan, 205
Grand Traverse County, Michigan, 205
Grant County Public Lands Natural Resources Plan, 298
Grant County, Oregon, 297, 298
Grant, Sheriff Bailey, 149
Granville County, North Carolina, 271
Gray, Freddie, 197
Gray, John E., 281
Greater Newburyport Chamber of Commerce, 202
Greely, Colorado, 60
Green, Daniel, 264
Green, Sheriff Pat, 266
Green, Tony, 294
Greenblatt, Alan, vi
Greene, Ronald, *393*
Greenhut, Steven, 40
Greensburg, Louisiana, 153
Greensburg, Pennsylvania, 305
Greenville County, South Carolina, 310
Greenville News, 316
Greenwell, Sheriff David, 138
Greenwich, NJ, Township Police Department, 246
Grewal, Attorney General Gurbir, 244

Griffin, Landon, 216
Griffith, Rusty, 186
Griggers, District Attorney Greg, 11
Griner, Ryan, **89**
Grisham, Gov. Michelle, vii
Grubb, Cody, 343
Gruda, Jessica, 237
Grundy County, Tennessee, 321
Gualtieri, Bob, v
Gualtieri, Sheriff Bob, 70
Guerra, Sheriff Reymundo, 332
Guevara, Jose Luis, 335
Guffey, Eric Duane, 137
Guidry, Robert, 161
Guidry, Shane, 166
Guilford, U.S. District Judge Andrew, 45
Guinness Book of World Records, 262
Gulf of Mexico, 68, 334
Gulf War, 241
Gulrola, U.S. District Judge Louis, 213
Gun Owners of America, xii
Gun Trace Task Force, the, 195, 196
Gundu, Krishnaveni, *359*
Guste, Attorney General William, 187
Guthrie, Sheriff J.W., *355*
Gwinnett County, Georgia, **89**

Hackensack, New Jersey, 243
Hagan, Jason, 225
Hagan, Laura, 225
Haidl, Don, 47
Haidl, Gregory, 42
Haidl, Lt. Don, 42
Haimes, Nicole Lucas, 263
Hain, Sheriff Ron, 115

Halat, Mayor Pete, 323
Halat, Pete, 212
Hall, Lee M., 351
Hall, Roger, 137
Hamblen County, Tennessee, 321
Hamilton County, Kansas, 125
Hamilton, Bruce, 189
Hamilton, Sheriff Hank, 348
Hammond, Indiana, 119
Hammond, Louisiana, 190
Hammond, Louisiana, Police Department, 190
Hanchett, Sheriff Seth, **105**
Hancock County Courthouse, *385*
Hancock County, West Virginia, *385*
Hanlin, Sheriff John, 299
Hanna, Sheriff Thomas, 60
Hannah, Justin, *371*
Hanson Brandy, 167
Hanson, David, 166
Happy, Texas, 343
Haralson, Allen, 215
Harden, Sheriff Kenny, 2
Hargrove, Thomas, 172
Harlan County, Kentucky, 131, 133
Harmon, Special Prosecutor Don, 36
Harper's magazine, *392*
Harris County jail, 341
Harris County Sheriff's Department, 339
Harris County Sheriff's Office, 339
Harris County, Texas, 331, 339
Harris, Dewayne, 132, 133
Harris, Edna, 133
Harris, Raymond, 133
Harris, Sheriff Brian, 11
Harrison County, 212
Harrison County Adult Detention Center, 214
Harrison County Sheriff's Office,

413

213
Harrison County, Mississippi, 211, 212
Harvard College, 191
Harvey Gulf, 166
Harvey, Joe, 30
Haskell, Sheriff Stephen, *391*
Hatch, Kenneth, 194
Hatfields and McCoys, *383*
Hathaway, Sheriff Randy, 272
Hattiesburg, Mississippi, 214
Haughton, Louisiana, 148
Hawaii, ix, xv, 206,
Hawes, Robert, **89**
Hawkins, Sheriff, 259
Hawks, Brandon, 272
Hawley, Attorney General Josh, 222
Hawman, Jay, 74
Haynes, Colt, 284
Hays, John, *399*
Healey, Massachusetts Attorney General Maura, 202
Healey, Sheriff Harry, xv
Hebbronville, Texas, 333
Hebert, Toby, 172
Held, Sheriff Jonathan, 304
Helena, Montana, 228
Helms, Erika, 70
Hendershott, Maricopa County Chief Deputy David, 20
149Hendrix, Evodio, 198
Hendry County Sheriff's Department, 79
Hendry County, Florida, v, 79, 80
Henrico County, Virginia, *360*
Henry County, Virginia, *373*
Henry, Don, 35
Henry, Sheriff Knox, 324
Hernandez, Joseph Anthony, 338
Herren, Jeanette, *397*

Herrera, Federal District Judge Judith, 248
Herrera, Leon, 249
Hersl, Daniel, 195
Hewett, Sheriff Ronald, 268
Hewitt, Curt, 146, 148
Hickman, Sheriff Ron, 340
Hidalgo County High Intensity Drug Trafficking Area Task Force, 332
Hidalgo County, Texas, 331—334
High Intensity Drug Task Force, 115
Highland Park, Michigan, 206
Highland Park, Michigan, police department, 206
Hilbert, Sheriff Eddie, *383*
Hilburn, Wiley, *398*
Hill, Erica, 44
Hill, Sheriff Samuel, *365*
Hill, Sheriff Victor, **88, 100**
Hillsborough County, Florida, 65
Hillsborough, North Carolina, 259
Hilton, Roger Ray, 285
Hilton, Sheriff William, 190
Hines, Aris Lamont, 261
Hines, David, 172
Hingle, Irvin "Jif", 159
Hingle, Sheriff Irvin "Jif", 158, 160
Hinojosa, Jose Carlos, 332
Hinton, Maggie, *397*
Historic Richmond Foundation, *375*
HistoryLink.org, *377*
Hoard, Floyd, **93**
Hobbs Act, 280
Hobbs, Sheriff Leroy, Sr., 211
Hobby, Sheriff Jeff, **94**
Hodge, Sheriff Lawrence, 129
Hodgson, Sheriff Thomas, 202
Hoffman, Acting Attorney General John, 244
Hoffman, Debra, 42—45

Hoffman, Peter, **105**
Hofstadter Committee, 255
Hogan, Jeane, 288
Hogan, Sheriff Joe, 287
Holbert, Akymzee, 315
Holcomb, Jonathan, *385*
Holden Beach, North Carolina, 268
Holding, U.S. Attorney George, 265
Holiwell, Alicia, *379*
Holiwell, Darrion Keith, *362, 378—381*
Holland, Sheriff Eugene, 153
Holland, Wesley, **85**
Holley, Clay, *357*
Holliman, Earl, 340
Holly, Sheriff Melvin, 285
Holman, Mirya, vii Holmes, Linda, **110**
Holmes, Ted, 236
Holt, Benton County, Ark. Lt. Robin, 33
Homeland Security and Justice Training grants, 68
Homeowners Association multi-million-dollar scandal, 240
Hook, Sheriff Wayne, **88**
Hoover, Todd, *393*
HOPE Team, 288
Hopper, Dennis, 348
Hopson, Debra, 11
Horn, Joe, 227
Hornyak, Undersheriff Joseph, 244
Horton, Sandy, 124
Horton, Sheriff Jonathon, 6
Houma Police Department, 181
Houma, Louisiana, 181, 184
House of Representatives, U.S., 276
Houston Chronicle, The, 353
Houston Police Department's Criminal Investigation Division, 332
Houston, Texas, 147, 160, 190, 238, 331, 339, 340, 346
Howard, Sheriff Tim, 259
Howard, Tim, v
Howard, U.S. District Judge Malcolm, 270
Hoyle, Mark Ray, 269
Huber, U.S. Attorney John, 28
Hudson County, Pennsylvania, 302
Hudson, Rock, 348
Hudspeth County, 349
Hudspeth County, Texas, 247, 349
Huffington Post, 23
Huffingtonpost.com, 8
Hughes, Karen, 237
Human Resources Commission, Vermont, *366*
Humboldt County Sheriff's Department, 241, 242
Hunter, Lonnie, 286
Hunterdon County, New Jersey, 245
Huntsman, Inspector General Max, 56
Hurst, Ian, 126
Hutchens, Sheriff Sandra, 48
Hutcheson, Sheriff Cory, 222
Hutchins, Sheriff Sandra, 47
Hydrotex Industries, 147

Iberia Parish, 167, 170
Iberia Parish Jail, 171
Iberia Parish Sheriff's Department, 168, 172
Iberia Parish Sheriff's Office, 168, 172, 174
Iberia Parish, Louisiana, v, 167, 170, 172
ICE, 261, 270, 359
Idaho County, Idaho, **102**

Idaho Press-Tribune, **105**
Idaho Territory, x
Illinois, **105**
Illinois Secretary of State, **113**
Illinois State Board of Elections, **113**
Illinois State Police, 115
Immigration and Customs Enforcement (ICE), 203, 260, 270, 359
Incredible Hulk, 247
Independence, Kansas, 126
Independence, Missouri, 222
Indian River County, Florida, 74
Indiana, 117, 138
Indianapolis Star, 118
Infelise, Rocco, **113**
Infowars, *388*
Ingle, Sheriff Rodney, 5
Ingram, James, *339*
Innocents, the, x
Inslee, Gov. Jay, *378*
Institute for Justice, 242
Institute for Justice, the, 345
Internal Revenue Service Criminal Investigation Division, 157
investigative holds, 177–180
Iowa, 121
Iowa State Patrol, 123
Iran, 114
Iran-Contra, 218, 370
Iroquoian Mingo Native American tribe, *383*
IRS, 119, 164, 332
Irwin, Dustin, 274
Isakson, Robert, 158
Isenberg, Andrew, 39
Isham, Sheriff Russ, 291
Isom, Sheriff John R., *369*
Israel, Sheriff Scott, 87
Ives, Kevin, 35

Ives, Linda, 36
Ivey, Gov. Kay, 6

Jackson County Board of Commissioners, 207
Jackson County Sheriff's Department, 69
Jackson County, Georgia, **93**
Jackson County, Michigan, 207
Jackson County, Mississippi, 213
Jackson County, Missouri, 222
Jackson, Cory, 270
Jackson, Dwayne, 241
Jackson, Gen. Andrew, 174
Jackson, James, 154
Jackson, Jesse, 31
Jackson, Kelly, 236
Jackson, Mississippi, 143
Jackson, Myra, 156
Jacobs, Ikeisha, 270
JailCigs, LLC, 26
Jails on Demand, 158
James, Attorney General Letitia, 257
Janovich, Sheriff George, *379*
Jaramillo, George, 42, 44
Jarvis, Sheriff Pat, 82
Jasler, Natalie, 252
Jeff Davis 92
Jeff Davis County, Georgia, **92**
Jefferson County, Alabama, 1
Jefferson County, Idaho, **102**
Jefferson County, Ohio, 278
Jefferson Davis Parish jail, 189
Jefferson Davis Parish, Louisiana, 189
Jefferson Parish Sheriff's Department, 191
Jefferson Parish Sheriff's Office,

161—166
Jefferson Parish, Louisiana, vii, 13, 161—166, 184, 191, 247
Jeffersonville, Indiana, 117
Jenkins County, Georgia, **95**
Jenkins County, Georgia, Jail, **95**
Jenkins, Wayne, 195
Jenne, Sheriff Ken, 65
Jerome Combs Detention Center, **113**
Jim Crow, 143
Jinkins, Sheriff Chuck, 199
Joe Arpaio, v, 13, 23, 164
John Birch Society, xii
John Curtis High School, 165
John Day, Oregon, 297
John Day, Oregon, Police Department, 297
John Jay College, 49
John, Ron, 133
Johnson County, Kansas, 124, 127
Johnson, Marques, 79
Johnson, Northwest District Judge Benjamen, 271
Johnson, Robert, 340
Johnson, Sheriff Greg, **113**
Johnson, Sheriff Michael L., 306
Johnson, Sheriff Terry, 260
Jolly, Sheriff Clem, 83
Jonathan, Kingsley, 2629
Jones, Alex, *188*
Jones, DeKalb County CEO Vernon, 83
Jones, Heather, 124
Jones, Richard, v
Jones, Scott, v
Jones, Sheriff Richard K., 281
Jones, Sheriff Scott, 40, 51
Jones, Sheriff Terry, 287
Jordan, Glen, *157*
Jordan, James, 261
Jordan, Michael, 259
Jordan, State Sen. Maryanne, **104**
Joseph, Steve, 126
Josephine County Sheriff's Department, 287
Josephine County, Oregon, 287
Joye, Michael, 274
Judd, Sheriff Grady, 76
Juneau, District Court Judge Jeanne, 179
Justia, **xix**
Justice Department, U.S., 146, 170, *354*
Justice for Victor White III Foundation, 172

Kagenyera, Kenneth, 264
Kane County Sheriff's Department, 118
Kane County, Illinois, 117
Kankakee County Sheriff's Office, **116**
Kansas, 125, 129
Kansas Bureau of Investigation, 126, 130
Kansas City Chiefs, 167
Kansas Commission on Peace Officers' Standards and Training (CPOST), 129
Kansas Highway Patrol, 130
Kansas Sheriffs Association, 126
Katrina, Hurricane, 158, 160, 177
Kealoha, Katherine, **xviii**
Kealoha, Police Chief Louis, **xviii**
Kearbey, Steffanie, 222
Keating, Lt. James, **111**
Keefe Commissary Network, 33
Keen, Clifford "Skip", 166

Keen, Jarret, 167
Keener, Melanie, 235
Keeter, Judge Harold, 343, 3344
Keine, Ron, vii
Kellerman, Sheriff Keith, 221
Kelley, Police Chief T.P., 187
Kelly, Sheriff Pat, 276
Kemler, Sheriff John, 245
Kemp, Georgia State Sen. Rene, **97**
Kemp, Gov. Brian, 85
Kendrick, Corene, *371*
Kennedy, President John F., *383*
Kennedy, Robert F., 144
Kennedy, Sean, 56
Kenner, Louisiana, 157
Kenney, Dennis, 49
Kentucky, 47, 129, 131—139, *383*
Kentucky Fried Chicken, 129
Kentucky State Reformatory, 137
Kermit, West Virginia, *383*
Kern County, California, v, 51
Kern, U.S. District Judge Terence, 290
Kewanee Star Courier, **113**
KGUN-TV, 29
Kilkenny, Sheriff Sean, 305
Kim, Benjamin, 240
Kimball, William, 185
Kimble County, Texas, *356*
Kimbrough, Sheriff Kem, **88**
King County Sheriff Office, *364*
King County Sheriff's Department, *378*
King County Sheriff's Office, *378*,
King County, Washington, *378*
King George II, x
King, Larry, 41
King, Rodney, *370*
King, Ronnie, 321
King, Ruby, **87**

King, Sheriff William L., Jr., 193
King, Timothy, Jr., **91**
King, Tony, **88**
Kingsley, Jonathan, 262
Kinman, Jamie, 138
Kinzie, Sheriff John, **105**
Kirby, Jason, 329
Klamath County, Oregon, 295
Kleberg County, Texas, 337
Knoxville, Tennessee, 324
Koch, Curtis, *362*
Kogut, Stanley, 115
Kolb, Matt, **106**
Korea, 327
Kosciusko County Sheriff's Office, 120
Kosciusko County, Indiana, 120
KPNX TV, 21
Kristofferson, Kris, 335
Ku Klux Klan, 144, 150
Kubitskey, Arizona Deputy Sheriff Association President, Kevin, 24, 26
Kubitskey, Pima County Sgt. Kevin, 24
Kuhn, Undersheriff Dan, 75
Kukowski, Sheriff Steven, 274
Kurtz, Michael, 141
Kwas, Taylor, 319
Kyle, Sheriff Mike, **95**

La Cosa Nostra, 279
La Grange, Kentucky, 137
La Tuna federal prison, 248
Lacey & Larkin Frontera Fund, 16
Lacey, Mike, 16
Lafayette Parish, 170
Lafayette Parish, Louisiana, 170
Lafayette, Louisiana, 169
 Lafourche Novelty Company, 184
Lafourche Parish, Louisiana, 152,

153
Lafrance, Acting Sheriff Michael, 159
Lagano, Frank, 243
Lagerkvist, Mark, 245
Lail, Blake, 273
Lake Charles, Louisiana, xvii, 186
Lake County Sheriff's Police, 119
Lake County, California, 54
Lake County, Indiana, 118
Lake County, Montana, 227
Lake Michigan, 118
Lake Providence, Louisiana, 155
Lake Superior, 322
Lake, Frankie, **106**
Lakefront Tavern, 321
Lamoille County Sheriff's Office, 365
Lamoille County, Vermont, 365, 367
Landersman, David, 350
Landersman, Mark, 351
Landis, Brian, 193
Landry, Attorney Gen. Jeff, 166
Landry, Nelson, Jr., 172
Lane, Pulaski County deputy Kirk, 35
Langenberg, SAC James C., 249
Langley, Judge Glenn, 321
Lanza, Adam, xv
Laredo, Texas, 335
Larkin, Jim, 16
Larpenter, Sheriff Jerry, 180, 183
Larson, Gordon, 298
Larson, Undersheriff James R., 256
Lartigue, Police Chief Neal, 180
Las Cruces, New Mexico, 247
Las Vegas Metro Police Department, 238
Las Vegas Metropolitan Police Department, 241
Las Vegas Metropolitan Police Department/Clark County Sheriff's Office, 241
Las Vegas, Nevada, 14, 43, 68, 100, 237—241, 288, 309, 339
LaSalle, Byron Benjamin, 169
Last Western, The, 292
Latimer County Jail, 285
Latimer County, Oklahoma, 285
Laurens County Sheriff's Office, 311
Laurens County, South Carolina, 311
Laurino, Anthony, **110**
Laux, Sheriff Charles, 231
Law Enforcement Institute, LSU, 185
Lawman, 13
Lawrence County, Alabama, 5
Lawson, Scott, 76
Lawson, Sheriff Johnny "Zip", 273
Laxalt, Attorney General Adam, 235
LCS Corrections Services Inc., 338
Leaf, Sheriff Dar, xviii, 205
Leche, Daniel, 152
LeDoux, Sheriff Adler, 142
Lee County Sheriff's Office, 77
Lee County, Florida, 76
Lee County, Kentucky, 135—142
Lee County, South Carolina, 312
Lee, Anna, 316
Lee, Georgia State Sen. Daniel, **97**
Lee, Harry, vii, 161
Lee, Martiny and Caracci Law Firm, 162
Lee, Rev. Robert, Jr., 144
Lee, SAC Carol K.O., 251
Lee, Sheriff Harry, vii, 161
Lee, Sheriff Roy, 308
Leon County, Texas, *358*
Leon County, Texas, District Court,

358
Leonard, Terry, 228
Leroy, Jenis, *373*
Leslie, Jim, 7, 185, 187
Leslie, Sheriff Larry, 123
Letten, U.S. Attorney Jim, 157, 1600
Levett, Sheriff Eric, **86**
Lewis, Charlotte, *397*
Lewis, Jerry Lee, 142
Lewis, Sheriff Will, 310
Lexington County, South Carolina, 312
Liddel, Sheriff Moses Wesley, Jr., 285
Life magazine, *392*
Lincoln County Drug Court, 224
Lincoln County Jail, 234
Lincoln County Sheriff's Office, 195
Lincoln County, Maine, 194
Lincoln County, Missouri, 224
Lincoln, Nebraska, 234
Lipfird, Carrie, 134
Lipfird, Sheriff Marvin J., 134
Lipkovitch, Tiffany, 206
Little, Sheriff Albert D. "Bodie", 160
Livingston Parish School Board, 188
Livingston Parish, Louisiana, 187, 188
Llano County, Texas, *357*
Logan County, West Virginia, *385*
Lohman, Joseph C., **107**
Lombardo, Sheriff Joe, 238
Lone Star Justice, *358*
Long, Earl K., 141, 182
Long, Huey P., 141
Long, Sheriff Gary, 85
Longoria, Homero Arturo, 332
Lonoke County Circuit Court, 35
Lonoke County, Ark, 34

Lonoke County, Arkansas, 35
Lonoke, Arkansas, 34
Lopez, Leonard, 338
Lopez, Nancy, 337
Lopez, Sheriff Ralph, 337
Los Angeles County Civilian Oversight Commission, 56
Los Angeles County Intelligence Unit, 49
Los Angeles County Sheriff's Department, xi, 57
Los Angeles County, California, xii, 40, 49, 57
Los Angeles Police Department, 47
Los Angeles Times, 46, 49
Los Angeles, California, *370*
Lost Nation Airport, 278
Lostutter, Deric, 279
Lott, Sheriff Leon, 313
Lotter, John, 231
Loudoun County Board of Supervisors, *371*
Loudoun County Sheriff's Office, *370*
Loudoun County, Virginia, *369—371*,
Louisiana, v—ix, xiii, xv, xvii, 141—192, 245—247, 291, 323, 331, 337, 358
Louisiana Association of Business and Industry (LABI), 185
Louisiana Attorney General, 160
Louisiana Department of Public Safety and Corrections (LDOC), 154
Louisiana House of Representatives, 157
Louisiana Legislature, 186
Louisiana Secretary of State, 155, 167
 Louisiana Sheriffs' Association, 158

Louisiana Sheriffs' Association (LSA), xiii
Louisiana Sheriffs' Association Risk Management Program, 162
Louisiana Sheriffs' Law Enforcement Program (LSLEP), 172
Louisiana Stadium and Exposition District, 164
Louisiana State Penitentiary at Angola, 148, 323
Louisiana State Police, 161, 170, 191
Louisiana State Police Troop G, 346
Louisiana State Senate, 124
Louisiana State Trooper, *viii, 161*
Louisiana Tech Journalism Department, *398*
Louisiana Tech University, *397*
Louisiana's Rogue Sheriffs: A Culture of Corruption, xvii
Louisville, Kentucky, 117
Love County, Oklahoma, 283, 285
Love, Hartwell, 143
Lovin, Steven Ray, 265
Loving County, Texas, 331
Lovingier, Brad, 61
LSLEP (Louisiana Sheriffs Law Enforcement Program), 172
LSU, 159
Lucarelli, Paul, 244
Lucas County Jail, 281
Lucas County, Ohio, 250
Lujan, Tom, 252
Lumbee Indians, 262
Lynch, Attorney General Loretta, 168
Lynch, Richard, 328
Lynde, Christine, 224
Lynn Haven, Florida, 71

M.D. Anderson Cancer Center, 160
Mack, Sheriff Richard, 298, *354, 362, 388*
Madera, Elbert, 347
Madera, Elbert "Jack", 347
Madigan, Illinois Attorney General Lisa, **112**
Madison Square Garden, 147
Madonna, G. Terry, 303
Maez, Stephanie, vii
Mafia, 145, 184
Maggs, Sheriff Mark, 319
Maginnis, John, 142
Mahnomen County Sheriff's Office, 210
Mahnomen County, Minnesota, 210
Mahoning County, Ohio, 279—281
Maine, x, 193
Maine Sheriffs' Association, 193
Maitland, Jeff, 326
Major Investigations Unit, **107**
Maketa, Sheriff Terry, 59, 60
Malheur County, Oregon, 295
Malheur National Wildlife Refuge, 297
Mallory, Tarus, 315
Mandan, Hidatsa and Arikara Nation, 274
Mangham, Louisiana, 143
Manley, Allison Haley, 311
Mann, Sheriff Jeff, 83
Mann, Sheriff Johnny, 135
Manning, Douglas, 72
Manning, Leah, 72
Manor, James, 240
Marcello, Carlos, 145, 146, 161, 184, 185, 212
Marcoux, Sheriff Robert, *365*

Marfa, Texas, 348
Maricopa County Sheriff's Office, 21, 164
Maricopa County, Arizona, v, 13—27, 166, 247, *354*, *387*
Marine, U.S., 174
Marion County Sheriff, 75
Marion County, Florida, 75
Marion County, Oregon, 291
Marjory Stoneman Douglas High School, 66
Marmolejo, Sheriff Brig, Jr., 334
Marshal's Office, U.S., *369*
Marshall County, Alabama, 1
Marshall, Adam, 295
Marshall, Bill, 217
Marshall-Jones, Charlotte, 65
Marshals' Service, U.S., *370*
Martin County Sheriff's Office, 68
Martin, Chicago Police Superintendent, Leroy, **111**
Martin, Investigator Brian, 209
Martin, Sheriff Brian, 55
Martin, Sheriff J. Lamar, 83
Martin, Sheriff Lamar, **96**
Martinez, U.S. Attorney Damon, 251
Martiny, Daniel, 162
Marx, FBI Special Agent Leah, 50
Maryland, 195, 269
Maryland Natural Resources Police, 197
Mason, Greta, 38
Massachusetts, ix, 199, 201, 206, 345
Massey, Jesse Aaron, 339
Massimiano, Sheriff Carmen, Jr., 199
Mastronardy, Sheriff Michael, 245
Matamoros, Mexico, 331

Mathews, Joe, 39
Matrisciana, Patrick, 36
Mattingly, Chris, 138
Mauney, Sheriff Gary, 217
Maverick County, Texas, 351
Mayfield, Caroll County, Ark. Sheriff Randy, 33
Maynard, Tennis, *384*
Maynor, Sheriff Glenn, 264, 266
Mayorkas, Secretary of Homeland Security Alejandro, 203
McAllen, Texas, 333
McAllister, U.S. Attorney Stephen, 126
McArthur, William, 38
McBride, Harry, 135
McBroom, Robert, 281
McCabe, Sheriff Bob, *371*
McCain, U.S. Sen. John, 23
McCarthy, Police Chief Hugh, **107**
McCarty, Assemblyman Kevin, 52
McCarty, Kevin, 40
McClary, Daryl, *377*
McClendon, Marshall, 152
McConigle, Sheriff John, 199, 201
McCormick County Sheriff's Office, 308
McCormick County, South Carolina, 308
McCown, Danny, 137
McCutchen, Johnny, 312
McDaniel, Gary, 323
McDonald, Jennifer, *376*
McDowell, Sheriff James, 56
McEathron, Sheriff Daniel, *376*
McFadden, Sheriff Garry, 267 Mc-Farlin, Sheriff Theodore "Big Mac", 314
McFarlin, South Carolina, 3314
McGhee, Sheriff John, 322

422

McKay, Christina, 341
McKeithen, Gov. John, 181, 191
McKenzie County Sheriff's Department, 274
McKenzie County, North Dakota, 210, 273
McKinley, Sheriff Todd, 298
McKinney, Jerry, Sr., 190
McKnight, Joe, 164
McLaughlin, Sheriff Kevin, *366*
McLean, Virginia, *370*
McMahon, Jack, 305
McMillian, Walter, 9
McMinn County, Tennessee, 323
McNairy County, Tennessee, 323
McSally, Martha, 23
Mears, Sheriff Terry, 4
Mebane, North Carolina, 261
Mecklenburg County Sheriff's Office, 270
Mecklenburg County, North Carolina, 270
Medford, Sheriff Bobby Lee, 267
Medicaid, 338
Meeks, Dennis, 4
Meeks, Sheriff Dennis, 3
Meier, Sheriff, 227
Melendez, William, 206
Melton, John Daniel, 84
Melton, Sheriff Greg, 221
Melvin, Sheriff Edward Jerome "E.J.", 311
Memphis, Tennessee, 323, 327
Men's Central Jail, Los Angeles, 49,
Mendez, Sheriff Johnny "Big John", *385*
Mendoza, Daniel, 239
Meneley, Sheriff David, 127
Menton, Judge Paul, 200
Mercer County, New Jersey, 245

Mercer County, NJ, Sheriff's Office, 245
Mercer, Elizabeth, 237, 238
Merrillville, Indiana, 119
Metropolitan Correction Center, 115
Metropolitan Crime Commission (MCC), 174
Metropolitan Crime Commission, New Orleans, 158
Metts, Sheriff James, 312
Mexico, 23, 49, 112, 202, 331–350, 396
Meyering, Sheriff William, **106**
MgtGp, Inc., 123
Miami, Florida, 324
Miami-Dade County, Florida, 40
Michigan, 43, 205. 208
Michigan Campaign Finance Network, 207
Michigan Department of Transportation, 205
Michigan Eastern District Federal Court, 208
Mid-America Services, 347
Middlesex County Sheriff's Office, 199, 244
Middlesex County, Massachusetts, 199
Middlesex County, New Jersey, 243, 245
Midwest Wood Flooring, *389*
Mike Carona Foundation, 44
Mikhaeil, Adel, 302
Miles, Shannon, 340
militia, 299
Millard County, Utah, *363*
Millard, April, 237
Miller, Misty, 284
Miller, Sheriff Charles M., 246
Miller, Sheriff Phil, **86**
Miller, William, 240

Milwaukee County Deputies Union, *389*
Milwaukee County, Wisconsin, *387*
Milwaukee Journal-Sentinel, The, *387*
Milwaukee, Wisconsin, *387*
Mineo, Sal, 348
Mingo County, West Virginia, *383*
Minneapolis, Minnesota, 209, 296, 393
Minnesota, 51, 209
Minor, Adam Gene, 137
Miranda, 281
Miranda rights, *385*
Mirkarimi, Sheriff Ross, 51
Mission, Texas, 334
Mississippi, 211, 322, 369, 370
Mississippi Bureau of Narcotics, 217
Mississippi County, Missouri, 222
Mississippi Delta, 191, 217
Mississippi Gulf Coast, 211
Mississippi River, 142, 165
Mississippi Supreme Court, 217
Missouri, 33, 148, 221, 225
Missouri Highway Patrol, 223
Missouri River, 319
Mitchell, Michelle B., *375*
Mitchell, Sheriff Gene, 5
Mitchell, Sheriff Tim, 216
Mobile County, Alabama, 7
Mobile, Alabama, 1, 158, 322
Molina, Albert, 296
Monk, Brandon, *358*
Monroe Athletic Club, 151
Monroe County, Alabama, 8
Monroe Mountain, Utah, *361*
Monroe News Star, 150
Monroe Regional Airport, 151
Monroe, Craig, 212
Monroe, Louisiana, *156*, *393*

Monroeville dry cleaners, 9
Montana, 227, 345
Montana Attorney General's Office, 228
Montana Department of Justice, 228
Montana Fish, Wildlife and Parks, 228
Montana Police Standards and Training (POST) Commission, 228
Montana Vigilantes, the, x
Monterey Klan unit, 145
Monterey, Louisiana, 145
Montgomery County, Kansas, 126
Montgomery County, Pennsylvania, 305
Montgomery, Alabama, 153
Montgomery, District Attorney Warren, 166
Moody, Florida Attorney General Ashley, 73
Moody, U.S. District Judge James, 119
Moore, Sheriff-Coroner Steve, 41
Moore, Timothy Brandon, 213
Mordaga, Michael, 243
Morgan County, Alabama, 8
Morgan County, Kentucky, 134
Morgan County, Tennessee, v
Morgan, Bruce, 314
Morgan, District Attorney Tom, 82
Morgan, Sheriff David, 71, 74
Morgel, Dorothy, 155
Morina, Sheriff Carmel M., 246
Morning Paper, *397*
Morris County, New Jersey, 245
Morris, Frank, 143
Morris, Jeff, 137
Morris, Michael Patrick, *385*
Morris, NJ, Township Police Department, 245
Morris, Sheriff Charlie, 68

Morrison, Patrick, 21
Morrison, Ronda, 9, 10
Morrison, Sabrina, 21
Mortensen, Ron, 239
Morville Lounge, 145, 147
Mosca's Restaurant, 184
Mount Olive, NJ, Township Police Department, 246
Mouriz, Brandon, 158, 159
Mudgett, Ebenezer, x
Muleshoe, Texas, *356*
Multnomah County, Oregon, 293, 297
Munnell, Maricopa County Deputy Frank, 16
Munsell, Michael, 333
Murakami, Undersheriff Timothy, 56
Murchek, Daniel, 119
Murder Accountability Project, 172
Murkerson, Sheriff Jimmie, **96**
Murphy, Gov. Phil, 244
Murphy, Michael, 267
Murray, Capt. Christine, 46
Mustang Ranch, 235

NAACP, 315
Nabors, Savana, 31
Nagyiski, Kevin John, 197
Nanos, Pima County Sheriff Chris, 24
Napier, Mark, 27, 30
Napoleon, Sheriff Benny, 207
Napoli, Louis, *375*
Napoli, Sheriff Louis, *393*
Narcan, 281
Narramore, Sheriff Giles, 322
Narum, Judge Daniel, 275
Nashville, Tennessee, 322

Natchez, Mississippi, 142, 146
Natchitoches Parish, xi
National Geographic, 134
National Police Officers Association of America, 185
National Public Radio (NPR), 49
National Reporters Committee for Freedom of the Press, 295
National Sheriffs' Association, 158, 307
Navy intelligence office, 350
Neal, Don, 308
Neal, Johnny, 309
Nebraska, 60, 124, 319, 345, 396
Nebraska Supreme Court, 231
Negron, Chris, *358*
Nehls, Sheriff Troy, 352, *354*
Nehls, Trever, *354*
Nelson, Willie, vii, 164
Nemeth, Sheriff Ed, 279
Neshoba County, Mississippi, 144
Ness County, Kansas, 125
Nevada, 235, 242, 297
Nevada City, California, x
Nevada Commission on Ethics, 235
Nevada Highway Patrol, 239
Nevada State Prison, 241
New Hampshire, ix
New Haven County, Connecticut, xv
New Iberia Police Department, 172
New Iberia, Louisiana, 170, 173
New Jersey, ix, **105,** 243
New Jersey State Police, 245
New Jersey State Treasury, 246
New Mexico, vii, ix, 14, 213, 247
New Mexico A&M, 248
New Mexico State Police, vi, 248, 249
New Orleans, 124, 323
New Orleans Advocate, 167

New Orleans Police Department, 210
New Orleans Times-Picayune, vii, 143
New Orleans, Louisiana, vii, 131, 159, 163, 166, 176, 211, 214
New York, 52, 206, 332
New York City, 149, 311, *374*
New York City, New York, 253
New York County, New York, 253
New York Jets, 167
New York Times, The, 366
New Zealand, 213
Newburyport, Massachusetts, 204
Newman, Karl Emmett, 193
Newport Beach, California, 44, 46
Newport Police Department, 313
Newport, Tennessee, 313
Newsome, Levar, 269
Newtown, Connecticut, 293
Nguyen, Kayden, 166
Nicholson, Brian, 238
Nightline, 22
Nipp, James Conn, 279
Nissen, Tom, 230
Nix, Kirksey McCord, 213, 312
Nixon, President Richard, **110**
Noblin, Sheriff Charles R., Jr., 268
Nocco, Sheriff Chris, 79
Nodaway County Sheriff's Department, 226
Nodaway County, Missouri, 226
Noe, Police Chief Omer, 138
Noel, Sheriff Jamey, 120
Norfolk County Sheriff's Office, *355*
Norfolk County, Virginia, *355*
Norfolk, Virginia, *356*
Norman, John, 241
Normand, Sheriff Newell, 165, 166

Normangee, Texas, *345*
Norris, Sheriff Robert, *350*
North Carolina, 156, 256, 264, 267, 308, 312, 313, 332, *358*
North Carolina ACLU, 258
North Dakota, 269
North, National Security Advisor Oliver, 220
North, Oliver, *354*
North, Sammy, *361*
Northhampton County North Carolina, 267
Northhampton County, North Carolina, 266
Norton, Lisa, 18
Nowata County Sheriff's Department, 285
Nueces County, Texas, 325
Null, Michael, 206
Null, Pamela Denise, 217
Null, Teddy, 217
Null, William, 206
Numi Financial, 33
Nungesser, Lt. Gov. Billy, 167, 177
Nuzum, Jerry, 248
Nye County Sheriff's Department, 235
Nye County, Nevada, 235

O.K. Corral, 14
O'Brien, Sheriff Thomas, **109**
O'Brien, Teresa, 287
O'Connor, Patrick, 228
O'Grady, Undersheriff James, **111**
O'Leary, Steven, 69
O'Malley, U.S. District Judge Kathleen, 276
O'Mary, Derek, 263
O'Nesti, Charles, 275
Oak Grove, Louisiana, 157, *158*

Oakland County, Michigan, 207
Oath Keepers, *371*
Oath Keepers, The, 292
Obama, President Barack, xx, 24
Obstruction of Justice: The Mena Connection, 38
Occupy Steubenville, 275
Ocean City, NJ, Police Department, 246
Ocean County, New Jersey, 245
Oconee County, Georgia, **90**
Ode to Billie Joe, 217
Office of Pre-Crime, Pasco County, 79
Ogilvie, Sheriff Richard, 117
Ogilvie, Sheriff Richard B., **110**
Ohio, 271
Ohren, Richard, 211 Okaloosa County, Florida, 68 Oklahoma, viii, 129, 280, 285
Oklahoma County Jail, 284
Oklahoma County public defender's office, 285
Oklahoma County Sheriff's Office, 284
Oklahoma County, Oklahoma, 284
Oklahoma Sheriffs' Association, 285
Olivarez, Sheriff Larry, 325
Oliver, Lt. Gov. Sheila, 245
Olsen, Sheriff Blair, **105**
Omaha, Nebraska, 231
Open Meetings Act, Texas, *342*
Open Public Records Act, 246
Operation Carlito's Weigh, 320
Operation Prickly Pear, 323
Operation Rockfish, 266
Operation Rolling Thunder, 307, 308
Operation Rose Thorn, 313
Operation Safe Bet, **111**
Operation Tarnished Badge, 262

Optimist Club, 324
Orange Beach, Alabama, 7
Orange County Register, 48
Orange County Sheriff's Department, 51
Orange County Sheriff's Department (OCSD), 50
Orange County Sheriff's Office, 58
Orange County Weekly, 50, 51
Orange County, California, 43, 47, 50
Orange County, North Carolina, 267
Orange County, Vermont, *351*
Orangeburg County, South Carolina, 299
Ordway, Colorado, 61
Oregon, 287, 291
Oregon Attorney General, 288
Oregon Firearms Federation, 292
Oregon State Police, 287
Oregon State Trooper, 287
Oregonian, The, 291, 292
Orendorff, Judge Matt, 281
Orlando, Florida, 294
Ortega Melendres, Manuel de Jesus, 19
Osborne, Judge Roxanne, 289
Osteen, Judge William, Jr., 259
Ouachita Parish Sheriff's Office, 152
Owens, Casey, **93**
Owens, Sheriff Jack, 316
Owens, Sheriff Johnie, *366*
Owsley County, Kentucky, 138
Oxford County, Maine, 196

Packenham, Gen. Edward, 177
Padgett, District Attorney Louis H., 148

Padgett, District Attorney Louis H., Jr., 147
Padila, Jose, 334
Page County, Virginia, *374*
Page, Tom, 76
Palm Beach County, Florida, 77
Palmer, Sheriff Glenn, 297
Pamerleau, Sheriff Susan, 338
Pan, California State Sen. Richard, 40
Panama City, Florida, 6
Panola County, Texas, *358*
Panola County, Texas, Treasurer's Office, *358*
ParaTech, 1768
Parish Oilfield Services LLC, 175
Park, Clift, **93**
Parker, Gary, 346
Parker, Glenda, 272
Parker, Sheriff James C. "Humpy", 346
Parker, Sheriff Sam, 310
Parker, Thomas, 49
Parkland, Florida, 66
Parrish, Floyd, xii
Pasadena Independent School District, 340
Pascagoula, Mississippi, 213
Pasco County Sheriff's Office, 78
Pasco County, Florida, 70, 79
Passaic County, New Jersey, 245
Patton, Gen. George, **108**
Pawlowski, Mayor Ed, 305
Paxton, Ken, xii
Payne, Sheriff George, 212
Peace Officer Standards and Training (POST), xii, 210
Pennington, Judee, *393*
Pennsylvania, 43, 279, 301, 305
Pensacola Naval Air Station, 71
Pentagon, the, 350
Penzone, Paul, 22
Pereira, A.B., 184
Perez, Cristobal, 339
Perkins, Cynthia, 188
Perkins, Dennis, 188, 190
Perrodin, Assistant District Attorney Janet, 171
Perry County, Missouri, 221
Perry Township, Ohio, 275
Perry, Georgia, **92**
Perry, Gov. Rick, 345
Perry, Ohio, Township Police Department, 275
Peter, Laurence J., 352
Peterson, Associate Magistrate Judge Linda, **98**
Peterson, Scot, 67
Peterson, Sheriff Winston, **98**
Peterson, Virgil, **108**
Pettway, Sheriff Mark, 1
Pfeifer, John, 146
Phelan, Robert, 239
Philadelphia, Mississippi, 144
Philadelphia, Pennsylvania, 209, 301, 374,
Phillips, Sheriff Chaney, 153
Phoenix E, 14
Phoenix New Times, 16, 18, 20
Pickering, Stacey, 215
Piedra, Margarito, 332
Pierce County, Washington, *377*
Pierce, Julia, 263
Pierce, Julian, 262
Pignatalli, State Rep. William "Smitty", 199
Pike County, Ohio, 275
Pima County Sheriff's Office, 23, 28
Pima County, Arizona, 23
Pima County, Arizona Sheriff's Auxiliary Volunteers (SAV), 24

Pinedale, Wyoming, *391, 393*
Pinellas County Sheriff's Office, 71, 80
Pinellas County, Florida, v, 70, 79
Piper, Sheriff Duane, 84
Pitts, Sheriff LaVelle, 71, 74
Pittsburgh Steelers, 248
Pittsburgh, Pennsylvania, 279
Pittsfield, Massachusetts, 199
Piute County, Utah, *361*
Plaquemines Parish, 176
Plaquemines Parish Sheriff's Office, 157
Plaquemines Parish, Louisiana, 157, 159
Plazio, Nicholas, 197
Plummer, Sheriff Henry, x
Poe, Donald, *376*
Pointer, Cassie, 343
Poissot, O.C. "Coonie", 144
Police Officer Standards and Training (P.O.S.T.)., 4
Police Officer Standards and Training (POST), xiii, 85, 89, 210
Police Policy Committee, BPSST, 293
Policing for Profit, 242, 345
Polk County Sheriff's Office, 75
Polk County, Florida, 75, 308
Pontchartrain Cadillac, 184
Portland, Oregon, 297
Post-Intelligencer, *380*
Potter County jail, 347
Potter County, Texas, 347
Powell, Sheriff Mickey, 4
Prairieville, Louisiana, 337
Premier Management Enterprise, 337
Presgraves, Sheriff Daniel, *374*
Presidio County, Texas, 348

Price, State District Judge O.E., 147, 149
Priest, William Jeffrey, 213
Prior Lake Police Department, 210
Prison Law Center, *371*
Prison Legal News, v, 328
Privett, Thomas, 35
Pro, Mark, 84
ProPublica, 192, 345
Provenzano, Sheriff Frank J., 245
Provident Capital, **97**
Prue, Sheriff Sheila, *367*
Puana, Gerald, **xvi**
Public Employees Retirement System, Ohio, 276
Pulaski County, Ark., 35
Pulaski County, Arkansas, 35
Pulaski County, Kentucky, 136
Pulitzer Prize, 145
Pusser, Pauline, 323
Pusser, Sheriff Buford, 321, 323
Putnam County, Tennessee, 328

Quigley, John, x
Quimby Inn, **x**

Racketeer Influenced and Corrupt Organizations (RICO), 24
Racketeer Influenced and Corrupt Organizations (RICO) Act, 280
Radmanovich, Steven, 241
Radtke, Pima County Chief Deputy Christopher, 24, 29
Ramirez, Michael, 239
Ramirez, Sheriff Romero R., 355
Ramsey, Sheriff D.C., 325
Ramsey, Taylor, 325
Rand, Sheriff Steven, 207
Randall County, Texas, 343
Randall, Willie, Jr., 314

Rankine, FBI agent James, 77
Raritan, NJ, Township Police Department, 245
Rashid, Jamal "Mally Mall", 237
Rather, Dan, *392*
Rawson, Lyle, **113**
Ray, Ned, xi
Rayam, Jernell, 195
Rayville, Louisiana, 143
Read, District Attorney Richard, **86**
Reader, Sheriff Charles, 275
Reagan, Ronald, 37
Reardon, Sheriff Charles, 201
Reason.com, 40
Reece, Florence, 132
Reece, Sam, 132
Reed, Kenneth, 341
Reed, Tyrone, 80
Reeves County, Texas, 345
Rehnquist, US Supreme Court Chief Justice William, 9
Reid, Sheriff George, 308
Reno County jail annex, 123
Reno County, Kansas, 123
Reno, Nevada, 307, 325
Republican Central Committee, Delaware County, Ohio, 275
Republican Party, Massachusetts, 201
Reserve Deputy program, Oklahoma County, 289
Reyes, Amy, 333
Reyes, Bobby Lee, 333
Reynolds, Frank, v
Reynolds, John, 337
Reynolds, Karey, 228
Reynolds, Roy, 130
Reynolds, Sheriff Don, 311
Reynolds, Sheriff Frank, **100**
Reynosa, Mexico, 332
Rhode Island, ix, 206, 348

Rhoden family, 275
Rhoden, Christopher, Jr., 275
Rhoden, Christopher, Sr., 275
Rhoden, Clarence "Frankie", 276
Rhoden, Dana, 275
Rhoden, Gary, 276
Rhoden, Kenneth, 276Rhodes, Assistant. U.S. Attorney. Lizabeth, 51
Rhodes, Regina Lynn, 213
Richardson County, Nebraska, 231
Richardson, Chad, 331
Richardson, District Attorney John, 187
Richardson, Sheriff Todd, *362*
Richey, Mr. and Mrs. W.H., 147
Richland County Sheriff's Office, 3312
Richland County, South Carolina, 312
Richmond County, Georgia, **86**
Richmond County, Virginia, *375*
Richmond Police Department, 352
Richmond, Texas, 352
Richmond, U.S. Rep. Cedric, 168
Richmond, Virginia, *375* 307, 325
Rigal, John, Jr., 395
Rigden, Shane, 342
Rinehart, Sheriff Charles, 215
Rinicker, Sheriff Dale, 154, 157, *158*
Rio Arriba County, New Mexico, 250
Rio Grande, 331, 350
Rio Grande basin, 350
Rio Grande City, Texas, 333
Rio Grande Valey, 311
Risinger, Assistant U.S. Attorney Katy, 327

River Ridge, Louisiana, 165
Rivera, Richard, 233
Rivero, Sheriff Frank, 51, 55
Riverside County, California, 51, 53
Rizzolo, Rick, 43
Roach, Sheriff Terry, **88**
Roane County, Tennessee, 322
Roane County, West Virginia, *385*
Roanoke, Virginia, *374*
Roberts County, South Dakota, 310
Roberts, Duncan, *357*
Robeson County Sheriff's Department, 24
Robeson County, North Carolina, 262—268
Robicheaux, Marcus, 173
Robinson, Pulaski County, Ark. Sheriff, 37
Rochford, Sheriff Edward V., 245
Rock Island County Sheriff's Office, **112**
Rock Island County, Illinois, **112**
Rock Springs, Wyoming, *391*
Rock, Vermont State Auditor Randy, *367*
Rockdale County, Georgia, **86**
Rockefeller Commission, *370*
Rodden, Sheriff Danny, 117
Roddey, Allegheny County Chief Executive Jim, 303
Rodella, Sheriff Tommy, 250
Rodella, Thomas, 250
Rodgers, Jimmy, 115
Rodriguez, Manny, 348
Rodriguez, Rumaldo, 335
Roemer, William F., 114
Rogers, Sheriff Brad, vi
Rogers, Sheriff James W., 308
Rolling Stone, 23
Romanek, Philip, 302

Romanowski, Erika, 304
Rooks County Fairgrounds, 124
Rooks County, Kansas, 124
Roosevelt, Gov. Franklin D., 255
Rosa, Mike, *391*
Rosen, Alan, 342
Roston, Jacquar, 241
Rotter, Craig, **92**
Roundtree, Sheriff Richard, **86**
Rovenstine, Sheriff Aaron, 120
Rowland, Sheriff Craig, **101**
Rozands, Mae, 182
Rozands, Sheriff Charlton P., 182
Ruffin, Tobe, 272
Russell, George "Willie", 284
Russell, Joe, II, 326
Russell, Sheriff Joe, 283
Russell, Superior Court Judge Richard B., III, **93**
Russian Mission, Alaska, xiv
Ruston High School, *395*
Ruston, Louisiana, *395*
Rutherford County, Tennessee, 326
Rutiaga, Ramiro, 343
Ryals, Faulkner County, Ark. Sheriff Tim, 34
Ryan, House Speaker Paul, 23
Ryland, Earvin, *379*

Saadi Haberdashery, 184
Saadi, George, 184
Sacramento Bee, 52
Sacramento County Board of Supervisors, 52
Sacramento County, California, v, 51
Sacramento, California, 39
Sain, Sheriff Frank, **107**
Sain, Sheriff Frank G., **108**
Salazar, Sheriff Javier, 338

Salem County, New Jersey, 246
Sales, Loyd, 287
Saline County, Ark., 35
Saline County, Missouri, 224
Sallet, Special Agent in Charge Jeffrey, vi
Salt Lake City, Utah, *392*
Saluda County, South Carolina, 313
Sam's Club, 31
San Antonio del Bravo, Mexico, 348
San Antonio, Texas, 186, *356*
San Clemente, California, 232
San Francisco, 322
San Francisco Chronicle, 39
San Francisco County, California, 51
San Francisco, California, 207, *322, 377*
San Jacinto County, Texas, 346
San Joaquin County, California, 41, 51, 53
San Juan County, Utah, *361*
San Quentin Prison, x
San Quentin, California, x
Sanders, Bill, Sr., 286
Sanders, Scott, 47
Sanders, Sheriff Max, 5
Sanders, Will, **87**
Sandman, Roy, 248
Sandoval, Sheriff Vidal, 248
Sands, Maricopa County Sheriff Chief Brian, 19
Sandy Creek, North Carolina, 259
Sandy Hook Elementary School, xv, 299
Santa Clara County, California, 39, 51, 53
Saratoga County Deputy Sheriff's Police Benevolent Association, 256
Saratoga County Sheriff's Office, 256
Saratoga County, New York, 255

Sargeant, Mike, 228
Sarpy County Sheriff's Department, 233
Sarpy County, Nebraska, 233
Saudino, Sheriff Michael, 244
Saville, James, 17
Savoy, Gerald "Bubba", 168, 169
Scalzitti, Richard, **114**
Schafer, Alan, 308
Schaffer, Sheriff Gary, 246
Schmeltz, Jay M., 281
Schmerber, Sheriff Tom, 351
Schoonover, Andy, *386*
Schroeder, U.S. District Judge Thomas, 258
Schrunk, Sheriff Terry, 297
Schuler, Marsha, 187
Schuster, Simon, 207
Scott County, Tennessee, 321
Scott, Chad, 190
Scott, Florida Gov. Rick, xii, 67
Scott, Interim Sheriff John L., 55
Scott, Roger, xiii
Scott, Sheriff Mildred S., 245
Scott, U.S. District Judge Nauman, 147
Screven County, Georgia, **95**
Seabury investigations, 255
Seabury, Judge Samuel, 255
Seagal, Steven, 13, 163, 247, 350
Seagraves, Maricopa County Sgt. Kim, 20
Seattle Post-Intelligencer, 380
Sedgwick County, Colorado, 60
Sedgwick County, Kansas, 125, 127
Sedillo, Dan, 248
Seibert, Kristan, 214
Sellers, Derrick, 173
Sellers, Lance, 70
Sellersburg, Indiana, 117

Senanayake, Janine, 275
Seneca County, New York, 256
Sessions, Attorney General Jeff, 23
Sessions, US Senator Jeff, 10
Seven Days Blog, 365, 366
Sewall, Art, 232
Seward County, Nebraska, 232
Seymour, Thomas, 286
Shamrock Motel, 147
Sharkey County, Mississippi, 219
Sharp, Sheriff Mike, 222
Shawnee County, Kansas, 127
Sheahan, Sheriff Michael F., **111**
Shelby County, Tennessee, 327
Shelley, Danny, 137
Shelley, Judge Vincent, 323
Shelley, Margaret, 323
Sheridan, Maricopa County Chief Deputy Jerry, 19, 20
Sheriff's Education and Training Standards Commission, North Carolina, 260
Sheriff's Posse Association, 15
Sheriffs' Association of Texas, 348
Sheriffs' Association, South Carolina, 307
Sheriffs' Pension and Relief Fund, Louisiana, 160
Sherman, Texas, 285, 287
Sherry, Judge Vincent, 212
Sherry, Margaret, 212
Shield Land, 153
Shipley, Howard, 124
Shoob, U.S. District Judge Marvin, **997**
Shoupe, Oddie, v
Shoupe, Sheriff Oddie, 328
Showtime, 189
Shreveport police, 161
Shreveport Times, The, 185, 187, *397*
Shreveport, Louisiana, 147, 161, 187, 346
Shumate, Sheriff Mike, 336
Sicily Island, Louisiana, 143
Siembra, North Carolina, 260
Sigman, Sheriff James, 223
Sikh, 244
Simmons, Jaquaree, 342
Simmons, Kevin, 154
Simpson, Kevin, 309
Simpson, O.J., 67
Sims, Sheriff Phil, 1
Sims, Thetis "Scoop", **113**
Sisolak, Gov. Steve, 235
Skilling, Jeffrey, 46
Skosnik, Dennis, 303
Skrah, Sheriff Frank, 295
Slidell Work Release Center, 16
Smith County, Texas, *345–358*
Smith, Cara, 115
Smith, Dawn, 121
Smith, Federal Judge Laurie, 234
Smith, Gerald, 247
Smith, Gulfport, Mississippi, Police Chief Larkin, 212
Smith, H. Allen, 333
Smith, Howard K., 142
Smith, Ken, 242
Smith, Mark, 72
Smith, Nicole, 73
Smith, Randy, 166
Smith, Robert, 124
Smith, Sheriff Bill, **96**
Smith, Sheriff Billy Wayne, 321
Smith, Sheriff J.B., *358*
Smith, Sheriff Laurie, 51
Smith, Sheriff Nick, 4
Smith, Sheriff Rob, **96**
Smith, Sheriff Tyrone, 2

Smith, Undersheriff Brian, 244
Smith, Valerie, 126
SNAP, 338
Sniff, Sheriff Stan, 53
Snow, U.S. District Judge G. Murray, 18
Snyder, Lorraine, 372
Snyder, Sheriff William, 69
Snyder, Undersheriff Travis, 295
Socorro County, New Mexico, 247
Solis, Nazario, III, 333
Somerset County, New Jersey, 245
Songe, Elmore, 182
Sorrento, Louisiana, 189
Soto, Mark, 120
South Carolina, vii, 189, 262, 269, 307—316
South Carolina Criminal Justice Academy, 308
South Carolina Federal Credit Union, 308
South Carolina State Law Enforcement Division (SLED), 319
South Dakota, 319
South Dakota Law Enforcement Standards and Training Commission, 319
Southern California, University of, 165
Southern Center for Human Rights, 9
Southern Methodist University, 185
Southern Mississippi, University of, 214
Southern Poverty Law Center, xviii, 298
Southwestern Legal Foundation, 185
Spalding County Board of Commissioners, **87**
Spalding County Sheriff Department, **87**
Spalding County Sheriff's Department, **87**
Spalding County, Georgia, **87**
Spanish Harlem, *392*
Sparks, Michael, *384*
Sparks, Sheriff Kelly, *363*
Spartanburg County, South Carolina, 315
Spartanburg Herald-Journal, 315
Spartanburg, South Carolina, 316
Special Emergency Response Team, 339
Special Investigations Unit, **108**
Spector, Nicole Audrey, v, 328
Spencer Police Department, *385*
Spencer, Arthur Leonard, 144
Spencer, Sheriff Dean, 135
Spencer, West Virginia, *385*
Sperling, U.S. Attorney Sheldon J., 288
Spicuzzo, Sheriff Joseph C., 243
Sprinkle, George, 267
Sprouse, Robert, 309
St. Bernard Parish, Louisiana, 174, 177
St. Francis Medical Center, 153
St. Helena Parish Sheriff's Office, 154
St. Helena Parish, Louisiana, 153 St. James Parish, Louisiana, xiii
St. Landry Parish, Louisiana, 141
St. Louis County, Missouri, 40
St. Martinville Police Department, 171
St. Petersburg Times, 76
St. Tammany Parish, Louisiana, 166
St. Tammany Workforce Solutions, 167
Stamp, U.S. District Court Judge Frederick, *385*
Stanford Stadium, 54

Stanford, Ian, 145
Stanislaus County, California, 34
Stark, Sheriff James, *392*
Starr County, Texas, 331, 335, 348
State Bureau of Investigations, North Carolina, 265
State Corporation Commission, 248
State Ethics Commission, Massachusetts, 200
State Law Enforcement Division (SLED), 305
State Line Mob, 310
Staten, Pima County Deputy Terry, 25
Staubach, Roger, 71
Stebbins, Alaska, xiv
Stephens, Sheriff Jack, 174, 177
Sterling, Virginia, *369*
Sterner, Brian, 65
Steubenville Big Red football team, 279
Steubenville High School, 279
Steven Seagal, Lawman, 13, 163
Stevens, George, 348
Stewart, Martha, 304
Stinson, Buck, x
Stockton, California, 53
Stolze, Karl Walter, 213
Stone, Kevin, 263
Stone, Sheriff Hubert, 263, 265
Stone, Wilson, 135
Stonecipher, Elliott, 187
Storey County, Nevada, 235
Stovall, Kansas Attorney General Carla, 127
Strada, Sheriff Michael, 246
Strain, Sheriff Jack, 166
Strange, Alabama Attorney General Luther, 10
Strassheim, Sheriff Chris, **105**

Strickland, Charles Thomas, 265
Strickland, Sheriff Andy, 310
Strollo, Lenine "Lenny", 279
Strommen, Luke, 227
Strong, Sheriff Herman, 268
Sublette County, Wyoming, *391*
Suiter, Sean, 196
Sulfridge, Adam, 129, 130
Sullivan, Shaun, 53
Sullivan, Sheriff Patrick, 59
Sumpter County, Alabama, 10, 11
Sunlaw Energy Corp., 53
Superdome Commission, 166
Superior Court, North Carolina, 268
Sussex County, Delaware, 63
Sussex County, New Jersey, 246
Swaggart, Jimmy, 142
Swank, Hilary, 231
Swanson Services Corp., 31
SWAT, 188, 268
Sweeney, James, 243
Sweetwater County, Wyoming, *392*
Swindler, Samantha, 129, 130
Swisher County jail, 344
Swisher County Sheriff's Department, 343
Swisher County, Texas, 342, 3443
Switzer, Barry, 352
Sycamore, Georgia, **92**
Syracuse University, 262
Systems Analysts, 337
Szarmach, William, 119

Tacoma Police Department, *376*
Tacoma, Washington, *376*
Taffaro, Craig, Sr., 175
Taffaro, Sheriff Craig, 165
Taffaro, St. Bernard Parish President Craig, Jr., 175

Tallahatchie Bridge, 216
Tallahatchie County, Mississippi, 216
Tammany Hall, 255
Tan Nguyen, 242
Tanaka, Undersheriff Paul, 50, 52, 55, 59
Tangipahoa Parish Sheriff's Office, 190
Tangipahoa Parish, Louisiana, xiii, 190
Tanksley, Georgia State Sen. Charlie, **97**
Tanner, Steven, **88**
Tapper, Jake, 67
Tardo, Sheriff Cyrus "Bobby", 152
Tarrant County Sheriff's Office, *359*
Tarrant County, Texas, v, *359*
Tarver, U.S. Attorney Edward, **91**
Tate, Sheriff Thomas, xx, 8
Taylor, Elizabeth, 348
Taylor, Marcus, 195
Taylor, Roger Hugh, 265
Taylor, State Sen. Lena, *387*
Tea Party, xii, 63
Teel, Ryan Michael, 213
Telb, Sheriff James, 281
Telfair County, Georgia, **90**
Tempest, Rone, *392*
Tennessee, 129, 133, 211, 321, 328
Tennessee Highway Patrol, 328
Tennessee Sheriffs' Association, 323, 328
Terrebonne Parish Sheriff's Office, 183
Terrebonne Parish, Louisiana, 180, 183
Terrell, Renea, 326
Terry, Jevon, *389*
Texarkana, Texas, 146, 148

Texas, v, xxiv, 31, 81, 146, 184, 190, 211, 223, 247, 261, 262, 285, 323, 331—359, 97
Texas Commission on Jail Standards, 353
Texas Commission on Law Enforcement (TCOLE), xii
Texas County, Missouri, 223
Texas Jail Project, the, *359*
Texas Monthly, 348
Texas Rangers, *357*, *359*
Than, Michael, 61
The Arizona Daily Star, 24
The Clinton Chronicles, 36
The Concordia Sentinel, 144
The Kansas Commission on Peace Officers' Standards and Training (CPOST), 127
The Last Hayride, 142
The Los Angeles Times, 357
The New York Times, 23, 383
The Peter Principle, 352
The Wall Street Journal, 36
The Washington Post, 281
Theiss, Nate, 3328
Theobald, Greg, 241
Thibodaux, Louisiana, Civic Center, 152
Thomas, Andrew, 16
Thomas, David, 80
Thomas, Sheriff Pat, 233
Thomas, Sheriff Paul, 326
Thomas, Terrill, *388*
Thomas, Walter Michael, Jr., 72
Thomason, Brandi Kauilani, 261
Thompson, Daquentin, 171
Thompson, Georgia State Sen. Steve, **97**
Thompson, Lt. Greg, 49
Thompson, Morgan Lee, 213

Thompson, Sheriff Richard Dee, 348
Thornsbury, Circuit Court Judge Michael, *384*
Thrash, U.S. District Judge Thomas, 83
Three Rivers Wildlife Management Area, 186
Thurmond, Strom, Jr., 313
Tidwell, Mitchell, 154
Tillman, Sheriff Jack, 7
Tingle, Allen, 167
Tippah County, Mississippi, 217
Tisdale, Justin, 75
Toler, Dallas, *384*
Toman, Sheriff John, **106**
Tomaszewski, Jennifer, 223
Toms River, NJ, Township Police Department, 245
Toney, Sheriff Royce, 150
Tony, Sheriff Gregory, 67
Torrance County, New Mexico, 250
Torres, Janet, *372*
Torres, Ramon, 189
Townsend, Santana Monshea, 216
Traffic Records Electronic Data System, 48
Traficant, U.S. Rep. James, 280
Trapp, Sheriff J.W., 287
Traubel, Steve, **103**
Travis County, Texas, 352
Traynor, U.S. District Judge Daniel, 273
Tremaine, Todd, 130
Treutlen County, Georgia, **88**
Treviño, Armando, 338
Treviño, Jonathan, 334
Trevino, Luis Rodriguez, 281
Treviño, Sheriff Guadalupe "Lupe", 334

Trimble, Kentucky Commonwealth Attorney Allen, 131
Tripp, Todd Eric, 188
Trosclair, Howard, 171
Trotter, Sheriff Dennis, 321
Troyer, Ed, *377*
True West magazine, *391*
Truman, President Harry, 222
Trump, Donald, vi, 13
Trump, President Donald, 10, 23, 99, 202, 235, 270, 281, 326, 352
Tucker, Keith, 239
Tucson, Arizona, 23
Tulane University, vi
Tulia, Texas, 343
Tullier, John, Jr., 152
Tulsa, Oklahoma, 148, 290
Tunnell, Gay, 71
Turman, Sheriff Blake, 4
Turner County, Georgia, **92**
Turner, Tyler, **94**
Twitter, *387*
U.S. Attorney's Office for the Western District of Arkansas, 37
U.S. Constitution, vi, xi, 63, 181, 298
U.S. Court of Appeals, **99**
U.S. Court of Appeals for the Ninth Circuit, 16
U.S. Court, Eastern District of North Carolina, 267
U.S. Department of Justice, 18, 56, 245, 293
U.S. District Court for the Northern District of Alabama, 11
U.S. District Court, Northern District of Indiana, 119
U.S. Drug Enforcement Agency, 161
U.S. Justice Department, 17, 20, 168
U.S. Marshal's Service, 218
U.S. Representative, 279, 352

U.S. Supreme court, xx, 9
Uinta County Sheriff's Department, *393*
Uinta County, Wyoming, *393*
Umpqua Community College, 299
Uncle Sam's Restaurant, 17
Underwood, Sheriff Alex "Big A", 309—313
Underwood, Sheriff Jim, 4
Union County, South Carolina, 313
United States Postal Service, 215
University of Chicago, **107**
University of New Mexico, vii
University of Oklahoma, 352
University of Texas Pan American, 331
Unsolved Mysteries, *355*
Upshaw, Sheriff Leroy, 2
Urquhart, Sheriff John, *380, 381*
USA Today Network, 79
Utah, *361*
Utah Attorney General's Office, *361*
Utah County jail, *363*

Valdez, Sheriff Lupe, 348
Vale, Andrew W., 256
Valley County, Montana, 227
Van Tatenhove U.S. District Judge Gregory, 134
Vance, U.S. District Judge Sarah, 159
Vandenham, Derek, 313
Vanderveer, John, 326
Vasquez, Alberto, 302
Vaughan, Robert, 115
Vaught, James A., *374*
Velky, David, *355*
Venus, D.J., III, 212

Vermont, *355*
Vidalia, Louisiana, 142, 147
video poker, 162, 267, 325
Vietnam, 71, 327
Villanueva, Alex, vi
Villanueva, Sheriff Alejandro, 56, 57
Ville Platte Police Department, 177
Ville Platte, Louisiana, 177
Vincent, Edward, 294
Vincent, Wardie, Jr., 270
Vineland, NJ, Police Department, 246
Virginia, 133, 211, 217, 269, 345, 350, 369, 371, 373
Virginia Beach, Virginia, *376*
Virginia City, Montana, x
Virginia Law Review, 40
Virginian-Pilot, *372*
Volstead Act, **106**
Volusia County, Florida, 74
Volz, U.S. Attorney John, 152

Waco, Texas, 336
Wade, Neal, 217
Wade, Sheriff Mike, *375*
Waggonner, Sheriff Willie, 147
Waggonner, U.S. Rep. Joe, 147
Wagner, Angela, 276
Wagner, Billy, 276
Wagner, David, 239
Wagner, George, 276
Wagner, Jake, 276
Wagner, Janet, 239
Wagon Mound, New Mexico, 249
Wagoner County, Oklahoma, 285
Wainwright, Chris, 193
Wake County Detention Center, 271
Wake County Sheriff's Department, 259

Wake County, North Carolina, 259, 271
Walker County, Georgia, **85**
Walker Police Department, 188
Walker, Louisiana, 188
Walker, Scott, 75
Walking Tall, 322
Wall, Kathleen, *3453*
Wallace, Faulkner County, Ark. deputy Keenan, 34
Wallace, Torrell, 286
Walls, Sheriff Scott, 1
Walmart, 31
Walsh, Elmer Michael, **107**
Walter Cronkite School of Journalism and Mass Communication, 16
Walter, U.S. District Judge Donald E., 170
Walters, Ivadella, 309
Walton County, Florida, 75
Wamhoff, Coroner Janice, **113**
Ward County jail, 274
Ward County, North Dakota, 274
Ward, Maurice, 195
Ware, Sheriff Korey J., 319
Warren County, Mississippi, 217, *369, 376*
Warren County, New Jersey, 245
Warren County, New York, 255
Warren County, Virginia, *376*
Warren, Sgt. James, 68
Warsaw, Indiana, 120
Wasden, Idaho Attorney Gen. Lawrence, **102**
Washington, *361*
Washington County District Attorney's Office, 295
Washington County Sheriff's Office, 295
Washington County, Oregon, 289, 290
Washington County, Vermont, *365, 367*
Washington Post, 241
Washington Post, The, 281, 350, 371, 376
Washington, D.C., 14, 207, 209, 362, 369
Watonwan County, Minnesota, 209
Waybourn, Bill, v
Waybourn, Sheriff Bill, *359*
Wayne County Sheriff's Office, 206
Wayne County, Michigan, 207
WBZ-TV, 201
Webb County, Texas, 345
Webb, Ray, 294
Webre, Sheriff Bobby, 189
Webster County, Mississippi, 216
Wehrly, Sheriff Sharon, 236
Welker, Special Agent in Charge David, 158
Wellpath, LLC, *370*
Wells County, North Dakota, 273
Wells, James B., 148
Wells, Sheriff Burnie, 343, 344
Wells, Sheriff Howard, 313
Wentworth, Gov. John, x
West Central Ohio Crime Task Force (WCOCTF), 277
West New York, New Jersey, 233
West Palm Beach, Florida, 77
West Virginia, 345, 383, 386
West Virginia Senate, *386*
West, Sheriff Arvin, 349, 351
Westbrook, Wesley, **106**
Wester, Zachary, 69
Westmoreland County, Pennsylvania, 303, 304
Westwego, Louisiana, 184
Wethington, Sheriff Warren, 121

Wever, Dennis, 234
Wever, Nancy, 234
Wheeler, Tommy, **99**
Whetsel, Sheriff John, 288
Which Side Are You On, 132
Whidden, Sheriff Steve, 79
Whidden, Steve, v
Whiddon, Deidra, **94**
Whipple, Sheriff Bryan, 125
White County, Tennessee, v, 322, 328
White House, 36, 51
White House, the, *388*
White, Carl Douglas "Towhead", 323
White, Kenneth, 137
White, Lawson, 323
White, Miles, 76
White, Sheriff Darren, 224
White, Sheriff Heath, 250
White, Victor, III, 167, 171
White, Victor, Jr., 169, 171
Whiteman, Alexander, 125
Whiting, Sheriff Benjamin, x
Whitley County Sheriff's Department, 130
Whitley County, Kentucky, 129
Whitlock, Craig, 351
Whitmer, Gov. Gretchen, xviii, 205
Whitney, Maricopa Capt. Steve, 20
Whitten, Donald, *385*
Wicca, *356*
Wicks, Jared, 239
Wiggins, Jim, **88**
Wilcox County Jail, **91**
Wilcox County, Georgia, **91**
Wilcox, Robert, *361*
Wiley, Sheriff Roy, **92**
Wilkins, Ira Lee, 290
Wilkins, Sheriff Brindell, 271

Willets, Jeffrey, 74
Willets, Kathy, 74
Williams, Chonda Shalett, 341
Williams, Chris, 69
Williams, Jessie Lee, Jr., 213
Williams, Mat, 75
Williams, Sheriff Bo, *385*
Williams, Sheriff Clarence, Jr., *375*
Williams, Sheriff James H., 309
Williams, Sheriff Jewell, 302
Williams, Sheriff Larry, 308
Williams, Stephanie, 295
Williams, Ted, 71
Williams, Thomas Lee "Ty", 314
Williamsburg County, South Carolina, 314
Williamsburg, Kentucky, 130
Williamson, Ian, 337
Williamson, Jimmie, **90**
Williamson, West Virginia, *384*
Williston, North Dakota, 274
Willoughby, Ohio, 278
Wills, Chill, 348
Wills, Preston Thomas, 213
Wilmington, Delaware, 209
Wilson, Sheriff Gary, 61
Wilson, Sheriff Gilbert, 246
Wilson, Sheriff Steve, **85**
Windham County, Vermont, *367*
Windsor County, Vermont, *365*
Winham, Steve, *397*
Winn Parish, Louisiana, 160, 161
Winnsboro, Louisiana, 143
Winona Lake, Indiana, 120
Wintrow, State Rep. Melissa, **101**
Wintters, Charles Everett, *358*
Wisconsin, 345, *387*
Wisner, Louisiana, 143
Wolfe County, Kentucky, 135
Wolfe, Sheriff Brian, 295

Wolfson, District Attorney Steve, 238
Womack, Sheriff Bobby, **95**
Wood, Buck, *354*
Woodland, Jerry, 215
Woods, Ben, 228
Woods, Joseph, **108**
Woods, Lester L., 315
Woods, Rosemary, **108**
Wooton, Sheriff Ernest, 157
World's Deadliest Prosecutor, 262
Worth County High School, **94**
Worth County, Georgia, **94**
Wright, Adam, 340
Wright, Sheriff Chuck, 315
WWL-TV, 176
Wyly, Jack "Captain Jack", 155, *156*
Wyoming, 345, 391, 393
Wyoming State Police, *374*
Wyoming State Supreme Court, *373*

Yakish, Bryce, 122
Yale Law Journal, 80
Yale Law School, 47
Yankton, South Dakota, 224
Yant, Bryan, 240
Yates, Donald Lee, 148, 149
Yeghiazarian, Raymond, 239
Yerby, Sheriff Byron, 5
Yonkin, Dan, 228
York County, Maine, 193
Youngblood, Donny, vi
Youngblood, Sheriff Donny, 51
Youngstown, Ohio, 279, 280

Zaitz, Les, 295
Zapata County, Texas, 331, 335, 348
Zinke, Kimberly, 115
Zoldan, Bruce, 280

Zurik, Lee, 158
Zurlo, Sheriff Michael H., 256

Author's Notes

Prologue

1. Spector, Nicole Audrey, "The 10 Worst Sheriffs in America," *Prison Legal News*, June 2021.
2. Greenblatt, Alan, "Why There Are So Many Bad Sheriffs," *Governing Magazine*, March 22, 2018.
3. Zoorob, Michael, "There's (Rarely) a New Sheriff in Town: The Incumbency Advantage for County Sheriffs," Department of Government, Harvard University, Nov. 12, 2019.
4. Ibid.
5. "300 unique New Orleans moments: Harry Lee first elected as sheriff of Jefferson Parish in 1979," *New Orleans/Baton Rouge Advocate*, Dec. 15, 2017.
6. Selby, Daniele, "New Mexico is the Second State to Ban Qualified Immunity," *Innocence Project*, April 7, 2021.
7. *The National Registry of Exonerations*.
8. Kindy, Kimberly, "Dozens of states have tried to end qualified immunity. Police officers and unions helped beat nearly every bill," *The Washington Post*, Oct. 7, 2021.
9. English, T.J., *Where the Bodies Were Buried*, HarperCollins Publishers, 2015.

Introduction

1. Maginnis, John, *The Last Hayride*, Gris Gris Press, 1984.
2. North Carolina Sheriffs' Association, *History of the Sheriff*, undated,
3. *Sheriff*, Wikipedia, undated,
4. Ibid.
5. *National Sheriff's Association*, Wikipedia, undated,
6. *Sheriffs in the United States*, Wikipedia, undated, Sheriff, Wikipedia, undated,
7. Harte, Julia, "The Army to set our nation free," The Center for Pub-

lic Integrity, April 18, 2016.
8. Schweers, Jeffrey, "Man freed by Sheriff Nick Finch accused of murder," *Tallahassee Democrat*, Sept. 26, 2016.
9. Mancimer, Stephanie, "He was a Board Member of the Oath Keepers. Now He's Holding State-Approved Trainings for Law Enforcement in Texas," *Mother Jones*, Oct. 29,2021.
10. Murphy, Tim, "Montana Bill Would Let Sheriffs Arrest FBI Agents for Arresting People," *Mother Jones*, Feb. 21, 2013.
11. Anthony G. "Tony" Falterman, Assumption Parish Sheriff (ret.), interview, March 2019.
12. Ibid.
13. Ibid.
14. Neiwert, David, "'Constitutional Sheriffs' Want to Seize Dominion Voting Machines," *Daily Kos*, June 25, 2022.
15. Ibid.
16. Ibid.
17. Potok, Mark, Lenz, Ryan, "A radical and growing organization of 'constitutional sheriffs' is promoting defiance of federal laws it doesn't like," the *Intelligence Report*, Southern Poverty Law Center, June 13, 2016.
18. Chemerinsky, Erwin, "Against Sovereign Immunity," Duke Law School, June 8, 2004.
19. Blum, Karen M. "Support your Local Sheriff: Suing Sheriffs Under § 1983," Suffolk University Law School, 2005.
20. Ibid.
21. Ibid.
22. Ibid.
23. Commission on Accreditation for Law Enforcement Agencies (CALEA).

Alabama

1. Sheets, Connor, "Wasted Funds, Destroyed Property: How Sheriffs Undermined their Successors After Losing Reelection," *AL.com*,

ProPublica, June 12, 2019.
2. Sheets, Connor, "How Nine Sheriffs Who Lost Reelection Made Life Harder for Their Successors," *AL.com. ProPublica*, June 12, 2019.
3. Ibid.
4. Sheets, Connor, "The Sheriff Lost Reelection. Then the Spending Spree Began," *AL.com. ProPublica*, June 28, 2019.
5. Sheets, Connor, "Wasted Funds, Destroyed Property: How Sheriffs Undermined their Successors After Losing Reelection," *AL.com*, *ProPublica*, June 12, 2019.
6. Sheets, Connor, "How Nine Sheriffs Who Lost Reelection Made Life Harder for Their Successors," *AL.com. ProPublica*, June 12, 2019.
7. Ibid.
8. Ibid.
9. Ibid.
10. Sheets, Connor, "Etowah sheriff pockets $750k in jail food funds, buys $740k beach house," *AL.com*, March 7, 2018.
11. Strassmann, Mark, "Sheriff defiant amid claims he turned jail into his personal piggy bank," CBS News, March 23, 2018.
12. Ferner, Matt, "Alabama Sheriff Who Pocketed $750,000 From Jail Food Budget Loses GOP Primary," *Politics*, June 6, 2018.
13. Reeves, Jay, "Federal judge arrests sheriff over jail food scandal," Associated Press, January 8, 2009.
14. Whitmire, Kyle, "49 Alabama sheriffs hide jail food funds, flout open records law," AL.com, March 6, 2018 and Nicholson, Lucy, "Alabama sheriffs accused of profiting from jail food funds," Reuters, May 25, 2018.
15. Tron, Gina, "Alabama Sheriff Accused Of Having Sex With Underage Girls in the '90s," *Oxygen.com*, July 17, 2018, and Adl-
16. Tabatabai, Sean, "Alabama Sheriff Accused Of Running Pedophile Ring," *News Punch*, July 19, 2018.
17. Pruitt, Sharon Lynn, "What Happened to Law Enforcement After Walter McMillian's Wrongful Conviction?" Oxygen.com, Dec. 26, 2019.
18. "McMillian v. Monroe County, Alabama," United States Supreme Court, June 2, 1997.
19. Cason, Mike, "Alabama sheriff impeached for corruption, neglect of duty," al.com, July 27, 2016.
20. Ibid.

21. Brackin, John, "Ex-Alabama Sheriff Sued for Sexual Harassment," courthousenews.com, April 12, 2017.
22. "Ex-Sumter County sheriff pleads guilty to criminal charges," WALA-TV, Mobile, Alabama, Nov. 27, 2018.

Alaska

1. Hopkins, Kyle, Demarban, Alex, five-part series in *ProPublica*, October 2018; May, June and July 2019.
2. Hopkins, Kyle, "After the Last Cop Killed Himself, All the Criminals Have to Do Is Hide," *Anchorage Daily News*, October 24, 2019.

Arizona

1. Johnny Behan biography, Wikipedia
2. Peralta, Eyder, "Arizona Sheriff Uses a Tank and Steven Seagal to Arrest Cockfighting Suspect," NPR, March 23, 2011.
3. "OSIA Honors Sheriff Arpaio," Encyclopedia.com, April 1, 2008.
4. "Re-elect Sheriff Joe Arpaio 2012," Encyclopedia.com.
5. "Arpaio's travel agency offers 'affordable' bookings on space flights," azcentral.com.
6. Scott, Eugene, *"Temperatures rise to 145 inside Tent City". Azcentral.com.* July 3, 2011.
7. Shorey, Ananda, "Phoenix is sizzling through what could be the hottest July on record," *signonsandiego.com*, July 25, 2003.
8. "Ninth Circuit Court of Appeals Orders Sheriff Arpaio to Fix Unconstitutional Conditions in Maricopa County Jail," American Civil Liberties Union, October 13, 2010.
9. Santos, Fernanda, "When a Taste for Publicity Bites Back," *The New York Times*, August 1, 2012.
10. Ortega, Tony, "Blowing his Cool," *Phoenix New Times*, May 27, 1999.
11. Collom, Lindsey, Hensley, J.J., "Judge backs county inmates in jail

case," *The Arizona Republic*, May 17, 2010.
12. Wingett, Yvonne, "Joe Arpaio's staff misspent $99.5 million, budget officials say," *The Arizona Republic*, April 13, 2011.
13. Lemons, Stephen, "Joe Arpaio's Watergate: Read MCSO Deputy Chief Frank Munnell's Memo Here," *Phoenix News*, September 16, 2010.
14. Wingett, Yvonne, "Joe Arpaio aide's misconduct allegations investigated by the U.S. Attorney's Office, FBI," October 6, 2010, *azcentral.com*.
15. Lacey v. Maricopa County, 693 F.3d. 896 (9th Cir. 2012) (en banc).
16. "Maricopa County Feud: What happens next?", *The Arizona Republic*, August 15, 2009.
17. Lemons, Stephen, "Andy Thomas Needs a Perp Walk with his Papi, Sheriff Joe Arpaio," *Phoenix New Times*, April 19, 2012.
18. Conder, Chuck, "Arizona sheriff under investigation for alleged abuse of power," CNN, July 10, 2010.
19. Billealid, Jacques, "Restauranteur whose business was raided by sheriff gets $5M," Associated Press, Oct. 20, 2021.
20. Dougherty, John, "The Plot to Assassinate Arpaio," *Phoenix New Times*, August 5, 1999.
21. Bommersbach, Jana, "Will Sheriff Joe Stop at Nothing?", *Phoenix Magazine*, February 2005.
22. Dickerson, John, "A Phony Murder Plot Against Joe Arpaio Winds Up Costing Taxpayers $1.1 million," *Phoenix New Times*, October 28, 2008.
23. Lemons, Stephen, Joe Arpaio's Victim Deborah Braillard: Family Agrees to $3/2 million settlement," *Phoenix New Times*, October 17, 2012.
24. "Ortega Melendres, et al. v. Arpaio, et al," *American Civil Liberties Union*, September 25, 2012.
25. "District Court Judge Grants Over $4 million in Attorney Gees to Civil Rights Groups in Landmark Lawsuit Against Sheriff Joe Arpaio and Maricopa County Sheriff's Office (MCSO), *American Civil Liberties Union*, September 11, 2014.
26. Lemons, Stephen, "Joe Arpaio's Investigating Federal Judge G. Murray Snow, DOJ, Sources Say, and Using a Seattle Scammer to Do It," *Phoenix New Times*, June 4, 2014.
27. "Arpaio immigration case attorney quits, citing ethical conflicts," *Arizona Daily Star*, April 28, 2015.
28. Lemons, Stephen, "Snow Blasts Arpaio's 'Bogus Conspiracy Theory,'" *Phoenix New Times*, May 15, 2015.

29. "Sheriff Joe Arpaio in contempt of federal court, judge rules," *The Arizona Republic*, May 13, 2016.
30. Cassidy, Megan, Former Maricopa County Sheriff Joe Arpaio found guilty of criminal contempt of court," *The Arizona Republic*, July 32, 2017.
31. Atkinson, Paul, "Scandals Plague Controversial Arizona Sheriff," NPR, May 27, 2011.
32. Stern, Ray, "Sheriff Joe Arpaio's Sex-Crime Scandal After Five Years: No One Disciplined, Report Still Unfinished," *Phoenix New Times*, January 17, 2013.
33. De la Paz, Noelle, "What Arpaio Didn't Do This Time: Over 400 Sex Crimes Ignored," *Colorlines.com*, December 8, 2011, reprinted in *Truthout.org*, December 10, 2011.
34. Fenske, Sarah, "How the MCSO Neglected a 14-year-Old Rap Victim, *Phoenix New Times*, May 28, 2009.
35. Gabrielson, Ryan, "Reasonable Doubt: Public pays the price," *East Valley Tribune*, July 23. 3008.
36. Fenske, Sarah, "How the MCSO Neglected a 14-year-Old Rap Victim, *Phoenix New Times*, May 28, 2009.
37. Dana, Joe, "Many MCSO cases solved without arrests," azcentral.com, January 19, 2010.
38. Bernstein, Josh, "Sexual assault victim claims MCSO failed to do its job," KNXV-TV, Phoenix, Arizona, May 21, 2009.
39. "Sheriff Joe Arpaio Unapologetic About Tactics, Illegal Immigrant Crackdowns," ABC News, July 23, 2009.
40. "Goldwater Institute: Arpaio's crime clearance rate a sham," *AzCapitolTies.com*, May 22, 2009.
41. Billeaud, Jacques, "Critics: 'Tough' sheriff botched sex-crime cases," Boston.com, December 4, 2011.
42. Lemons, Stephen, "Rape victim opens up about botched MCSO investigation," *Phoenix New Times*, September 28, 2012.
43. Stern, Ray, "Maricopa County to Pay $3.5 Million for Botched Sheriff's Office Rape Investigation," *Phoenix New Times*, April 9, 2015.
44. "Arpaio's office continues to investigate sex-crime cases," *Casa Grande Dispatch*, October 2, 2012.
45. "Arizona Sheriff Joe Arpaio is officially charged with criminal con-

tempt in racial profiling case," Associated Press, October 25, 2016.
46. Cassidy, Megan, "Former Maricopa County Sheriff Joe Arpaio found guilty of criminal contempt of court," *The Arizona Republic*, July 31, 2017.
47. Porter, Tom, "Trump asked Sessions to stop Joe Arpaio racial profiling investigation: report," *Newsweek*, August 27, 2017.
48. *@realDonaldTrump*, "I am pleased to inform you that I have just granted a full Pardon to 85-year-old American patriot Sheriff Joe Arpaio. He kept Arizona safe!." Tweet, August 25, 2017.
49. Logan, Bryan, "Trump pardons former Arizona sheriff Joe Arpaio," *Business Insider*, August 26, 2017.
50. "Critics: Trump pardon his latest affront against judiciary," *Washington Post*, August 27, 2017.
51. "Arizona Primary Election Results," New York Times, August 29, 2018.
52. Fogey, Quint, "Ex-Sheriff Joe Arpaio files libel suit against NYT," Politico, October 16, 2018.
53. Rozsa, Matthew, "After Being Pardoned by Trump, Joe Arpaio Will Seek Seventh Term as Sheriff," Salon.com, August 26, 2019.
54. Schmidt, Caitlin, "Sheriff official's relative ran department cafes rent-free," *Arizona Daily Star*, November 21, 2015.
55. Ibid.
56. Ibid.
57. Cavazos, Valerie, "FBI investigation into alleged misuse of RICO money by Pima County Sheriff's Department," WGUN-TV, October 11, 2016.
58. Ibid.
59. Duarte, Carmen, "Bradley Gagnepain, chief of staff for Sheriff Nanos, dies," *Arizona Daily Star*, June 20, 2016.
60. "Under FBI Investigation, Pima County Sheriff Chief Gagnepain Takes Own Life," *Arizona Independent News Network*, June 20, 2016.
61. "Nanos Handling of Chief of Staff Death Raising Questions for Pima County Public," *ADI News Services*, June 25, 2016.
62. Ibid.
63. Ibid.
64. Ibid.

65. Cavazos, Valerie, "Indictment released in case of Deputy Chief Chris Radtke," WGUN-TV, October 12, 2016.
66. Cavazos, Valerie, "FBI Indictment: Details released and Sheriff Nanos responds publicly," WGUN-TV, October 13, 2016.
67. Schmidt, Caitlin, "Mark Napier defeats Chris Nanos in race for Pima County Sheriff," *Arizona Daily Star*, November 9, 2016.
68. Foster, Bud, "Nanos retires as Pima County Sheriff," KOLD-TV, December 21, 2016.
69. Cavazos, Valerie, "Former chief deputy pleads guilty in PCSD money laundering case," WGUN-TV, February 10, 2017.
70. Schmidt, Caitlin, "Ex-Pima sheriff's official gets probation, fine in theft case," *Arizona Daily Star*, May 5, 2017.
71. Cavazos, Valerie, "Secret Audio Recordings: New memo surfaces in PC Sheriff's Dept. money laundering case," KGUN-TV, September 1, 2017.
72. Steller, Tim, "Steller: Dissent surges over Pima sheriff's handling of inherited scandal," *Arizona Daily Star*, September 9, 2017.

Arkansas

1. De la Garza, "Sheriff Took Kickbacks for Card Fees, Class says," *Prison Legal News*, April 12, 2013, and "Arkansas Sheriff Took Kickbacks for Card Fees, Class-Action Suit says," May 15, 2013.
2. Adams v. Benton County Sheriff, U.S. District Court Western District, No. 5:13-cv-05074-PKH.
3. Clarke, Matt, "Jails Face Backlash, Class-action Lawsuits Over Debit Card Fees," *Dallas Morning News*, September 15, 2014.
4. 4. Gray, Katti, "Fee-Based Debit Cards for Ex-Inmates 'Unlawful': Lawsuit," *The Crime Report*, June 19, 2017.
5. Gilna, Derek, "Settlements in Arizona DOC, BOP Lawsuits Over Release Debit Card Fees," *Prison Legal News*, March 6, 2018.
6. Ibid.

7. De la Garza, "Sheriff Took Kickbacks for Card Fees, Class says," *Prison Legal News*, April 12, 2013.
8. Salinger, Tobias, "Arkansas sheriff arrested, charged with felony and misdemeanor tampering in probe into jail deputy's hiring," *New York Daily News*, January 19, 2016.
9. Ibid.
10. "Benton County Sheriff Kelley Cradduck arrested," KHBS/KHO-TV News, January 21, 2016.
11. Neal, Tracy, "Former Sheriff Cradduck pleads no contest to misdemeanor," *Arkansas Democrat-Gazette*, April 29, 2016.
12. Brantley, Max, "Convicted ex-Benton County sheriff hired in Carroll County," *Arkansas Times*, September 28, 2017.
13. "Former Benton County Sheriff's Wife Accused of Harassment, Communicating False Alarm," KFSM-TV news, February 8, 2018.
14. Chaitin, Daniel, "Arkansas sheriff's deputy fired after shooting dog," *Washington Examiner*, January 5, 2019.
15. May, Ashley, "Police officer who shot a Chihuahua during a service call loses job, Arkansas sheriff says," *USA Today*, January 7, 2019.
16. Hunter, Gary, "Arkansas Mayor, Sheriff, Wife Jailed for Burglary, Drugs, Sex and More," Prison Legal News, October 15, 2006.
17. "Ex-Lonoke chief sees conviction reversed,' Associated Press, November 5, 2009.
18. Hofheimer, John, "Prosecutor wasn't told Campbell's a free man," The Arkansas Leader, June 1, 2010.
19. Hunter, Gary, "Arkansas Mayor, Sheriff, Wife Jailed for Burglary, Drugs, Sex and More," Prison Legal News, October 15, 2006.
20. Hoagland, Hunter, "Family of Arkansas teen killed by deputy during traffic stop demands justice," KARK-TV, June 23, 2021.
21. "Sheriff of Franklin County, Arkansas, Found Guilty of Assaulting Two Individuals in Custody," news release, U.S. Attorney, Western District of Arkansas, Aug. 9, 2021.
22. "Tommy Franklin Robinson," *Encyclopedia of Arkansas*, undated.
23. Ibid.

24. Ibid.
25. "Tommy F. Robinson," fampeople.com, undated

California

1. Mathews, Joe, "Time to get rid of sheriffs in California," *San Francisco Chronicle*, January 27, 2019; "Sheriffs in all 58 counties have too much power, and do pretty much as they please," *USA Today*, January 28, 2019.
2. Ibid.
3. Ibid.
4. Pishko, Jessica, "Are Sheriffs Necessary?", *The Appeal*, April 24, 2019.
5. Greenhut, Steven, "California Senate Bill 1303 would fix glaring conflict of interest in sheriff-coroner offices," *Orange County Register*, August 4, 2018.
6. Reza, H.G., Hanley, Christine, and Martelle, Scott, "O.C. Sheriff Dogged by Scandals," *Los Angeles Times*, March 28, 2004.
7. Moxley, R. Scott, "Who Shot the Sheriff?", Orange County Weekly, April 14, 2005.
8. Moxley, R. Scott, "Sheriff Loses Battle to End Federal Case," *Orange County Weekly*, October 5, 2007.
9. Lowe, Peggy, Welborn, Larry, "Sheriff Mike Carona indicted on corruption charges," *Orange County Register*, October 30, 2007.
10. Lowe, Peggy, "The career of Sheriff Mike Carona," *Orange County Register*, October 30, 2007.
11. Therolf, Garrett, Pfeifer, Stuart, Hanley Christine, "The mistress, the wife, and the O.C. sheriff," *Los Angeles Times*, December 29, 2007.
12. "Former Orange County Sheriff Carona Sentenced to Federal Prison," United States Department of Justice, April 27, 2009.
13. "Indicted California Sheriff Resigns to Fight Federal Corruption Charges," *Prison Legal News*, July 15, 2008.
14. Hanley, Christine, Pfeifer, Stuart, Goffard, Christopher, "Ex-OC Sheriff Carona guilty on 1 count, cleared on 5," *Los Angeles Times*, January 17, 2009.
15. Hanley, Christine, "Scolding and a stiff sentence for Carona," Los Angeles Times, April 28, 2009.

16. Mentor, Marvin, "Corruption in Orange County, CA sheriff's Department Revealed; Sheriff Resigns, Convicted on Criminal Charges," *Prison Legal News*, February 15, 2009.
17. Lithwick, Dahlia, "You're All Out," Slate.com, May 28, 2015.
18. Balko, Radley, "The jaw-dropping police/prosecutor scandal in Orange County, Calif.," Washington Post, July 13, 2015.
19. "Orange County Judge Blasts Sheriff in Jail Informant Scandal: 'What Is Going On Over There?', The Bagspost.com., December 17, 2016.
20. Frere, Eileen, "OC assistant public defender accuses OC sheriff's department of improperly recording jail calls," KABC-TV, October 3, 2018.
21. Moxley, R. Scott, "New Orange County Sheriff Don Barnes Runs A Toxic Agency," *Orange County Weekly*, June 5, 2019.
22. Rudolf, John, "Los Angeles County Sheriff's Department Hit by Corruption Allegations," *Huffpost*, August 9, 2012.
23. "'New Level' of Scandal with LA Sheriff's Department," *NPR News*, December 22, 2013.
24. Palta, Rina, "LA jail scandal: All 6 Sheriff's Department officials found guilty on all counts," KPCC Radio, July 1, 2014.
25. "Six Current and Former Los Angeles Sheriff's Deputies Sentenced to Federal Prison for Obstructing Federal Civil Rights Investigation," U.S. Attorney's Office, September 23, 2014.
26. Wynter, Kareen, "Paul Tanaka, Former L.A. County Undersheriff, Sentenced to 5 years in Prison for Obstructing FBI Probe," *Los Angeles Times*, June 27, 2016.
27. Melley, Brian, Myers, Amanda Lee, "Ex-LA sheriff pleads guilty to lying during corruption probe," Associated Press, February 10, 2016.
28. "Ex-LA County Sheriff Lee Baca convicted in jail corruption case, Associated Press, CBS-TV, March 15, 2017.
29. Ibid.
30. Stevens, Matt, "Ex-Los Angeles Sheriff Lee Baca Is Sentenced to 3 Years in Prison," *New York Times*, May 12, 2017.
31. "The only 'spectacular failure' is Sheriff Scott Jones forgetting whom he represents," *Sacramento Bee*, March 21, 2018.
32. Wiley, Hannah, Ashton, Adam, "'Literally, our sheriff locked the

doors': Sacramento County grand jury calls for new oversight," Sacramento Bee, July 5, 2019.
33. "County Sheriff Pleads Guilty in Power Plant Scandal," *California Planning & Development Report*, February 1, 2005.
34. "Amid Scandals Surrounding Sheriff Candidates Sniff and Brown, Riverside Deputy Sheriffs Give $300,000 to Lt. Chad Blanco," political ad for Chad Blanco, February 16, 2018.
35. Wyloge, Evan, Kelman, Brett, "Riverside County sheriff's cheating scandal threatens prosecution, challenges investigator's credibility," *The Desert Sun*, May 16, 2018.
36. "First California female sheriff is accused by three former officers of sexual harassment," *The Daily Mail*, June 4, 2018.
37. "Frank Rivero recall, Lake County, California (2013)," *Ballotpedia*.
38. Levin, Sam, "California sheriff warns officers not to join far-right extremist groups, records reveal," The Guardian, June 4, 2021.
39. "Former L.A. County Sheriff Lee Baca Sentenced to 3 Years in Federal Prison for Leading Scheme to Obstruct Investigation into Jails," U.S. Attorney's Office, Central District of California, news release, May 12, 2017.
40. Kennedy, Sean, "Los Angeles County Sheriff Civilian Oversight Commission Memorandum," May 27, 2021.
41. Letter from Sheriff Alex Villanueva and Undersheriff Timothy Murakami to Brian K. Williams, Executive Director, County of Los Angeles, July 14, 2021.
42. Levin, Sam, "'The sheriff who went rogue': Alex Villanueva's scandal-plagued tenure ends in LA," The Guardian, November 16, 2022

Colorado

1. Frosch, Dan, "Ex-Sheriff Is Accused in Sex Case Tied to Drug," *New York Times*, November 30, 2011.
2. Gurman, Sadie, "Ex-sheriff in Colorado gets prison in meth-for-sex case," Associated Press, June 19, 2014.
3. "Former Sheriff Pat Sullivan to be released from prison Wednes-

day," KCNC-TV, March 17, 2015.
4. "Judge Dismisses All Charges Against Terry Maketa," KCNC-TV, February 27, 2018.
5. Campbell, Greg, "Vocal Colorado Sheriff Snared in Sex-for-Promotion Scandal," *Daily Caller*, May 23, 2014.
6. Ibid.
7. Ibid.
8. "Former Sedgwick County sheriff sentenced for misconduct," KMGH-TV, July 13, 2018.
9. Ibid.
10. Zoukis, Christopher, "Scandals Rock Denver Sheriff's Department," *Prison Legal News*, July 20, 2017.
11. Antonio Vargas, Ramon, "Colorado sheriff honors deputy after he killed man who mistakenly got in wrong car," *The Guardian*, Feb. 25, 2023.

Connecticut

1. Weizel, Richard, "High Noon for Sheriffs," *New York Times*, April 30, 2000.
2. Hoffman, Christopher, "Connecticut voters decide to abolish controversial sheriff system," *The Middletown Press*, November 8, 2000.
3. Weizel, Richard, "High Noon for Sheriffs," *New York Times*, April 30, 2000.
4. Hoffman, Christopher, "Connecticut voters decide to abolish controversial sheriff system," *The Middletown Press*, November 8, 2000.
5. Weizel, Richard, "High Noon for Sheriffs," *New York Times*, April 30, 2000.
6. Daly, Matthew, "Sheriff reform plan has powerful foes," *The Hartford Courant*, April 12, 2000.
7. Letter from the Judicial Branch of the Court Operations Division to deputies in Connecticut's eight sheriffs' offices, November 24, 2000.

Delaware

1. "The Battle for the Sheriff in Delaware Takes a Bad Turn, Associated Press, October 7, 2013.
2. Shannan, Pat, "Sheriffs Bushwhacked," *American Free Press*, April 8, 2012.

Florida

1. Calizic, Mike, "Deputy dumps paralyzed man out of wheelchair," *Today*, February 13, 2008.
2. McMahon, Paula, "Former sheriff sentenced, 10 months for corruption," *South Florida Sun-Sentinel*, November 17, 2007.
3. Ibid.
4. "Broward Sheriff's Office bogus crime stats," *Broward-Palm Beach New Times*, undated.
5. Mayo, Michael, "Ken Jenne gone as sheriff but signs of presence remain," *South Florida Sun-Sentinel*, September 5, 2007.
6. Jaeger, Max, "Sheriff's officer who did 'nothing' to stop Florida shooter resigns," *New York Post*, February 22, 2018.
7. Brown, Ruth, "Disgraced deputy ignored tip about school massacre," *New York Post*, February 23, 2018.
8. Wallman, Brittany, O'Matz, Megan, "Stoneman Douglas student warned school that Nikolas Cruz could become shooter," *South Florida Sun-Sentinel*, November 9, 2018.
9. Moore, Mark, "Florida sheriff refuses to resign during heated CNN interview," *New York Post*, February 25, 2018.
10. "Florida sheriff under growing pressure over handling of Parkland shooting,' CBS/AP, February 25, 2018.
11. Huriash, Lisa, Man, Anthony, Trishitta, Linda, Wallman, Brittany, "Sheriff Scott Israel dumped over Parkland shooting failures; new sheriff is Gregory Tony," *South Florida Sun-Sentinel*, January 11, 2019.
12. "New arrests in Panhandle sheriff's office scandal," *The Lakeland Ledger*, July 30, 2009.

13. "Former president of Florida Sheriffs' Association enters plea in kickback scheme," *Prison Legal News*, October 15, 2009
14. O'Connor, Meg, "Florida woman faced 10 years for 'meth' that was 'just a rock,'" *The Appeal*, March 26, 2019.
15. Flynn, Meagan, "A Florida cop planted meth on random drivers, police say. One lost custody of his daughter," *Washington Post*, July 11, 2019.
16. Conlon, Kendra, "Pinellas deputy, 7 recruits busted in cheating scandal," *USA Today*, January 25, 2016.
17. Stiteler, Rowland, "Scandal in the sheriff's office," *The Orlando Sentinel*, September 18, 1988.
18. Lithwick, Dahlia, "David Morgan is Wrong, Terribly Wrong," Slate, August 15, 2013.
19. Bonvillian, Crystal, "Lawsuit: Sheriff 'tolerated' sex ring in which twin girls were abused by parents, deputy," Cox Media Group, October 27, 2017.
20. "Escambia County Sheriff David Morgan denies involvement in alleged sex ring," WKRG-TV, Mobile, Alabama, July 3, 2019.
21. "Sheriff Morgan, concerned About Child Porn, Seeks to Limit Access to Evidence in 'Sex Ring' Lawsuit," NorthEscambia.com, July 6, 2019.
22. Butler, Scott, "Clay County sheriff apologizes for 'embarrassment,'" *The Florida Times-Union*, May 17, 2019.
23. Patrick, Steve, "Letter asks governor to remove Sheriff Daniels; FDLE ups its investigation," WJXT-TV, June 26, 2019.
24. Clary, Mike, Baum, Geraldine, "Sex Scandal Heats Up Florida—Accused Woman Uses 'Nympho Defense,'" *The Seattle Times/Los Angeles Times*, September 22, 1991.
25. Lambiet, Jose, "Married Florida sheriff's deputy, 25, and mother-of-two high school counselor, 36, lose their jobs for 'having sex in patrol car following school football game,'" *Daily Mail*, January 11, 2019.
26. "Sheriff: 2 deputies ousted over drug court sex scandal," Associated Press, October 17, 2017.
27. "Undersheriff resigns amid affair allegations," WESH-TV, October 4, 2012.
28. McLaughlin, Tom, "5 fired in Sheriff's Office sex scandal," *North-

west *Florida Daily News*, February 6, 2019.
29. Tron, Gina, "Deputy Allegedly Fondled Trainee, Said He 'Owed' Him Oral Sex for Teaching Him to Write Reports," *Crime Time*, October 9, 2018.
30. "Why Didn't Sheriff's Office Investigate Deputy's Role in Crash?" The St. Petersburg Times," Aug. 29, 2008
31. Dulaney, Cody, "Former Lee County sheriff's deputies to talk corruption with FBI," *Fort Myers News-Press*, December 22, 2017.
32. "An FDLE probe into PBSO handling of Epstein incarceration is warranted," editorial by the Palm Beach Post editorial board, July 28, 2019.
33. Madrak, Susie, "Dept. of Pre-Crime: Florida Sheriff Harassing Pre-Criminals," Tampa Bay Times, July 26, 2021.
34. "Threats, extortion alleged in 400-page suit against Pasco Sheriff's Office employees," WTVT-TV, June 21, 2019.
35. "Civil Rights Lawsuit Filed Against Pasco Sheriff," press release by attorney Kwall Barack Nadeau, June 15, 2020.
36. Gilna, Derek, "Pinellas County, Florida Sheriff's Office Sued in Federal Court for Treatment of Transgender Prisoner," Prison Legal News, February 2021.
37. Patel, Devan, "Dozens of deputies lied, cheated and stole. This Florida sheriff hired them anyway," *Fort Myers News-Press*, Jan. 7, 2021.
38. DesOrmeau, Taylor, "Embattled sheriff losing vehicle, nearly $11,000 a year in benefits," milive.com, Jan. 30, 2019.
39. Weidmayer, Marie, "Judge dismisses lawsuit against former Jackson County sheriff, allows county suit to continue," milive, Jan. 5, 2021.

Georgia

1. Stokes, Stephannie, "Why Ga. Has the second highest number of counties in the US," National Public Radio's *All Things Considered*, April 4, 2014.
2. Roig-Franzia, Manuel, "Ex-Sheriff Convicted in Murder of Succes-

sor," *Washington Post*, July 11, 2002.
3. Green, Josh, "Corruption in DeKalb is nothing new—remember Pat Jarvis?" *Atlanta Magazine*, March 18, 2015.
4. Torpy, Bill, "Torpy at Large: This is no walk in the park for DeKalb sheriff," *The Atlanta Journal-Constitution*, May 10, 2017.
5. Sharpe, Joshua, "DeKalb sheriffs: Getting in trouble with the law since 1951," *The Atlanta Journal-Constitution*, June 1, 2017.
6. "Sheriff unapologetic over controversial campaign flyer," WXIA-TV, May 18, 2016.
7. Bynum, Russ, "Georgia sheriff charged with grabbing 75-year-old by throat," Associated Press, May 30, 2019.
8. Davis, Michael, "Six deputies ousted from Butts County sheriff's office," *Jackson Progress-Argus*, January 24, 2014.
9. "Georgia sheriff says lack of dash cams isn't a priority," Associated Press, June 10, 2019.
10. "Walker County deputy fired, arrested in sexual misconduct investigation," *Walker County Messenger*, May 13, 2016.
11. "Georgia Jail Staffers Face Inmate Sex Scandal," Associated Press, December 24, 2002.
12. Cook, Rhonda, "Rockdale sheriff's investigators suspended for possible cheating," *The Atlanta Journal-Constitution*, September 3, 2014.
13. Wiley, Kelly, "Lieutenant fired after gaming machine incident," WAGT-TV, October 30, 2018.
14. Travis, Randy, "Cover-up of Sheriff Sex Scandal?" WAGA-TV, September 28, 2015.
15. Bell, Bret, "The law and a community in disorder," Savannah Morning News, February 3, 2004.
16. Dawson, Wendell, "Georgia Sheriff Convicted in Federal Court—Again," AVOC, February 3, 2004.
17. Cook, Rhonda, "Clayton Sheriff Victor Hill acquitted of all charges," *The Atlanta Journal-Constitution*, August 15, 2013.
18. Prince, Chelsea, "Clayton County Sheriff Victor Hill's police certification put on probation," *Clayton News*, March 21, 2017.
19. Kemp, Robin, "Ex-CCSO Deputy Hawes granted $26K bond; Hill alleges Hawes wrote fake ticket for stripper," *Clayton News*, August 28, 2018.

20. Georgia public safety news, "Telfair county sheriff sentenced to 36 months…"
21. 21. Manley, Rodney, "Former Telfair sheriff pleads guilty in federal court," *The Telegraph*, January 8, 2009.
22. 22. Manley, Rodney, "Ex-Dodge sheriff gets 18 months for voter fraud," The Telegraph, June 29, 2010.
23. 23. "Former Dodge County Sheriff and Deputy Plead Guilty in 2004 Election Fraud," U.S. Attorney's Office, Southern District of Georgia, March 12, 2010.
24. 24. "Former Wilcox County, Georgia, Sheriff and Others Sentenced for Assaulting Inmate, U.S. Department of Justice, Middle District of Georgia, May 8, 2013.
25. 25. Everson, Latasha, "Former Turner Co. sheriff pleads guilty," The Tifton Gazette, August 23, 2011.
26. 26. Bynum, Russ, "Ga. Sheriff pleads guilty to fraud charges," *Law.com Daily Report*, September 8, 2008.
27. "County was forever changed 48 years ago," *Jackson Herald*, August 15, 2015.
28. Burns, Asia Simone, "Students to split $3 million after winning lawsuit against Georgia sheriff over illegal body searches," *Atlanta Journal-Constitution*, August 1, 2018.29
29. Schrade, Brad, "Ga. Sheriff indicted for sexual battery in high school drug search," *Atlanta Journal-Constitution*, October 4, 2017.
30. Rigby, Michael, "Georgia Sheriffs Illegally Profit From Captive Workforce," *Prison Legal News*, June 2005.
31. 31. Marcelo, Courtney Elizabeth, "Sheriffs: Prohibit Sheriffs from Engaging in Private Security, Private Investigation, or Bail Bond Businesses," *Georgia State University Law Review*, fall 2003.
32. Reutter, David M., "Fulton County Jail under Federal Control," *Prison Legal News*, March 15, 2005.
33. "Fulton County Reinstates Deputies Fired in Killing Rampage," *Prison Legal News*, February 15, 2007.
34. "Georgia Sheriff, Judges, Other Officials Face Misconduct, Criminal Charges," *Prison Legal News*, July 15, 2008.
35. Ibid.
36. Zoukis, Christopher, "Eleventh Circuit Slams Douglas County,

Georgia Sheriff's Office for Retaliation Against Whistleblower," *Prison Legal News*, September 6, 2017.
37. Bailey v. Wheeler, Case No. 15-11627 (Ct. App. 11th Cir., 2006).
38. Reutter, David M., "Prison, Jail and Law Enforcement Corruption Continues in Georgia," *Prison Legal News*, December 15, 2009.
39. Kornfield, Meryl, Knowles, Hannah, "Sheriff's official who said spa shooting suspect had 'bad day' posted shirts blaming 'CHY-NA' for virus," The Washington Post, March 17, 2021.
40. Thanawala, Sudhin, "3 jail guards in Georgia charged in beating of detainee," Associated Press, November 23, 2022.

Hawaii

1. Nakaso, Dan, Perez, Rob, Pang, Gordon Y.K., "Katherine and Louis Kealoha are convicted of conspiracy and obstruction," *Honolulu Star Advertiser*, June 28, 2019.
2. Kelleher, Jennifer Sinco, "Hawaii law enforcement power couple mired in corruption case," Associated Press, April 29, 2019.
3. Nakaso, Dan, Perez, Rob, Pang, Gordon Y.K., "Katherine and Louis Kealoha are convicted of conspiracy and obstruction," *Honolulu Star Advertiser*, June 28, 2019.
4. Dockterman, Eliana, "Hawaii Police Won't Get to Have Sex With Prostitutes Anymore," *Time Magazine*, March 26, 2014.
5. Eifling, Sam, "Above the Law, Under the Sheets," The New Republic, January 28, 2015.
6. Colb, Sherry F., "Should the Law Permit Sexual Contact Between Police and Suspects?" *Justia*, September 13, 2017.

Idaho

1. Paquette, Danielle, "The rape myth that lives on in Idaho," *The Washington Post*, March 18, 2016.
2. Ibid.

3. Carlson, Mia, "Idaho County Sheriff's Office sued after deputy has relationship with minor," KXLY TV, Spokane, Washington, April 29, 2014.
4. Brentzel, Chelsea, "Former Jefferson County sheriff makes public apology," KIFI-TV, Idaho Falls, Idaho, June 22, 2015.
5. Neiwert, David, "Sheriff Finalist for Idaho's Largest County Blames Jews for Communism," Daily Kos, July 21, 2021.

Illinois

1. Flood, John J., "A Police Department Held Hostage by Politics: A History, part 1."
2. Ibid.
3. Ibid.
4. Flood, John J., "A Police Department Held Hostage by Politics: A History, part 2."
5. O'Connor, Matt, "Dvorak sentenced to 41-month term," *Chicago Tribune*, April 29, 1994.
6. Gorman, John, "Operation Safebet pays off for FBI," *Chicago Tribune*, August 21, 1990.
7. "Corruption is Charged in Chicago Sheriff's Office," Associated Press, August 20, 1989.
8. Dold, R. Bruce, "Mob tape may be kiss of death for O'Grady," *Chicago Tribune*, February 11, 1990.
9. Galica, Larry, "Federal grand jury indicts O'Grady business associate, NWI.com, August 2, 1991.
10. Rehkamp, Patrick, "Sheriff's Ex-Secretary Resigns Over Timekeeping Irregularities," Better Government Association, September 21, 2014.
11. "Illinois sheriff: No foreclosure evictions on m watch," CNN, October 8, 2008.
12. Nelson, Shellie, Minor, Chris, "Sheriff pleads guilty to charge based on cyber-stalking," WQAD-TV, September 11, 2014.
13. Gregory, Ted, "In central Illinois, sheriff under a cloud," *Chicago Tribune*, December 7, 1999.
14. Gilna, Derek, Illinois Sheriff Settles Federal Class-action Suit Over Strip Searches," *Prison Legal News*, March 6, 2018.

15. "Crime: Double-Dealer's Death, *Time Magazine*, January 7, 1974.
16. "Lawman Who Joined Mobsters Is Gunned to Death in Chicago," *The New York Times*, December 22, 1973.
17. "Backstabbers, Reader, April 12 2001.
18. McCoppin, Rogert, Berger, Susan, "Kane County sheriff's deputy charged with drug possession: officials," *Chicago Tribune*, June 24, 2016.
19. Jones, Megan, "Kane County Sheriff's sergeant charged with cocaine possession, *Aurora Beacon News*, December 5, 2019.
20. "Ill. Deputy kills self after corruption sting arrest," CBS News, Nov. 5, 2014.

Indiana

1. Fountaine, Heather, "Former Clark County Sheriff accuse of paying for a prostitute again," WHAS-TV, May 18, 2017.
2. White, Charlie, "Clark County sheriff Rodden indicted," *Lafayette Courier & Journal*, July 29, 2014.
3. Ibid.
4. Ibid.
5. "Boone County Sheriff to retire after allegations of misconduct." WTHR-TV, April 14, 2015.
6. Clark, Kirsten, Gross, Lexy, "TV show sparks firings at Clark County jail," *Lafayette Courier & Journal*, May 21, 2016.
7. Dolan, Bill, "Lake County Sheriff guilty of bribery, other crimes. What happens now?" *Hammond Times*, August 24, 2017.
8. "Northwest Indiana sheriff convicted in bribery case," WTTV-TV, August 24, 2017.
9. "United States of America v. Daniel Murchek," Cause No. 2:18 CR 49, U.S. District Court Northern District of Indiana, Hammond Division.
10. Dolan, Bill, "A federal judge sentences a former high-ranking Lake County policeman," *Northwest Indiana Times*, August 27, 2018.
11. Franklin, Tom, "Kosciusko County Sheriff Aaron Rovenstine sentenced to probation," May 23, 2017.

Iowa

1. Foley, Ryan J., "In rural Iowa feud, sheriff won't honor small town's arrests," Associated Press, June 13, 2019.
2. "Iowa officer resigns after video shows him striking biker," Associated Press, July 23, 2019.
3. Magee, Dennis, "Athey receives deferred judgment for assault charges," *Waterloo-Cedar Falls Courier*, May 6, 2015.

Kansas

1. 0Kenefake, Mary, "Ex-Kan. Sheriff sentenced on drug charges," Associated Press, April 11, 2013.
2. Hittle, Shaun, "Court documents in case against Franklin County sheriff reveal drug allegations against former county attorney," *Lawrence (Kan.) Journal-World*, April 1, 213.
3. "Kansas sheriffs executive says arrests offensive, Associated Press, September 23, 2013.
4. Ibid.
5. Stavola, Michael, "Sedgwick jail deputy arrested in thefts, including one against another deputy," *Wichita Eagle*, September 27, 2019.
6. 'Sedgwick County Sheriff's Office suspends 8 deputies for using, selling steroids," KWCH-TV, February 12, 2020.
7. "Ness County Sheriff Pleads Guilty, Agrees to Resigns," U.S. Attorney's Office, District of Kansas, October 22, 2018.
8. Strader, Stacie, "Dierks officially ousted as Sheriff for misconduct," KOAM-TV, January 7, 2020.
9. Tidd, Jason, "Sheriff interfered with deputies arresting his girlfriend after DUI stop, KBI says," Wichita Eagle, March 15, 2019.
10. 11.Hrenchir, Tim, Van Dyke, Aly, "For a community, ousting elected officials hurts," *Topeka Capital-Journal*, April 23, 2014.
11. "Deputy Loses 'False Light' Privacy Claim When Statement Issued by Department Proves to be True," Labor Relations Information System, October 1, 2005.

12. Morrison, Oliver, "Kansas cracks down on misbehaving cops, "*Wichita Eagle*, December 30, 2016.

Kentucky

1. "Corrupt Kentucky sheriff brought down by reporters," CBS News, May 6, 2012.
2. "How 2 twentysomething journalists brought down a corrupt Kentucky sheriff," *60 Minutes*, CBS News, May 7, 2012.
3. Ibid.
4. "Reporters risk lives to expose corruption," CBS News, May 3, 2012.
5. Ibid.
6. "Corrupt Kentucky sheriff brought down by reporters," CBS News, May 6, 2012.
7. White, Mark, "Former Sheriff Hodge sentenced to 17 years in Whitley County case," Corbin *News Journal*, November 1, 2013.
8. Ibid.
9. Ibid.
10. Ibid.
11. Ibid.
12. Ibid.
13. Hevener, John W., *Which Side Are You On?: The Harlan County Coal Miners, 1931-39*.
14. "Harlan County sheriff sentenced to prison," UPI, December 6, 1982.
15. Alford, Roger, "Ex-Sheriff Videotaped Taking Cash," Associated Press, April 9, 2002.
16. Estep, Bill, "Ex-Harlan deputy admits role in murder," *Lexington Herald-Leader*, November 19, 2009.
17. "Ex-deputy sentenced to prison," *Media Awareness Project*, March 23, 2005.
18. Opinion of Court of Appeals, Commonwealth of Kentucky, November 9, 2018.

19. Estep, Bill, "From lawman to felon, former Eastern Kentucky sheriff sentenced in corruption case," *Lexington Herald-Leader*, December 19m 2017.
20. Barron, James, "Drug case rocks political establishment in a Kentucky town," *The New York Times*, March 29, 1986.
21. "United States of America v. Roger Benton," U.S. Court of Appeals for the Sixth Circuit, July 22, 1988.
22. "Jury finds 5 law officers guilty of accepting bribes in Kentucky," Associated Press, August 17, 1991.
23. "United States of America v. Billy McIntosh, Johnny Mann, Wilson Stone, Lester Drake, Omer Noe," U.S. Court of Appeals for the Sixth Circuit, December 29, 1992.
24. "4 Kentucky sheriffs arrested as FBI closes drug-protection trap," Associated Press, August 17, 1990.
25. Ibid.
26. "Kentucky law officials are arrested in drug sting," *The New York Times*, August 17, 1990.
27. "United States of America v. Billy McIntosh, Johnny Mann, Wilson Stone, Lester Drake, Omer Noe," U.S. Court of Appeals for the Sixth Circuit, December 29, 1992.
28. Clines, Francis X., "In Eastern Kentucky, Politics Extends a Bloody Legacy," The New York Times, June 2, 2002.
29. "Candidate for Ky. Sheriff linked to slaying of incumbent," Associated Press, April 15, 2002.
30. Ibid.
31. Slavey, Carla, "Man who plotted Catron's murder dies," *Somerset Commonwealth Journal*, December 14, 2018.
32. "Candidate for Ky. Sheriff linked to slaying of incumbent," Associated Press, April 15, 2002.
33. "Ex-sheriff convicted of witness tampering reports to prison," Associated Press, June 6, 2015.
1. "Criminal complaint details charges against Kinman," Madison (Kentucky) *Courier*, March 24, 2017.
34. Wolfson, Andrew, "Sheriff avoids prison in tough Carroll County," *Louisville Courier-Journal*, April 4, 2017.
35. Wolfson, Andrew, "Ex-Bullitt County sheriff acquitted of aiding drug trafficking scheme," *Louisville Courier-Journal*, November 8,

2018.
36. "Former Bullitt County, KY sheriff faces Federal charges," News release, U.S. Attorney's Office, U.S. Department of Justice, Western District of Kentucky, May 3, 2017.

Louisiana

1. Nelson, Stanley, Barnidge, Matt, and Stanford, Ian, "Cold Case: Connected by violence—the mafia, Klan & Morville Lounge," *The Concordia Sentinel*, July 16, 2009.
2. Johnson, William, "St. Landry deputy retires after 50 years with sheriff's office," *Gannett Louisiana*, Dec. 28, 2014.
3. Noah W. Cross—Cross as Sheriff,
4. Aswell, Tom, "On 50th anniversary of Ferriday civil rights killing, read journalist Stanley Nelson's Concordia Sentinel series," *LouisianaVoice*, December 10, 2014,
5. Nelson, Stanley, Barnidge, Matt, Stanford, Ian, "Cold case: connected by violence—the mafia, Klan and Morville Lounge," *Concordia Sentinel*, July 16, 2009.
6. Noah W. Cross—Cross as Sheriff,
7. Nelson, Stanley, Barnidge, Matt, Stanford, Ian, "Cold case: connected by violence—the mafia, Klan and Morville Lounge," *Concordia Sentinel*, July 16, 2009.
8. "Frank Morris Case," The Civil Rights Cold Case, undated,
9. Jack G. Favor v. C. Murray Henderson, May 16, 1972,
10. "List of Louisiana wrongful convictions overturned since 1966," *Baton Rouge Advocate*, November 23, 2003.
11. "State will not prosecute former Texas rodeo star Jack Favor on the second of two murder charges," *Brownwood (Texas) Bulletin*, May 11, 1974.
12. "Jack Graves Favor," Wrongly Convicted Database Record, *Forejustice*,
13. Lane, Emily, "Public corruption in Louisiana 'can't get much worse,' says outgoing FBI New Orleans director," *New Orleans Times-Picayune*, November 6, 2017.

14. Cold case file of Federal Bureau of Investigation dated April 29, 2010, obtained by LSU School of Mass Communications,
15. Cold case file of Federal Bureau of Investigation dated April 29, 2010, obtained by LSU School of Mass Communications,
16. U.S. Department of Justice press release, Feb. 25, 2012,
17. Temple, Stacy, Leader, Barbara, "FBI Raids Ouachita Parish, LA Sheriff's Office," *Monroe News-Star*, Feb. 9, 2011.
18. "Woman Scorned Caused Royce Toney Trainwreck," *Monroe Free Press*, Feb. 26, 2012.
19. "Former sheriff charged in bomb plot to kill successor," United Press International, Feb. 3, 1989.
20. Gyan, Joe Jr., Semien, John, "Former sheriff held in bombing," *Baton Rouge Advocate*, Feb. 3, 1989.
21. *Baton Rouge Advocate*, May 1, 1992.
22. Hackenburg, Liz, "Duffy Breaux, notorious Lafourche ex-sheriff, dies," *Houma Courier*, Dec. 14, 2005.
23. Gill, James, "Sheriffs run afoul of law and order," *New Orleans Times-Picayune*, March 4, 2012,
24. Colona, Dora, "Residents not surprised about sheriff's indictment," *Hammond Daily Star*, August 27, 1997
25. "Mayor takes over as St. Helena sheriff, Associated Press, April 23, 1988,
26. Hunter, Gary, "Louisiana work-release prisoners used by sheriff in chop shop," Prison Legal News, February 15, 2008.
27. Gates, Paul, "Former sheriff 'Gun' Ficklin sentenced to 63 months," WAFB-TV, Baton Rouge, February, 2005.
28. Ibid.
29. Louisiana Sheriff Busted in Private Prison Scheme, *Prison Legal News*, July 15, 2000,
30. Louisiana Secretary of State corporate records.
31. Records of U.S. Fifth Circuit Court of Appeals, Oct. 13, 1999.
32. U.S. Attorney's Office, Western District of Louisiana, news release, April 1, 2014.
33. Joint press release by FBI and U.S. Attorney's Office, October 5, 2011,
34. Zurik, Lee, "Emails paint a picture of parties and potential corruption," WVUE Fox 8, New Orleans, undated

35. Zurik, Lee, "Will feds raise the pressure on Hingle?" WVUE Fox 8, New Orleans, March 30, 2012,
36. News release by U.S. Attorney for the Eastern District of Louisiana Jim Letten, Nov. 30, 2011.
37. Alexander-Bloch, Benjamin, "Former Plaquemines Parish Sheriff Jiff Hingle sentenced to nearly 4 years on corruption charges," *New Orleans Times-Picayune*, Feb. 25, 2016.
38. "Former Winn Parish sheriff convicted in drug case," Associated Press, Feb. 25, 2012,
39. Finley, Stephanie A, "Former Winn Parish sheriff sentenced 13+ years in prison," Press release, U.S. Attorney's Office, Western District of Louisiana, Aug. 17, 2012,
40. Pompilio, Natalie, "Lee ignores rule against associating with criminals," *New Orleans Times-Picayune*, Nov. 16, 1999.
41. Opinion No. 92-132, Louisiana Board of Ethics for Elected Officials, Oct. 27, 1994.
42. Warren, Bob, "Lee goes to bat for Caracci—defends connections at hearing on a.-Ace," *New Orleans Times-Picayune*, April 1, 1994.
43. Samples of Harry Lee quotes, *New Orleans Times-Picayune*, April 2, 2000.
44. "Sex scandal could cost Steven Seagal his fake badge," *New York Post*, April 26, 2010,
45. Lemons, Stephen, "Steven Seagal resigned rather than face an IA investigation, according to Sheriff Newell Normand," *Phoenix New Times*, March 18, 2011,
46. Vargas, Ramon Antonio, Sledge, Matt, "Joe McKnight killing probe defended by police; questions mount over confessed shooter's release," *New Orleans Times-Picayune*, Dec. 2, 2016
47. Lane, Emily, "Jefferson Parish Sheriff Newell Normand announcement retirement," *New Orleans Times-Picayune*, July 25, 2017,
48. Rhoden, Robert, "Ex-Sheriff Jack Strain arrested; accused of rape and incest," *The New Orleans Advocate*, June 11, 2019.
49. Pagones, Sara, "Former St. Tammany sheriff spent nearly $500K on work-release facility before handing it over to friends," *New Orleans Advocate*, Nov. 7, 2016.
50. Richmond, U.S. Rep. Cedric L., letter to U.S. Attorney General Loretta Lynch, May 19, 2015.

51. "Acquittal for Louisiana sheriff whose deputies beat inmates," *New Orleans Times-Picayune,* Nov. 5, 2016.
52. Broussard, Donald D., e-mail to author dated March 25, 2017.
53. Author's interview with Victor White, Jr., June 2018.
54. Hargrove, Thomas, Murder Accountability Project.
55. Simerman, John, "$3 million in new payouts as Iberia Parish Sheriff's Office settles more abuse suits," Acadiana Advocate, March 2, 2019.
56. Barker, Kim, "Spillionaires: Profiteering and mismanagement in the wake of the BP oil spill," *ProPublica,* April 13, 2011,
57. "Head of the Metropolitan Crime Commission says his group is interested in a possible study of the St. Bernard Parish criminal justice system," news release from St. Bernard Parish Sheriff's Office, January 23, 2015.
58. Purpura, Paul, "Former St. Bernard Parish sheriff's deputy indicted in corruption probe," *New Orleans Times-Picayune*, Aug. 4, 2015,
59. Myers, Ben, "Indictment against former St. Bernard sheriff's deputy quashed," *New Orleans Times-Picayune,* May 31, 2016,
60. "St. Bernard Sheriff Jack Stephens retires, says he's 'seen it all,'" New Orleans Times-Picayune, July 1, 2012.
61. *Investigation of the Ville Platte Police Department and the Evangeline Parish Sheriff's Office*, Report of U.S. Department of Justice, Civil Rights Division, Dec. 19, 2016.
62. Mustian, Jim, "In Evangeline Parish arrest scandal, civil liberties took back seat to decades of tradition," *Baton Rouge Advocate*, Dec. 31, 2016,
63. *Investigation of the Ville Platte Police Department and the Evangeline Parish Sheriff's Office*, Report of U.S. Department of Justice, Civil Rights Division, Dec. 19, 2016.
64. Quinn, Rob, "Sheriff Raids House to Find Online Critic," *Newser* Web page, August 5, 2016,
65. Author interview with former Louisiana Governor Edwin Edwards, October 2016
66. Editorial, *Houma Daily Courier*, August 7, 2016
67. Moore, Katie, "Terrebonne Sheriff reaches 'compromise' with blogger in 1st Amendment lawsuit over illegal search," WWL-TV, September 7, 2017.

68. "Authement v. State of Louisiana,' Court of Appeal of Louisiana, First Circuit, 97 CA 0579 and 97 CA 0580, May 15, 1998 decision,
69. Official Oath of Office, December 18, 1981,
70. Author interview with Denham Springs, Louisiana, City Judge Jerry Denton, June 2018
71. Kozak, Brad, "When cops go bad I: the tale of George D'Artois," The Truth About Guns, October 19, 2011
72. *The Shreveport Times*, May 19, 1974.

Maine

1. Valigra, Lori, "Maine sheriff on lewd photo taken at work: 'I did nothing illegal,' *Bangor Daily News*, November 22, 2017.
2. Ibid.
3. Hoey, Dennis, "Head of Main Sheriff's Association steps down after admitting to sending sexually explicit photo of himself in uniform to woman," *Portland Press-Herald*, November 22, 2017.
4. Bleiberg, Jake, "Oxford County sheriff resigns amid sexual misconduct allegations," Bangor Daily News, December 6, 2017.
5. Chrisos, Jon, Lampariello, Dan, "FBI investigates allegations of sexual harassment against former sheriff, chief deputy," WGME-TV, July 26, 2018.
6. "Ex-Deputy of the Year accused of abusing girls is fired," Law Report..org, January 10, 2018.

Maryland

1. Schuppe, Jon, "Members of rogue Baltimore police unit found guilty of corruption charges, MSNBC, February 12, 2018.
2. "Baltimore Police Officers Convicted I Corruption Scandal," NPR, February 12, 2018.
3. Schuppe, Jon, "Disgraced Baltimore officer says detective slain before testifying was also corrupt," MSNBC, February 5, 2018.
4. Poppa, Doug, "Police corruption and misconduct is just as bad as it

was in the 1960s," Baltimore Post-Examiner, May 8, 2015.
5. McDonell-Parry, Amelia, Barrow, Justine, "Death of Freddie Gray: 5 things you didn't know," *Rolling Stone*, April 12, 2017.
6. Englar, Brian, "Deputy charged with sex abuse," *The Frederick News-Post*, March 25, 2011.
7. Byrnes, Kym, "Former sheriff's major pleads guilty to misconduct charges," *Patch.com*, January 8, 2013.
8. "Sheriff's sergeant charged with rape on boat in Maryland," Associated Press, March 15, 2019.

Massachusetts

1. Fanto, Clarence, "There's no question that Massachusetts sheriffs have power. But is it too much? *The Berkshire Eagle*, Aug. 8, 2010.
2. "Mass. Sheriff sentenced on fed charges, UPI, Feb. 8, 1995.
3. Beals, Jeff, "Sheriff Guilty of Tax Evasion," *The Harvard Crimson*, Oct. 14, 1994.
4. "Retirement board ordered to stop pension for convicted former sheriff," Associated Press, Dec. 17, 2010
5. Ellement, John, "Ex-captain faces embezzlement, drug charges," The Boston Globe, Nov. 23, 2004
6. Guilfoil, John M., Estes, Andrea, Smith, Stephen, "Middlesex sheriff kills self, police say," *The Boston Globe*, Nov. 28, 2010.
7. Murphy, Matt, "Coakley closes DiPaola probe," *Commonwealth Magazine*, Jan. 25, 2012.
8. "Massachusetts Sheriff Pleads Guilty in Federal Court," Associated Press, Sept. 17, 1996.
9. Lorant, Richard, "Essex County sheriff resigns in corruption," Associated Press, Jan. 10, 2011.
10. Rizzuto, Robert, "Mass. Democratic Party calls for investigation of sheriff accused of using intimidation to solicit campaign contributions from employees," Masslive.com, Feb. 15, 2012.
11. Eddings, Keith, "Report: As sheriff, Cousins allowed widespread abuse of sick time," *The Newbury Port Daily News*, Dec. 20, 2017.
12. Crimaldi, Laura, "Bristol sheriff violated immigration detainees'

civil rights during May melee, attorney general says," *Boston Globe*, Dec. 15, 2020.
13. Crimaldi, Laua, "Biden administration terminates ICE contract with Bristol Sheriff Thomas Hodgson," Boston Globe, May 20, 2021.

Michigan

1. McLaughlin, Kelly, "A Michigan sheriff defended the group of men accused of plotting to kidnap Gov. Gretchen Whitmer," *Business Insider*, Oct. 14, 2020.
2. Ibid
3. Ibid
4. "Michigan Sheriff Surprised to Hear Ticket Quotas Were Illegal, Claims Ignorance," Truthvoice.com, undated.
5. Schaefer, Jim, Kaufman, Gina, "How problem cops stay on Michigan's streets," Detroit Free Press, July 9, 2017.
6. Ibid.
7. Ibid.
8. Burns, Gus, "Accidentally exposed court records reveal new names in corruption probe," mlive.com, Dec. 27, 2017.
9. Ibid.

Minnesota

1. Goodrich, Kristine, "Minnesota sheriff kills himself during child sex-abuse probe," *Twin Cities Pioneer-Press*, Sept. 26, 2017.
2. Furst, Randy, "Years before George Floyd's death, Minneapolis police chief spoke of difficulty of stopping misconduct by a veteran cop," *Minneapolis Star-Tribune*, Aug. 23, 2020.
3. Bjorhus, Jennifer, Webster, Mary Jo, "Over the past two decades, hundreds of Minnesota law enforcement officers have been convicted of criminal offenses. Most were never disciplined by the state," Minneapolis Star-Tribune, Oct. 1, 2017.

Mississippi

1. Nicholson, Chet, *Dream Room: Tales of the Dixie Mafia* (*Mississippi Sound Publishing*, 2009).
2. "FBI Top Stories: Murder and the Dixie Mafia," *Criminal Justice News*, Sept. 5, 2012.
3. "Convicted ex-sheriff files for job," *Memphis Commercial-Appeal*, Jan. 27, 2007.
4. Ibid.
5. "Former Harrison County Sheriff dies at 73," WLOX-TV, Biloxi, MS., March 4, 2008.
6. "Former Harrison County, Mississippi, Corrections Officer Found Guilty of Criminal Civil Rights Violations, Obstruction of Justice," U.S. Department of Justice news release, Aug. 17, 2007.
7. "Former Jailer Ryan Teel Sentenced To Life In Prison," WLOX-TV, Biloxi, MS., Nov. 1, 2007.
8. Williams, Bob, "Millions Paid in Mississippi Jail Deaths; Ten Guards Sentenced for Abuses; Corruption Continues," *Prison Legal News*, Sept. 2008.
9. Jonsson, Patrik, "Mississippi indictment highlights pitfalls of power for sheriffs," *Christian Science Monitor*, Aug. 31, 2013.
10. "Mississippi Gulf Coast sheriff indicted on corruption charges," *New Orleans Times-Picayune*, Aug. 31, 2013.
11. Havens, April M., "Jackson County Sheriff Mike Byrd indicted on 31 counts including embezzlement, fraud, extortion," *Mississippi Press*, Pascagoula, MS., Aug. 30, 2013.
12. Kulo, Warren, "Former Jackson County Sheriff Mike Byrd ordered to pay $260,000 in sexual harassment suit," *Gulflive.com*, Sept. 17, 2015.
13. "Former Forrest Co. sheriff's chief deputy terminated," *Mississippi Business Journal*, Sept. 20, 2016.
14. Beveridge, Lici, "Charles, Linda Bolton sentenced for tax crimes," *Hattiesburg American,* March 17, 2017.
15. Davidson, Robert, "Former Sheriff Gets House Arrest," WCBI-TV, Columbus, MS., Dec. 7, 2016.
16. Arnold, Ed, "State auditor announces arrest of Alcorn County Sheriff," *Memphis Business Journal*, June 23, 2015.

17. "Former Sheriff of Tallahatchie County Sentenced to Federal Prison for Accepting Bribes," U.S. Attorney's Office, Northern District of Mississippi, April 18, 2019.
18. Amy, Jeff, "Trafficking, embezzlement: Mississippi sheriff admits guilt. Prison next," *Jackson Clarion Ledger*, June 13, 2019.
19. Harrist, Ron, "Three Convicted Felons to Serve as Mississippi Sheriffs," Associated Press, Dec. 21, 1995.
20. "United States v. Cartlidge," U.S. Court of Appeals, 5th Circuit, Jan. 14, 1987.
21. "Mauney v. State Moore," Supreme Court of Mississippi decision, Feb. 26, 1998.
22. "United States v. Barrett," U.S. Court of Appeals, District of Columbia Circuit, May 2, 1997.
23. Daly, Ilyssa, Mitchell, Jerry, "Sex Abuse, Beatings and an Untouchable Mississippi Sheriff," *The New York Times*, April 11, 2023.
24. Mitchell, Jerry, "State's lack of jail inspections a disaster in the making, lawyer says," *Mississippi Today*, April 18, 2023.
25. Niemeyer, Kenneth, "Rankin County Sheriff Bryan Bailey, who oversaw 'goon squad' that tortured Black men in Mississippi, is running for reelection unopposed," *Insider*, Aug. 19, 2023.
26. Goldbert, Michael, "Six former Mississippi officers plead guilty to state charges for torturing two Black men," Associated Press, Aug. 14, 2023.
27. Goldberg, Michael, Deputies accused of shoving guns in mouths of 2 Black men," Associated Press, Mar. 27, 2023.
28. Daly, Ilyssa and Mitchell, Jerry, "Where the Sheriff is King, these women say he coerced them into sex," Mississippi Center for Investigative Reporting, July 19, 2023.

Missouri

1. Sulzberger, A.G., "Sheriff in southeast Missouri faces meth allegations," *New York Times*, May 6, 2011.
2. "Former Carter County Sheriff and Deputy Sentenced for Possession and Sale of Stolen Firearms," U.S. Attorney's office, Eastern

District of Missouri, July 9, 2012.
3. Pistor, J.C., "Perry County Sheriff cited in Caseyville for alleged public sex act," *St. Louis Post-Dispatch*, Dec. 19, 2011.
4. "Former Missouri sheriff sentenced to 6 months in fed prison," Associated Press, April 30, 2019.
5. Ibid.
6. Bailey, R., "Missouri Sheriff Who Vowed to Clean Up Crime Faces Criminal Charges, Lawsuits," *Columbia Tribune*, Dec. 7, 2018.
7. Vockrodt, Steve, Hendricks, Mike, "Missouri sheriff to step down today as scandal with administrative assistant revealed," *Kansas City Star*, April 19, 2018.
8. "Southern Missouri sheriff, subordinate indicted on multiple felonies," Associated Press, July 21, 2018.
9. Ibid.
10. Ibid.
11. "Longtime Saline County Sheriff Pleads Guilty to Stealing $79,000 in Public Funds," U.S. Attorney's Office, Western District of Missouri, Feb. 9, 2016,
12. "Ex-sheriff sentenced to 9 months for embezzling state checks," Associated Press, Feb. 7, 2017.
13. "Former Lincoln County, Missouri, Sheriff's Office Detective Sentenced on Sexual Abuse Charges," U. S. Department of Justice news release, Dec. 14, 2012.
14. Olson, Kyle, "Homeschooling family tasered, arrested after being accused of having a 'messy' house," Eagnews.org.

Montana

1. Weiser, Kathy, *Legends of America*, February 2020.
2. Wilson, Sam, "Write-in candidate wins Eastern Montana sheriff's race after sex-abuse allegations sink 2 opponents," *Billings Gazette*, Nov. 7, 2018.
3. Tollefson, Phoebe, Etherington, A.J., "Ex-undersheriff guilty of raping teen, Valley County jury finds," *Glasgow Courier*, July 17, 2020.
4. Rosenbaum, Traci, "Complaints: Valley County should have pro-

tected victims from ex-Glasgow undersheriff," *Great Falls Tribune*, Nov. 6, 2020.
5. Myers, Reece, "Misguided Brotherhood," *Flathead Beacon*, Nov. 23, 2011.
6. Ibid.
7. Devlin, Vince, "In lawsuit, workers claim corruption in Lake County Sheriff's Office," *The Missoulian*," Sept. 12, 2013.
8. Devlin, Vince, "Lake County undershiff resigns amid office's corruption allegations," *The Missoulian*, Jan. 11, 2012.
9. Devlin, Vince, "Lake County sheriff's deputy embroiled in controversy resigns," The Missoulian, Mar. 11, 2014.

Nebraska

1. Friedman, Herb, attorney for Teena Brandon's mother, undated.
2. "100K Ruled Enough For 'Boys' Mother, CBS News, Dec. 6, 2002.
3. Ibid.
4. Sallah, Michael, O'Harrow, Robert Jr., Rich, Steven, Silverman, Gabe, "Stop and seize," *The Washington Post*, Sept. 6, 2014.
5. Ibid.
6. Ibid.
7. Nebraska Legislature, Legislative Document, 2017.
8. "Former cop falls victim to police misconduct; ACLU of Nebraska claims discrimination," ACLU of Nebraska news release, Nov. 14, 2001.
9. U.S. Court of Appeals, Eighth Circuit, Nov. 4, 2004.

Nevada

1. *Nevada Appeal*, April 11, 2017.
2. Wikipedia.
3. DeHaven, "Laxalt finds no crimes committed by embattled Storey County sheriff Gerald Antinoro," *Reno Gazette-Journal*.
4. Wikipedia.

5. DeHaven, James, "Ethics panel dismisses a pair of complaints against embattled Storey County Sheriff Antinoro," *Reno Gazette-Journal*, Aug. 21, 2019.
6. Hart, Joe, "Report shows Storey County Sheriff violated sex harassment laws," KRNV-TV, Sept. 7, 2016.
7. Botkin, Ben, "Nye County Sheriff's Office faces two lawsuits alleging hostile work environment," *The Pahrump Valley Times*, January 10, 2017.
8. Juhl, Wesley, "Lawsuit alleges Nye County police sergeant used evidence for 'pornographic matinees' at station," Las Vegas Review-Journal, March 2, 2016.
9. Hansen, Kyle B., "Nye County detective accused of harassment turns self in," *Las Vegas Sun*, May 21, 2010.
10. Poppa, Doug, "Did Las Vegas D.A. Steve Wolfson and Sheriff Joe Lombardo cover up corruption?" *Baltimore Post-Examiner*, Feb. 9, 2019.
11. Ibid.
12. Wikipedia.
13. Ibid.
14. Sallah, Michael, O'Harrow, Robert Jr., Rich, Steven, Silverman, Gabe, "Stop and Seize," *Washington Post*, Sept. 6 2014.
15. Sibilla, Nick, "Cops Use Traffic Stops To Seize Millions From Drivers Never Charged With A Crime," Institute for Justice, March 12, 2014.
16. Ibid.
17. "The Abuse of Civil Asset Forfeiture, 2nd Edition," Policing for Profit, 2014 report.

New Hampshire

1. New England Historical Society, undated.
2. Mortensen, Michael, "Ex-sheriff's deputy recharged with sexually assaulting prisoner," *The Laconia Daily Sun*, Nov. 8, 2020.
3. Blackman, Jeremy, "Lawyers, authorities searching for answers as scandal grows over accused Belknap deputy," *Concord Monitor*, Feb. 25, 2016.
4. Fisher, Damien, "So, what's next for trans satanic anarchist who lost her bid for Cheshire County sheriff?" *Manchester Ink*, Nov. 8, 2020.

5. Caldwell, Thomas P., "Hilliard resigns as Merrimack County Sheriff," The Laconia Daily Sun, Feb. 19, 2020.

New Jersey

1. Rimbach, Jean, "Ten years after killing, a bizarre mob story continues," Northjersey.com, April 16, 2017
2. Ibid.
3. "Former Middlesex County Sheriff Joseph Spicuzzo Sentenced to Nine Years in State Prison for Collecting Bribes for Jobs," news release from Office of the New Jersey Attorney General, Sept. 20, 2013.
4. Haydon, Tom, "Former Middlesex County sheriff's officer gets 3 years probation for collecting bribe," NJ Advance Media for NJ.com, Oct. 4, 2013.
5. "Former Middlesex County Sheriff Joseph Spicuzzo Sentenced to Nine Years in State Prison for Collecting Bribes for Jobs," news release from Office of the New Jersey Attorney General, Sept. 20, 2013.
6. "New Jersey sheriff resigns after racist remarks caught on tape, CBS News, Sept. 21, 2018.
7. Lagerkvist, Mark, "The List: New Jersey's 16 'Double-Dipping County Sheriffs," NJSpotlight.com, Sept. 19, 2016.

New Mexico

1. Borunda, Daniel, "Like any good action-movie hero, he's back," *El Paso Times*, Jan. 23, 2013.
2. "'The Incredible Hulk' actor Lou Ferrigno to become deputy in Socorro County," *El Paso Times*, Jan. 12, 2020.
3. Moore, Paula, *Cricket in the Web: The 1949 Unsolved Murder that Unraveled Politics in New Mexico*, University of New Mexico Press, 2008.
4. Ibid.
5. "The Waitress Who Shook New Mexico, Parts One and Two, *Frontera NorteSur*, New Mexico State University, Nov. 24 and 25,

2013.

6. "Former Deputy Sheriff in Colfax County sentenced to 87 months in federal prison for drug trafficking and theft of government property," news release by Department of Justice, U.S. Attorney's Office, District of New Mexico, Feb. 20, 2020.
7. "Former Colfax County Sheriff's Deputy Pleads Guilty to Federal Drub Trafficking and Theft of Government Property Charges,' news release by Department of Justice, U.S. Attorney's Office, District of New Mexico, July 13, 2016.
8. "Former Deputy Sheriff in Colfax County sentenced to 87 months in federal prison for drug trafficking and theft of government property," news release by Department of Justice, U.S. Attorney's Office, District of New Mexico, Feb. 20, 2020.
9. "Embezzlement charges vs ex-Torrance County sheriff dismissed," Associated Press, Oct. 27, 2019.
10. Kent, Jackie, "State requesting judge revisit sheriff's embezzlement case," KRQE-TV, Jan. 4, 2020.
11. Laflin, Nancy, "New Mexico judge who used to be a sheriff now charged with embezzlement," KDAT-TV, May 2, 2019.
12. Haywood, Phaedra, "Former Rio Arriba County sheriff won't get out of prison early," Santa Fe New Mexican, Jan. 24, 2020.
13. "Former Rio Arriba County Sheriff Thomas R. Rodella Sentenced to Ten Years in Federal Prison for Criminal Civil Rights and Firearms Conviction," news release by Department of Justice, U.S. Attorney's Office, District of New Mexico, Jan. 21, 2015.
14. Kolb, Joseph, "New Mexico sheriff guilty of violating motorist's civil rights," Reuters News Service, Sept. 26, 2014.
15. "Former Rio Arriba County Sheriff Thomas R. Rodella Sentenced to Ten Years in Federal Prison for Criminal Civil Rights and Firearms Conviction," news release by Department of Justice, U.S. Attorney's Office, District of New Mexico, Jan. 21, 2015.
16. "New Mexico Citizens Live in Fear of Their Police," Realcrimes.com, undated.

New York

1. "Farley is removed: unexplained funds sole basis of action," *New York Times*, Feb. 25, 1932.
2. Allen, Oliver E., *The Tiger: The Rise and Fall of Tammany Hall*, Addison-Wesley Publishing Co., 1993.
3. "Farley, Former N.Y. Sheriff, succumbs," *San Pedro News Pilot*, April 3, 1934.
4. "Former Saratoga County Deputy Sheriff Sentenced to Five Years on Drug Charge," news release by U.S. Attorney's Office, Northern District of New York, June 25, 2014.
5. Lyons, Brendan I, "Ex-deputy pays steep price for vices," *Albany Times-Union*, Dec. 18, 2014.
6. "Saratoga County Sheriff's Deputy Arrested in FBI Sting," news release by U.S. Attorney's Office, Northern District of New York, Feb. 28, 2014.
7. Fox, Craig, "Larson gets 21 months," *Finger Lake Times*, Feb. 14, 2008.
8. York, Michelle, "Indictment of a Sheriff Unsettles a Region's Calm," *The New York Times*, Sept. 4, 2007.
9. Stith, John, "Jury finds former Seneca County Sheriff Leo Connolly innocent of misconduct charges," *The Syracuse Post- Standard*, Aug. 13, 2010.
10. Baggerman, Mike, "NY Attorney General sues Erie County Sheriff for failing to address sexual misconduct at jails," WBEN-TV, March 17, 2021.
11. Goshgarian, Mark, "Erie County Sheriff Tim Howard Speaks Candidly About DOJ Report, Holding Center Deaths in 1-on-1," Spectrum News 1, Oct. 23, 2019.

North Carolina

1. Kickler, Troy L., Ph.D., "Hillsborough Confrontation," North Carolina History Project, undated.

2. "Regulators Hanged in Hillsborough," North Carolina Department of Natural and Cultural Resources, undated.
3. *Prison Legal News*, undated
4. Browder, Cullen, "More than 1,000 NC officers have lost their certifications, but reasons usually not made public," WRAL-TV, June 12, 2020.
5. "Suspension, Revocation, or Denial of Officer Commission," North Carolina Administrative Code 021.0212.
6. McDowell, Ian, "Sheriff Terry Johnson tells woman 'you're breaking the law' by being an activist, *Yes! Weekly*, Aug. 19, 2020.
7. Terry, Grace, "Elon students hold sit-in outside the Alamance County Sheriff's Office," *Elon News*, July 10, 2020.
8. Ball, Billy, "Federal judge dismisses lawsuit against Alamance Sheriff Terry Johnson," *Durham Indy Weekly*, Aug. 11, 2015.
9. Ibid.
10. Ibid.
11. Haimes, Nicole Lucas, "Who killed Julian Pierce?" *Mel Magazine*, April 25, 2017.
12. Hubert Stone obituary, *Rocky Mount Telegram*, Feb. 13, 2008.
13. Ibid.
14. Ibid.
15. Blythe, Anne, "Did Robeson sheriff hide evidence in Jordan investigation?" *Raleigh News & Observer*, Dec. 20, 2016.
16. "Ex-sheriff gets prison time for corruption," WRAL-TV, June 19, 2008.
17. Barnes, Greg, "Some not surprised by Robeson lawmen's arrests," *Fayetteville Observer*, June 18, 2006.
18. Woolverton, Paul, "Feds resume asset forfeiture with Robeson Sheriff's Office following Tarnished Badge corruption probe," *Fayetteville Observer*, Nov. 21, 2019.
19. "Former Durham deputy sentenced for embezzlement," WRAL-TV, June 7, 2011.
20. "Former Durham deputy surrenders on embezzlement charges," WRAL-TV, Sept. 8, 2010.
21. "Former Franklin sheriff pleads guilty to embezzlement," WRAL-TV, Aug. 17, 2012.
22. Boyle, John, "Former Sheriff Bobby Medford dies of COVID-19 in

federal custody," *Asheville Citizen-Times*, June 3, 2020.
23. "Fourth Circuit Upholds North Carolina Sheriff's Bribery Conviction," *Prison Legal News*, Oct. 15, 2012.
24. McAllister, Denise, "Disgraced Sheriff Accused of Frame-Up Job, *Courthouse News Service*, Sept. 26, 2014.
25. Boyle, John, "Former Sheriff Bobby Medford dies of COVID-19 in federal custody," *Asheville Citizen-Times*, June 3, 2020.
26. Curran, Caroline, "Operation N.C. Gateway stings Brunswick's former sheriff in early 80s," *The Brunswick Beacon*, Oct. 10, 2008.
27. "The rise and fall of Ronald Hewett," *The Brunswick Beacon*, Oct. 10 2008.
28. Curran, Caroline, "Former Brunswick sheriff arrested on federal firearm charge; ATF agents seize guns from Hewett's home," *Port City Daily*, July 9, 2014.
29. Sloan, Renee, "Autopsy: Tasing not the cause of former sheriff Ronald Hewett's death in jail," *State Port Pilot*, Dec. 3, 2014.
30. Turbyfill, Diane, "Cops get 1 to 3 years in federal prison," *Shelby Star*, Feb. 27, 2014.
31. Saul, Josh, "How the FBI Took Down a Dozen Crooked Cops, Jail Guards in Drug Smuggling Conspiracy, *Newsweek*, June 21, 2017.
32. Thomason, John, "A North Carolina sheriff doubled down on cooperation with ICE – so voters gave him the boot," *The Intercept*, May 9, 2018.
33. Kalmbacher, Colin, "North Carolina Sheriffs Clash with ICE Officials After Series of Unwanted Immigration Raids," *Law & Crime*, Feb. 9, 2019.
34. "New sheriff named after predecessor accused of plot to kill," Associated Press, Jan. 7, 2020.
35. Browder, Cullen, "Suspended Granville sheriff facing more charges, WRAL-TV, June 22, 2021.
36. Shaffer, Josh, "North Carolina sheriff urged killing ex-deputy over racist recording, records allege," *Raleigh News-Observer*, Sept. 18, 2019.
37. "Sheriff, three deputies charged with embezzlement in Gates County corruption investigation," WTKR-TV, Jan. 22, 2018

North Dakota

1. Olson, Chris, "Former Wells County sheriff charged with drug, bribery offenses, Forum News Service, May 31, 2017.
2. Hurtado, Daniela, "Federal charges for theft posted against former Wells County Sheriff, KFYR-TV, Mar. 1, 2019.
3. Fundingsland, Kim, "Former Wells County Sheriff Johnny Lawson guilty of theft of government property," *Minot Daily News*, June 2, 2020.
4. Kelly, Jamie, "Former police officer gets suspended sentence in corruption of a minor case," *Winston Herald*, March 4, 2019.
5. Skurzewski, Joe, "Steven Kukowski resigns, Bob Barnard named new Ward County Sheriff," KFVR-TV, April 13, 2017.

Ohio

1. New stories of April 5, April 8, April 9, April 24 and May 3, 2012, WBNS-TV, Columbus, Ohio.
2. Caniglia, John, "Pike Co. sheriff, face of mass-murder investigation, accused of misappropriating funds," *Cleveland.com*, May 17, 2020.
3. Francisco, Curtney, "Ex-Pike County sheriff Charles Reader sentenced to three years in prison," WCPO-TV, March 24, 2021.
4. Caniglia, John, "Pike Co. sheriff, face of mass-murder investigation, accused of misappropriating funds," *Cleveland.com*, May 17, 2020.
5. Ibid.
6. Lane, Mary Beth, "Ex-sheriff sentenced to 7 years, insists he did nothing wrong," *Columbus Dispatch*, March 20, 2015.
7. Ibid.
8. Swygart, J., "Sam Crish sentenced in federal court for extortion, bribery," *Lima News*, Sept. 27, 2019.
9. "Former Allen County Sheriff indicted for soliciting bribes, extor-

tion, making false statements," U.S. Department of Justice news release, June 18, 2018.
10. "Law officers rounded up on drug charges," CNN, Jan. 21, 1998.
11. Quinn, Christopher, "Badge of Dishonor," *Cleveland Plain Dealer*, Jan. 22, 1998.
12. Graves, Amy Beth, "Ohio Agents Sentenced in FBI Sting," Associated Press, Aug. 19, 1998.
13. 13. Simpson, Connor, "Occupy Steubenville: Anonymous vs. the Sheriff," *The Atlantic*, Jan. 3, 2013.
14. Kushner, David, "Anonymous vs. Steubenville," *Rolling Stone*, November 27, 2013.
15. "United States v. Chance," U.S. Court of Appeals, Sixth Circuit, No. 99-4437, Sept. 19, 2002.
16. Schudel, Matt, "James A. Traficant Jr., colorful Ohio congressman expelled by House, dies at 73," Washington Post, Sept. 27, 2014.
17. "United States v. Chance," U.S. Court of Appeals, Sixth Circuit, No. 99-4437, Sept. 19, 2002.
18. "Lucas County, Ohio, Sheriff's Sergeant Sentenced for Civil Rights Violations and Falsifying Written Reports," U.S. Department of Justice news release, Jan. 28, 2011.
19. Wootson, Cleve R. Jr., "Why this Ohio sheriff refuses to let his deputies carry Narcan to reverse overdoses," *The Washington Post*, July 8, 2017.
20. Golick, Keith Biery, "Sheriff Rick Jones: The making of Ohio's mini-Trump," *Cincinnati Enquirer*, Jan. 6, 2018.
21. Nill Sanchez, Andrea, "Ohio Sheriff Charged with Violating the Constitutional Rights of Local Immigrant," *ThinkProgress*, Jan. 27, 2010.
22. "Ohio Sheriff Agrees to Pay $100,000 After Illegal Immigration Raid," *Prison Legal News*, April 15, 2011

Oklahoma

1. Lee, David, "Oklahoma Sheriff Accused of taking Sexual Bribes, *Courthouse News Service*, June 17, 2016.

2. "Former Sheriff Milton Anthony makes plea deal to avoid jail time," KTEN-Tv, Nov. 7, 2016.
3. "Former Oklahoma sheriff accepts plea deal to corruption charge," KFOR-TV, March 6, 2017.
4. Reed, Jason, "Oklahoma sheriff arrested after allegations of meth use & strippers at his home," Reuters, July 25, 2016.
5. Clay, Nolen, "Son of suspended Love County sheriff is sentenced in meth distribution case," *Tulsa World*, Aug. 25, 2016.
6. Briquelet, Kate, "How Police Corruption Poisoned this American City," The Daily Beast, Oct. 8, 2018.
7. Russell, Doug, "Holly gets 25 years," *McAlester News-Capital*, Nov. 25, 2005.
8. Russell, Doug, "Appeals court overturns ex-sheriff's federal conviction," *McAlester News-Capital*, June 13, 2007.
9. Marler, Ralph W., "Latimer County sheriff charged with having sex with inmates," *Tulsa World*, Oct. 21, 2004.
10. Belkin, Lisa, "Oklahoma Officers Acquitted Of Conspiring to Kidnap Man," The New York Times, Oct. 19, 1989.
11. Burton, Wendy, "Former sheriff Bob Colbert pleads to new charge after felony dismissal," *Muskogee Phoenix*, Sept. 8, 2017.
12. Vicent, Samantha, "Former Wagoner County sheriff receives deferred sentence on reduced charge related to cash seizure during 2014 traffic stop," *Tulsa World*, Sept. 7, 2017.
13. Stogsdill, Sheila, "Delaware County sheriff resigns," *Tulsa World*, Nov. 4, 2011.
14. Reutter, David M., "Oklahoma Taxpayers Foot $13.5 Million Settlement Bill for Sexual Abuse by Jailers," *Prison Legal News*, July 2012.
15. Ruutter, David M., "$10 million settlement in suit over Oklahoma sheriff's sex abuse scandal," *Prison Legal News*, March 15, 2012.
16. "Former Custer County sheriff gets 79 years," *Enid News & Eagle*, May 24, 2009.
17. Swindell, Bill, "Choctaw County Ex-Sheriff Accused of Witness Tampering," *Tulsa World*, Oct. 20, 1995.
18. Faughts, Jamison, "McIntosh County Sheriff Resigns," Muskogee Politico,, March 1, 2010.
19. "Former McIntosh County Sheriff, Undersheriff Sentenced on

Civil Rights Charges," news release from U.S. Attorney's Office, Eastern District of Oklahoma, Sept. 22, 2009.
20. Banne, Adam, "Despite Errors Found in Audit and a Pending Investigation, Oklahoma Reelects Incumbent Sheriff," HuffPost, Nov. 14, 2016.
21. 21. Farzan, Antonia Noori, "An Oklahoma sheriff quit in protest over dangerous jail conditions. So did all the deputies," *Washington Post*, March 20, 2019.
22. Gilna, Derek, "Federal Lawsuit Filed Against Oklahoma Sheriffs – All of Them," Prison Legal News, May 8, 2018.
23. Order of Judge Terence Kern, U.S. District Court for the Northern District of Oklahoma, March 12, 2021.
24. "Oklahoma sheriff says recording of killing talk was illegal," Associated Press, April 18, 2023.
25. Ibid.

Oregon

1. Sulzberger, Arthur Gregg, Zaitz, Les, "Giusto's job tangled with his private life," *The Oregonian*, Oct. 27, 2007.
2. Furuichi, Miles, "Civil lawsuit alleges sexual harassment, discrimination at JoCo Sheriff's Office," KOBI-TV, July 17, 2019.
3. "Marion County Sheriff resigns over affair," KGW-TV, Aug. 19, 2009.
4. "Jury Finds Former Klamath County Sheriff Guilty on 5 charges," Associated Press, May 20, 2017.
5. Caldwell, Pat, "Malheur County officials ask sheriff to assess whether *Enterprise* reporters broke laws," *The Malheur Enterprise*, Aug. 19, 2019.
6. Wilson, Mark, "After $625,000 Settlement, Oregon Deputy Charged in Assault of Prisoner," *Prison Legal News*, February 2021.
7. Bailey, Everton Jr., "Washington County deputy suit claims sheriff's office rife with sexual harassment," *The Oregonian*, Jan. 20, 2017.

8. Genovese, Fran, "Politicians and scandal: a Portland-area tradition," The Oregonian, Feb. 19, 2009.
9. Zaitz, Les, "Sheriff Glenn Palmer makes his own rules," *The Oregonian*, Aug. 20, 2016.
10. Ibid.
11. Ibid.
12. Ibid.
13. "Stand with Oregon Sheriff Glenn Palmer," *Facebook* post of the Oath Keepers, May 3, 2016.
14. Cureton, Emily, "A new Grant County sheriff and the end of an era in Eastern Oregon," Oregon Public Broadcasting, Nov. 4, 2020.
15. Andrews, Becca, *Mother Jones*, Oct. 2, 2015.
16. Vanderhart, Dirk, Johnson, Kirk, Turkewitz, Julie, "Oregon Shooting at Umpqua College Kills 10, Sheriff Says," *The New York Times*, Oct. 1, 2015.
17. Letter from Sheriff John Hanlin to Vice President Joe Biden, Jan. 15, 2013.
18. Mortensen, Camilla, "Sheriff John Hanlin appears caught with his pants down, says online photo posted by his ex," *Eugene Weekly*, April 11, 2018.

Pennsylvania

1. McCoy, Craig R., "Longest-serving Philly sheriff is sentenced to 5 years in prison for $675k bribery scheme," *Philadelphia Inquirer*, Aug. 1, 2019.
2. Sahn, Michelle, "Authorities: Former Sheriff's Officer Sentenced in Pennsylvania Bounty Hunter Bribery Scheme., *Patch*, May 11, 2015.
3. Reed, Bill, "Ex-deputy sheriff convicted of hitting suspect, perjury," *Philadelphia Inquirer*, June 29, 2012.
4. McGinnis, James, "Bucks pays $85,000 to Bristol Twp. Couple claiming false arrest," *Bucks County Courier Times*, Oct. 2, 2014.
5. Wereschagin, Mike, Vellucci, Justin, "DeFazio macing a relic of

old style of Pa. corruption," *Pittsburgh Tribune-Review*, Nov. 26, 2006.
6. Ibid.
7. Reed Ward, Paula, "Judge confines former sheriff DeFazio to home," *Pittsburgh Post-Gazette*, Feb. 23, 2007.
8. Wereschagin, Mike, Vellucci, Justin, "DeFazio macing a relic of old style of Pa. corruption," *Pittsburgh Tribune-Review*, Nov. 26, 2006.
9. News releases by the U.S. Attorney's Office, Western District of Pennsylvania, July 25, 2018, and Nov. 14, 2018.
10. "Ex-Sheriff's Office Employee Sentenced To 1 Day In Prison For Obstruction Of Justice," KDKA-TV, March 18, 2019.
11. Hays, Constance L., "Martha Stewart's Sentence: the Overview; 5 Months in Jail, and Stewart Vows, 'I'll Be Back'," *New York Times*, July 17, 2004.
12. Cholodofsky, Rich, Signorini, Renatta, "State attorney: Sheriff Jonathan Held made staff solicit gifts, merchandise while in uniform, county car," *Pittsburg Tribune-Review*, Feb. 26, 2018.
13. "Mistrial declared in Westmoreland Co. sheriff's trial after juror questions verdict," WPXI-TV, Dec. 7, 2018.
14. Cholodofsky, Rich, "Albert knocks off Held in Westmoreland sheriff's race," *Monongahela Valley Independent*, Nov. 6, 2019.
15. "Montco sheriff gets spotlight in Allentown corruption case," Yahoo News, Aug. 7, 2017.
16. Hall, Peter, Opilo, Emily, "Former Allentown Mayor Ed Pawlowski stunned by 15-year prison sentence that lawyer calls 'cruel,'" *The Morning Call*, Oct. 23, 2018.
17 "Montco sheriff gets spotlight in Allentown corruption case," Yahoo News, Aug. 7, 2017.
18 Melwert, Jim, "Montgomery County Sheriff Testifies In Corruption Trial of Allentown Mayor," KDKA-TV, Jan. 29, 2018.

Rhode Island

1. Hillinger, Charles, "Top Sheriff of Tiny State Keeps Traditions

Alive," *Los Angeles Times,* May 11, 1986.
2. White, Tim, "Large number of sheriffs out for years collecting full salary," WPRI-TV, Nov. 12, 2018.

South Carolina

1. "5 Orangeburg deputies among 7 S.C. officers charged with taking bribes," *The Sumter Item*, March 31, 2019.
2. "Lawsuit: Dead sheriff stole money from Midlands County," WIS-TV, May 24, 2012.
3. Bartelme, Tony, "In Orangeburg, a sheriff dies – and the secrets spill out," *Charleston Post and Courier*, March 16, 2019.
4. "Reid Wins McCormick Sheriff's Race," *Criminal Justice Chronicle*, April 1987.
5. "Coroner Facing Bribery Charge To Meet Pardoned Felon in Run-off for Sheriff," Associated Press, December 31, 1986.
6. Hagey, Steve, "Dillon County Democratic chairman Alan H. Schafer and six others plead guilty," United Press International, October 12, 1981.
7. Bartelme, Tony, Cranney, Joseph, "SC sheriffs fly first class, bully employees and line their pockets with taxpayer money," *Charleston, S.C. Post and Courier*, March 16, 2019.
8. "Guilty Plea Entered by Sheriff," *Charleston, S.C. Post and Courier*, May 5, 1972.
9. Wilks, Avery G., Cranney, Joseph, "Former SC sheriff guilty in corruption case, faces years in prison," *Columbia Post and Courier*, April 23, 2021.
10. Ibid.
11. Francisco, Courtney, "Controversy Resurfaces with Ex-Sheriff's Prison Release," WCCB-TV, April 7, 2015.
12. Bartelme, Tony, "Suspended Colleton County Sheriff Andy Strickland pleads guilty to 3 charges, gets probation," *Charleston Post and Courier*, October 23, 2020.
13. Collins, Jeffrey, "Sheriff admits stealing public money; avoids pris-

on," Associated Press, January 8, 2020.
14. Gross, Daniel J., "Former Greenville Sheriff Will Lewis's 12 remaining criminal charges have been dismissed," *Greenville News*, March 31, 2021.
15. "Sheriff, county settle suit over affair, abortions," WYFF-TV, April 16, 2012.
16. Dominguez, Damian, Henley, Matthew, "Don Reynolds: Text allegations tarnish Ricky Chastain's authority as Laurens County sheriff," *Greenwood Index-Journal*, My 3, 2016.
17. Clayton, John, "Chastain enters race for sheriff," *The Laurens County Advertiser*, March 4, 2020.
18. "Laurens County Sheriff Don Reynolds wins 4-way race for GOP nod," *Greenwood Index-Journal*, June 9, 2020.
19. "Ex-Lee Co. Sheriff sentenced to 17 years," WACH-TV, March 17, 2011.
20. Barr, Jody, "Melvin deputy wore wire, helped FBI build case against former sheriff," WMBF-TV, October 29, 2010.
21. Barr, Jody, "Former Lee County sheriff moved to Texas prison," April 16, 2011.
22. Kinnard, Meg, "Ex-South Carolina sheriff sentenced: 1 year, 1 day in prison," Associated Press, April 27, 2015.
23. Burke, Minyvenne, "South Carolina cop charged with soliciting minor for sex in sting set up by his own department," NBC News, August 14, 2019.
24. Collins, Jeffrey, "Questions about convicted Saluda County sheriff remain unanswered as SLED report kept secret," *The Augusta Chronicle*, September 23, 2012.
25. "Ex-Saluda County sheriff loses bid to regain his seat," WIS-Tv, June 14, 2016.
26. U.S. Attorney's Office, District of South Carolina, September 21, 2010.
27. "Former S.C. County Sheriff Dies in Federal Prison," *Florence Morning News*, October 30, 2002.
28. "Cyrus Sentenced to Life Without Parole," Florence Morning News, August 10, 2001.
29. Hagey, Steve, "Gov. Dick Riley Saturday suspended Theodore McFarlin," United Press International, Oct. 23, 1982.

30. "Mistrial is Declared by Judge in South Carolina Sheriff Case," *The New York Times*, May 26, 1983.
31. "Williamsburg County Sheriff, Columbia Man Sentenced for Fraud," U.S. Attorney's Office, Columbia, S.C., March 25, 201.
32. "Wyatt, Dustin, Montgomery, Bob, "Sheriff refuses to apologize for saying deputies had opportunity to kill Black men but didn't," *Spartanburg Herald-Journal*, September 22, 2020.
33. Cary, Nathaniel, Lee, Anna, Ellis, Mike, various stories published in the *Greenville News* between January 27 and February 5, 2019.
34. Field, Caria, "Man files lawsuit against Sheriff Chuck Wright, wants his money back," WYFF-TV, August 12, 2016.
35. 35. "Former Berkeley Co. Sheriff sentenced for DUI," WCSC-TV, Jan. 11, 2016.

South Dakota

1. "Former Roberts County sheriff gets jail time, community service for assault," *Aberdeen News*, July 3, 2019.
2. "South Dakota Sheriff Loses Re-Election, Fires Winning Deputy," KELO-TV, June 7, 2018.

Tennessee

1. "Tennessee's 1980 'Outstanding Sheriff of the Year' pleaded guilty to selling cocaine," United Press International, June 15, 1984.
2. Baker, Steve, "Two Tennessee sheriffs arrested in corruption probe," Associated Press, March 26, 1986.
3. "United States of America v. John Mcghee," U.S. Court of Appeals for the Sixth Circuit, August 22, 1988.
4. Baker, Steve, "Tennessee sheriffs grapple with corruption in their midst with crooked sheriffs," United Press In
5. Serena, Kate, "The Cold-Blooded Revenge of Buford Pusser," *All That's Interesting*," February 8, 2018.

6. Ibid.
7. Budanovie, Nikola, "The Battle of Athens – when WWII veterans stood up to the corrupt local government in Tennessee, *War History Online*, December 20, 2017.
8. "Former FBI agent recalls Cocke County corruption," WBIR-TV, July 24, 2014.
9. "Strategy, stealth key for FBI in Cocke County investigative work," Knoxville News, October 5, 2008.
10. "Patrick Taylor sentenced to two years in federal prison," *The Newport Plain Talk*, April 7, 2008.
11. Thomas, Craig, "Ex-sheriff Chuck Arnold pleads guilty, won't go to jail," *Jackson Sun*, October 21, 2016.
12. Hidell, Alek, "Corruption in Tennessee sheriff's office leaves a dozen officials behind bars," AnonHQ.com.
13. Lessmiller, Kevin, "Former Tennessee sheriff gets 4 years on corruption charges," *Courthouse News Service*, May 4, 2017.
14. "Joe Russell sentenced in JailCigs scheme," WTVF-TV, Nov. 16, 2017.
15. Broden, Scott, "Former Sheriff Robert Arnold completes prison sentence," *Murfreesboro Daily News-Journal*, April 15, 2020.
16. Beres, Nick, "Disgraced former Rutherford County sheriff Robert Arnold on track for early prison release," WTVF-TV, Feb. 11, 2019.
17. "Former Fentress County Sheriff sentenced to federal prison," United States Attorney, Middle District of Tennessee, August 23, 2017.
18. Barchenger, Stacey, "Tennessee sheriff sent to prison for sex with inmates," *The Nashville Tennessean*, August 23, 2017.
19. "Tennessee sheriff shoots self dead," United Press International, May 5, 1990.
20. Hall, Ben, "Sheriff tells deputies to change their stories about what happened after pursuit," WTVF-TV, Dec. 17, 2018
21. Hall, Ben, "Tennessee sheriff wrongly told mom her son was killed by officers," WTVF-TV, Feb. 12, 2018

Texas

1. Reinhold, Robert, "Dispute over murder heightens border tensions," *The New York Times*, Aug. 31, 1986.
2. Katz, Jesse, "Jailed sheriff takes a shot at redemption," *The Los Angeles Times*, July 25, 2000.
3. "Former sheriff sentenced to prison for providing protection to drug traffickers in exchange for cash," U.S. Attorney's Office, Southern District of Texas, Aug. 27, 2009.
4. "Starr County, Texas, sheriff's deputy arrested and detained on bribery, extortion and drug charges," U.S. Department of Justice, Southern District of Texas, news release, July 20, 2012.
5. "Former Starr County deputy sheriff pleads guilty to drug trafficking," U.S. Attorney's Office, Southern District of Texas, news release, Feb. 10, 2015.
6. Aguilar, Julian, "Border corruption back in focus after guilty plea," *The Texas Tribune*, April 17, 2014.
7. del Bosque, Melissa, "Former border sheriff sentenced for money laundering," *Texas Observer*, July 17, 2014.
8. Price, Bob, "Texas border sheriff's office raided in corruption investigation," *Breitbart*, March 2014.
9. Lemieux, Josh, "Sheriff gets 7 years for influence peddling," Associated Press, November 22, 1994.
10. Brezosky, Lynn, "Former sheriff sentenced to more than 24 years," Associated Press, Dec. 12, 2005.
11. Balli, Cecilia, "The bad guy with the badge," *Texas Monthly*, August 2006.
12. Howe Verhovek, Sam, "A town's leaders stand accused (but stand tall)," The New York Times, April 22, 1994.
13. Stiles, Matt, "Buyers Behind Bars," *The Texas Tribune*, April 8, 2010.
14. Ibid.
15. FCI Commissary List, Bureau of Prisons, undated.
16. Clarke, Matt, "San Antonio Sheriff Pleads No Contest to Corruption Charges, Resigns," *Prison Legal News*, March 2008.
17. "Private Commissary Contracts Lead to Corruption in Bexar County," *texasprisonbidness.org*, Aug. 1, 2007.

18. "Bexar bribery allegations over jail commissary widen to other counties," *Grits for Breakfast,* Sept. 9, 2007.
19. "BCSO: Detention officer arrested while making drug deal in uniform," KSAT-TV, May 27, 2019.
20. Lisheron, Mark, "Bexar County Sheriff's Department plagued by criminal misbehavior," *The Texas Monitor*, April 19, 2018.
21. Martinez, Mary Ann, "BCSO sex scandal could cost four deputies their jobs," KENS-TV, April 7, 2016.
22. "FBI investigating corruption allegations at Bexar Sheriff's narcotics unit," *Grits for Breakfast*, Jan. 6, 2010.
23. Flynn, Meagan, "It's official: Harris County Sheriff's Deputies can't have sex with witnesses, victims," *Houston Press*, Feb. 9, 2016.
24. "Det.'s firing upheld over sex with witness in deputy's murder," CBS News, July 21, 2016.
25. Barned-Smith, St. John, "Sheriff's office fires third deputy in sex scandal tied to Goforth case," *Houston Chronicle*, Feb. 12, 2016.
26. "3 Harris County deputies fired in sex scandal," KPRC-TV, Feb. 5, 2013.
27. Glenn, Mike, "Deputy, detention officers fired in sex probe at county jail," *Houston Chronicle*, Oct. 5, 2012.
28. Fischer, Curtney, "Harris County deputy charged with sexually assaulting woman in March," KTRK-TV, July 21, 2020.
29. "Deputy, dispatcher charged in child sex abuse case after Harris Co. Pct. 1 deputy commits suicide, constable says," KPRC-TV, May 21, 2021.
30. Vasquez, Lucio, "Female Harris County Deputies Accuse Superiors of Sexual Misconduct in New Lawsuit," *Houston Public Media*, May 24, 2021.
31. Harah, Matt, "11 Fired, 6 Suspended at Harris County Sheriff's Office Following Death of Inmate in February," *Houston Public Media*, May 28, 2021.
32. "Former Harris County Deputy Sentenced to Prison for Extortion," news release by U.S. Attorney's Office, Southern District of Texas, Aug. 18, 2011.
33. Cortez, JC, "Former sheriff pleads guilty to charges," *Amarillo Globe News*, Aug. 18, 2014.

34. "Timeline of Corruption in Swisher County, Texas," *copblock.org*, March 27, 2015.
35. "Ex-Swisher County sheriff gets 30 days for oppression," *Lubbock Avalanche-Journal*, Aug. 20, 2014.
36. Datar, Saurabh, Dooling, Shannon, "Massachusetts Police Can Easily Seize Your Money. The DA of One County Makes it Nearly Impossible to Get it Back," WBUR Public Radio, Aug. 18, 2021
37. Williams, Marian, Holcomb, Jefferson, Kovandzic, Temisiav, *Policing for Profit: The Abuse of Civil Asset Forfeiture*, Institute for Justice, March 2010.
38. Walters, Edgar, McCullough, Jolie, "Texas police made more than $50 million in 2017 from seizing people's property. Not everyone was guilty of a crime," *The Texas Tribune*, Dec. 7, 2018.
39. Texas Code of Criminal Procedure, Chapter 59, Forfeiture of Contraband.
40. Reddell, Valerie, "Humpy Parker's Hwy. 59 terrorism put lasting stain on San Jacinto County," interview with author Steve Sellers, Feb. 28, 2019.
41. "Texas sheriff's guilty plea shuts a road trap," *The New York Times*, March 27, 1983.
42. "Potter County sheriff convicted in public corruption case," *Greenville Herald-Banner*, June 13, 2008.
43. Wilonsky, Robert, "Potter County Sheriff Clearly Didn't Learn a Thing from Dallas County," *Dallas Observer*, June 13, 2008.
44. Dallas County sheriff subpoenaed in vendor inquiry," *My Plainview*, Oct. 30, 2003.
45. "Vendor paid for Sallas County sheriff's meals, trips," *My Plainview*, Sept. 20, 2003.
46. Sweany, Brian, "There's a New Sheriff in Town," *D Magazine*, Feb. 2005.
47. West, Richard, "The Last Frontier," *Texas Monthly*, November 1977.
48. "About the Rio Grande," International Boundary & Water Commission, undated,
49. MacCormack, John, "Corrupt Texas sheriff soon to be released from prison," *San Antonio Express-News*, April 6, 2018.
50. Suro, Roberto, "Drug Traffickers Are Reopening Old Routes in

Texas Badlands," *The New York Times*, Dec. 7, 1992.
51. MacCormack, John, "Corrupt Texas sheriff soon to be released from prison," *San Antonio Express-News*, April 6, 2018.
52. Grissom, Brandi, "In the Jailhouse Now," *The Texas Tribune*, Dec. 1, 2010.
53. Whitlock, Craig, "How a high-profile Texas sheriff is tied to a rogue Navy unit facing a criminal probe," *The Washington Post*, September 30, 2016.
54. Weiner, Rachel, "Former Navy official suffers seizure for 2nd time in 4 days while on trial," *The Washington Post*, March 2, 2017.
55. Collier, Dillon, "Footage shows Maverick County deputies tackling man who recorded them, asked for their names," KSAT-TV, October 29, 2020.
56. "9-year-old son of triple-murder suspect sought driver's help after shooting, police say," KEYE-TV, April 20, 2021.
57. Thebault, Reis, Shammas, Brittany, "Gunman who police say killed 3 in Austin is a former sheriff's detective accused of child sexual assault," *The Washington Post*, April 18, 2021.
58. Floyd, John, "'People's Sheriff' Troy Nehls is a bad cop," John T. Floyd Law Firm blog, Oct. 22, 2020.
59. Lannelli, Jerry, "A Trumpist Texas sheriff is running for congress. If he wins, his brother might take over the sheriff's office," *The Appeal*, Oct. 23, 2020.
60. Hannaford, Alex, "Above the Law," Texas Observer, May 2, 2016.
61. Ibid.
62. "J.W. Guthrie garners win in sheriff's race," *Rocksprings Record*, March 5, 2020/
63. Zarate, Eric, "Junction sheriff no-billed," *Kerrville Daily Times*, June 14, 1990.
64. Ellison, Richard L., *Lawyers Hall of Shame* blogpost, published 2018.
65. Barr, Jody, "Series of indictments nearly wipes out Llano Police Department," KXAN-TV, Aug. 27, 2018.
66. Hart, Lianne, "Corruption Case Swallows the Police Force of a Texas Town," *The Los Angeles Times*, March 20, 2006.
67. "Smith County Sheriff J.B. Smith posted bond Monday," UPI, July 13, 1981.

68. "Lone Star Justice: Former Smith County sheriff J.B. Smith gets TV show on *Investigation Discovery*," KYTX-TV, May 6, 2019.
69. Holden, Sarah, "Leon County Sheriff's deputies indicted on charges of misuse of official information," KBTX-TV, March 13, 2017.
70. "Panola Co. sheriff pleads guilty to tampering, removed from office," KLTV-TV, May 16, 2013.
71. Mathew, Teresa, "Will Texas Democrats' gains topple a Trumpian sheriff?" *The Appeal*, Oct. 15, 2020

Utah

1. Marcello, Molly, "Eldredge off the hook in San Juan gun allegations," The Moab Times-Independent, November 22, 2017.
2. Roth, Max, "Piute County Sheriff threatens arrest of Forest Service personnel," KSTU-TV, Feb. 23, 2016.
3. Thompson, Jonathan, "The rise of the Sagebrush Sheriffs," *High Country News*, Feb. 2, 2016.
4. McKellar, Katie, Reavy, Pat, "Controversial Davis County sheriff won't seek re-election," *Desert News*, March 15. 2018.
5. Klopfenstein, Jacob, "Davis County sheriff 'deeply saddened' by employees' actions following sexual harassment investigation," KSL-TV, May 11, 2018.
6. Flores, Cristina, "More trouble at the Davis Co. Sheriff's Office, this time it's money," KUTV-TV, May 22, 2018.
7. Shenefelt, Mark, "Davis Sheriff's Office's finances back in order two years after blistering audit," *The Provo Daily Herald*, Feb. 3, 2020.

Vermont

1. Free, Alicia, "For Vermont's Sheriffs, Policing Is a Lucrative Business," *Seven Days* blog, Sept. 5, 2018.

2. Robinson, Stuart, "State officials say partial closure of Grand Isle courthouse is part of a statewide problem," *VTDigger*, Aug. 22, 2021.
3. Blaisdell, Eric, "Sheriff says he can't cover inmate transports due to lack of staff," *Barre Montpelier Times-Argus*, Sept. 3, 2019.
4. "Edson pleads guilty, resigns as sheriff," Vermont Public Radio, April 12, 2004.
5. Ring, Wilson, "Sheriff resigns after pleading guilty," Associated Press, June 24, 2006.
6. Ring, Wilson, "Ex-Sheriff Complains of Candidate's Ad," Associated Press, Oct. 27, 2006.
7. "Ex-sheriff deputy charged with seeking nude photos, sex," Associated Press, Aug. 25, 2021.

Virginia

1. United States of America, Appellee, v. J.C. Herbert Bryant, Jr., Appellant, U.S. Court of Appeals for the District of Columbia Circuit, Sept. 15, 1977.
2. "Outlaws run Virginia sheriff's dept. that worked to frame up candidate," *Executive Intelligence Review*, May 22, 1992.
3. O'Harrow, Jr., Robert, "U.S. probe faults marshals over ties to ARGUS leader," *The Washington Post*, Dec. 3, 1992/
4. Morrison, Aaron, "Virginia sheriff seeking re-election took campaign donations from healthcare provider for jail he oversees," *The Washington Post*, Oct. 17, 2019.
5. Greene, Renss, "Sheriff's Inmate Medical Provider Involved in FBI Investigation in Norfolk," Loudoun Now, Aug. 16, 2017.
6. Daugherty, Scott, Eberly, Tim, "Feds probing ex-Norfolk Sheriff Bob McCabe's ties to jail contractor. What is Correct Care Solutions?" The Virginian-Pilot, Feb. 10, 2017.
7. Eberly, Tim, "Allegations of sexual harassment, cronyism and impropriety: Did ex-Sheriff Bob McCabe abuse his power?" *The Norfolk Virginian-Pilot*, April 14, 2017.
8. "Patrol Car Tape Leads to Lawsuit Against Ex-Loudoun County Sheriff's Deputy," Associated Press, Feb. 14, 2012.

9. "Former Chesapeake sheriff's deputy gets 30 months for drug smuggling, "WVEC-TV, Aug. 26, 2019.
10. Lindsey, Sut, "Ex-Virginia Sheriff Gets 8 Months for Corruption," Associated Press, Sept. 11, 2007.
11. Newman, Maria, "A Virginia Sheriff is Charged with Selling Seized Evidence," The New York Times, Nov. 3, 2006.
12. Kunkie, Fredrick, "Corruption wrecked career of Page County, Va., sheriff," *The Washington Post*, Dec. 20, 2009.
13. Burton, Lonnie, "Virginia Sheriff Investigated for Misuse of Prisoner Funds," *Prison Legal News*, November 2002.
14. Nolan, Jim, "Henrico hires former Richmond sheriff," *Richmond.com* blog, Dec. 12, 2007.
15. Olivo, Antonio, "Millions of dollars are missing, the sheriff is dead, a small Virginia town wants answers," *The Washington Post*, Sept. 24, 2019.

Washington

1. Hagey, Jason, "Elected-sheriff amendment easily passes," *The Tacoma News-Tribune*, Nov. 8, 2020.
2. McClary, Daryl C, "Federal grand jury indicts 15 men in Pierce County for racketeering on December 8, 1978," essay written for *HistoryLink.org*, posted April 5, 2011.
3. "Ex-Pierce County sheriff, jailed for corruption, dies," Associated Press, June 23, 2005.
4. "Newspaper carrier confronted by Pierce County Sheriff Ed Troyer files a $5 million tort claim," Associated Press, June 16, 2021.
5. "Sheriff describes 'police corruption' after deputy arrest," KIRO-TV, June19, 2014.
6. Bill of Information, filed by Prosecuting Attorney Daniel T. Satterberg in Superior Court of Washington for King County, June 19, 2014.
7. Cohen, Bryan, "Seatle sheriff's deputy arrested for drugs, theft, prostitution," Reuters, June 19, 2014.

8. Rebik, Dana, "Former King County deputy gets 366 days in jail for pimping wife, drug dealing, theft.
9. "Prosecutors: Deputy busted for prostitution crimes defrauded court," KOMO-TV, Aug. 25, 2014.
10. "How Could Anyone Have Known About Darrion Holiwell?" *The Seattle Post-Intelligencer*, June 22, 2014.

West Virginia

1. Snyder, Timothy, *The Road to Unfreedom: Russia, Europe, America, London, U.K.*, Tim Duggan Books, 2018.
2. Stone, Gene, "Almost Heaven? This Corrupt Corner of West Virginia Was More Like the Other Place," *People Magazine*, Nov. 14, 1988.
3. "West Virginia Sheriff Quits in Plea Bargain," *The New York Times* April 19, 1988.
4. "15 charged with buying spots on ballot," *The Washington Post*, April 8, 1984.
5. "Corrupt officials jailed for abusing justice system," FBI news release, Aug. 5, 2014.
6. "Former Mingo Chief Magistrate Sentenced to 27 Months in Federal Prison," news release, U.S. Attorney's Office, Southern District of West Virginia, March 10, 2014.
7. Coyne, Caity, "Five years after sheriff's murder, corruption probe, Mingo marches on," Charleston Gazette-Mail, Mar. 31, 2018.
8. "Former Roane sheriff Bo Williams sentenced to up to 10 years of home confinement," Associated Press, March 28, 2017.
9. "Two Former Lincoln County Officials Sentenced to Federal Prison on Election Fraud Charges," news release, U.S. Attorney's Office, Southern District of West Virginia, Aug. 29, 2012.
10. Metzner, Janet, "Former Hancock County Deputy Mark Cowden Sentenced to 18 Months in Federal Case," Wheeling Intelligencer-News Register, Jan. 19, 2017.
11. Dedaj, Paulina, "One-armed former West Virginia state senator sues over being handcuffed wrist-to-ankle," Fox News, May 17, 2019.

12. Weaver, Bob, "Logan Sheriff Resigns after Vote Buying," *The Hur Herald*, July 20, 2004.

Wisconsin

1. Neiwert, David, ?Ex-Sheriff Clarke urges far-right followers to 'take to the streets,' defy coronavirus measures," Daily Kos, March 16, 2020.
2. Bice, Daniel, "David A. Clarke Jr. resigns as Milwaukee County sheriff," *Milwaukee Journal-Sentinel*, Aug. 31, 2017.
3. Ibid.
4. Neiwert, David, "With DHS Position, Clarke Would Be the First 'Patriot' Leader to Hold a Federal Post," Southern Poverty Law Center, May 18, 2017.
5. Bice, Daniel, Diedrich, John, "Sheriff David Clarke promotes captain despite misconduct case," *Milwaukee Journal-Sentinel*, March 10, 2014.

Wyoming

1. Schrock, Lillian, "Sublette County sheriff faces criminal charges," *Casper Star-Tribune*, Jan. 19, 2016.
2. "Deputy retires over Wyoming sheriff's ban on Western attire," *LEO Affairs*, Feb. 3, 2015.
3. Ufford, Joy, "Haskell sentenced," *Pinedale Roundup*, Sept. 24, 2021.
4. "Ed Cantrell, Rock Springs and Boom-time Crime," *WyoHistory.org*, July 28, 2020.
5. Tempest, Rone, *The Last Western* (2020).
6. "Wyoming Sheriff Granted Qualified Immunity for Jail Guard's Sexual Assault," *Prison Legal News*, Dec. 15, 2013.

www.ingramcontent.com/pod-product-compliance
Lightning Source LLC
Chambersburg PA
CBHW050132240426
43673CB00043B/1638